D1042216

American
State *and* Local
Government

THE CENTURY
POLITICAL SCIENCE SERIES

CLYDE F. SNIDER

in collaboration with
SAMUEL K. GOVE
both of the University of Illinois

American
State and *Local*
Government
second edition

 *New York*

APPLETON-CENTURY-CROFTS
division of Meredith Corporation

Copyright © 1965 by
MEREDITH PUBLISHING COMPANY

All rights reserved. This book, or parts
thereof, must not be used or reproduced
in any manner without written permission.
For information address the publisher,
Appleton-Century-Crofts, Division of
Meredith Corporation, 440 Park
Avenue South, New York, N. Y. 10016

712-11

Library of Congress Card Number: 64-25813

Copyright © 1950 by Appleton-Century-Crofts, Inc.

PRINTED IN THE UNITED STATES OF AMERICA
E-82822

UNIVERSITY LIBRARY
Lethbridge, Alberta
95228

PREFACE

Many important developments have occurred in the field of state and local government since the first edition of this book appeared in 1950. Two new states have joined the Union; another state has adopted a new constitution; and several constitutions have been amended in significant respects. Traditional governmental services have been expanded and new service programs have been inaugurated. State and local expenditures have tripled, and the problem of obtaining additional revenue to meet mounting expenditures has become more acute. The position of the states in the federal system has been accorded increasing attention. Growing interest in this problem, and in problems of intergovernmental relations generally, is evidenced by the establishment by Congress of the Commission on Intergovernmental Relations (Kestnbaum Commission) and more recently of the permanent Advisory Commission on Intergovernmental Relations. The rapid growth of suburban populations has intensified metropolitan problems. The overall number of local governmental units has been drastically reduced through the consolidation of school districts, but special districts of certain other types have multiplied rapidly. Organizational improvements at the state level have been effected in numerous instances, and there has been some improvement in the traditional forms of local government. Certain decisions of the United States Supreme Court, notably those relating to racial segregation and legislative apportionment, have had a significant impact on the states and on their local governments, as have such federal statutes as those concerning civil rights.

It has been our objective in this revision to update the subject matter of the book thoroughly and to take account of recent developments. The original chapter organization has been retained with little change, though there has been some rearrangement of materials. A section on metropolitan adjustments has been added to the chapter on local-government reorganization, and the discussion of natural resources has been expanded to include a section on state and local planning. Other new sections have been added at appropriate points. Several new maps and charts have been included.

We are obligated to many people for their aid in preparing this revision. Comments and suggestions from instructors and students who have used the book in its original edition have been most helpful. Public officials and staff members of legislative councils and reference bureaus have been generous in supplying information concerning individual states. To authors of the books, articles, and other published materials which have served as sources of information and guidance, our obligation is heavy, as we have sought to indicate in the reference lists and footnotes. Advice or assistance at various points has been provided by Professors Glenn W. Fisher, Neil F. Garvey, Charles M. Kneier, Jack W. Peltason, and Gilbert Y. Steiner, all of the University of Illinois; Jack F. Isakoff of Southern Illinois University; Austin Ranney of the University of Wisconsin; Andrew E. Nuquist of the University of Vermont; John E. Stoner and David R. Derge of Indiana University; and James W. Drury of the University of Kansas. Lois Riley Snider has made many contributions to the project throughout its several stages. Ronald B. Bailey, graduate student in political science at the University of Illinois, has rendered invaluable library assistance. Sincere gratitude is extended also to Mrs. Catherine VonRiesen and Mrs. Helen Cropp for their diligence and proficiency in typing the manuscript. Responsibility for errors of fact or judgment is of course ours alone.

C.F.S.
S.K.G.

CONTENTS

III. POPULAR CONTROL OF GOVERNMENT

IV. STATE ORGANIZATION AND POWERS

pal corporations versus municipal corporations proper. Powers of local units. Legal liability of local governments.

VI. STATE AND LOCAL FUNCTIONS

arbitration services. Municipal adjustment plans. Unions and collective bargaining. Yellow-dog contracts and anti-injunction laws. Labor relations acts. Fair employment practices laws. Employment agencies. Regulation of private employment agencies. State employment services. Unemployment compensation. Administrative organization.

VII. STATE AND LOCAL FINANCE

I

Fundamental Laws

1

State Constitutions and Local Charters

Every government, whatever its nature, rests upon some basic law. This law may have its source in anything from the fiat of an autocratic ruler to the will of a sovereign people. It may be written or unwritten, or partly one and partly the other. In the United States, these fundamental laws of government are all in written form, though custom and interpretation are influential in their actual operation. In the case of the nation and the states they are called *constitutions*, whereas the basic laws of local governmental units are known as *charters*.

Nature of State Constitutions

The constitution of an American state is a written instrument through which the inhabitants of the state, as a political entity, establish a government and prescribe its powers and limitations. The United States Constitution lays down the framework of our national government and divides governmental powers between nation and states.[1] That constitu-

[1] In conformity to common usage, the terms *national government* and *federal government* are employed in this book interchangeably to designate the general government with headquarters in the nation's capital. Strictly speaking, *national government* is the more accurately descriptive term. Together, the general and state governments constitute the *federal system* of government established by the United States Constitution.

3

tion also requires that state governments be republican in form[2] and imposes certain restrictions upon the powers which may be exercised by the states. Within these broad limits, however, each state is free to determine, by provisions in its own constitution, what its internal organization shall be and what powers shall be conferred upon its various governmental agencies. Actually, all governments established by the state constitutions consist of three branches—legislative, executive, and judicial. "The government" of a particular state at a given time is composed, therefore, of the state legislature, the governor and other executive officers, the state courts, and the employees of these various agencies. Since the government is established by the constitution, it is subject at all times to limitations imposed by that instrument, as well as to popular control according to constitutional provision. In the hierarchy of political authority the citizen occupies a dual position. As an *individual* each citizen is subject, at any given time, both to rules laid down in the constitution and to all lawful statutes and regulations emanating from the government. If he violates any of these he does so at his peril and may be called upon to pay the legal consequences of his action. On the other hand, the citizens of the state in their *collective* capacity constitute the body politic which has ultimate power to determine, either directly or indirectly, both the personnel and the policies of the government, and even to change the forms of government by altering the constitution in the manner provided by that organic law.

Early Constitutions and Subsequent Trends

When the English colonies in America declared their independence and proceeded to make that declaration effective by force of arms, it was necessary that they frame instruments for their self-government. Between 1776 and 1780, therefore, constitutions were framed and put into effect by all but two of the thirteen original states.[3] The two exceptions were Connecticut and Rhode Island. Their colonial charters had conferred broader powers of self-government than were enjoyed by the other colonies and those charters, with some modifications, served the new states as constitutions until 1818 and 1843, respectively.

Most of the constitutions of this Revolutionary period were framed and adopted by methods which today would be considered irregular. In a majority of the states the constitution was framed by an ordinary legislative body rather than by a convention of delegates chosen specifically for the purpose;[4] and in several instances the new document was put into

[2] The nature of this requirement is discussed below, Chap. II, "Guarantee to States of Republican Government."

[3] The colonies became states upon gaining their independence.

[4] In several instances the constitution-making body was the popularly-elected branch of the colonial legislature, continuing in session extralegally after the governor had ordered its dissolution.

effect without being submitted to popular vote. The Massachusetts constitution of 1780, however, in being framed by a convention chosen for that sole purpose and having its effectiveness made contingent upon approval of the voters, presaged what was to become the generally accepted method of state constitution-making.

These early constitutions differed from present-day state constitutions in several respects. One of the most obvious was the matter of length. The early documents were comparatively brief, rarely containing more than 5,000 words.[5] Most present-day constitutions are from two to five times that length and several are still longer. It is estimated that California's constitution as amended now comprises some 70,000 words, and that of Louisiana upwards of 200,000. The tendency of state constitutions to increase in length has been the result of various factors. One of these is the increasing complexity of government made necessary by modern social and economic conditions, and another is the fact that constitutional conventions have been all too prone to incorporate into their handiwork governmental machinery and procedures which might better have been left to legislative determination. It is of interest, however, and perhaps of significance, that the newest constitutions now give evidence of a trend toward curtailment of length, those of Alaska and Hawaii running to only some 12,000 words each.[6]

An extremely important difference between the provisions of early and more recent constitutions concerns the powers of the legislative and executive branches, respectively. The framers of the first constitutions seem to have had implicit faith in the elective legislative bodies, placing very few restrictions upon their action. On the other hand the governor, because of unhappy experiences with colonial governors appointed by the British king, was reduced to a position of relative weakness. Such appointments as the governor was authorized to make were subject to confirmation by the legislature or an executive council; he usually had no power to veto legislative acts; and in most states he was elected to his office by the legislature, this fact tending to make him subservient to that body. Experience was soon to prove, however, that the placing of unlimited confidence in the legislature had not been justified. As the legislatures, especially during the middle decades of the nineteenth century, plunged the states into debt to subsidize railroads and other public improvements, enacted great masses of special legislation at the behest of special interests, and demonstrated generally their unfitness to exercise the almost limitless powers conferred upon them, constitutions were amended to impose restrictions upon legislative action, and as new constitutions were framed they were made to include such restrictions. These limitations con-

---

[5] Sister M. Barbara McCarthy, *The Widening Scope of American Constitutions*, v.

[6] For comparative data on length of state constitutions, see *The Book of the States* (Council of State Govts., Chicago), 1964-65, p. 12. Cf. Alfred de Grazia, "State Constitutions—Are They Growing Longer?" *State Govt.*, XXVII, 82-83 (Apr., 1954).

cerned various matters, but of particular importance were those restricting the legislature's power to enact special legislation and to tax, spend, and borrow money.[7] So numerous were the restrictions imposed upon the legislative bodies that they constituted one factor in the growing length of state constitutions. As the legislature lost in power, the governor gained. He soon came to be chosen by direct popular election rather than by the legislature, his power of appointment was increased, and he was given the veto power. Indeed, one of the most significant trends in American state government over the years has been a shifting in relative power from the legislative branch to the office of the chief executive.

Early state constitutions differed from those of modern times also in the stringent limitations imposed upon the voting privilege.[8] Yet another difference was the lack, in several of the early instruments, of a bill of rights and specific provisions for amendment, both of which are now considered essential elements of a constitution.

Contents of Present-Day Constitutions

Present-day state constitutions naturally vary a great deal in detail, but their principal provisions fall into three categories: (1) the bill of rights; (2) provisions relating to governmental structure, powers, and procedures; and (3) provisions for amendment and revision. Each constitution usually also includes, though they are of distinctly minor importance, an introductory clause or statement known as the "preamble," and a concluding "schedule" of temporary provisions for the inauguration of the new government.

The Bill of Rights. Every state constitution now includes a bill of rights[9]—an enumeration of certain fundamental civil liberties for their protection against governmental interference. The importance attached to the bill of rights by framers of state constitutions seems to be indicated by the prominent position which it is usually accorded in the constitutional document. Three-fourths of the states either make the bill of rights the first article of the constitution or, as in a few instances, place it between the preamble and the articles.[10] Though it is sometimes said that the purpose of the bills of rights is to *confer* civil liberties upon the people, such a statement is not strictly in accordance with history and theory. The liberties set forth in the first state bills of rights, and which have been copied and elaborated in subsequent constitutions, consisted of certain funda-

---

[7] See below, Chap. VIII, "Limitations on Legislative Powers: The State Constitutions."

[8] See below, Chap. V, "The Voting Privilege in American History."

[9] In about half of the states the official title is "declaration" of rights rather than "bill" of rights.

[10] Cf. Leila R. Custard, *Bills of Rights in American History,* 28; Robert S. Rankin, *State Constitutions: The Bill of Rights,* 1.

mental freedoms which early Americans claimed as the "rights of Englishmen." According to their views these rights—set forth in such historic English documents as Magna Charta, the Bill of Rights, the Petition of Right, and the Habeas Corpus Act—had been enjoyed by them or their forefathers before their emigration to America and had not been lost by the fact of emigration. Bills of rights in American constitutions were conceived, therefore, not as conferring new rights upon the people, but as protecting against governmental infringement rights already possessed.

The federal bill of rights, contained in the first eight amendments to the United States Constitution, was early construed by the United States Supreme Court to afford protection against the national government only,[11] and it was therefore considered essential to have similar bills of rights in state constitutions to protect individuals against arbitrary action by their state and local governments.[12] More recently the broad interpretation given by the Supreme Court to the "liberty" which is protected against state interference by the "due process" clause of the Fourteenth Amendment has operated to afford federal protection to many civil rights as against state action.[13] This fact has lessened the relative importance of state constitutional guarantees, but has by no means rendered them of no consequence.

State bills of rights usually include provisions of two general types. In the first place there are, particularly in the older constitutions, statements of political axioms and theories which, though high-sounding from the standpoint of rhetoric, are so vague and general as to afford, in practice, little or no actual protection to the individual against misuse of governmental power. These statements relate to the doctrines of inherent rights and popular sovereignty, and to various other matters. Thus, the Rhode Island constitution declares that "All free governments are instituted for the protection, safety and happiness of the people" and that "All laws, therefore, should be made for the good of the whole; and the burdens of the State ought to be fairly distributed among its citizens."[14] Other examples are afforded by the declarations of the Illinois constitution that "Every person ought to find a certain remedy in the laws for all injuries and wrongs which he may receive in his person, property or reputation," and that "A frequent recurrence to the fundamental principles of civil government is absolutely necessary to preserve the blessings of liberty."[15]

---

[11] *Barron v. Baltimore*, 7 Peters 243 (1833).

[12] Restrictions contained in state bills of rights apply to local governmental units as well as to the states. Local governments have only the powers delegated to them by the state, and it follows that any power which is denied by the constitution to the state government itself cannot be delegated by that government to its local units.

[13] See below, Chap. II, "Due Process of Law."

[14] *Const. of R.I.* (1843), art. I, sec. 2.

[15] *Const. of Ill.* (1870), art. II, secs. 19, 20.

Secondly, and far more important, are the provisions which set forth, as immune from governmental infringement, various specific rights of the individual. Most of these fall into one or another of four categories depending upon whether they are designed to protect (1) religious freedom, (2) freedom of speech and press, (3) rights of persons accused of crime, or (4) property rights.[16]

All constitutions, in varying language, guarantee freedom of conscience and worship. In about a third of the states, it is expressly stated that the guarantee of religious freedom may not be used to excuse acts of licentiousness or justify practices inconsistent with the peace of the state; and, where not expressly stipulated, this limitation upon religious liberty usually exists by judicial interpretation. Thus an individual may not, as for example in practicing polygamy, violate a criminal law of the state in the name of religion. Many bills of rights prohibit the expenditure of state funds in aid of any religious or sectarian institution. About half of the states provide that there shall be no religious test for holding public office.

The constitutional guarantee of free speech and press generally means that, in normal times, the state may place no restriction upon what the individual may say, write, or publish. This does not imply, however, that individuals are relieved of responsibility for civil wrongs which may result from what they say or print; if they commit slander or libel, they are subject to civil suit for damages by the person or persons injured. Furthermore, the state may, in the exercise of its police power, prohibit the publication of obscene material on the ground that such publication would endanger the public morals. And in time of war the right to free speech and press may be restricted by governmental action in whatever degree the emergency requires. Persons will not be permitted, under the semblance of constitutional liberty, to interfere with the successful conduct of the war. Closely related to the rights of free speech and press are those of peaceable assembly and of addressing petitions to the government.

Constitutional provisions for the protection of persons accused of crime are numerous. One of the most common is the guarantee, at least in the case of serious offenses, of indictment by grand jury and trial by jury.[17] A unanimous verdict by the trial jury is usually required for conviction. An accused person is guaranteed the right to legal counsel in his defense. He may call witnesses in his behalf and may not be compelled to testify against himself. No person may be twice put in jeopardy for the same offense. There are usually also prohibitions of cruel or unusual punish-

---

[16] Cf. Frank G. Bates and Oliver P. Field, *State Government* (Harper, New York, rev. ed., 1939), 77-82; John M. Mathews, *American State Government* (Appleton-Century-Crofts, New York, rev. ed., 1934), 110-113.

[17] In some states the right to jury trial is guaranteed in civil cases also.

ment; the enactment of ex post facto laws;[18] and the suspension, except in case of rebellion or invasion, of the writ of habeas corpus.[19] Unfortunately, some of the constitutional requirements respecting judicial procedure operate to impede improvements in law enforcement. Thus, the use of the grand jury is still widely required in criminal proceedings, as is the unanimous verdict on the part of the trial jury, notwithstanding that the grand-jury system has pretty largely fallen into disrepute and the requirement of a unanimous verdict often defeats the ends of justice.[20]

Property rights are protected by such provisions as the prohibition of unreasonable searches and seizures and the requirement that compensation be paid for property taken by eminent domain.[21]

Not falling within any of the above categories, because designed to protect both property rights and individual liberties, is the common provision that no person may be deprived of life, liberty, or property without due process of law.[22] This due-process clause is so general in phraseology that its actual meaning has necessarily been determined by judicial interpretation. The courts have consistently declined to give a precise definition of the concept, preferring to determine what constitutes due process and what does not by "inclusion and exclusion" as they decide specific cases in which the meaning of the constitutional provision is involved. In a general way, however, the view has been taken that the requirement of due process is one of *reasonableness*. When, therefore, governmental agencies take restrictive action concerning the life, liberty, or property of the individual, such action must be fair, reasonable, and in conformity to recognized standards of justice, or it will be overturned by the courts, if occasion arises, as wanting in due process. Although due-process clauses have at times produced wholesome results, especially in the field of judicial procedure, they have long operated as deterrents to the enactment of desirable social legislation. This has been particularly true when state legislatures have sought to regulate, in the public interest, such matters as business practices and the conditions of labor in industry. Legislation of this nature is enacted under what is known as the state's *police power*—a broad and largely undefined power of the legislature to take whatever

[18] An ex post facto law is a retroactive law which makes criminal an act which was not a crime when committed, increases the penalty for a previous act, or operates in any way to the disadvantage of a person previously accused of crime. The constitutional prohibition does not apply to retroactive statutes of a civil nature.

[19] A writ of habeas corpus is a court order requiring that a person who is held in custody be brought before the court for a determination of the legality of his detention.

[20] See below, Chap. XVII, "Preferring of Charges," "The Trial Jury."

[21] Eminent domain is the power of the government to take private property for public use. Compensation for property so taken by state or local governments is now required also by the Fourteenth Amendment to the United States Constitution.

[22] Some constitutions use the phrase "law of the land" instead of "due process of law."

action is necessary to protect and promote the health, safety, morals, and general welfare of the state's inhabitants—and the requirement of due process is the principal constitutional limitation upon the exercise of that power.

For many years the state courts, steeped in the old laissez-faire philosophy of the relationship between government and business, tended to look upon all but the most elementary regulatory action in the fields of business and labor as unreasonable interference with individual liberty, and therefore lacking in due process. More recently, however, courts generally have adopted a more liberal view of the matter and upheld much legislation of types formerly held unconstitutional. This change in judicial attitude may be illustrated by two decisions of the supreme court of Illinois. In 1895 that court declared invalid, as violative of the due-process clause of the state constitution, an act of the state legislature fixing a maximum work day of eight hours for women in industry. The court reasoned that the privilege of entering into contracts was both a liberty and a property right, and that the legislative act was an unreasonable interference with the exercise of that privilege by women workers and their employers. Fifteen years later, in 1910, a ten-hour-day law for women was upheld. The court at this time was prepared to recognize the fact that the health and well-being of women workers were matters of concern to the state, and that it was not unreasonable to take necessary measures to protect those workers from exploitation.[23] But while the general tendency has been for the courts to take more liberal views than formerly respecting the constitutional competence of the legislature to deal with social and economic problems, the judicial attitude varies from state to state and within the same state from time to time. Even today, seemingly wholesome legislation sometimes falls a prey to the judicial veto as being in violation of the due-process requirement.[24]

In conclusion it may be suggested that present-day bills of rights might be improved in several ways.[25] For one thing, flowery but meaningless statements of theory should be eliminated. Also deleted should be those provisions which, like the prohibition of ex post facto legislation,

[23] *Ritchie v. People*, 155 Ill. 98 (1895); *Ritchie v. Wayman*, 244 Ill. 509 (1910). Though it is true that the act upheld was somewhat less stringent than the earlier statute, fixing the maximum work day at ten hours rather than eight, it would seem that the real reason for the different decision in the second case was a change in the view of the court as to what the state could constitutionally accomplish under its police power.

[24] The requirement of due process in state governmental action is imposed also by the Fourteenth Amendment to the United States Constitution. This federal requirement of due process on the part of the states is considered in the following chapter. The distinction made in that discussion between the *procedural* and *substantive* aspects of due process is applicable also to the due-process clauses of state constitutions.

[25] Cf. Bates and Field, *op. cit.*, 82-86; Herbert F. Goodrich, "Does the Bill of Rights Need Revision?" *Annals of Amer. Acad. of Polit. and Soc. Sci.*, CLXXXI, 27-38 (Sept., 1935).

merely duplicate restrictions placed upon the states by the federal constitution. Various provisions, such as those concerning juries, should be
revised to bring them in line with modern needs; and constitutional protection might well be accorded certain "newer" rights, such as the right
of employees to organize and freedom from discrimination on account of
race, creed, color, or national origin.[26] Finally, the careful rephrasing of
many provisions should result in a considerable reduction of verbiage and
added clarity of expression. Some bills of rights embrace as many as forty
or more sections.[27] It seems reasonably certain that many of the longer
enumerations could well be shortened without in any way impairing the
civil liberties of the individual.

Governmental Structure, Powers, and Procedures. The purposes of
a constitution are to set up a government; to confer powers upon that government; and, by the imposition of appropriate limitations, to protect individuals against arbitrary governmental action. The fact that the bill of
rights, which restricts all agencies of state and local government, almost
universally precedes the constitutional provisions establishing governmental agencies and conferring powers upon them, serves to emphasize
the concept of *limited* government prevailing in this country.

Following the bill of rights, many constitutions have a brief article
—sometimes called the "distributive" article—which declares that the government is to be divided into three branches or departments and that the
officers of one department shall never exercise powers rightfully belonging
to either of the others. Though the phrasing of the distributive article
differs slightly from state to state, its essence is the same everywhere. The
Illinois article, which may be taken as typical, declares that "The powers
of the government of this State are divided into three distinct departments
—the legislative, executive and judicial; and no person, or collection of
persons, being one of these departments, shall exercise any power properly
belonging to either of the others, except as hereinafter expressly directed or
permitted."[28]

Whether or not there is a special distributive clause formally pro-
claiming the doctrine of separation of powers, it is customary for state
constitutions to devote a separate article to each of the three departments
of government, prescribing its structure and conferring appropriate powers upon it. These articles provide for the principal officers in the respective departments, prescribe their qualifications and terms, specify the
method of their selection and how they may be removed, and sometimes
even fix their compensation. In addition to grants in general terms of

[26] Some recently-framed constitutions do give constitutional recognition to
some of these newer rights. Cf. W. Brooke Graves, "A New Bill of Rights?" *Nat. Mun.
Rev.*, XLVI, 238-244 (May, 1957).

[27] Cf. Custard, *op. cit.*, 28.

[28] *Const. of Ill.* (1870), art. III.

legislative, executive, and judicial powers, respectively, the articles contain certain more specific provisions relative to the powers and duties of the departments and their officers. Thus it is usual to confer the power of impeachment upon the house of representatives and the power to try impeachments upon the senate; to assign appointing and veto powers to the governor; and to prescribe the jurisdiction of the various courts. In connection with the provisions relative to powers will be found others prescribing the procedures to be followed in their exercise; and there will be imposed, in addition to the restrictions contained in the bill of rights, certain limitations upon the departments and officers. Limitations are most numerous in the case of the legislative branch. In most constitutions, for example, the legislative article includes a section prohibiting the enactment of special legislation on a lengthy list of subjects, as well as limitations upon the legislature's control over finance and other matters. Articles other than those concerning the three major departments vary in number and subject matter from state to state. Commonly included are articles dealing with such matters as suffrage, education, finance, corporations, and local government.

Most of the more significant constitutional provisions relating to governmental structure, powers, and procedures will be considered at some length at appropriate points in subsequent chapters.

Provisions for Amendment and Revision. The wisest of constitution-makers cannot hope to build for all time.[29] An essential element in any constitution, therefore, is the establishment of means whereby changes may be made in an orderly manner as particular provisions prove unsatisfactory or are rendered obsolete by social and economic developments. The task of providing satisfactory methods of constitutional change is by no means simple. Basically, the problem is one of balancing stability and flexibility. As the *fundamental* law of the state, the constitution should serve as a stabilizing force in government, and this requires that alteration should not be effected too easily. Yet if the method of modification is too difficult, the instrument becomes a bar to progress. Most state constitutions today provide two alternative methods of change, and some provide three. There is considerable diversity in these various procedures, but more constitutions err in the direction of providing procedures which are too difficult than in that of permitting changes to be made too easily.

In considering methods of constitutional change and their operation, it is usual to distinguish between two types of alteration—*amendment* and *revision*. By amendment is meant the making of a single specific

[29] Problems of constitutional obsolescence in illustrative states are considered in Charles S. Hyneman, "The Illinois Constitution and Democratic Government," *Ill. Law Rev.*, XLVI, 511-574 (Sept.-Oct., 1951); Mark S. Matthews, "Under an 1818 Cloud" [in Connecticut], *Nat. Mun. Rev.*, XLIV, 352-358 (July, 1955); Manning J. Dauer and William C. Havard, "The Florida Constitution of 1885—A Critique," *Univ. of Fla. Law Rev.*, VIII, 1-92 (Spring, 1955).

change, or at most a relatively small number of changes; whereas revision implies a more thorough overhauling—perhaps even a complete rewriting—of the document. The difference between amendment and revision being one of degree only, it is not always possible to apply the distinction with absolute accuracy, and it occasionally happens that changes of one kind are made by procedures designed primarily for the other. Nevertheless, the general distinction is useful and will be observed in the discussion which follows.[30]

Proposal of Amendments

The amending process involves two steps—the proposal or initiation of the amendment and its ratification.[31] In New Hampshire, amendments as well as revisions may be proposed only by convention action. Elsewhere two methods of proposal are in use: (1) legislative proposal; and (2) proposal by popular initiative.

Legislative Proposal. In every state save New Hampshire amendments to the constitution may be proposed by the state legislature.[32] In thirty-six states only a single legislature need act on a proposal, while the remaining thirteen states[33] require approval by two successive legislatures. The latter requirement is designed in theory to serve a dual purpose: (1) to assure mature and deliberate consideration of proposals; and (2) to permit issues to be made of proposed amendments in the election at which the second legislature is chosen. In practice, however, its principal effect seems to have been merely to diffuse responsibility and impose undue delay. The vote required in the legislature for proposing amendments is in eighteen states[34] a simple majority of the members of each house, this group including most of the states which require action by two legislatures. In nineteen states[35] the required vote is two-thirds of the members, and in seven states[36] three-fifths. Under the constitution of two

[30] For a comprehensive treatment of the subject in general, see Albert L. Sturm, *Methods of State Constitutional Reform.*

[31] The one state which might be considered an exception to this statement is Delaware, where favorable action by two successive legislatures completes the amending process without popular referendum. Even here, however, first legislative action might be considered as proposal and action by the second legislature as ratification.

[32] The provisions for amending and revising the constitutions of the various states are summarized in tabular form in *The Book of the States,* 1964-65, pp. 13-15.

[33] Connecticut, Delaware, Indiana, Iowa, Massachusetts, Nevada, New York, Pennsylvania, Rhode Island, Tennessee, Vermont, Virginia, and Wisconsin.

[34] Arizona, Arkansas, Indiana, Iowa, Massachusetts, Minnesota, Missouri, Nevada, New Mexico, New York, North Dakota, Oklahoma, Oregon, Pennsylvania, Rhode Island, South Dakota, Virginia, and Wisconsin.

[35] Alaska, California, Colorado, Delaware, Georgia, Idaho, Illinois, Kansas, Louisiana, Maine, Michigan, Mississippi, Montana, South Carolina, Texas, Utah, Washington, West Virginia, and Wyoming.

[36] Alabama, Florida, Kentucky, Maryland, Nebraska (unicameral legislature), North Carolina, and Ohio.

states, proposal may be either by an extraordinary majority vote (three-fifths in New Jersey and two-thirds in Hawaii) in a single legislative session or by simple majority vote in each of two successive legislative years.[37] Connecticut requires a majority vote of the house of representatives in one legislature and a two-thirds vote of each house in the next; Tennessee a majority vote of each house in one legislature and a two-thirds vote of each house in the next; and Vermont two-thirds of the senate and a majority of the house of representatives in one legislature, and a majority vote of each house in the next.

A few states limit the number of amendments which may be submitted to the voters at any one election, Kansas and Montana fixing the maximum at three and Kentucky at two. No single legislative session may propose amendments to more than three articles in Illinois, or to more than six in Colorado. Still other types of limitations upon the power of the legislature to propose amendments are found in individual states.

In occasional instances state legislatures have prepared and submitted to the voters comprehensive constitutional revisions. However, in at least one state—Indiana—the courts have held that it is beyond the constitutional power of the legislature to prepare and submit a general revision.[38] Of interest in this connection is a provision of the Hawaiian constitution which expressly authorizes the legislature to propose revisions as well as amendments.

Proposal by Popular Initiative. Thirteen states[39] provide a second method of proposing amendments in the form of the popular initiative. Under this plan the voters may propose directly, by petition, amendments which they think desirable and for which legislative proposal has not been forthcoming. The number of voters who must sign the initiative petition is usually fixed as a certain percentage of the votes cast in the last election for a designated state officer, the requirement ranging from 8 to 15 percent.[40] In North Dakota, however, a definite number of signers—20,000— is required. Some states make requirements concerning the geographic distribution of signers. Thus the petitioners must include a certain number of voters, in Arkansas from each of fifteen counties, and in Nebraska from each of two-fifths of the state's counties.

[37] Legislative sessions in New Jersey and Hawaii are held annually.

[38] *Ellingham v. Dye,* 178 Ind. 336 (1912).

[39] Arizona, Arkansas, California, Colorado, Massachusetts, Michigan, Missouri, Nebraska, Nevada, North Dakota, Ohio, Oklahoma, and Oregon.

[40] The requirement in Missouri is 8 percent of the legal voters in each of two-thirds of the state's congressional districts. Initiated proposals in Massachusetts need be signed by only 3 percent of the number of voters voting for governor in the preceding biennial election but must, before being submitted to the voters in a referendum election, be approved by two successive legislatures by vote of one-fourth of all members in joint sessions of the two houses.

Ratification of Amendments

Amendments proposed either by the legislature or by initiative petition must, in all states except Delaware,[41] be ratified by the voters of the state before they become effective.[42] Ordinarily proposed amendments are submitted to the voters at the general elections held for electing state officers, though in some cases submission is at primary or special elections.[43] The vote required for ratification is in most instances merely a majority of the votes cast *on the amendment.* However, a few states, including Minnesota, Mississippi, and Oklahoma, require a majority of those voting *in the election.*[44] This latter requirement makes it extremely difficult to secure ratification and seems indefensible. When a proposed amendment is submitted at an election for the choice of officers, it almost invariably happens that more persons vote for candidates than on the amendment. Voters are more interested in candidate personalities than in the seemingly prosaic matter of constitutional change, and therefore many of them, while voting for officers, ignore the constitutional question. Since the amendment, to secure adoption, must receive in its favor a majority of all votes cast in the election, the vote of a person who votes in the election but not on the constitutional amendment operates as effectively to secure the amendment's defeat as if a negative vote had actually been cast. Where this ratification requirement prevails, it frequently occurs that a proposed amendment is defeated, notwithstanding that more votes are actually cast for than against it. Under such circumstances, amendments are defeated, not by voters who are actually opposed to them, but by those who are not sufficiently interested to express an opinion one way or the other. For this reason, the more common provision for ratification of amendments by a majority vote of those voting thereon is distinctly to be preferred.[45]

[41] See above, footnote 31.

[42] In South Carolina *final* ratification, after a favorable popular vote, rests with the legislature.

[43] In Connecticut and Rhode Island amendments are submitted to the voters in town meeting.

[44] Still other requirements are found in several states. Illinois, for example, provides for ratification by either a majority of those voting in the election or two-thirds of those voting on the amendment. Nebraska requires that the favorable majority for the amendment equal at least 35 percent of the total vote cast in the election. Hawaii imposes a like requirement where submission is at a general election, and provides that where submission is at a special election the favorable majority must constitute at least 35 percent of the registered voters. Tennessee provides for ratification by a majority of those voting for governor. Amendments in Rhode Island are ratified by "three-fifths of the electors of the state present and voting thereon in town and ward meetings."

[45] In some states the requirement for ratification, as stated in the constitution, has been the subject of judicial interpretation. The Mississippi constitution, for example, stipulates that amendments shall be ratified by "a majority of the qualified

Frequency of Amendment

There is much variation among the states regarding frequency of constitutional amendment. In general, as would be expected, states with more difficult amending procedures tend to have fewer amendments. Tennessee's constitution remained unamended from its adoption in 1870 down to 1953; and the Illinois instrument, also adopted in 1870, was amended only seven times prior to 1950. Throughout this period, it may be noted, Illinois required for ratification of amendments a majority of all votes cast in a general election, while the Tennessee requirement was a majority of those voting for state representatives. As among constitutions having similar amending procedures, the longer ones tend to be amended more frequently than the briefer documents. This, too, is only natural, since the provisions of the longer documents are more detailed, and details require more frequent change than fundamentals. Louisiana's constitution, the longest of all, though dating only from 1921 has undergone more than 400 amendments. The California constitution of 1879, second longest, has been amended more than 300 times; and the South Carolina constitution of 1895, another of the longer documents, has undergone more than 200 amendments.[46] Georgia's long constitution of 1877 was amended 301 times before its replacement by a new instrument in 1945.[47] It is worthy of note that in some of the longest constitutions much of the textual matter is actually in the nature of special legislation, many provisions applying to but a single city or town. This appears to have been particularly true in Georgia and South Carolina, in each of which a large percentage of the amendments have been of a similar special-legislation character. The necessity in such cases of securing approval of the voters of the state before change can be made in legislative matter of local application emphasizes the folly of attempting to deal with individual units of local government by constitutional provision.[48]

---

electors voting," and this has been interpreted by the courts to mean a majority of the votes cast in the election at which the amendment is submitted. *State v. Powell*, 77 Miss. 543 (1900). Indiana's constitution provides for ratification by a majority of the "electors of the state." For many years the Indiana supreme court interpreted this provision to mean a majority of those voting in the election, but in 1935 the court modified its former stand and held that the required vote for ratification was only a majority of those voting on the amendment. *State v. Swift*, 69 Ind. 505 (1880); *In re Todd*, 208 Ind. 168 (1935).

[46] Cf. *The Book of the States*, 1964-65, p. 12.

[47] Alden L. Powell, "Constitutional Growth and Revision in the South," *Jour. of Politics*, X, 354-384 (May, 1948).

[48] If subject matter of strictly local concern is to be retained in state constitutions, much can be said in favor of an amendment provision similar to that inserted in Georgia's 1945 constitution by a 1956 amendment. Under this provision a proposed amendment which is not of general statewide concern is submitted for ratification only to the voters of the political subdivision or subdivisions directly affected thereby.

In states which permit the proposal of amendments by popular initiative as well as by legislative action, the simple fact that two methods of proposal are available has probably resulted in some instances in a slight increase in the frequency of amendment. Any such increase, however, has never been unduly large. From 1904, when the first popularly-initiated amendment was adopted in Oregon, down through 1938, 109 amendments in eleven states were adopted as the result of initiative proposals. The number in individual states ranged from 3 in Nebraska to 24 in Oregon. Massachusetts and Nevada, though authorizing the use of initiative proposal, had adopted no popularly-proposed amendments.[49]

Revision by Convention[50]

Where a reasonably workable amending procedure exists, individual amendments may serve satisfactorily to keep a constitution up to date over a considerable period of time. Eventually, however, numerous amendments may result in a patchwork of provisions which do not work well together; and where the amending procedure is virtually unworkable many provisions of the constitution inevitably become obsolete. In either case it may be desirable, at intervals of some years, to carry out a general revision of the constitutional document. Though legislative action and popular initiative may serve satisfactorily for the proposal of individual amendments, they are not generally considered to be appropriate means of making a comprehensive revision. Legislatures are elected for other purposes and do not have the necessary time to devote to constitutional revision. Moreover, in American theory the revision of a constitution has traditionally been viewed as a task of such fundamental importance that it should be entrusted only to a body chosen by the people for that specific purpose. Accordingly, it is now possible in every state to assemble a convention of popularly-elected delegates to propose constitutional changes. Approximately three-fourths of the state constitutions expressly provide procedures for calling conventions, and in the remaining states the power to provide for such bodies has been established by practice and judicial interpretation.[51]

Ratification requires a favorable vote in each such subdivision. Determination of whether a proposed amendment is general in nature and, if not, what subdivision or subdivisions are directly affected, is made by the governor, the attorney general, and the secretary of state.

[49] Winston W. Crouch, "The Constitutional Initiative in Operation," *Amer. Polit. Sci. Rev.*, XXXIII, 634-645 (Aug., 1939). See also George H. Hallett, Jr., "The Constitutional Initiative Starts a New Advance," *Nat. Mun. Rev.*, XXIV, 254-257 (May, 1935).

[50] Cf. John P. Wheeler, *The Constitutional Convention: A Manual on its Planning, Organization and Operation.*

[51] During the 1880's, the supreme court of Rhode Island ruled in an advisory opinion that a convention could not lawfully be held in that state, but a half century

The usual procedure in assembling a convention is for the legislature, by resolution, to submit to the voters the question of whether they wish a convention, and then to call the convention only if the voters, in the referendum election, express themselves, by the necessary majority, in its favor.[52] The vote in the legislature required for submitting to the voters the question of calling a convention is ordinarily, but not always, the same as that required in the particular state for legislative proposal of amendments. However, action by two successive legislatures is usually not required even in those states where such a requirement applies to amendments.[53] Several constitutions provide that the question of calling a convention shall be submitted to the voters at regular intervals. Thus, the question is to be submitted in Maryland, Missouri, New York, Ohio, and Oklahoma every twenty years; in Michigan every sixteen years; in Iowa every ten years; and in New Hampshire, where the convention is the only means of proposing constitutional changes, every seven years. In several of these states the constitutional provision is merely to the general effect that the question "shall be submitted," thereby presumably imposing a duty enforceable against state election officials. However, the duty of submitting the question is imposed specifically in Maryland upon the legislature and in Missouri upon the secretary of state. Alaska requires submission of the question by the secretary of state at the end of any ten-year period during which a convention has not been held, and each ten years thereafter; and in Hawaii it is the duty of the lieutenant governor to submit the question at the end of any ten-year period during which it has not been submitted by the legislature.

The vote required for popular approval of a convention call is in most instances either a majority of the votes cast on the question or a majority of those cast in the election, several states having a different requirement from that for ratification of amendments. A proposal for a convention having been approved by the voters, the actual "call" therefore is issued by the legislature in the form of a statutory enactment. This act, except insofar as the matters are covered by constitutional provision, fixes the time and place (which is usually the state capital) of the convention, prescribes the

---

later the court abandoned that view. *In re the Constitutional Convention,* 14 R. I. 649 (1883); *In re the Constitutional Convention,* 55 R. I. 56 (1935). Cf. Clifford C. Hubbard, "The Issue of Constitutional Amendment in Rhode Island," *Amer. Polit. Sci. Rev.,* XXX, 537-540 (June, 1936). The difficulties, legal and otherwise, which must commonly be overcome in securing constitutional conventions, are discussed in Wilbert L. Hindman, "Road-Blocks to Conventions," *Nat. Mun. Rev.,* XXXVII, 129-132, 144 (Mar., 1948).

[52] In Alaska, Georgia, and Maine the legislature may call a convention without referendum.

[53] Kentucky requires that the convention call be approved by two legislatures even though a single legislature may propose amendments. In Oregon the question of calling a convention may be submitted to the voters by initiative petition as well as by legislative action.

number of members and the manner in which they shall be chosen, and makes provision for members' pay. The number of constitutional conventions which have been held in the different states naturally shows a great deal of variation. About a third of the states, for the most part those of the "younger" group, have had but a single convention each and hence are still operating under their original constitutions as amended. On the other hand, some twenty states have had as many as five conventions and a few have had ten or more.[54] In all, some 200 state constitutional convention: have been held, though of course some of the instruments framed or revised by these bodies were rejected by the voters when submitted for their approval.

The composition of the constitutional convention is in some states prescribed by constitutional provision and in others left to legislative determination. Conventions have varied in size from less than a hundred members to more than four hundred.[55] Members are ordinarily elected from state legislative districts (representative or senatorial), though in some instances they are chosen from counties or congressional districts. Occasionally a part of the membership is elected at large. The Missouri convention of 1943-44, for example, consisted of eighty-three members— fifteen elected at large and sixty-eight from state senatorial districts.[56] Conventions customarily organize themselves into committees, each of which is charged with primary responsibility for revising particular parts— commonly one or more articles—of the constitution. The "draft" revisions made by the various committees are then considered by the convention as a whole, which of course must approve the complete revision in its final form.

Some conventions, and especially several of the most recent ones, have been vastly aided in their work by the advance compilation and publication, primarily for use by the delegates, of information concerning problems with which the convention will be confronted. This preparatory work, usually done by competent researchers, has been variously sponsored by "constitutional convention committees" established by the legislature or governor, and by other public and civic agencies.[57] Preliminary to the Illinois convention of 1920-22, for example, the state legislative ref-

[54] The number of conventions held in each state down to 1955 is indicated in a table in *The Book of the States*, 1956-57, pp. 70-74.

[55] Cf. Arthur W. Bromage, *State Government and Administration in the United States* (Harper, New York, 1936), 86.

[56] The constitution framed by this convention was ratified by the voters in 1945. On the convention and the new constitution, see Charlton F. Chute, "The New Missouri Constitution," *The Book of the States*, 1945-46, pp. 81-84; William L. Bradshaw, "Missouri's Proposed New Constitution," *Amer. Polit. Sci. Rev.*, XXXIX, 61-65 (Feb., 1945); Tess Loeb, "Constitution by Convention," *Nat. Mun. Rev.*, XXXIII, 14-16, 26 (Jan., 1944).

[57] Preparatory research activities in representative states are described in Kimbrough Owen, "Blazing the Constitutional Trail," *Nat. Mun. Rev.*, XXXVII, 140-144 (Mar., 1948).

erence bureau prepared a series of fifteen "constitutional convention bulletins" on as many subjects for use by the convention. The reports of the New York Constitutional Convention Committee preparatory to that state's convention of 1938 comprise twelve volumes totalling some 8,000 pages. For the Missouri convention of 1943-44 eight convention "manuals" were prepared under the auspices of a statewide Committee for the Revision of the Missouri Constitution.[58] A Constitutional Convention Committee prepared materials for the Hawaiian convention of 1950; and the Alaska Statehood Committee contracted with a professional research organization to prepare a series of twelve studies for that state's convention of 1955-56. In anticipation of Michigan's convention of 1961-62, the governor appointed a Constitutional Convention Preparatory Commission representative of business, labor, agriculture, and other groups. This commission established a research staff for the purpose of preparing studies and reports on problems with which the convention would have to deal. The research staff undertook the preparation of eighteen studies relating to such matters as the bill of rights, the elective franchise, the legislature, the executive branch, the judiciary, local government, and taxation. Most of these studies were completed, printed, and distributed to delegates either before the meeting of the convention or shortly after its opening.[59] Today there appears to be general recognition of the fact that background research and preparation of materials for use of the delegates are essential if a constitutional convention is to perform its work most effectively.[60]

A problem which confronts the convention at the conclusion of its labors is that as to whether it shall submit its recommendations to the voters in the form of a revised *constitution* to be voted on as a single proposition, or as a series of proposals or amendments to be voted on separately. In support of the latter plan it is sometimes pointed out that a new constitution submitted as a whole for a straight "yes or no" vote may be defeated by the combined negative votes of persons who are opposed only to particular and different provisions of the document. Thus, some may object to the judiciary article, others to the revenue article, and still others to the article on education, but all vote "no" on the constitution, since their only alternative is to vote approval of the provisions to which they are opposed. Were the proposed changes submitted as a series of amendments, so the reasoning goes, there might not be enough opposition to any single amendment to defeat it, or at any rate some of the proposals might gain approval. When a plan of piecemeal submission is followed, however,

---

[58] The respective titles were: *Organization Manual; County Government Manual; Manual on Federal-State Relations; Manual on the Executive Article; Manual on Education; Manual on the Legislative Article; Manual on the Bill of Rights, and Suffrage and Elections;* and *Manual on the Amending Procedure and the Initiative and Referendum.*

[59] Albert L. Sturm, *Constitution-Making in Michigan, 1961-1962,* 32-34.

[60] Cf. Wheeler, *op. cit.,* 15-16.

great care must be exercised to make certain that, if some proposed changes are ratified and others rejected, a balanced and coordinated document will nevertheless remain. Moreover, if the proposed changes constitute anything approximating a thorough revision, the submission of a new document as a single proposition becomes virtually a necessity, except that perhaps a strictly limited number of proposals, if highly controversial and readily separable from the remainder of the constitution, might be submitted separately. The recent ratification of six new constitutions[61] submitted as single propositions exemplifies the practical possibility of securing ratification in this manner.

Limited Conventions

The convention method of proposing constitutional changes is designed primarily for use in the making of general revisions, and most conventions are in no wise restricted with respect to the changes which they may propose. However, "limited constitutional conventions" have been held on various occasions and during recent decades have been used with some frequency. These are bodies which, by the terms of the legislative act submitting to the voters the question of calling the convention, have either (a) had their powers confined to matters specifically stated or (b) been expressly denied power over specific matters. The limited convention, thus, affords a means whereby restrictions may be imposed in advance upon those changes in the existing constitution which may be considered.[62]

During the 1940's limited conventions were employed in Rhode Island to propose, and in Virginia to make,[63] constitutional changes to facilitate voting by members of the armed forces; and conventions were subsequently held in Rhode Island in 1951 and 1955 to propose amendments dealing with other specified subjects. Both Rhode Island and Virginia require that legislative proposals for amendments be approved by two successive legislatures; and resort was had to the limited convention in order to expedite adoption of the specific changes desired by the legislature and at the same time assure that other changes would not be made. Of the amendments proposed by the second and third Rhode Island conventions, some were ratified by the voters and some were rejected.

The convention of 1947 which framed New Jersey's new constitution was forbidden to propose changes in legislative representation—a limitation demanded by small-county legislators who otherwise might

---

[61] Those of Missouri, Georgia, New Jersey, Alaska, Hawaii, and Michigan. Alaskans voted in addition upon two "ordinances" submitted by the constitutional convention.

[62] Cf. "Constitutional Revision by a Restricted Convention," *Minn. Law Rev.*, XXXV, 283-297 (Feb., 1951).

[63] Convention action in Virginia does not require popular ratification.

have stood to lose their dominance in the senate;[64] and in Tennessee a limited convention of 1953 proposed eight amendments, all of which were ratified by the voters.[65] This, it may be noted, was the first time since its adoption in 1870 that the Tennessee constitution had been amended, all attempts at amendment through legislative proposal having failed.

Whether it is within the constitutional competence of a legislature, with voter approval, to restrict the authority of a constitutional convention, will depend upon the situation in the particular state concerned. If the constitution contains a provision which operates as a prohibition of such action, the device of course may not be used. But in states whose constitutions contain no provision regarding constitutional conventions, and in those with provisions containing nothing which may be construed as a prohibition, the limited convention would appear to be quite in order.[66] The legality of the 1945 Virginia convention was specifically upheld by the state supreme court.[67] In Tennessee, the supreme court in 1949 upheld convention limitations;[68] and under one of the amendments proposed by the limited convention of 1953 the constitution of that state now expressly provides that a convention may be called to propose changes in the constitution or "any specified part or parts of it." On the other hand, Alaska's constitution expressly forbids the imposition of limitations.

Revisory Commissions

An alternative to convention revision of state constitutions is revision by commission.[69] Under this plan, in its usual form, a special commission is established by legislative action to prepare a revision and report the same to the legislature.[70] The legislature may then submit the revision to

[64] Cf. Bennett M. Rich, "A New Constitution for New Jersey," *Amer. Polit. Sci. Rev.*, XLI, 1126-1129 (Dec., 1947).

[65] H. L. Trewhitt, "Tennessee Amends Her Constitution," *State Govt.*, XXVII, 119-122, 128 (June, 1954). A more extensive account of the Tennessee convention is to be found in Tip H. Allen, Jr., and Coleman B. Ransone, Jr., *Constitutional Revision in Theory and Practice*, Chaps. 2-4.

[66] Walter F. Dodd, "State Constitutional Conventions and State Legislative Power," *Vanderbilt Law Rev.*, II, 27-34 (Dec., 1948). For earlier expressions of views on the matter generally, see John A. Jameson, *A Treatise on Constitutional Conventions* (4th ed.), 362 ff; Walter F. Dodd, *Revision and Amendment of State Constitutions*, Chap. 3.

[67] *Staples v. Gilmer*, 183 Va. 613 (1945).

[68] *Cummings v. Beeler*, 189 Tenn. 151 (1949). Cf. Henry N. Williams, "The Calling of a Limited Constitutional Convention," *Tenn. Law Rev.*, XXI, 249-256 (Apr., 1950).

[69] Cf. W. Brooke Graves, ed., *Major Problems in State Constitutional Revision*, Chap. 6; Sturm, *Methods of State Constitutional Reform*, Chap. 6; Bennett M. Rich, "Revision by Commission," *Nat. Mun. Rev.*, XL, 201-206 (Apr., 1951); Lloyd M. Short, "Constitutional Revision for Minnesota," *State Govt.*, XXIII, 97-99 (May, 1950). A commission may be used for suggesting individual amendments as well as general revisions.

[70] Some commissions have been established by the governor rather than by

the voters, with whatever changes it may see fit to make therein, under its constitutional power to propose amendments. It is to be emphasized that under the commission plan the legislature retains complete control over the changes to be referred to the voters, exercising both revisory and veto authority over commission action. Though no constitution expressly authorizes revision by commission, there appears to be no constitutional bar to the legislature's employment of such an advisory agency to aid it in carrying out its constitutional function of initiating amendments for submission to the electorate. Professor Albert Sturm reports that during the first half of the present century constitutional commissions of various types were employed 21 times by 15 states.[71] Since 1950 commissions of one kind or another have been used in a growing number of states, including Kansas, Kentucky, New York, North Carolina, Oregon, Pennsylvania, and Wisconsin.[72]

The commission method of revision is well illustrated by the procedure followed in framing Georgia's new constitution of 1945. The Georgia revision commission consisted of twenty-three members: the governor, the president of the senate, the speaker of the house of representatives, three members of the senate appointed by the president, five members of the house appointed by the speaker, a justice of the supreme court and a judge of the court of appeals designated by their respective courts, the attorney-general, the state auditor, and eight members appointed by the governor. The appointive members were required to include two judges of the superior courts, three practicing lawyers, and three laymen. Subcommittees were established to make preliminary studies of designated articles, public hearings were held, and experts were consulted. The revision prepared by the commission was reported to the legislature, which made several changes.[73] The legislature then submitted the final revision to the voters in the form of a single amendment to the constitution of 1877, which struck out all of the old constitution after the preamble and inserted the articles of the new instrument.

Certain advantages are claimed for the commission plan of constitutional revision. In the first place, it is less expensive than the convention

legislative action. In such cases it is usual for the commission to report its recommendations to the governor who may then, if he wishes, transmit them to the legislature.

[71] Sturm, *Methods of State Constitutional Reform*, 126.

[72] A tabular analysis of commissions established in the various states, down to 1960, is to be found in Graves, ed., *op. cit.*, 90-91. An excellent report of one recent commission is Walter E. Sandelius, *Report of the Second Commission on Revision of the Kansas Constitution Submitted to the Governor and the Legislature of the State of Kansas* (Gov't'l. Research Center, Univ. of Kan., Lawrence, 1963).

[73] Albert B. Saye, "Georgia's Proposed New Constitution," *Amer. Polit. Sci. Rev.*, XXXIX, 459-463 (June, 1945). A case study of the Georgia commission is reported in Allen and Ransone, *op. cit.*, Chaps. 5-7. See also Albert B. Saye, ed., *Records of the Commission of 1943-1944 to Revise the Constitution of Georgia* (2 vols., 1946).

method. Again, the personnel of the commission, selected in most instances by the governor or legislature, should be better qualified for the task of constitutional drafting than are the elected members of the typical convention. This latter factor, together with its relative smallness, should enable the commission to act both more expeditiously and more efficiently than the convention. The objection most frequently voiced to the commission is to the effect that it is undemocratic both because of its small size and because its members have not been elected by the people specifically for the task of constitutional revision. This objection, however, loses much of its weight when it is remembered that the popularly-elected legislature reviews the work of the commission and finally decides what proposals shall be referred to the voters.

If the success of constitutional commissions is to be judged solely on the basis of the number of constitutional revisions drafted by them which have received popular approval, their record is by no means impressive. It appears certain, however, that their efforts on various occasions have resulted directly or indirectly in the adoption of individual amendments or the effecting of improvements in statutory law. Furthermore, commissions serve an important function as educational agencies in informing the public concerning the need for constitutional change.[74] Though there is no reason to believe that the special commission is destined to supplant the convention as the usual agency for revising state constitutions, it seems likely that commissions will be used frequently in the future in connection with both general revisions and less extensive constitutional alterations.[75]

Ratification of Revisions

Revisions prepared by commissions and approved by the legislature must, of course, be submitted to the voters for ratification in the same manner as individual amendments proposed by legislative action. Convention revisions are also usually submitted to popular referendum. This is required by constitutional provision in some states and is the practice in most others. However, in a few states, including Virginia and Louisiana, revisions or amendments framed and approved by conventions become effective without action thereon of the voters. In most states the requirement for ratification of convention proposals is a majority of the votes cast thereon, though some states require a majority of the votes cast in the election. The referendum is in some cases at the general election and in others

[74] Cf. Rich, "Revision by Commission," *loc. cit.*

[75] By having the commission's recommendations reviewed and submitted to the voters by a constitutional convention instead of by the legislature, commission revision might well be employed to supplement rather than supplant the convention system. This procedure would seem to be particularly appropriate in states where the legislature is constitutionally incompetent to propose a general revision for voter action.

at a special election.[76] Use of the special election is particularly desirable in those states which require for ratification a majority vote of those voting in the election. Every person voting in a special election held for this purpose votes on the matter of constitutional revision since that is the only question submitted. Thus the proposed revision cannot meet defeat, as so often happens in such states to amendments submitted at general elections,[77] at the hands of persons who vote in the election but ignore the constitutional question.

The Model State Constitution

In 1921, the National Municipal League published the first edition of a Model State Constitution prepared by the League's Committee on State Government. This document, which has now been revised five times, represents the opinion of some of the country's ablest students of state government as to what the provisions of a state constitution *should* be. "Strictly speaking," as pointed out in the introduction to the sixth edition, "there can be no such thing as a 'Model State Constitution' because there is no model state."[78] This being the case, the model has not been, and is not expected to be, adopted in its entirety by any state. Nevertheless, some of its provisions in original or modified form have been incorporated into recent amendments and revisions. As a source of suggestions, the model is useful both to constitution-makers and to students of government.

Local Charters

Units of local government in the United States, whatever their nature, are created by the respective states, or pursuant to state authority, and possess no inherent powers of self-government. Both the framework of local government and the extent of local powers are subject to state control.[79] The basic laws of the local governments, corresponding to the constitution in the case of the state, emanate from the state, and consist either of enactments of the state legislature or of instruments of government locally framed and adopted under authority of state constitutional provisions. These basic laws are the *charters* of the respective local units, and from what has been said it will be noted that local charters are of two general types—"legislative" and "home-rule." The term *charter* is sometimes used in a restricted sense to include only documents of the

[76] Convention proposals in New Hampshire are referred to the voters in the annual town meetings with the requirement, for ratification, of a two-thirds vote of the qualified voters present and voting on the subject.

[77] See above, "Ratification of Amendments."

[78] National Municipal League, *Model State Constitution* (6th ed., 1963), vii.

[79] See below, Chap. XII, "Legal Nature of Local Units," "Powers of Local Units."

home-rule type. Again, it is at times applied to all fundamental laws governing *municipalities*,[80] but not, except in the few cases of home-rule charters, to the laws governing other types of local units. In this discussion, however, the term is used in a broad sense to mean the basic law prescribing the structure and powers of any unit of local government.

Legislative Charters

A legislative charter consists of all the statutory provisions concerning the structure and powers of a local governmental unit, whether contained in a single legislative enactment or scattered among many. Legislative charters are granted to local units in the various states by four different methods: (1) special legislation; (2) general law; (3) a classification system; and (4) optional laws.

Under the first of these plans each local unit is created by, and has as its charter, a special act of the state legislature. Any subsequent changes in such a charter must, of course, be effected by other special acts amendatory to the first. This was once the prevailing method of granting and amending local-government charters in this country, and it is still commonly used in several eastern and southern states.[81] In practice, however, the special-legislation plan has certain disadvantages, not the least of which is the burden which it imposes upon the legislature; and the constitutions of most states now prohibit the chartering or regulation of local governments in this manner.[82]

Under the second plan, a single statute or code of state-wide application serves as the charter of all local units of a given kind. This plan serves to eliminate undesirable discrimination as between different units, but at the same time prevents the legislature from permitting desirable variations. Counties, townships, and school districts are in many states governed under general codes, and some states use the plan for municipalities and certain types of special districts.

Under the classification system, governmental units of a given type are divided on the basis of population into different classes or groups (usually numbering from three to five), and different statutory provisions are enacted for governing the units of each class. This plan represents a

[80] On the general subject of municipal charters, see Nathan Matthews, *Municipal Charters;* Harold Zink, *Government of Cities in the United States* (Macmillan, New York, rev. ed., 1948), Chap. 7; Charles M. Kneier, *City Government in the United States* (Harper, New York, 3rd ed., 1957), Chap. 5.

[81] The states usually considered as being special-law states are Maine, New Hampshire, Vermont, Connecticut, Rhode Island, Delaware, Maryland, Florida, Georgia, and Tennessee. See Norman N. Gill and Mary S. Benson, "Classes and Forms of Municipal Government," *The Municipal Year Book* (Int. City Mgrs.' Assn., Chicago), 1945, pp. 90-96.

[82] See below, Chap. VIII, for discussion of state constitutional limitations on special legislation.

compromise between special legislation and general codes, permitting more variation of treatment than the latter but less than the former. Many states deal with municipalities on a classification basis, and some classify counties and townships.

The optional-charter system permits local units to make a selection, by popular vote, from among two or more forms of government provided by statute. A substantial number of states, for example, permit most or all of their cities to choose from among the three principal forms of municipal government—mayor-council, commission, and manager; and several states—including Montana, New York, North Carolina, North Dakota, Oregon, and Virginia—provide optional forms of government for counties.

In conclusion it may be noted that a particular state does not ordinarily use any single method of charter-granting to the complete exclusion of all others. Most states employ *primarily* either special legislation, general laws, or classification; but many provide, as alternatives, either optional-charter laws, or the privilege of framing home-rule charters, or both.

Home-Rule Charters

Nearly half of the states have constitutional provisions under which some or all cities are permitted to frame and adopt their own charters, and thirteen states extend a similar privilege to some or all counties.[83] These home-rule provisions confer upon the local units concerned a substantial degree of freedom in determining the structure of their government and the manner in which they will regulate matters of local concern. A home-rule charter is usually framed by a charter commission, sometimes called a "board of freeholders," which is in all but name a miniature constitutional convention. The commission varies in size from three to twenty-five members, with a membership of around fifteen being fairly common. Members are ordinarily elected by popular vote, but in a few instances are appointed by the courts. An election for the choice of a charter commission may usually be called either by the governing body of the local unit concerned (city council or county board) or by initiative petition, though in some states there must be a preliminary referendum on the question of whether a commission shall be chosen. Home-rule charters must in every instance be referred to the local voters and receive their approval, by a stipulated majority, before becoming effective. Charter amendments may in most states be proposed either by the local governing body or by popular initiative. However proposed, amendments, like the charters themselves, must be ratified by the voters before taking effect.[84] Home-rule charters are ordinarily published in pamphlet form, and

[83] See below, Chap. III, "Municipal Home Rule," "County Home Rule."

[84] Cf. William Anderson and Edward W. Weidner, *American City Government* (Holt, New York, rev. ed., 1950), 145-155; Austin F. Macdonald, *American*

a copy of any such charter may usually be secured from the clerk of the city or county concerned.

Model Charters

Similar in purpose to the Model State Constitution are the model charters prepared under the auspices of the National Municipal League. The *Model City Charter,* now in its sixth edition, and the *Model County Charter,* suggest provisions which, in the opinion of students of local government, might appropriately be included in the basic laws of local governmental units.

REFERENCES

ALLEN, Tip H., Jr., and RANSONE, Coleman B., Jr., *Constitutional Revision in Theory and Practice* (Bur. of Pub. Admin., Univ. of Ala., University, Ala., 1962).

BURDINE, J. Alton, "Basic Materials for the Study of State Constitutions and State Constitutional Development," *Amer. Polit. Sci. Rev.,* XLVIII, 1140-1147 (Dec., 1954).

CALLENDER, Clarence N., CARTER, Edward W., and ROHLFING, Charles C., eds., "The State Constitution of the Future," *Annals of Amer. Acad. of Polit. and Soc. Sci.,* CLXXXI (Philadelphia, Sept., 1935).

CAPE, William H., *Constitutional Revision in Kansas* (Govtl. Research Center, Univ. of Kan., Lawrence, 1958).

———, *Constitutional Revision in South Dakota* (Govt'l. Research Bur., State Univ. of S. D., Vermillion, 1957).

Columbia University Legislative Drafting Research Fund, *Constitutions of the United States: National and State* (2 vols., Oceana Publications, Dobbs Ferry, N. Y., 1962).

———, *Index Digest of State Constitutions* (Oceana Press, New York, 2nd ed., 1959).

CUSTARD, Leila R., *Bills of Rights in American History* (Univ. of Southern Calif. Press, Los Angeles, 1942).

DEALEY, James Q., *Growth of American State Constitutions* (Ginn, Boston, 1915).

DISHMAN, Robert B., *A New Constitution for New Hampshire?* (Univ. of N. H. Bookstore, Durham, 1956).

———, *State Constitutions: The Shape of the Document* (Nat. Mun. League, New York, 1960).

DODD, Walter F., *The Revision and Amendment of State Constitutions* (Johns Hopkins Press, Baltimore, 1910).

City Government and Administration (Crowell, New York, 6th ed., 1956), 60-72. In a few states home-rule charters, after popular approval thereof, must be approved by a designated state authority (legislature or governor). In practice, however, such state approval, where required, appears to be granted as a matter of course.

GRAVES, W. Brooke, ed., *Major Problems in State Constitutional Revision* (Pub. Admin. Service, Chicago, 1960).

HOAR, Roger S., *Constitutional Conventions: Their Nature, Powers, and Limitations* (Little, Brown, Boston, 1917).

IRVINE, Charlotte, and KRESKY, Edward M., *How to Study a State Constitution* (Nat. Mun. League, New York, 1962).

JAMESON, John A., *A Treatise on Constitutional Conventions: Their History, Powers, and Modes of Proceeding* (Callaghan, Chicago, 4th ed., 1887).

KEITH, John P., *Methods of Constitutional Revision* (Bur. of Mun. Research, Univ. of Tex., Austin, 1949).

MATTHEWS, Nathan, *Municipal Charters* (Harvard Univ. Press, Cambridge, 1914).

McCARTHY, Sister M. Barbara, *The Widening Scope of American Constitutions* (Catholic Univ. of America, Washington, 1928).

McCLURE, Wallace, *State Constitution-Making with Especial Reference to Tennessee* (Marshall & Bruce Co., Nashville, 1916).

National Municipal League, *Model City Charter* (Nat. Mun. League, New York, 6th ed., 1963).

————, *Model County Charter* (Nat. Mun. League, New York, 1956).

————, *Model State Constitution* (Nat. Mun. League, New York, 6th ed., 1963).

O'ROURKE, Vernon A., and CAMPBELL, Douglas W., *Constitution-Making in a Democracy: Theory and Practice in New York State* (Johns Hopkins Press, Baltimore, 1943).

PELEKOUDAS, Lois M., ed., *The Illinois Constitution* (Inst. of Govt. and Pub. Affairs, Univ. of Ill., Urbana, 1962).

RANKIN, Robert S., *State Constitutions: The Bill of Rights* (Nat. Mun. League, New York, 1960).

STURM, Albert L., *Constitution-Making in Michigan, 1961-1962* (Inst. of Pub. Admin., Univ. of Mich., Ann Arbor, 1963).

————, *Methods of State Constitutional Reform* (Univ. of Mich. Press, Ann Arbor, 1954).

THORPE, Francis N., ed., *The Federal and State Constitutions, Colonial Charters, and other Organic Laws of the States, Territories, and Colonies now or heretofore Forming the United States of America* (7 vols., U. S. Govt. Printing Office, Washington, 1909). This compilation, published under congressional authorization, includes for each state both the current constitution as of the date of publication and all earlier constitutions, if any. Also included are various other fundamental laws such as congressional enabling acts authorizing organized territories to frame state constitutions and congressional resolutions admitting territories to statehood.

UHL, Raymond, STOUDEMIRE, Robert H., and SHERRILL, George R., *Constitutional Conventions: Organization, Powers, Functions, and Procedures* (Bur. of Pub. Admin., Univ. of S. C., Columbia, 1951).

United States Bureau of the Census, *State Constitutions: A Bibliography* (U. S. Bur. of the Census, Washington, 1944).

University of Chicago Libraries, Document Section, *Official Publications relating to American State Constitutional Conventions* (Wilson, New York, 1936). Bibliography.

WHEELER, JOHN P., *The Constitutional Convention: A Manual on its Planning, Organization and Operation* (Nat. Mun. League, New York, 1961).

————, ed., *Salient Issues of Constitutional Revision* (Nat. Mun. League, New York, 1961).

II

Intergovernmental Relations

2

The States in
the Federal Union

Nature of the Federal System

American government, as concerns the interrelations of nation and states, is federal in nature. A federal system is one wherein governmental powers are divided by the terms of a written constitution between a general government and the governments of territorial subdivisions. Federalism involves the operation at the same time and within the same territory of two governments, the one central or general and the other of a more localized character, each of which is supreme within a sphere marked out for it by the constitution. Since the system postulates constitutional protection of each government from infringement by the other, a federal constitution in its truest form will not be amendable by either the general government or the subdivisional governments alone, but only by the concurrent action of both.[1]

The fundamental purpose of federalism is to provide for centralized control over matters of general concern to the nation as a whole, while at the same time permitting the subdivisional governments to regulate matters of more localized concern. In actually setting up the distribution of powers, it is customary for the framers of a federal constitution to *delegate* to either the central government or the subdivisional governments certain powers by positive enumeration, and to *reserve* to the other government or governments authority to act in all other matters.[2] The

[1] Amendments to the United States Constitution must be proposed by a national agency—Congress or constitutional convention—and ratified by three-fourths of the states acting either through their legislatures or through ratifying conventions.

[2] Except, of course, that power to take action of certain types may be denied to *both* the general and the subdivisional governments by bills of rights or other constitutional prohibitions.

33

more common plan, and the one followed in the United States Constitution, is that of establishing the central government as an organ of delegated powers and reserving all other powers to the subdivisions. In accordance with this procedure, powers are delegated to the various branches of our national government and it is provided, in the Tenth Amendment, that "The powers not delegated to the United States by the Constitution, nor prohibited by it to the states, are reserved to the states respectively, or to the people." It should be noted in this connection that the delegation of a particular power to the national government does not deny to the states the right to exercise the same power within their respective spheres, unless the power is expressly prohibited to the states or is such that it can be exercised only by the national government. It thus happens that many powers, such as that of taxation, may be exercised by the national and state governments concurrently.

No matter how carefully a federal constitution is framed, its delegations and reservations cannot be sufficiently detailed to prevent disputes arising, on occasion, as to whether the power to act in a particular situation belongs to the general government or to the subdivisions. There is needed, therefore, an official "umpire" to settle such controversies, and this function in the United States is performed by the United States Supreme Court. The nature of the method followed in distributing powers under the United States Constitution—i.e., delegation to the national government and reservation to the states—would indicate that doubts regarding the location of power under the constitution should be resolved in favor of the states and against the central government. In practice, however, the Supreme Court, itself an organ of the national government, has throughout most of our history given an extremely liberal interpretation to national powers; and as a result there has been a notable increase through the years, largely without constitutional amendment, in the powers exercised by the national government.[3] Nevertheless, the rule that the national government possesses only those powers *delegated* to it either expressly or by implication, and that all other powers are *reserved* to the states, still stands as a cardinal principle of American constitutional law and government.[4]

Admission of States to the Union

The thirteen original states became members of the Federal Union by ratifying the United States Constitution. Power to admit new states is vested by the Constitution in Congress, subject to the provision that no state may be erected within the jurisdiction of any other state, or formed by the junction of two or more states or parts of states, except with the

[3] See below, "Expansion of National Power."
[4] Cf. below, Chap. VIII, "Powers of the State Legislature: Residual Character."

consent of the legislature of each state concerned.[5] Of the thirty-seven states admitted under this power, five were carved from older states;[6] Texas was an independent republic prior to its admission; and California was admitted without passing through the customary territorial stage. Each of the remaining thirty states had been an organized federal territory prior to its admission. The usual procedure in these cases was for the territorial legislature to petition Congress for the passage of an "enabling act" authorizing the inhabitants of the territory to hold a convention for framing a proposed state constitution. Such an act having been passed and a convention having been held, the constitution framed therein, after approval by the territorial voters, was submitted to Congress. If Congress found the proposed constitution acceptable, it then adopted a joint resolution, sometimes called a "statehood bill," admitting the territory into the Union as a state. Some territories, including those of Alaska and Hawaii, have framed proposed constitutions for submission to Congress without waiting for the passage of enabling legislation. Though this is at variance with the usual procedure, the passage of a statehood bill validates whatever procedure has been followed in framing the constitution concerned.[7]

No new state was admitted to the Union after New Mexico and Arizona were admitted in 1912, until the admission of Alaska and Hawaii in 1959. The peoples of the two latter territories had long sought admission, and proposed statehood legislation had several times been introduced in Congress. Opposition based on various factors, however, had succeeded, year after year, in defeating these proposals.[8] Never before had a new state been admitted which was not contiguous, geographically, to older states or to federal territory. Alaska, though having an area more than twice the size of Texas and being rich in natural resources, had relatively few people; and the populations of both territories were of diverse composition. Certain business interests which felt that they would be adversely affected by statehood also stood in opposition. Gradually, however, objections were overcome and statehood forces gained strength. Beginning in 1944, the national platforms of the Democratic party in-

[5] *Const. of U.S.*, art. IV, sec. 3.

[6] Vermont from New York, Kentucky and West Virginia from Virginia, Tennessee from North Carolina, and Maine from Massachusetts. In the case of West Virginia, which was admitted during the Civil War, the consent of the Virginia legislature was not obtained. However, consent was given by a newly-organized body in the western portion of the state which claimed to be the legal legislature, and this consent was considered by Congress to be sufficient. See John M. Mathews, *The American Constitutional System* (2nd ed.), 52.

[7] Cf. *Ibid.*, 51-57.

[8] Arguments for and against admission are considered in Marvin Meade, "Statehood for Alaska and Hawaii," *Your Govt.* (Govtl. Research Center, Univ. of Kan.), Vol. VII, No. 7 (Mar. 15, 1952); Ernest Gruening, "Statehood for Alaska," *Harper's Mag.*, Vol. CCVI, No. 1236 (May, 1953), 72-77; Symposium, "The Question of Granting Statehood to Hawaii," *Cong. Digest*, XXXVIII, 3-32 (Jan., 1959).

cluded planks urging immediate statehood for both territories, and in this demand the Republicans joined in 1956. A statehood bill for Alaska was finally enacted in July of 1958, and one for Hawaii in March of 1959; and both were admitted as states during the latter year by presidential proclamations issued pursuant to the statehood legislation.

At present the only remaining territory which appears to be a potential candidate at some future date for statehood (or perhaps for independence on the Philippine model) is Puerto Rico. Both major political parties, at one time or another, have declared in favor of eventual statehood for this island possession. Since 1952, however, Puerto Rico has operated under a "commonwealth" constitution which was framed by the island's inhabitants and which provides for a substantial measure of self-government in internal affairs. Another factor which tends to lessen the demand of Puerto Ricans for statehood is their exemption, under present law, from the federal income tax. Though there is perennial discussion of the possibility of erecting as separate states certain metropolitan areas within the present United States, such as those containing New York City and Chicago, action of this nature, as has been noted, would require the consent of the legislatures of the present states concerned as well as of Congress, and seems unlikely in the foreseeable future.

Reciprocal Duties of Nation and States

American federalism presupposes that the nation and the states owe certain duties and obligations to each other. Since the Constitution contemplates, in the words of the Supreme Court, "an indestructible Union, composed of indestructible States,"[9] the states owe to the nation a duty to refrain from secession—a duty enforced by arms in the Civil War—and the nation owes to the states the correlative duty of respecting their territorial integrity. The latter duty is given constitutional recognition in the provision, previously noted, that no state or part thereof may be used by Congress in the formation of a new state without the consent of the state legislature. Other duties owed by the states to the nation include those of holding elections for representatives and senators in Congress, choosing presidential electors, and considering amendments to the United States Constitution when duly proposed by Congress or a national constitutional convention.[10] The national government, on its part, is obliged to guarantee to every state a republican form of government; and to protect each state against invasion and, on proper application by the state government, against domestic violence.[11]

[9] *Texas* v. *White*, 7 Wall. 700 (1869), 725.
[10] Cf. *Const. of U.S.*, art. I, secs. 2-4; art. II, sec. 1; art. V; amdt. XVII.
[11] *Ibid.*, art. IV, sec. 4.

Guarantee to States of Republican Government

The "republican" form of government which the nation is obliged to guarantee to the states is not defined in the Constitution. However, James Madison, one of the most influential members of the convention which framed the Constitution, defined a republic in the famous *Federalist* papers as "a government which derives all its powers directly or indirectly from the great body of the people, and is administered by persons holding their offices during pleasure, for a limited period, or during good behavior."[12] Madison referred to the then *existing* state governments—most of which consisted of a popularly-elected legislature, a governor chosen by the legislature, and courts whose members were elected by the legislature or appointed by the governor—as being republican in character. He pointed out also that "other republican forms" might undoubtedly be substituted for those then existing and be entitled to protection under the constitutional guarantee, the purpose of which was to prevent "aristocratic or monarchial innovations."[13] These contemporary interpretations, reinforced by the generally accepted meaning of the term *republican,* indicate rather clearly that what the Constitution intends is an assurance that the states shall maintain *popular* governments, in the sense of governments under which laws are made by the people, either directly or through representatives of their choosing, and also perhaps in which the chief executive is elected by the people directly or indirectly.[14] The duty of guaranteeing to the states a republican form of government is imposed by the Constitution merely upon the United States, with no indication as to what branch or branches of the government shall be responsible for its performance. However, the Supreme Court has taken the view that the question of what is and what is not republican government is political rather than judicial in nature, and that its determination therefore rests not with the courts but with Congress.[15] It is also incumbent upon Congress, or the president acting under congressional authorization, to enforce the constitutional guarantee. The House of Representatives and the Senate have means of enforcement ready at hand in their constitutional power to deny seats to members-elect from any state whose government they deem nonrepublican in form; and the President could, if necessary, use the armed forces of the nation to carry out the guarantee. One interesting problem under the constitutional provision arose in a case challenging the use of the popular initiative and referendum by the states. It

[12] *The Federalist* (Tudor, New York, 1937), No. 39.

[13] *Ibid.,* No. 43.

[14] Cf. Hugh E. Willis, *Constitutional Law in the United States,* 451.

[15] *Luther* v. *Borden,* 7 How. 1 (1849); *Pacific States Telephone and Telegraph Co.* v. *Oregon,* 223 U.S. 118 (1912).

was argued that these devices, in permitting the people of the states to legislate directly rather than through elected representatives, were *democratic* rather than *republican* in character, and therefore unconstitutional. The Supreme Court, however, on the ground that the question was political rather than judicial, dismissed the case;[16] and the houses of Congress, in continuing to admit members-elect from states employing the initiative and referendum, have indicated that they do not consider those devices nonrepublican in character.[17]

Protection of States against Invasion and Domestic Violence

The duty of the United States to protect member states against invasion is an absolute one, to be performed without waiting for a request from the state or states concerned. In the case of action by foreign forces, the invasion of any state would, of course, constitute an invasion of the United States which the national government would of necessity take measures to repel even without the constitutional requirement.

With respect to internal disorder or domestic violence, the national government is duty-bound to act only upon application from the state authorities, such application to be made by the legislature of the state concerned or, when the legislature is not in session and cannot be convened, by the governor. Applications of this nature have not been numerous, though on some occasions state authorities have felt themselves incompetent to deal with internal disturbances and have requested federal assistance. For example, in the case of Dorr's rebellion in the early 1840's, the governor of Rhode Island asked the President for military assistance in preventing the seizure of power by a rival government led by Dorr. When it became known that the President intended to act in support of the existing government under a statute empowering him, on application of a state, to employ the militia of any other state or states in suppressing insurrection, the uprising collapsed.[18] It is to be noted that, while the Constitution *requires* national action to suppress internal disorder only upon state request, the national government *may* act on its own initiative and responsibility whenever necessary to protect federal activities or individual rights guaranteed by the Constitution. Thus, without request from state authorities or even over their protest, the national government may take steps to quell domestic disorder or violence if such action is necessary to remove obstructions to the flow of interstate commerce or the mails,[19] or to protect federal property or enforce federal

---

[16] *Pacific States Telephone and Telegraph Co.* v. *Oregon,* cited above.
[17] On the nature and use of the initiative and referendum, see below, Chap. VI.
[18] See *Luther* v. *Borden,* cited above.
[19] *In re Debs,* 158 U.S. 564 (1895).

law. For the suppression of disorder, the President may use either the National Guard units of the respective states, or regular federal troops, or both. In 1957, for example, President Eisenhower employed both federalized units of the Arkansas National Guard and regular federal troops for the suppression of disorder arising in Little Rock in connection with school desegregation. In 1962 United States marshals, the Mississippi National Guard, and federal troops were used by President Kennedy to enforce a federal court order requiring the admission of a Negro student to the University of Mississippi. And in 1963 efforts of the governor of Alabama to use the National Guard of that state to prevent desegregation of the University of Alabama and public schools in several Alabama cities were blocked when the President federalized the guard units concerned.

Constitutional Limitations on the States

Although, as we have seen,[20] the federal bill of rights restricts the national government only, the United States Constitution contains, in the original document and various amendments, numerous limitations upon the states. Most of those in the original constitution are to be found in section 10 of Article I. Some of the provisions are in the nature of absolute prohibitions of state action, whereas others permit the states to act but only with congressional consent. Thus, no state may without the consent of Congress lay any duty on imports or exports except such as may be absolutely necessary for executing its inspection laws. Moreover, any such levies are subject to revision and control by Congress, and the net proceeds therefrom must be paid into the United States treasury. Again, no state may, without congressional consent, lay any tonnage duty; keep troops or ships of war in time of peace; enter into any agreement or compact with another state[21] or with a foreign power; or engage in war, unless actually invaded or in such imminent danger as will not admit of delay. Among the absolute prohibitions are the provisions that no state shall enter into any treaty, alliance, or confederation; coin money; emit bills of credit (i.e., paper money); make anything but gold and silver coin a tender in payment of debts; or pass any bill of attainder,[22] ex post facto law,[23] or law impairing the obligation of contracts.

Impairment of Contracts

The contract provision is designed to prevent a state legislature from enacting any law applicable to preexisting contracts which would

---

[20] Above, Chap. I, "The Bill of Rights."

[21] See below, Chap. IV, "Interstate Compacts."

[22] A bill of attainder is a legislative act which imposes a criminal penalty without a judicial trial.

[23] On the nature of of ex post facto laws, see above, Chap. I, footnote 18.

make it impossible, or more difficult, for a party to such a contract to enforce against the other party or parties thereto the obligations due him thereunder. The contracts thus protected against impairment are not only those between individuals, but include as well those to which the state itself, or one of its governmental subdivisions, or a corporation, may be a party. In the famous Dartmouth College Case,[24] it was held by the Supreme Court that a charter granted by the state to a private corporation is a contract between the state and the corporation within the meaning of the constitutional provision. Therefore, a corporate charter may not be changed by the state during the term for which it runs unless the corporation gives its consent or unless, at the time the charter is granted, the state specifically reserves the right to make changes therein.

It should be noted, however, that, notwithstanding constitutional protection against impairment, contracts are merely a form of property and, like all other property, are subject to reasonable regulation by the state under the police power.[25] Also to be noted is the fact that, unlike charters to private corporations, charters granted by the state to corporations of a *public* or governmental nature do not enjoy the status of contracts within the meaning of the impairment clause.[26] As far as this provision of the United States Constitution is concerned, state legislatures are therefore free to modify or revoke at their pleasure the charters of municipalities and other local governmental units.[27]

The Fourteenth Amendment

The most important limitations imposed upon the states by the various amendments to the United States Constitution are contained in the first section of the Fourteenth Amendment, reading as follows:[28]

All persons born or naturalized in the United States, and subject to the jurisdiction thereof, are citizens of the United States and of the state wherein they reside. No state shall make or enforce any law which shall abridge the privileges or immunities of citizens of the United States; nor shall any state deprive any

[24] *Trustees of Dartmouth College* v. *Woodward*, 4 Wheat. 518 (1819).
[25] *Fertilizing Co.* v. *Hyde Park*, 97 U.S. 659 (1878); *Home Building and Loan Assn.* v. *Blaisdell*, 290 U.S. 398 (1934).
[26] *Hunter* v. *Pittsburgh*, 207 U.S. 161 (1907).
[27] For a comprehensive discussion of the contract clause, see Benjamin F. Wright, *The Contract Clause of the Constitution.* See also John G. Hervey, "The Impairment of Obligation of Contracts," *Annals of Amer. Acad. of Polit. and Soc. Sci.,* CXCV (Jan., 1938), Supp., 87-120; Robert L. Hale, "The Supreme Court and the Contract Clause," *Harvard Law Rev.,* LVII, 512-557, 621-674, 852-892 (Apr., May, July, 1944). Much the same protection of contractual rights against state impairment that was at one time afforded only by the contract clause is now available also under the "due-process" clause of the Fourteenth Amendment.
[28] The other principal limitations are those of the Fifteenth, Nineteenth, and Twenty-fourth Amendments concerning the voting privilege. These are discussed in Chap. V, below.

person of life, liberty, or property, without due process of law; nor deny to any person within its jurisdiction the equal protection of the laws.

Analysis of this section discloses a definition of citizenship, followed by three provisions designed to protect civil rights. These latter provisions are commonly referred to as (1) the "privileges-and-immunities" clause, (2) the "due-process" clause, and (3) the "equal-protection" clause. The amendment was adopted at the close of the Civil War to confer citizenship upon the recently liberated Negroes and to protect the freedmen in their civil rights; and apparently it was generally supposed, at the outset, that the provisions would be used for no other purpose. In its first opinion construing the amendment, the Supreme Court itself said of the equal-protection clause: "We doubt very much whether any action of a state not directed by way of discrimination against the Negroes as a class, or on account of their race, will ever be held to come within the purview of this provision."[29] Subsequent developments, however, demonstrated this to be a rash prophecy indeed. The various provisions of the amendment have now been interpreted by the high court in well over a thousand opinions, and in many cases state action has been invalidated under the due-process and equal-protection clauses.[30] Only a comparatively small proportion of these cases have involved Negroes. Members of all races, and corporations as well as natural persons, have long since been brought within the purview of the amendment by judicial interpretation. Each of the three civil-rights clauses of the amendment will now be considered in turn.

Privileges and Immunities of United States Citizens

In interpreting the privileges-and-immunities clause[31] the Supreme Court from the beginning has emphasized the fact that the Fourteenth Amendment distinguishes between United States citizenship and state citizenship,[32] and that it is only the privileges enjoyed by virtue of the former which are protected against abridgment by state action. In other words, the clause was not designed to protect all personal rights and

[29] *Slaughter-House Cases*, 16 Wall. 36 (1873), 81. Cf. F. Lyman Windolph, "The Two Fourteenth Amendments," *Annals of Amer. Acad. of Polit. and Soc. Sci.*, CXCV (Jan., 1938), Supp., 12-31.

[30] Cf. Windolph, *op. cit.*; William B. Cudlip, "The Function of the States," *Mich. Law Rev.*, XLIII, 95-112 (Aug., 1944).

[31] There is another privileges-and-immunities clause, concerning interstate relations, in Article IV of the Constitution. This latter provision, in order to distinguish it from the one in the Fourteenth Amendment, is often referred to as the "interstate citizenship" clause. See below, Chap. IV, "Interstate Citizenship."

[32] In most instances the two citizenships go together, but there are many United States citizens who reside permanently in the District of Columbia or elsewhere outside the states and are therefore without state citizenship.

privileges against state interference, but only those which are peculiarly related to national, as distinguished from state, citizenship.

The clause was first construed in the famous Slaughter-House Cases,[33] in which certain independent butchers challenged the validity, under the privileges-and-immunities clause, of an act of the Louisiana legislature granting a designated corporation a monopoly of the slaughtering business in New Orleans. The Supreme Court took the view, however, that any right which the complaining butchers might have to engage in slaughtering in New Orleans was a privilege of state rather than United States citizenship, and therefore was not entitled to protection under the constitutional provision specified. In subsequent cases various other alleged rights have been held by the court *not* to be privileges of United States citizenship. Thus, it is not a privilege of national citizenship to use the American flag for advertising purposes, to attend the public schools or a state university, or to be a member of a Greek-letter fraternity while attending a state educational institution.[34] Down to 1935, at least 44 cases in which state statutes were attacked as violating the privileges-and-immunities clause had been taken to the Supreme Court, but in not a single instance had the Court held that the clause had been infringed.[35] In the year mentioned the Court, in the case of Colgate v. Harvey, struck down as violating the provision a Vermont income-tax statute which levied a tax upon interest received by residents of the state from loans made outside the state but not upon that from loans made within the state. Four years later, however, the Colgate case was expressly overruled.[36]

Except as it is necessary in deciding cases, the courts have declined to determine what privileges *are* to be considered as inhering in United States citizenship. In the Slaughter-House Cases, however, the Supreme Court "suggested" certain privileges, among them the following, as being included: the right to travel to the seat of government; free access to seaports; protection by the national government while on the high seas or in a foreign country; use of the navigable waters of the United States; the right to assemble peaceably and petition for redress of grievances; and the right to become a citizen of any state by establishing residence therein. In recent cases some members of the Court have indicated their belief that the privileges of national citizenship include the right to

[33] Cited above. For a discussion of these cases and their historical background, see Mitchell Franklin, "The Foundations and Meaning of the Slaughterhouse Cases," *Tulane Law Rev.*, XVIII, 1-88, 218-262 (Oct., Dec., 1943).

[34] *Halter v. Nebraska*, 205 U.S. 34 (1907); *Cumming v. Board of Education*, 175 U.S. 528 (1899); *Hamilton v. Regents of the University of California*, 293 U.S. 245 (1934); *Waugh v. Board of Trustees*, 237 U.S. 589 (1915).

[35] The cases are listed in a footnote to the dissenting opinion of Mr. Justice Stone in *Colgate v. Harvey*, cited below.

[36] *Colgate v. Harvey*, 296 U.S. 404 (1935); *Madden v. Kentucky*, 309 U.S. 83 (1939).

assemble freely for the discussion of national legislation,[37] and the right to migrate freely from state to state. Thus, in declaring unconstitutional a California statute which made it a misdemeanor to bring into the state, knowing him to be such, an indigent person not a resident thereof, five of the Supreme Court justices held that the act was invalid as an obstruction to interstate commerce, but the other four, in two concurring opinions, preferred to consider it an infringement of the privileges-and-immunities clause.[38]

From what has been said it will be evident that the privileges-and-immunities clause of the Fourteenth Amendment has not operated as an effective check on state action. Indeed, throughout most of its history, the clause has been little more than a dead letter. This does not mean, however, that the states have been permitted to ride roughshod over the rights of citizens, but only that the very broad interpretation given to the due-process and equal-protection clauses has made available under those provisions protection which otherwise might reasonably have been expected under that concerning privileges and immunities.[39]

Due Process of Law

It would be difficult to overemphasize the importance of that clause in the Fourteenth Amendment which provides that no state shall deprive any person of life, liberty, or property without due process of law.[40] Unlike the privileges-and-immunities clause, the provisions of which apply to citizens only, but like the equal-protection requirement and most other constitutional provisions concerning civil rights, the due-process clause protects all *persons*—citizens and aliens alike, and corporations as well as natural persons. In common with the privileges-and- immunities and equal-protection provisions, the due-process clause limits only the *states* and their subdivisions, and does not operate as a restraint upon the action of individuals or of the national government. It is furthermore to be noted that the clause is only a qualified, and not an absolute, prohibition of interference with life, liberty, or property. In the day-by-day conduct of their affairs the states take private property in the form of fines as punishment for criminal acts, as taxes for the support of government, and under the power of emi-

[37] *Hague* v. *Committee for Industrial Organization*, 307 U.S. 496 (1939).

[38] *Edwards* v. *California*, 314 U.S. 160 (1941).

[39] On the privileges-and-immunities clause in general, see Bruce R. Trimble, "The Privileges of Citizens of the United States," *Univ. of Kansas City Law Rev.*, X, 77-88 (Feb. 1942); Lucile Lomen, "Privileges and Immunities under the Fourteenth Amendment," *Wash. Law Rev. and State Bar Jour.*, XVIII, 120-135 (July, 1943); S. P. Meyers, "Federal Privileges and Immunities: Application to Ingress and Egress," *Cornell Law Quar.*, XXIX, 489-513 (June, 1944).

[40] A due-process clause in the Fifth Amendment, like other provisions of the first eight amendments, is a restriction upon the national government but not upon the states.

nent domain for public use. They deprive individuals of their liberty in punishment for crime, limit personal freedom in innumerable ways, and even, on occasion, deprive persons of their very life for the commission of major offenses against society. All these things may be done constitutionally *if* the requirement of due process is observed.

The due-process clause of the Fourteenth Amendment has been the subject of more litigation than any other restriction imposed upon the states by the United States Constitution. In attempting to determine its meaning, the federal courts, like the state courts in construing similar provisions in state constitutions,[41] have insisted upon proceeding by "inclusion and exclusion" and have adopted the touchstone of reasonableness for determining what does, and what does not, comply with the constitutional standard. As the result of numerous court decisions, there have developed two rather distinct aspects or phases of the due-process requirement—the one *procedural* in nature and the other *substantive.* In its procedural aspect the requirement operates principally, though not exclusively, as a limitation upon the executive and judicial branches of government, and is a restriction upon the *manner* in which deprivation of life, liberty, or property may be effected. In its substantive aspect the requirement operates for the most part to restrict the legislative branch with respect to *what* it may constitutionally do in the direction of regulating or taking the life, liberty, or property of individuals. The clause is thus a limitation upon both the procedures of state governmental agencies and the substance of state legislation. So many questions concerning the due-process clause have been presented to the courts for determination, and the meaning of the requirement is still so inexact and incapable of comprehensive definition, that only a few illustrative cases can be mentioned here.

On the procedural side, many cases have concerned the standards which must be observed by state courts and law-enforcement officers in criminal proceedings. In an early case, for instance, the question was raised as to whether, in order to comply with the due-process requirement, a person tried in a state court for a capital offense must first be indicted by a grand jury instead of being charged with the crime merely by "information" filed by the prosecuting attorney. The Supreme Court answered that grand-jury indictment in such cases is *not* essential to due process. Proceeding by information, the court held, is a fair method and in accordance with recognized standards of justice, and therefore constitutes due process notwithstanding that grand-jury indictment (which of course also constitutes due process) is an older method of proceeding and one more generally used.[42] Again, it has been held that state courts may, without violating the due-process requirement, use trial juries of

---

[41] See above, Chap. I, "The Bill of Rights."

[42] *Hurtado* v. *California,* 110 U.S. 516 (1884). The indictment and information, as alternative methods of preferring criminal charges, are considered at some length in Chap. XVII, below.

less than twelve members notwithstanding that at common law the jury is a twelve-member body.[43] On the other hand, it *is* essential to due process that indigent persons charged with criminal offenses be provided with legal counsel.[44] It is also necessary that the tribunal before which judicial proceedings take place be of an impartial nature. Thus, a state law providing that a mayor, when sitting as judge of a minor court in a criminal case, shall receive a fee for his services in the event of conviction but not in case of acquittal, tends to prejudice the court against the defendant and therefore constitutes a denial of due process.[45]

In taxation and eminent domain proceedings, due process usually requires that the parties concerned be given proper notice of the proceedings and opportunity for a hearing; and, when property is taken by eminent domain, just compensation must be paid therefor.[46]

It is to be noted that due process does not necessarily require jury trial, or for that matter trial before any judicial tribunal. In the case of taxation, for instance, proceedings are usually before administrative agencies rather than the courts. What is necessary to constitute due process varies with the circumstances of particular situations. About all that can be said in the way of generalization is that due process, as a procedural matter, requires *fair and reasonable* proceedings, including notice and opportunity for a hearing, before an impartial tribunal, judicial or otherwise, which has lawful jurisdiction over the subject matter.

In substantive matters the due-process clause of the Fourteenth Amendment operates as a potent check upon state and local legislation and upon the activities of state and local governmental agencies.[47] The term *liberty* as used in the clause has been interpreted by the courts very broadly, to include much more than freedom from bodily restraint. Indeed, it is said to embrace all those freedoms which are "implicit in the concept of ordered liberty."[48] In a series of decisions beginning in the 1920's the United States Supreme Court has adopted the view that the due-process clause of the Fourteenth Amendment operates to protect against state and local abridgement many of the liberties protected against the national government by the federal bill of rights. The rights thus "absorbed" into the concept of due process include all of the freedoms enumerated in the First Amendment—i.e., freedom of religion, speech, press, assembly, and petition—as well as certain others.[49] In a series of decisions in 1962-63, for example, the United States Supreme

[43] *Maxwell* v. *Dow*, 176 U.S. 581 (1900).

[44] *Gideon* v. *Wainwright*, 372 U.S. 335 (1963).

[45] *Tumey* v. *Ohio*, 273 U.S. 510 (1927). But see below, Chap. XI, "Justices of the Peace."

[46] Cf. Mathews, *op. cit.*, Chaps. 28, 29.

[47] Like similar clauses in state constitutions, this provision has often prevented the enactment of socially-desirable legislation.

[48] Cf. *Palko* v. *Connecticut*, 302 U.S. 319 (1937).

[49] Cf. William J. Brennan, Jr., *The Bill of Rights and the States* (Center for the Study of Democratic Institutions, Santa Barbara, Calif., 1961).

Court held that a requirement by a state legislature or local school board that the opening exercises in public schools include prayer or Bible-reading violates the First Amendment's prohibition of an "establishment of religion" as applied to the states through the Fourteenth Amendment.[50]

Property rights as well as personal liberties are protected by the due-process clause. For example, public utility companies have many times, and often successfully, attacked as violative of the due-process requirement rates of charge fixed for their services by state regulatory agencies. If the rates so fixed are found by the courts to be insufficient to enable the utility to pay its operating costs and make a fair profit, they will be overturned as arbitrary and unreasonable and hence wanting in due process.[51]

Although most of the rights protected by the due-process clause are, it is true, also guaranteed against state infringement by bills of rights in the respective state constitutions, their guarantee under the Fourteenth Amendment makes them enforceable in the federal as well as the state courts. Indeed, the due-process and equal-protection clauses go a long way toward placing the whole field of civil rights under federal protection.

Equal Protection of the Laws

The provision in the Fourteenth Amendment that no state shall deny to any person within its jurisdiction the equal protection of the laws is sometimes said to require "equality before the law" or "protection of all persons by equal laws." The essence of the requirement is nondiscrimination. This does not mean, however, that all laws must be of universal application or that all persons must be treated alike under all circumstances. The provision permits legislative classification of persons and things, provided that the classification is reasonable and for a proper purpose, and provided that all persons or things within a given class are accorded equal treatment.[52]

Under long-established practice in the South, state laws have required that white and Negro passengers in public conveyances occupy separate coaches or compartments, and that children of the two races attend separate schools. For many years such segregation was upheld by the courts as constitutional if equal, though separate, facilities were provided

---

[50] *Engel* v. *Vitale*, 370 U.S. 421 (1962); *Abington School District* v. *Schempp* and *Murray* v. *Curlett*, 374 U.S. 203 (1963). The Engel decision and earlier federal and state cases concerning religion in the schools are discussed in Donald E. Boles, *The Bible, Religion, and the Public Schools* (Ia. State Univ. Press, Ames, 2nd ed., 1963).

[51] See *Smyth* v. *Ames*, 169 U.S. 466 (1898).

[52] On the subject in general, see Noel T. Dowling, "Equal Protection of the Laws," *Annals of Amer. Acad. of Polit. and Soc. Sci.*, CXCV (Jan., 1938), Supp., 65-78.

for the members of both races.[53] In passing upon the matter of equality, the courts long displayed an attitude of extreme leniency, with the result that in practice the facilities provided for Negroes, particularly in the field of education, in many instances were notoriously inferior to those provided for whites. Beginning in the 1930's, however, the United States Supreme Court began to examine more closely the situation with respect to equality and to insist that the accommodations provided for the two races be equal in fact as well as in theory. Finally, in the school-segregation decision of 1954, the Court abandoned entirely the "separate but equal" doctrine in its application to the public schools and held that segregation *in and of itself* is unconstitutional. In the opinion of the Court "separate educational facilities are inherently unequal," since the mere fact of segregation gives Negro children a feeling of inferiority which affects adversely the learning process; and therefore a requirement of segregation constitutes a denial of equal protection of the laws in violation of the Fourteenth Amendment. In an implementing decision of 1955, the Supreme Court directed the school authorities, under supervision of the federal district courts, to make a prompt and reasonable start toward compliance with the new ruling and to achieve full compliance at the earliest practicable date.[54] Since the school-segregation decisions, the "separate but equal" doctrine has been abandoned also in its application to transportation and public-recreation facilities.[55] And recent decisions of the Court indicate that even racial discrimination by private individuals, if perpetrated pursuant to state or local law or at the direction of public officers, may run afoul of the equal-protection clause. Thus the Court reversed, as violative of the Fourteenth Amendment, trespass convictions of Negroes who refused to leave southern lunch counters after being refused service, where segregated service was required by city ordinance or directed by city officials.[56]

In a criminal proceeding, a Negro defendant is denied equal protection of the laws if members of his race are deliberately excluded from the grand jury which indicts him or the petit jury which tries him. Such a defendant has no right to demand that one or more Negroes be included in the grand or petit jury, but he is entitled to assurance that Negroes are not prevented by arbitrary and discriminatory practices from being drawn

[53] See, for example, *Plessy* v. *Ferguson*, 163 U.S. 537 (1896).

[54] *Brown* v. *Board of Education of Topeka*, 347 U.S. 483 (1954); *Brown* v. *Board of Education of Topeka*, 349 U.S. 294 (1955). Progress in implementation of the school-segregation decisions up to 1961 is recounted in J. W. Peltason, *Fifty-Eight Lonely Men: Southern Federal Judges and School Desegregation* (Harcourt, New York, 1961). Overall progress was extremely slow during these early years and has continued to be so more recently.

[55] Cf. George W. Spicer, *The Supreme Court and Fundamental Freedoms* (Appleton-Century-Crofts, New York, 1959), 101-115.

[56] *Peterson* v. *Greenville*, 373 U.S. 244 (1963); *Lombard* v. *Louisiana*, 373 U.S. 267 (1963).

for jury duty.[57] Again, a state statute prohibiting Negroes from voting in the primary election of a political party is unconstitutional as a denial of equal protection.[58]

The question of equal protection is frequently raised in connection with matters of taxation. With respect to property taxation the state may, as far as the equal-protection clause is concerned, classify property in a reasonable manner and impose different rates of levy upon property in different classes, or assess different classes of property at different percentages of their value.[59] However, classifications which the courts feel to be arbitrary or unreasonable will be overturned as denying equal protection.

Still another field in which the question of equal protection often arises is that of city zoning. Municipal zoning ordinances divide the city into districts for the purpose of regulating building and the use which may be made of buildings and land. They forbid, for example, the establishment of industrial or commercial enterprises in residential districts, and the erection of apartment houses in districts designated for single-family dwellings only. Zoning ordinances, if authorized by the state and reasonable in their provisions, are upheld as valid regulations of liberty and property under the police power;[60] but property owners whose rights are affected unreasonably or with undue harshness may secure relief under the due-process and equal-protection clauses.

In 1962 a new dimension was added to the guarantee of equal protection of the laws when the United States Supreme Court, in the now famous Tennessee Reapportionment Case, held that invidious discrimination in state legislative apportionment may violate the equal-protection clause of the Fourteenth Amendment.[61] This decision and its results are discussed in the chapter on legislative structure and organization.[62]

Intergovernmental Tax Immunity

In interpreting the United States Constitution, the courts early adopted the principle that neither the national government nor the states could constitutionally tax instrumentalities of the other.[63] The basis of this doctrine was found in the very nature of federalism which, as we have

---

[57] *Norris* v. *Alabama*, 294 U.S. 587 (1935); *Smith* v. *Texas*, 311 U.S. 128 (1940). In like manner, a defendant of Mexican ancestry was held to have been denied equal protection of the laws where qualified persons of his ancestry were systematically excluded from jury service. *Hernandez* v. *Texas*, 347 U.S. 475 (1954).

[58] *Nixon* v. *Herndon*, 273 U.S. 536 (1927). See below, Chap. V, "The White Primary and Its Legal Demise."

[59] Cf. Mathews, *op. cit.*, 487, and cases there cited.

[60] *Village of Euclid* v. *Ambler Realty Co.*, 272 U.S. 365 (1926).

[61] *Baker* v. *Carr*, 369 U.S. 186 (1962).

[62] Below, Chap. VII, "Reapportionment and the Courts."

[63] *McCulloch* v. *Maryland*, 4 Wheat. 316 (1819); *Collector* v. *Day*, 11 Wall. 113 (1871). The latter case was overruled in 1939 by *Graves* v. *New York*, cited below.

seen, involves the concurrent operation of two distinct and largely independent governments over the same persons and territory. If, it was
reasoned, either the general government or that of the states were allowed
to tax the other, the government so taxed might be impeded in the proper
exercise of its functions and ultimately even destroyed.[64] For many years,
under the application of this principle, neither the national government
nor that of the states was permitted to tax the other's property, its bonds
or income therefrom, or even the salaries paid to its officers and employees. Local governmental units, of course, enjoyed the same immunity
from federal taxation as did the states, and labored under the same disability to tax federal agencies.

More recently, however, the doctrine of intergovernmental tax immunity has undergone substantial change.[65] In decisions handed down in
1938 and 1939, the Supreme Court modified its previous stand by holding
that salaries paid by state and local governments are subject to the federal
income tax and that there is no constitutional bar to nondiscriminatory
taxation by the states of the salaries of federal officers and employees
resident therein.[66] Following these decisions, Congress enacted the Public
Salary Tax Act of 1939 which provided expressly that the federal income
tax should apply to state and local salaries, and gave congressional consent to state and local taxation of federal salaries on a nondiscriminatory
basis.[67] Since the enactment of this statute, serious consideration has been
given to the feasibility of federal legislation which would subject to the
federal income tax interest received from state and local bonds subsequently issued, and authorize the states and local governmental units to
tax the interest on future issues of United States bonds. As yet, however,
such legislation has not been enacted, though there is good reason to believe, on the basis of the Supreme Court's decisions relative to the taxation
of salaries, that its constitutionality would be sustained.[68]

Federal property and activities of every kind have always been
considered to be immune from state taxation.[69] On the other hand, the

[64] It is to be observed that the doctrine of intergovernmental tax immunity has
no application to the power of either the national government or a state government
to tax its own instrumentalities, but only to their respective powers to tax each other.

[65] See Thomas Reed Powell, "The Waning of Intergovernmental Tax Immunities," *Harvard Law Rev.*, LVIII, 633-674 (May, 1945); B. U. Ratchford, "Intergovernmental Tax Immunities in the United States," *Nat. Tax Jour.*, VI, 305-332 (Dec.,
1953).

[66] *Helvering* v. *Gerhardt*, 304 U.S. 405 (1938); *Graves* v. *New York*, 306 U.S.
466 (1939).

[67] 53 *U.S. Stat. at L.* 574.

[68] The pros and cons of permitting intergovernmental taxation of government
securities are discussed in Edward H. Foley and Henry Epstein, "Shall We Tax Government Bonds?" *Nat. Mun. Rev.*, XXX, 674-688 (Dec., 1941). See also Alfred G.
Buehler, "Discriminations in Federal Taxation of State and Local Government Securities," *Amer. Polit. Sci. Rev.*, XXXVI, 302-312 (Apr., 1942).

[69] Congress of course may, and sometimes does, waive this immunity and permit taxation of federal property by state and local governments. See below, "Cooperation between Nation and States." Real estate which has been sold by the federal gov-

rule was established early in the present century that business or commercial enterprises operated by the states, such as state-owned liquor stores, were not exempt from federal taxes.[70] More recent decisions seem to indicate a disposition on the part of the Supreme Court, or at least some of its members, to reject the traditional distinction between governmental and business activities as a basis for applying the doctrine of immunity, and to take the view that state property or activities of whatever character may be subjected to federal taxation, provided that private property and activities of similar nature are taxed in like manner, and provided also that the tax will not actually interfere with the performance of the state's governmental functions. Thus, in a case decided in 1946, a majority of the Court upheld a federal excise tax on the sale of bottled mineral water as applied to water sold by the state of New York from state-owned mineral springs, as against the contention that, since the state was here disposing of its natural resources, the function was governmental in nature.[71]

It should be emphasized, of course, that the Supreme Court has not abandoned the doctrine of intergovernmental tax immunity but has only narrowed its application. The narrowing process has thus far been confined for the most part to the matter of public salaries, though it may eventually be extended to other fields. What the Court did in its decisions modifying the earlier rule with respect to salaries was to take the view— a very sensible one—that for the national government or a state to tax salaries of officers and employees of the other government in the same manner and at the same rate that it taxes salaries from private sources does not, in fact, endanger the existence or functioning of the government paying the salaries, and therefore could not be destructive of the federal system. It seems safe to predict that, whenever the Court is convinced that any tax imposed by one government upon instrumentalities of the other would actually jeopardize the proper functioning of the latter, it will apply the doctrine of intergovernmental immunity in its original vigor and invalidate the levy.

Cooperation between Nation and States

It would be a grave mistake to think of national-state relations as comprising only those contacts between the two levels of government which flow from duties and limitations imposed by constitutional provision. Over the years, and especially during the present century, numerous

---

ernment to a private party on instalment payments has been held to be subject to state and local taxation when possession has passed to the purchaser, notwithstanding that legal title remains in the United States until all instalments of the purchase price have been paid. *S.R.A., Inc.* v. *Minnesota,* 327 U.S. 558 (1946).

[70] *South Carolina* v. *United States,* 199 U.S. 437 (1905).

[71] *New York* v. *United States,* 326 U.S. 572 (1946).

voluntary relationships of a cooperative nature have evolved, until today these are quite as important, and in some respects more so, than the relations definitely prescribed by the Constitution. These voluntary relationships are of almost infinite variety, and only a few can be mentioned here for illustrative purposes.[72]

One field in which much cooperation has been evident is that of legislative action. A great deal of legislation has been enacted by Congress and the state legislatures, respectively, to supplement and strengthen laws passed by the other. When, in 1933, Congress enacted the National Industrial Recovery Act (later declared unconstitutional) providing for establishment of "codes of fair competition" for industries engaged in or affecting interstate commerce, a number of states followed with statutes making similar provision with respect to intrastate business. Enactment by Congress of the National Labor Relations (Wagner) Act, to protect the right of labor in interstate commerce to bargain collectively, was followed by the passage in several states of "baby Wagner acts" to guarantee collective bargaining in intrastate transactions. During World War II a few states and many municipalities, through "little O.P.A. acts," imposed criminal penalties for the violation of price, rent, and rationing regulations of the federal Office of Price Administration.[73]

Under its power to regulate interstate commerce, Congress has enacted many statutes designed to strengthen state legislation. Among the earlier ones are the Lacey Act of 1900, which makes it a federal offense to take or send from any state wild game killed in violation of state law, and the Dyer Act of 1919 which imposes a federal penalty for interstate transportation of stolen motor vehicles. More recent examples are the Kidnapped Persons (Lindbergh) Law of 1932 and the Stolen Property Act of 1934 penalizing the interstate transportation, respectively, of kidnapped persons, and of stolen property valued at $5,000 or more. The Fugitive Felon Law of 1934 makes it a federal crime to move from one state to another to avoid prosecution by the state fled for murder, kidnapping, burglary, robbery, or certain other specified felonies, or to avoid the giving of testimony in any case involving such offenses. Under the Connally Act of 1935, it is a federal offense to transport in interstate commerce oil pro-

[72] Many aspects of cooperative relationships between the national and state governments are discussed in Jane Perry Clark's *The Rise of a New Federalism*. A comprehensive discussion of relationships based upon a single constitutional provision will be found in Joseph E. Kallenbach's *Federal Cooperation with the States under the Commerce Clause*. See also Emerson D. Fite, *Government by Cooperation*, Chap. 3; W. Brooke Graves, "State Constitutional Provision for Federal-State Cooperation," *Annals of Amer. Acad. of Polit. and Soc. Sci.*, CLXXI, 142-148 (Sept., 1935).

[73] Jane Perry Clark, "State Industrial Recovery Acts and State Codes," *Amer. Bar Assn. Jour.*, XX, 343-347 (June, 1934); Samuel Mermin, " 'Coöperative Federalism' Again: State and Municipal Legislation Penalizing Violation of Existing and Future Federal Requirements," *Yale Law Jour.*, LVII, 1-26, 201-218 (Nov., Dec., 1947). The state labor relations acts are discussed below, Chap. XXIII.

duced or withdrawn from storage in violation of state law.[74] A federal law of 1951 prohibits the interstate shipment of slot machines or related gambling devices into states where their possession or use is illegal.

On the administrative side, federal law-enforcement officers, especially through the Federal Bureau of Investigation, cooperate with state and local authorities in the apprehension of criminals. The federal Food and Drug Administration frequently commissions state or local officials to conduct food, drug, and cosmetics investigations for the national agency; and the United States Secretary of Agriculture licenses state grain inspectors to make inspections under the federal Grain Standards Act. "In the programs aimed at livestock diseases and plant pests, it is not infrequent for employees to hold appointments under both the United States Department of Agriculture and a State regulatory agency."[75] Federal and state agencies cooperate in civil-defense programs and programs for dealing with natural disasters.[76]

In the field of finance numerous cooperative relationships have developed. Though federal property is constitutionally exempt from state and local taxation, Congress has voluntarily waived this exemption in the case of real estate owned by various federal agencies, and made this property taxable by the states and local governmental units on the same basis as if it were privately owned. The federal agencies whose property is thus made taxable are for the most part credit agencies, and the property concerned has usually been acquired as a result of lending operations. In addition to these waivers of tax exemption, the federal statutes provide in numerous instances for the making of cash contributions to states and local units from revenues derived from federal properties located therein. These contributions are sometimes called "payments in lieu of taxes," since their purpose is to replace, wholly or in part, revenues lost because of the property's tax exemption. Thus, a portion of the grazing fees derived from public-domain lands under the Taylor Grazing Act is paid to the states for benefit of the counties in which the lands are situated; the Tennessee Valley Authority pays to the state and counties in which its power property is located a percentage of its receipts from the sale of electric power; and many federal housing projects pay a portion of their receipts from rentals to the states and local units in which they are situated.[77] State

[74] Cf. Kallenbach, *op. cit.*, Chap. 9. See also articles in symposium entitled "Extending Federal Powers over Crime," *Law and Contemp. Probs.*, Vol. I, No. 4 (Oct., 1934). A 1934 amendment to the Lindbergh law provides that whenever a kidnapped person is not released within seven days a presumption shall be created that he has been moved across state lines.

[75] Commission on Intergovernmental Relations, *A Report to the President for Transmittal to the Congress*, 81.

[76] See below, Chap. IX, "Civil Defense."

[77] *Federal Contributions to States and Local Governmental Units with respect to Federally Owned Real Estate* (House Doc. No. 216, 78th Cong., 1st Sess., U.S. Govt. Printing Office, Washington, 1943). Concerning T.V.A. payments, see also

agencies withhold federal income tax from the salaries of their employees; and federal agencies are authorized, pursuant to agreements between the Secretary of the Treasury and the respective states, to withhold state income taxes from federal salaries. To aid the states in collecting their cigarette taxes, federal law requires that persons shipping cigarettes in interstate commerce, to consignees other than licensed distributors, report such shipment to the tax authorities of the state into which the cigarettes are sent. One of the most important aspects of fiscal cooperation is found in the federal grants-in-aid discussed in the following section.

All in all, national-state cooperation on a voluntary basis bulks large in the everyday conduct of American government.

Federal Grants-in-Aid

The federal grant-in-aid, in its most common present-day form, is a conditional grant of federal funds to the states[78] to be used for a specified purpose.[79] Some early federal grants of land and money, especially for the support of education, were made with no conditions attached other than the requirement that they be used for the purposes specified. However, beginning with the Weeks Act of 1911 in aid of forest-fire prevention, grants have ordinarily been made subject to additional conditions of two types. In the first place, the states have been required, with respect to the activity subsidized, to conform to standards fixed by a federal supervising agency and to submit to federal inspection and control. The federal supervising agency varies with the function concerned, being, for example, the Bureau of Public Roads in the case of federal aid for highways, and the Social Security Administration in the case of aid in caring for the aged, the blind, the disabled, and dependent children. Secondly, the states, either alone or together with their local governments, must contribute a designated proportion—most commonly half—of the total cost of the function or project. This "match-fund" requirement, though customary in the financing of federal-aid activities, has never been universal. During the depression years of the 1930's the matching requirement was relaxed in numerous instances, especially with respect to grants for relief purposes, and at present there are several programs that do not require

Tennessee Valley Authority, *Progress in the Valley; TVA, 1947* (U.S. Govt. Printing Office, Washington, 1947), 77-78; Alexander T. Edelmann, "The T.V.A. and Inter-Governmental Relations," *Amer. Polit. Sci. Rev.*, XXXVII, 455-469 (June, 1943).

[78] Federal grants to local governmental units are discussed below, Chap. III, "National-Local Relations"; Chap. XXIV, "Federal Aid."

[79] For general discussions, see Austin F. Macdonald, *Federal Aid;* Council of State Governments, *Federal Grants-in-Aid;* Henry J. Bittermann, *State and Federal Grants-in Aid;* V. O. Key, Jr., *The Administration of Federal Grants to States;* Charles Warren, *Congress as Santa Claus;* Jane Perry Clark, *The Rise of a New Federalism,* Chaps. 6-8; Joseph P. Harris, "The Future of Federal Grants-in-Aid," *Annals of Amer. Acad. of Polit. and Soc. Sci.,* CCVII, 14-26 (Jan., 1940).

matching on a 50-50 basis. Under the federal-state program for constructing a national system of Interstate Highways, for example, the federal government bears 90 percent of construction costs. A further condition was imposed by the Civil Rights Act of 1964, which provides that no person shall
be excluded from participation in federally aided programs on the ground
of race, color, or national origin. Federal agencies administering aid programs are directed to effectuate this provision—if necessary, by the withholding of federal funds.

The activities for which federal-aid funds are available to the states
are quite varied. They include, in addition to those already mentioned and
still others not listed: agricultural experiment stations and extension work,
agricultural and mechanical colleges, veterans' services, state employment
offices, vocational education, vocational rehabilitation, services to crippled
children, child welfare services, maternity and child hygiene, and venereal
disease control. Federal expenditures in connection with these programs
vary from year to year, but have shown a distinct tendency to increase. In
1961, federal expenditures in connection with some 64 grant-in-aid and
related programs amounted to $7 billion.[80]

The grant-in-aid, by its conditional nature, makes it possible for the
national government to exercise substantial control over many state activities. The national government cannot directly compel the states to build
highways in certain locations, and of certain widths and materials; but it
can and does say that *if* these and other conditions are met a designated
portion of the costs will be paid from the federal treasury. Again, the national government has no authority to require directly that state and local
personnel engaged in administering old-age assistance, aid to dependent
children, and other specified welfare services be selected under a merit
system; but it can and does stipulate that *unless* the merit system is used
in such cases federal aid in financing the activities will not be forthcoming.
Theoretically, of course, the acceptance of federal aid with its concomitant
conditions is entirely optional with the respective states. If a state does
not wish to submit to federal supervision, it may avoid doing so by merely
declining federal assistance. Actually, however, the element of option is
little more than nominal. The residents of a particular state must pay their
share of federal taxes, and unless they are prepared to meet the requirements for federal aid their tax money will be spent in other states which
do meet those requirements. As a practical matter, therefore, an individual
state has scarcely any alternative but to accept federal assistance and submit to federal control.

Concerning the basic merits of the federal-aid system there is con-

[80] Annual Report of the Secretary of the Treasury for Fiscal Year 1961, excerpt
in *Intergovernmental Relations* (Report of the Senate Committee on Government Operations made by its Subcommittee on Intergovernmental Relations, Sen. Rept. No.
84, 88th Cong., 1st Sess., U.S. Govt. Printing Office, Washington, 1963), 123-134. See
also below, Chap. XXIV, "Federal Aid."

siderable difference of opinion. On the one hand, it is said to stimulate states to desirable action and to enable the poorer states to maintain better services than would otherwise be possible. On the other hand, it is argued that federal aid unjustly robs the richer states for the benefit of the poorer, and that the system is merely a means of bribing the states to submit to federal dictation. Regardless of its relative merits, however, the federal grant-in-aid has become firmly established in our system of government and its widespread use seems certain to continue.[81] For several years now, Congress has been giving serious consideration to extension of the federal-aid program to include grants in general support of elementary and secondary schools, and it appears not unlikely that legislation to that end will ultimately be enacted.[82] There is also considerable current support for modification of grant-in-aid programs to permit the percentage of total costs borne by the federal government to vary inversely with per capita income in the recipient states. In states with high per capita income, for example, the federal government might pay only one-third of the cost of the service concerned, while paying perhaps as much as two-thirds in the "poorest" states. Although the principle of the variable grant has as yet been accorded only limited application in federal-aid programs, it was written into the Hospital Survey and Construction Act by a 1949 amendment, and by 1958 amendments to the Social Security Act was introduced into the programs of categorical assistance given federal support under that law.[83]

Expansion of National Power

A comparison of present-day federal activities with those of the national government in the early days of the Republic reveals that the number and variety of those activities have increased astoundingly. This increase has come about in part from the popular demand, because of the growing complexity of social and economic conditions, for the performance of more functions by government at all levels; but it is also due to the entry of the national government into many fields of activity which, supposedly, had been reserved by the Constitution to the states. This expansion of national authority has come about in several ways.

The most obvious method of increasing the power of the national government is, of course, through amendment of the Constitution, since it is that instrument which makes the basic distribution of authority between nation and states. In practice, however, this method has been used surprisingly little. Of the twenty-four amendments only two—the Six-

[81] J. Kerwin Williams, "Federal Aid Due to Continue," *Nat. Mun. Rev.*, XXXVII, 86-90 (Feb., 1948).

[82] See below, Chap. III, "National-Local Relations—Other Relationships."

[83] See below, Chap. XVIII, "Categorical Assistance: The Federal-State Programs;" Chap. XIX, "Government Hospitals."

teenth, which empowers Congress to levy income taxes without their apportionment among the states according to population, and the Eighteenth, which established national prohibition—directly augmented national authority, and of these the Eighteenth was subsequently repealed by the Twenty-first. Another means of introducing national action in fields of activity hitherto considered as belonging to the states, which as yet has been little used but seems to be of some potential importance, is through the federal treaty power. Some years ago, for example, after the lower federal courts had declared unconstitutional a congressional act regulating the killing of migratory birds, the national government entered into a treaty with Great Britain under the terms of which the United States and Canada were reciprocally obliged to protect such birds. A statute *then* enacted by Congress, with regulatory provisions similar to those of the earlier statute but more elaborate, was upheld by the Supreme Court as a means of implementing the treaty.[84] An extremely important means, in practice, of extending national control, has been the system of federal grants-in-aid discussed in the preceding section. Fully as effective a means of control as the grant-in-aid, though of a somewhat different nature, is the tax-offset scheme used in the field of unemployment compensation.[85]

But undoubtedly the most important single factor in expanding national power at the expense of the states has been the liberal interpretation by the courts of those powers which are expressly conferred by the Constitution upon the national government. Though there has been a tendency to interpret all such grants broadly, the most significant expansion has taken place under the powers of Congress to regulate interstate commerce and to tax—and therefore spend—to provide for the general welfare. Under the commerce clause, for example, the Supreme Court has sustained the power of Congress to regulate the hours and wages, not only of employees actually engaged in interstate commerce, but also of those engaged in the production of goods for such commerce; and to require employers to bargain with their employees collectively, even in the case of employees who are themselves engaged in local production, where refusal to bargain might impede the flow of interstate commerce.[86] And under the power of Congress to tax and spend, the Court has upheld a broad social security program, including not only a purely national system of old-age insurance but also federal-state programs in unemployment compensation and various other fields.[87]

Two decisions of the United States Supreme Court—that of 1954 invalidating racial segregation in public schools and the decision of 1962

---

[84] *Missouri* v. *Holland,* 252 U.S. 416 (1920).
[85] This scheme is explained in Chap. XXIII, below.
[86] *United States* v. *Darby,* 312 U.S. 100 (1941); *National Labor Relations Board* v. *Jones and Laughlin Steel Corp.,* 301 U.S. 1 (1937).
[87] *Steward Machine Co.* v. *Davis,* 301 U.S. 548 (1937); *Helvering* v. *Davis,* 301 U.S. 619 (1937). The social security program, as it relates to state and local government, is discussed below, Chaps. XVIII and XXIII.

upholding the jurisdiction of federal courts in cases concerning state legislative apportionment—have recently engendered considerable criticism of the Court and the federal government in general and brought about a revival, in some quarters, of the old "states' rights" doctrine. As a result, the General Assembly of the States, which is sponsored by the Council of State Governments, in 1962 endorsed three proposals for amendments to the United States Constitution designed to curtail federal authority, and urged the state legislatures to petition Congress to submit the proposals to the states for ratification or call a national constitutional convention for their proposal. One of the proposals would establish a "Court of the Union," composed of the chief justices of the 50 states and empowered to review and reverse judgments of the Supreme Court relating to rights reserved to the states by the Constitution; another would specify that no provision of the Constitution shall restrict any state in the apportionment of representation in its legislature and would deny to federal courts jurisdiction over controversies relating to state legislative apportionment; and the third would enable the state legislatures to propose and ratify amendments to the Constitution without approval by Congress or a national convention. Adoption of these proposals, which have been referred to as the "disunion" amendments, would in effect destroy our federal system of government and establish in its stead a weak confederation of sovereign states. Although the legislatures of several states have adopted resolutions calling upon Congress for action on one or more of the proposals, it appears highly improbable that they are destined to gain widespread support.[88]

Future of the States

As a result of the marked shift in the balance of power toward Washington, concern has inevitably arisen as to the future of the states.[89]

---

[88] Jefferson B. Fordham, "To Foster Disunity," *Nat. Civic Rev.*, LII, 418-421, 433 (Sept., 1963); William F. Swindler, "Congressional Bypass," *Ibid.*, 422-429; John R. Schmidhauser and Richard L. McAnaw, "Calhoun Revisited," *Ibid.*, 430-433. The text of the proposals may be found in *State Govt.*, XXXVI, 10-15 (Winter, 1963).

[89] On the subject generally, see Leonard D. White, *The States and the Nation;* William Anderson, *The Nation and the States, Rivals or Partners?;* Nelson A. Rockefeller, *The Future of Federalism;* Edward A. Harriman, "The Twilight of the States," *Amer. Bar Assn. Jour.*, XVI, 128-132 (Feb., 1930); Lester B. Orfield, "What Should Be the Functions of the States in Our System of Government?" *Ibid.*, XXIX, 480-488 (Sept., 1943); Julian P. Alexander, "The Waning Power of the States," *Georgetown Law Jour.*, XXXIV, 288-301 (Mar., 1946); Richard L. Neuberger, "The Decay of State Governments," *Harper's Mag.*, Vol. CCVII, No. 1241, pp. 34-41 (Oct., 1953); Arthur B. Langlie, "States' Rights, Duties," *Nat. Mun. Rev.*, XLIV, 408-417 (Sept., 1955); Arthur B. Langlie, "Stronger States in the Federal Union: Why and How," *State Govt.*, XXVIII, 267-270, 286 (Dec., 1955); Richard C. Welty, "Are the States Obsolete?" *Midwest Quar.*, I, 87-100 (Autumn, 1959); Mark O. Hatfield, "The Role of the States," *Nat. Civic Rev.*, XLVIII, 562-567 (Dec., 1959); Vernon C. Myers, "Who'll Save the States?" *Ibid.*, XLIX, 11-15 (Jan., 1960); Jefferson B. Fordham, "The States in the Federal System—Vital Role or Limbo?" *Va. Law Rev.*, XLIX, 666-674 (May, 1963).

Some students of American institutions appear to believe that the states as originally conceived are rapidly approaching oblivion and will eventually be completely overshadowed by the national government. Again, the suggestion is sometimes made that the states should be subordinated to regional governments serving larger areas or, perhaps, abolished altogether and replaced by such governments of wider territorial jurisdiction.[90] Still other observers, however, point out that government at all levels, including that of the states, is growing and expanding its activities, and that any decline in state government is relative only, with expansion in state activities suffering in comparison with the vast growth during recent decades of activities of the national government in the fields of defense and foreign affairs. Professor William Anderson, for example, maintains that, if defense functions and expenditures are excluded from consideration, state and local activities have increased far more during the last half-century than national. "If anyone will candidly lay the facts about state powers and functions today alongside the comparable facts of forty to sixty years ago," Professor Anderson writes, "I do not see how he can reach the conclusion that the states are weaker today than they were then." [91]

Concern by the national government over the states and their place in the federal system is evidenced by the creation by Congress in 1953 of a temporary Commission on Intergovernmental Relations "to study the proper role of the Federal Government in relation to the States and their political subdivisions . . . to the end that these relations may be clearly defined and the functions concerned may be allocated to their proper jurisdiction;" [92] and by the establishment in 1959, also by congressional action, of a permanent Advisory Commission on Intergovernmental Relations designed to study intergovernmental relations in all of their aspects and to "recommend, within the framework of the Constitution, the most desirable allocation of governmental functions, responsibilities, and revenues among the several levels of government." [93]

The Commission on Intergovernmental Relations, as a result of its studies, concluded that the trend toward centralization has been due not only to overzealousness on the part of the national government to enter new fields and expand existing programs, but also to an unreadiness or unwillingness on the part of state and local governments to perform services demanded by their citizens. In other words, nonuse of state and local authority has been fully as important a factor in centralization as has overuse of national power. As a deterrent to further undesirable centraliza-

[90] Various regional proposals are summarized in Howard W. Odum and Harry E. Moore, *American Regionalism* (Holt, New York, 1938), especially Chaps. 8 and 10. Cf. also Frank R. Strong, "The Future of Federalism in the United States," *Tex. Law Rev.*, XXII, 255-285 (Apr., 1944).

[91] Anderson, *op. cit.*, 140, 197-198.

[92] 67 *U.S. Stat. at L.* 145.

[93] 73 *U.S. Stat. at L.* 703.

tion, the Commission recommended the strengthening and improvement of state and local governments through such means as modernization of state constitutions and state governmental machinery, more use of interstate cooperation, and the continued reorganization of local government.[94]

The permanent Advisory Commission on Intergovernmental Relations consists of 26 members and is constituted on a broadly representative basis. Included in its membership are members of both houses of Congress, officers of the executive branch of the national government, state legislators and governors, county and municipal officials, and lay citizens. Meetings of the Commission are held periodically and between meetings its operations are carried on through working committees and a permanent professional staff. Research is conducted on intergovernmental problems and the results thereof are published. On the basis of these studies the Commission formulates its recommendations for submission to the President and Congress in its annual reports. Among the numerous recommendations made thus far are those for periodic review of grant-in-aid programs by congressional committees and executive agencies, and the exchange of tax records and information by national and state officials. Currently the Commission is devoting a substantial portion of its efforts to encouraging and stimulating implementation of its recommendations by the authorities of the governments concerned.[95]

Whatever the degree to which state government has suffered a loss in relative status, the states are firmly imbedded in our constitutional system and continue to perform many essential functions. As of first-rate importance among such functions may be mentioned the control of local government, broad regulatory functions under the police power, the enactment and administration of civil and criminal law, and the performance of extensive services in such fields as those of education, highways, and mental health. One major reason for the present subordination of state government lies in the fact that the states are inevitably overshadowed by the national government in times of war or national emergency. During the past half-century, the First World War, the depression of the 1930's, World War II, and the prolonged "cold war" with Russia have occurred in such rapid succession as to keep state government virtually in constant eclipse. To rescue the states from this condition will be a major task for the future if our federal system is again to operate in something like its fullest vigor.

In conclusion, it may be suggested that the loss by the states to the

[94] Commission on Intergovernmental Relations, *A Report to the President for Transmittal to the Congress.* Cf. Editorial Comment: "It's Up to the States," *Nat. Mun. Rev.*, XLIV, 344-345 (July, 1955).

[95] Advisory Commission on Intergovernmental Relations, *The Advisory Commission on Intergovernmental Relations* (a descriptive booklet, U.S. Govt. Printing Office, Washington, 1962); Charles A. Joiner, "A Permanent Advisory Commission on Intergovernmental Relations," *The County Officer*, XXIV, 366-367 (Dec., 1959). See also The Commission's *Annual Reports.*

national government of a part of their original power and prestige is not, in itself, necessarily to be deplored. The line between matters of national and state control, respectively, cannot be static. It was the intent of those who framed the Constitution that the nation be given control over matters which can best be performed by a central government, and that there be left to the states those functions which *they* can best perform. As the *actual* line between these two groups of functions changes with changing social and economic conditions, there should be a corresponding shift in the *constitutional* line. In the words of an eminent historian, "The true principle of federalism is that it be adjusted to realities." [96]

REFERENCES

Advisory Commission on Intergovernmental Relations, *Annual Reports* (The Commission, Washington).

ANDERSON, William, *The Nation and the States, Rivals or Partners?* (Univ. of Minn. Press, Minneapolis, 1955).

BITTERMANN, Henry J., *State and Federal Grants-in-Aid* (Mentzer, Bush & Co., Chicago, 1938).

CLARK, Jane Perry, *The Rise of a New Federalism; Federal-State Cooperation in the United States* (Columbia Univ. Press, New York, 1938).

Commission on Intergovernmental Relations, *A Report to the President for Transmittal to the Congress* (U.S. Govt. Printing Office, Washington, 1955).

Council of State Governments, *Federal Grants-in-Aid* (The Council, Chicago, 1949).

Federal-State-Local Relations: Federal Grants-in-Aid (Thirtieth Report of the Committee on Government Operations, House Rept. No. 2533, 85th Cong., 2d Sess., U.S. Govt. Printing Office, Washington, 1958).

FITE, Emerson D., *Government by Cooperation* (Macmillan, New York, 1932).

FRAENKEL, Osmond K., *Our Civil Liberties* (Viking, New York, 1944), especially Chaps. 14, 21.

GRAVES, W. Brooke, *American Intergovernmental Relations* (Scribner, New York, 1964).

——, *The Coming Challenge in Federal-State Relations: A Preliminary Report* (Chamber of Commerce of the United States, Washington, 1957).

——, ed., "Intergovernmental Relations in the United States," *Annals of Amer. Acad. of Polit. and Soc. Sci.*, CCVII, pp. 1-43, 111-143 (Philadelphia, Jan., 1940).

KALLENBACH, Joseph E., *Federal Cooperation with the States under the Commerce Clause* (Univ. of Mich. Press, Ann Arbor, 1942).

KEY, V. O., Jr., *The Administration of Federal Grants to States* (Pub. Admin. Service, Chicago, 1937).

MACDONALD, Austin F., *Federal Aid* (Crowell, New York, 1928).

[96] Henry Steele Commager, "Nation or the States: Which Shall Dominate?" *N.Y. Times Mag.*, Nov. 28, 1937, pp. 4-5, 22, 24, at 24.

MATHEWS, John M., *The American Constitutional System* (McGraw-Hill, New York, 2nd ed., 1940), especially Chaps. 5, 25-31.

PATTERSON, Ernest Minor, ed., "Federal versus State Jurisdiction in American Life," *Annals of Amer. Acad. of Polit. and Soc. Sci.*, CXXIX, Philadelphia, Jan., 1927.

ROCKEFELLER, Nelson A., *The Future of Federalism* (Harvard Univ. Press, Cambridge, 1962).

WARREN, Charles, *Congress as Santa Claus, or National Donations and the General Welfare Clause of the Constitution* (Michie Co., Charlottesville, Va., 1932).

WHITE, Leonard D., *The States and the Nation* (La. State Univ. Press, Baton Rouge, 1953).

WILLIS, Hugh E., *Constitutional Law of the United States* (Principia Press, Bloomington, Ind., 1936), especially Chaps. 7, 20-25.

WRIGHT, Benjamin F., *The Contract Clause of the Constitution* (Harvard Univ. Press, Cambridge, 1938).

————, *The Growth of American Constitutional Law* (Reynal, New York, 1942).

3

State-Local and National-Local Relations

STATE-LOCAL RELATIONS

The Unitary Relationship

The outstanding characteristic of the relationship between the states and their local governments is its *unitary* character. In contrast with federalism, wherein governmental powers are divided between the general and subdivisional governments by constitutional provision,[1] under a unitary system powers are conferred upon subdivisional governments by the legislature of the general government. State constitutions establish the state governments and confer broad powers upon them; the state legislatures, in turn, create units of local government and delegate certain powers thereto.[2] Since the powers of the local units are derived from state legislative action, those units are accorded no protection in their powers against the state legislatures comparable to that enjoyed by the respective states, under the United States Constitution, against congressional action. To the general rule that the state-local relationship is unitary in nature there is one major exception. This is found in the fact that in many states, cities, and in some instances counties as well, are granted certain powers of local government by constitutional provision.

[1] See above, Chap. II, "Nature of the Federal System."
[2] Counties are established in a few states by constitutional provision, but even in such instances county powers are derived from legislative delegation.

62

These "home-rule" provisions, which involve a limited application of the federal principle in the relation between the states and their subdivisions, are discussed in a subsequent section of this chapter.

Broad Power of State Legislatures; Constitutional Limitations

As a result of the unitary relationship just noted, state legislatures possess extremely broad powers over local government. Subject to whatever specific limitations the state constitution may impose, it is the legislature which creates local governmental units, prescribes the form of their organization, and confers powers upon them. By the same authority and procedure that the legislature grants powers to local governments, it may take away those powers; as it creates local units, so it is legally competent to abolish them at its pleasure; and, while units of local government exist and operate, they do so subject to state control of whatever form and degree the legislature may see fit to impose.[3] This broad power over local government is exercised by the legislature through the enactment of ordinary statutes in the performance of its general lawmaking function.

The most common type of constitutional limitation on the power of the state legislature over local government is that which prohibits the enactment of *special* legislation concerning counties, cities, and other local units. Such prohibitions, which are found in a majority of the states, have as their purpose the prevention of favoritism and discrimination. In practice, however, many legislatures have found it possible, notwithstanding provisions of this nature, to enact what is special legislation in all but name. This is done by classifying cities or other units, usually on the basis of population, in such a manner that a particular "class" contains but a single governmental unit or at most a small number of units. Legislation then enacted for units of this class, while general in form, is so limited in its application as to be in reality special.[4]

Other constitutional restrictions are of varied character. A common type of limitation with respect to counties consists of constitutional provisions establishing various county offices, such as those of sheriff and coroner, and stipulating that their incumbents shall be chosen by popular election. Provisions of this nature make it impossible for the legislature either to abolish the offices concerned or to make them appointive. Other constitutional provisions of frequent occurrence forbid the establishment of counties having less than a specified minimum area, or the reduction of the size of existing counties to less than that area; and require that changes of county boundaries have the approval of the local voters. Some state

---

[3] Cf. below, Chap. XII, "Powers of Local Units."
[4] See below, Chap. VIII, "Limitations on Special Legislation."

constitutions limit the power of local governmental units to levy taxes and to incur indebtedness, and in such cases the legislature is powerless to confer upon the local governments taxing or borrowing powers in excess of the constitutional prescriptions.[5] Constitutional provisions conferring home-rule powers upon cities and counties operate to limit the competency of the legislature in regulating local affairs. Although the combined effect of these and other constitutional restrictions is of considerable importance, the fact remains that, even in home-rule states, the state legislature possesses broad powers of control over most local governmental units.

Forms of State Control

All measures of state control over local government have their ultimate basis either in constitutional provisions or in enactments of the state legislature. Depending upon the means by which these measures are actually executed or carried out, it is helpful to distinguish two broad forms of control, namely, judicial and administrative.[6] In judicial control, constitutional and statutory provisions relating to local government are enforced directly by the courts in suits properly instituted therein. Administrative control, on the other hand, involves the primary enforcement of such provisions by officers, boards, and commissions within the executive or administrative branch of the state government. It is to be noted, however, that the action taken by administrative agencies in such matters is frequently subject to ultimate appeal to the courts for judicial determination.

Judicial Control [7]

One of the most direct forms of judicial control over local government and its officers is exercised through the writs of mandamus and injunction. A writ of mandamus is a court order directing a public officer to perform some duty imposed upon him by law, while an injunction is an order prohibiting the committing of an illegal act. If, for example, a city council is required by statute to impose a tax levy of a prescribed amount for health purposes and the council refuses to act in the matter of its own

---

[5] Limitations of this character are, however, frequently circumvented in practice by establishing within a given area two or more overlapping governmental corporations, each with its own taxing and borrowing powers. See below, Chap. XII, "Special Districts."

[6] What is here designated as judicial control is called by some writers legislative control. However, since administrative control also has its basis in legislation, the term *judicial control* seems preferable.

[7] Since the local courts are, strictly speaking, units in the state judicial system, judicial control over local government, even when exercised through such lesser courts, is properly considered a form of state control.

accord, it may be required by mandamus to make the levy. If a county board proposes to issue bonds in excess of a debt limit imposed upon the county by constitutional or statutory provision, resort may be had to an injunction suit to prevent such unlawful action. Suits for mandamus or injunction are usually instituted by local taxpayers, because of their financial interest, or by other private persons or public officers who have some direct and substantial interest in the matter concerned. Violation of a writ of mandamus or injunction constitutes contempt of court, for which the offender may ordinarily be punished summarily by fine or imprisonment, or both. Other judicial writs sometimes used to control the action of local officers are those of quo warranto and habeas corpus. A quo warranto action may be employed, for example, to test the legal right of a person in possession of a local office to hold the same, or to determine whether a community acting as a public corporation has been lawfully organized. Quo warranto suits are sometimes filed by private individuals who have an interest at stake, but are more often instituted by the prosecuting attorney in the name of the state. Habeas corpus proceedings are commonly used by or on behalf of persons held in jail or otherwise restrained by law-enforcement officers, to determine the legality of their detention.

These "extraordinary" writs, however, do not provide the only means of judicial control over local officers. If such officers commit any acts of a criminal nature, they are subject to prosecution in the criminal courts in the same manner as private individuals. Courts frequently construe the powers and duties of local officers in ordinary civil suits instituted by or against those officers or involving their official actions. Decisions of local administrative agencies are in many instances subject to appeal to the courts for final determination; and local officials are sometimes subject to removal from office by judicial proceedings.[8]

Administrative Control: Advice and Assistance

State administrative control over local government takes a great variety of forms, only the more important of which, with some typical examples, can be touched upon in this brief discussion.[9] Of considerable present-day importance, though not in the strict sense constituting *control*, since the element of compulsion is wanting, is the rendering to local governments by state administrative agencies of various kinds of advice, information, and service. Many state departments and boards give advice and assistance to local agencies either voluntarily or by statutory require-

[8] Cf. Clyde F. Snider, "State Control over Counties and Townships in Indiana," *John Marshall Law Quar.*, III, 556-569 (June, 1938).
[9] Cf. Schuyler C. Wallace, *State Administrative Supervision over Cities in the United States;* Clyde F. Snider, *Local Government in Rural America*, 91-104.

ment. In several states, for example, the state tax commission or an equiva-lent agency holds annual "schools" or short courses for local assessors at which the latter are instructed in the duties of their office and the proper procedures to be followed in performing those duties. Short courses simi-lar in purpose are sometimes provided by other state agencies, such as departments of health, welfare, and highways, for the benefit of local officers in their respective fields. In some states local governmental units are permitted to purchase materials and supplies through the state pur-chasing office, thus benefiting from scientific purchasing procedures and the lower prices which result from large-scale buying. State police depart-ments often aid local officers in the apprehension of criminals and in other law-enforcement activities.

Inspection

Inspection of local-government facilities and activities by state agencies is a widely-used form of administrative control. Representatives of a state department of education inspect local schools in many states with respect to both physical plant and instruction. Municipal water and sewerage systems are often inspected by the state department of health. Inspectors of the latter department commonly investigate community health and sanitary conditions to determine whether local health officers are performing their duties in a satisfactory manner. Local jails and wel-fare institutions are often subject to inspection by the welfare department or some other state agency. In many states, the accounts of some or all local officers who collect and disburse public funds are audited annually, or at some other regular interval, by state examiners. When, as a result of state inspection in any field, practices on the part of local officers are dis-covered which are inefficient, irregular, or illegal, it is ordinarily the duty of the state agency concerned to take whatever steps are necessary to cor-rect the situation. This can usually be accomplished through suggestions or orders of the state agency, but if need be resort may be had to the courts. If a shortage is found in the accounts of a local officer and is not made good voluntarily, a civil suit may be instituted against the officer or his bondsman to recover the amount of the deficit. If evidence is found of criminal intent, the matter may be referred to the regular law-enforcement authorities for prosecution.

Regulations

Another method of control is by means of regulations prescribed by state agencies, under statutory authority, for governing the conduct of local officers. A major form of control in this category is the prescribing in many state of accounting and budgeting forms for use by local governmental units.[10] Health, welfare, and other state departments frequently prescribe record and reporting forms to be used by, and procedures to be followed in carrying on the work of, local administrative departments in corresponding fields. Public-school curricula are in most states prescribed by state educational authorities.

Appointment and Removal

Although such power is by no means the general rule, there are numerous instances in which authority to appoint and remove certain local administrative officers is vested in a state agency. Coroners and justices of the peace, for example, are appointed in a few states by the governor; and in some half dozen states local health officers are appointed by the state health authorities. Several states make designated classes of local officers subject to removal by the governor or some other administrative officer or agency. The state removal power applies most commonly to law-enforcement officers, but is sometimes applicable to local officials engaged in financial, health, educational, and other activities.[11]

Approval and Review

Provisions for approval or review of local action by state administrative authorities are common, and constitute an effective means of state control. Local budgets in New Mexico and New Jersey, for example, and local bond issues in Louisiana and Michigan, must have the approval of designated state agencies. In Indiana, the state board of tax commissioners, on appeal by ten taxpayers of the local governmental unit concerned, will review any proposed local budget and tax levy, or any proposal of local fiscal authorities to issue bonds in an amount exceeding $5,000. After a public hearing in the locality concerned on any proposal appealed from, the state board may approve the proposal in its original form, reduce it in amount and approve it as thus reduced, or disapprove it entirely.[12] Iowa provides for the review of local budgets and tax levies by a state appeal board along lines similar to the Indiana system. Plans and specifications

[10] On this and other forms of state control in the financial field, see Wylie Kilpatrick, *State Supervision of Local Budgeting*, and the same author's *State Supervision of Local Finance*.

[11] Cf. Snider, *Local Government in Rural America*, 94-96.

[12] This "Indiana plan" of state control over local finance has been widely publicized. An excellent account is Frank G. Bates, "State Control of Local Finance in Indiana," in Charles G. Haines and Marshall E. Dimock, eds., *Essays on the Law and Practice of Governmental Administration* (A Volume in Honor of Frank Johnson Goodnow, Johns Hopkins Press, Baltimore, 1935), 229-268. See also Carl R. Dortch, "The 'Indiana Plan' in Action," *Nat. Mun. Rev.*, XXVII, 525-529 (Nov., 1938); Edwin E. Warner, "A Study of the Indiana Plan of Budgetary Review," *Legal Notes on Local Govt.*, IV, 279-295 (Mar., 1939).

for the construction of local roads and bridges sometimes require the approval of the state highway department. Local property assessments in the various states are commonly subject to review by a state board of equalization. Many states require state approval of plans for the construction and operation of municipal water and sewerage plants.[13] States in which local welfare departments administer federal-aid funds for old-age assistance, aid to the blind, disability aid, and aid to dependent children, provide that decisions of the local departments denying applications for assistance, or approving such applications only in reduced amounts, may be appealed to a state supervisory agency.

Grants-in-Aid

The conditional grant-in-aid, which was discussed in the preceding chapter as a means of national control over the states, is also used widely in the field of state-local relations. State grants to local units are employed most extensively, though by no means exclusively, in the fields of education, health, welfare, and highways.[14] As the price of state financial assistance, the local units receiving grants are usually required to meet standards of service prescribed by state administrative agencies, to submit to state inspection with respect to the activity concerned, and to make a stipulated contribution to the support of the service from local funds. In view of the unitary character of the state-local relationship,[15] the state in reality is not obliged to purchase in this manner local compliance with its standards, since it is legally competent to impose directly upon local governmental units whatever requirements it may see fit. However, the grant-in-aid frequently affords a practical means of equalizing governmental services and costs as among different localities; and local citizens are likely to accept state regulation with less complaint when it is accompanied by a cash consideration.[16]

Substitute Administration

The most drastic form of administrative control is that in which some local service, the performance of which by local officials has proved for some reason to be unsatisfactory, is actually taken over by a state agency and administered directly by its own personnel, but usually at the expense of the local taxpayers. This device is sometimes called "direct state administration" and sometimes, since it involves a substitution of

[13] Cf. W. Brooke Graves, *American State Government* (Heath, Boston, 4th ed., 1953), 823-824.

[14] For comprehensive discussions, see Russell J. Hinckley, *State Grants-in-Aid;* Henry J. Bittermann, *State and Federal Grants-in-Aid.*

[15] See above, "The Unitary Relationship."

[16] On revenue aspects of state grants-in-aid, see below, Chap. XXIV, "State Aid to Local Governments."

state for local personnel in conducting the service concerned, "substitute administration." This type of state control is intended only as a temporary expedient, and provision is ordinarily made for returning the function's administration to local officials when the situation which occasioned state assumption of control has been corrected. Substitute administration is most widely used in the public-health field, some forty states providing that local health activities may be taken over by the state in the event that local health officers fail to perform their duties satisfactorily.[17] The Indiana statute on this subject, which is fairly typical, provides as follows:[18]

> When, in the opinion of the state board of health, any local health authority shall fail or refuse to enforce the laws and regulations necessary to prevent and control the spread of communicable or infectious disease declared to be dangerous to the public health, or when, in the opinion of the state board of health, a public health emergency exists, the state board of health may enforce the rules and regulations of the state board within the territorial jurisdiction of such local health authorities, and for that purpose shall have and may exercise all the powers given by law to local health authorities. All expenses so incurred shall be a charge against the respective counties or cities. . . .

There are various circumstances in which state law-enforcement officials may supersede local officers. Thus, if local officers prove incapable of dealing with emergency situations arising from fire, flood, or other disaster, units of the National Guard, by order of the governor, may assume control. Substitute administration is sometimes used in financial matters. For example, several states, including Maine, New Jersey, and Alabama, have statutes which provide what is virtually a state administrative receivership for local governmental units unable to meet their financial obligations.[19] These laws vary greatly in detail, but the general import of their provisions is everywhere the same. If a local unit defaults on the payment of principal or interest on its obligations, the state supervisory agency may assume control of the collection and disbursement of some or all of the unit's revenues, and continue its supervision until the default has been removed. In some instances, unsound financial conditions short of actual default provide occasion for the state's assumption of control.

Extent of Administrative Control

Administrative control over local government has long been common in England and on the continent of Europe, and is now firmly estab-

[17] Cf. Graves, op. cit., 821.
[18] Burns Ann. Ind. Stats. (Bobbs, Indianapolis, 1949 Replacement), sec. 35-216.
[19] Some laws of this nature apply to any local unit within the state which is in default, while others are applicable only to units of one or more designated classes, such as cities or counties.

lished in the United States. Though scarcely any field of local activity in this country is now completely free from it, the device is employed most widely, as the illustrations in preceding paragraphs may have suggested, in the fields of finance, education, highways, health, and welfare. Since the spread of administrative control has been dependent upon its adoption by the legislatures of the individual states, it has inevitably made more progress in some states than in others. As a general rule, administrative control over local-government departments is exercised by the regular state departments operating in corresponding fields. In some instances, however, and especially in the field of finance, special state supervisory agencies have been established. Examples of agencies of this nature are Maine's emergency municipal finance board, North Carolina's local government commission, and New Jersey's department of local government.[20] In 1959 the New York legislature established a somewhat different sort of agency in the form of an office for local government in the executive department. The office is administered by a director appointed by the governor and an advisory board comprised of representatives of both the state and local governments. Included among the duties of the office are those of assisting in coordination of the activities of various state agencies providing services to local governments, serving as a clearinghouse of information on local-government problems, and advising and assisting local governments in the solution of their problems.[21] The Tennessee legislature in 1963 created an office of local government with functions substantially similar to those of the New York office.[22] Alaska's constitution provides specifically that an agency to advise and assist local governments shall be established in the executive branch of the state government; and, pursuant to this provision, a local affairs agency has been established by statute.[23]

Merits of Administrative Control

The rapid spread of administrative control during recent decades is to be attributed in large measure to certain advantages of this form of supervision over the older judicial form. In the first place, administrative

---

[20] John W. Fleming and Roy H. Owsley, "Maine's Emergency Municipal Finance Board," *Nat. Mun. Rev.*, XXVII, 143-147, 184 (Mar., 1938); Samuel D. Hoffman, "A State Department of Local Government," *Ibid.*, XXVIII, 348-354 (May, 1939); James W. Fesler, "North Carolina's Local Government Commission," *Ibid.*, XXX, 327-334 (June, 1941).

[21] Frank C. Moore, "New York State's New Office for Local Government," *State Govt.*, XXXIII, 227-231 (Autumn, 1960).

[22] *Nat. Civic Rev.*, LII, 443 (Sept., 1963).

[23] *Const. of Alaska* (1959), art. X, sec. 14. On the subject generally, see John G. Grumm, *A State Agency for Local Affairs?* (Bur. of Pub. Admin., Univ. of Calif., Berkeley, 1961).

control, or at least the possibility of its application, is continuous. Legislative requirements and restraints which are enforced only by the courts through the ordinary judicial process are applied only intermittently as interested officers or citizens institute suits for their enforcement. In contrast, a state administrative agency charged with enforcing statutory controls is on duty at all times and may usually go into action on its own initiative as well as at the request of interested parties. Again, administrative action is likely to operate more expeditiously. Judicial procedure is slow and complicated, and court dockets are frequently so crowded as to entail long delays. Administrative agencies ordinarily are free to follow simpler procedures, and if properly staffed should be able to handle their business promptly. In the third place, administrative control is more flexible than judicial. Regulatory statutes are usually enacted in general terms, and courts in interpreting statutory provisions lean heavily upon precedent. But the needs of local government vary as among different units and with differences in time. Administrative agencies, if granted adequate discretion by the legislature, are in a position to deal with individual problems of supervision as they arise, treating each according to its own merits. Finally, the administrative branch is the only department of government having trained, professional personnel in the fields of activity where state control is exercised. Legislators are elected from the general public to represent the voters in the formation of policy; and the principal qualities to be desired in judges are judicial temperament and knowledge of the law. Administrators, on the other hand, are or should be chosen because of their competence, gained through training or experience or both, in the fields in which they are to work. Local governmental problems, such as those of health and education, are largely technical in nature. The legislature is, of course, the proper agency for determining general policies of control; but of the three branches of state government, only the administrative is equipped to provide the element of "expertness" desired in the day-by-day supervision of local affairs.

Notwithstanding the various advantages just indicated, the success of administrative control over local government depends largely, in the final analysis, upon the personnel of the state agencies in which control powers are vested. If the supervising agencies are headed by politicians and staffed under the spoils system, the theoretical benefits of administrative controls are unlikely to be realized in practice. On the other hand, agencies headed by competent administrators and staffed by personnel recruited on a merit basis will go far toward assuring a control system gratifying alike to the local governmental units and to the state as a whole.

Constitutional Home Rule

Constitutional home rule is a form of state-local relationship in which local governments are granted, by state constitutional provision, authority to exercise certain local powers free from control by the state legislature. Some of the constitutional provisions are self-executing in nature, in the sense that they confer home-rule authority directly upon the units concerned, while others merely require or permit the legislature to confer such authority. Although provisions of the self-executing type place the local units in a stronger position than those necessitating legislative implementation, both types are generally considered as providing home rule of the constitutional variety.[24]

The powers constitutionally conferred upon local units fall into two general categories: (1) power to determine the form and organization of local government through the framing and adopting of local charters;[25] and (2) power to determine and regulate, free from state interference, matters which are of local concern as distinguished from those of general statewide interest. Home-rule provisions applicable to municipalities usually confer powers of both types; those pertaining to counties ordinarily are confined to matters of charter-making and organizational forms though in some instances they confer substantive legislative authority as well. As was suggested earlier in this chapter, constitutional home rule involves, in states where it exists, a limited degree of federalism in state-local relations. The United States Constitution divides governmental authority between nation and states with a view to permitting national control over matters of nationwide interest while reserving to the states control over other affairs. A state home-rule provision similarly attempts to divide authority between the state government and the local units in such manner as to permit state regulation in matters of statewide concern and local control in affairs of a local nature. In each instance, the subdivisional governments possess certain powers as the result of constitutional provision and are accorded constitutional protection against the usurpation of those powers by the general government. A fundamental difference is to be noted, however, in the manner in which the distribution of powers is made, on the one hand between nation and states and on the other between the state and local governments. Whereas the United States Constitution delegates certain powers to the general (national) government and reserves all others to the subdivisions (states), under state home-rule provisions the general (state) government is the agency of re-

[24] Cf. John R. Kerstetter, "Municipal Home Rule," *The Municipal Year Book* (Int. City Mgrs'. Assn., Chicago), 1956, pp. 255-256.
[25] The procedure for framing, adopting, and amending home-rule charters has been discussed in an earlier connection. See above, Chap. I, "Home-Rule Charters."

served powers, possessing all authority not delegated to the subdivisional (local) governments.

Municipal Home Rule

Beginning with Missouri in 1875, twenty-six states have now adopted constitutional provisions for municipal home rule.[26] In some of these, including Minnesota and Michigan, the home-rule provision is applicable to all municipalities, whereas in others home-rule powers are extended only to cities with populations in excess of a specified minimum. Thus, the home-rule provision is limited in West Virginia to municipalities of over 2,000 inhabitants, in Nebraska and Texas to those over 5,000, in Missouri to those over 10,000, and in Washington to those of 20,000 or more.

Altogether, it appears that more than 5,000 American municipalities are now eligible to frame and adopt home-rule charters, and that perhaps as many as 1,000 have actually done so.[27] While some home-rule municipalities are relatively small, the list includes many of the country's larger cities. New York City, in 1938, inaugurated a new charter which had been drafted by a local charter commission[28] and adopted by the city's voters. Other major home-rule cities include Baltimore, Cleveland, Cincinnati, Dayton, Detroit, Denver, Kansas City (Missouri), Los Angeles, Philadelphia, Portland (Oregon), and St. Louis.[29]

[26] The states are Alaska, Arizona, California, Colorado, Hawaii, Kansas, Louisiana, Maryland, Michigan, Minnesota, Missouri, Nebraska, Nevada, New Mexico, New York, Ohio, Oklahoma, Oregon, Pennsylvania, Rhode Island, Tennessee, Texas, Utah, Washington, West Virginia, and Wisconsin. In addition, Idaho's constitution confers upon municipalities local legislative authority but no charter-making power; and the constitution of Georgia authorizes the legislature to provide for municipal self-government. A few state legislatures have granted home-rule powers to cities without constitutional authorization. Such "legislative home rule," however, affords municipalities no constitutional protection against the legislature, for whatever powers that body grants it may take away. Moreover, home-rule statutes have been declared invalid by the courts in certain states as unconstitutional attempts on the part of the legislature to delegate its powers to the local voters. On the subject of legislative home rule, see Charles M. Kneier, *City Government in the United States* (3rd. ed.), 69-71.

[27] If home rule of the legislative type is included, the numbers of home-rule states and home-rule municipalities are somewhat larger than those suggested in this discussion. Furthermore, as broader or narrower concepts of constitutional home rule are applied, varying numbers are arrived at. Cf. John R. Kerstetter, "Municipal Home Rule," *The Municipal Year Book*, 1956, pp. 256-266; John R. Kerstetter, "Status of Municipal Home Rule," *Pub. Management*, XXXVIII, 74-76 (Apr., 1956).

[28] The commission was appointed by the mayor pursuant to statutory authorization.

[29] On the general subject of home rule for cities, see Howard L. McBain, *The Law and the Practice of Municipal Home Rule;* Joseph D. McGoldrick, *Law and Practice of Municipal Home Rule, 1916-1930;* Rodney L. Mott, *Home Rule for America's Cities;* Jefferson B. Fordham, *Model Constitutional Provisions for Municipal Home Rule;* Wallace Mendelson, "Paths to Constitutional Home Rule for Municipalities," *Vanderbilt Law Rev.,* VI, 66-78 (Dec., 1952); Arthur W. Bromage, "Home-

County Home Rule

County home rule developed later than home rule for cities and has made less progress.[30] Thus far, thirteen states have adopted constitutional provisions conferring home-rule powers upon counties or requiring or permitting the legislature to do so.[31] The first such provision was adopted by California in 1911. In addition to California, Hawaii, Maryland, Michigan, Ohio, Washington, Minnesota, and Oregon now have provisions applicable to all counties. New York's provision applies to all counties outside New York City, the Texas provision to counties having a population of 62,000 or more,[32] and that of Missouri to counties having more than 85,000 inhabitants. Florida's provision applies to Dade county only and that of Louisiana to Jefferson parish only. Of the 500 or so counties empowered under these provisions to frame and adopt home-rule charters, only some twenty—ten in California, three in New York, two each in Maryland and Oregon, and one each in Missouri, Louisiana (parish), and Florida—have actually done so.[33] In at least 20 other counties, home-rule charters have been drafted but have failed to receive the necessary popular vote for ratification. It is significant, though not surprising, that, even in those states which extend the home-rule privilege to all counties, the most active interest in home-rule charters has been displayed in the relatively populous counties.

Rule—NML Model," *Nat. Mun. Rev.*, XLIV, 132-136, 158 (Mar., 1955); Jefferson B. Fordham, "Home Rule—AMA Model," *Ibid.*, 137-142; Arthur W. Bromage, "The Home Rule Puzzle," *Ibid.*, XLVI, 118-123, 130 (Mar., 1957).

[30] On county home rule, see Arthur W. Bromage, *American County Government*, Chap. 5; Snider, *Local Government in Rural America*, 104-113; Gladys M. Kammerer, *County Home Rule;* John P. Keith, *City and County Home Rule in Texas*, Chap. 5; Arthur W. Bromage and Kirk H. Porter, "County Home Rule: Pro and Con," *Nat. Mun. Rev.*, XXIII, 514-519, 535 (Oct., 1934); Earl L. Shoup, "Judicial Abrogation of County Home Rule in Ohio," *Amer. Polit. Sci. Rev.*, XXX, 540-546 (June, 1936); Earl L. Shoup, "Constitutional Problems of County Home Rule in Ohio," *Western Reserve Law Rev.*, I, 111-132 (Dec., 1949); W. E. Benton, "The County Home Rule Movement in Texas," *Southwestern Soc. Sci. Quar.*, XXXI, 108-120 (Sept., 1950); David T. Kenney, "County Home Rule Today," *The County Officer*, XVI, 74-76, 81 (Mar., 1951); John P. Keith, "County Home Rule for Michigan," *Ibid.*, XVII, 234-240, 245, 252 (Aug., 1952); John Alexander McMahon, "County Home Rule and Local Legislation: A Case Study in North Carolina's Programming," *Ibid.*, XXII, 100-105 (Apr., 1957).

[31] In addition, the Idaho constitution confers certain local legislative powers upon counties, but no charter-making authority. Alaska's constitution extends the home-rule privilege to boroughs.

[32] The legislature may, by a two-thirds vote, authorize any smaller county to adopt its own charter.

[33] The California counties of Los Angeles, San Bernardino, Butte, Tehama, Alameda, Fresno, Sacramento, San Diego, San Mateo, and Santa Clara; Erie, Oneida, and Onondaga counties in New York; Montgomery and Baltimore counties in Maryland; Lane and Washington counties in Oregon; St. Louis county, Missouri; Jefferson parish, Louisiana; and Dade county, Florida.

Extent of Home-Rule Powers

Constitutional grants of legislative authority to local units ordinarily take one of two forms. Under the older and more prevalent form, a single grant in broad terms is made of authority to legislate in matters of local concern. Municipalities in California and West Virginia, for example, are given control over "municipal affairs"; Wisconsin cities and villages are given authority to determine their "local affairs and government"; and Ohio municipalities are granted "powers of local self-government." Although the various provisions thus differ somewhat in phraseology, their general import is in all instances the same. Their intent is to enable local governments to deal as they wish with matters primarily local in character, while reserving to the state legislature jurisdiction over state-wide matters. But their terms are so general that all detailed determination of what is of local and what of statewide concern, respectively, becomes a task for the courts. A city traffic ordinance conflicts with the state motor vehicle code. Is traffic regulation a matter of local or of statewide concern? If the former, the city ordinance must be enforced; if the latter, the state statute. A city council sets a streetcar fare by franchise provision and the state public service commission fixes a different rate. Which rate is the transportation company entitled to collect? A board of county commissioners fixes the county clerk's salary at $4,000 and a state statute provides that county clerks shall receive $5,000. Can the clerk of the county concerned collect the higher salary? Questions such as these, in almost infinite number, must be decided by the courts as they arise in the process of litigation.

The second form of provision, now found in several states, *begins* with a general grant of authority in local affairs, similar to the provisions just noted, but *then* proceeds to enumerate specifically certain matters as being definitely local in character. The Utah constitution, for example, confers upon home-rule cities power over "municipal affairs" and then lists various powers, including the following, as falling within the "municipal" category: assessment and collection of taxes; borrowing money; furnishing local public services, including public utilities; granting local utility franchises; and the power of eminent domain. Provisions of this nature, it will readily be seen, require somewhat less judicial interpretation than those of the type first considered, but still leave much to court determination. No attempt is ever made, for indeed it would be impracticable, to enumerate *all* matters which are to be considered as being of a local nature.

In classifying as local or statewide in character those governmental functions concerning which the constitution is not explicit, the courts of home-rule states have reached substantial agreement on some functions, but are in hopeless disagreement with respect to the proper classification of others. For example, the qualifications, terms, and salaries of municipal officers are usually held to be local in nature, whereas education and the regulation of public utilities are quite generally held to be of statewide concern. On the other hand, many matters, including finance and taxation, special assessments, and eminent domain, are held in some states to be local and in others to be of statewide interest.[34]

Merits of Home Rule

Home rule is of course not without its disadvantages. For one thing, as we have seen, the system tends to flood the courts with litigation. Again, as is always the case under federalism, it is extremely difficult, if not impossible, to devise a thoroughly satisfactory distribution of authority between the general government and the subdivisions. In the final analysis, it is doubtful whether any function of government is *solely* of either local or statewide concern; the most that can reasonably be said is that the interest of the local community or the state at large is *paramount*.[35] Moreover, the line between matters primarily local and those in which the state's interest is predominant cannot logically be fixed and static, but should change with the times and circumstances. Many activities such as health protection, which a half-century ago were largely of local interest, have now become of statewide and even national concern; and it is quite possible that some matters which today are considered primarily local may in the future come to be of concern to the entire state.

These disadvantages of home rule, however, seem to be outweighed by its positive merits. The plan tends to make local government more flexible and better adapted to local conditions and needs. Again, it relieves the state legislature of some of the burden of dealing with local problems, leaving the body free to give more attention to matters of statewide importance. But perhaps the greatest merit of home rule lies in the fact that it enables the inhabitants of the community concerned to have the kind of local government they desire, both as to form of organization and as to the exercise of local powers.[36] Every community must, of course, be subject to the state legislature in matters of statewide concern. In the absence of home rule, however, cities, counties, and other local units must secure state authorization before they can make the slightest change in their organization or undertake any additional local functions. Local inhabitants, especially in the larger cities, feel humiliated by this necessity, the more so because state legislatures are themselves usually controlled

[34] Cf. McGoldrick, *op. cit.*, Chap. 14.
[35] Cf. *Ibid.*
[36] Cf. Illinois Constitutional Convention Bulletin No. 6: *Municipal Home Rule* (Ill. Legis. Ref. Bur., Springfield, 1920), 420.

by representatives from rural areas.[37] Although many relatively small municipalities are operating successfully under home-rule charters, the plan is especially adapted to populous cities and counties. The urban populations of such communities are likely to be better satisfied under local governments based upon self-determination than under institutions imposed by a rural-dominated legislature; and past experience indicates that this concession to the democratic principle does not result, in practice, in any loss in governmental efficiency.

The Trend Toward Centralization

In the preceding chapter there was noted a tendency for the national government to increase in power and prestige at the expense of the states.[38] Constitutional home rule, which we have just considered, involves a degree of decentralization in the relation between the states and their local governmental units. On the whole, however, the state-local relationship is characterized by the same tendency toward centralization as that existing at the higher level.[39] For one thing, certain functions, as for example that of providing highways, have during recent decades been transferred in some states from local units to the state government.[40] Even more significant, as well as more widespread, has been the expansion of state administrative control over local government both by increasing the element of compulsion employed in the control mechanism and by extending control into additional fields. State centralization has naturally progressed further in some states than in others[41] but, even where it has made most headway, local government retains much importance. Indeed, the effect of state administrative control has often been an improvement and revitalization of local institutions.

NATIONAL-LOCAL RELATIONS

The United States Constitution makes no mention of local government, and consequently the power to establish and control local governmental units is reserved to the several states by the Tenth Amendment. Congress provides for governing the District of Columbia, and for establishing

[37] See below, Chap. VII, "Urban Under-Representation."

[38] Above, Chap. II, "Expansion of National Power."

[39] A comprehensive discussion of centralization within the states, covering the years down to the early 1930's, will be found in Leonard D. White, *Trends in Public Administration*, Chaps. 5-9. See also Paul W. Wager, "State Centralization in the South," *Annals of Amer. Acad. of Polit. and Soc. Sci.*, CCVII, 144-150 (Jan., 1940).

[40] See below, Chap. XVI, "Transfer of Functions."

[41] For discussion of the centralization movement in one of the states where it has proceeded furthest, see Paul V. Betters, ed., *State Centralization in North Carolina*; Paul W. Wager, "Effects of North Carolina's Centralization," *Nat. Mun. Rev.*, XXVI, 572-577 (Dec., 1937).

local governments in federal territories, but the creation and regulation of political subdivisions within the states is a state function. Over the years, nevertheless, numerous contacts between the national and local governments have developed, until today any discussion of intergovernmental relations in the United States must include some consideration of national-local relationships.

Older Federal Services

Prior to the depression of the 1930's, national-local relations were relatively informal in nature, consisting for the most part of advice, information, and services offered to the local units by various federal agencies. A few examples will indicate the general character of the federal services inaugurated during this earlier period. The United States Bureau of Standards made federal specifications available to local purchasing officers and published various informational pamphlets on local planning and zoning; the Office of Education issued numerous publications of interest to local school officers and teachers, conducted local school surveys upon request, and provided a consultative and advisory service for local boards of education; the Public Health Service made health surveys for local governments upon request, and assisted in the organization of local health departments; the Bureau of Public Roads assisted local highway officers on problems of road construction and maintenance; and the United States Civil Service Commission made its examinations available for use by local personnel agencies.[42]

More Recent Developments

During more recent years, these older federal services have been continued and expanded and, in addition, many new contacts, some of

---

[42] The predepression services offered by the national government to cities are catalogued and discussed in Paul V. Betters, *Federal Services to Municipal Governments.* On more recent developments in the relations of the national government to cities, see Paul V. Betters, J. Kerwin Williams, and Sherwood L. Reeder, *Recent Federal-City Relations;* Wylie Kilpatrick and Others, "Federal Relations to Urban Governments," in *Urban Government* (Volume I of the Supplementary Report of the Urbanism Committee to the National Resources Committee, Washington, 1939), 55-160; E. H. Foley, Jr., "Recent Developments in Federal-Municipal Relationships," *Univ. of Pa. Law Rev.,* LXXXVI, 485-516 (Mar., 1938); Paul V. Betters, "The Federal Government and the Cities: A Problem in Adjustment," *Annals of Amer. Acad. of Polit. and Soc. Sci.,* CXCIX, 190-198 (Sept., 1938); Raymond S. Short, "Municipalities and the Federal Government," *Ibid.,* CCVII, 44-53 (Jan., 1940); Frances L. Reinhold, "Federal-Municipal Relations—The Road Thus Far," *Nat. Mun. Rev.,* XXV, 452, 458-464 (Aug., 1936); Morton L. Wallerstein, "Federal-Municipal Relations— Whither Bound," *Ibid.,* 453-457. Developments in the relations of the national government to rural local units during a period of a dozen years, beginning in the mid-1930's, are discussed briefly in annual articles on "County and Township Government" in the *American Political Science Review.*

which involve a direct contractual relationship, have developed between the nation and the local governmental units. The immediate occasion for this noteworthy development was the economic maladjustment and widespread unemployment of the depression period. Confronted with an urgent need for vastly increased relief expenditures, and at the same time with dwindling tax revenues, the local governments appealed to the states and the nation for financial assistance. But the expenditures required were of such magnitude that they could not practicably be financed from current revenues, and most of the state governments, like the local units, operate under legal debt limitations. Since the borrowing power of Congress is constitutionally unlimited,[43] it was inevitable that the problem of supplying a large part of the needed funds should ultimately be passed on to the federal government. Recognizing that the depression was a calamity of nationwide extent, Congress embarked upon a national borrowing program to raise funds for the assistance of the hard-pressed states and local governments.

Public Works and Housing

For a brief period during the early years of the depression, federal funds were made available to the local governmental units, through state channels, for direct relief purposes.[44] Of more lasting importance, however, were the various federal work-relief programs—especially the making of federal loans and grants to the state and local governments for public-works purposes.

The best-known federal agency operating in this field was the Public Works Administration, established in 1933 for a two-year period but extended by subsequent legislation. The Public Works Administration made loans and grants to states and local governments for a great variety of projects, including school buildings, county court-houses and city halls, hospitals, streets and highways, sewerage systems, and electric and water utilities.[45] Originally the Administration was authorized to make grants of 30 percent of the cost of approved projects and loans for the remaining 70 percent; but in 1935 the statutory provisions were liberalized to permit grants of 45 percent and loans of 55 percent. As is usual in the case of financial assistance given by one government to another, federal loans and grants to local units under these provisions were not made uncondition-

[43] From time to time Congress establishes *statutory* debt "ceilings," thereby limiting, for the time being, the borrowing authority of the Treasury Department. Such limitations, however, are subject to statutory modification at any time.

[44] See Edward A. Williams, *Federal Aid for Relief;* Bittermann, *op. cit.*,

[45] Jack F. Isakoff, *The Public Works Administration;* J. Kerwin Williams, *Grants-in-Aid under the Public Works Administration.* The Public Works Administration was consolidated in 1939 into the new Federal Works Agency, which in turn was abolished in 1949 with its functions transferred to the General Services Administration. Chap. 11.

ally. When an allotment of federal funds was made, a formal contract was entered into between the Public Works Administration and the local government concerned, setting forth the terms and conditions under which the contemplated project was to be constructed. The conditions thus imposed upon the local units were numerous. The Administration reserved the right to inspect the construction to see that all terms of the loan and grant were complied with; all construction work was usually required to be done under contracts let on the basis of open competitive bidding; in selecting labor, designated classes of applicants, including ex-servicemen and their dependents, were to be given preference; certain stipulations were made concerning wages and hours of labor, and proper safety appliances for the protection of laborers were required; the use of materials produced by convict labor was prohibited; and funds for the payment of construction costs were required to be deposited in a banking institution protected by the Federal Deposit Insurance Corporation.[46] A special phase of the federal works program was the subsidy for low-cost housing provided by the United States Housing Act of 1937. Under this legislation, many city and county housing authorities organized under state law received federal loans and grants for the construction and operation of housing projects.[47]

These public-works and housing programs continued in active operation until, with the development of defense and war activities in the early 1940's, most of the previously unemployed were able to secure jobs in industry, and building materials were no longer available for nonmilitary construction. During the war years the federal government provided funds to local units for the construction, in military and defense-industry areas, of recreational buildings and other facilities designed to promote the welfare of military and naval personnel. Both loans and grants were provided for this purpose through the Federal Works Agency, into which the Public Works Administration had by then been consolidated. Though the construction of housing projects by local housing authorities was for the most part suspended, the federal government itself constructed many projects for housing military personnel and workers in war industry. Some of these federally-built projects were assigned to local authorities for management; and local authorities continued to receive federal subsidies for operating their completed projects.[48] After the war's end, local construction of federally-subsidized housing was resumed, and today housing and urban-renewal projects continue to constitute an important cooperative program of the national and local governments.

[46] Cf. Isakoff, *op. cit.*, 111-127.
[47] See below, Chap. XIX, "Local Housing Authorities."
[48] See Roy H. Owsley, "Federal-City Relations in 1941," *The Municipal Year Book*, 1942, pp. 204-216.

Municipal-Bankruptcy Legislation

A special type of national-local relationship growing out of the depression results from the federal municipal-bankruptcy or municipal-debt-adjustment legislation.[49] Some states, as we have seen,[50] provide administrative receiverships for defaulting local governments. Since, however, the United States Constitution forbids the states to pass laws impairing the obligation of contracts,[51] the authority of state legislatures to provide for the composition of local indebtedness is subject to serious restriction, and effective provision for debt-adjustment plans of a compulsory nature can be made only by the federal government in pursuance of its power over bankruptcy.[52] Faced with mounting local defaults, Congress in 1934 enacted the first Municipal Debt Adjustment Act. This statute was declared unconstitutional by the United States Supreme Court, on the ground that it constituted an attempt to use the bankruptcy power for the unlawful purpose of interfering with the reserved power of the states to control their local governmental units, but subsequent legislation of substantially similar nature was sustained.[53] Under the present law, dating in most of its features from 1946, a defaulting city, county, or other local unit may propose a plan for the composition or adjustment of its indebtedness. If this plan is approved by creditors of the defaulting unit holding two-thirds in amount of the claims affected by the plan, and by a federal court having bankruptcy jurisdiction, it becomes binding upon all creditors. The local units which have actually taken advantage of the federal law have not been numerous, and have consisted for the most part of irrigation, drainage, and other special districts.[54] However, the mere existence

[49] See Carl H. Chatters and John S. Rae, *The Federal Municipal Debt Adjustment Act: A Guide to Municipalities* (Pub. Admin. Service, Chicago, 1934); A. M. Hillhouse, "The Federal Municipal Debt Adjustment Act," *Nat. Mun. Rev.*, XXV, 328-332, 368 (June, 1936); Wylie Kilpatrick, "Federal Regulation of Local Debt," *Ibid.*, XXVI, 283-290, 298 (June, 1937); Giles J. Patterson, "Municipal Debt Adjustments under the Bankruptcy Act," *Univ. of Pa. Law Rev.*, XC, 520-532 (Mar., 1942).

[50] Above, "State-Local Relations—Substitute Administration."

[51] See above, Chap. II, "Impairment of Contracts."

[52] In a 1942 case the United States Supreme Court held that, notwithstanding the contract clause, a state composition law could, within appropriate limits, provide for debt adjustments which would be compulsory upon minority creditors. *Faitoute Iron & Steel Co. v. City of Asbury Park*, 316 U.S. 502 (1942). The municipal bankruptcy act of 1946, however, stipulates that no composition effected under state law shall be binding upon any creditor who does not consent to it, so that in practice minority creditors can now be forced into line only by recourse to the federal legislation. Jefferson B. Fordham, *Local Government Law* (The Foundation Press, Brooklyn, 1949), 693-694.

[53] *Ashton v. Cameron County Water Improvement District*, 298 U.S. 513 (1936); *United States v. Bekins*, 304 U.S. 27 (1938).

[54] Kilpatrick, *State Supervision of Local Finance*, 41.

of the law has doubtless been a factor in stimulating the unanimous agreement of creditors to voluntary compositions.

Other Relationships

Certain other illustrative national-local relationships may be mentioned briefly. From federal-aid funds received by the states for highway purposes, substantial sums have, especially during recent years, been expended on county and township roads and city streets. Federal funds have been made available to local governmental units for aid in the construction of airports, sewerage facilities, and water-supply systems. The Tennessee Valley Authority sells electric power to a number of cities and counties in the Valley area, and by contract with the local governments fixes resale rates to consumers.[55] Various western municipalities purchase from the Department of the Interior water and electric power from Boulder, Grand Coulee, Bonneville, and other federal dams. Federal grants are made to local health departments to aid in the support of qualified, full-time personnel, this assistance being especially important to county and district health departments in rural areas. Under the Hill-Burton Act, federal grants are made to local governmental units to assist in the construction of hospitals and health centers. The National Police Academy of the Federal Bureau of Investigation provides short-course training for select representatives of state and local police forces.[56] Aid in the form of technical assistance, materials, and equipment is extended by the United States Department of Agriculture to local soil conservation districts. That department also cooperates, through the state colleges of agriculture, in supporting the office of county agricultural agent. Federal aid has long been available to local schools for purposes of vocational education, and there is now federal support of school lunch programs. Though as yet no provision has been made for federal participation in the *general* costs of maintaining local schools throughout the country, Congress for some years has provided for grants to "federally-impacted" districts where the location of military or defense establishments has resulted in extraordinary increases in the school population. The federal Office of Civil Defense assists state and local authorities in providing air-raid shelters and formulating plans for protection of civilians in the event of enemy attack.[57] Federal funds are available in aid of city-planning ac-

[55] For discussion of numerous other contacts of the Authority with local governments, see Lawrence L. Durisch, "Local Government and the T.V.A. Program," *Pub. Admin. Rev.*, I, 326-334 (Summer, 1941); M. H. Satterfield, "TVA-State-Local Relationships," *Amer. Polit. Sci. Rev.*, XL, 935-949 (Oct., 1946).

[56] J. Edgar Hoover, "FBI Cooperation in Police Schools," *Pub. Management*, XXVII, 177 (June, 1945). The primary purpose of the Academy program is to train police instructors and executives who, in turn, will make the training available to their fellow officers.

[57] See below, Chap. IX, "Powers of the Governor—Civil Defense."

tivities. The Bureau of the Census publishes data on revenues, expenditures, and debt of local governmental units of all classes; issues periodic reports on employees and payrolls of state and local governments; and makes special local-government studies. So numerous, indeed, are present-day contacts of the national government with the local governmental units, and especially with municipalities, that the American Municipal Association has recommended the establishment of a Federal Department of Urban Affairs, of cabinet status, to be concerned with problems of local government and to organize national-local relations more efficiently.[58] However, proposed legislation to accomplish this objective was defeated in Congress in 1962.

Present Outlook

In view of past developments, the question naturally arises as to the probable future of national-local relations. Contacts between the national and local governments have tended to increase both in number and in directness, especially in times of national emergency whether due to economic depression or to war or threat of war. Observing this trend, some students of the subject have feared an insidious extension of national authority into local affairs which would undermine the states and ultimately result in a breakdown of the federal system. Careful examination of the facts, however, fails to justify any such dire foreboding. National policy toward the local governments has been principally one of assistance and cooperation—not of dictation. To be sure, conditions are usually attached to loans and grants of federal funds to local units, but this has long been the practice in federal aid to the states without disastrous results. It is significant, in this connection, that local governmental units must, almost invariably, have the consent of the state before entering into relationships with the national government involving the assumption of any direct obligation or any possible impingement of state authority. Thus, local governments in a given state can enter into contracts for federal aid for public works or housing, or take advantage of the Municipal Debt Adjustment Act, only if there is state legislation authorizing them to do so. Congress seems, indeed, to have exercised particular care, when enacting legislation affecting local government, to safeguard, at least

---

[58] "Federal Department of Urban Affairs Proposed," *Nat. Mun. Rev.*, XLVI, 139-140 (Mar., 1957). Cf. William L. C. Wheaton, "A New Cabinet Post?" *Nat. Civic Rev.*, XLVIII, 574-578 (Dec., 1959). Some scholars, opposing a Department of Urban Affairs, have argued that what is needed is a Council on Metropolitan Areas operating as a staff agency in the Executive Office of the President. See Robert H. Connery and Richard H. Leach, "U.S. Council on Metro," *Ibid.*, 292-297 (June, 1959); Robert H. Connery and Richard H. Leach, *The Federal Government and Metropolitan Areas* (Harvard Univ. Press, Cambridge, 1960).

nominally, state sovereignty over the local units.[59] Yet it cannot be denied that an individual state is under economic pressure to permit its local governments to participate in federal-aid programs since refusal to do so would result in federal funds, to which its citizens have contributed, being channeled to local units in other states.

With the tasks of all governments as interrelated as they are today, it appears reasonably certain that, unless something is done to check the present trend, contacts between the highest and lowest of our three governmental levels will continue to increase in both number and importance. Those who are fearful of further centralization of control in the hands of the national government would do well to seek improvements in state and local governmental services which might reduce the necessity of looking to Washington for the solution of local problems. All in all, however, there seems to be little reason to believe that some further extension of national-local relationships along present lines will seriously endanger our federal form of government.

REFERENCES

Advisory Commission on Intergovernmental Relations, *State Constitutional and Statutory Restrictions on Local Government Debt* (U.S. Govt. Printing Office, Washington, 1961).

———, *State Constitutional and Statutory Restrictions on Local Taxing Powers* (U.S. Govt. Printing Office, Washington, 1962).

———, *State Constitutional and Statutory Restrictions upon the Structural, Functional, and Personnel Powers of Local Government* (U.S. Govt. Printing Office, Washington, 1962).

BENSON, George C. S., *The New Centralization* (Holt, New York, 1941), Chaps. 7, 9.

BETTERS, Paul V., *Federal Services to Municipal Governments* (Mun. Admin. Service, New York, 1931).

———, ed., *State Centralization in North Carolina* (Brookings Inst., Washington, 1932).

———, WILLIAMS, J. Kerwin, and REEDER, Sherwood L., *Recent Federal-City Relations* (U.S. Conf. of Mayors, Washington, 1936).

BITTERMANN, Henry J., *State and Federal Grants-in-Aid* (Mentzer, Bush & Co., Chicago, 1938).

BROMAGE, Arthur W., *American County Government* (Sears Pub. Co., New York, 1933), Chap. 5.

Commission on Intergovernmental Relations, *A Report to the President for Transmittal to the Congress* (U.S. Govt. Printing Office, Washington, 1955).

[59] Cf. J. Kerwin Williams, "The Status of Cities under Recent Federal Legislation," *Amer. Polit. Sci. Rev.*, XXX, 1107-1114 (Dec., 1936).

Council of State Governments, *State-Local Relations* (The Council, Chicago, 1946).

The Federal Government and the Cities (School of Govt., Bus., and Int. Affairs, The George Washington University, Washington, 1961).

FORDHAM, Jefferson B., *Model Constitutional Provisions for Municipal Home Rule* (Amer. Mun. Assn., Chicago, circa 1953).

FRYE, Robert J., *Federal-Municipal Relations: An Overview* (Bur. of Pub. Admin., Univ. of Ala., University, Ala., 1963).

GOODALL, Leonard E., *State Regulation of Local Indebtedness in the United States* (Bur. of Govt. Research, Ariz. State Univ., Tempe, 1964).

GRAVES, W. Brooke, ed., "Intergovernmental Relations in the United States," *Annals of Amer. Acad. of Polit. and Soc. Sci.*, CCVII, 44-53, 144-160 (Philadelphia, Jan., 1940).

HEIN, Clarence J., *State Administrative Supervision of Local Government Functions in Kansas* (Govtl. Research Center, Univ. of Kan., Lawrence, 1955).

HINCKLEY, Russell J., *State Grants-in-Aid* (Special Rept. of the N.Y. State Tax Comsn., Albany, 1935).

ISAKOFF, Jack F., *The Public Works Administration* (Univ. of Ill. Press, Urbana, 1938).

KAMMERER, Gladys M., *County Home Rule* (Pub. Admin. Clearing Service, Univ. of Fla., Gainesville, 1959).

KILPATRICK, Wylie, *State Supervision of Local Budgeting* (Nat. Mun. League, New York, 1939).

————, *State Supervision of Local Finance* (Pub. Admin. Service, Chicago, 1941).

KNEIER, Charles M., *City Government in the United States* (Harper, New York, 3rd ed., 1957), Chaps. 4, 5, 7, 8.

LANCASTER, Lane, *Government in Rural America* (Van Nostrand, New York, 2nd ed., 1952), Chaps. 7, 14.

McBAIN, Howard L., *The Law and the Practice of Municipal Home Rule* (Columbia Univ. Press, New York, 1916).

McGOLDRICK, Joseph D., *Law and Practice of Municipal Home Rule, 1916-1930* (Columbia Univ. Press, New York, 1933).

McMILLAN, T. E., Jr., *State Supervision of Municipal Finance* (Inst. of Pub. Affairs, Univ. of Tex., Austin, 1953).

MILLSPAUGH, Arthur C., *Local Democracy and Crime Control* (Brookings Inst., Washington, 1936), Chap. 2.

MOTT, Rodney L., *Home Rule for America's Cities* (Amer. Mun. Assn., Chicago, 1949).

Nevada Legislative Counsel Bureau, *Home Rule in Nevada* (Nev. Legis. Counsel Bur., Carson City, 1952).

SNIDER, Clyde F., *Local Government in Rural America* (Appleton-Century-Crofts, New York, 1957), Chap. 4.

WALLACE, Schuyler C., *State Administrative Supervision over Cities in the United States* (Columbia Univ. Press, New York, 1928).

WHITE, Leonard D., *Trends in Public Administration* (McGraw-Hill, New York, 1933), Chaps. 5-10.

WILLIAMS, Edward A., *Federal Aid for Relief* (Columbia Univ. Press, New York, 1939).

WILLIAMS, J. Kerwin, *Grants-in-Aid under the Public Works Administration* (Columbia Univ. Press, New York, 1939).

4

Interstate and
Interlocal Relations

INTERSTATE RELATIONS

Constitutional Relationships

American federalism presupposes not only a close working relationship between nation and states, but also that the various states will cooperate among themselves and mutually respect the actions of each other. To foster interstate cooperation several specific provisions were included in the United States Constitution, and in practice many extra-constitutional contacts among the states have developed. The principal constitutional provisions concerning interstate relations are five in number. Three are found in Article IV of the Constitution and are commonly referred to as (1) the "full-faith-and-credit" clause, (2) the "interstate-citizenship" clause, and (3) the "interstate-rendition" clause. A fourth provision, in section 10 of Article I, relates to interstate compacts; and a fifth, in section 2 of Article III, confers upon the federal courts jurisdiction over interstate controversies.

Full Faith and Credit.[1] "Full faith and credit," declares the Constitution, "shall be given in each state to the public acts, records, and judicial

[1] Robert H. Jackson, *Full Faith and Credit: The Lawyer's Clause of the Constitution;* Edward S. Corwin, "The 'Full Faith and Credit' Clause," *Univ. of Pa. Law Rev.,* LXXXI, 371-389 (Feb., 1933); Bernard F. Cataldo, "Full Faith and Credit," *Annals of Amer. Acad. of Polit. and Soc. Sci.,* CXCV, Supp., 32-45 (Jan., 1938); James Wm. Moore and Robert Stephen Oglebay, "The Supreme Court and Full Faith and Credit," *Va. Law Rev.,* XXIX, 557-616 (Feb., 1943).

proceedings of every other state. And the Congress may by general laws prescribe the manner in which such acts, records, and proceedings shall be proved, and the effect thereof." Pursuant to this provision, Congress very early prescribed the method for authenticating state judicial records and proceedings and declared that records and proceedings so authenticated "shall have such faith and credit given to them in every court within the United States as they have by law or usage in the courts of the state from which they are taken." Methods have also been provided for authenticating and giving faith and credit to state legislative enactments and nonjudicial records.[2] It will thus be noted that the constitutional and statutory provisions relating to full faith and credit among the states cover three types of state action or instrumentality: (1) public acts; (2) public records, judicial or otherwise, and (3) judicial proceedings.

The public acts involved are state statutes or legislative enactments. In deciding cases before them, it is often the task of courts in one state to apply and enforce the statutes of other states. This is known in legal terminology as the "conflict of laws," and it is in such cases that the constitutional requirement is designed to assure full faith and credit. Suppose, for example, that a suit is brought in a Virginia court involving a contract made in North Carolina. Under such circumstances, the rights and obligations of the respective parties depend, not upon the law of contracts of the state in which the suit is brought, but upon the law of the state where the agreement was made. It thus becomes the duty of the Virginia court, in making its decision in the case, to apply, and to give full faith and credit to, the pertinent statutes of North Carolina.

Records entitled to full faith and credit include, among others, those involving such documents as wills, deeds, and mortgages. Many of these are to be found, in most states, in the office of the county recorder or register of deeds. When such instruments have been lawfully executed and made a matter of public record in any state, they must be given legal recognition in all other states. Thus, a will made and recorded in Illinois is entitled to full faith and credit in Nebraska, notwithstanding that the laws concerning wills may differ as between the states.

The judicial proceedings referred to in the clause are court judgments in civil cases.[3] Most common among these are money judgments and divorce decrees. Take, for illustration, a case in which X secures a valid money judgment against Y in Tennessee, but Y moves with his property to Kentucky before the judgment is satisfied. It is then the duty of the appropriate Kentucky court within whose jurisdiction Y or his property may be found, upon being presented by X with a certified copy of the

---

[2] *U.S. Code,* 1958 ed., Title 28, secs. 1738, 1739.

[3] For a discussion of the clause as applied to judgments, see Willis L. M. Reese and Vincent A. Johnson, "The Scope of Full Faith and Credit to Judgments," *Columbia Law Rev.,* XLIX, 153-179 (Feb., 1949).

judgment of the Tennessee court, to enforce the judgment against Y without retrying the case.

Because many persons seek divorces in states other than those in which they live, divorce decrees present a special problem with respect to full faith and credit.[4] The securing of a divorce is much more difficult in some states than others, and residents of states having strict laws frequently go to other states to secure divorces. In New York, for example, divorces will be granted only on the ground of adultery, whereas some states permit divorces on numerous grounds, including even an habitually violent temper or mere incompatibility.[5] Moreover, some states having liberal laws with respect to the grounds of divorce also require only a brief period of residence in the state before suit for divorce may be filed. Nevada, for example, permits the granting of divorces on some nine grounds and requires only six weeks' residence for divorce purposes. Now, a court can lawfully divorce only persons *domiciled* within its jurisdiction. A person's legal domicile is his home—his permanent abode. To be domiciled within a state a person must intend to live there permanently, or at least indefinitely. Clearly, persons who go to a state merely for the purpose of obtaining a divorce, without any real intention of remaining thereafter, do not acquire a bona fide domicile there. Divorce decrees granted under such circumstances may be denied recognition by other states on the ground that the courts granting them were without proper jurisdiction over the parties concerned, and that the decrees are therefore not entitled to full faith and credit.

A divorce granted by a court to parties both of whom are domiciled within the state is, of course, entitled to full faith and credit the same as any other civil judgment; and most states in practice accord full faith and credit to a divorce decree if one of the parties was legally domiciled in the granting state.[6] But a decree granted in a state where neither spouse is domiciled is not entitled to full faith and credit, and may be denied recognition by other states. It thus sometimes happens that a person is considered as married in one state and divorced in another—a situation which may result in numerous legal complications. Questions frequently arise, for example, concerning such matters as the validity of subsequent marriages, the legitimacy of children, title to property, and rights of inheritance.[7] The confusion and uncertainty flowing from the migratory divorce are well illustrated by a case decided by the United States Supreme

[4] See Dougal Herr, "The Migratory Divorce and the Full Faith and Credit Clause," *Temple Law Quar.,* XXI, 357-367 (Apr., 1948).

[5] Cf. Illinois Legislative Council, *Legal Grounds for Divorce* (Ill. Legis. Council, Springfield, 1944).

[6] Cataldo, *op. cit.*

[7] Maurice H. Merrill, "The Utility of Divorce Recognition Statutes in Dealing with the Problem of Migratory Divorce," *Tex. Law Rev.,* XXVII, 291-311 (Jan., 1949).

Court in 1945. A man and a woman, each married and domiciled in North Carolina, went to Nevada, remained the necessary six weeks, divorced their respective spouses in a Nevada court, and married each other. Upon returning to North Carolina and living as man and wife, they were prosecuted and convicted in the North Carolina courts of the crime of bigamous cohabitation. The North Carolina authorities took the view that the Nevada divorces were invalid, since in each case neither of the parties involved was actually domiciled in Nevada; that the defendants were still lawfully married to their original spouses; and that therefore their purported marriage to each other was bigamous and void. The conviction of the defendants was sustained by the Supreme Court, which held that the North Carolina courts were not obliged to give full faith and credit to the Nevada decrees.[8]

It is to be noted that the full-faith-and-credit provision does not apply to court judgments in criminal proceedings. One state is not obliged to enforce—indeed, has no authority to enforce—the criminal law of another. If a person convicted of a crime in one state escapes to another, the proper procedure is to secure the return of such person, for execution of the judgment, to the state in which he was tried. This is accomplished through the rendition process soon to be described.

Interstate Citizenship. The interstate citizenship clause provides that "The citizens of each state shall be entitled to all privileges and immunities of citizens in the several states." This provision, designed to prevent any state from discriminating unjustly against citizens of other states, requires that each state extend to citizens of every other the same privileges and immunities, with certain exceptions to be presently noted, which it extends to its own citizens. Ohio, for example, must permit citizens of Pennsylvania to engage in business in Ohio, to acquire property therein, and to bring suits in Ohio courts, on the same basis as Ohio citizens. Each state must accord to citizens of other states within its borders full protection of its laws; and property owned in one state by citizens of other states may not be taxed at a higher rate than that owned by the taxing state's own citizens. The constitutional provision, however, does not apply to political privileges. For instance, a citizen of New York who moves to New Jersey must comply with all constitutional and statutory qualifications of the latter state before being entitled to vote or hold public office there. Moreover, resources or institutions in which a state has a property right may be reserved by that state to its own citizens exclusively, or citizens of other states may be permitted to enjoy them only under special conditions. Thus it is quite permissible for states to charge higher fees to nonresidents than

[8] *Williams v. North Carolina*, 325 U.S. 226 (1945). Subsequent developments in the law of migratory divorce are considered in Herbert R. Baer, "The Aftermath of Williams vs. North Carolina," *N.C. Law Rev.*, XXVIII, 265-290 (Apr., 1950).

to their own citizens for hunting and fishing licenses, the use of state parks, or the privilege of attending state colleges or universities. It is to be noted also that corporations, though treated for some purposes as citizens of the state in which they are organized, are not considered as such within the meaning of the interstate citizenship provision. A corporation is "foreign" to all states except the one in which it is chartered, and states are quite free to impose upon foreign corporations higher license fees for doing business within their boundaries than are required of domestic corporations.

Interstate Rendition. An act constituting a state crime can be punished only by the state in which it is committed. Therefore, if no means were provided for the return of a person who commits a crime in one state and flees to another, criminals might readily escape punishment by merely crossing state lines. To prevent the defeat of justice in this manner, the Constitution provides that "A person charged in any state with treason, felony, or other crime, who shall flee from justice, and be found in another state, shall, on demand of the executive authority of the state from which he fled, be delivered up, to be removed to the state having jurisdiction of the crime." By act of Congress, the duty of "delivering up" such a fugitive is placed upon the governor of the refuge state. The process of returning fugitives as carried on between independent nations is known as *extradition,* and the same term is sometimes applied also to the process as between states of the American Union. For the latter, however, the term *rendition* seems preferable, in order to distinguish it the more clearly from the international process.[9]

The rendition process is relatively simple. The governor of the demanding state issues a formal "requisition" directed to the governor of the refuge state and requesting the return of the fugitive. This requisition is accompanied by a certified copy of the indictment or other essential documents in the case. If the governor of the refuge state honors the requisition, he issues a "warrant" of rendition directing the law-enforcement officers of his state to arrest the fugitive and turn him over to officers of the demanding state who will be sent to return him. In some instances, since it may be impossible to secure a requisition immediately, officers of the demanding state ask those of the refuge state to arrest the fugitive and hold him pending issuance of formal requisition papers. A fugitive whose rendition is sought may secure a judicial determination of the legality of his return by habeas corpus proceedings in the courts of the refuge state. In such proceedings, however, the court does not pass upon the guilt or innocence of the fugitive. It merely seeks to establish

[9] Cf. James A. Scott, *The Law of Interstate Rendition,* 1-5. This book is a comprehensive, though now rather old, treatise covering the entire subject.

that he is charged with a crime against the laws of the demanding state, that he was in that state when the crime was committed and is now in fact a fugitive from justice, and that he is actually the person whose rendition is sought.[10] When a fugitive has been returned through rendition proceedings to a particular state, he may be tried there not only for the crime for which his rendition was sought but also for any other criminal offense with which he may be charged.

Although the constitutional provision states that, on demand of the executive authority of the state fled, a fugitive *shall* be delivered up for return to that state, there is no legal means of compelling a governor to honor a rendition request. In the final analysis, the obligation imposed by the Constitution thus becomes a moral one only. A governor may, if he chooses to do so, deny rendition for any reason which he deems sufficient; and there have been some refusals to honor requisitions. Occasionally, for example, a governor will refuse to return a fugitive who, since the commission of the offense concerned, has lived for many years in the refuge state as a law-abiding citizen. Again, there have been instances of refusal where the governor of the refuge state has felt that the laws of the demanding state were unduly harsh, or that the fugitive would not receive a fair trial. But as a matter of interstate comity and practical administration, if not of enforceable law, requests for rendition are usually honored. The mere fact that a governor who is one day asked to return a fugitive to a sister state may the next day find it necessary to make a like request of the governor of that state, renders it unlikely that many rendition requests will be denied.

Interstate Compacts.[11] The Constitution contains no authorization of interstate agreements in positive terms. It provides, however, that "No state shall, without the consent of congress, . . . enter into any agreement or compact with another state . . . ," thus clearly implying that such agreements *may* be made *with* congressional consent. The courts have taken the view that the requirement of congressional consent was intended as a protection against interstate agreements of a "political" nature which might affect the power relationships among governments within the federal system, and especially agreements which might increase the power of the states and thereby encroach upon the supremacy of the national government. According to this doctrine, approval by Congress is not essential in the case of agreements which are "nonpolitical" in the sense that they do not disturb the established political balance and hence are not of national

[10] Other questions are occasionally considered by the courts. See "Scope of a Habeas Corpus Hearing on Interstate Extradition of Criminals," *Yale Law Jour.*, LIII, 359-364 (Mar., 1944).

[11] Since their basis is a specific constitutional provision, compacts are considered at this point rather than below with other forms of voluntary cooperation.

concern.[12] Pursuant to this interpretation of the constitutional provisions, some agreements have been concluded and put into effect without congressional approval.[13] In practice, however, it may be difficult to determine whether a particular agreement is political or nonpolitical in nature, and therefore most interstate agreements have been submitted as a matter of course for congressional consent.[14] Approval by Congress may either precede or follow the actual conclusion of an agreement. Consent may be given to an individual compact, or may be granted in blanket form to any and all compacts on a specified subject. An example of advance consent of a blanket nature is afforded by a 1934 statute which provided "That the consent of Congress is hereby given to any two or more states to enter into agreements or compacts for cooperative effort and mutual assistance in the prevention of crime and in the enforcement of their respective criminal laws and policies, and to establish such agencies, joint or otherwise, as they may deem desirable for making effective such agreements and compacts." [15] Some statutes granting advance consent nevertheless require that any compacts made pursuant thereto be submitted in their definitive form for final congressional approval.[16] This would seem to be a wise precaution, since advance consent is usually given in comparatively broad and general terms.

Though interstate compacts are sometimes made simply by the enactment of reciprocal state legislation,[17] the more common method is the conclusion of a formal instrument of agreement. The usual procedure is for commissioners representing the states concerned to negotiate and reach an agreement, which is subsequently ratified by the respective state legislatures and approved by Congress. A report of 1956 indicated that, over the years, no less than 101 compacts had been ratified by the

[12] Cf. *Virginia v. Tennessee*, 148 U.S. 503 (1893); *Dixie Wholesale Grocery, Inc. v. Martin*, 278 Ky. 705 (1939); *Roberts Tobacco Co. v. Department of Revenue*, 322 Mich. 519 (1948); Frederick L. Zimmerman and Mitchell Wendell, *The Interstate Compact Since 1925*, pp. 33-37.

[13] The southern regional education compact, for example, has been in operation for several years without specific congressional consent. Zimmermann and Wendell, *The Interstate Compact Since 1925*, pp. 8, 19-21, 39-41. The compact's provisions and their administration are described in John E. Ivey, Jr., "Southern Regional Education—A Progress Report," *State Govt.*, XXV, 207-210 (Sept., 1952).

[14] Some scholars, emphasizing the difficulty of determining whether or not a compact is political in nature, have argued that the proper test to apply in determining whether congressional consent is required is not the subject matter of the agreement but rather the degree and importance of its consequences. Cf. Leslie W. Dunbar, "Interstate Compacts and Congressional Consent," *Va. Law Rev.*, XXXVI, 753-763 (Oct., 1950).

[15] 48 *U.S. Stat. at L.* 909. Adoption of interstate crime compacts pursuant to this authorization has been widespread. See Council of State Governments, *The Handbook on Interstate Crime Control* (rev. ed., 1955), ii.

[16] See, for example, 54 *U.S. Stat. at L.* 261, authorizing any two or more of the fourteen Atlantic-coast states to enter into a compact concerning marine fisheries.

[17] Cf. Alice Mary Dodd, "Interstate Compacts," *U.S. Law Rev.*, LXX, 557-578 (Oct., 1936).

states. As of that date, every state was currently a party to some compacts, with the number of affiliations varying widely from state to state. New York was a party to 25 compacts, and each of three other states had ratified 17 or more. On the other hand, Iowa had ratified only three and each of seven other states had approved five or less.[18]

Most numerous, with respect to subject matter, are compacts settling boundary disputes between states and those allocating the rights to water from interstate rivers. Others concern such matters as stream pollution, flood control, forest fire prevention, oil conservation, interstate bridges, crime control, interstate transfer of patients in mental hospitals, the return of runaway juveniles, the pooling of educational resources, and even the development of nuclear industry. Many compacts have only two states, or at most a relatively small group of states, as parties. However, instances of broader participation are not unusual. Through the western regional education compact, for example, a dozen or so western states cooperate in providing professional education in medicine, dentistry, and veterinary medicine. By 1963 the interstate oil compact had been ratified by 30 oil-producing states, and by three additional states on an associate basis; and by 1953 all of the then existing 48 states had ratified the compact for interstate supervision of parolees and probationers.[19]

All in all, the interstate compact has proved to be in the past, and promises to be in the future, an extremely useful device for dealing with problems which concern more than a single state, and especially those with respect to which Congress is without jurisdiction.[20]

[18] Council of State Governments, *Interstate Compacts: 1783-1956.*

[19] *Oil Facts* (Committee on Pub. Affairs, Amer. Petroleum Institute), Vol. V, No. 6 (Nov.-Dec., 1963); B. E. Crihfield, "The Interstate Parole and Probation Compact," *Fed. Probation,* Vol. XVII, No. 2 (June, 1953), pp. 3-7. See below, Chap. XXI, "Oil and Gas."

[20] For further discussion of the subject, see Vincent V. Thursby, *Interstate Cooperation: A Study of the Interstate Compact;* Richard H. Leach and Redding S. Sugg, Jr., *The Administration of Interstate Compacts;* Frederick L. Zimmermann and Mitchell Wendell, *The Law and Use of Interstate Compacts;* Felix Frankfurter and James M. Landis, "The Compact Clause of the Constitution—A Study in Interstate Adjustments," *Yale Law Jour.,* XXXIV, 685-758 (May, 1925); Jane Perry Clark, "Interstate Compacts and Social Legislation," *Polit. Sci. Quar.,* L, 502-524, LI, 36-60 (Dec., 1935, Mar., 1936); Frederick L. Zimmermann and Mitchell Wendell, "New Experience with Interstate Compacts," *Western Polit. Quar.,* V, 258-273 (June, 1952); Richard H. Leach, "The Status of Interstate Compacts Today," *State Govt.,* XXXII, 134-139 (Spring, 1959); Richard H. Leach, "Interstate Agencies and Effective Administration," *Ibid.,* XXXIV, 199-204 (Summer, 1961). Authorities are not agreed concerning the enforceability of compacts. Some take the view that they impose, in the last analysis, a moral obligation only, but others believe that their provisions could be enforced by suit in the United States Supreme Court. Cf. *Federal, State, and Local Government Fiscal Relations* (Sen. Doc. No. 69, 78th Cong., 1st Sess.), 127; Herbert H. Naujoks, "Compacts and Agreements Between States and Between States and a Foreign Power," *Marquette Law Rev.,* XXXVI, 219-247 (Winter, 1952-53).

Settlement of Interstate Disputes. Controversies among neighboring governments are inevitable and, in recognition of this fact, the Constitution makes the United States Supreme Court the arbiter of interstate disputes. It provides that the federal judicial power shall extend "to controversies between two or more states," and that in all cases to which a state is a party the Supreme Court shall have original jurisdiction. Down to 1940, at least eighty suits were brought by one state against another in the Supreme Court, with every state except Maine being either plaintiff or defendant in at least one such suit.[21] These cases have involved a variety of subjects, but most numerous have been those concerning interstate boundaries and rights to water from interstate streams. Though many interstate disputes are now settled in practice by direct negotiation, through the conclusion of interstate compacts or otherwise, the Supreme Court is still the tribunal for the ultimate adjudication of such controversies if other means fail.[22]

Voluntary Cooperation

In addition to the various forms of interstate cooperation which flow directly from constitutional provisions, numerous means of voluntary cooperation have developed in practice. Some of these, such as uniform laws and state commissions on interstate cooperation, though originating merely in a desire that the states should work together in harmony, have crystallized into statutory form, while others remain quite extra-legal in both origin and operation. Voluntary cooperation of this character evolved slowly at first, but during recent years has developed at an accelerated pace.[23] Some of its more significant aspects will be considered in the sections which follow.

Uniform State Laws

There are many matters over which Congress has no jurisdiction, but with respect to which uniform legislation throughout the country is desirable. To promote uniform state legislation on such subjects, the National Conference of Commissioners on Uniform State Laws was organized in 1892. The Conference meets annually, and since 1912 has included representatives from all states and territories and the District of Columbia. Conference headquarters are now in the American Bar Cen-

[21] Charles Warren, "The Supreme Court and Disputes between States," *Internat. Concil.*, No. 366, pp. 20-42 (Jan., 1941).

[22] For a discussion of legal and procedural aspects, see Paul F. Good, "Judicial Determination of Interstate Disputes," *Neb. Law Rev.*, XXVI, 1-20 (Nov., 1946).

[23] Cf. Henry W. Toll, "Modern Machinery for Interstate Cooperation," *Ia. Law Rev.*, XXIII, 573-585 (May, 1938). For an interesting account of early examples of interstate cooperation see Albert S. Abel, "Interstate Cooperation as a Child," *Ibid.*, XXXII, 203-231 (Jan., 1947).

ter building, Chicago. Each state is represented on the Conference by commissioners, from one to five in number, appointed by the governor from the legal profession. Some commissioners are practicing lawyers, some judges, and some law teachers. To facilitate its work, the Conference has organized itself into seven sections, each dealing with legislation in a particular legal field: commercial law, property law, public law, social welfare, corporations, torts and criminal law, and civil procedure. In cooperation with the American Bar Association, the Conference drafts uniform statutes on subjects concerning which uniformity seems desirable and practicable, and recommends these drafts to the various state legislatures for enactment.[24] By the late 1950's, more than 100 uniform acts had been prepared under Conference auspices, and more than 50 of these were being currently recommended to the states. Of the recommended statutes, the Uniform Negotiable Instruments Act and the Warehouse Receipts Act had been adopted by all fifty states; and 14 others in the list had received more than 30 adoptions. The most significant achievement of the Conference to date is doubtless its comprehensive Uniform Commercial Code which replaces, wholly or in part, nine earlier uniform laws, including the Negotiable Instruments Act and the Warehouse Receipts Act. Approved by the Conference in 1952, the code had been enacted by 1963 in 18 states.[25]

In addition to its various *uniform* acts, the Conference drafts and recommends to the states *model* acts concerning matters with respect to which some degree of uniformity appears desirable but complete uniformity in phraseology is less essential.[26] Examples are the State Administrative Procedure Act and the Post-Mortem Examinations Act.[27]

The Governors' Conference

Important as agencies of voluntary interstate cooperation are various national organizations of state officials. Best known among these is the Governors' Conference, organized in 1908 and composed of all state, commonwealth, and territorial governors. The Conference holds

[24] W. Brooke Graves, *Uniform State Action*, Chap. 3; William A. Schnader, "Progress toward Uniform State Laws," *State Govt.*, XIII, 219-220, 231-232 (Nov., 1940); Walter P. Armstrong, Jr., "Uniform State Laws and the National Conference," *Ibid.*, XXXV, 185-190 (Summer, 1962); James Thomas Connor, "The Work of the National Conference of Commissioners on Uniform State Laws," *Tulane Law Rev.*, XXIII, 518-530 (June, 1949); Sigmund A. Cohn, "Georgia and the Uniform Laws," *Ga. Bar Jour.*, XIX, 457-471 (May, 1957). See also the annual issues of the Conference *Handbook*.

[25] Armstrong, *op. cit.*; William A. Schnader, "The Uniform Commercial Code: What Is Accomplished—What Remains," *State Govt.*, XXXVI, 49-53 (Winter, 1963).

[26] Connor, *op. cit.*

[27] A table showing what uniform and model acts have been adopted by each of the states may be found in George R. Richter, Jr., "Uniform State Laws," *The Book of the States* (Council of State Govts., Chicago), 1962-63, pp. 97-107.

annual meetings at which the chief executives explore matters of common concern to all of the states and adopt resolutions expressing official opinions of the organization. The Conference seeks to improve state government generally, giving particular attention to problems requiring interstate or federal-state cooperation.[28]

Other National Organizations of State Officers

Comparable in general purpose to the Governors' Conference, but more specialized in their activities and interests, are a number of other national organizations of state officials. Among these are the National Association of Attorneys General, the National Association of State Budget Officers, the National Association of State Purchasing Officials, the National Legislative Conference, and the Conference of Chief Justices.[29]

The Council of State Governments[30]

The present-day interstate organization of broadest scope is the Council of State Governments. Founded in 1925 as the American Legislators' Association, this organization, with expanded functions to serve administrative officials as well as state legislators, assumed its present name in 1935. Although nominally the American Legislators' Association continues in existence as a section of the Council of State Governments, for all practical purposes the two organizations may now be considered as one.[31]

The basic machinery of the Council consists of commissions on interstate cooperation established by the respective states.[32] Legislation creating these commissions usually provides that "The Council of State Governments is hereby declared to be a joint governmental agency of

[28] *The Book of the States*, 1962-63, p. 255. For further discussion, see Graves, *Uniform State Action*, Chap. 5; Joseph P. Harris, "The Governors' Conference: Retrospect and Prospect," *State Govt.*, XXXI, 190-196 (Summer, 1958). An excellent account of the role of the Conference in national affairs is Glenn E. Brooks, *When Governors Convene: The Governors' Conference and National Politics*.

[29] *The Book of the States*, 1962-63, pp. 256-261. Additional organizations of this character are discussed by W. Brooke Graves in his *American State Government* (Heath, Boston, 4th ed., 1953), 864-865.

[30] This description of the Council and its activities is based principally on accounts in various issues of *The Book of the States* and descriptive booklets published by the Council. See also *Federal, State, and Local Government Fiscal Relations*, 129-135.

[31] Concerning Council history, see Henry W. Toll and Frederick L. Zimmermann, "The Founding of the Council of State Governments," *State Govt.*, XXXII, 162-173 (Summer, 1959).

[32] See Hubert R. Gallagher, "Work of the Commissions on Interstate Cooperation," *Annals of Amer. Acad. of Polit. and Soc. Sci.*, CCVII, 103-110 (Jan., 1940); Frederick L. Zimmermann and Richard H. Leach, "The Commissions on Interstate Cooperation," *State Govt.*, XXXIII, 233-242 (Autumn, 1960).

this state and of the other states which cooperate through it." Virtually every state now has a commission on interstate cooperation or an equivalent agency. In most states, the commission, following the provisions of a model bill drafted by the Council, consists of five members from each of the two houses of the legislature and five administrative officials. The policy-determining body of the Council is its Board of Managers, consisting of delegate members from all of the states and Puerto Rico, nineteen ex-officio members, ten members-at-large, and one life member. State delegates are in most instances chosen by the respective state commissions on interstate cooperation. The ex-officio managers are the nine members of the executive committee of the Governors' Conference; the presidents or chairmen of nine national organizations of state officials;[33] and the Honorary President of the Council. Managers-at-large are elected by the Board of Managers itself for five-year staggered terms, and the life member is the immediate past executive director of the Council. Officers of the Council are elected by the Board of Managers and serve as members of the board's executive committee. The Council's executive director is appointed by the executive committee with the approval of the Board of Managers. The Board of Managers meets annually and on call, while the executive committee holds more frequent meetings. The Council maintains a central office in Chicago, an office in Washington, D.C., and regional offices in New York, Atlanta, and San Francisco.

The Council of State Governments has four principal objectives: (1) to serve the states as a clearinghouse for information and research; (2) to foster improvement in state legislative and administrative practices; (3) to promote cooperation among the states in the solution of interstate problems; and (4) to facilitate federal-state cooperation in matters of common concern. The Council encourages the adoption of interstate compacts, the enactment of uniform and reciprocal statutes, and informal cooperation among state officials. An Interstate Legislative Reference Bureau is maintained for the use of state legislators and administrative officials, and conferences on current governmental problems are sponsored. The Council serves as secretariat for the Governors' Conference; the Conference of Chief Justices; the American Legislators' Association; the national associations of state Attorneys General, Budget Officers, and Purchasing Officials; the National Legislative Conference; the Parole and Probation Compact Administrators' Association; the Juvenile Compact Administrators' Association; and the National Conference of Court Administrative Officers. In addition, the Council works in close co-

---

[33] The National Association of Attorneys General, National Association of State Budget Officers, National Association of State Purchasing Officials, Parole and Probation Compact Administrators' Association, National Legislative Conference, National Conference of Commissioners on Uniform State Laws, Conference of Chief Justices, Association of Juvenile Compact Administrators, and National Conference of Court Administrative Officers.

operation with the National Conference of Commissioners on Uniform State Laws. Thus the Council is enabled, as an important phase of its activity, to coordinate the work of a considerable number of interstate agencies. Regular Council publications include a quarterly magazine entitled *State Government,* a monthly newsletter entitled *State Government News,* a biennial manual of information known as *The Book of the States,* a monthly publication *States and Nation* reporting news of congressional and administrative activities of interest to the states, and a quarterly *Legislative Research Checklist.* There is also frequent publication of special studies dealing with state government and interstate and federal-state relations. The Council sponsors a biennial General Assembly of representative legislators and administrative officials from the various states for the discussion of common problems. Originally supported in part from private philanthropic funds, the Council is now financed entirely through state legislative appropriations.

Regional Organizations

In addition to the organizations of nationwide scope just discussed, there are certain organizations designed to foster interstate cooperation on a regional or sectional basis. Thus the New England Council, created in 1925, has sponsored various meetings of governors and administrative officials of the New England states for the discussion of common problems and agreement on common action. Among the matters dealt with have been agriculture, flood control, and industrial and recreational development.[34] Also on a regional basis are the Southeastern Governors' Council, a Western Governors' Conference, and, organized in 1962, a Midwest Governors' Conference.[35] In 1945, public officials in Washington, Oregon, and California organized a Pacific Coast Board of Intergovernmental Relations, consisting of representatives of cities, counties, the three cooperating states, and the western offices of certain federal agencies. Meetings of this organization are held quarterly for the discussion of regional problems at all governmental levels.[36]

Noncooperation: Interstate Trade Barriers

Thus far we have been concerned principally with organizations, practices, and constitutional provisions designed to foster cooperation

[34] Arthur W. Bromage, *State Government and Administration in the United States* (Harper, New York, 1936), 640; Toll, "Modern Machinery for Interstate Cooperation," *loc. cit.*

[35] Cf. Toll, "Modern Machinery for Interstate Cooperation," *loc. cit.* On other regional conferences, see Graves, *Uniform State Action,* Chap. 5.

[36] Miriam Roher, "Coast States Try Cooperation," *Nat. Mun. Rev.,* XXXIV, 484-487 (Nov., 1945); Stanley K. Crook, "The Pacific Coast Board of Intergovernmental Relations," *Pub. Admin. Rev.,* XI, 103-108 (Spring, 1951).

among the several states. At times, however, state action is noncooperative, or even positively hostile, toward sister states. Such noncooperation assumes a variety of forms, but especially significant is that of interstate trade barriers. A trade barrier has been defined as "a statute, regulation, or practice which operates or tends to operate to the disadvantage of persons, products, or commodities coming from sister states, to the advantage of local residents or industries." [37] Interstate trade barriers operate on the national scene much as do tariff walls in international trade.

Some of the more important interstate trade barriers result from the imposition of certain state taxes. About half of the states, for example, impose taxes upon oleomargarine, including annual license fees on manufacturers, dealers, and importers, and specific excises of from 5 to 15 cents per pound. Dairy states having such taxes usually impose them upon all margarine products, to prevent their competition with butter. On the other hand, nondairy states with products useful in the manufacture of margarine sometimes apply the tax only to that made of "foreign" products. Thus, some southern states exempt from the tax margarine containing cottonseed oil, corn oil, or peanut oil—all local products; and several cattle-producing states tax only margarine not containing specified minimum percentages of animal fats or oils. That oleomargarine levies are not imposed for revenue, but rather to protect domestic producers of butter or margarine, is clearly evidenced by the fact that in most states having such taxes the revenue therefrom is negligible.[38]

Even more widespread are trade barriers in the form of state liquor taxes. Under the Twenty-first Amendment to the United States Constitution, a state is free to pass whatever discriminatory legislation it may wish with respect to intoxicating liquor. Trade-barrier laws in most fields are enacted by the states under their police power or the taxing power. Since state action which *directly* obstructs interstate commerce is deemed unconstitutional, barrier legislation must be so framed that any interference with such commerce is, on its face at least, of *indirect* nature only. With respect to liquor legislation, however, the commerce clause of the Constitution does not operate as a limitation upon the states, and in that field therefore discriminatory action may be taken quite openly and

[37] Temporary National Economic Committee, *Interstate Trade Barriers*, 15739.

[38] This and the succeeding paragraphs in this section are based principally upon *Federal, State, and Local Government Fiscal Relations*, 252-268; F. E. Melder, *State Trade Walls;* and Raymond L. Buell, *Death by Tariff*. For further discussion, see Temporary National Economic Committee, *op. cit.;* F. E. Melder, *State and Local Barriers to Interstate Commerce in the United States;* Thomas S. Green, Jr., *Liquor Trade Barriers;* George R. Taylor, Edgar L. Burtis, and Frederick V. Waugh, *Barriers to International Trade in Farm Products;* Tax Institute, *Tax Barriers to Trade;* Margaret R. Purcell, *Interstate Barriers to Truck Transportation;* J. S. Hillman and J. D. Rowell, *Barriers to the Interstate Movement of Agricultural Products by Motor Vehicle in the Eleven Western States;* Joint Committee of the States to Study Alcoholic Beverage Laws, *Trade Barriers Affecting Interstate Commerce in Alcoholic Beverages.*

aboveboard. Many states have laws which make differentials, in license fees or gallonage taxes or both, in favor of liquor produced within their boundaries. License fees of large amounts have been exacted of nonresident manufacturers and wholesalers for the privilege of shipping liquor into certain states. Michigan, some years ago, taxed Michigan-produced wine only 4 cents per gallon though taxing other wines at the rate of 50 cents; and Georgia taxed dry wine only 5 cents per gallon if made from native grapes, but 40 cents if made from grapes grown in other states.[39] Some states even go so far as to discriminate, in the taxation of out-of-state liquor, in favor of the products of one state as against those of another— a practice which in some instances has led to "wars of retaliation" in the enactment of tax legislation.

Another field in which many interstate barriers are to be found is that of motor-vehicle laws. All states now practice reciprocity in recognizing the license plates of visiting passenger automobiles, but some require out-of-state trucks and buses to register and pay a license fee. Multiple-registration requirements naturally result in discrimination against interstate traffic. At one time it was reported, for example, that a five-to-six ton truck traveling from Alabama to South Carolina would have to pay fees of $400 in Alabama, $400 in Georgia, and $300 in South Carolina—a total of $1,100—whereas a truck operating entirely within one of the states would of course pay one fee only.[40] Action by one state in requiring registration of out-of-state trucks is frequently followed by retaliatory action on the part of sister states, and in some instances the ultimate result has been vicious "border wars" involving the wholesale arrest and detention of drivers of nonregistered "foreign" trucks. Impediments to interstate traffic also result from varying state regulations concerning safety requirements, and maximum weight and dimensions of vehicles and loads.

A particularly drastic form of motor-vehicle barrier is seen in the "port-of-entry" laws enacted, during the 1930's, by Kansas and some nine other western states. These statutes varied in detail, but the general import of all was the same. Commercial vehicles entering a state having such a law were required to do so through officially-designated "ports" established at intervals along the border. At the port of entry, each truck and bus was stopped and subjected to various forms of inspection. Thus lights and brakes might be examined, and the loaded vehicle weighed and measured to make certain that it complied with state restrictions. If the state required the carrying of liability insurance, the fact that such was carried would have to be demonstrated. A fee for use of the state's highways, frequently measured on a ton-mile basis for the proposed trip, was collected; and sometimes also the regular state tax upon whatever gasoline the vehicle carried in its fuel tank or elsewhere. All requirements

---

[39] Taylor, Burtis, and Waugh, *op. cit.*, 32-33.
[40] Temporary National Economic Committee, *op. cit.*, 15790.

having been complied with, the driver was supplied by port officials with formal papers or stickers indicating that his vehicle had properly "cleared" the port. The declared purposes of these port-of-entry laws included those of promoting traffic-safety, requiring out-of-state commercial users to bear a share of the cost of highway maintenance, and preventing the "bootlegging" of gasoline into the state. But whatever the motives of legislatures in enacting them, the statutes inevitably operate as impediments to interstate traffic. Where such laws are in force, the crossing of a state line takes on much the same character as the crossing of an international boundary, with port offices corresponding to customs stations, and the clearance papers supplied to drivers being comparable to visas from immigration officers. All this tends to give the states the appearance of being "foreign countries" to each other rather than sister commonwealths within a single nation.

Trade-barrier laws, it cannot be denied, confer certain benefits upon the states enacting them, or at least upon interest groups therein. But those benefits are often problematical, and in most cases are likely more than offset, in net results, by the ill feeling and retaliation which the measures engender. Wisconsin, for example, places a high tax on oleomargarine to protect her butter producers, but about 90 percent of the butter produced in Wisconsin is sold outside the state[41] and therefore cannot possibly benefit by the tax. Moreover, the tax encourages states producing oils used in the manufacture of margarine to retaliate against Wisconsin products. Some years ago the California legislature, faced with the virtual exclusion of California wines from Michigan by the latter state's high gallonage tax on out-of-state products, seriously considered enacting a law which would have prohibited the purchase of Michigan-made automobiles for public use in California. Though this proposal was dropped before it came to fruition, it is illustrative of the natural temptation on the part of states whose products are the victims of discriminatory action to seek retaliation.

The decade of the 1930's witnessed a phenomenal increase in the amount of trade-barrier legislation. This was doubtless due in part to the economic depression, which caused states to seek new sources of revenue and to promote the interests of local business in every way possible. In 1939, however, the Council of State Governments, recognizing the seriousness of the situation, made the elimination of interstate barriers a major point in its program, and sponsored a national conference on the subject at which most states were represented by members of their commissions on interstate cooperation. The conference adopted a resolution strongly opposing trade barriers; and subsequently several regional conferences were held to deal with barriers of particular types. In a follow-up program, the Council campaigned vigorously against the enactment of

[41] Melder, *State Trade Walls*, 26.

new trade-barrier legislation, and sought to secure, wherever possible, the elimination of existing barriers. As a result of these efforts, the further spread of state trade barriers was in large measure stopped. More recently little new legislation of the kind has been enacted and some of the earlier laws have been repealed. It is unfortunate, however, that much barrier legislation still remains on the statute books of the various states. Uniform legislation and interstate compacts offer much more promise than do discriminatory laws as means of solving interstate economic problems.[42]

INTERLOCAL RELATIONS

Local governmental units in the states are, for the most part, quite independent of each other. Each unit usually has its own officials and taxing power, and conducts its affairs with little regard for neighboring or overlapping governments. But with so many local units in each state, and various overlapping units operating within the same territory,[43] it has been inevitable that certain interrelationships, both legal and extralegal, should develop at the local level. Some of these relationships are of a competitive nature. This is often the case, for example, in revenue matters, with each of the various units or classes of units seeking as large a portion as possible of the public moneys. Thus, cities may contend with counties before the legislature for grants of taxing power or shares of state-distributed funds; and in states with overall tax-rate limits it is commonly necessary, because of intergovernmental competition, to establish at either the state or the county level an administrative agency to apportion the total rate among the various units within a given area.[44] Many interlocal relationships, however, are cooperative in character.

State Municipal Leagues

One of the oldest and most widely-used agencies of interlocal cooperation is the state municipal league, with its membership consisting of cities and villages[45] as corporate entities. The organization of municipal leagues began in the last decade of the 1800's. By 1962 leagues were operating in forty-five states, with total league membership at that time including nearly 13,000 municipalities.[46] Most of the leagues maintain perma-

[42] Cf. *The Book of the States*, 1941-42, pp. 1, 14, 17-18; *Ibid.*, 1943-44, pp. 40-41.

[43] See below, Chap. XII, "Number of Units," "Pyramiding and Overlapping of Units."

[44] Cf. Clyde F. Snider, "Fiscal Control at the County Level," *Nat. Mun. Rev.*, XXX, 579-586 (Oct., 1941).

[45] Some leagues also admit certain other local units to membership.

[46] Patrick Healy, "State Municipal Leagues in 1962," *The Municipal Year Book* (Int. City Mgrs.' Assn., Chicago), 1963, pp. 208-213, and similar annual summaries by various authors in earlier issues of the *Year Book*.

nent offices, under full-time secretaries, and some employ additional staff. One of the most important league activities is the holding of an annual convention at which officials representing member municipalities discuss current problems of municipal government. Leagues usually provide an information service, and often also a consultant service, to their members. Another major activity is the sponsoring of legislative programs through which measures deemed beneficial to municipalities are supported and those considered detrimental to municipal interests are opposed. Several leagues engage in municipal research in cooperation with their respective state universities; and some sponsor in-service training programs for municipal officials. In some instances the league provides centralized purchasing facilities through which small municipalities may pool their orders and thus economize through large-scale buying. More than half of the leagues publish official magazines, usually on a monthly basis, to publicize league activities and information of interest to members. Municipal leagues are financed primarily from dues of member municipalities.[47]

The American Municipal Association

State municipal leagues are federated on a national basis in the American Municipal Association. This federation, organized in 1924, promotes the organization of new leagues and the reorganization of any which become inactive, and attempts in general to expand and strengthen the league movement. It holds an annual convention, which is attended for the most part by staff members and field agents of state leagues; serves member leagues and municipalities as a clearinghouse of information; and publishes research bulletins. With offices in Washington, the Association seeks to safeguard the interests of municipalities in federal legislation, and publishes a weekly *Washington News Letter* reporting on proposed legislation and other matters of interest to municipalities. The Association is supported by dues payments from member leagues.[48]

The United States Conference of Mayors

The United States Conference of Mayors held its first meeting in 1932 and was formally organized the following year. The Conference was instituted by the mayors of some of the larger cities, primarily as a means of cooperation in dealing with current relief problems. Any municipality with a population of more than 50,000 is eligible for membership, and the executive committee of the Conference may invite any other city with a

---

[47] Harold D. Smith, "Associations of Cities and of Municipal Officials," *Urban Government* (Volume I of the Supplementary Report of the Urbanism Committee to the National Resources Committee, Washington, 1938), 179-245.

[48] Cf. *Ibid.* The American Municipal Association is to be distinguished from the National Municipal League. The League, with headquarters in New York City, is a national civic organization having interests much broader than those of the Association and being concerned with problems at all three levels of government.

population of at least 30,000 to join. By 1936, 150 cities had become Conference members. The purposes and activities of the Conference are in many respects similar to those of the American Municipal Association, but there are also important differences. Whereas the Association is a national federation of state municipal leagues, the Conference is a national organization of individual municipalities. While the Association, like the leagues which comprise it, is concerned with matters of interest to all municipalities, large and small, the Conference specializes in the problems of large cities. Finally, whereas the Association concerns itself chiefly with local and state-local problems, the relations of municipalities to the national government being only one of its many interests, the *primary* purpose of the Conference is that of representing the larger cities of the country before Congress and federal administrative agencies. The Conference holds annual meetings, maintains a permanent office in the nation's capital, and publishes a news letter, *The United States Municipal News,* circulated to several thousand city officials and other people interested in municipal government. Conference financing is from membership dues.[49]

Organizations of County and Township Officers

County and township officials are commonly organized on a state-wide basis. In various states will be found state-wide associations of township trustees or supervisors, county commissioners, county clerks, county treasurers, sheriffs, coroners, recorders, highway supervisors, assessors, surveyors, prosecuting attorneys, justices of the peace, and other local officers. In some instances there is a separate organization for the incumbents of each office, and in others a single association serves two or more offices. The principal activities of these various associations ordinarily consists of an annual convention and concerted action with respect to proposed legislation. In some states, the organizations serving individual offices or combinations of offices are joined together in a single statewide federation. Examples are the Indiana County and Township Officials Association and the Illinois Association of County Officials. Federations of this character usually hold annual conventions and in some instances publish official magazines. Such organizations do much to enhance the influence of county and township officers over the course of state legislation pertaining to local government. In 1936 there was organized a National Association of County Officials, with a membership consisting of county officers and employees in the various states. This organization, now known as the National Association of Counties, holds an annual convention and publishes an official monthly magazine entitled *The County Officer.*[50]

---

[49] Smith, *op. cit.*

[50] Cf. Dean Z. Haddick, "NACO and its Organization," The *County Officer,* XVII, 231-233 (Aug., 1952); Alastair McArthur, "State Associations of County Officials in 1962," *The Municipal Year Book,* 1963, pp. 64-69.

Professional Organizations of Local Administrators

Of a different nature, but deserving of mention in a discussion of intergovernmental relations, are various professional associations of local officials organized on a nationwide or international basis. One of the most important of these is the International City Managers' Association, the professional organization of city and county managers. This association holds an annual convention and, among its other activities, provides correspondence courses of instruction, for local officials and other interested persons, in various phases of municipal government and administration. Its publications include *Public Management*, a monthly journal; *The Municipal Year Book*, an annual compendium of municipal facts and developments; and a semi-monthly *City Managers' News Letter*. Among other organizations serving local officials are the Municipal Finance Officers Association of the United States and Canada, the International Association of Chiefs of Police, and the National Institute of Municipal Law Officers.[51] Organizations of this character exercise a substantial influence in the improvement of local administration and the promotion of intergovernmental cooperation.

Cooperative Performance of Local Functions

The organizations for interlocal cooperation described in the preceding paragraphs have developed for the most part extralegally, though some states now have statutes authorizing the payment of membership dues in certain of these organizations from public funds. A type of cooperation ordinarily based upon express constitutional or statutory provision is that in which two or more units of local government, of the same or different classes, collaborate in the performance of some common function. Cooperation of this character may take the form of joint performance of the function by the units involved, or may consist in one of the units providing the service for the other or others under contractual agreement. This cooperative performance of local functions, which during recent

---

[51] The two organizations last mentioned have their headquarters in Washington, D.C. The associations of managers and finance officers are two of more than a dozen organizations devoted to better government at the various levels which maintain national offices at 1313 East 60th Street on Chicago's Midway. On this "1313" group and the organizations comprising it, see "Improving Government from Within," *Pub. Management*, XX, 131-135 (May, 1938); Hal Hazelrigg, "The '1313' Group in Chicago," *Annals of Amer. Acad. of Polit. and Soc. Sci.*, CXCIX, 183-189 (Sept., 1938). The late Professor Leonard D. White once suggested that the "1313" group of offices might in a very real sense be called "the national capitol of state and local government in the United States," albeit "a capitol with no authority and no influence other than that derived from competence, good will, and high ideals." Leonard D. White, *The States and the Nation* (La. State Univ. Press, Baton Rouge, 1953), 55.

years has come to be of first-rate significance, is discussed in some detail in a subsequent chapter.[52]

REFERENCES

BROOKS, Glenn E., *When Governors Convene: The Governors' Conference and National Politics* (Johns Hopkins Press, Baltimore, 1961).

BUELL, Raymond L., *Death by Tariff: Protectionism in State and Federal Legislation* (Univ. of Chicago Press, Chicago, 1939).

Colorado Legislative Council, *Ports of Entry in Colorado*, Parts I and II (Colo. Legis. Council, Denver, 1954, 1955).

Council of State Governments, *Interstate Compacts: 1783-1956* (The Council, Chicago, 1956).

———, *The Handbook on Interstate Crime Control* (The Council, Chicago, rev. ed., 1955).

Federal, State, and Local Government Fiscal Relations (Sen. Doc. No. 69, 78th Cong., 1st Sess., U.S. Govt. Printing Office, Washington, 1943), Chaps. 2, 3.

FITE, Emerson D., *Government by Cooperation* (Macmillan, New York, 1932), Chaps. 4-6.

GOODWIN, George, *Intermunicipal Relations in Massachusetts* (Bur. of Govt. Research, Univ. of Mass., Amherst, 1956).

Governors' Conference, *Proceedings* (Governors' Conf., Chicago, annually).

GRAVES, W. Brooke, *Uniform State Action* (Univ. of N. C. Press, Chapel Hill, 1934).

GREEN, Thomas S., Jr., *Liquor Trade Barriers* (Pub. Admin. Service, Chicago, 1940).

HILLMAN, J. S., and ROWELL, J. D., *Barriers to the Interstate Movement of Agricultural Products by Motor Vehicle in the Eleven Western States* (Univ. of Ariz. Agr. Exp. Sta., Tucson, 1953).

JACKSON, Robert H., *Full Faith and Credit: The Lawyer's Clause of the Constitution* (Columbia Univ. Press, New York, 1945).

Joint Committee of the States to Study Alcoholic Beverage Laws, *Trade Barriers Affecting Interstate Commerce in Alcoholic Beverages* (The Committee, Cleveland, 1952).

LEACH, Richard H., and SUGG, Redding S., Jr., *The Administration of Interstate Compacts* (La. State Univ. Press, Baton Rouge, 1959).

MELDER, F. E., *State and Local Barriers to Interstate Commerce in the United States* (Univ. of Me., Orono, 1937).

———, *State Trade Walls* (Pub. Affairs Committee, New York, 1939).

National Conference of Commissioners on Uniform State Laws, *Handbook and Proceedings of the Annual Conference* (Nat. Conf. of Comsrs. on Uniform State Laws, annually).

[52] See below, Chap. XVI, "Functional Consolidation," "Intergovernmental Agreements." For discussion of interlocal cooperation in the Tennessee Valley Region, see M. H. Satterfield, "Cooperation Pays Dividends," *Nat. Mun. Rev.*, XXXI, 431-435 (Sept., 1942); James P. Pope, "Intercity Cooperation Increases," *Ibid.*, XXXIII, 287-291 (June, 1944).

PURCELL, Margaret R., *Interstate Barriers to Truck Transportation* (U.S. Dept. of Agriculture, Washington, 1950).

SCOTT, James A., *The Law of Interstate Rendition* (Sherman Hight, Chicago, 1917).

Tax Institute, *Tax Barriers to Trade* (The Institute, Univ. of Pa., Philadelphia, 1941).

TAYLOR, George R., BURTIS, Edgar L., and WAUGH, Frederick V., *Barriers to Internal Trade in Farm Products* (A Special Report to the Secretary of Agriculture by the Bureau of Agricultural Economics of the United States Department of Agriculture, U.S. Govt. Printing Office, Washington, 1939).

Temporary National Economic Committee, *Interstate Trade Barriers* (Part 29 of Hearings before the Committee, Congress of the United States, 76th Cong., 2nd Sess., U.S. Govt. Printing Office, Washington, 1941).

THURSBY, Vincent V., *Interstate Cooperation: A Study of the Interstate Compact* (Pub. Affairs Press, Washington, 1953).

United States Conference of Mayors, *City Problems* (Proceedings of the Conference, U.S. Conf. of Mayors, Washington, annually).

ZIMMERMANN, Frederick L., and WENDELL, Mitchell, *The Interstate Compact Since 1925* (Council of State Govts., Chicago, 1951).

———, *The Law and Use of Interstate Compacts* (Council of State Govts., Chicago, circa 1961).

III

Popular Control
of Government

5

Suffrage
and Parties

Under a form of government which, like our own, presupposes a high degree of popular control over public personnel and policy, the composition and functions of the electorate are problems of major importance. Who shall be entitled to vote? How shall the voters be organized into political parties for the exercise of their authority? Just what shall be the functions of the electorate in nominating and electing public officers and participating directly in the political process? These and similar questions will be the concern of this chapter and the one which follows.

The Voting Privilege in American History

The story in American history of the suffrage or voting privilege has been largely one of step-by-step expansion.[1] In the colonies, property and religious qualifications for voting restricted the electoral franchise to a very small portion of the population, and the earliest state constitutions did little to relax these restrictions. After the turn of the century, however, and especially during the period of "Jacksonian democracy" which began in the 1820's, constitutional amendments eliminated many of these qualifications and the constitutions newly adopted contained more liberal suffrage provisions. As a result of this tendency, by the outbreak of the Civil

[1] On the subject generally, see Kirk H. Porter, *A History of the Suffrage in the United States;* Dudley O. McGovney, *The American Suffrage Medley.* A briefer treatment of historical and legal aspects is to be found in Charles M. Boynton, "A Study of the Elective Franchise in the United States," *Notre Dame Lawyer,* XX, 230-302 (Mar., 1945).

War most adult white male inhabitants were entitled to vote. Since that
time two principal enlargements of the electorate have occurred as a result
of the Fifteenth and Nineteenth Amendments to the United States Constitution. The Fifteenth Amendment, which became effective in 1870, prohibited denial of the right to vote on account of race or color and thereby
made it illegal to withhold the suffrage from large numbers of Negroes
who had recently gained freedom and citizenship. The Nineteenth, or
Woman Suffrage, Amendment was adopted a half century later and nullified, where they still existed, state constitutional provisions which confined the suffrage to men. As will appear later, the vast extensions of the
voting privilege have been offset to some degree in practice by the literacy
tests adopted in some states and by other qualifications established in the
South as a means of reducing the Negro vote. Nevertheless, well over half
of the country's inhabitants are legally entitled to vote at the present time
as compared with perhaps 3 percent when the government under the federal constitution was established.[2] So far, indeed, has the suffrage now
been expanded that its abridgment in certain directions is sometimes suggested as a possible means of promoting intelligence and responsibility
in voting.

Regulation of the Suffrage

Regulation of the suffrage in the United States is primarily in the
hands of the respective states. The framers of the federal constitution
might have provided uniform suffrage standards for the entire nation, but
they chose instead to leave the matter to the states and adopt state suffrage qualifications for purposes of national elections. As originally
adopted, the Constitution stated that voters for members of the national
House of Representatives should "have the qualifications requisite for
electors of the most numerous branch of the state legislature"; and when
members of the United States Senate were made popularly elective by the
terms of the Seventeenth Amendment a like provision was inserted concerning voters for senator. Thus, whoever in a particular state is entitled
to vote for members of the state legislature (no state now requires different qualifications of voters for members of the two houses) may vote also
for members of Congress. The formal choice of president and vice president, who are the only other elective officers of the national government,
is vested by the Constitution in electors to be appointed by each state "in
such manner as the legislature thereof may direct." Today presidential
electors are popularly elected in every state by those persons who are
qualified to vote under the state's constitution and laws.

But while the original Constitution left regulation of the suffrage

[2] Cf. Woodrow Wilson, *A History of the American People* (5 vols., Harper, New
York, 1901), III, 120-121.

entirely to the states, certain constitutional amendments have imposed limitations upon state power to prescribe qualifications for voting. The Fourteenth Amendment, adopted in 1868, included a provision to the effect that when the right to vote at a national or state election in any state is denied to any male citizens twenty-one years of age "except for participation in rebellion, or other crime," then the representation of that state in the national House of Representatives shall be reduced in the proportion that the number of persons so disfranchised bears to the entire number of male citizens twenty-one years of age in the state. This provision was designed to confer suffrage upon the southern Negroes indirectly by penalizing their disfranchisement, but in practice was found to be unworkable and has never been enforced. For one thing, no practicable procedure exists for determining the number of persons actually denied the ballot in violation of the provision and therefore the extent to which the state's representation should be reduced. Even more important than this administrative difficulty has been the fact that the provision is broad enough to penalize not only the southern states for disfranchising the Negro, but also other states which deny the right to vote because of illiteracy or indeed for any reason other than crime or rebellion. When, on occasion, northerners have suggested that the constitutional penalty be enforced against the South, southerners have been quick to demand that it be enforced equally against those states outside the South which have literacy tests. For these reasons, the penalty clause of the Fourteenth Amendment has from the outset been a dead letter.

Negro enfranchisement thus failing to be effected by indirection, the Fifteenth Amendment was added to provide expressly that "The right of citizens of the United States to vote shall not be denied or abridged by the United States or by any state on account of race, color, or previous condition of servitude." Though this amendment has been circumvented in large measure in southern states, the constitutional prohibition against racial discrimination is clear and has not been wholly ineffectual. A second express limitation upon the states was imposed by the Nineteenth Amendment, adopted in 1920, which provides that the right of United States citizens to vote shall not be denied or abridged by the United States or by any state on account of sex. After the adoption of the latter amendment, it was generally assumed that the states were entirely free to prescribe whatever qualifications for voting they might wish as long as they did not deny the suffrage on account of race, color, or sex. In 1964 a third express limitation was added with the ratification of the Twenty-fourth Amendment. This amendment provides that the right of citizens to vote in any primary or other election for senators or representatives in Congress or for presidential electors, shall not be denied or abridged by the United States or any state by reason of failure to pay any poll tax or other tax.

Although suffrage qualifications vary from state to state, a single set of qualifications in each state ordinarily serves for state, national, and local elections. In occasional instances, voters who are not also taxpayers have been excluded from participation in municipal elections on bond issues or annexation proposals.[3] Recently some states have established shorter residence requirements for voting for presidential electors than those required with respect to other officers; while certain other states have provided that persons moving therefrom may retain for a specified period their privilege of voting in the state in presidential elections.[4] With allowance made for a few exceptions such as these, the voting qualifications in a given state are uniform for all elections.

Present-Day Suffrage Qualifications

Each state, in its constitution, lays down qualifications for voting which are supposedly designed to place the suffrage in the hands of those persons most capable of exercising the privilege in the public interest. The qualifications prescribed relate for the most part to four subjects: (1) citizenship; (2) age; (3) residence; and (4) literacy. Citizenship, age, and residence requirements exist in all states, while literacy tests are found in some states but not in others. Taxpaying requirements, once widespread, have now all but disappeared. Voting on proposed bond issues is restricted in a few states to electors who pay property taxes, and Virginia's legislature is authorized by constitutional provision to establish property qualifications for voting in certain local elections. However, with some minor exceptions such as these, the requirement that voters own property or pay property taxes has been eliminated. Five southern states[5] still (in 1964) have constitutional provisions making payment of a poll tax prerequisite to voting; but these provisions have now been nullified, in their application to congressional and presidential elections, by the Twenty-fourth Amendment to the United States Constitution.[6]

[3] See Charles M. Kneier, *City Government in the United States* (Harper, New York, 3rd ed., 1957), 321.

[4] Morris S. Ogul, "Residence Requirements as Barriers to Voting in Presidential Elections," *Midwest Jour. of Polit. Sci.*, III, 254-262 (Aug., 1959). By 1963, more than a dozen states had relaxed in some manner their residence requirements for voting in presidential elections. Included among these were Alabama, Arizona, California, Colorado, Connecticut, Idaho, Illinois, Kansas, Michigan, Missouri, New Jersey, North Carolina, Ohio, Oregon, and Vermont.

[5] Alabama, Arkansas, Mississippi, Texas, and Virginia.

[6] Several of the New England states associate the poll tax in some manner with voting (as, for example, by providing that voting lists shall be compiled from poll-tax lists), but not as a general and absolute prerequisite. Cf. Clarence A. Berdahl, "The American Electoral System: Constitutional and Political Aspects," *Parliamentary Affairs*, III, 162-178 (Winter, 1949), 168, footnote. In Vermont, payment of a poll tax is a prerequisite to voting in town meetings. A number of other states in various parts of the country impose a poll tax for revenue purposes but do not associate it in any way with the suffrage.

The nature of the present-day suffrage qualifications in each of the four principal categories will now be noted.[7]

Citizenship. At one time it was not uncommon for the states, as a part of their effort to attract new settlers, to permit voting by aliens who had taken out their "first papers" in the naturalization process. This practice, however, was gradually abandoned, and since 1926 full-fledged United States citizenship has been required of voters in every state.[8] The citizenship requirement limits to those persons who are actually members of the body politic the privilege of sharing formally in the selection of its officers and the determination of its policies. In general, persons who have lived from birth to voting age in the United States, or who have acquired the knowledge necessary for passing their final examination for naturalization, are better able to participate intelligently in public affairs than are aliens recently arrived. Reserving the suffrage to citizens may also serve as an incentive to some aliens to expedite their naturalization. It is clear, of course, that the mere possession of citizenship, or of any or all of the other formal legal qualifications, gives no assurance that the voting privilege will be exercised in an intelligent and public-spirited manner. In most states the citizenship requirement is fulfilled if the person concerned is a citizen on the date of the election, though a few provide that a voter must have been a citizen for ninety days or some other specified length of time.

Age. The minimum-age requirement for voting is designed to confine the suffrage to persons supposedly capable of exercising mature judgment in political matters. Down to World War II, every state fixed the voting age at 21—the age of majority at which a minor becomes legally an adult. In 1943, however, Georgia's constitution was amended to lower the voting age to 18, this action resulting at least in part from the feeling that persons "old enough to fight are old enough to vote" and thus to have a share in determining governmental policy.[9] Kentucky, in 1955, lowered the voting age to 18; and Alaska and Hawaii entered the Union in 1959 with voting-age requirements of 19 and 20, respectively. At present, therefore, a minimum voting age lower than 21 is provided in four of the fifty states.[10]

[7] For a tabular analysis of suffrage qualifications and registration requirements in the respective states, see *The Book of the States* (Council of State Govts., Chicago), 1964-65, pp. 24-25.

[8] Leon E. Aylsworth, "The Passing of Alien Suffrage," *Amer. Polit. Sci. Rev.,* XXV, 114-116 (Feb., 1931).

[9] For a summary of the arguments advanced for and against the proposed amendment during the election campaign, see Franklin L. Burdette, "Lowering the Voting Age in Georgia," *South Atlan. Quar.,* XLIV, 300-307 (July, 1945).

[10] On the subject generally, see Henry J. Abraham, "Reduce the Voting Age to 18?" *Nat. Mun. Rev.,* XLIII, 11-15 (Jan., 1954).

As long as representation in Congress and the presidential electoral college depends upon factors other than the number of eligible voters or number of votes cast, the fact that one state has a lower voting age than others creates no particular problem. Should the plan ever be adopted, as has sometimes been advocated, of electing the president by direct popular vote from one nationwide constituency, then a lower voting age in any state would correspondingly increase the influence of that state upon the election results. Such a situation might well lead other states to lower their age requirement, or even to the establishment, by means of an amendment to the United States Constitution, of a uniform voting age for the entire nation. In this connnection it is of interest to note that the President's Commission on Registration and Voter Participation, in its 1963 report, recommended that all states give serious consideration to reducing the minimum voting age to 18. Concerned over the low voter participation among the age group from 21 to 30, the commission believed that a major reason for this low turnout is that, by the time they have turned 21, many young people are so far removed from the stimulation of the educational process that their interest in public affairs has waned, and that some of these may be lost as voters for the rest of their lives.[11]

Residence. Residence requirements are based upon the principle that only those persons who live within a state or locality are sufficiently familiar with its people and problems, and have a sufficient stake in community affairs, to be qualified to participate in its government. Every state makes a specified period of residence within its boundaries prerequisite to voting, and most require, in addition, a shorter period within one, and frequently two, local areas. The period of required state residence varies from six months to two years, with about two-thirds of the states having a one-year requirement. The areas for which a local residence requirement is most commonly imposed are the county and the voting district. Several states, for example, require residence of one year in the state, ninety days in the county, and thirty days in the voting district.

It is to be noted that what is concerned in these qualifications is *legal residence* within the state and local areas, and not physical presence. A person's legal residence, according to the courts, is his domicile or permanent abode—the place where he actually makes his home. An individual may remain indefinitely in a particular state or community—indeed, may think of himself as "living" there—but if it is not the place of his legal residence he is not entiled to vote in its elections. On the other hand, a legal or voting residence may be maintained by a person at a place from which he is absent for prolonged periods of time. Many Americans, for example, spend most of their time in Washington, D.C., and still others

[11] President's Commission on Registration and Voting Participation, *Report* (U.S. Govt. Printing Office, Washington, 1963), 43.

abroad, while retaining legal residence in one of the states. Such persons may vote at the place of their legal residence by returning on election day, or by absentee ballot where the laws of the state so permit.

The question of voting residence is frequently raised in relation to students who are away from the homes of their parents attending college or university. Many such students are citizens of voting age, meet the state residence requirement, and have been staying at fraternity, sorority, or boarding house in the college community longer than the period required for local residence. Under these circumstances, students sometimes seek to vote in the college community or are urged to do so by local politicians. Whether they are entitled to vote in that community depends in each instance upon whether the individual concerned is in fact a *legal resident* of the locality. Some students *do* fulfill the requirements for local residence, and since World War II, particularly during the years of the GI educational program, the proportion of the student body meeting those requirements has been larger than formerly. Veteran students on the average are several years older than nonveterans, many of them are married, and large numbers have severed their formal connection with the parental home and established their own families in the college community for the duration of their educational period. Under normal circumstances, however, the great majority of college students do *not* qualify as legal residents of the community where the college is located. Such students therefore, if otherwise qualified to vote, should do so, either personally or by absentee ballot, at the place where their parents reside. Though mere intent is given some weight in determining the place of a person's residence, intent alone is insufficient and must be supported by positive facts. Among the matters which are sometimes considered by the courts in determining legal residence in the case of a student are whether he is self-supporting and whether he returns to the home of his parents at vacation time and in case of illness, but no single factor is in itself controlling. Contrary to what is seemingly a widespread opinion, the fact that a student is "working his way" through college, while a factor to be considered, is by no means conclusive in establishing residence. And the fact that a student does not expect to return home to live after he finishes school is not of great importance.[12]

Though residence qualifications are a practical necessity, their hard-and-fast nature is often productive of incongruous results. When a person changes his place of abode, he ceases at once to be a resident of the community which he leaves and ordinarily is no longer entitled to vote there either personally or as an absentee. Yet, though he immediately acquires residence at his new location, he is not legally qualified to vote there until his residence has continued for the length of time prescribed by the constitution of that state for suffrage purposes. Notwithstanding the

[12] Cf. *Anderson* v. *Pifer*, 315 Ill. 164 (1925).

recent relaxation in some states, as noted above, of residence requirements for voting in presidential elections, it is still widely possible for a person to lose his vote in such an election by moving from one state to another within a year of the election date. And moving even across a street, if the street constitutes a boundary line between local voting districts, will sometimes disqualify a person from voting in any and all elections—national, state, and local.[13]

Literacy. Among those who believe that the suffrage has been expanded too far and should now be curtailed, the device most widely favored for narrowing its scope in the interest of intelligent voting is the literacy or educational test. The idea of the literacy test for voting is by no means new in the United States. Connecticut and Massachusetts established literacy requirements as early as the 1850's for the purpose of excluding ignorant immigrants from the suffrage, and after the Civil War most of the southern states adopted tests of this nature as a means of disfranchising the Negro notwithstanding the provisions of the Fifteenth Amendment. Over the years, literacy requirements have been introduced in various other states, principally in the East and the Far West, until today more than a third of the states have this type of qualification.[14] The usual requirement under the literacy test is that voters be able to read and write English, though some of the southern states have "understanding tests," whereby a voter is required to demonstrate that he can "understand and give a reasonable interpretation of" a selection from the state or United States constitution when this is read to him. Provisions of this nature, by conferring broad discretion upon those who administer the tests to determine what is and what is not a reasonable interpretation, enable election boards to admit illiterates to the ballot box or deny them admission at will.

Literacy tests are administered in most instances by registration or election officers, but New York's test, adopted in the early 1920's, pioneered a new method by providing for administration by school authorities. Administration by the schools should be less political and more effective than administration by politically-constituted election boards, and New York's experience indicates that in practice this is the case. Before a new voter may be registered in that state he must present, as evidence of literacy, either a diploma showing completion of the eighth grade in an elementary school or a certificate of literacy issued by the school authorities. Literacy certificates are issued by school superintendents to persons who present credentials showing completion of the sixth grade in school and to others who pass a literacy test devised and administered by school

---

[13] Cf. Ralph M. Goldman, "Move—Lose Your Vote," *Nat. Mun. Rev.,* XLV, 6-9, 46 (Jan., 1956).

[14] Cf. Arthur W. Bromage, "Literacy and the Electorate," *Amer. Polit. Sci. Rev.,* XXIV, 946-962 (Nov., 1930).

officials. The effectiveness of the New York system in excluding illiterates from the suffrage is indicated by the fact that the test is failed by a substantial percentage of those who take it. On the whole the system appears to have been administered successfully and with little difficulty. A wholesome by-product has been a growing interest in evening schools on the part of foreign-born residents.[15]

Though literacy tests offer no promise of being a panacea for all suffrage ills, if administered vigorously and impartially they should improve the quality of the electorate perceptibly. No thinking person would seriously contend that an individual's civic competence necessarily varies in direct proportion to the amount of his formal education. Any college student can think of some acquaintances with little schooling who nevertheless are well informed on political matters, and of others with college degrees who have little knowledge of and take little interest in public affairs. Yet, nothwithstanding our present radio and television facilities, ability to read remains a valuable aid in securing information on public questions; and in view of our public school systems, evening schools, and adult education facilities, it is certainly not unreasonable to require ability to read and write as a prerequisite to voting.[16]

Disqualifications for Voting

In practically every state certain classes of persons are specifically excluded from the suffrage. Persons who have been convicted of felony are generally disqualified, as are also in some states those convicted of certain lesser offenses, particularly election crimes. Ordinarily idiots and the insane are disqualified, and a few states disqualify paupers. While there may be good reason for barring from the suffrage persons who are habitual paupers, it would be a rank injustice to disqualify all those who, in times of widespread economic depression, may find it necessary to accept public aid. This problem arose during the 1930's in some of the states having the pauper disqualification, and in a few communities relief recipients were temporarily denied the vote. Fortunately, however, this practice did not spread to any appreciable extent, the disqualification being generally interpreted as not applicable in such circumstances.[17]

Registration of Voters

The most careful definition of suffrage qualifications in state constitutions will not in itself prevent widespread voting by persons legally in-

---

[15] Bromage, *op. cit.;* Finla G. Crawford, "Operation of the Literacy Test for Voters in New York," *Amer. Polit. Sci. Rev.,* XXV, 342-345 (May, 1931).

[16] Cf. Bromage, *op. cit.*

[17] Peter H. Odegard and E. Allen Helms, *American Politics* (Harper, New York, 2nd ed., 1947), 371-373.

eligible. If in practice ineligibles are to be barred from the polls and election frauds such as impersonation and repeating reduced to a minimum, some means must be provided for determining, with due deliberation and in advance of election day, what persons will be entitled to cast ballots at that time. Lists of eligible voters must be prepared, means provided whereby those persons can be identified by election officials, and provision made that only those whose names appear on such lists shall be permitted to vote. These ends are best achieved through a well-planned and efficiently administered system of voter registration.

Registration systems are of two general types—periodic and permanent. Under the former, existing registration lists are discarded at regular intervals and completely new lists compiled. The period between registrations varies in length, but quadrennial registrations are most common. Under the permanent plan, on the other hand, a voter, once registered, remains registered until he moves his residence, dies, becomes legally disqualified, or fails to vote for a specified period.[18] Where the interval between registrations is short, the periodic system, if properly administered, has the advantage of being highly accurate and at all times relatively up to date. It is disadvantageous, however, in its costliness and in requiring that the voter present himself again and again for reregistration. Because it is more economical and especially because of its greater convenience to the voter, the permanent plan is now generally preferred, provided that the registration lists are kept up to date by continuous revision.

Registration is now required of some or all voters in every state except Arkansas and Texas.[19] Constitutional and statutory provisions concerning registration, however, show a great deal of variation. Since the evils which registration is designed to minimize are more prevalent in urban communities than in rural areas where most voters are known personally to the election officials, it is not surprising that many of the earlier laws applied only to the larger cities. Even today registration in some states is still limited to the more populous communities, though the present tendency is toward a statewide registration requirement. Most of the more recent statutes provide for registration of the permanent type. A number of states, however, still use either the periodic system, or a "mixed" system under which the periodic plan is employed in certain localities and the permanent plan in others. Some laws require registration for voting in any election, whereas others exempt certain local elections

[18] Ordinarily reregistration is also required when a voter's name is changed by marriage or otherwise.

[19] The most comprehensive treatise on the subject is Joseph P. Harris, *Registration of Voters in the United States* (1929). For more recent data, see Council of State Governments, *Registration for Voting in the United States* (rev. ed., 1946); O. Douglas Weeks, "Permanent Registration of Voters in the United States," *Temple Univ. Law Quar.*, XIV, 74-88 (Nov., 1939); *The Book of the States*, 1964-65, p. 25.

from the registration requirement. Some states permit voters who are absent from their place of residence or physically disabled to register by mail. In a few instances this privilege of absentee registration is confined to members of the armed forces, but more often it extends to qualified electors generally. Registration systems are usually locally administered, with the administrative agency either a registration board or a single registrar. Where the latter plan is used, it is fairly common for county or city clerks to be designated as registrars ex officio.[20] Under some systems, the means provided for identification of voters at the polls is a personal description of each voter placed in the registration record and including such items as age, height, weight, and color of eyes and hair. A more effective method, and one which is gaining in favor, is that of signature comparison. Under this system, the voter is required to sign the registration record when he registers and an application for ballot when he presents himself at the polls on election day, with his identification then made by the election officials through a comparison of the two signatures.[21]

Under registration systems of the permanent type, a major problem is that of keeping the lists of voters up to date. In the absence of effective procedures for constant revision, lists soon become loaded with the names of persons who have died, moved away, or become disqualified, and on election day these names may be "voted" by the party machines. The means which are employed, in sundry combinations, for the revision and purging of registration lists, are numerous and varied. Some states employ the house-to-house canvass. It is fairly common to require that official notices of deaths, and sometimes also of criminal convictions, be transmitted to the registration officials. Registrations may be challenged in most states by any voter, and in some by registration officials and party watchers as well. Many states provide for suspension or cancellation of registrations for failure to vote for a specified period. Keepers of lodging houses are required in some instances to make periodic reports to the registration officials of persons residing in their establishments. Some jurisdictions provide for cancellation, after notice and opportunity for hearing, of the registration of persons believed by the registration officials, on the basis of inquiries mailed to all registrants, to have moved away or become ineligible.[22]

Under the earlier permanent registration laws it was usual for registration and the revision of registration lists to be confined to designated periods of time between elections. The more recent tendency, however, has been to provide for a system of continuous registration and

[20] Council of State Governments, *Registration for Voting in the United States,* 1-8; James K. Pollock, *Absentee Voting and Registration* (Amer. Council on Pub. Affairs, Washington, 1940), 10-11.

[21] Cf. Harris, *op. cit.,* 232-238.

[22] Council of State Governments, *Registration for Voting in the United States,* 14-17 and summaries of state laws.

revision under which new registrations may be made, registrations cancelled, changes of address filed, and corrections made at any time, except during brief periods when the registration books are closed, as is commonly the case for a certain number of days preceding each primary and general election.[23] The spread of continuous revision, as of various other improvements in registration technique, has been due in no small measure to the influence of the "model" system of permanent registration prepared by a committee of the National Municipal League and first published in 1927.[24] Recent state statutes establishing permanent registration on a statewide basis and making registration and revision a continuous process represent a striking advance over the early laws providing periodic registration, and that only for populous communities. The best of registration laws can of course accomplish little in the absence of efficient administration. But, when honestly and vigorously administered, a good registration statute has proved to be an effective means of reducing voting frauds and raising the general tone of elections.

Negro Suffrage in the South

From the time of the Civil War, Negro suffrage in the southern states has constituted a serious problem. The Fifteenth Amendment attempted at one fell stroke to secure full enfranchisement of the freedmen. Since Negroes at that time outnumbered the white population in several states, the effect of the amendment, had its provisions been carried out as intended by its sponsors, would have been to place the governments of those states under the control of an uneducated people fresh from slavery and utterly inexperienced in political affairs. Indeed, for a time during the Reconstruction period, Negro-controlled legislatures manipulated by northern "carpetbaggers" actually functioned in some instances and carried on the public business with deplorable corruption and excesses. In the face of this situation, it is not surprising that southerners contrived a series of devices intended to disfranchise the Negro population in practice without violating the letter of the federal constitution. State constitutional and statutory provisions to achieve this end became an established part of the South's legal system and were successful in disfranchising all but a negligible number of the Negro voters. Unfortunately, these restrictions upon Negro suffrage for many years were not relaxed in any appreciable measure as Negroes gained in education and experience. Only within recent decades have some of the more important of these provisions been

[23] Weeks, "Permanent Registration of Voters in the United States," *loc. cit.*
[24] "A Model Registration System," *Nat. Mun. Rev.,* XVI, 45-86 (Supp. to Jan., 1927). This report has now been revised several times, a partial revision of the fourth edition appearing as a pamphlet publication of the National Municipal League in 1957.

repealed or invalidated by judicial decision, and the number of southern Negroes actually participating in the electoral process, though now growing, still constitutes but a small part of the adult Negro population.

Although outright intimidation has been a factor in Negro disfranchisement from the beginning, it is less common now than formerly, and principal reliance has always been upon legal stratagem. As we have seen, most of the southern states in the years following the Civil War adopted literacy requirements for voting; and at one time poll-tax requirements were also widespread in the South.[25] These tests effectively barred large numbers of Negroes from the ballot box, but, had they been enforced against all persons equally, would also have disfranchised many poor and illiterate whites. To forestall such a result, resort has been had to various forms of discrimination in the administration of the requirements. Among the literacy tests, those of the "understanding" variety in particular lend themselves readily to discriminatory administration, since election officials are free to reject as unreasonable, when proffered by a Negro, a constitutional "interpretation" which would be accepted if tendered by a white person.[26] Poll-tax requirements also served as instruments of discrimination. Election officials might easily "forget" to require white persons to show their poll-tax receipts while always "remembering" in the case of Negroes; and, notwithstanding laws forbidding the practice, it appears that many political machines regularly paid the poll taxes of white voters *en bloc* in order to qualify them for voting.[27]

As a means of reducing the disfranchisement of white persons through literacy and poll-tax requirements, several states at one time placed in their constitutions some form of the so-called "grandfather clause." According to these provisions, any person unable to qualify under the literacy or poll-tax test was nevertheless to be permitted to register permanently as a voter if he or his ancestors were entitled to vote on a specified past date, fixed always at some point prior to the adoption of the Fifteenth Amendment. Though the grandfather-clause device was ultimately declared invalid by the United States Supreme Court as a violation of that amendment,[28] this was only after such provisions had served their purpose of placing on permanent voters' lists the names of many white persons who otherwise would have been disqualified under literacy or poll-tax requirements.

[25] For a comprehensive discussion, see Frederic D. Ogden, *The Poll Tax in the South* (Univ. of Ala. Press, University, Ala., 1958).

[26] See above, "Present-Day Suffrage Qualifications—Literacy." An "understanding" test inserted in Alabama's constitution in 1946 by the Boswell Amendment was declared unconstitutional by the federal courts as a violation of the equal-protection clause of the Fourteenth Amendment. *Davis* v. *Schnell*, 81 F. Supp. 872 (1949), affirmed in *Schnell* v. *Davis*, 336 U.S. 933 (1949).

[27] Virginius Dabney, *Below the Potomac* (Appleton-Century-Crofts, New York, 1942), 118.

[28] *Guinn* v. *United States*, 238 U.S. 347 (1915).

The White Primary and Its Legal Demise

A favorite means of Negro disfranchisement for many years was the white primary. The South being essentially a one-party region, exclusion of Negroes from the Democratic primary effectively barred them from participation in the choice of public officers, since the general election served merely to give formal confirmation to the Democratic candidates. Federal constitutional provisions concerning elections were long regarded as inapplicable to nominating primaries, and thus it was possible to perpetrate in the primary discriminatory practices which would not have been countenanced in the general election. At one time Negroes were excluded from Democratic primaries in some eleven southern states either by statutory provision or, more commonly, by party rule.[29] However, in a series of decisions beginning in 1927, the United States Supreme Court has now held that white primaries are invalid whether established by law or merely by party action.

In the 1927 case it was held by the Court that a state statute which by its own express terms prohibited Negroes from participating in Democratic primaries was a violation of the provision of the Fourteenth Amendment that no state shall deny to any person within its jurisdiction the equal protection of the laws.[30] Five years later a more common form of white primary was held also to violate the equal-protection clause. This was the form in which Negro exclusion was accomplished, not by direct statutory provision, but by rule of the party's executive committee adopted pursuant to authority conferred upon the committee by statute to prescribe qualifications for party membership and primary participation. In the opinion of the Court, party action taken under statutory authority was tantamount to state action and therefore fell equally within the constitutional prohibition.[31] Finally, in the *Allwright* case of 1944, the Court overruled an earlier decision to the contrary and held that exclusion of Negroes from Democratic primaries by resolution of the state party convention, on its own responsibility and without statutory authority, was a violation of the Fifteenth Amendment. In taking this position, the Court accepted the view that, since the party primaries and conventions were provided for and their procedures regulated by state law, the action of the convention amounted to state action even though taken without an express statutory grant of authority.[32]

The *Allwright* decision naturally met with considerable disfavor in

---

[29] On the history and forms of the white primary, see O. Douglas Weeks, "The White Primary," *Miss. Law Jour.*, VIII, 135-153 (Dec., 1935).

[30] *Nixon* v. *Herndon,* 273 U.S. 536 (1927).

[31] *Nixon* v. *Condon,* 286 U.S. 73 (1932).

[32] *Smith* v. *Allwright,* 321 U.S. 649 (1944), overruling *Grovey* v. *Townsend,* 295 U.S. 45 (1935).

the South, and several states attempted in one way or another to circumvent its intended effect. A drastic form of action with this end in view was taken by South Carolina, which proceeded to repeal all constitutional and statutory provisions relating to party organization and primaries. In the *Allwright* case, Negro exclusion had been invalidated because the primaries were organized and conducted under provisions of state law, and South Carolina now sought, by dissociating party machinery and primaries completely from the state's legal system, to make of the political party a strictly private organization not subject to the limitations imposed upon state action by the Fourteenth and Fifteenth amendments. Having thus been freed from legal control, the Democratic state convention of South Carolina proceeded to readopt a former rule barring Negroes from party membership and primary voting. But this action fared no better at the hands of the courts than that contested in the *Allwright* and previous cases. A federal district court, relying upon the *Allwright* case and related decisions, held the exclusion rule invalid, this decision was affirmed by the circuit court of appeals, and the Supreme Court declined to review the judgment of the latter tribunal.[33] In the opinion of the judges, mere repeal of the constitutional and statutory provisions had not materially altered the actual situation. The same party membership by the same methods was attempting to accomplish the same results as before. Action of the party remained the equivalent of state action in the constitutional sense and therefore fell under the same constitutional prohibitions. Subsequent attempts by the Democratic party in South Carolina and elsewhere to disfranchise Negroes by placing control of primary elections in the hands of private clubs to which only white persons are admitted have likewise been invalidated by the courts.[34]

Federal Civil Rights Acts

The civil rights legislation recently enacted by Congress is designed, among other things, to extend some degree of protection to Negro suffrage. Under the terms of the 1957 act, a bipartisan Commission on Civil Rights is authorized to investigate cases of alleged violation of civil rights, including the right to vote, and to recommend corrective measures to Congress. Furthermore, the Department of Justice is empowered to institute in the federal courts, on its own initiative, injunction suits on behalf of persons who are being unlawfully denied the right to vote.[35]

[33] *Elmore* v. *Rice*, 72 F. Supp. 516 (1947); *Rice* v. *Elmore*, 165 F. 2d 387 (1947); certiorari denied, 333 U.S. 875 (1948).

[34] *Brown* v. *Baskin*, 78 F. Supp. 933 (1948); *Baskin* v. *Brown*, 174 F. 2d 391 (1949); *Terry* v. *Adams*, 345 U.S. 461 (1953). Cf. George W. Spicer, *The Supreme Court and Fundamental Freedoms* (Appleton-Century-Crofts, New York, 1959), 93-94.

[35] Jack W. Peltason, "Congressional Government 1957-1959," in *American Government Annual: 1959-1960* (Holt, New York, 1959), 44-68 at 60-62.

In 1960, the Civil Rights Act of that year included additional provisions relating to elections and voting. In an effort to prevent the destruction of evidence of voting discrimination, this statute makes it a federal crime for local election officers to destroy the records of any congressional or presidential primary or general election within twenty-two months of the election date; and requires that such records be made available to the Attorney General or his representatives for inspection, reproduction, and copying. It is further provided that federal judges or voting referees appointed by them may register qualified voters who are denied registration by local election officials.[36]

The Civil Rights Act of 1964 prohibits discrimination in the application of voting qualifications in any federal election; and provides that, where a literacy test is used, it must be conducted wholly in writing with completion of the sixth grade in school raising a rebuttable presumption of literacy.[36a]

Present Status of Negro Voting

Although the white primary in all of its forms has now been invalidated by the courts, and Congress has enacted statutory provisions designed to afford some protection against voting discrimination, it was not to be expected that full enfranchisement of southern Negroes would follow immediately. Literacy tests remain, and the practices and habits of generations are not to be lightly set aside. Still, a major rent has been made at last in what was long an almost solid front of disfranchisement. As yet, little use has been made of the protective provisions of the civil rights statutes, and the adequacy of these provisions to effect a widespread enfranchisement of Negroes appears at best to be problematical. Of more significance thus far in lessening the traditional discrimination has been the fact that southerners themselves in increasing numbers are taking a more liberal attitude toward Negro suffrage. During recent years, southern Negroes have voted in larger numbers than ever before in both primaries and general elections. It is true that the increase in Negro voting has been less in rural areas than in the larger cities, and markedly less in some of the southern states than in others, yet the overall gain has been considerable. At this point it appears beyond doubt that, as the result of a combination of legal action and changes in southern attitudes, Negro participation in public affairs will continue to increase and at a constantly-rising tempo.[37] Should the two-party system be reestablished in the South

[36] 74 *U.S. Stat. at L.* 86.
[36a] 78 *U.S. Stat. at L.* 241.
[37] Cf. O. Douglas Weeks, "The White Primary: 1944-1948," *Amer. Polit. Sci. Rev.*, XLII, 500-510 (June, 1948); Donald S. Strong, "The Rise of Negro Voting in Texas," *Ibid.*, 510-522. On the extent of Negro voting in the respective states as of the late 1940's, see V. O. Key, Jr., *Southern Politics in State and Nation*, 517-522.

—and the remarkable Republican gains in the region in recent elections suggests a definite trend in that direction—the two parties will inevitably compete for the Negro vote, and Negroes will then be in a position to strengthen still further their influence upon southern and national politics.[38] And to the extent to which they obtain and exercise the suffrage, Negro citizens will be aided immeasurably in their endeavors to secure elimination of discriminatory practices other than those in connection with voting.

The Voter's Task

The task imposed upon the American voter is a heavy one—so onerous, in fact, that its performance in an intelligent manner is for the average person quite impossible. A typical voter is expected to participate in the election, and in most instances the nomination, of a multitude of national, state, and local officials and also to pass judgment upon a large variety of propositions. Included in the list of elective officers are United States senators, representatives, and presidential electors; state legislators and judges, governors, and various other state administrative officials; and a plethora of officers serving counties, townships, school districts, municipalities, and special-purpose districts. Among the questions of policy commonly submitted to the electorate are proposals for state constitutional amendments and for the authorization of state and local bond issues. Where the initiative, referendum, and recall are used, the voter may also be asked to express himself as favoring adoption or rejection of proposed state statutes or city ordinances and as favoring or opposing the removal of designated officers.

In an effort to reduce the demands placed upon the voter at any one time, and to lessen the confusion of local and national issues, local elections in many instances have now been separated from those for national and state officers. This separation, however, complicates the voter's task in another direction by increasing the number of elections. The average voter today is likely to be called to the polls for one purpose or another several times each year, and still many ballots remain unduly long. A single ballot sometimes carries the names of a hundred or more candidates, and at the same election several propositions may also be submitted. Manifestly, the ordinary voter is in no position to express an informed and intelligent judgment on so many candidates and issues. Even if we assume sufficient interest on his part, he has neither the time nor the facilities for

[38] Cf. "Negro Disenfranchisement—A Challenge to the Constitution," *Columbia Law Rev.*, XLVII, 76-98 (Jan., 1947); Virginius Dabney, "What the G O P is Doing in the South," *Harper's Mag.*, Vol. CCXXVI, No. 1356 (May, 1963), 86-88, 91-92, 94.

securing the necessary information upon which to base such a judgment.[39] Confronted with so hopeless a task, many voters absent themselves from the polls, and those who do vote must, in large measure, do so in a random and haphazard manner. An individual voter may be well enough informed concerning the candidates for a few of the higher offices, and perhaps even those for occasional other offices in which he may be especially interested, to express a reasoned judgment; but certainly this is not the case with respect to most of the offices and questions involved. Analysis of primary and election results has shown that substantially more votes are cast for offices appearing at or near the top of the ballot than for those farther down on the list. For example, many persons who cast votes for governor or United States senator do not vote for lesser state officers or for representative in Congress, and a still larger number—sometimes more than half—fail to vote for some of the county offices appearing at the bottom of the ticket. This element of "voter fatigue," as it has been aptly characterized by Professor James Pollock, is further evidence of the inability or unwillingness of voters to pass judgment on the qualifications of candidates for each of the many offices now appearing on the typical ballot.[40]

Need for a Shorter Ballot

Political scientists have long advocated a shortening of the ballot as a means of promoting democracy in government. The present long ballot, by discouraging voter participation in primaries and elections, often makes it possible for a political machine, through its ability to "deliver" even a small if solid bloc of votes, to control the choice of elective officers. If only a few top officials were popularly elected, and these given authority to appoint subordinate officers, the voter's task would be simplified to a point where he could reasonably be expected to inform himself properly regarding the qualifications of candidates and to vote intelligently. The top officers so elected would be directly accountable to the voters for their own actions and for those of their appointees as well. Thus, though fewer officers would be chosen directly by the voters, responsibility in government would be fostered rather than impaired.

The short-ballot principle envisages the popular election of those officers concerned primarily with the formulation of public policy and the appointment of all others. In practice, this would mean the election

[39] A few states attempt to supply information concerning issues and, less frequently, candidates, through official voters' bulletins known as "publicity pamphlets," issued and distributed to the voters at public expense. See William L. Josslin, "Oregon Educates its Voters," *Nat. Mun. Rev.*, XXXII, 373-379 (July, 1943).

[40] James K. Pollock, "New Thoughts on the Short Ballot," *Ibid.*, XXIX, 18-20, 47 (Jan., 1940); James K. Pollock, *The Direct Primary in Michigan, 1909-1935* (Bur. of Govt., Univ. of Mich., Ann Arbor, 1943), 32-35

in any governmental unit of few if any officers other than members of the legislative body and the chief executive. Where an appointive executive is provided, as under the city manager plan, the ballot may be shortened even further. The principle of the short ballot, it is to be noted, has always been observed in the national government, where the only elective officers are the president, vice-president, and members of Congress. In a few states the ballot has been shortened somewhat during recent years as a result of administrative reorganization,[41] and the short ballot exists in some cities, especially among those which have adopted either the commission or the manager form of government.[42] But in most states, practically all counties, and thousands of other local governments, the long ballot still prevails. A drastic reduction both in the number of elective offices and in the frequency of elections might go far toward stimulating active and intelligent citizen participation in public affairs.

Nonvoting

Americans have been more anxious to possess the suffrage than to exercise it. Nonvoting in this country has always been extensive. The ratio of ballots cast to number of qualified electors varies from place to place and from election to election, depending in some measure upon personalities and issues involved, but is almost universally low. Even in presidential elections, where the largest votes are returned, the percentage of potential voters who actually cast ballots has at times been less than 50 and rarely if ever, during the present century, more than 70.[43] In local elections the percentage of voter participation is sometimes pitifully small. Because of Negro disfranchisement and the one-party system, the smallest votes, in proportion to population, are cast in the South; but even in the northern states, though the record there is somewhat better, nonvoting is ordinarily high.

The causes of nonvoting are many. Every election finds some persons disqualified because of recent changes in residence. Absence from home on election day at one time prevented many from voting, but absent-voters' laws[44] now enable most absentees to cast ballots by mail or otherwise. Some electors are unable to go to the polls because of sickness or other physical disability, though more and more states are extending their absent-voting statutes to cover such cases. While all of these factors are of some significance, case studies have indicated that the most important

---

41 See below, Chap. X.
42 See below, Chap. XIV.
43 Cf. Howard R. Penniman, *Sait's American Parties and Elections* (5th ed.), 510; Austin Ranney, *The Governing of Men* (Holt, New York, 1958), 266; President's Commission on Registration and Voting Participation, *op. cit.*, 67.
44 See below, Chap. VI, "Absentee Voting."

causes of nonvoting are mere indifference and inertia.[45] The largest single group of nonvoters by far consists of those who simply are not sufficiently interested to register and go to the polls.

As to whether nonvoting really constitutes a serious problem and, if so, what can be done about it, there is considerable diversity of opinion. Some people believe that widespread nonvoting is actually a menace to our democratic institutions, while others think it no cause for worry.[46] Among those who subscribe to the first of these views, compulsory voting is sometimes suggested as a possible remedy.[47] Systems of compulsory voting under which electors are fined for failure to participate in elections have been tried in various countries in Europe and elsewhere, and when effectively administered have been markedly successful in reducing abstentions.[48] But compulsion does not appear to be the answer to nonvoting in this country.[49] While threat of penalty doubtless would cause many to vote who otherwise would not do so, compulsion cannot assure careful and intelligent voting. Instead, there is no way to prevent the mere dropping of blank ballots into the ballot box. There would seem, moreover, to be grave doubts as to the constitutionality of compulsory voting in the United States. Some years ago a provision in the home-rule charter of Kansas City, Missouri, which imposed a poll tax in election years upon male persons over twenty-one years of age, but exempted from payment of the tax those who voted in the city election, was invalidated by the Missouri supreme court. The court took the view that the suffrage is a sovereign right which the citizen must be free to exercise or not as he chooses and that therefore the charter provision concerned, being clearly designed to impose a penalty for nonvoting, was unconstitutional. For the performance of such civic duties as that of voting, said the court, "reliance must be placed only on the enlightened conscience of intelligent and patriotic freemen."[50] And, regardless of the matter of constitutionality, compulsory voting seems hardly to square with the American concept of free government.

Those who take the view that the "slacker vote" constitutes no threat to democracy point out that, contrary to common impression, nonvoting is most prevalent among the politically unintelligent.[51] The princi-

[45] Charles E. Merriam and Harold F. Gosnell, *Non-Voting;* Harold F. Gosnell, *Getting Out the Vote.*

[46] Cf. Charles E. Merriam and Harold F. Gosnell, *The American Party System* (4th ed.), 456.

[47] See, for example, Robert Cobb Myers, "A Proposal to Tax Those Who Don't Vote," *N.Y. Times Mag.,* Nov. 6, 1949, pp. 12, 75-76, 78-79.

[48] William A. Robson, "Compulsory Voting," *Polit. Sci. Quar.,* XXXVIII, 569-577 (Dec., 1923); Henry J. Abraham, "One Way to Get Out the Vote," *Nat. Mun. Rev.,* XXXIX, 395-399 (Sept., 1950).

[49] Cf. Henry J. Abraham, "What Cure for Voter Apathy?" *Nat. Mun. Rev.,* XLI, 346-350, 357 (July, 1952).

[50] *Kansas City* v. *Whipple,* 136 Mo. 475 (1896).

[51] William B. Munro, "Is the Slacker Vote a Menace?" *Nat. Mun. Rev.,* XVII, 80-86 (Feb., 1928).

pal cause of nonvoting, as we have seen, is sheer indifference, and indifference is most widespread among the illiterate and uninformed. Studies of nonvoting have shown that voter participation is highest among the well-to-do and better educated, and lowest among the residents of poorer neighborhoods and those with little or no education.[52] In general, therefore, it appears that nonvoting is most prevalent among those groups least able to participate intelligently in the governmental process.

An interesting but somewhat unusual theory of nonvoting regards failure to vote as signifying approval of existing conditions in public affairs.[53] According to this view, all that is necessary in a democratic system is that the *opportunity* of voting be preserved so that every elector will have the means of registering a protest if he wishes to do so. While this theory may have elements of validity, students of democratic government seem generally to agree that a high rate of voter participation in the electoral process, at least if informed and intelligent in nature, is desirable. To be sure, it is doubtful whether there is any virtue in *number* of votes alone. What is needed is more intelligent voting on the part of those who do go to the polls, coupled with some means of stimulating interest in public affairs so that more people will want to vote. Much has been said of the need for "educating" the voter and potential voter for the proper performance of the electoral task, and certainly anything that can be done along this line in the way of clarifying issues and providing adequate information concerning candidates is all to the good. But educating the average voter so as to enable him to express a reasoned judgment on all the candidates and propositions with which he is now confronted is a feat which can never be accomplished. A shorter ballot is an essential element in any practicable approach to the problem of nonvoting.[54]

Political Parties

The principle medium through which voters seek to influence their government is the political party. Electors inevitably entertain varying opinions concerning who should hold public offices and what governmental policies should be pursued, yet complete independence of action on the part of individuals could result only in chaos and an utter lack of consensus. It is therefore only natural that voters should associate themselves together in some kind of organization for concerted action in choosing officers and determining policy. Though voter influence on government is also exerted through various types of pressure groups, these groups

[52] Merriam and Gosnell, *The American Party System* (4th ed.), 452; Gordon M. Connelly and Harry H. Field, "The Non-Voter—Who He Is, What He Thinks," *Pub. Opinion Quar.*, VIII, 175-187 (Summer, 1944).

[53] Francis G. Wilson, "The Pragmatic Electorate," *Amer. Polit. Sci. Rev.*, XXIV, 16-37 (Feb., 1930). See also Connelly and Field, *op. cit.*

[54] Clyde Eagleton, "A Defense of the Non-Voter," *South Atlan. Quar.*, XXVII, 341-354 (Oct., 1928).

may be distinguished from political parties, in a general way, by the fact that they ordinarily do not nominate candidates for office but are concerned primarily with the influencing of policies.[55]

Political parties are not mentioned in the United States Constitution and originally developed outside the framework of constitutional and statutory law. Today, however, parties in most states have a definite legal status. About a third of the state constitutions contain provisions of one kind or another relating to political parties, but much more important is existing statutory regulation. While in a few states, principally in the South, statutory regulation is meager or nonexistent, in a large majority party membership, organization, and activities are now regulated in some detail by direct primary laws and other statutes.[56]

During most of our national history there have been two major parties in the country, and since the Civil War these have been the Democratic and the Republican. Numerous minor or "third" parties have come and gone, with the issues for the promotion of which they were organized frequently taken over by one of the major parties. Two present-day minor parties—the Prohibition and the Socialist—have been in existence over a long period; but the present Republican party, organized during the 1850's as an anti-slavery third party, is the only minor party ever to achieve "major" status.

Although some persons are "independents" in the sense of having no party affiliation, and although independence in voting, even among party members, is on the increase, most voters think of themselves as being adherents of some political party. Various factors are influential in determining the individual's choice of party. Many voters are Republicans or Democrats simply because of family tradition. Other determinants include place of birth or residence, occupation, and economic self-interest. For most of us, party affiliation is largely a matter of fortuitous circumstances. Some persons, no doubt, calmly weigh the leadership and policies of the respective parties and then deliberately align themselves with that party which they believe most likely to further the general welfare of the community, state, or nation. But the number of such persons, though perhaps slowly increasing, probably represents a very small portion of the entire electorate.

Some minor parties have a relatively cohesive and determinable membership. Persons seeking admission to membership are required to make a formal application and declare their belief in and support of the party's principles. There is a dues-paying requirement, and provision is made for expulsion of delinquent members. The major parties, on the other hand, are extremely loosely organized insofar as membership is concerned.

---

[55] Cf. V. O. Key, Jr., *Politics, Parties, and Pressure Groups* (4th ed.), 170-177.
[56] Joseph R. Starr, "The Legal Status of American Political Parties," *Amer. Polit. Sci. Rev.*, XXXIV, 439-455, 685-699 (June, Aug., 1940).

In general, party membership is merely a matter of voting affiliation. A party member is supposed to vote in the primary of his own party and is expected to support all or most of that party's nominees in the general election. Yet in some states any qualified voter is legally entitled to vote in the primary of any party without even being required to reveal the identity of the party in whose primary he participates. Under such a system the voter may keep his party affiliation a secret, and even the officials of a given party have small means of knowing what persons are party "members." Other states, it is true, provide that a voter whose right to participate in the primary of a particular party is questioned must declare under oath that he has supported the party's nominees in the past or expects to do so in the future. In many instances, however, these tests of party affiliation are so lax and easily met that they still leave to the voter a large measure of freedom to change his party affiliation at will. Unlike other organizations and associations, the major political parties, which are ordinarily the only parties to which the primary laws apply, are not free to determine their own membership rules. The primary statutes now quite generally prescribe that any qualified voter, by complying with certain simple requirements, may become a "member" of any party he wishes and thereby entitled to vote in that party's primary. It will thus be seen that little relation exists between actually working for one of the major parties and being a voting member thereof, a fact which makes it exceedingly difficult to determine the numerical strength of the respective parties. The most accurate checks upon actual membership are probably those provided by the party lists in those states where public registration as a party member is a legal prerequisite to participation in primary elections. Such registration requirements, however, do not exist in all states, and even where they are available the registration lists afford little indication of the number of *working* party members.[57]

State Party Systems

Party organization in the United States is commonly characterized as a *two-party* system and, in view of the extent to which possession of the presidency and the control of Congress have alternated between Republicans and Democrats, this characterization as applied to parties at the national level is quite acceptable. In approximately half of the states, furthermore, there is sufficient alternation in party control of state offices to render the two-party designation not inappropriate. There are other states, however, in which, though both major parties maintain organizations and regularly contend for office, one of the two wins office only on

[57] Clarence A. Berdahl, "Party Membership in the United States," *Amer. Polit. Sci. Rev.*, XXXVI, 16-50, 241-262 (Feb., Apr., 1942); E. E. Schattschneider, *Party Government*, 55-56. The different types of primaries are discussed in the following chapter.

rare occasions. And in yet another group of states one party so clearly predominates that the other maintains a mere "shadow" organization and seldom nominates candidates. The principal purpose of the lesser party in maintaining any organization at all in such states would appear to be that of having facilities in existence for dispensing federal patronage when the party is in control of the national government.[58]

In view of this varying situation among the states, Professors Austin Ranney and Willmoore Kendall have suggested that actually we have at the state level three types of party systems: (1) the two-party type, (2) the modified one-party type, and (3) the one-party type. These they distinguish as follows:[59]

The two-party type. To this type belongs any system in which at most elections in the fairly recent past (a) two parties have shared the bulk of the votes and public offices between them, (b) the winning party has gained a majority of the votes and offices, and (c) the two dominant parties have alternated in winning majorities.

The modified one-party type. To this type belongs any system in which at most elections in the recent past (a) one party has won all or almost all the offices, but (b) the second party, though it has seldom won any offices, has normally received a substantial percentage of the votes and thus constitutes a significant center of organized party opposition.

The one-party type. To this type belongs any system in which at most elections in the recent past (a) one party has won all or nearly all of the offices, and (b) the second party has usually received only a small percentage of the popular votes.

Though the distinction made in this classification is significant, the line of demarcation between the respective types is not always distinct. Different persons, therefore, in applying the classification, might assign a given state to different classes. Furthermore, a state may move from one class to another with changes in the political climate. Thus recent gains of the Republicans in the South and of the Democrats in upper New England suggest that some of the states which traditionally have deserved assignment to the one-party or modified one-party groups are now trending in the direction of establishing two-party systems.[60]

[58] Austin Ranney and Willmoore Kendall, "The American Party Systems," *Amer. Polit. Sci. Rev.*, XLVIII, 477-485 (June, 1954).

[59] *Ibid.*, 481.

[60] For a criticism of the Ranney-Kendall method of classification and the suggestion of an alternative method, see Joseph A. Schlesinger, "A Two-Dimensional Scheme for Classifying the States According to Degree of Inter-Party Competition," *Amer. Polit. Sci. Rev.*, XLIX, 1120-1128 (Dec., 1955). In some instances, a situation strongly resembling two-party competition has developed in one-party states through the rivalry of two distinct and well-organized factions within the dominant party. See, for example, Allan P. Sindler, "Bifactional Rivalry as an Alternative to Two-Party Competition in Louisiana," *Ibid.*, 641-662 (Sept., 1955). On the general subject of state parties and politics, see Duane Lockard, *The Politics of State and Local Government*, especially Chap. 8.

Party Functions

The best known and one of the most important functions of political parties is the nomination of candidates for public office and the support of those candidates in the general election. By nominating procedures described in the next chapter the respective parties make a preliminary sifting of candidates and select, frequently from large numbers of aspirants, the nominees which they propose to support for the various elective offices. Where any one party is strongly predominant, the general election may amount to nothing more than a means of giving formal confirmation to the nominees of that party. Otherwise the election constitutes an interparty contest in which a final selection of public officers is made from among the nominees of the various parties. Nor is it to be supposed that party participation in the selection of government personnel is limited to elective officers. Party leaders offer abundant advice concerning the selection of appointive personnel, and an appointing officer who has been nominated and elected as a party candidate, or himself appointed with party support, is likely to give considerable weight to that advice.[61]

A second function of parties, less generally recognized than their part in the choice of official personnel, is that of presenting policy issues to the public and sharing in the formulation of public opinion on those issues. Positions on current problems are taken in party platforms and by candidates in campaign speeches, and arguments are presented in support of those positions. Where the major parties align themselves on opposite sides of an issue, the voters hear the problem debated and, from the respective arguments presented, may decide which point of view they wish to endorse at the polls. To be sure, instances in which the two parties take definite and opposing stands on vital issues are nowadays relatively few. Too often platform planks are of the "straddling" variety and candidates are evasive. But even with party positions indefinite, or where as sometimes happens the positions of both parties are essentially alike, the public discussion of issues, even for partisan and propagandist purposes, may be of real assistance to the voter in his task of formulating judgments concerning policies involved.

When a political party has won an election, it is the duty of that party, insofar as its control of public offices enables it to do so, to put into effect the program embodied in its platform and campaign promises. During the interim between elections, the party of the "outs" can perform a useful public service by keeping vigilant watch over the conduct of the

[61] On this and other party functions, see Merriam and Gosnell, *The American Party System* (4th ed.), Chap. 21. A case study of party influence upon selection of appointive highway personnel in a Pennsylvania county is reported in Frank J. Sorauf, "State Patronage in a Rural County," *Amer. Polit. Sci. Rev.*, L, 1046-1056 (Dec., 1956).

government and offering constructive criticism whenever it is honestly believed that mistakes have been made. Such criticism tends to keep the "ins" on their mettle and thus to have a wholesome effect upon governmental administration.

Still another function of the party system is that of providing a means for enforcing some degree of continuing responsibility in the conduct of public affairs. When a public officer who has been elected as an independent makes an unsatisfactory record, the voters of course may refuse to reelect him. This, however, may be scarce recompense for his official failure and, in the event that he does not desire further continuance in office, fear of repudiation at the polls is no stimulus to efficient service during his official term. A political party, on the other hand, is bidding for office year after year. When an officer elected with party endorsement fails to give satisfaction, the voters are in a position to hold the party responsible by refusing to support its candidates in succeeding elections. For this reason, party leaders are under some compulsion to choose able candidates and to exercise constant surveillance, during their terms of office, over officials elected or appointed with party endorsement.

Finally, where the separation-of-powers principle prevails, as it does in our national and state governments and many of our cities, the party system may play an important role in promoting the smooth and orderly functioning of the governmental process. Because of their constitutional checks upon each other, either the chief executive or the legislative body is generally in a position to block measures favored by the other. When, however, the chief executive and a majority of the legislators are members of the same party, this common affiliation is likely to facilitate cooperative action. Thus the party in control is in a position, for the time being, to determine in large measure the course of public policy and to assume responsibility therefor.

In practice, of course, there are many instances in state government where a party in opposition to the governor controls one or both houses of the legislature. This situation may arise from any of several causes. In some cases it is a result of the fact that gubernatorial and legislative terms are nonconcurrent. Again, division in party control may flow from legislative malapportionment. In a given state, for example, an urban majority may elect a Democratic governor at the same time that apportionment provisions and practices assure that rural Republicans, though in the minority throughout the state as a whole, will control one or both legislative chambers. In circumstances such as these, the party system clearly cannot function to mesh the respective governmental organs.[62]

[62] V. O. Key, Jr., *American State Politics: An Introduction,* Chap. 3.

Party Organization

Whether prescribed by state primary law or by party rules, the formal machinery of party organization is, in general pattern, fairly uniform throughout the country. This organization consists of a series of party committees, with, ordinarily, a committee for each area from which officers are elected and a "committeeman" for each voting district or precinct.[63] In each state there will usually be found a state central committee, congressional district committees, legislative district committees, county committees, township committees where township government exists, city committees, and precinct committeemen. Members of the different committees are selected in a variety of ways, but most often are elected by the party voters in the primary election or chosen by party conventions. Sometimes the members of one set of committees, or the chairmen thereof, serve ex officio as members of one or more higher committees. The tendency in recent years has been to make increasing use of elective committees, and since the advent of woman suffrage provision has been made in some instances for equal representation of the sexes in committee membership. Ordinarily each committee selects a chairman from among its members.

Each major party in each state is represented on the party's national committee by two members—a man and a woman. These national committeemen are variously chosen, depending upon law or practice in the respective states, by the state delegation to the national convention, the state convention, the state central committee, or the party voters in the primary.[64] While the members of party committees are usually experienced in politics and have some influence in party councils, actual control of party affairs may rest in the hands of a political "boss" who, though he may hold neither public nor party office, is able, through personal influence derived from varying sources, to determine the personnel and policies of the party organization.[65]

The members of the committee hierarchy constitute the central

[63] Edward B. Logan, ed., *The American Political Scene* (rev. ed.), Chap. 2; Merriam and Gosnell, *The American Party System* (4th ed.), Chap. 8. At times parties actually operate in large measure through extra-legal "voluntary" committees and other informal organs rather than through the formal hierarchy of statutory committees. See, for an excellent example, Frank J. Sorauf, "Extra-Legal Political Parties in Wisconsin," *Amer. Polit. Sci. Rev.*, XLVIII, 692-704 (Sept., 1954).

[64] Senatorial and congressional campaign committees also operate at the national level.

[65] There are many good books on bosses and bossism. See, for example, Samuel P. Orth, *The Boss and the Machine* (Yale Univ. Press, New Haven, 1919); Harold Zink, *City Bosses in the United States* (Duke Univ. Press, Durham, N.C., 1930); Frank R. Kent, *The Great Game of Politics* (Doubleday, New York, 1930), especially Chaps. 13-18; William L. Riordon, *Plunkitt of Tammany Hall* (Knopf, New York, 1948).

working force of the party. Each committee is responsible for party affairs in the area where it functions. During the interim between elections it is the job of the various committees to keep the party, together with public officers whom it has sponsored and potential candidates for future office, in as favorable a light as possible before the voters. Sometimes "slates" of candidates to be supported by the "organization" for nomination in the primaries are prepared by the party committees; and, whatever candidates are nominated by the party, it is the duty of the committees to work for their victory in the general election. To this end, the committees are charged with planning and conducting the election campaign and getting out the vote on election day. When party nominees have been placed in public office, party committeemen are frequently active in advising those officers on appointments and matters of policy, and in serving in a liaison capacity between officials and private citizens.[66]

When local elections are held at a time apart from state and national, as is often the case in cities, primary responsibility for conducting the campaign falls upon the local committee of the area concerned, though higher committees may give financial or other assistance. County elections are ordinarily held concurrently with those of the state, and at such times both state and county committees are active. In presidential years, national, state, and county committees are activated all along the line and their energies mobilized into one grand campaign effort. Though the committee hierarchy is organized in an extremely loose manner, with committees at one level having little or no formal responsibility to those above, the various agencies ordinarily cooperate with each other in their work, intercommittee harmony frequently being promoted by the over-lapping of committee personnel.

To a large degree, the effectiveness of the entire party organization depends upon the precinct committeemen. These lowly party officials, sometimes called precinct executives, leaders, or captains, constitute the very backbone of the party's working force.[67] Whereas other committees function actively only with respect to particular elections, the precinct

---

[66] Party organization also extends into legislative bodies, where through caucuses, steering committees, and floor leaders efforts are made to secure unified party action with respect to proposed legislation. See below, Chap. VII, "Party Organization in the Legislature."

[67] On the precinct committeeman and his work, see Sonya Forthal, *Cogwheels of Democracy: A Study of the Precinct Captain* (William-Frederick Press, New York, 1946); Hugh A. Bone, *Grass Roots Party Leadership: A Case Study of King County, Washington* (Univ. of Wash. Press, Seattle, 1952); J. T. Salter, *Boss Rule* (Whittlesey House, New York, 1935); Kent, *op. cit.*, Chaps. 1-6; Harold F. Gosnell, *Machine Politics: Chicago Model*, Chaps. 3, 4; Sonya Forthal, "The Small Fry and the Party Purse," *Amer. Polit. Sci. Rev.*, XXXIV, 66-76 (Feb., 1940); Leon Weaver, "Some Soundings in the Party System: Rural Precinct Committeemen," *Ibid.*, 76-84; Sonya Forthal, "The Precinct Worker," *Annals of Amer. Acad. of Polit. and Soc. Sci.*, CCLIX, 30-45 (Sept., 1948); William J. Keefe and William C. Seyler, "Precinct Politicians in Pittsburgh," *Soc. Sci.*, XXXV, 26-32 (Jan., 1960).

committeeman is active in every election as well as between elections. It is he who maintains direct contact with the voters. Many precinct committeemen hold minor public jobs, but regardless of their regular vocation they ordinarily spend a substantial portion of their time on activities connected directly or indirectly with politics. They aid precinct residents in securing employment, public or private; give temporary assistance to the needy without the red tape and delay incident to publicly administered relief; lend a helping hand to those who become involved with the law; and in countless other ways perform small services for ordinary people. In return for these services, the precinct committeeman naturally hopes that those whom he has befriended will remember him at election time and vote for the candidates suponsored by him and his party. It is the duty of the precinct committeeman to see to it that qualified voters in his precinct who are likely to support the slate or ticket endorsed by the party organization are properly registered and that they vote in the primaries and general elections. If the precinct committeemen do their job well, the organization tends to function in the manner of a well-oiled machine; if they fall down on the job, the party cause is likely to be lost.

Before leaving the matter of party organization, emphasis should be given to the essentially democratic basis of that organization in law and in theory. Precinct committeemen are now generally elected by the party voters in the primaries and many of the higher committees are composed either of precinct committeemen ex officio or of other elective members. If the personnel of party committees is substandard, that is largely because too many citizens take little interest in the choice of party officials in the primaries and themselves refuse to accept the responsibilities of party service. Those who habitually complain that the party organization is corrupt and inefficient would do well to remember that ultimate authority rests with the party voters to "turn the rascals out" and elect in their stead persons who might have the public interest more at heart.

Party Finance

The financing of party activities requires large sums of money, and one of the principal responsibilities of party committees is that of raising and spending campaign funds.[68] Practically every party committee is engaged to some extent in fund-raising. In a particular election, however, the task is often centralized in some measure in the hands of the highest committee concerned, with a part of the funds raised being subsequently apportioned to the lesser committees and precinct committeemen. Purposes

---

[68] On party finance generally, see James K. Pollock, Jr., *Party Campaign Funds* (Knopf, New York, 1926); Louise Overacker, *Money in Elections* (Macmillan, New York, 1932); Edward B. Logan, ed., *op. cit.*, Chap. 5; Merriam and Gosnell, *The American Party System* (4th ed.), Chap. 17.

of party expenditures are legion. Headquarters must be maintained and staffed; campaign literature prepared and distributed; newspaper advertisements paid for; and speakers secured and halls rented for meetings. Election-day workers must be paid, and sometimes automobiles are hired to transport voters to the polls. Printing, postage, telephone bills, and traveling expenses bulk large in campaign expenditures. Nowadays the purchase of radio and television time is a major, and sometimes the largest, item.

Minor parties secure their necessary funds in large part from members in the form of dues, but the major parties rely upon contributions from various sources. Public officers and employees, elective or appointive, who owe their tenure to the party, are expected to do their part in financing party activities; contributions from this source, though perhaps nominally voluntary, being virtually assessments. Frequently, a specified percentage of their salaries is designated as the minimum amount which will be acceptable from such office-holders. Political assessment of employees who are under the merit system is forbidden by the civil service laws, and some states also prohibit the solicitation of political funds from various other classes of public employees.[69] These prohibitions, however, are not always strictly enforced, and in any event voluntary contributions from such persons are legal. Candidates for office on the party ticket are expected to make contributions in proportion to their ability and the importance, monetary and otherwise, of the office which they seek.

After account is taken of the contributions of candidates and office-holders, parties must often still rely heavily upon donations from members and friends of the party. Indeed, these donations not infrequently constitute the greater part of the total campaign fund. Some of the contributors in this category are motivated merely by the desire for civic betterment. Many, however, and perhaps most, are businessmen and others who believe that they stand to gain in some pecuniary or other manner from the success of the party concerned. Persons who contribute substantially to the campaign chest of a party are likely to have some influence in public affairs and may be able to secure personal favors from officials if that party obtains control of the government. Some contributors, in order to make certain of being on the safe side, make a practice of donating to both of the major parties. In general, it may be said that the funds of the major parties are derived from a relatively small number of large contributors rather than in the form of small donations from the rank and file of the party membership—a situation which is not without its disadvantages. During recent years the national committees of both parties have

---

[69] The 1940 federal Hatch Act forbids state and local officers and employees whose principal employment is in connection with any activity financed wholly or in part from federal funds to coerce, command, or advise other such officers and employees to make contributions to any person or organization for political purposes. 54 *U.S. Stat. at L.* 767.

made deliberate efforts to democratize party finance by securing larger numbers of small contributions and thereby making it unnecessary to rely so heavily on large gifts. These efforts, however, appear as yet to have been of little practical effect.[70]

Corrupt-Practices Legislation

In an effort to lessen or prevent some of the more prevalent abuses, both the states and the federal government have enacted legislation regulating the raising and spending of party campaign funds. These statutes are commonly called corrupt-practices acts, and every state now has some legislation of this nature.[71] The provisions of the statutes vary widely, but may be considered as falling into two general categories: (1) those which provide merely for giving publicity to campaign receipts and expenditures; and (2) those which impose limitations upon contributions or expenditures or both.

The most common type of provision is that which requires candidates for elective office, and in most instances party committees as well, to file as a matter of public record statements of their receipts and disbursements for campaign purposes. Requirements of this nature exist today in nearly all of the states. Statements are required to show the names of all persons from whom contributions have been received and to whom payments have been made, together with the amount of each contribution and payment. The public official with whom the statement must be filed is ordinarily the secretary of state in the case of candidates for statewide office and the county or city clerk in the case of local candidates. The required filing takes place in some states before, and in others after, the primary or election concerned. Preelection filing is definitely preferable, since the voters can then be advised of the information contained in the statements before they go to the polls.

Limitations on expenditures and contributions take a variety of forms. Every state prohibits the offering or giving of bribes in connection with elections, and most states also prohibit the accepting of a bribe. Though these prohibitions are usually contained in statutes apart from the corrupt-practices laws, they deserve mention at this point. In a majority of the states the corrupt-practices act lists in greater or less detail the specific purposes for which campaign expenditures may lawfully be made. Typical of the expenditures commonly included in such lists are those for travel, stenographic work, preparation and distribution of campaign literature, newspaper advertising, radio and television publicity,

[70] Cf. John W. Lederle, "Party Finance in a Presidential Year," *Annals of Amer. Acad. of Polit. and Soc. Sci.*, CCLIX, 64-74 (Sept., 1948).

[71] S. Sydney Minault, *Corrupt Practices Legislation in the 48 States* (Council of State Govts., Chicago, 1942). See also Earl R. Sikes, *State and Federal Corrupt-Practices Legislation* (Duke Univ. Press, Durham, N.C., 1928).

postage, telephone, and office and hall rent. Most states limit the amount which may be spent for campaign purposes by candidates for some or all elective offices, and a few place limitations upon party expenditures as well. Three-fourths of the states prohibit altogether political contributions from corporations, but only an occasional state limits the amount which may be contributed by an individual.

In general, the results of the corrupt-practices laws have been disappointing. Many of the statutes fail to include adequate enforcement provisions, and both state and federal experience has revealed that regulations in this field are easily circumvented. Prohibitions of corporate contributions may be evaded through donations by corporation officers as individuals. Where limitations are imposed upon the expenditures of candidates or party committees, "clubs" to promote various candidacies may be formed and a part of the funds channeled through those organizations. Limitations on the amount of individual contributions may be evaded by having several members of a family make donations, each giving a sum within the statutory maximum. Despite such weaknesses, however, corrupt-practices legislation has not been wholly ineffective. Publicity concerning campaign financing, at least when made available in advance of the election, doubtless has some wholesome effect; and some of the more stringent regulatory provisions, when well administered, appear to have raised somewhat the general tone of elections. Yet it must be admitted that the problems of eliminating financial abuses and the handicap of the impecunious candidate remain largely unsolved.[72]

REFERENCES

ABRAHAM, Henry J., *Compulsory Voting* (Pub. Affairs Press, Washington, 1955).

BERDAHL, Clarence A., *Our Two-Party System* (Bur. of Pub. Admin., Univ. of Miss., University, Miss., 1951).

BONE, Hugh A., *American Politics and the Party System* (McGraw-Hill, New York, 2nd ed., 1955).

Council of State Governments, *Registration for Voting in the United States* (The Council, Chicago, rev. ed., 1946).

CRESAP, Dean R., *Party Politics in the Golden State* (Haynes Found., Los Angeles, 1954).

EPSTEIN, Leon D., *Politics in Wisconsin* (Univ. of Wis. Press, Madison, 1958).

FENTON, John H., *Politics in the Border States* (Hauser Press, New Orleans, 1957).

[72] For an account of one of the more recent statutes and its initial effectiveness, see Elston E. Roady, "Florida's New Campaign Expense Law and the 1952 Democratic Gubernatorial Primaries," *Amer. Polit. Sci. Rev.*, XLVIII, 465-476 (June, 1954).

GOODMAN, William, *The Two-Party System in the United States* (Van Nostrand, Princeton, N.J., 2nd ed., 1960).

GOSNELL, Harold F., *Getting Out the Vote* (Univ. of Chicago Press, Chicago, 1927).

———, *Machine Politics: Chicago Model* (Univ. of Chicago Press, Chicago, 1937).

GREENSTEIN, Fred I., *The American Party System and the American People* (Prentice-Hall, Englewood Cliffs, N.J., 1963).

HARRIS, Joseph P., *Registration of Voters in the United States* (Brookings Inst., Washington, 1929).

HINDERAKER, Ivan, *Party Politics* (Holt, New York, 1956).

HUTHMACHER, J. Joseph, *Massachusetts People and Politics* (Harvard Univ. Press, Cambridge, Mass., 1959).

JONAS, Frank J., ed., *Western Politics* (Univ. of Utah Press, Salt Lake City, 1961).

KEY, V. O., JR., *American State Politics: An Introduction* (Knopf, New York, 1956).

———, *Politics, Parties, and Pressure Groups* (Crowell, New York, 4th ed., 1958).

———, *Southern Politics in State and Nation* (Knopf, New York, 1949).

LOCKARD, Duane, *New England State Politics* (Princeton Univ. Press, Princeton, N.J., 1959).

———, *The Politics of State and Local Government* (Macmillan, New York, 1963).

LOGAN, Edward B., ed., *The American Political Scene* (Harper, New York, rev. ed., 1938).

McGOVNEY, Dudley O., *The American Suffrage Medley* (Univ. of Chicago Press, Chicago, 1949).

MERRIAM, Charles E., and GOSNELL, Harold F., *Non-Voting* (Univ. of Chicago Press, Chicago, 1924).

———, *The American Party System* (Macmillan, New York, 4th ed., 1949).

MITAU, G. Theodore, *Politics in Minnesota* (Univ. of Minn. Press, Minneapolis, 1960).

MOSCOW, Warren, *Politics in the Empire State* (Knopf, New York, 1948).

National Municipal League, *Model Voter Registration System* (Nat. Mun. League, New York, partial revision of 4th ed., 1957).

PENNIMAN, Howard R., *Sait's American Parties and Elections* (Appleton-Century-Crofts, New York, 5th ed., 1952).

PORTER, Kirk H., *A History of Suffrage in the United States* (Univ. of Chicago Press, Chicago, 1918).

RANNEY, Austin, *Illinois Politics* (N.Y. Univ. Press, New York, 1960).

———, and KENDALL, Willmoore, *Democracy and the American Party System* (Harcourt, New York, 1956).

SCHATTSCHNEIDER, E. E., *Party Government* (Holt, New York, 1942).

6

The Voters at Work

Voter participation in government takes two principal forms: (1) the choice of elective public officers and (2) the approval or rejection of propositions concerning matters of public policy. Elective officers, as noted in the preceding chapter, include members of Congress, presidential electors, and a host of state and local officials. Where the popular recall exists, the electoral process may also be invoked to effect the removal of officers. Policy propositions submitted to the voters are extremely varied in nature. Except in Delaware, state constitutional amendments must have voter approval. Proposals to establish new local governmental units, to change the boundaries of existing units, to adopt optional forms of local organization, or to establish or amend home-rule charters, are ordinarily subject to popular referendum. Other matters frequently submitted to the voters include propositions to issue bonds, levy special assessments, or increase the taxing power of local authorities. Additional phases of voter participation in some states and localities are the enactment of statutes or ordinances through the initiative, and the popular veto, by referendum procedure, of measures enacted by legislative bodies.

Use of the initiative and referendum in the adoption and amendment of constitutions and charters was discussed in an earlier chapter.[1] In the present chapter consideration will be given to the nomination and election of public officials, the popular recall as a means of removing offi-

[1] Above, Chap. I.

144

cers, and the voter's direct participation in legislation through the statutory initiative and referendum.

NOMINATION AND ELECTION OF OFFICERS

Nomination and Its Importance

The procedure for choosing elective officers ordinarily involves two distinct steps: (1) the nomination of candidates for the offices concerned; and (2) the final selection, from among the candidates so nominated, of persons to fill the respective posts. The importance of the first of these steps is too generally not recognized. Actually, nomination constitutes a preliminary sifting or "weeding out" process, following which the voter's choice at the general election is virtually limited to a selection from among the candidates previously nominated. Votes for "write-in" candidates, to be sure, may be permitted at the election, but occasions on which such candidates have any substantial chance of winning are rare. Indeed, since independent and minor-party candidates also in most instances have little likelihood of success, the voter in the general election is often limited, for all practical purposes, to a choice between the candidates of the two major parties. If, under such circumstances, both parties nominate able and honest candidates, high-grade officers will be obtained regardless of who wins in the general election. On the other hand, if both parties nominate candidates with inferior qualifications, incompetent officers are bound to be the result. Thus the nominating process generally assumes an importance equal to, if not greater than, that of the election which follows. And where, as frequently happens, one party clearly and consistently predominates in a state or community, the choosing of that party's nominees becomes the only step of real importance in the entire electoral process, since the general election amounts to nothing more than a means of giving formal confirmation to those candidates.[2]

In view of its prime importance, it is most unfortunate that the nominating step in the election process is so lightly regarded by the voters. Many persons who make a practice of voting in general elections decline to participate in the primaries or other nominating procedures. Nonvoting, except in the South where the one-party system has traditionally prevailed, is commonly more widespread in primaries than in general elections. Until voters can be made to understand the significance of the nomination as a means of sifting potential candidates for public office, and to assume a more active role in the making of nominations, they are likely all too often to be faced, at the general election, with the unhappy

[2] Cortez A. M. Ewing, "Primaries as Real Elections," *Southwestern Soc. Sci. Quar.*, XXIX, 293-298 (Mar., 1949).

task of merely choosing between candidates who are not properly qualified for the office concerned.

Nominating Methods

Four principal methods of nominating candidates for public office
have developed in the United States: (1) the caucus, (2) the convention,
(3) the primary election, and (4) the petition. Long the prevalent nominating devices, caucus and convention have in large measure been superseded since the turn of the century by the direct primary, though they
still continue to be used to some extent. Nomination by petition, though
of considerable present-day importance, has never been used as extensively as the other methods.

Caucuses and Conventions

Down to the beginning of the present century, caucuses and conventions constituted the normal means for nominating candidates for public office.[3] The nominating caucus is a meeting of voters for the purpose
of designating local candidates, and in some instances also for selecting
delegates to nominating conventions serving larger areas. Though some
caucuses are nonpartisan, consisting of voters who, without regard to
party affiliation, seek to agree upon candidates to whom they will give
their united support, the device is more generally used for making party
nominations, each party holding a caucus of its own members for the
purpose.

In its heyday the caucus system developed various evils, caucus
control tending to fall into the hands of ruling cliques or "machines"
within the parties. Typical of these evils were the "snap" caucus and the
"packed" caucus. The snap caucus was held on such short notice that
most of the party members were unaware of the meeting or could not
arrange to attend, thus making it possible for the inner circle to control
caucus deliberations and dictate nominations. Caucus packing was accomplished in a variety of ways. Under one method, the meeting was held
in a small room or hall with word passed out in advance to members of
the inner clique to come early with their friends and occupy the seats.
Where, by such practices as these, party machines controlled caucus nominations, their control extended also to any nominations made by conventions composed of delegates selected at the caucuses. In an effort to eliminate these evils, many states enacted legislation designed to regulate caucus
proceedings, but in practice means were usually found of circumventing
the regulatory measures.

[3] On early nominating methods, see Frederick W. Dallinger, *Nominations for
Elective Office in the United States;* Ernst C. Meyer, *Nominating Systems: Direct
Primaries versus Conventions in the United States.*

Regulation proving generally unsuccessful, the caucus system was eventually supplanted to a large extent by the direct primary election, though candidates for certain local offices are still nominated by the caucus method in some states. A variant form of caucus found in some places is that in which polls are kept open at a designated place for several hours and party voters, instead of assembling together at a specified time, appear individually during the polling period and vote by ballot for the candidates of their choice. This type of caucus bears close resemblance to the direct primary election and indeed in some states and localities is called a primary. It is, however, conducted in a less formal manner than the direct primary, as the latter term is employed generally and in this chapter, and subject to a lesser degree of public regulation.[4]

Whereas party caucuses for nominating purposes are composed of the party voters themselves, nominating conventions consist of delegates representative of the voters. Convention delegates are variously chosen by caucuses, subsidiary conventions, or the party voters directly in primary elections. The convention system was once widely used for making both state and local nominations. Like the caucus, however, the convention lent itself readily to machine domination and for this reason ultimately fell into disrepute. Over the years, state after state has abandoned convention nomination wholly or partially in favor of the direct primary system. Several states, however, while using primary nomination for some offices have retained convention nomination for others; and under Connecticut's law primaries are held only if candidates defeated in convention so demand. As will appear presently a few states, while employing the primary system, provide for preprimary conventions as a part of their regular nominating procedure. At the national level, the convention method is used to nominate candidates for the presidency and vice-presidency, but in most states the party convention is now limited in its functions to the formulation of party policy and the adoption of party platforms.[5]

The Direct Primary

Most widely used, by far, of all nominating methods at the present time is the direct primary election. The direct primary system was devised

[4] P. Orman Ray, *An Introduction to Political Parties and Practical Politics* (Scribner, New York, 3rd ed., 1924), Chap. 4. During our early constitutional history, party nominations for elective state offices were frequently made by the legislative caucus, composed of the members of the state legislature who were also members of the political party concerned. As a nominating device, however, the legislative caucus soon gave way to the more democratic delegate convention. Charles E. Merriam and Harold F. Gosnell, *The American Party System* (Macmillan, New York, 4th ed., 1949), 302-303.

[5] Cf. V. O. Key, Jr., *Politics, Parties, and Pressure Groups* (Crowell, New York, 4th ed., 1958), 407-413. Another function of the state convention in some states is the selection of delegates to the national nominating convention.

in an effort to overcome the evils of the caucus-convention system and to bring the nominating process under direct control of the party voters. Though various states had previously experimented with the direct primary idea, the real *movement* for establishment of the primary system did not develop until the early years of the present century. The first statewide primary law was enacted by Wisconsin in 1903. Thereafter the plan was adopted by other states in rapid succession until, by 1917, forty-four states had enacted primary legislation, mandatory or optional, applicable to nominations for some or all offices.[6] Since 1955, with the enactment of Connecticut's legislation, every state has had a primary law of some sort.[7] As we have seen, however, some states still employ the caucus or convention for the making of party nominations to certain offices.

Nature of the Primary

As used for making party nominations, the direct primary is an *intraparty* election for the selection of candidates who will compete for public office in the succeeding general election with the nominees of other parties and with independent candidates. Primary laws ordinarily apply only to parties whose candidates received a specified percentage of the total vote cast in the last general election, this percentage varying widely but being frequently in the neighborhood of 5 or 10 percent. In many states, because of these limitations, only the two major parties hold primary elections, with minor-party and independent nominations being made in some other manner, frequently by the petition method discussed at a later point. Primary elections in some southern states are conducted by party committees with the cost thereof being paid by the parties or candidates. In most states, however, the primaries are conducted at public expense, by publicly-appointed election officials, and according to much the same procedure as that followed in general elections. This public management of primary elections, and the common practice of holding the primaries of both parties at the same time and place, sometimes tend to obscure the basic facts that there is a separate primary for each party and that the primary is, in theory at least, a strictly intraparty affair. Yet these facts must be kept in mind if the operation of the primary system is to be understood. Each voter is entitled to vote in the primary of only one party,

---

[6] Charles E. Merriam and Louise Overacker, *Primary Elections*, Chap. 5. This volume is the standard treatise on the history and operation of primary elections up to 1928, the date of its publication.

[7] Under the Connecticut system, sometimes referred to as a "primary by challenge," a primary election is held only when request therefor, supported by petition of party members, is filed by a candidate who, though receiving a specified percentage of the convention vote, failed to win convention nomination. Concerning the law's initial operation, see Duane Lockard, "Connecticut Tries its New Primary," *Nat. Mun. Rev.*, XLV, 494-496 (Nov., 1956). For an evaluation of the system after several years of operation, see National Municipal League, *Seven Years of Connecticut's Challenge Primary* (Supplement to the "Model Direct Primary System," Nat. Mun. League, New York, 1963).

and "split-ticket" voting, in the sense of voting for some candidates of each of two or more parties, is therefore impossible at this point in the election process. The voter must choose to participate in the primary of a single party or none at all. An interesting exception to this general rule is found in the state of Washington where, under a unique "blanket" form of primary, a voter may vote in the primaries of different parties for the nomination of candidates for different offices. Candidates' names in that state are grouped on the primary ballot according to office sought, with the party designation after each name, and the voter is permitted to vote for one candidate for each office without regard to party.[8]

Names of persons desiring to become candidates for nomination under the primary system are usually placed on the primary ballot pursuant to petition signed by party members in number as prescribed by statute and filed with a designated public official. Ordinarily only party members are entitled to enter the primary of a given political party as candidates for party nomination. A few states, however, permit "double" or "cross" filing in the primaries and thereby make it possible for a candidate to seek the nomination of two or more parties for a particular office. In California, where a system of cross filing existed for nearly a half-century, it was at one time not uncommon for a single candidate for an office to win both Republican and Democratic nominations. Cross filing was abandoned in California, however, in 1959.[9]

In addition to serving as a nominating agency, the primary is the election in which elective party officials—committeemen and convention delegates—are chosen, and this function further enhances its importance. In presidential-election years, the primary in some states also includes the "presidential preference" feature through which party voters are permitted to indicate the candidate whom they wish their delegates to the national nominating convention to support for the presidential nomination.[10]

Open and Closed Primaries

Party primaries are usually considered as being of two general types, depending upon whether or not a test of party affiliation is applied to persons seeking to participate. These types are known, respectively, as

[8] Claudius O. Johnson, "The Washington Blanket Primary," *Pacific Northwest Quar.*, XXXIII, 27-39 (Jan., 1942); Daniel M. Ogden, Jr., "The Blanket Primary and Party Regularity in Washington," *Ibid.*, XXXIX, 33-38 (Jan., 1948); Daniel M. Ogden, Jr., "Parties Survive Cross-Voting, " *Nat. Mun. Rev.*, XXXIX, 237-241 (May, 1950).

[9] Evelyn Hazen, *Cross Filing in Primary Elections* (Bur. of Pub. Admin., Univ. of Calif., Berkeley, 1951); Key, *Politics, Parties, and Pressure Groups* (4th ed.), 429-431; Dean E. McHenry, "Invitation to the Masquerade," *Nat. Mun. Rev.*, XXXIX, 228-232 (May, 1950); Gordon E. Baker and Bernard Teitelbaum, "An End to Cross-Filing," *Nat. Civic Rev.*, XLVIII, 286-291 (June, 1959).

[10] Nevada Legislative Counsel Bureau, *A Study of the Presidential Primary* (Nev. Legis. Counsel Bur., Carson City, 1958); Charles B. Judah, *The Presidential Primary* (Dept. of Govt., Univ. of New Mex., Albuquerque, 1953).

the "open" primary and the "closed" primary. In the open primary, no test of party affiliation is provided and each voter may participate, at his option, in the primary of any party. Thus the primary of each party is "open" to any and all qualified voters who may desire to participate. Ballot forms and procedures under the open primary are not uniform.[11] In some states, the voter is given the primary ballots of all parties with instructions to mark only one and to deposit all others in a special box for unmarked ballots. Another plan is that of the "blanket" ballot in which the names of candidates for nomination in all parties appear on a single large ballot but in separate columns. Voters are then instructed to use only one column and warned that the placing of marks in more than a single column will invalidate their ballots. In any case, under the open primary plan the voter's selection of the primary in which he is to vote is made in the secrecy of the polling booth and the identity of that primary need not be disclosed. This element of secrecy is deemed by some to be desirable, and indeed constitutes the principal alleged advantage of the open, as opposed to the closed, primary. On the other hand, a major disadvantage of the open primary lies in the fact that it facilitates "raiding"—the practice whereby members of one party sometimes vote in the primary of another in an effort to bring about the nomination of weak candidates who can easily be defeated in the general election.

The closed form of primary seeks, through a declaration or test of party affiliation, to "close" the primary of each party to all voters other than those properly affiliated with that party. Tests provided for this purpose may be lax or stringent in any degree, and thus vary widely in their effectiveness. An occasional state merely requires the primary voter, at the polls, to declare his adherence to a particular party in order to receive the primary ballot of that party, making no provision for the challenging of any such declaration. In practice this may amount to nothing more than the voter's asking for the ballot of one party or the other. Under such a system, the closed primary differs from the open only in requiring a public statement of party affiliation and thus eliminating any degree of secrecy in that respect. Most closed-primary states, however, provide either a challenge system or an enrollment system as a means of administering the party-affiliation test. Where the challenge system is used, the voter's declaration of party affiliation at the polls is subject to challenge by election officials, party watchers, or other voters. When thus challenged, a voter must demonstrate the bona fide character of his declared affiliation by making an affidavit in the form required by law. As employed in the various states, these affidavits concern, singly or in some sort of combination, such matters as the voter's past allegiance, present affiliation, and future

[11] On forms of primary ballots, see Illinois Legislative Council, *The Direct Primary Ballot* (Ill. Legis. Council, Springfield, 1940); Spencer D. Albright, *The American Ballot*, Chap. 6.

intention. Thus the voter may be required to swear that he supported the party's candidates, or a majority thereof, in the last general election, that he now believes in the party's principles or program, or that he intends to support the party's candidates in the next election. Under the enrollment system, which is now gaining in favor, only those persons may vote in the primary of a particular party who have been enrolled in advance as party members, with enrollment ordinarily taking place at the time of registration.[12]

Because it tends to discourage raiding[13] and thereby to promote party responsibility, the closed type of primary has been more generally favored than the open, and about three-fourths of all state primary statutes today provide systems of the closed variety. Several states have tried first one type of primary and then the other, and it may be of some significance that most of the states which now use the open primary have adopted that form within recent years. Some voters resent the necessity, under the closed type of primary, of revealing their party affiliation, feeling that this impairs the secrecy of the ballot, and this may explain at least in part the recent shifts to the open type. The Washington primary, mentioned above, provides for no test of party affiliation, but differs so drastically from the ordinary open primary as to justify being placed in a class by itself. Indeed, this unusual system, which permits the voter "to roam at will among the different parties at the same time," resembles in some measure the nonpartisan primary which will now be discussed.[14]

The Nonpartisan Primary

Some state and local officers are elected by the so-called nonpartisan method, using ballots which carry no indication of the candidates' party affiliation.[15] Municipal officers in many cities, various school and

[12] Howard R. Penniman, *Sait's American Parties and Elections* (Appleton-Century-Crofts, New York, 5th ed., 1952), 377-379; Clarence A. Berdahl, "Party Membership in the United States," *Amer. Polit. Sci. Rev.*, XXXVI, 16-50, 241-262 (Feb., Apr., 1942).

[13] Raiding may, of course, take place not only under the open form of primary, but also in primaries of the closed type where tests of party affiliation are lax or not rigidly enforced. Moreover, cross-party voting in primaries does not always have as its purpose the nomination of weak candidates by a party whose primary is raided. Voters of one party may, and sometimes do, enter the primary of another party for the purpose of supporting candidates whose success in the general election they genuinely desire. For examples of this type of raiding, see Berdahl, *op. cit.*, 39-44.

[14] *Ibid.*, 23.

[15] Robert E. Cushman, "Non-Partisan Nominations and Elections," *Annals of Amer. Acad. of Polit. and Soc. Sci.*, CVI, 83-96 (Mar., 1923); Charles R. Adrian, "Some General Characteristics of Non-Partisan Elections," *Amer. Polit. Sci. Rev.*, XLVI, 766-776 (Sept., 1952); Oliver P. Williams and Charles R. Adrian, "The Insulation of Local Politics under the Non-Partisan Ballot," *Ibid.*, LIII, 1052-1063 (Dec., 1959); C. C. Ludwig, "No Place for Parties," *Nat. Civic Rev.*, XLVIII, 237-240 (May, 1959).

other local officers, some state and local judges, superintendents of public instruction in a few states, and members of the state legislature in Minnesota and Nebraska are chosen in this manner. More extensive use of nonpartisan elections for local officers and judges than for other officers is to be explained by the rather widespread assumption that national party lines have no legitimate place in local government or in judicial administration.

Nominations for nonpartisan elections are usually made either by petition or by the primary. Where the latter method is used, the primary as well as the election is of the nonpartisan type. Under the partisan primary system, as we have seen, a separate primary is held for each party concerned. The nonpartisan system, on the other hand, involves but a single primary in which all qualified voters are entitled to participate whatever their party and indeed whether or not they have any party affiliation. Names of persons seeking nomination are placed on the primary ballot by voter petition and appear without party designation. The two candidates polling the largest votes for each office usually compete with each other in the election which follows. In some instances, however, any candidate for nomination who receives an absolute majority of all votes cast in the primary for the office which he seeks is declared elected without any subsequent "run-off" election.

Actually, nonpartisan primaries and elections are often less free from partisan influence than the name would imply. Though the ballots carry no party designation, the party affiliation of candidates may be a matter of common knowledge and party organizations may "pass the word around" as to whom the party members should support. In Chicago, for example, where members of the city council are nominated and elected by nonpartisan ballot, party politics continues to dominate city elections, and after each primary and election the voters are informed by their newspapers that so many Democratic aldermen, and so many Republican, have been chosen. Notwithstanding such instances, however, nonpartisan elections seem generally to have lessened, even if they have not eliminated, the influence of the regular political parties, this being especially true with respect to local elections. And it must be remembered that those who favor nonpartisanship do not ordinarily maintain that local government should be *nonpolitical*. It is generally recognized that, at all levels of government, *politics* in the sense of competition among interests and groups in influencing the formulation of public policy is well-nigh inevitable and indeed is desirable. What the advocates of nonpartisanship object to is the injection of *partisan* politics of the Democratic-Republican variety into local affairs.[16]

[16] An excellent recent analysis of nonpartisan elections in a single state is set forth in Eugene C. Lee, *The Politics of Nonpartisanship: A Study of California City Elections.*

Nonpartisanship in local elections has been widely supported by students of government on the ground that national and local issues are entirely different and readily separable. There is no Republican or Democratic way of building streets and highways or performing other local services, so the reasoning goes, so why should national party lines have any place in local-government affairs? There have always been some scholars, however, who have doubted the alleged advantages of nonpartisanship. The notion that national and local issues are unrelated is, some present-day critics believe, becoming obsolete as county and city officials develop more and more contacts with national governmental agencies.[17] Furthermore, local governments operating under the usual party system may find themselves in a better position to secure sympathetic consideration of their problems by state legislatures, all but two of which are organized on a partisan basis, than are units operating under the nonpartisan plan. Whatever the merit of these lines of reasoning, there appears to be little doubt that in many localities the nonpartisan system of nominations and elections has had a wholesome effect upon local government.

Merits and Weaknesses of the Primary System

The direct primary was devised as a means of democratizing the nominating process, and in some measure this objective has been accomplished. Ultimate control of nominations is exercised directly by the party voters rather than by party leaders, and a larger proportion of party members vote in the primary than participated, under the former system, in the making of caucus and convention nominations. Yet it should not be supposed that primary nominees are always the choice of a majority of the party members, or that machine domination of primaries is by any means nonexistent. As noted in the preceding chapter, nonvoting is notoriously extensive in primary elections, and a small primary vote makes it relatively easy in many instances for an active group within the party to secure the nomination of candidates of their choice. In practice it is not unusual for groups of party leaders, who may or may not constitute the membership of the official party committees, to prepare "slates" of candidates whom they propose to support in the primary and then to work zealously in the primary campaign for the nomination of those candidates. Such a "regular" or "organization" slate, if endorsed and supported by influential party leaders, is likely to carry the primary and win nomination notwithstanding any "rebel" opposition on the part of less influential leaders or even in the face of minor uprisings within the party membership. Indeed, "machine" pressure may be exerted to prevent independents

[17] Cf. Samuel K. Gove, "Interparty Competition," in Lois M. Pelekoudas, ed., *Illinois Political Parties* (Inst. of Govt. and Pub. Affairs, Univ. of Ill., Urbana, 1960), 29-39.

within the party from filing for nomination, or to prevail upon such persons, after they have filed, to withdraw before the date of the primary and thereby leave the field clear for organization candidates. Thus it is often possible, under the primary system, for the party leadership or machine to control nominations quite as effectively as under the old caucus-convention system. Nevertheless, since primary nominations are formally made by the party members themselves, the leaders are enabled to escape even that degree of responsibility which was theirs in the public mind when nominations were made by procedures which they more obviously controlled.

While actual *control* of nominations by party machines is contrary to the public interest, it may well be argued that some degree of *leadership* within the party in the matter of nominations is highly desirable, and that the primary system is weak in failing to recognize the need for such leadership and to make provision for its formal exercise. Persons active in politics are in many respects in a better position than the rank and file of the electorate to make a wise selection of candidates. A useful purpose might therefore be served by permitting party leaders, through convention or otherwise, to recommend candidates to the party voters, provided that the voters were then free to endorse the recommended candidates in the primary or to nominate others in their stead. It is in recognition of these circumstances that some use is made of the preprimary convention. Under this plan, a party convention held in advance of the primary election makes recommendations of candidates for consideration of the primary voters. Two or more candidates may ordinarily be endorsed by the convention for the same office, and additional aspirants for nomination may usually have their names placed on the primary ballot by petition. Party slate-making is thus brought out into the open, and responsibility of the "organization" for candidates whom it endorses is given official recognition. In a measure, the plan combines the advantages of the convention system with those of the primary, with conventions, after a preliminary sifting, recommending candidates whom the party members may then endorse or displace in the primary election. Preprimary conventions now constitute a part of the regular nominating procedure in several states, including Colorado, Massachusetts, New Mexico, and Utah.[18] Similar in purpose to the preprimary convention is the plan employed in Rhode Island where, under the primary law, endorsement of candidates is made by party committees rather than by conventions. A central feature of the

---

[18] Schulyer C. Wallace, "Pre-Primary Conventions," *Annals of Amer. Acad. of Polit. and Soc. Sci.*, CVI, 97-104 (Mar., 1923); Rene N. Ballard, *The Primary Convention System in Utah*. Under the Utah law voters are limited in the primary election to a choice between two candidates for each office previously named by "primary conventions," no provision being made for placing additional names on the primary ballot by petition.

model primary system prepared by a committee of the National Municipal League is its provision that party organizations, acting through committees or conferences of party officers, be authorized by statute to propose candidates for nomination, with the candidates so proposed being
clearly identified by asterisk or otherwise on the primary ballot.[19]

Most state primary laws make it extremely easy for any aspirant
to nomination to have his name placed on the primary ballot. Under the
petition plan used in most states, the requirement as to number of signatures is usually so low that it can readily be met by any party member
whether or not he has substantial backing. In a few states mere declaration of candidacy, without the filing of a petition, is sufficient to place a
name on the ballot. Because of these lax requirements, primary ballots
tend to become cluttered with the names of persons who have no conceivable chance of winning nomination, but who, for publicity purposes
or other reasons, decide to become candidates. Not infrequently a half
dozen or more candidates will contend for a single nomination. This situation is of course not universal—indeed, in some instances there is actually a dearth of primary contenders[20]—but multiplicity of candidates appears to be a widespread concomitant of the primary system in this country. Primary ballots, as a consequence, often become so long that it is
impossible for the average voter to express an intelligent choice among the
candidates. Another common result of the multiplicity of candidates is
minority nomination. In most states a mere plurality vote in the primary
is sufficient to nominate; that is to say, the candidate who receives the
largest number of votes for a particular office wins the nomination regardless of how small that number may be. Where this is the case, and
there are three or more contenders for a particular nomination, the vote
is often so divided that the winning candidate is nominated by less than a
majority, indeed sometimes by a relatively small fraction, of the total vote
cast. Under these circumstances, it not infrequently happens that a person
is nominated to an office notwithstanding that many more persons voted
against him (that is, voted for other candidates) than for him.

For the purpose of preventing minority nominations, two principal
devices have been employed: (1) preferential voting, and (2) the second
or "run-off" primary.[21] Under the preferential voting plan, each voter is
permitted to express not only a first choice for each office concerned, but

---

[19] National Municipal League, *A Model Direct Primary System;* Richard S.
Childs, "A New Model Primary Law," *Nat. Mun. Rev.*, XXXIX, 225-227, 266 (May,
1950); Joseph P. Harris, "A Model Direct Primary Election System," *State Govt.*,
XXIV, 135-138 (May, 1951).

[20] See, for example, Kirk H. Porter, "The Deserted Primary in Iowa," *Amer.
Polit. Sci. Rev.*, XXXIX, 732-740 (Aug., 1945).

[21] A third device, the post-primary convention, has been used by an occasional
state. See Penniman, *op. cit.*, 380.

also a second choice and sometimes additional choices. If no candidate
for a particular nomination receives a majority of all first choices, subsequent choices are then taken into consideration in an effort to secure a
nominee for whom a majority of all the primary voters have voted, either
as their first or as some subsequent choice. Preferential voting, where it
works as intended, often makes it possible to secure a majority nomination
where this could not be done under ordinary voting methods. Its successful operation, however, requires the expression of second choices, and in
practice large numbers of voters fail to indicate more than a single choice.
Moreover, the system is somewhat complicated both for the voter in casting his ballot and in the method by which the results of the election must
be canvassed. For these reasons, the plan has not won permanent popularity. It has been tried at one time or another by eleven states, only to
be eventually abandoned, and it is not now employed in any state primary
system.[22] Under the run-off primary plan, if no candidate for a particular
office receives a majority vote in the regular primary election, a second
primary is held in which the two candidates polling the largest votes compete for the nomination. With only the two candidates contending, one is
then certain of securing a majority vote. The run-off primary is employed
rather generally in the South and has been used at one time or another
in a few other states. The plan has the disadvantage of calling the voters
to the polls an additional time when no candidate receives a majority
vote in the first primary. But in the southern states, where Democratic
nomination is usually tantamount to election, this added requirement of
the voter may well be justified.

As previously noted, the typical primary ballot tends to become
overloaded with names of persons who have no chance whatever of winning nomination. Any measure operating to keep such nonentities off the
ballot, while it would not assure majority nominations, would tend to
lessen vote scattering and facilitate intelligent voting. One means of discouraging frivolous candidacies would be to increase the number of signatures required on nominating petitions. The signature requirement
should, of course, remain low enough to enable every aspirant with any
considerable popular support to obtain a place on the ballot, but present
requirements in many states could be raised and this standard still preserved. Another possible approach to the problem is a requirement that
each candidate either pay a nonreturnable filing fee or make a deposit of
money which will be forfeited if he fails to receive a specified percentage
of the primary vote. Since even unknown candidates, through the employment of paid "petition pushers," may readily secure signatures in almost any number, the fee or deposit is sometimes urged as being more

22 O. Douglas Weeks, "Summary of the History and Present Status of Preferential Voting in State Direct Primary Systems," *Southwestern Soc. Sci. Quar.*, XVIII,
64-67 (June, 1937); Penniman, *op. cit.*, 380-381.

practicable than the higher petition requirement. Several states require filing fees, though these are usually relatively small,[23] and during recent decades there has been some interesting experimentation with the deposit plan in certain county, municipal, and legislative primaries in Michigan. For the most part, the deposit plan in that state has been authorized merely as an alternative to the petition requirement, with candidates permitted to obtain places on the ballot by either method; though the plan has been mandatory since 1935 for municipal candidates in Detroit and for a brief period was mandatory for county and state legislative candidates in Wayne county. Deposits required have not been large, rarely if ever exceeding $100, and provision has usually been made for return of their deposits to winning candidates as well as to losers polling prescribed minimum votes. Contrary to expectations, the deposit plan in Michigan, whether in optional or mandatory form, has failed to effect any material reduction in the number of primary candidates. Indeed, there is some evidence that, particularly in urban areas, the plan has served to increase the number of publicity seekers and other nuisance candidates on the ballot. To be sure, increasing the amount of deposits and the risk of forfeiture might render the plan more effective, but at the same time might operate to deter bona fide candidacies. On the whole, Michigan's experience does not presage a bright future for the deposit plan. The plan, nevertheless, has certain merits, such as eliminating the difficult task of checking signatures on petitions, and experience with its operation has as yet been too limited to justify its condemnation as definitely a failure.[24]

Opponents of the primary system of nomination make much of the fact that it involves additional cost both to the public and to candidates. It is of course true that a nominating election, where its cost, as is generally the case, is a public charge, does constitute an additional item of expense to the taxpayers. But election costs in their entirety account for only a very small portion of public expenditures, and the expense of conducting a primary can scarcely be considered unduly burdensome if that is felt to be the most satisfactory method of nominating official candidates. Moreover, it must not be forgotten that nominating conventions also cost money, though convention expenses are borne by the party or its members, as indeed are primary expenses in some of the southern states. Perhaps more serious is the element of expense to individual candidates. Under the primary system, an aspirant for public office must be prepared to finance two campaigns—one preceding the primary and a second, if he is successful in securing nomination, preceding the general election. Here

---

[23] Merriam and Overacker, op. cit., 77.
[24] Harold M. Dorr, "Candidates Won't Stay Out," Nat. Mun. Rev., XXXVIII, 224-229 (May, 1949); Harold M. Dorr, "Nomination by Money Deposit," Ibid., XLIII, 288-292 (June, 1954); John R. Owens, "Nothing Stops Them," Nat. Civic Rev., XLVIII, 458-461, 466 (Oct., 1959).

again, however, it should be remembered that candidates for convention nomination may incur expense in campaigning for delegate support, and it is probable that the convention system lends itself more readily than does the primary to manipulation and control through the corrupt use of funds.

Whatever its shortcomings, the direct primary appears now to have been permanently established as the predominant—perhaps one might almost say the normal—method of making nominations for public office in the United States. Where the primary system has been established, it has rarely been abandoned. Occasional reversions to older nominating methods have occurred here and there, but the distinct tendency has been toward ever-wider use of primary nominations. The primary avoids some of the more serious abuses of the caucus-convention system, and places ultimate authority and responsibility for nominations directly in the hands of the rank and file of party voters. While the primary has developed problems of its own, these are not fatal to the system nor do they seem, in most instances, to be insurmountable. With continued use and experimentation, improvements will doubtless be made, perhaps in some instances along lines suggested in preceding paragraphs. One of the most serious present-day problems is the excessive length of the primary ballot—a problem which flows in large measure, not from any inherent defect of the primary system, but from the large number of elective officers. The much-needed shortening of the general election ballot,[25] if it could be effected, should go far toward facilitating intelligent primary voting by reducing the number of offices for which nomination would be required. Another major problem is that of convincing the average voter that the primary is fully as important as, and indeed in many instances more important than, the general election. Could this be accomplished, and the primary ballot shortened so that the voter would be confronted with a less formidable task than at present, a long step would have been taken toward solution of the problem of nonvoting in primary elections.

Nomination by Petition

Nomination by voter petition has been used to some extent in this country for many years and seems likely to be continued as a supplementary nominating procedure. A petition for nomination is to be clearly distinguished from a petition for a place on the primary ballot. The petition under the primary system results merely in placing the name of an aspirant on the primary ballot, whereas the names which appear on the general election ballot are there as the result of winning in the primary elections. Under the system of nomination by petition, on the other hand,

[25] See above, Chap. V, "Need for a Shorter Ballot."

the effect of the petition is to place the candidate's name directly on the general election ballot. Petition procedure is much the same in both cases, though the nominating petition ordinarily requires a larger number of signatures than the primary petition. The petition method of nomination is used for various local offices. It is also commonly employed for the nomination of independent candidates, as distinguished from party candidates, for both state and local offices; and, where use of the direct primary is confined to the major parties, is frequently used for making minor-party nominations. Participation in a primary for the nomination of major-party candidates usually disqualifies a voter from signing nominating petitions for independent or minor-party candidates for the same offices; and some states provide that a person who has been defeated in a party primary may not then be nominated by petition as an "independent" candidate for the ensuing election.[26]

Election Administration

Election administration is primarily a local responsibility.[27] State statutes prescribe in detail the procedures to be followed in general elections, and in most states in the primaries as well, but the actual conduct of elections is left to local authorities and election expenses are usually a charge on local treasuries. Local responsibility in election matters is widely scattered. Counties in most states have important responsibilities in the conduct of both state and local elections, and in some instances have almost exclusive charge of their management. City elections, however, are frequently under the jurisdiction of municipal authorities; and elections for the choice of township, school, and other special-district officers are often conducted by the governing authorities of the respective units concerned. In New England the town is an important unit for election administration. Some use is made, for administrative purposes, of special election boards, but more frequently election duties are devolved upon other local officers. Among the officers and agencies thus charged with election functions in various states are county, city, and town clerks, county governing boards, county courts, and city councils.

Activities in the field of election administration are quite varied. Voting precincts must be laid out, polling places designated, booths and ballot boxes provided, ballots printed, and precinct officials appointed to preside at the polls on election day. For polling places, the tendency to-

[26] Cf. Austin F. Macdonald, *American State Government and Administration* (Crowell, New York, 6th ed., 1960), 282.

[27] A comprehensive treatise on the subject is Joseph P. Harris, *Election Administration in the United States*. See also Committee on Election Administration of the National Municipal League, "A Model Election Administration System," *Nat. Mun. Rev.*, XIX, 629-671 (Sept., 1930, Supp.).

day in many localities is to make use wherever possible of school buildings, fire and police stations, city halls, county court-houses, and other
public buildings. Since polling-place rentals ordinarily constitute a substantial item in election costs, the use of public buildings may effect a
considerable saving to taxpayers. Precinct election boards are usually required by law to be bipartisan. Board members—inspectors, judges,
clerks, or whatever they may be called in the various states—are appointed
by public authority, but law or custom usually decrees that the appointing agency merely confirm nominations made by the local committees of
the respective parties.[28] In effect, therefore, precinct officials are party
appointees, and the positions are frequently viewed as minor patronage
and used as rewards for party service. Generally, the precinct board which
receives ballots during voting hours also serves, after the close of the
polls, as a counting board to determine and certify the results. Several
states, however, provide for the use in some precincts of separate counting boards, thus permitting voting and counting to proceed concurrently
and making the results of the election available several hours earlier. This
system of "double" boards appears to have given rather general satisfaction where tried. Its failure to secure more widespread adoption has
probably been due to its tendency to increase election costs and a reluctance to divide responsibility.[29]

When the vote in the precinct has been counted and tabulated, the
results of the count are certified to the appropriate canvassing officer or
board. In cases of city elections, this may be a city canvassing agency
charged with making the final canvass and issuing certificates of election
to the winning candidates. Where county and state offices are at stake,
precinct certification is ordinarily to a county canvassing agency which
issues certificates of election to those persons elected to county offices and
certifies to a designated state officer, usually the secretary of state, the returns from the entire county on state offices. The final canvass for state
offices is then made, and election certificates issued to winning candidates,
by a state canvassing board. Canvassing agencies, at whatever level, have
no authority to examine or recount the ballots, but are limited in their
function to a compilation and certification of returns on the basis of the
precinct count. However, the result of an election as finally certified by
the canvassing authorities is usually subject to contest through a procedure prescribed by statute, and in the course of determining a contest
a recount may be ordered and carried out. Election contests are heard
and determined in some instances by the election authorities, in others

[28] Precinct officials in Pennsylvania and a few other states are elected by the
voters. Harris, op. cit., 138. On methods of choosing such officials in the larger cities
of the country, see Murray H. Shusterman, "Choosing Election Officers," Nat. Mun.
Rev., XXIX, 185-193, 199 (Mar., 1940).
[29] Illinois Legislative Council, Improved Election Precinct Returns (Ill.
Legis. Council, Springfield, 1955), 8-10.

by the courts, and, in the case of legislative office, ordinarily by the legislative body itself.[30]

Ballot Forms

At one time it was customary for election ballots to be provided by the political parties, the ballot of each party containing the names of its own candidates only. A "straight" ticket was voted by merely securing a ballot of the preferred party and placing it in the ballot box; while the voting of a "split" ticket required that the voter draw lines through the names of candidates not favored and write in the names of their opponents. Since the various parties ordinarily used ballots of different colors little secrecy in voting was possible, both election officials and bystanders being able to determine at a glance which party ballot was used by each voter. From time to time legislation was enacted in various states in an effort to overcome some of the most flagrant evils of the party-ballot system—a number of states, for example, requiring that all ballots voted be printed on plain white paper—but it was only with the adoption of the Australian ballot, named for the country of its origin, that genuine ballot reform made substantial progress.

The Australian ballot is characterized by two essential features: (1) it is official, and (2) it is secret. Ballots containing the names of candidates of all parties, and of independents as well, are prepared by public officials at public expense and cast in such a manner as to safeguard the secrecy of the voter's choice. Beginning with Kentucky in 1888, adoption of the Australian ballot by the American states made steady progress, and today every state requires its use in some form.[31]

Australian ballots are of two principal types: (1) the party-column, and (2) the office-group. Under the party-column plan, names of the candidates of each party appear on the ballot in a separate vertical column. At the head of each column, along with the name of the party, there is usually a party circle or square for use in voting a straight ticket, and sometimes also a party emblem or vignette. This type of ballot, by enabling the voter to vote a straight ticket by making a single cross in the party square or circle, encourages straight party voting and for that reason is generally favored by politicians. On the office-group ballot, candidates are grouped according to the office sought with each candidate's party indicated alongside his name, and it is necessary for the voter to make a separate cross-mark for each individual candidate for whom he wishes to vote. Thus, the number of marks required to vote a split ticket is no greater than for a straight ticket, and this form of ballot is therefore sup-

[30] Key, *Politics, Parties, and Pressure Groups* (4th ed.), 682.
[31] Cf. Eldon C. Evans, *A History of the Australian Ballot System in the United States;* Albright, *The American Ballot,* Chap. 1.

posed to encourage independent voting. At present, some two-thirds of
the states use ballots which may be classified as of the party-column type,
with the remaining third using the office-group pattern. In several states,
however, the ballot form is actually of a hybrid type, but with one or the
other of the principal patterns predominating.[32]

Voting Machines

In some areas, paper ballots have now been replaced by voting
machines.[33] Operating on the principle of the cash register or adding
machine, the voting machine permits votes to be cast, recorded, and automatically counted without the use of ballots in the ordinary sense.[34] Candidates' names appear on the face of the machine and a vote is cast by
the manipulation of keys or levers—an individual key being provided for
each candidate and, in states which use the party-circle plan, a party
lever for casting a straight party vote. Additional spaces and keys are
provided for voting on policy propositions. More than two-thirds of the
states now authorize the use of machines, the laws usually making their
use optional with the various local units. In most of the states having permissive legislation, machines are actually used, if at all, only in some of
the larger cities, though in some states they are employed in certain rural
areas as well. In New York, Rhode Island, and Connecticut machines are
used in all precincts, both rural and urban.

Voting machines offer certain advantages over paper ballots. The
average time required for casting a vote, once the voters have become
familiar with the operation of the machines, is somewhat reduced, and
therefore it is practicable to use larger and fewer precincts. Invalid and
defective ballots are eliminated, since the machines are so constructed as
to make the casting of such ballots impossible. The count is accurate, automatic, and available promptly after the close of the polls, and recounts
are for the most part avoided. Perhaps the most important advantage of
all is in the fact that various types of voting fraud, especially ballot-box
stuffing and fraudulent counting, tend to be reduced or eliminated. On
the other hand, objections to the machines have been raised on various
grounds. Some of these center about the allegation that voters dislike the
machines and find them difficult to operate. Apparently the most widespread objections, however, have concerned the costliness of the initial

---

[32] Albright, *The American Ballot*, Chap. 3. On methods of marking ballots, see
also Spencer Albright, "Legislation on Marking Ballots," *Southwestern Soc. Sci.
Quar.*, XXI, 221-226 (Dec., 1940). Facsimile reproductions of representative ballots,
both American and foreign, will be found in Carl O. Smith, *A Book of Ballots*.

[33] T. David Zukerman, *The Voting Machine;* Albright, *The American Ballot*,
Chap. 4.

[34] Cf. Merriam and Gosnell, *The American Party System* (4th ed.), 439.

installation of machines and of their subsequent maintenance and operation.[35]

Data concerning the relative costs of voting machines and paper ballots are somewhat contradictory. Certain savings through the use of machines are fairly clear. With fewer precincts, expenses for polling-place rental and the hire of precinct officials are reduced. The cost of printing official paper ballots is eliminated, and expensive recounts are avoided. On the other hand, the original cost of the machines is high and there are recurring expenses incidental to their use, such as those for storage, drayage, and insurance. Some studies of comparative costs have indicated that, when consideration is taken of both amortization of original cost and operational expenses, the total cost of voting with machines is greater than with paper ballots.[36] Other reports, on the contrary, indicate a reduction in election costs through the use of machines.[37] In the final analysis, however, voting machines must find their principal justification not in reduced election costs, since economies in particular instances may be negligible or nonexistent, but in the fact that they reduce election frauds and promote accuracy in the count. It is primarily because of these advantages that voting machines are tending to be used more and more extensively, particularly in urban areas.

Absentee Voting

Election laws now quite generally contain provisions under which qualified voters absent from their place of residence on election day may cast "absentee" ballots. Every state permits absentee voting by members of the armed forces, and all but perhaps two or three of the states permit absentee voting by civilians.[38] Furthermore, most states now extend the privilege of casting absentee ballots to persons who, though not absent from their place of residence, are unable to go to the polls because of illness or physical disability. Some states restrict the application of their absent-voting laws to certain classes of elections, but most permit absentee voting in elections and primaries generally.

Absent-voting procedures vary from state to state. Under the plan

[35] Harris, *op. cit.*, Chap. 7.

[36] *Ibid.*, 268-271.

[37] Penniman, *op. cit.*, 547-548.

[38] Cf. Illinois Legislative Council, *Civilian Absentee Voting Laws* (Ill. Legis. Council, Springfield, 1958). Since the publication of this survey, Pennsylvania has provided for civilian absentee voting; and a proposed constitutional amendment to permit absentee voting by civilians is to be submitted to New Mexico's voters in 1964. Apparently Mississippi and South Carolina were the only states, other than New Mexico, which did not have laws in 1963 permitting absentee voting by civilians generally. Concerning voting by service personnel, see *Voting in the Armed Forces* (House Doc. No. 407, 82d Cong., 2d Sess., U.S. Govt. Printing Office, Washington, 1952); "Findings and Recommendations of the Special Committee on Service Voting," *Amer. Polit. Sci. Rev.*, XLVI, 512-523 (June, 1952).

now used in most states, however, a person expecting to be absent from his place of voting residence on the day of a primary or election secures and marks his ballot sufficiently in advance of that day so that it may be transmitted to his home precinct for inclusion in the regular count. The first step required of a voter under the prevalent form of procedure is the filing, under oath, of a formal application for absentee ballot in which the applicant declares that he is a qualified voter of the county and precinct specified and entitled to vote under the state's absent-voting statutes. This application is filed with a designated local election officer (frequently the county clerk) within whose jurisdiction the voter resides and from whom the official application blank is ordinarily first secured. Application for absentee ballot may usually be made either in person or by mail, and most states prescribe a time limit within which the application must be filed. Upon securing his ballot from the election officer, the voter marks it, in accordance with formal instructions which accompany the ballot, in the presence of an election officer, notary public, or other officer authorized to administer oaths, but in such manner that the officer or notary cannot see for what candidates or propositions it is marked. The marked ballot is then sealed in an official envelope on the back of which the voter must execute an affidavit, attested by the officer or notary, to the effect that he is a duly-qualified voter and that he marked the enclosed ballot in secret. The envelope containing the marked ballot is then delivered, personally or by mail, to the election officer from whom it was obtained, and transmitted by him, at the appropriate time, to the election board of the voter's precinct. Here the ballot is removed from its envelope and placed in the regular ballot box.[39]

Under normal circumstances, the absentee ballots cast in a given election constitute a relatively small portion of the total vote. Nevertheless, in the interest of democratic government it is only appropriate that absentee and disabled voters be permitted to participate in elections, and especially desirable when large numbers of voters are absent from home as members of the armed forces that every reasonable measure be taken to enable such persons to cast their ballots. And instances are by no means wanting in which the final result of an important election has actually turned on the count of the absentee ballots.

THE POPULAR RECALL

If popular government is to function most effectively, appropriate means must be provided for holding public officials responsible for the

[39] Cf. Paul G. Steinbicker, "Absentee Voting in the United States," *Amer. Polit. Sci. Rev.*, XXXII, 898-907 (Oct., 1938). Laws relating to service personnel frequently waive registration requirements and permit application for absentee ballot on a special postcard form supplied by the federal government.

proper performance of their duties and removing from office those who prove faithless or incompetent. The methods of removal most commonly provided are impeachment, judicial process, and executive action. Executive removal, however, is limited for the most part to appointed officials, while impeachment and judicial removal are cumbersome processes which can ordinarily be invoked only for crime or gross misconduct and not for mere inefficiency.[40] Elective officials, if they wish to continue in office, must of course stand for reelection from time to time and thereby render to the voters some measure of accounting for the conduct of their offices. This method of enforcing official responsibility is, however, available to the electorate only at regularly recurring intervals. Since the turn of the century, a new method of removal has been developed which is designed to make public officers responsible to the voters directly and continuously during their official terms—namely, the popular recall. Under this plan, a specified number of voters may, by petition, demand and secure a special election to determine whether a designated officer shall continue in office to the end of his term or be immediately removed therefrom.

The recall was introduced in this country in the Los Angeles city charter of 1903, and was first applied to state officers by Oregon in 1908. Today, elective state officers are removable by recall procedure in 13 states,[41] though in five of these[42] judges are excepted from the recall provision. Kansas applies the recall to appointive as well as elective officers.[43] It is at the local level, however, and especially among municipalities, that the recall has spread most widely. Most of the constitutional provisions for the recall of state officers apply also to some or all local officers, and many states without such provisions have extended the recall to various local officers by statute. At the present time, three-fourths or more of the states provide for the recall in some or all cities, with the device particularly common among municipalities which have adopted commission or manager government.[44] In local government, as at the state level, the re-

---

[40] See below, Chap. VIII, "Judicial Power: Impeachment;" Chap. IX, "Powers of the Governor—Appointment and Removal."

[41] Alaska, Arizona, California, Colorado, Idaho, Kansas, Louisiana, Michigan, Nevada, North Dakota, Oregon, Washington, and Wisconsin.

[42] Alaska, Idaho, Louisiana, Michigan, and Washington.

[43] The most thorough study of the recall, though with reference primarily to a single state, is Frederick L. Bird and Frances M. Ryan, *The Recall of Public Officers: A Study of the Operation of the Recall in California.* More recent data concerning California will be found in Winston W. Crouch, Dean E. McHenry, John C. Bollens, and Stanley Scott, *California Government and Politics* (Prentice-Hall, Englewood Cliffs, N.J., 1956), 127-133. An early study of the system in Oregon is James D. Barnett, *The Operation of the Initiative, Referendum and Recall in Oregon.* On the subject generally, see Bird and Ryan, *op. cit.,* Chap. 1; Arnold B. Hall, *Popular Government,* Chap. 9.

[44] Cf. J. Otis Garber, "The Use of the Recall in American Cities," *Nat. Mun. Rev.,* XV, 259-261 (May, 1926).

call usually applies only to elective officials, though there are occasional instances of its application to appointive officers as well.

Recall proceedings involve two distinct steps: (1) the petition, and (2) the recall election. A recall petition must be signed by a specified percentage of the qualified voters of the state or local area concerned. The required percentage varies from 10 to 55, and is usually based upon the total number of votes cast for the office affected at the last general election.[45] The petition must set forth a statement of the charges against the officer whose removal is sought and a demand for an election to determine whether he shall be permitted to continue in office. When the petition has been signed by the necessary number of voters, it is filed with the secretary of state, the county or city clerk, or some other designated election official. If the petition is found to meet all legal requirements as to form and signatures, the recall election is ordered.

Recall elections take various forms. Under one plan, the name of the official against whom the recall is directed merely appears on the ballot, along with the names of other candidates nominated by petition, as a candidate for the office for the remainder of the term. If the incumbent receives more votes than any other candidate, he retains his office; otherwise he is removed and succeeded by the winning candidate. A variant of this plan is that in which the voter votes separately on two questions: the recall of the incumbent and the choice, from among candidates nominated by petition, of a successor. Under this plan, if there are more votes for than against the recall of the incumbent, he relinquishes his office to the person who, as a candidate, has received the largest vote. If, on the other hand, more votes are cast against than for the recall, the incumbent remains in office. Both of these forms of recall election are open to criticism on the ground that the official whose removal is sought must, if he is to retain his office, overcome not only the criticisms of his own record but also the personal and political popularity of opposing candidates. Another, and perhaps the most satisfactory, type of election is that in which the voter is asked to vote on the single question of whether or not the officer concerned shall be recalled. If the election goes against the incumbent, he is removed from office and a second election is held to choose his successor; or, in some states, the vacancy created by his removal is filled in the same manner as if the vacancy had occurred from any other cause. Whatever the form of recall election, provision is ordinarily made that an officer may not be recalled until he has held the office for a specified minimum length of time, varying from three months to a year. The purpose of such a provision is, of course, to give the official at least a brief opportunity, before subjecting him to a recall election, to demonstrate to the voters the manner in which he can and will conduct his office. Furthermore, provision is often made that, if an officer wins a recall election and

[45] Bird and Ryan, *op. cit.*, 17.

thereby retains his office, he may not be subjected to another such election until the lapse of a specified period of time. In some instances, a second recall election within a single term of office is prohibited altogether.[46]

Considering the large number of jurisdictions in which it is available, the recall has not, in practice, been used extensively. Only a very few state officers, including but a single governor and an occasional state legislator, have been removed by the method. At the local level the device has been employed somewhat more frequently, but even there it has been used but sparingly. Perhaps the most wholesome effect of such occasionally been recalled, the great majority of recall elections have been in cities. Mayors have been recalled in Los Angeles, Detroit, and Seattle, and there have been several instances of the recall of city councilmen. Indeed, the entire council of Pasadena, California, was recalled in 1932, as was that of Long Beach in 1934.[47] On the other hand, many recall elections in cities and elsewhere have resulted in victories for the officials against whom they were directed.

The merits of the recall are difficult to evaluate. There is substantial agreement that the device is best adapted to elective officers, and especially to those, such as legislators and chief executives, who are concerned at least to some extent with policy determination. As applied to appointive officers, the recall violates the administrative principle of the responsibility of an appointee to his appointing officer. It is felt by some that removal by recall is less appropriate in the case of judges than in that of legislative and executive officers[48] and, as has been pointed out, several of the states which provide the recall for state officials exempt judicial officers from its operation. Judges, it is true, are not considered as being concerned primarily with the determination of policy. Yet, when they exercise the power of judicial review their work does partake of policy determination and, in any case, the question may well be raised whether the recall procedure as applied to judges is not as justifiable as their popular election in the first place.

As previously indicated, recall provisions where they exist have been used but sparingly. Perhaps the most wholesome effect of such provisions springs from the mere fact of their existence. Public officials who are subject to recall know that they may be called to account by the voters at any time and thus may be stimulated to constant vigilance in the performance of their duties. The recall is sometimes criticized on the ground that it involves a further lengthening of the ballot. On the other hand, it has been contended that, without the recall as a means of holding to account officials vested with wide appointing powers, the short

[46] *Ibid.*, 18.
[47] Crouch, McHenry, Bollens, and Scott, *op. cit.*, 131.
[48] See below, Chap. XI, "Removal of Judges."

ballot would not be practical.[49] Provision for the recall may make it possible to lengthen official terms without impairing popular control, but may also be used by factions defeated in an election to continue the election fight or to harass the winners while in office.

Doubtless some of the removals which have been effected by the recall have been wise and others unwise; and, whatever merits the device may have, it is not spreading appreciably at the present time. Of the thirteen states which authorize the recall of state officers, ten adopted the system within a half dozen years of Oregon's lead in 1908, and there was not a single addition to the list between Wisconsin's adoption in 1926 and Alaska's provision of 1959. At the local level the commission form of city government, in connection with which the recall has achieved most popularity, spread rather rapidly during the early years of the century, but today is no more than holding its own, if indeed it is not actually losing ground.[50] Though the recall will certainly be retained in some states and many local governments, there is no indication that it is destined to gain appreciably in popularity in the foreseeable future.

DIRECT LEGISLATION

Introduction of the popular recall in this country came as a result of the Populist and Progressive movements which, during the 1890's and the first two decades of the present century, were an important factor in American politics, particularly in the western states. Closely associated with the recall in this democratic upsurge, and adopted somewhat more widely, was the provision for direct popular participation in lawmaking through the initiative and referendum. The initiative is a device which permits a specified number of voters, by petition, to propose a statute or local ordinance and secure its submission to the electorate for adoption or rejection. The referendum, or "popular veto" as it is sometimes called, enables the voters, also by petition, to demand that a statute or ordinance enacted by a representative legislative body be submitted to the electorate for a determination of whether it shall or shall not take effect. It will thus be noted that the purpose of the initiative is positive in nature, seeking to provide a means whereby the voters may enact directly legislative measures which they desire, but which they have been unable to secure from the regular legislative agencies. The referendum, on the other hand, has the negative purpose of enabling the electors to nullify undesirable measures which legislative bodies have enacted. Each device provides the voters with a measure of direct control over the legislative process, the

[49] Cf. Barnett, op. cit., 217.
[50] See below, Chap. XIV.

initiative affording a remedy for the legislature's "sins of omission" and the referendum a remedy for its "sins of commission."[51]

The initiative and referendum for state legislation were first adopted by South Dakota in 1898, and during the twenty years which followed various other states took similar action. Today twenty states[52] make provision for these instruments of popular control in some form, with two additional states—Maryland and New Mexico—providing for the referendum only.[53] At the local level, and particularly in the cities, the initiative and referendum have gained even wider acceptance. In more than half of the states having constitutional provisions for the initiative and referendum as applied to state legislation, those provisions also make the devices available to the voters of some or all local governments; and elsewhere the local initiative and referendum have been authorized by statutory and charter provisions. Like the recall, the initiative and referendum have become fairly standard features of the commission form of municipal government, and they are provided in many manager and mayor-council cities as well. Indeed, all but a very few of the states

[51] An analysis and discussion of constitutional provisions appears in Armand B. Coigne, *Statute Making* (Commerce Clearing House, New York, 1948), Chaps. 2, 3. For studies of the initiative and referendum in individual states, see James D. Barnett, *The Operation of the Initiative, Referendum, and Recall in Oregon;* V. O. Key, Jr., and Winston W. Crouch, *The Initiative and the Referendum in California;* Winston W. Crouch, *The Initiative and Referendum in California;* James K. Pollock, *The Initiative and Referendum in Michigan;* Joseph G. LaPalombara, *The Initiative and Referendum in Oregon: 1938-1948;* N. D. Houghton, "The Initiative and Referendum in Missouri," *Mo. Historical Rev.,* XIX, 268-299 (Jan., 1925); Waldo Schumacher, "Thirty Years of People's Rule in Oregon: An Analysis," *Polit. Sci. Quar.,* XLVII, 242-258 (June, 1932); David Y. Thomas, "The Initiative and Referendum in Arkansas Come of Age," *Amer. Polit. Sci. Rev.,* XXVII, 66-75 (Feb., 1933); C. I. Winslow, "The Referendum in Maryland," *Ibid.,* 75-79; Edwin A. Cottrell, "Twenty-five Years of Direct Legislation in California," *Pub. Opinion Quar.,* III, 30-45 (Jan., 1939); Max Radin, "Popular Legislation in California," *Minn. Law Rev.,* XXIII, 559-584 (Apr., 1939); Claudius O. Johnson, "The Initiative and Referendum in Washington," *Pacific Northwest Quar.,* XXXVI, 29-63 (Jan., 1945); Max Radin, "Popular Legislation in California: 1936-1946," *Calif. Law Rev.,* XXXV, 171-190 (June, 1947); Arthur A. Schwartz, "Initiative Held in Reserve" [in Ohio], *Nat. Mun. Rev.,* XLI, 142-145, 174 (Mar., 1952); Hubert D. Henry, "Popular Law-Making in Colorado," *Rocky Mt. Law Rev.,* XXVI, 439-449 (June, 1954). An appraisal based upon experience in five states will be found in Joseph G. LaPalombara and Charles B. Hagan, "Direct Legislation: An Appraisal and a Suggestion," *Amer. Polit. Sci. Rev.,* XLV, 400-421 (June, 1951).

[52] Alaska, Arizona, Arkansas, California, Colorado, Idaho, Maine, Massachusetts, Michigan, Missouri, Montana, Nebraska, Nevada, North Dakota, Ohio, Oklahoma, Oregon, South Dakota, Utah, and Washington. A provision for the initiative and referendum in Mississippi was invalidated by the courts.

[53] Tabular analyses of the constitutional provisions will be found in Illinois Legislative Reference Bureau, *The Initiative, Referendum, and Recall,* 81-82; Pollock, *op. cit.,* 87-94; Coigne, *op. cit.,* 37-40, 44-47. Kentucky, in addition to Maryland and New Mexico, is considered by Coigne as a "referendum" state, though the referendum there may be invoked only on certain taxing and borrowing measures.

now permit the use of one or both of these devices in certain classes of cities.[54]

Initiative Procedures

Individuals or groups wishing to propose legislation through the initiative must first prepare a formal draft of the proposed statute or ordinance and secure proper petition blanks.[55] The petition forms, with a copy of the proposed measure attached to each, are then circulated for voters' signatures. The required number of signatures is usually expressed as a percentage of the number of votes cast in the last preceding election for a specified public office. In the case of the statewide initiative, the office most commonly used for this purpose is that of governor, and the percentage required varies from five to ten.[56] An occasional state, on the other hand, sets the minimum number of signatures at a specific figure, North Dakota, for example, requiring 10,000 signatures to a state-wide petition. Where the percentage formula is used, the requirement for local petitions is frequently higher than for statewide, but is based on the vote for a local rather than a state office. Several states, in the case of statewide petitions, impose requirements concerning the geographic distribution of signatures, Arkansas, for example, providing that the 8 percent of the state's voters required as signers of initiative petitions must include at least 4 percent of the voters in each of fifteen counties.

When signatures in the necessary number have been obtained, the initiative petition is filed with a designated officer, commonly the secretary of state in the case of proposed state statutes and the clerk of the county, city, or other local unit in the case of local measures. From this point, the course of procedure depends upon whether the *direct* or the *indirect* form of the initiative is employed. Under the first of these forms, the proposed measure is referred directly to the voters for enactment or rejection, the proposition being placed on the ballot at a general or special election as may be required in the jurisdiction concerned. In this type of initiative procedure the representative legislative body, be it state legislature, city council, or local governing board, has no part. Under the indirect form of initiative, on the other hand, the initiated measure is referred first to the state or local legislature. If the legislature enacts the measure within a specified period of time, a popular vote on the proposition is un-

[54] Winston W. Crouch, "The Initiative and Referendum in Cities," *Amer. Polit. Sci. Rev.*, XXXVII, 491-504 (June, 1943).

[55] In some jurisdictions the initiative procedure is inapplicable to certain types of legislation such as appropriation measures and statutes of local application.

[56] Under Ohio's provision for the indirect initiative, only 3 percent of the voters for governor need sign an original initiative petition to the legislature but, in case of legislative inaction on the measure, a supplementary petition signed by an additional 3 percent of the voters must be filed in order to secure a popular vote on the proposal.

necessary. Should the legislature, however, fail to enact the proposed measure, it is then referred to the voters. The significance of the terms *direct* and *indirect* initiative is thus apparent. Under the one form, petitioners make proposals of legislative measures *directly* to the voters for acceptance or rejection at the polls; while, under the other, proposals go first to the legislative body and reach the electorate, if at all, only *indirectly* via the legislature.

Two advantages may be claimed for the indirect initiative over the direct type: (1) it fosters careful and mature deliberation by making the benefits of legislative discussion and action available prior to popular vote; and (2) where the legislative body enacts an initiated measure, the trouble and expense involved in a popular referendum election on the question are eliminated. Of the states and local units which employ the initiative, some use the direct form and some the indirect, whereas still others permit the use of either type. Where both forms are available, the initiating voters determine which procedure is to be used by directing their petition to the electors or the legislative body as the case may be. Under such circumstances, the number of signatures required on the initiative petition may be smaller for the indirect initiative than for the direct. This is true, for example, in the case of the statutory initiative in California, where 8 percent of the electors, based on the vote for governor, must sign a petition for the direct initiative and only 5 percent a petition of the indirect type.

The popular vote required for enactment of statutes or ordinances proposed by the initiative is most commonly a simple majority of the votes cast on the question, with the provision in some instances that the total number of votes cast for and against the proposition must equal a specified percentage of all the votes cast at the election. Ordinarily a measure enacted by initiative procedure may be amended or repealed only by subsequent popular vote and not by mere legislative action.

The Referendum

Popular referenda of several different types are employed in connection with state and local government. Amendments to constitutions and home-rule charters, for example, usually require approval of the voters in referendum elections. Proposals for public borrowing, or for the imposition or increase of tax levies for certain purposes, must often be submitted to the voters for acceptance or rejection. Referendum elections, as we have seen, constitute an integral part of the initiative procedure through which legislative measures may be enacted by petition and popular vote. Some states and local units have an optional form of referendum under which the legislative body may, of its own volition, refer measures to the electorate for final action. The form of referendum with which we are here concerned, however, is that under which voters who are opposed to a measure enacted by a legislative body may, by petition, secure a popular vote on the question of whether the measure shall become effective or be "vetoed" by voter action. This "petition referendum," as previously noted, is now available to the voters of twenty-two states and many cities and other local units.

As the plan ordinarily operates, statutes or ordinances enacted by the legislative body do not become effective for a specified number of days, usually sixty or ninety, from the time of their passage or the time of legislative adjournment. If, prior to the expiration of that period, a referendum petition is filed in proper form, effectiveness of the measure against which the petition is directed is further suspended until the voters have had an opportunity, at a general or special election, to approve or veto the legislation. Emergency measures are usually exempt from the referendum, as also in many instances are appropriations for current governmental expenses. Some jurisdictions exempt local or special laws, certain tax measures, and various other specific categories of legislation. In an effort to prevent legislative abuse of the "emergency" exemption, it is often provided that measures carrying emergency clauses must be enacted by the legislative body by an extraordinary majority (frequently two-thirds) vote, or that emergencies may not be declared on enumerated types of legislation. In some instances both varieties of safeguard are provided.

The required number of signatures is ordinarily somewhat smaller for referendum than for initiative petitions. For statewide referenda, the most common requirement is 5 percent of the voters, based upon a previous vote for the governorship or some other state office. As in the case of the initiative, the signature requirement is sometimes in terms of a definite number, such as 10,000 in Maryland and 7,000 in North Dakota, and some jurisdictions make requirements concerning the geographic distribution of signatures. When a referendum petition has been signed by the required number of electors, it is filed with the official, usually the secretary of state or local clerk, whose duty it is to see that the measure is submitted to popular vote. Acceptance or rejection of the measure is ordinarily determined by a simple majority of the votes cast on the question.

Merits of Direct Legislation

From the first, the advantages and disadvantages of the initiative and referendum have been warmly debated, and even now there is little if any consensus regarding their merits. The devices were instituted in the hope of breaking the power of selfish "interest groups" which frequently dominate legislative bodies, and placing control over legislation directly in the hands of "the people." That hope has not been realized. Experience has shown that most initiative and referendum petitions originate with pressure groups representing special interests. Groups of this nature ordinarily have the organization and funds necessary to circulate petitions for the placing of measures on the ballot, whereas spontaneous citizen groups interested in good government usually lack those facilities. Organizations exist which, at so much per signature, will secure signers to any petition, and interest groups without sufficient organization of their own, if well financed, can readily secure the services of such professional "petition pushers." While pressure groups have thus had to adapt their methods to the new procedures, they are probably no less able to influence the course of legislation than before.[57]

Opponents of direct legislation have contended that the voters are not properly qualified to act upon legislative proposals and that use of the initiative and referendum will result in a large amount of radical or "crack-pot" legislation. Experience, again, has scarcely sustained this contention. To be sure, some ill-advised measures have been adopted by the voters, but such measures are also enacted at times by representative legislative bodies; and the voters in some instances—perhaps as frequently as legislatures—have subsequently corrected their indiscretions. Available data indicate that more than half of the proposals referred to the electorate through the initiative and referendum have been defeated, and there would seem to be little if any evidence that the voters in choosing what to approve and what to reject have been less sane and discriminating than their elected representatives.[58]

It is argued, on the one hand, that the initiative and referendum have an educative effect upon the voters and stimulate interest and participation in government and, on the other, that because of lack of popular interest they result in minority legislation. Actually, direct legislation probably does have some educational effect, particularly in those jurisdictions which provide publicity pamphlets,[59] though such educational value, because of its very nature, cannot be accurately measured. In regard to the interrelated matters of voter interest and minority legislation, it must be admitted that in general elections fewer votes are ordinarily cast on initiative and referendum propositions that on candidates, and that for this reason legislation is frequently enacted or vetoed by less than a majority vote of all those participating in the election concerned. While this may be unfortunate, it should be remembered that legislation is not infrequently enacted by legislative bodies by the vote of members who represent a minority of the electorate, this being especially true in states where urban areas are grossly underrepresented in the state legislature.

[57] Cf. Pollock, *op. cit.*, 69; Key and Crouch, *op. cit.*, 565; Schumacher, *op. cit.*
[58] Pollock, *op. cit.*, 66; Radin, "Popular Legislation in California: 1936-1946," *loc. cit.*
[59] See above, Chap. V, footnote 39.

Minority legislation, therefore, is not confined to that enacted through the initiative. Moreover, though it is true that some persons who cast ballots for candidates fail to vote on legislative propositions, the degree of voter participation in direct legislation has, in some jurisdictions, been surprisingly high. Opponents of direct legislation have also alleged that provision for the initiative and referendum lessens legislative responsibility and thereby discourages some of the best qualified potential candidates from seeking or accepting legislative office. It seems extremely doubtful, however, that introduction of these instrumentalities of popular control has lowered the caliber of legislative personnel.

Perhaps the most valid objection to the initiative and referendum lies in their lengthening of the ballot. Where the instruments of direct legislation are used only occasionally, this presents no serious problem, but where they are employed extensively ballot length becomes a matter of genuine concern. In practice, the use made of the initiative and referendum has varied widely from one jurisdiction to another. In Michigan, for example, the devices have been used quite moderately. During the three decades from 1910 to 1939, the people of that state were called upon to vote on only eighty-four propositions, including constitutional amendments proposed by the legislature. This was an average of only three propositions per election, and never were there more than eight proposals on the ballot at one time.[60] California voters, on the other hand, were called upon, during the period from 1912 to 1942, to pass upon no less than 390 propositions. Of these, 357 were submitted at the regular biennial elections—an average of more than 20 propositions per election.[61] As a result, it has been clearly impossible for any large percentage of the voters in that state to be adequately informed on all of the measures submitted to them.[62] In both Michigan and California, it is only appropriate to note, a large majority of the propositions submitted to the voters have consisted of legislative proposals for constitutional amendment. While, therefore, initiative measures are not in themselves the principal cause of the overburdened ballot in California, such measures do complicate still further the voter's task. It may also be surmised that more constitutional amendments are proposed by the legislature than would be the case were the initiative not available for proposing constitutional amendments as well as statutes. In an effort to determine themselves the form which proposed amendments shall take, the legislators may submit proposals on matters which they believe would otherwise be the subject of initiative proposals. At the local level, various California cities, particularly Los Angeles and San Francisco, rather consistently have ballots made unduly long by the inclusion of numerous propositions. Here again, however, the great major-

---

[60] Pollock, *op. cit.*, 17-18.
[61] Crouch, *The Initiative and Referendum in California*, 23.
[62] Cottrell, *op. cit.*

ity of the propositions referred have been council proposals for charter amendments, with initiative measures and petition referenda constituting but a small percentage of the total.[63]

All in all, it is difficult, on the basis of the record, to make a strong case either for or against the initiative and referendum. They have neither been the boon to democracy contemplated by their friends nor produced the dire consequences predicted by their enemies. Actually, it seems doubtful that they have exerted any profound influence upon the course of legislation.[64] It is true that they provide potential checks, both positive and negative, upon the elected legislature, and for that reason their existence as a "gun behind the door" may have some wholesome effect upon legislative action. But they have proved to be no panacea for legislative ills and, where used excessively, their effect has been to lengthen the ballot unduly and thereby impede responsible government. It may well be wondered whether those genuinely interested in legislative improvement might not better, instead of promoting the initiative and referendum, devote their efforts to raising the standards of personnel and procedure in our elected legislative bodies.

REFERENCES

ALBRIGHT, Spencer D., *The American Ballot* (Amer. Council on Pub. Affairs, Washington, 1942).

BALLARD, Rene N., *The Primary Convention System in Utah* (Inst. of Govt., Univ. of Utah, Salt Lake City, 1947).

BARNETT, James D., *The Operation of the Initiative, Referendum, and Recall in Oregon* (Macmillan, New York, 1915).

BECKETT, Paul, and McNUTT, Walter L., *The Direct Primary in New Mexico* (Div. of Research, Dept. of Govt., Univ. of N.M., Albuquerque, 1947).

BIRD, Frederick L., and RYAN, Frances M., *The Recall of Public Officers; a Study of the Operation of the Recall in California* (Macmillan, New York, 1930).

CROUCH, Winston W., *The Initiative and Referendum in California* (Haynes Found., Los Angeles, 1943).

DALLINGER, Frederick W., *Nominations for Elective Office in the United States* (Longmans, New York, 1897).

EVANS, Eldon C., *A History of the Australian Ballot System in the United States* (Univ. of Chicago Press, Chicago, 1917).

EWING, Cortez A. M., *Primary Elections in the South: A Study in Uniparty Politics* (Univ. of Okla. Press, Norman, 1953).

[63] Crouch, "The Initiative and Referendum in Cities," *loc. cit.;* Winston W. Crouch, "Direct Legislation Laboratory," *Nat. Mun. Rev.,* XL, 81-87, 99 (Feb., 1951).
[64] Cf. Pollock, *op. cit.,* 67; Key and Crouch, *op. cit.,* 575.

GRIMES, Marcene, *Kansas Primaries: Our Nominating Process* (Govtl. Research Center, Univ. of Kan., Lawrence, 1954).

HALL, Arnold B., *Popular Government* (Macmillan, New York, 1921).

HARRIS, Joseph P., *Election Administration in the United States* (Brookings Inst., Washington, 1934).

HOLLAND, L. M., *The Direct Primary in Georgia* (Univ. of Ill. Press, Urbana, 1949).

Illinois Legislative Reference Bureau, *The Initiative, Referendum, and Recall* (Constitutional Convention Bull. No. 2, Ill. Legis. Ref. Bur., Springfield, 1919).

KEY, V. O., Jr., and CROUCH, Winston W., *The Initiative and the Referendum in California* (Univ. of Calif. Press, Berkeley, 1939).

KING, Clyde L., ed., "The Initiative, Referendum, and Recall," *Annals of Amer. Acad. of Polit. and Soc. Sci.*, XLIII (Philadelphia, Sept., 1912).

LaPALOMBARA, Joseph G., *The Initiative and Referendum in Oregon: 1938-1948* (Ore. State Coll., Corvallis, 1950).

LEE, Eugene C., *The Politics of Nonpartisanship: A Study of California City Elections* (Univ. of Calif. Press, Berkeley and Los Angeles, 1960).

MARTIN, Boyd A., *The Direct Primary in Idaho* (Stanford Univ. Press, Stanford University, Calif., 1947).

MERRIAM, Charles E., and OVERACKER, Louise, *Primary Elections* (Univ. of Chicago Press, Chicago, 1928).

MEYER, Ernst C., *Nominating Systems: Direct Primaries versus Conventions in the United States* (Author, Madison, Wis., 1902).

MILLER, George F., *Absentee Voters and Suffrage Laws* (Daylion Co., Washington, 1948).

National Municipal League, *A Model Direct Primary System* (Nat. Mun. League, New York, 1951).

POLLOCK, James K., *The Direct Primary in Michigan, 1909-1935* (Bur. of Govt., Univ. of Mich., Ann Arbor, 1943).

———, *The Initiative and Referendum in Michigan* (Bur. of Govt., Univ. of Mich., Ann Arbor, 1940).

SALTER, J. T., ed., "The Direct Primary," *Annals of Amer. Acad. of Polit. and Soc. Sci.*, CVI (Philadelphia, Mar., 1923).

SMITH, Carl O., *A Book of Ballots* (Detroit Bur. of Govtl. Research, Detroit, 1938).

ZUKERMAN, T. David, *The Voting Machine* (Pol. Research Bur., Repub. County Com. of N.Y., New York, 1925).

See also political parties textbooks included in the reference list at the end of the preceding chapter.

IV

State Organization and Powers

7

State Legislatures: Structure and Organization

The Legislative Function

The function of the state legislature, as of other legislative bodies, consists essentially in the determination of public policy. Although it is usual in the United States to speak of three functions of government—legislative, executive, and judicial—it is sometimes helpful, and quite as logical, to think of the governmental process as involving but two functions or steps, namely the determination of public policy and the carrying out or execution of that policy.[1] When viewed in this light, the work of the courts, as well as that of executive and administrative officials, falls within the category of policy execution, whereas policy determination is the function of the legislative branch. Policy determination in the governmental field involves making decisions as to what services are to be provided by the government, the nature of the organization or machinery through which those services are to be provided, the amount of money to be expended upon the various services, and the manner in which that

[1] This idea of two ultimate functions of government, the one concerned with the expression of the will of the state and the other with the execution of that will, was set forth at the turn of the century by Professor F. J. Goodnow, who gave to the respective functions the names "politics" and "administration." Frank J. Goodnow, *Politics and Administration* (Macmillan, New York, 1900).

179

money is to be raised. Since democracy involves government based upon the will of the people, the legislative function in a democratic state resolves itself into the task of ascertaining the public will relative to governmental matters and giving expression to that will in the form of law. To put it figuratively, the function of the legislature consists in "blueprinting" or planning the governmental program. Having been given the stamp of legislative approval, the plans for a particular course of action, in the form of legislative enactments, are turned over to the executive and judicial branches of government to be carried out. It is for the legislature to determine, for example, the general nature of the state's highway program, the amount of money to be expended, and the manner in which the necessary funds are to be raised; but, those determinations having been made, the task of actually constructing and maintaining the highway system, including preparation of plans for specific projects and the letting of necessary contracts, falls to the appropriate executive or administrative agencies to be carried out in accordance with the legislative will. In practice, of course, it is impossible to draw a precise line of separation between the making of public policy and its execution, since the two inevitably intermingle in some degree. Nevertheless, the two aspects of government differ in the matter of emphasis, and the general distinction between policy-formulation and administration remains useful.

Bicameralism

With the single exception of Nebraska, each of the fifty states has a two-house or bicameral legislature.[2] The *official* name of the legislative body varies from state to state. About half the states use *legislature* as the official name; most of the others use the name *general assembly*, although a few use *legislative assembly* and in Massachusetts and New Hampshire the official title is *general court*. Regardless of official names, however, the name *legislature* is commonly used in a generic sense to designate the legislative branch of the state government, and is so used in this book. The upper house of the legislature is uniformly given the official designation of *senate*. The official name of the lower house is in most states *house of representatives*, but in a few instances is *assembly* or *house of delegates*. In New Jersey, where the name *legislature* is used for the two branches together, the name *general assembly* is used for the lower house.[3]

The widespread adoption of bicameralism in the field of American

[2] On the subject generally, see Charles B. Hagan, "The Bicameral Principle in State Legislatures," *Jour. of Pub. Law*, XI, 310-327 (1963).

[3] A list of the official names of the legislative bodies and their respective houses in the various states will be found in *The Book of the States* (Council of State Govts., Chicago), 1964-65, p. 42.

state government is to be explained in large part upon historical grounds. Following the precedent of the British Parliament, the legislatures of most of the English colonies in America were bicameral; and when, with the break from the mother country, the colonies became states, it was only natural that most of the new state constitutions should follow colonial precedent in establishing legislatures of two houses.[4] Moreover, the establishment of a bicameral Congress by the Federal Constitution of 1787 was a strong influence in bringing about the incorporation of the bicameral plan in state constitutions framed thereafter. It was apparently assumed that, since a legislative body of two chambers seemed feasible in the general government, similar organization of the legislative branch was desirable also in the respective states.

But historical precedent was not the sole reason for the adoption of bicameralism. There was some feeling that a legislature of two houses might be made more widely representative of the various interest groups within the state by providing means whereby different interests would find representation in the respective houses. With this purpose in view, some of the earlier constitutions fixed higher qualifications—with respect to age and property ownership, for example—for both the members of the upper house and the electors entitled to vote for such members. It was thus intended that the senate should be chosen by and from, and hence be representative of, the more prosperous and conservative classes. A broader suffrage, and less rigorous qualifications for membership, were provided for the house of representatives. Now, however, most of these early differences in the two houses no longer exist. With uniform suffrage requirements throughout the state, the same voters elect the members of both houses; and, except that minimum age and residence requirements for senators are frequently somewhat higher than those for representatives, there is little difference in the qualifications required of members of the respective chambers. Thus the two houses, other than in size and length of terms, tend to become virtually duplicates one of the other, and the earlier argument that they would represent different interests is no longer of any validity. Indeed, in a few states the members of the two houses are chosen from a single set of districts.[5] In some instances representation of different interests in the respective houses still results, to a certain extent, from constitutional provision that counties or towns shall be represented as such in one house whereas the other chamber shall be directly representative of population. The effect of provisions of this na-

[4] The colonial legislatures were unicameral in Delaware and Pennsylvania, and early state constitutions provided for unicameral legislatures in Georgia, Pennsylvania, and Vermont. Georgia and Pennsylvania changed to the bicameral plan in 1789 and 1790, respectively, but Vermont did not abandon unicameralism until 1836. W. Brooke Graves, *American State Government* (Heath, Boston, 4th ed., 1953), 190-191.

[5] See below, "Apportionment and Districting."

ture will be considered in connection with the discussion of urban representation.

Still more important as a factor in fostering the adoption of bicameralism was the belief that the two-chamber arrangement would make an important contribution to a desirable system of "checks and balances," since each house would operate as a check upon the other. Thus pernicious measures enacted by one house might be defeated in the other. Moreover, the mere fact that every piece of legislation would have to be considered and approved by both houses would tend to prevent hasty action and the enactment of carelessly-drawn or "half-baked" measures. It was also felt that a two-house legislature would be less susceptible to corruption from the outside since it would be more difficult to exert influence or pressure upon two chambers than upon one.

In practice, however, it seems doubtful that the supposed advantages of bicameralism in the direction of checks and balances have actually been realized.[6] To be sure, some measures passed by one chamber are killed or revised by the other. But there is scarcely a practical method of determining the extent to which measures thus killed are pernicious proposals which *should* be killed, or that to which the revision effected actually *improves* the quality of legislation. A large percentage of the bills presented to the legislature are killed by the house in which they are introduced, and to this extent a second chamber is superfluous. Conversely, some bills are passed in as irresponsible manner by one house with the expectation that the other house will kill them. Also, the large number of bills passed by the second house without any amendment or revision whatsoever suggests doubt that a second chamber functions effectively as a revising agency.

Unicameralism

For almost exactly a century—from the abolition of unicameralism by Vermont in 1836[7] to its adoption by Nebraska in 1934—every state legislature consisted of two houses. During this period the operation of bicameralism was not altogether satisfactory, and in several states serious consideration was given to the possibility of inaugurating the unicameral system. Interest in unicameralism became especially marked in the second decade of the present century, with several governors strongly endorsing

---

[6] As to the results of bicameralism in particular states, see David L. Colvin, *The Bicameral Principle in the New York Legislature;* Dorothy Schaffter, *The Bicameral System in Practice* [in Iowa]; Thelma I. Griswold, *Bicameralism in Ohio;* John E. Hall, "The Bicameral Principle in the New Mexico Legislature," *Nat. Mun. Rev.,* XVI, 185-190, 255-260 (Mar., Apr., 1927); May Wood-Simons, "Operation of the Bicameral System in Illinois and Wisconsin," *Ill. Law Rev.,* XX, 674-686 (Mar. 1926).

[7] For an analysis and evaluation of Vermont's experience with the unicameral system, see Daniel B. Carroll, *The Unicameral Legislature of Vermont.*

the plan. Various cities which had formerly used bicameral councils were changing to the unicameral system with good results; and it was felt that the states, several of which had less population than some of the larger cities with single-chambered councils, might also profit from the adoption of this simpler form of legislative organization. However, conservatism is strong in the American states and the bicameral principle had become well rooted in tradition. Hence it was not until 1934 that Nebraska, under the leadership of the late George W. Norris,[8] became the first state to break with precedent by amending her constitution to establish a one-house legislature. As a result of this beginning, interest in the unicameral plan again became more pronounced for a time. In 1937, of the forty-three state legislatures in session, no less than twenty-one considered proposals for constitutional amendments to inaugurate the unicameral system;[9] though a mere two years later the number of legislatures considering such proposals dropped to seven.[10] A popularly-initiated amendment which would have established the unicameral system in Missouri was submitted to the voters of that state in 1944 but was defeated. Since then there has been little interest in this "reform," and it may be worthy of note that the two newest states, Hawaii and Alaska, established bicameral legislatures.

Relative Merits of Bicameralism and Unicameralism

The principal arguments in favor of the bicameral system have already been suggested in explaining why that form of legislative organization was so widely adopted. It is said that bicameralism facilitates the representation of differently based areas and groups; that the two houses tend to serve as checks upon each other, thereby providing protection against the passage of selfish or dangerous measures; that consideration of proposed legislation by two different branches slows down the legislative process, thus fostering mature and careful consideration of all measures before they become law; that the two-house system prevents the concentration of too much power in a single agency; and that a bicameral legislature is less susceptible to corruption than a legislature composed of a single house.

On the other hand, weighty arguments are offered in favor of unicameralism. One important advantage of this system, according to its proponents, is the elimination of "buck-passing" and shifting of responsibility as between the two houses. The single house must accept full responsibil-

---

[8] For Senator Norris' own account of his part in the campaign for unicameralism in Nebraska, see *Fighting Liberal: The Autobiography of George W. Norris* (Macmillan, New York, 1945), Chap. 32.

[9] For a tabular analysis of these proposals, see Alvin W. Johnson, *The Unicameral Legislature* (Univ. of Minn. Press, Minneapolis, 1938), 152-155.

[10] Alvin W. Johnson, "Unicameralism Marks Time," *State Govt.*, XII, 101-102, 108 (June, 1939).

ity for all measures passed. Moreover, it is contended that, since public attention will be focused upon the single chamber, legislators will be less, rather than more, readily corrupted than under the bicameral plan. Again, it is urged that actual practice has failed to demonstrate that one house acts to kill unwise legislation enacted by the other; and that the governor's veto power is a more effective check upon rash legislative action than is bicameralism. It is further pointed out that, since a unicameral legislature will usually consist of fewer members than a bicameral one, fewer bills are likely to be introduced—a fact which will make it possible for each bill to receive more, rather than less, careful consideration than under the bicameral system. Still another argument is that the one-house system should result in substantial savings of money, since not only will there be fewer members to be paid but the smaller membership will make possible a reduction in the number of employees as well as in the amounts required for stationery, postage, and other supplies.[11] A final and important factor in unicameralism urged by proponents of the plan as one of its outstanding advantages is its elimination of the conference committee. This committee, consisting of a designated number of members from each house, is used in the bicameral legislature for the purpose of settling disagreements between the respective houses in regard to pending legislation.[12] The conference committee works in secret and without recorded votes. Since agreements reached by it must be accepted or rejected by the legislative houses without change, the final form of many important laws is determined by this small committee. Indeed, so powerful can be the conference committee under bicameralism that it has been called a "third branch" of the legislature and characterized as the most powerful of the three.[13] Under the bicameral system, disagreements between the two houses on major legislation are almost inevitable, and the conference committee has proved to be the only practicable way of reconciling them. Under unicameralism, such disagreements cannot arise, and legislation is, in substance as well as form, given its final shape and sanction in a session of the entire membership of the legislative body.

On the whole, it seems questionable whether the record of bicameralism in state legislatures justifies its retention. Such case studies as have been made of the operation of the bicameral system raise grave doubt that the benefits which are alleged to flow from two houses are achieved in practice. From a theoretical standpoint, the merits of unicameralism seem to be fully as great as those of bicameralism; and in the one state where the unicameral system is actually used it seems to have given satisfaction. All in all, it would appear that, given a single legislative

[11] Cf. Alvin W. Johnson, *The Unicameral Legislature*, Chap. 3; John P. Senning, *The One-House Legislature*, Chap. 4.

[12] See below, Chap. VIII, "The Conference Committee."

[13] George W. Norris, "The One-House Legislature," *Nat. Mun. Rev.*, XXIV, 87–89, 99 (Feb., 1935).

chamber which is adequately representative and provided with appropriate procedural safeguards, and considering that the executive veto is available as a check upon legislative action, a second chamber is scarcely necessary as a means of protecting the public interest.[14] If, as the result of recent court decisions considered at a subsequent point in this chapter, the states are now to be required to apportion both houses of their bicameral legislatures on the basis of population, the case for the retention of bicameralism is further weakened.

Nebraska's One-House Legislature

The constitutional amendment establishing unicameralism in Nebraska was proposed by popular initiative after the bicameral legislature of the state had several times refused to approve such a proposal for submission to the voters. Since adoption of the unicameral plan in any state is likely to involve a substantial reduction in the number of legislative seats, it is hardly to be expected that a bicameral legislature will be eager to propose such a change. Nebraska's experience seems therefore to suggest that, in those states where popular initiative is available as a means of proposing constitutional amendments, the initiative is more practicable than legislative proposal as a means of securing a popular vote on the proposition of adopting the unicameral system.

The Nebraska amendment was approved by the voters in the November election of 1934, and the first session of the unicameral legislature began in January, 1937. The amendment provides that the legislature shall consist of not less than thirty nor more than fifty members, chosen from single-member districts in nonpartisan elections. The task of fixing the number of members, within the prescribed limits, and of dividing the state into a like number of legislative districts, is left to the legislature itself. The last bicameral legislature provided that the succeeding unicameral body should consist of forty-three members, and divided the state into districts accordingly. The constitution stipulates that, unless other provision is made by law, the unicameral legislature shall hold regular biennial sessions. These sessions convene in January of odd-numbered years,[15] and there is no constitutional limitation upon their length. The lieutenant governor is the presiding officer of the legislature.

Unicameralism has now been operating in Nebraska well over two

[14] Further analysis of the advantages and disadvantages of unicameralism, with comments upon the early operation of the system in Nebraska, is to be found in Belle Zeller, ed., *American State Legislatures*, Chap. 4. The experience of American colonies and states with the unicameral system, as of 1937, is summarized in Charles W. Shull, *American Experience with Unicameral Legislatures*. Several articles on unicameralism appear in the Dec., 1942, issue of the *University of Kansas City Law Review*.

[15] Members are elected in November of non-presidential even-numbered years. sessions therefore meet in January of odd-numbered years.

decades and the one-house system appears, on the whole, to be enjoying marked success. Legislative responsibility has been definitely centralized. Though reduction in the size of the legislature has not altered in any appreciable degree the ratio of representation of the various occupational groups, there has been a general improvement in personnel. Many of the more able members of the former bicameral body were elected to the first unicameral legislature; and in the membership of subsequent sessions the level of education and of experience in public affairs has been higher, and the rate of turnover lower, than under the old system. Nebraskans generally seem well pleased with their one-house legislature. It appears that unicameralism has actually increased in popularity during the years of its operation and that, notwithstanding occasional criticism of the new system, there has been no widespread demand for reversion to the bicameral plan.[16]

The Problem of Size

What is the proper size of a state legislature? This is a problem which has caused the framers of state constitutions more than a little difficulty and which, it must be admitted, has not always been solved in a satisfactory manner. As a general guiding principle, it may be suggested that the legislature's membership should be large enough so that the major interest groups within the state may be represented, yet not so large as to be unwieldy in its actions. On the whole, the legislatures of the various states as constituted at present are probably too large for maximum efficiency. Senates vary in size (as of 1964) from 21 members in Delaware and Nevada to 67 in Minnesota, with an average of about 36; while lower houses range from 35 in Delaware to 400 in New Hampshire, with an average of approximately 117.[17] Curiously enough, the four largest lower houses are found in the New England states of New Hampshire (400), Vermont (246), Massachusetts (240), and Connecticut (294), a fact to be attributed in part at least to a tendency to give representation to every town, however small its population.[18] The combined membership of these four chambers comprises approximately one-fifth of the total membership

---

[16] A. C. Breckenridge, *One House for Two: Nebraska's Unicameral Legislature;* Zeller, ed., *op. cit.,* appendix A: "Unicameral Lawmaking in Nebraska;" John P. Senning, "Nebraska's First Unicameral Legislative Session," *Annals of Amer. Acad. of Polit. and Soc. Sci.,* CXCV, 159-167 (Jan., 1938); Lane W. Lancaster, "Nebraska's Experience with a One-House Legislature," *Univ. of Kansas City Law Rev.,* XI, 24-30 (Dec., 1942); Richard C. Spencer, "Highest Score Sheet," *Nat. Mun. Rev.,* XLVI, 502-505, 510 (Nov., 1957); Richard C. Spencer, "Nebraska 'Unicam' Operates Smoothly," *Nat. Civic Rev.,* L, 424-425 (Sept., 1961).

[17] *The Book of the States,* 1964-65, p. 43.

[18] In New Hampshire, some of the least populous towns have members of the house of representatives in some, but not all, legislative sessions. The New Hampshire constitution provides, however, that each town shall be entitled to representation in at least one session in every ten years.

of the forty-nine lower houses. Other than these four states, only Georgia and Pennsylvania have lower houses of as many as two hundred members. The membership of the New Hampshire chamber, it may be noted, falls only thirty-five short of that of the United States House of Representatives. Why that state, with a population (in 1960) of some 600,000 should require a legislature of 424 members (including the 24 senators) while New York, with nearly 17 million inhabitants, gets along with a membership of 208, it is difficult to understand. An inevitable result of having legislative bodies the size of the larger state legislatures is that most of the actual work of legislation will, as a matter of necessity, be delegated to committees.

But while most of the present state legislatures seem to err in the direction of excessive size, some of the proposals for legislative reorganization have swung too far in the other direction. Thus Governor Hodges of Kansas once proposed the establishment for that state of a single-chamber legislature of eight, or at most sixteen, members (one or two members from each of the state's congressional districts).[19] In proposing a legislative body of so few members, the Kansas governor appears to have ignored the fact that a legislature, in addition to being of manageable size, should be large enough to reflect and represent the different shades of opinion within the state. It seems extremely doubtful that a body of the size suggested would be large enough to meet the latter requirement even in a relatively homogeneous state.

Election Methods

Members of the legislature are elected in every state by popular vote. Elections are in most states of a partisan character, candidates being nominated by the respective political parties in primaries preceding the general election. However, members of both legislative houses in Minnesota, and of the unicameral legislature in Nebraska, are nominated and elected on a nonpartisan basis.

In general, legislative elections are conducted according to the simple plurality method. Each voter is entitled to vote for as many candidates as there are members to be chosen from his district, and the candidate or candidates receiving the greatest number of votes are elected. Illinois, however, employs a unique system of "cumulative voting" for the choice of members of its house of representatives. Three representatives are elected from each district. Each voter has three votes, which he may distribute among two or three candidates or may cumulate and give to a single candidate. Under this system, any party which controls more than

[19] The governor's message embracing this proposal is reprinted from the Kansas Senate Journal in John M. Mathews and Clarence A. Berdahl, *Documents and Readings in American Government* (Macmillan, New York, 1928), 674-677.

25 percent of the votes within a district is able, by nominating a single candidate and prevailing upon party members to cast all their votes for that nominee, to elect one of the three legislative members. In this manner the minority party in a district usually succeeds in electing one member of the house of representatives, while the majority party elects two.[20] Since 1940 there have been only six instances when one party has won all three seats in a district. Although designed primarily for the purpose of affording minority representation, an incidental result of the system seems to have been a stabilization of the membership of the house. When voting is by the usual method, representatives from districts in which the two principal parties are of nearly equal strength may lose their seats by a very slight shifting of voter support. In a "close" district under the Illinois system, each of the major parties is likely in any event to elect one representative, the fate of only the third being at stake in a given election. Since there is a tendency for parties to renominate incumbent representatives, cumulative voting has thus operated to foster reelection.[21]

Apportionment and Districting

Every state is divided into legislative districts for the purpose of choosing members of the state legislature. In most states there will be found two separate and distinct sets of districts, one for the choice of senators and another for choosing members of the lower house. A few states, however, use a single set of districts for electing members to both houses. Thus, North Dakota and Minnesota elect representatives as well as senators from senatorial districts, though in the latter state representatives are in some instances assigned to individual counties within the senatorial districts or to specified subdivisions of those districts. Both single-member and multimember legislative districts are widely used. Taking the country at large, some 88 percent of all state senators and 55 percent of lower-house members are elected from single-member districts, with the remainder being chosen from multimember constituencies.[22] In laying out legislative districts, county boundaries or, in New England, town boundaries, are commonly followed. Thus in most states a typical legislative district consists of a single county or of two or more contiguous counties. When a single county has sufficient population to entitle it to more than one representative, some states follow the plan of electing the entire number from the county at large, whereas others divide the county into as many districts as there are members to be elected therefrom. In a few states the boundaries of legislative districts are prescribed by the

[20] An analysis of the operation of the Illinois system may be found in George S. Blair, *Cumulative Voting: an Effective Electoral Device in Illinois Politics.*

[21] See Blair, *op. cit.,* Chap. 4.

[22] Maurice Klain, "A New Look at the Constituencies: The Need for a Recount and a Reappraisal," *Amer. Polit. Sci. Rev.,* XLIX, 1105-1119 (Dec. 1955).

constitution. Most states, however, confer upon the legislature authority to lay out the districts and to change their boundaries from time to time.

In laying out legislative districts and apportioning members among them, the factor given most general consideration is that of population.[23] Many states, however, give some recognition to subdivisional areas. Thus it is provided in seven states that the senate shall consist of one member from each county, while the lower house in Vermont is composed of one member from each organized town. A fairly common provision with respect to one or both legislative chambers is that each county shall have at least one member thereof. In some instances it is provided, with respect to the senate, that no county shall have more than one member. Overall, of the 99 separate state legislative chambers, the basis of representation is population alone in 32, population with weighted ratios in 8, combinations of population and area considerations in 45, equal representation for each unit in 8, and state tax payments in 1 (New Hampshire senate). Five chambers have a fixed constitutional apportionment.[24]

Since population within a state is continually shifting, most constitutions make provision for periodic reapportionment of legislative members. The duty of making this reapportionment, together with that of redrawing district boundaries when necessary, is usually devolved upon the legislature. Several states, however, provide for the performance of those duties—in some instances as a matter of course and in others in event of legislative inaction—by a reapportionment commission composed of designated state administrative officers and sometimes including the governor. A 1954 amendment to the Illinois constitution provides that, if the Illinois general assembly fails to reapportion the house of representatives (reapportionment of the senate is apparently not contemplated), a special bipartisan commission will be created for the purpose. If the commission fails to act within a specified time, all members of the house of representatives are to be elected from the state at large.[25] Missouri's constitution of 1945 and Michigan's constitution of 1963 remove the reapportionment function entirely from legislative hands. In Missouri, senatorial reapportionment is made by a bipartisan board appointed by the governor, while representatives are apportioned among the counties by the secretary of state. Michigan provides for reapportionment by a commission consisting of members selected by the state organizations of the re-

[23] There are several states in which apportionment is made upon some basis other than *total* population. Thus some states exclude aliens for apportionment purposes, while a few apportion the members of one or both houses according to the number of voters. A table of the constitutional provisions relating to legislative apportionment in the various states may be found in *The Book of the States*, 1964-65, pp. 62-66. Constitutional provisions are analyzed in National Municipal League, *Compendium on Legislative Apportionment*.

[24] Gordon E. Baker, *State Constitutions: Reapportionment*, 5.

[25] *Const. of Ill.* (1870 as amended), art. IV, sec. 8. An at-large election was held under this provision in 1964.

spective political parties. Hawaii places responsibility for reapportionment solely upon the governor.[26] In general, it may be said that there is a growing disposition to make use of executive or administrative agencies in the reapportionment process. The frequency of the periodic reapportionment envisaged by state constitutions varies from state to state, with the provision for decennial action being most common. Some states provide for reapportionment on the basis of the federal census and some upon that of a state enumeration, while still others permit the use of either the federal or a state census.[27]

State constitutions commonly stipulate that legislative districts shall be composed of "compact and contiguous" territory. Though the requirement of contiguity is usually complied with, in letter if not always in spirit, that of compactness is frequently ignored. The latter fact is a result of a practice known as "gerrymandering," whereby the political party in control of the legislature at the time of redistricting draws the boundaries in such a manner as to give that party a voting plurality in as many districts as possible. Such partisan redistricting has sometimes resulted in the creation of districts of fantastic shapes. Thus the Massachusetts state senatorial district established early in the nineteenth century during the governorship of Elbridge Gerry, and from which the practice of gerrymandering derived its name, was said to resemble a salamander. Other examples of gerrymandered districts, legislative or congressional, have been popularly known, because of their unusual shapes, as "shoestring," "dumb-bell," "saddlebag," and "belt-line" districts.[28]

Urban Underrepresentation

In general it may be said that, in our state legislatures, rural areas are overrepresented and urban areas underrepresented. Urban legislative districts commonly have larger populations than do rural districts electing the same number of members. Most of the large metropolitan centers in the country, and many other urban communities as well, are the victims of underrepresentation. New York, Chicago, St. Louis, Detroit, Los Angeles, Atlanta, and Birmingham are only a few of the large cities which are underrepresented in one or both houses.[29] Though the underrepresentation of cities is commonly emphasized, some of the most extreme inequities in existence today affect heavily-populated areas suburban to

[26] *Const. of Mo.* (1945), art. III, secs. 2, 7; *Const. of Mich.* (1963), art. IV, sec. 6; *Const. of Hawaii* (1959), art. III, sec. 4.
[27] Cf. Alfred Z. Reed, *The Territorial Basis of Government under the State Constitutions*, 145-146, 199-200.
[28] Cf. Paul S. Reinsch, *American Legislatures and Legislative Methods*, 202; Robert Luce, *Legislative Principles*, 399.
[29] Cf. Gordon E. Baker, *Rural versus Urban Political Power*, 18.

central cities.[30] Many large cities now have relatively stable populations, and in some the population is actually declining, while the population in surrounding suburban areas is in many instances increasing at a phenomenal rate. A 1955 study reported that, as of that date, urban areas suffered severe discrimination in 8 states, substantial discrimination in 22, and at least moderate discrimination in 16. Of the 48 states then in existence, only Wisconsin and Massachusetts were considered as providing unmistakable representative equality for urban residents.[31] Although varying degrees of improvement have been made in some states during the decade since this study, gross inequities continue to be widespread.[32]

Underrepresentation of urban areas has come about as a result of the operation of one or both of two causes: (1) constitutional provisions, and (2) failure of the legislature to reapportion as directed by the constitution. There are at least four types of constitutional provision, each found in several states, which curtail urban representation. One of these consists of provisions excluding from the general population for apportionment purposes certain classes of persons who are more numerous in urban than in rural areas. Since aliens are more numerous in cities, their exclusion for apportionment purposes operates to the disadvantage of urban areas. Basing apportionment upon the number of voters has much the same effect since, aside from persons not yet of voting age, aliens constitute the largest single group of nonvoters. The view is sometimes expressed that, since aliens are without the right to vote, they are not entitled to representation. On the other hand, it may be argued that, though they are denied the suffrage, aliens are entitled to representation inasmuch as they pay taxes and, in many respects, engage in business upon the same basis as citizens. A second type of constitutional provision which fosters urban underrepresentation is that requiring equal representation of counties or towns, regardless of population. In Nevada, where each county has one senator, senatorial districts vary in population from less than 600 to 127,000; and in Vermont, where one member of the house of representatives is allotted to each town, the range of district population is from 38 to 33,000.[33]

A third type of restrictive constitutional provision limits urban representation indirectly by providing that each county or town shall have at least one member. Since a provision of this type is commonly accom-

[30] Cf. Robert S. Friedman, "Reapportionment Myth," *Nat. Civic Rev.*, XLIX, 184-188 (Apr., 1960).

[31] Baker, *Rural versus Urban Political Power*, 15-18.

[32] Cf. Ralph Eisenberg, "Power of Rural Vote," *Nat. Civic Rev.*, LI, 489-492, 530 (Oct., 1962).

[33] Comparative data on the population of legislative districts in the respective states may be found in National Municipal League, *Compendium on Legislative Apportionment,* and in Advisory Commission on Intergovernmental Relations, *Apportionment of State Legislatures.*

panied by a limitation upon the total membership of the house concerned, its usual effect is to allot so many of the members to rural areas that too few remain to afford adequate representation to the more populous communities. The Kansas constitution, for example, provides for a house of representatives not exceeding 125 members and stipulates that each county shall have at least one member. There being 105 counties in the state, only twenty members are available for apportionment to the more populous counties. As a result, under the 1961 apportionment house districts vary in population from 2,000 to 68,000. The fourth type of provision sets an upper limit upon the number of legislative members which any county or town may have. Illustrative of this type is the New York provision that no county may have more than a third of the total membership of the senate, nor any two adjoining counties more than half. Several other states go even further and provide that no county may have more than one senator. As the result of such a provision in California's constitution, Los Angeles county, with 6 million inhabitants, has only one of the state's forty senators, while three rural counties with a combined population of less than 15,000 together have a senator. Approximately 10 percent of the state's population elects a majority of the senators, while 65 percent of the population, residing in the six most populous counties, elects only 15 percent of the senate membership.[34]

But even more common than constitutional restrictions as a cause of urban underrepresentation is legislative failure to carry out the reapportionment provision of the constitution. Although state constitutions usually stipulate that the legislature *shall* make a reapportionment at specified intervals,[35] this duty is frequently disregarded by the legislature for long periods of time. The reason underlying such legislative inaction is, of course, fairly obvious. Since urban centers grow in population more rapidly than rural districts, reapportionment normally involves increasing the number of members allotted to the urban areas and decreasing correspondingly the number of rural respresentatives. For a rural representative to vote for such a reapportionment and thereby, perhaps, vote himself out of the legislative body, takes, to say the least, considerable courage. It is therefore not surprising that rural-controlled legislatures have hesitated to take action which would weaken rural control over the legislative body or perhaps transfer that control to urban areas. And notwithstanding that the duty to reapportion periodically is in form mandatory, the courts until recently have declined to compel the performance of the duty.

Overrepresentation of rural areas naturally arouses resentment on

[34] Gordon E. Baker, "The California Senate," in Malcolm E. Jewell, ed., *The Politics of Reapportionment*, 51-63.
[35] See above, "Apportionment and Districting." In a few states the constitution purports to do no more than *authorize* the legislature to reapportion.

the part of the urban districts and frequently precipitates sectional conflicts and ill feeling both within the legislature and outside. A special reason for urban resentment over control of the legislature by rural elements is the fact that, in most states, the legislature determines the form of city government and exercises broad regulatory power over the municipalities. City dwellers naturally dislike having to seek needed authority and desired changes in their governmental organization from a "farmer" legislature. The situation is not so serious where only one of the two houses is dominated by a rural minority, since if the urban districts control the other house they are in a position to block enactment of measures which they consider inimical to their interests. But the problem becomes acute indeed where the rural inhabitants, though in the minority numerically, control both chambers.

Reapportionment and the Courts

Over the years, state apportionment statutes have occasionally been invalidated by the courts on the ground that they failed to comply with constitutional requirements that legislative districts be composed of contiguous territory, compact, and approximately equal in population. But will the courts, in the event that the legislature neglects or refuses to reapportion periodically in conformity to constitutional provisions, attempt to compel legislative action? Until quite recently, the answer to this question has been generally "no." Time and again the courts, both state and federal, declined to order state legislatures to perform their reapportionment duties. Frequently this declination was based upon the doctrine that the matters involved were not justiciable in character (i.e., were not adapted to judicial settlement) but rather were "political" in nature and as such must be resolved by those branches of government which are primarily concerned with policy formation, namely, the executive and legislative branches. In other instances, judicial declination was justified on the ground that intervention by the courts would constitute violation of the separation-of-powers principle, or that action by the federal courts would involve an impingement upon state sovereignty.

Eventually, however, some courts began to take a different view of judicial competence in this field.[36] Thus a federal court in Minnesota, in 1958, and the supreme court of New Jersey, in 1960, accepted jurisdiction over suits brought by urban residents to secure reapportionment of the Minnesota and New Jersey legislatures, respectively. In these cases the courts refused to act until the legislatures were given another opportunity to perform their constitutional duties, but retained jurisdiction and

[36] See James E. Larson, *Reapportionment and the Courts* (Bur. of Pub. Admin., Univ. of Ala., University, Ala., 1962); Charles A. Barrett, "Reapportionment and the Courts," *State Govt.*, XXXV, 138-143 (Summer, 1962).

indicated that they *would* take appropriate judicial measures to secure reapportionment in the event that the legislatures persisted in their inaction. In each case the state legislature responded by enacting a new apportionment statute.

Then, early in 1962, the United States Supreme Court in the case of Baker v. Carr handed down a decision which was destined to constitute a landmark in the law of legislative apportionment. The Supreme Court in this case was reviewing the decision of a lower federal court in Tennessee in a case in which urban residents sought reapportionment of the Tennessee legislature. Plaintiffs in the case contended that, as a result of failure to reapportion, the votes of urban dwellers had in effect been debased, in relation to the votes of rural residents, to a point where urbanites were being denied the equality protected by the provision in the Fourteenth Amendment to the United States Constitution that no state shall "deny to any person within its jurisdiction the equal protection of the laws." The trial court dismissed the case on the ground that the subject matter was political in nature. In reversing the lower tribunal, the Supreme Court held that (1) the subject matter of the case was justiciable, (2) the lower federal courts had jurisdiction, and (3) the plaintiffs were entitled to challenge the existing apportionment in the federal courts as an infringement of the equal-protection clause. Consequently, the suit was returned to the lower federal court with directions to try the case upon its merits.[37]

The decision in Baker v. Carr precipitated a rash of suits in both state and federal courts seeking judicial intervention to secure reapportionment; indeed, within a year suits of one kind or another had been filed in more than three-fourths of the states.[38] Some of the suits merely asked the court to declare the existing apportionment unconstitutional and order that legislative elections be held in the state at large until a valid apportionment was enacted; others went so far as to ask that the court itself reapportion the state in the event of continued legislative inaction. As a result of these and more recent suits, some degree of reapportionment has now been achieved in a substantial number of states. In only a few instances has a court itself formulated a reapportionment plan and ordered it into effect. More often the court has accepted jurisdiction in the case and warned the legislature that judicial action would be forthcoming if the legislature persisted in its refusal to act. Faced with this threat of judicial action, some states have enacted reapportionment statutes. In several instances, however, these statutes appear to have increased urban representation to the minimum degree which it was believed the

---

[37] *Baker* v. *Carr,* 369 U.S. 186 (1962).

[38] For an account of some of these early cases, see Paul T. David and Ralph Eisenberg, *State Legislative Redistricting: Major Issues in the Wake of Judicial Decision* (Pub. Admin. Service, Chicago, 1962).

courts would accept, and some of them have already been, or are being, contested.

For some months following the Baker decision it was believed by many persons that the ruling in that case might require only that one chamber of a bicameral legislature be apportioned on the basis of population and that apportionment of the other chamber might be made on the basis of area or some other consideration. In 1964, however, in the case of Reynolds v. Sims concerning the Alabama legislature, the Supreme Court held that the equal-protection clause requires that *both* legislative houses be apportioned on a population basis and that a state "make an honest and good faith effort to construct districts, in both houses of its legislature, as nearly of equal population as is practicable." The court recognized that it is impracticable to attempt to establish legislative districts which are *precisely* equal in population but held that they must be substantially so. Factors other than population may be taken into account in the apportionment of one or both houses only to the extent that they do not significantly encroach upon the basic population principle.[38a]

It is still too early to evaluate the ultimate effectiveness of the new judicial doctrine in securing more equitable representation for the residents of populous areas. There can be no doubt, however, that a pronounced impetus has been given to the reapportionment movement. It appears likely that the greatest effectiveness of the new doctrine will continue to lie in a stimulus to legislative action flowing from the knowledge of legislators that there may be judicial intervention if they refuse to act. In any event, the principle is now definitely established that the courts are open to those suffering "invidious discrimination" as a result of state malapportionment. It may be noted also that a few constitutions, including those of Alaska, Hawaii, Michigan, and Texas, now expressly provide that the state courts may compel the governor or members of the apportionment commission to perform their reapportionment duties.

Qualifications of Members

Qualifications prescribed by state constitutions for members of the legislature usually relate to age, citizenship, and residence. The minimum age most commonly prescribed for membership in the lower house is twenty-one, although a few states have a higher requirement. Age require-

---

[38a] *Reynolds* v. *Sims* 377 U.S. 533 (1964). In another 1964 decision the court held that the provision in Article I of the United States Constitution that members of the national House of Representatives shall be chosen "by the people of the several states" requires that the *congressional* districts established in any state be substantially equal in population. *Wesberry* v. *Sanders*, 376 U.S. 1 (1964). Following the Reynolds decision, a proposed amendment to the United States Constitution was introduced in Congress which, if approved by Congress and ratified by the states, would expressly permit one house of a bicameral state legislature to be constituted on a basis other than population.

ments for the senate range from twenty-one to thirty, with twenty-five most common. In some states the same age requirement applies to members of both houses, but a higher requirement for senators than for representatives is usual. United States citizenship is required of legislators in all states, either expressly or through a provision that members must be qualified electors. Although a few states permit election to the legislature of any person, otherwise qualified, who resides in the district concerned at the time of his election, most require a specified minimum period of residence in the district immediately *prior* to election. This period varies from sixty days to two years, with one year most common. In addition to the prescribed period of residence within the district, many states require a longer period of residence, ranging from one year to six, in the state. Residence requirements are in some instances longer for senators than for representatives.

Some state constitutions enumerate specific disqualifications for legislative office. In various states, for example, conviction of bribery, perjury, or embezzlement disqualifies. Several states go further by prescribing as a disqualification conviction of any "infamous" crime. Most state constitutions either stipulate that no federal or state officer may, during his continuance in such office, serve in the state legislature, or enumerate specific federal and state offices the holding of which shall disqualify from legislative membership. In some states the holding of certain local offices disqualifies. Other miscellaneous disqualifications are found in occasional states. It is usual for each house to be made the judge of the qualifications of its members.

Terms of Members

Members of the lower house of the legislature are usually elected for a term of two years. Indeed, the two-year term is found in 45 of the 49 states having bicameral legislatures, with the remaining 4—Alabama, Louisiana, Maryland, and Mississippi—having a four-year term. Where legislatures meet in regular session only biennially, the two-year term means that all members of the lower house are elected anew prior to each regular session. In state senates, the term of office is four years in 36 states and two years in 13.[39] Where the four-year senatorial term prevails, a common, though not universal, practice is to renew only half of the membership every two years. Such provision for overlapping terms is believed to foster stability and afford protection against abrupt changes in policy. The scheme also assures that in each session at least half of the members

[39] *The Book of the States*, 1964-65, p. 43. The states with two-year senate terms are Arizona, Connecticut, Georgia, Idaho, Maine, Massachusetts, New Hampshire, New York, North Carolina, Rhode Island, South Dakota, Tennessee, and Vermont.

will be experienced, and further, makes it possible for the senate to operate under continuous organization. Complete reorganization following each election becomes unnecessary, the only need being to fill such vacancies as may have occurred in senate offices and committee posts. In the event of a shift in party control, a more general shakeup in organization is of course to be expected. The term of members of Nebraska's unicameral legislature is four years.

Tenure and Turnover: The Problem of Reelection

Is it a wise practice, when an incumbent legislator is doing a reasonably satisfactory job of representing his constituents, to reelect that person, perhaps again and again, rather than to retire him from office in favor of someone inexperienced in legislation? That a person who has already served in one or more sessions is a more effective member of a legislative body there can be little doubt. The typical state legislator, when elected to his first term, is a novice in dealing with legislative problems and procedure, and it takes some time for him to "learn the ropes" and acquire a fair degree of skill in participating in the legislative process. This fact is amply indicated by the testimony of legislators and ex-legislators to the effect that they were pretty much bewildered at the outset of their legislative career and that their effectiveness and usefulness increased with experience.[40] Furthermore, since the more important committee posts, as well as positions of leadership in general, are often assigned on the basis of seniority, districts which return the same representatives again and again thereby increase their influence in legislative counsels. This is not, by any means, to suggest that the voters should reelect members who are clearly out of accord with the views of their constituents, but merely to emphasize the fact that, as long as a legislator continues to reflect in substantial measure the will of the voters who elect him, his past legislative experience makes him a more valuable member of the legislative body. As one writer has put it: "Experienced members too far out of sympathy with their constituents must be ousted in favor of newcomers more responsive to the wants of the times and the demands of their constituents. But a wise public will temper its impatience by realization that it sacrifices something when it exchanges experienced lawmaker for novice." [41] These views, of course, are not accepted by those persons who believe, and not without some reason, that long-continued service in public office breeds arrogance and contempt for the wishes of the voters; and that, with respect to legislative office in particular, frequent turnover is essential if

[40] See, for example, Charles S. Hyneman and Edmond F. Ricketts, "Tenure and Turnover of the Iowa Legislature," Ia. Law Rev., XXIV, 673-696 (May, 1939).

[41] Charles S. Hyneman, "Tenure and Turnover of the Indiana General Assembly," Amer. Polit. Sci. Rev., XXXII, 51-67, 311-331 (Feb., Apr., 1938), 53.

the legislature is to reflect, at a given moment, the attitudes and desires of the electorate.

In practice, many individual legislators do see long continuous service. Yet such actual studies of legislative turnover as have been made seem to indicate that reelection is much less frequent than might be supposed or desired. A recent study found that over half of the state legislators are new at each session, the lower chamber having the greater percentage of new members. States with higher pay scales tend to have less turnover. Also, as might be expected, one-party states have less turnover than states with considerable interparty competition.[42] Professor Charles Hyneman, in a study of six successive regular sessions of the Indiana general assembly, found that, in a house of representatives of 100 members, 414 different individuals saw service during the six sessions. The 314 representatives who served at some time during the first five sessions, but were not present in the sixth, had seen service ranging from one to ten sessions. The average length of service for the 314, however, was only 1.7 sessions; and 187 of the number, or approximately 60 percent, had served in but a single session. Only 19 of the 314 had completed as many as four sessions, and only 5 had served for six sessions or more. In the senate, with members elected for a four-year term covering two sessions, the average number of sessions completed by retiring members during the same period was naturally larger than for the lower house—3.1 as against 1.7. However, of the 102 retiring senators, 59 quit at the end of a first term (two sessions) or earlier; while only 37 completed at least two terms and only 12 three terms or more.[43] A six-session survey of ten states, by the same investigator, revealed that in the lower chambers, on the average, 39.6 percent of the members were serving their first term, 23.8 percent their second, and 12.9 percent their third. Thus less than one-fourth of the members were serving a fourth or subsequent term.[44]

Reasons for the relatively rapid turnover in legislative personnel are numerous and varied. Particularly significant, it would seem, are the results of studies showing that a large percentage of the legislators who retire from service after one or a few years do so voluntarily. Defeat at the polls seems to be a less important factor in legislative retirement than has been generally supposed. In a five-session survey of eight state legislatures, Professor Hyneman found that, of 2,476 persons retiring from

[42] Zeller, ed., op. cit., 65-73. Also see Bruce B. Mason, "Turnover, Tenure and Occupation in the Arizona Legislature," Pub. Affairs Bull. (Bur. of Govt. Research, Ariz. State Univ., Vol. 1, No. 2, 1962).

[43] Hyneman, "Tenure and Turnover of the Indiana General Assembly," loc. cit. Other studies of legislative turnover made under the direction of Professor Hyneman are reported in Charles S. Hyneman and others, "Legislative Experience of Illinois Lawmakers," Univ. of Chicago Law Rev., III, 104-118 (Dec., 1935); Hyneman and Ricketts, "Tenure and Turnover of the Iowa Legislature," loc. cit.

[44] Charles S. Hyneman, "Tenure and Turnover of Legislative Personnel," Annals of Amer. Acad. of Polit. and Soc. Sci., CXCV, 21-31 (Jan., 1938).

legislative service, only 15.9 percent retired because of defeat in the general election and another 15.6 percent because of defeat in the primaries.[45] This means that more than two-thirds of the retiring legislators did not even seek renomination, and the question is thus raised as to why legislative service is so unattractive. Doubtless many individual members dropped out for such reasons as ill health or the press of personal business, but many others seem to have chosen not to run merely because they had "had enough of it." Some retirements were probably due to the fact that the legislators felt their honest efforts had been unappreciated, or indeed even censured, by their constituents. Another factor seems undoubtedly to be the widely prevalent inadequacy of compensation.[46]

Compensation of Members

Some states pay their legislators on a per diem basis while others pay a fixed salary per month, session, year, or term.[47] The per diem allowed for time spent in session ranged, in 1964, from $5 in North Dakota and Rhode Island to $50 in Louisiana. Several "per diem" states limit the number of days per session for which the per diem may be paid. Salaries paid varied, in 1964, from $100 per year in New Hampshire[48] to $10,000 per year in New York. A number of states provide a somewhat greater compensation for the presiding officers of the respective houses than for other members. In addition to their salary or per diem, legislators usually receive an allowance for travel to and from the state capital, a few states providing for payment of actual traveling expenses but most allowing mileage at a specified rate. In several states where the legislative salary or per diem is relatively low, an additional sum is allowed for living expenses or maintenance.[49] The compensation of legislators is fixed in some states by constitutional provision and in others by statute. Where

---

[45] *Ibid.*

[46] See below, "Compensation of Members." Mr. Hyneman found "no conclusive proof" that an increase in the per diem of Indiana legislators from $6 to $10 "had any substantial effect on willingness to continue service"; yet it was his opinion, based upon the results of his studies to the date of publication, that inadequate compensation is *probably* one important cause of instability of legislative personnel. Hyneman, "Tenure and Turnover of the Indiana General Assembly," *loc. cit.*, 328-331. See also Hyneman, "Tenure and Turnover of Legislative Personnel," *loc. cit.*, 30-31; Hyneman and Ricketts, "Tenure and Turnover of the Iowa Legislature," *loc. cit.*, 695-696. Substantial increases have been made in legislative compensation in Indiana since the dates of the studies here cited. The problem of turnover in Washington is considered in Paul Beckett and Celeste Sunderland, "Washington State's Lawmakers: Some Personnel Factors in the Washington Legislature," *Western Polit. Quar.*, X, 180-202 (Mar., 1957).

[47] A few states provide a fixed salary per regular session and a per diem during special sessions.

[48] Expressed as $200 per two-year term.

[49] A table showing compensation and allowances to legislators in the various states may be found in *The Book of the States,* 1964-65, pp. 46-47.

the matter is left to legislative determination, it is usual for the constitution to stipulate either that no increase shall take effect during the session at which it is made or that no increase shall become effective during the terms of the members making it.

During recent years, legislators' pay has been increased in many states. Though a number of states now provide reasonably adequate compensation, in others legislative service still entails financial sacrifice. If the legislator takes his task seriously, it means that for several weeks or months each year or every two years he must neglect his private business or profession to attend to his public task. Moreover, while staying at the state capital during legislative sessions he is inevitably at considerable expense. Most legislators feel obliged to stay at one of the better hotels where they can readily be found by constituents and colleagues, and in such a hotel living expenses are likely to consume most or all of the compensation paid in several states. Where compensation is lowest, the legislator may have to pay a part of his living expenses from his private funds, to say nothing of the fact that he is also donating his time. Under such circumstances it is inevitable that some able and public-spirited citizens who would otherwise be willing or anxious to serve their state in a legislative capacity will feel that they cannot make the necessary financial sacrifice. It is doubtless true that legislative pay should not be so high that the office will be sought because of the large salary. But only when the pay at least covers legitimate expenses will many persons of moderate means feel justified in seeking legislative office. And it seems questionable that even the well-to-do should be expected to pay a considerable part of their own expenses while serving the state. Either the Biblical avowal that "the labourer is worthy of his hire" is being ignored by many states or it must be assumed that the legislator performs little labor.

The inadequacy of legislative pay is in some instances attributable to the fact that the rate of compensation is fixed by constitutional provisions which are difficult to change.[50] Though several states have recently effected pay increases by constitutional amendment, this action in most instances did not take place until it was long overdue. On the whole, the practice of leaving the matter of compensation to legislative determination seems much to be preferred. Over the years public salaries should rise and fall with the general level of prices, and hence it seems unwise to fix the amount of such salaries by constitutional provisions which can be changed only with difficulty if at all. To those who fear "salary grabs" if compensation is left to legislative regulation, it may be pointed out that the experience of states employing that method indicates that there is little ground for such apprehension. Adequate safeguards

---

[50] A few of the states with low rates of compensation fixed by constitutional provision have found it possible, in periods of increased living costs, to make statutory grants of additional expense money to legislative members.

against such reprehensible measures seem to have been found in the pressure of public opinion and constitutional stipulations that pay increases shall not be immediately effective.

Legislative Sessions

As of 1964, regular sessions of the legislature were held biennially in 31 states and annually in 19.[51] Most of the states providing for annual sessions have changed from biennial since 1950. The two newest states—Alaska and Hawaii—provide for annual sessions, and the national trend is clearly toward yearly meetings. A principal reason for changing from biennial to annual sessions has been the difficulties encountered, under the biennial system, in planning state expenditures and revenues two years in advance. With the facilitating of fiscal planning thus a main objective of the change, 9 of the annual-session states confine their sessions in alternate (usually the even-numbered) years to adoption of the annual budget and, in some instances, the consideration of matters falling within a few other specified categories.[52] In Alabama, in addition to regular biennial sessions, there is a brief "organization session" following the quadrennial legislative election for the purpose of canvassing the election returns, electing legislative officers, and appointing standing committees.[53] Of the states having biennial sessions all but three—Kentucky, Mississippi, and Virginia—hold their sessions in odd-numbered years. In most states, regular sessions convene on a designated date in January. However, the legislatures of Hawaii and North Carolina, and the even-year "budget sessions" in California, Delaware, and Maryland, meet in February. The Florida legislature meets in April, and the legislatures of Alabama and Louisiana in May.[54]

More than half of the states have constitutional provisions limiting the length of regular legislative sessions. Budget sessions in California, Delaware, Kansas, Louisiana, Maryland, and West Virginia, and even-year sessions in South Dakota, are limited to thirty days' duration, while Alabama's organization session is limited to ten days. With these exceptions, maximum length varies from thirty-six days in Alabama to six and a

[51] The annual-session states are Alaska, Arizona, California, Colorado, Delaware, Georgia, Hawaii, Kansas, Louisiana, Maryland, Massachusetts, Michigan, New Jersey, New York, Pennsylvania, Rhode Island, South Carolina, South Dakota, and West Virginia. A table on legislative sessions and limitations on their length may be found in The Book of the States, 1964-65, pp. 44-45. For a discussion of arguments for and against annual sessions, see Illinois Legislative Council, Annual Legislative Sessions (Ill. Legis. Council, Springfield, 1956).

[52] The budget-session states are California, Colorado, Delaware, Hawaii, Kansas, Louisiana, Maryland, Pennsylvania, and West Virginia.

[53] Bureau of Public Administration, University of Alabama, A Manual for Alabama Legislators (Bur. of Pub. Admin., Univ. of Ala., University, Ala., 3rd ed., 1945), 1.

[54] Alabama's organization session convenes in January.

half months in Missouri, with a sixty-day limit most common.[55] A few states limit the length of sessions indirectly by stopping or reducing the per diem of members after a specified number of days. In Illinois, although there is no direct constitutional limitation upon length of sessions, a provision that all laws, other than those containing an emergency clause and passed by a two-thirds vote, shall take effect upon July first after passage, generally operates to fix June 30 as the closing date of regular sessions.

Constitutional limitations upon the length of legislative sessions seem, in general, unwise. In most instances a session of sixty days or less is hardly enough to enable the legislature to deal properly with the many problems which confront it under modern conditions. This is especially true since a majority of the legislatures meet in regular session only once in two years, and since each regular session normally includes many new members who must familiarize themselves with legislative problems and procedure before they are ready to take an active and intelligent part in legislative work. Moreover, even when the number of days allowed is more liberal, the mere fact that there is a set time at which adjournment is required opens an opportunity for obstructionists, near the end of the session, to block the passage of needed legislation or to exact concessions for permitting such measures to become law. The wiser practice seems to be to pay legislative members a fixed salary regardless of the number of days they are actually in session, and then to leave to the discretion of the members themselves the determination of the length of time necessary to complete the session's business. But if the fixing of a specific date for the required termination of legislative sessions is unwise, proposals that the legislature remain in *continuous* session[56] seem to be equally ill-advised. Though there should be provision for regular sessions of adequate length, and for special sessions when necessary, business interests and the public in general appreciate recurring periods of certainty during which, since the lawmaking body is not in session, it may reasonably be expected that the "rules of the game" will not be changed.

Special Sessions

Every state constitution provides that special sessions of the legislature may be called by the governor. Although the constitutional phraseology varies from state to state, a common provision is that the chief executive may convene the legislature in special session "on extraordinary

---

[55] Limitations expressed in terms of days apply in some states to calendar days and in others to meeting or legislative days. Missouri's legislature convenes on the Wednesday after the first day of January and is required to adjourn by July 15th. *The Book of the States,* 1964-65, pp. 44-45.

[56] See, for example, Read Bain, "Technology and State Government," *Amer. Sociol. Rev.,* II, 860-874 (Dec., 1937).

occasions." Such provisions are generally interpreted as making the governor the sole judge as to when an "extraordinary" occasion exists, and thereby conferring upon him full discretion as to when a special session shall be called. In certain states having executive councils, however, it is provided that the governor's power to call special sessions shall be exercised "with advice of council." [57] The constitutions of Arizona, Georgia, Louisiana, New Jersey, New Mexico, Virginia, and West Virginia, in addition to empowering the governor to call special sessions at his discretion, make it his *duty* to call such sessions upon application therefor by a stipulated proportion[58] of the membership of each house; and in Nebraska it is the statutory duty of the governor to call special sessions of the unicameral legislature on petition of two-thirds of the members. Alaska, Connecticut, Florida, Massachusetts, and New Hampshire, in addition to providing for regular legislative sessions and for special sessions on executive call, authorize their legislatures to assemble at such other times as they shall judge necessary; and in Georgia and New Mexico the legislature may convene itself in special session if the governor fails or refuses to call such a session upon proper application of the legislators. Some state constitutions limit the length of special sessions while others do not. In some states the business which may be considered by special legislative sessions is determined by the governor.[59]

Split Sessions

A few states have made use of what is known as the "split session." Under this plan the legislature meets for a specified number of days, recesses for a prescribed period, then meets again to conclude its deliberations. During the initial session, bills are introduced and referred to committees. The recess period permits members to consider the merits of the various measures, secure information concerning them, and determine the wishes of their constituents. The final session is devoted to discussion and enactment of measures introduced in the initial period, the introduction of additional bills being permitted only with the consent of an extraordinary majority of the members.

California had a long, but apparently unhappy, experience with the split session.[60] The device was approved by constitutional amendment in

[57] This is the case in Massachusetts, New Hampshire, and North Carolina. The nature of the executive council is discussed below, Chap. IX.

[58] Majority in New Jersey, two-thirds in Arizona, Louisiana, Virginia, and West Virginia, and three-fifths in Georgia and New Mexico. In Louisiana if the governor fails to act upon proper application, the call may be issued by either the lieutenant-governor or the speaker of the house of representatives.

[59] See below, Chap. IX, "Control over Special Legislative Sessions."

[60] Originally this practice was considered quite successful. See Victor J. West, "California—the Home of the Split Session," *Nat. Mun. Rev.*, XII, 369-376 (July, 1923). But later it was widely criticized. See Thomas S. Barclay, "The Split-Session

1911, and abolished in the same manner in 1958. The constitution of that state now provides for a 120-day session at which "no bill, other than the budget bill, shall be heard by any committee or acted upon by either house until 30 calendar days have elapsed following the date the bill was first introduced." This provision may be dispensed with by a three-fourths vote.[61]

West Virginia experimented with the split session for a few years during the 1920's, as did New Mexico in the 1940's, but in each instance the device met with little success and was abandoned after a brief trial.[62] Georgia, which now has annual legislative sessions, adopted a constitutional amendment in 1962 providing that sessions in odd-numbered years shall be split, with a brief initial meeting in January being followed by a recess and then a longer meeting beginning on the second Monday in February.[63]

Only a few states have ever sought, as in the case of those mentioned, to make the split session mandatory by constitutional provision. In many others, however, there is no constitutional obstacle to the legislature's obtaining any benefits which may flow from this device by adjourning, after an initial period in session, to a specified time several days or weeks in the future, and completing its deliberations at the "adjourned" session. As a matter of fact, the device of the adjourned session has actually been used at various times in several states.[64]

Legislative Personnel

What occupational groups are most prominent in our state legislatures? The answer seems to be that businessmen now constitute the largest such group, followed by lawyers or farmers. Rarely, however, does any single group constitute a *majority* of a legislative chamber. A 1954 survey found that, of the 7,475 members serving in 1949, 1,063 were listed as merchants, 311 as engaged in insurance, 212 as real estate dealers, 142 as bankers and investors—a total of 1,728 businessmen. Lawyers made up the next largest group, with a total of 1,674 while 1,468 were classified as farmers. The study cautioned that these numbers should not be used to overemphasize the influence of occupation on a legislator's vote. "Any careful analysis will show that farmers do not always support farm pro-

---

in California: Theory versus Practice," *State Govt.*, V, 5-6 (Apr., 1932); Thomas S. Barclay, "The Split Session of the California Legislature," *Calif. Law Rev.*, XX, 42-58 (Nov., 1931); Winston W. Crouch and others, *State and Local Government in California* (Univ. of Calif. Press, Berkeley, 1952), 48-49.

[61] *Const. of Calif.* (1879 as amended), art. IV, sec. 2.

[62] See Martin L. Faust, "Results of the Split-Session System of the West Virginia Legislature," *Amer. Polit. Sci. Rev.*, XXII, 109-121 (Feb., 1928); Thomas C. Donnelly, *The Government of New Mexico* (Univ. of N.M. Press, Albuquerque, 1947), 95-96.

[63] *Const. of Ga.* (1945 as amended), art. III, sec. 4.

[64] See Graves, *American State Government* (4th ed.), 221.

grams, businessmen do not all vote to protect the interest of business, and that laborers do not see only the interest of labor." In this connection it should be noted that a lawyer or businessman may represent a rural constituency while a farmer may represent an urban community.[65]

Considering the importance of business and agriculture as factors in the national economy, it is scarcely surprising to find that businessmen and farmers constitute important groups in most state legislatures. More remarkable perhaps is the prominence of lawyers. Their number, however, is not to be interpreted as necessarily meaning that lawyers as an occupational group are greatly overrepresented. In a real sense the lawyer, in the legislature as elsewhere, is a professional representative of the interests of others. Nonlawyers may prefer to be represented in the legislature by men with legal training, believing that the lawyer can promote their interests better than they could do if they themselves were members of the legislative body. Another probable factor in accounting for the large number of lawyer members is the value commonly attached by young lawyers to the publicity which is to be gained from legislative campaigns and service.[66]

Whether or not the large number of lawyers in our legislatures is to be deprecated seems open to controversy. There are those who believe that the nature of his training, stressing as it does the importance of precedent, makes it difficult for the lawyer to think in terms of the progressive social legislation which modern life requires.[67] On the other hand, it is suggested that little or no actual evidence has ever been presented to demonstrate that lawyer legislators slavishly follow their professional ways of thinking when considering proposed legislation.[68] This much, however, seems certain: Insofar as lawyers have been sent to the legislature with the thought that legal training makes the legislator adept at drafting legislative proposals and securing information regarding the probable effect of pending measures, the practice is unwarranted. For one thing, many practicing lawyers are by no means expert bill-drafters. Furthermore, the technical services now supplied to legislators in most states through legislative reference bureaus and research departments of legislative councils make it quite unnecessary that the individual legislator be skilled in these respects.[69]

[65] Zeller, ed., *op. cit.*, 70-73.

[66] Cf. Charles S. Hyneman, "Who Makes Our Laws?" *Polit. Sci. Quar.*, LV, 556-581 (Dec., 1940).

[67] Cf. Graves, *American State Government* (4th ed.), 195-196.

[68] Cf. Hyneman, "Who Makes Our Laws?" *loc. cit.* This point is substantiated in a recent study of the Illinois and Missouri legislatures. See David R. Derge, "The Lawyer as Decision-Maker in the American State Legislature," *Jour. of Politics*, XXI, 408-433 (Aug., 1959).

[69] In the matter of legislative personnel it is to be noted that, as in other fields of the public service, participation by women is increasing. In 1959 it was reported that 347 women were serving in state and territorial legislatures. Cf. Illinois Legislative Council, *Between Sessions* (Newsletter 72), Oct., 1959.

Organization of the Legislature

Each newly-elected legislature, before actually beginning its work, is faced with the task of organization. The organization of a legislative body normally involves (1) the election of officers, (2) the election or appointment of committees, and (3) the adoption of a set of rules. In the lower chambers of state legislatures, and in those senates of which the entire membership is renewed at one time, there must be a reorganization following each election notwithstanding that in many instances the same persons may be placed again and again in the same positions. In senates where the terms of members are staggered, only a part of the membership being renewed at any one time, organization may be continuous. Where it is continuous, it is necessary after an election only to fill vacancies occurring in offices and committee posts.

Officers and Employees. The presiding officer of the lower house is in every instance known as the speaker and is elected by the house. Some states require by constitutional provision that the speaker be chosen from among house members, and even where there is no such requirement custom decrees that the selection be made from the membership. In states having a lieutenant governor[70] that officer is, except in Massachusetts, president of the senate, it being customary for the senate to elect from its membership a president *pro tempore* to serve in the absence of the lieutenant governor. Elsewhere the senate elects its president in much the same manner that the house elects its speaker. The lieutenant governor is the presiding officer of Nebraska's unicameral legislature.

The power and influence of the presiding officer varies from state to state as well as between the two chambers in a single state. In general it may be said that the speaker of the lower house occupies a relatively influential position. He is usually a leader in the majority party, which fact alone makes his wishes carry considerable weight. His power, in most states, to appoint standing committees and to decide, within broad limits prescribed by the rules, the committees to which particular bills shall be referred, gives him a vital part in determining the fate of legislative proposals. No member may address the house without first securing "recognition" from the speaker. As a member of the chamber, the speaker is entitled to vote on any question and to participate in debate. In most states the speaker exercises freely his right to vote, but less frequently engages in debate. When, on occasion, a speaker does choose to participate in debate, it is ordinarily considered appropriate procedure for him to designate some other member to preside for the time being, so that the speaker may address the house from the floor, like an ordinary member, rather than from the speaker's rostrum.

[70] See below, Chap. IX, "The Lieutenant Governor."

In those states in which the senate elects its president from among its members, the position of the president, with respect to power and influence, is little different from that of the speaker of the house. The lieutenant-governor as presiding officer of the senate occupies, however, a distinctly less influential position. Since he is chosen by the voters of the state rather than by the senate, there is no assurance that he will be a member of the majority party. Although senate committees are in some states appointed by the lieutenant governor, in most of the states wherein that official acts as presiding officer committees are either elected by the senate or appointed by the president *pro tempore*. Since the lieutenant governor is not a senate member[71] he has no right to vote or enter into debate unless such right is specifically conferred upon him by the constitution or, in the case of debate, by special action of the senate. In no instance has he been clothed with the power to vote generally on all questions. Most states provide that he may vote to break a tie, although Minnesota does not confer even that limited voting power. In a few states the lietenant governor is authorized to debate and vote when the senate is in committee of the whole.[72]

Certain officers other than its presiding officer are required by every legislative chamber. Those most commonly found are the secretary or chief clerk, sergeant-at-arms, doorkeeper, and chaplain. In addition there are numerous employees. These may include, for example, reading clerks, roll clerks, engrossing clerks, enrolling clerks, assistant doorkeepers, janitors, messengers, and pages. The Illinois statutes authorize appointment by the senate of "such employees as may be necessary," but limit the number to be appointed by the speaker, except in emergencies, to ninety-seven.[73] Whether such minor officers and employees in the various states are elected by the respective chambers or appointed, they are usually chosen from nonmembers of the legislature who are found to be "deserving" at the hands of the majority party. The number of employees has been declared in many states to be excessive. In Indiana, some years ago, it was "estimated that one-third of the employees could do the work."[74] An Iowa governor once described the situation with respect to legislative employees in that state as "reprehensible and indefensible." Declaring that much of the legislative "help" was "pure, unadulterated 'graft'," the governor observed that "A dozen doorkeepers are used in the two houses where none at all are needed," and that clerks sit "around these chambers in luxurious ease from one end of the session to the other, doing practically nothing at all."[75] Wisconsin has acted to establish a career legisla-

[71] In Rhode Island, contrary to the practice elsewhere, the lieutenant-governor is a member, as well as president, of the senate.
[72] See Warren Rex Isom, "The Office of Lieutenant-Governor in the States," *Amer. Polit. Sci. Rev.*, XXXII, 921-926 (Oct., 1938). Nebraska's lieutenant-governor, as presiding officer of the unicameral legislature, may vote only in case of a tie.
[73] *Ill. Rev. Stat.*, 1961, Chap. 63, sec. 18.
[74] H. W. Dodds, *Procedure in State Legislatures*, 23.
[75] *Biennial Message of George W. Clarke, Governor of Iowa, 1915.*

tive service by requiring that legislative employees be appointed from civil service eligible lists.[76]

The Committee System.[77] Every state legislature, as an important part of its organization, has a rather elaborate system of standing committees. Set up when a newly-elected legislature organizes, such committees have as their primary function the study of legislative proposals referred to them; the securing of information relative to the need for such legislation and its probable effects if enacted; and the making of recommendations to the legislative body as to what course of action should be taken thereon.[78] The purpose of the committee system is twofold: (1) It expedites the legislative process by making possible the consideration, by various committees, of a number of legislative proposals simultaneously; and (2) it makes possible some degree of specialization, since a member of a particular committee, though perhaps at the time of his appointment not especially competent in the subject matter with which the committee deals, may be expected to acquire some degree of proficiency through committee service. In 46 states each of the two houses has its own set of standing committees. The Nebraska unicameral legislature has of course but a single set of committees, while the bicameral legislatures of Connecticut, Maine, and Massachusetts have systems of *joint* committees.

Committees of the lower house usually are appointed by the speaker, whereas the method of choosing senate committees varies more widely from state to state. In states where the senate elects its own president, it is usual for the president to appoint senate committees. Where the lieutenant governor is president of the senate, committees are in some instances appointed by that officer, in others appointed by the president *pro tempore* or by a committee of selection, and in still others elected by the senate membership.[79] Committees of the unicameral legislature in Nebraska are chosen by a committee on committees. Regardless

[76] *Wis. Stat.*, 1955, sec. 13.14.

[77] The most comprehensive study of the comittee system in state legislatures is C. I. Winslow, *State Legislative Committees*. A more recent analysis is to be found in Zeller, ed., *op. cit.*, 95-103. For good studies relating to particular states, see Robert F. Karsch, *The Standing Committees of the Missouri General Assembly* (Bur. of Govt. Research, Univ. of Mo., Columbia, 1959); Jay Doubleday, *Standing and Interim Committees of the California Legislature* (Bur. of Pub. Admin., Univ. of Calif., Berkeley, 1959); Dean E. Mann, "The Legislative Committee System in Arizona," *Ariz. Rev. of Bus. and Pub. Admin.*, Vol. XI, No. 8, pp. 1-10 (Aug., 1962).

[78] In addition to the regular *standing* committees, legislative chambers set up from time to time *special* or *select* committees to perform a particular, designated function. Thus special committees are frequently created to make investigations, or to draft resolutions expressing the sentiment of the house concerned on stated matters. Rarely are legislative proposals referred to special committees for consideration and report.

[79] Winslow, *op. cit.*, 11-15. A recent table showing methods of committee selection in the various states will be found in *The Book of the States*, 1964-65, p. 51. This table is the main source for the information on committees which follows.

of the method of selection, seniority may play an important part in the allotment of committee posts, positions on the more important committees usually going to members with the longest legislative service. Where the party system prevails, it is usual for the party which is in the majority in the chamber to receive the chairmanship as well as a majority of the members of each committee.

The number of committees found in the respective houses varies considerably from state to state, and to some extent in the same state from time to time. In 1964 the number of committees in the lower house varied from eight in South Carolina to fifty-one in Florida, while the number of senate committees ranged from seven in New Mexico to forty-six in Mississippi. Committees also vary considerably in size. In Illinois at the 1959 session, the number of members of house policy or bill-considering committees varied from twenty-six (four committees) to forty, and the number of members of senate policy committees from fifteen (ten committees) to thirty. The operational or "housekeeping" committees had smaller memberships.[80] Nebraska's unicameral legislature, in 1964, had fourteen standing committees, varying in size from one to eight members.

The large number of committees and their large size combine to make it necessary that each member of the legislature serve on several committees. The average number of committees on which members serve varies widely. A few years ago the number ranged in the lower house from one in Maine and New Hampshire to twelve in North Carolina, and in the senate from two in Indiana, Maine, and Rhode Island to fourteen in Tennessee. The mean of the state averages was 4.37 committees in the house and 6.09 in the senate.[81] With each legislator ordinarily serving on a number of committees it is difficult if not impossible to secure full attendance at committee meetings, since several committees are likely to be meeting simultaneously, and the degree of specialization which can be achieved is limited. Some committees are, in practice, overworked while others have relatively little to do. In the 1961 legislative session in Illinois, 299 bills were referred to the house judiciary committee and 250 measures to the corresponding committee of the senate. At the same time there were several committees in each house to which few bills were referred.[82] Recent years have seen a substantial reduction in the number of committees in one or both legislative chambers in several states. Nevertheless, the median number of standing committees in the forty-nine states having bicameral legislatures stood, in 1961, at twenty for the senates and twenty-three for the lower chambers.[83]

---

[80] Illinois Legislative Council, *Lawmaking in the Illinois General Assembly* (Ill. Legis. Council, Springfield, 1960), 13.

[81] Zeller, ed., *op. cit.*, 101.

[82] Illinois Legislative Council, *Final Status of Bills, 72nd General Assembly, 1961 Regular Session* (Ill. Legis. Council, Springfield, 1962).

[83] Herbert L. Wiltsee, "Structure and Procedures" [of State Legislatures], *The Book of the States*, 1962-63, pp. 33-39.

In the three states having the joint committee system[84]—Connecticut, Maine, and Massachusetts—a single set of committees, consisting of members from each of the two houses, serves both chambers. In Massachusetts, for example, a bill is referred by the house in which it is introduced to the appropriate joint committee. After committee consideration the bill is reported to either house,[85] an effort being made to distribute business equally between the chambers. If passed by the house to which it is reported, the bill is placed directly upon the calendar of the other house without a second consideration by committee.[86] Such a system effects a saving of legislators' time and effort. It is particularly advantageous in eliminating the necessity for two hearings on a bill, one by a committee of each chamber. The single hearing also operates to the advantage of citizens and organizations interested in proposed legislation, since they need present their views but once. Moreover, with the legislature's membership organized into a single set of committees rather than two sets, the individual member is not required to serve on as many different committees. This fact tends to promote specialization and the avoidance of conflicts in the scheduling of committee meetings.

The system of standing committees in the state legislature regularly includes, in addition to the committees charged with considering the *substance* of proposed legislation, certain committees whose work is of a *procedural* character. These committees are sometimes referred to as operational or housekeeping committees. Examples are committees on printing, engrossment of bills, enrolling of bills, and bill revision and style.[87] Most important among the procedural committees is the committee on rules, the work of which will be considered in the next chapter.

Rules of Procedure.[88] In addition to officers and a system of committees, a legislative chamber must have, if it is to function properly, a set of rules governing its procedure. Such rules exist for the threefold purpose of (1) expediting business, (2) assuring deliberate and adequate consideration of proposed measures, and (3) protecting the rights of minority members. Certain matters of procedure are governed by constitutional provision. For example, state constitutions not infrequently fix

---

[84] Many legislatures have joint committees for specific purposes, though rarely for the consideration of proposed legislation; while a few house and senate committees are to be found in the "joint committee" states. The latter states differ from others, however, in that the joint system is the *usual* means of giving committee consideration to legislative proposals. For a discussion of joint committees in Connecticut, Maine, and Massachusetts, see Zeller, ed., *op. cit.*, appendix B.

[85] All money bills are reported to the house of representatives.

[86] See John W. Plaisted, *Legislative Procedure in the General Court of Massachusetts* (Wright & Potter Printing Co., Boston, 1948).

[87] Cf. Winslow, *op. cit.*, 35-36.

[88] For a critique of state legislative rules of procedure, see Zeller, ed., *op. cit.*, Chap. 7. See also Paul Mason, "Procedure in State Legislatures: The Nature of Rules," *State Govt.*, XXXVI, 101-107 (Spring, 1963).

the number of members which will constitute a quorum, require that bills be read three times before passage, and stipulate that the final vote shall be by roll call and recorded in the official journal. Subject to such constitutional requirements, each house is free to determine its own rules of procedure, and in practice each operates under a set of rules which it has drawn up and adopted. These rules concern such matters as the method of choosing officers and employees, what committees shall be established and the means by which their membership shall be selected, the order in which business shall be taken up and disposed of, and the maximum length of speeches in the course of debate. Although each newly-elected chamber is legally free to adopt a completely new set of rules, what actually happens in most instances is that a new chamber adopts the rules of the last preceding chamber with any modifications therein which it may see fit to make. Changes may, of course, be made in the rules of a legislative body at any time, but in practice changes after the completion of formal organization are infrequent. When made, such changes usually come about as the result of recommendation by the rules committee. In senates having continuous organization as the result of staggered terms of members, it generally is not necessary at any time to adopt or readopt a complete set of rules, but merely to make from time to time such changes as may seem, on the basis of experience, to be desirable.

Party Organization in the Legislature.[89] In the state legislatures division of opinion and votes along strictly "party" lines is much less common than in Congress, and it is therefore natural that party organization in the state legislative chambers should be correspondingly weaker. Nevertheless, some use is made in the states, more frequently by the majority party but on occasion by the minority as well, of the party caucus, the party steering committee, and the party floor leader.[90]

The caucus is a meeting of the members of a legislative chamber who are also members of a given party. In the national Congress the caucus is extremely important as a means of determining what policy, if any, the party is to pursue with respect to various legislative proposals, but this function is of relatively minor importance in state legislatures. The principal function of the caucus in most states seems to be the nomination of the party's candidates for chamber offices (speaker, sergeant-at-arms, etc.) which are to be filled by election.[91] Since, where caucus nomination is used, the chamber normally elects the slate of nominees presented by the majority party, the officers are, for all practical purposes,

[89] See Zeller, ed., *op. cit.,* Chap. 12.

[90] For a good discussion of a legislature organized along factional rather than party lines, see Robert E. Riggs, "The Legislative Process in Arizona," *Ariz. Rev. of Bus. and Pub. Admin.,* Vol. XI, No. 12, pp. 1-22 (Dec., 1962).

[91] Cf. W. F. Willoughby, *Principles of Legislative Organization and Administration,* 621-622.

chosen by the majority caucus. A 1954 report stated that "in only thirteen states do majority caucuses meet frequently and exert or attempt to exert any significant control over their members or the program of the legislature." [92] Minority caucuses were reported to be less numerous and less important. Factional caucuses, especially in one-party states, were not unknown.

The steering committee, which is rarely found except in the majority party, is usually composed of a small number of the more influential party members of the chamber. This agency may be formally appointed by the party caucus or may be merely an informal but generally-recognized group of party leaders. Indeed, the name of steering committee is not always applied to the group.[93] The function of this group of leaders, regardless of its name, consists in "steering" through the various steps in the legislative process measures in which the party's members or leaders are particularly interested. In doing this the steering committee of the majority party normally expects and receives cooperation from the majority floor leader, the majority members of the rules committee, and (where that official is a member of the majority party) the presiding officer of the chamber. It should be emphasized that the steering committee is not an official committee of the house or senate, but solely a *party* organ established to further the policies or program of the party concerned.

The floor leader is the member who leads his party's forces in debate on the floor of the chamber. Like the steering committee, the floor leader may or may not be formally designated or recognized by the party caucus. Usually himself active in debate, the floor leader also exercises some degree of supervision over the participation of his colleagues therein. Thus, he may be called upon to decide which members are to speak for the party in the course of debate; and, if a time limitation has been imposed, to divide the allotted time among such speakers. The floor leader is frequently the one who presents to the chamber important motions designed to advance his party's program. In some states, as in New York, the position of majority floor leader is one of considerable power and prestige. In other states, however, the floor leader plays a relatively minor role in actual leadership, a fact which seems to be due, in part at least, to the prominent position of party leadership commonly assumed by the speaker.[94]

[92] Zeller, ed., *op. cit.*, 194. See also Malcolm E. Jewell, *The State Legislature: Politics and Practice*, 89-92.

[93] Cf. H. W. Dodds, *Procedure in State Legislatures*, 103; Joseph P. Chamberlain, *Legislative Processes, National and State*, 142-145; Jewell, *The State Legislature: Politics and Practice*, 85-89.

[94] Dodds, *op. cit.*, 102-104.

See References, Chapter 8, p. 243.

8

State Legislatures: Powers and Procedures

Powers of the State Legislature: Residual Character

The state legislature is, under the American federal system, the ultimate repository of all governmental powers which are not delegated to some other governmental agency. The United States Constitution delegates certain powers, some in express words and others by implication, to the national government, and reserves all other powers to the respective states. Of the powers thus reserved to the states, some are delegated by the respective state constitutions to the executive and judicial branches of the state government. All governmental powers remaining, after these delegations to national and state agencies, belong to the state legislature, subject to such specific limitations as may be imposed upon the legislature by constitutional provisions, national and state. The legislature is thus the possessor of a broad and largely undefined residuum of governmental authority.

The *residual* character of the legislature's powers is extremely important from the standpoint of constitutional law. When the United States Congress, which is a legislative body of delegated authority, seeks to exercise a particular power, it must be able to point to specific constitutional provisions which, expressly or by implication, confer the power concerned. On the other hand, when a state legislature attempts to exercise authority in a particular field, it need only show that the power concerned has not been *denied* to the state or its legislature by some constitutional provision and that it has not been delegated *exclusively* to some organ of government other than the legislature.

Outstanding among the residual powers of the state legislature is what is commonly called the "police power." Though incapable of exact definition, the police power may be described in general terms as the power to protect and promote the health, safety, and welfare of the state and its people. Under this broad authority a state legislature, for example, may regulate child labor even though this subject is not mentioned in any way in either the United States Constitution or that of the state concerned. On the other hand, since the federal constitution does not expressly confer the necessary power upon Congress, that body has found it impossible to provide for any comprehensive regulation of child labor throughout the nation.[1]

Powers of the Legislature Classified

In the preceding chapter it was pointed out that the primary function of the state legislature consists in the formulation of public policy and the expression of that policy in the form of law. Thus the foremost power with which the legislature is endowed is that of enacting laws; indeed, the legislature is often referred to in popular parlance as the "lawmaking" branch of the state government.[2] But every legislature possesses, in addition to its lawmaking authority, certain other important powers. For purposes of classification, it is therefore appropriate to divide the powers of the legislature into two broad categories: (1) lawmaking and (2) nonlawmaking. The process by which the lawmaking power is exercised will be described in some detail in subsequent portions of this chapter. It will be helpful at this point to consider briefly the powers of a nonlawmaking nature. These fall rather naturally into three groups: (a) executive powers, (b) judicial powers, and (3) investigatory powers.

Executive Powers. The principal executive power is that by which the legislature, or the upper house thereof, participates in the appoint-

---

[1] Limited regulation of child labor has been achieved by Congress under its delegated authority over interstate commerce.

[2] The term *law* is here used in a sense synonymous with *statute*, and therefore includes measures relating to the organization and financing of government as well as those which are laws in the narrower sense of constituting regulations of individual conduct.

ment and removal of state officers. The requirement is quite widespread, though by no means universal, that appointments made by the governor have the approval of the senate. In some states the legislature itself appoints or elects certain executive officers or judges. Less common, but still significant, is the legislature's share in the power of removal. In a few states the governor may exercise the removal power only on address of both legislative houses or of the senate alone; while in still other instances removals made by the governor must have senatorial confirmation. Several states vest in the legislature itself power to remove certain executive officers and judges by concurrent vote of both houses, removal in this manner usually requiring the vote of an extraordinary majority—commonly two-thirds—in each house.

Judicial Power: Impeachment. A more common method by which the legislature may remove executive or judicial officers is that of impeachment. Since impeachment procedure is essentially judicial in nature, the power of impeachment is considered as a judicial power of the legislature. The impeachment process, as provided in most states, involves two distinct steps: (1) the preferring of charges by the lower house of the legislature (the step which, strictly speaking, constitutes *impeachment*), and (2) the subsequent trial of those charges by the senate sitting as an impeachment court.[3]

Impeachment as a method of removal is available to the legislature in almost every state.[4] Usually the grounds upon which impeachment charges may be based are prescribed by constitutional provision, though in a few states they are not so stipulated. The grounds most frequently specified are crime, and corruption or malfeasance in office. In only a few instances is mere incompetency included among the grounds for impeachment.

Impeachment proceedings are instituted in the lower house of the legislature by the introduction of a resolution of impeachment. Such a resolution may be introduced by any house member, whereupon the matter is referred to a committee for investigation and report. On the basis of the committee's findings and recommendations, the house decides whether or not to vote charges in the form of "articles of impeachment." In most

[3] In New York the judges of the court of appeals (the highest state court) sit with the members of the senate as a court of impeachment. In Nebraska impeachment charges are preferred by the unicameral legislature and tried before the state supreme court. Impeachments in Missouri are tried before the supreme court, except in the cases of the governor and supreme court judges, those being tried before a commission of jurists elected by the senate. In Alaska impeachment is by the senate and trial by the house of representatives with a justice of the supreme court presiding.

[4] The constitution of Oregon (art. VII, sec. 6) forbids removal by impeachment but provides that incompetency, corruption, malfeasance, or delinquency in office may be tried in the same manner as criminal offenses and that the judgment in such cases may include dismissal from office.

states a simple majority vote in the house is sufficient to impeach, although a few states require a two-thirds vote. If the house votes in favor of impeachment, it transmits a copy of the charges to the senate, which resolves itself into an impeachment court to try the case. A "board of managers" is constituted by the house from among its members to prosecute the proceedings before the senate. The accused official is entitled to be represented by counsel, and the entire proceedings are conducted in a manner similar to procedure before the regular courts. When the taking of testimony and the presentation of evidence have been concluded, the senate votes upon the question of conviction or acquittal. A two-thirds vote—in some states of all members and in others merely of those present— is ordinarily necessary to convict. The state constitutions prescribe the judgment which may be imposed if the accused official is convicted. In a few states the judgment is limited to removal from office, but more commonly it may also include disqualification from holding any state office in the future. Most constitutions expressly except impeachment cases from the governor's pardoning power. Moreover, a person who has been impeached may, whether or not he is convicted on the impeachment charges, be prosecuted in the ordinary courts for any criminal act which he may have committed.

It will readily be seen that impeachment, particularly as it relates to the executive branch of government, is effective only as an *extraordinary* method of removal, and does not at all afford an adequate means of purging the public service of inefficient officers. The weakness of impeachment flows from the facts that: (1) the process can be used only when the legislature is in session; (2) the procedure is lengthy and cumbersome, and consumes time which the legislature may sorely need for other work; and (3) in most states, mere incompetency does not constitute ground for removal. Because of the inadequacy of impeachment as a sole method of removing executive officers, it has been quite generally supplemented by a power of removal placed, though sometimes subject to important limitations, in the hands of the governor.[5]

Investigatory Powers. Another type of power which deserves special mention, though in a sense it is merely incidental to other powers of the state legislature, lawmaking or otherwise, is the power of investigation. Unlike the legislature's powers of an executive or judicial nature, which are conferred by express constitutional provision, the investigatory power is not expressly conferred but inheres in the legislature as a necessary means of enabling that body to make law and perform its other functions in a proper manner. Seldom is there a regular legislative session which does not set up one or more committees—house, senate, or joint— for investigatory purposes. Sometimes the subject of investigation is the

[5] See below, Chap. IX.

administration of a designated office or institution. In such cases the purpose of the investigation may be to secure information upon which to base remedial legislation; or, perhaps, to determine whether impeachment proceedings should be instituted against the officer or officers concerned. Again, the investigation may concern alleged fraud in elections or in the handling of public funds. At times the matter to be investigated is extremely broad in scope, as, for example, when a legislative committee is established to study the executive branch of government in its entirety and to make recommendations respecting its reorganization. Legislative investigations, in addition to procuring information which aids the legislature directly in its own work, often serve a useful purpose in focusing public attention upon conditions requiring remedial action.[6]

Limitations on Legislative Powers: The Federal Constitution

As has already been suggested, the powers of the state legislature, though very broad, are limited by restrictions imposed by the federal and state constitutions. The more important limitations imposed upon state legislatures by the United States Constitution as originally adopted appear in the tenth section of Article I. There the states are forbidden, among other things, to make treaties, coin money, pass bills of attainder or ex post facto laws, or make any law impairing the obligation of contracts. Of the restrictions imposed upon state legislative action by amendments to the United States Constitution, the most important are those contained in the Fourteenth, and especially in that article's "due-process" and "equal-protection" clauses. These clauses operate to require that state legislatures, in regulating persons and property under the police power, do so in a reasonable and nondiscriminatory manner. Moreover, the requirement of due process has been construed by the United States Supreme Court in such a way as to protect against state interference various civil rights, such as freedom of press and religion, which the federal bill of rights in the first ten amendments protects only against interference by the national government. These and other restrictions imposed upon the states by the federal constitution have already been considered at some length in an earlier chapter.[7]

[6] On the general subject of legislative investigations, see Joseph P. Chamberlain, *Legislative Processes, National and State,* Chap. 7; Harvey Walker, *The Legislative Process,* 222-224; Theodore W. Cousens, "The Purposes and Scope of Investigations Under Legislative Authority," *Georgetown Law Jour.,* XXVI, 905-929 (May, 1938); Bernard Schwartz, "Legislative Powers of Investigation," *Dickinson Law Rev.,* LVII, 31-45 (Oct. 1952).

[7] Above, Chap. II. See especially the sections entitled "Impairment of Contracts," "Due Process of Law," and "Equal Protection of the Laws."

Limitations on Legislative Powers:
The State Constitutions[8]

Limitations imposed upon state legislatures by state constitutional provision are numerous and varied, and are the result in large measure of abuse by early legislatures of the almost unlimited authority which they enjoyed under the first state constitutions.[9] It will be recalled[10] that the provisions of state bills of rights restrict the legislatures in their regulation of persons and property. Typical of such provisions are those which prohibit the legislature from abridging freedom of speech, press, or religion; abolishing jury trial; or taking private property for public use without compensation. Aside from the bill of rights, the constitutional restrictions most generally imposed upon state legislatures are those relating to (1) finance, (2) special legislation, and (3) legislative procedure.

Financial Limitations. The legislature is the fiscal authority of the state and, except as it may be restrained by constitutional provision, is free to raise and spend state funds as it sees fit. Early state constitutions imposed few restrictions upon legislative authority in financial matters, and the early period of legislative history is replete with instances of profligate spending accompanied by unwise taxation and borrowing. As a result, present-day constitutions quite generally subject the fiscal powers of the legislature to various limitations, the most important of which relate to taxation and borrowing.

Limitations upon the taxing power may have to do with what may be taxed, or with the method or rate of taxation. Most state constitutions at one time virtually required that the greater part of state and local revenue be raised by the taxation of property, and furthermore that the rate of taxation be "uniform and equal" on all property regardless of its nature or productivity.[11] That this so-called "general property tax" is unsatisfactory under modern conditions is widely recognized, and a majority of the states now confer upon their legislatures some degree of power to classify property and to tax different classes at different rates.[12] The constitutional requirement of uniformity in taxation is in some states not limited to

---

[8] For an excellent analysis, see Byron R. Abernethy, *Constitutional Limitations on the Legislature.*

[9] See above, Chap. I, "Early Constitutions and Subsequent Trends."

[10] See above, Chap. I, "The Bill of Rights."

[11] Certain classes of property, such as that used exclusively for educational, religious, or charitable purposes, are in many states exempted from taxation either by constitutional provision directly or by statute under constitutional authorization. For an excellent analysis of these provisions, see Illinois Legislative Council, *Constitutional Mandates for Uniformity of Taxation* (Ill. Legis. Council, Springfield, 1959).

[12] See below, Chap. XXIV, "Criticisms of the General Property Tax," "Classified Property Taxes."

property taxation alone. Thus when the Illinois legislature attempted to place an occupational (sales) tax upon retailers, but to exempt retailers of gasoline and those of farm products produced by the seller, the act was declared invalid by the state supreme court as violative of a constitutional requirement that occupational taxes be uniform.[13] In the same state it has been found impossible, because of the uniformity requirement, to levy a state income tax at progressive rates. The Illinois courts have held that income is property and may be taxed as such but, if it is so taxed, the rate must be uniform regardless of the amount of income.[14] Several other states have found it impossible, because of constitutional restrictions, to levy an income tax. Some states have written into their constitutions limitations upon the *rate* of property taxation, these limitations applying in some instances to state rates only, in others to local rates only, and in still others to both state and local levies.[15]

Constitutional restrictions upon the power of the legislature to incur indebtedness are now quite common. Professor B. U. Ratchford, in his comprehensive study of state borrowing,[16] suggests that the states, with respect to the legislature's power to borrow, fall into three groups. In the first group there are constitutional provisions which, with minor exceptions,[17] prohibit the incurring of any state debt. In such states indebtedness can be incurred only through the adoption of constitutional amendments. In the second group of states the constitution requires, again with minor exceptions, that acts of the legislature which authorize borrowing be submitted to popular referendum for approval. In states of the third group the legislature may borrow on its own authority, virtually without quantitative limit. Well over half of the states fall within one or the other of the first two groups, thus requiring that every proposal to incur indebtedness in substantial amount secure popular approval through either the ratification of a constitutional amendment or the approval of a legislative act.[18]

Limitations on Special Legislation. The earliest state legislatures, unrestrained by constitutional limitations, enacted not only statutes of

---

[13] *Winter* v. *Barrett*, 352 Ill. 441 (1933).

[14] *Bachrach* v. *Nelson*, 349 Ill. 579 (1932). For a critique of this decision and subsequent developments in the Illinois courts and general assembly, see Rubin G. Cohn, "Constitutional Limitations on Income Taxation in Illinois," *Univ. of Ill. Law Forum*, Vol. 1961, pp. 586-613 (Winter, 1961).

[15] Mabel Newcomer, "The Growth of Tax Limitation Legislation," in Glenn Leet and Robert M. Paige, eds., *Property Tax Limitation Laws* (Pub. Admin. Service, Chicago, 1934), 38-40. See also below, Chap. XXIV, "The Taxing Power and its Limitations."

[16] B. U. Ratchford, *American State Debts* (Duke Univ. Press, Durham, N.C., 1941), Chap. 17.

[17] The most common exceptions are those which permit borrowing for casual deficits, to refund existing indebtedness, to repel invasion, to suppress insurrection, and to defend the state in case of war.

[18] Cf. below, Chap. XXV, "The Borrowing Power and Its Limitations."

general application but also large numbers of special acts applicable to individual persons or places. Thus there was an abundance of special acts granting divorces, changing names, creating or regulating particular cities, and the like. Such a system inevitably opened the door to favoritism at the hands of the legislature, and caused legislators to devote to special legislation a great deal of time which may have been needed for the consideration of matters of statewide concern. In consequence, most of the states have now inserted in their constitutions restrictions upon the enactment of special laws.[19] Such restrictions are of two general types, either or both of which may be found in a particular state. One type prohibits special legislation in all cases where a general law can be made applicable. Since such provisions have usually been interpreted as vesting in the legislature itself final determination as to when a general law can be made to apply,[20] limitations of this type have been for the most part ineffective. The second type of restriction lists specifically certain subjects upon which special legislation is forbidden. This list in the Illinois constitution, for example, includes twenty-three subjects, and that in the Indiana constitution seventeen. Subjects upon which special legislation is most frequently prohibited by such provisions include granting of divorces, changing of names of persons, and regulating the affairs of cities and counties. Though some restrictions of this nature are effective, those relating to the regulation of local government are often circumvented by the device of classification. The courts take the view that prohibition of special legislation in such cases does not prevent classification of cities or counties and the application of different regulations to different classes, provided that the classification is reasonable and that all units within a particular class are accorded like treatment. Classification is usually based upon population, and in exercising the power of classification legislatures not infrequently establish classes which contain but a single city or county. When that is the case the legislature, by providing regulations applicable to the units within such a class, actually legislates for a particular city or county. In some instances, where the legislature has clearly used the guise of classification as a mere cloak for special legislation, the courts have held such measures unconstitutional. In general, however, courts are loath to overturn legislative classifications as being unreasonable.

Procedural Limitations. Finally, most state constitutions impose certain restrictions upon the procedure which must be followed by the legislature in the enactment of laws. Such restrictions have as their purpose a reasonable assurance that legislative proposals will be carefully

---

[19] There are, however, several states, chiefly in New England and the South, which still permit special legislation.

[20] Cf. John M. Mathews, *American State Government* (Appleton-Century-Crofts, New York, rev. ed., 1934), 248.

considered before their enactment into law, and that legislators and the public will be correctly advised concerning their subject matter. Provisions of this nature, which are to be found in the constitutions of many states, include those requiring that a bill relate to but a single subject, which shall be clearly expressed in its title; fixing the number of legislative members which shall constitute a quorum; providing that bills shall be read three times in each house before passage; and providing that an amendatory act must set forth in full the section or sections amended. Although the courts will presume that these procedural requirements have been observed by the legislature, this presumption may be overcome by specific evidence to the contrary; and, on occasion, legislative acts are declared invalid because of the legislature's failure to follow procedural requirements.

Forms of Legislative Action: Bills and Resolutions

Formal action by state legislative bodies takes one of two forms, namely, that of a *bill* (which, when passed, is usually designated as an "act") or that of a *resolution*. A proposal for the enactment of an ordinary law or statute is usually introduced in the form of a bill. Indeed, about half of the state constitutions specifically provide that no law shall be enacted except by bill.[21] Legislative resolutions are of three kinds—simple, concurrent, and joint. A simple resolution may be adopted by either chamber of the legislature and is known as a "house" or "senate" resolution, as the case may be. Such a resolution relates to some matter within the competence of the house concerned and requires no action by the other chamber or the governor. It may be used, for example, to establish a house or senate investigating committee. As regards concurrent and joint resolutions, practice varies widely among the states as to the difference between these forms of action and the purposes for which they are employed. Each form requires action by both houses. In most states resolutions in neither form are presented to the governor for his approval or disapproval. However, some twenty states require that joint resolutions other than those concerning adjournment be submitted to the governor; and in several states certain concurrent resolutions are subject to the same requirement. Concurrent and joint resolutions are used for such purposes as proposing amendments to the state constitution, ratifying amendments to the United States Constitution, establishing joint investigating committees, and memorializing Congress.[22]

---

[21] Robert Luce, *Legislative Procedure*, 557.

[22] Cf. Harvey Walker, *Law Making in the United States*, 317-318; Luce, *Legislative Procedure*, 553-558; Robert E. Moore, "Legislative Resolutions: Their Function and Effect," *Tex. Law Rev.*, XXXI, 417-429 (Apr., 1953).

Steps in the Legislative Process

Having considered the powers of the state legislature and noted the forms of action through which those powers are exercised, we now turn to a consideration of the procedure followed by the legislature in the performance of its lawmaking function. In formulating public policy and expressing that policy in law, most of the legislature's time is devoted to the introduction, consideration, and approval or rejection of legislative proposals in the form of bills. What, then, are the steps in the process by which a bill becomes a law?

Although the different steps vary somewhat in nature and order as among the states, the general pattern of legislative procedure is much the same wherever the bicameral system prevails. The usual steps in the process by which a bill becomes a law are substantially as follows: (1) introduction and first reading; (2) reference to committee; (3) committee consideration and report; (4) second reading; (5) engrossment and third reading; (6) transmission to other house, where substantially the same steps are repeated; (7) conference committee, when necessary, to adjust differences between the two chambers; (8) enrollment and presentation to the governor; and (9) signature by the governor, or veto and repassage over veto by the required legislative majority.[23]

A bill may be introduced in either house by any member or committee thereof, except that in several states revenue bills must originate in the lower house.[24] A member desiring to introduce a bill takes it, or sends it by page, to the reading clerk, who reads the bill's title, this constituting "first reading" of the bill. The bill is then referred by the pre-

[23] On state legislative procedure in general, see H. W. Dodds, *Procedure in State Legislatures;* Council of State Governments, *American Legislatures: Structures and Procedures.* There are several studies of procedures and processes in individual states. As examples, see Frederic H. Guild, *Legislative Procedure in Kansas* (Govtl. Research Center, Univ. of Kan., Lawrence, rev. 1956); George A. Bell and Jean E. Spencer, *The Legislative Process in Maryland* (Bur. of Govtl. Research, Univ. of Md., College Park, 2nd ed., 1963); Cecil H. Underwood, *The Legislative Process in West Virginia* (Bur. for Govtl. Research, Univ. of West Va., 1953); Donald H. Webster and others, *The Legislature and the Legislative Process in the State of Washington* (Bur. of Govtl. Research and Services, Univ. of Wash., Seattle, rev. 1960); Perry Sentell, Jr., *Handbook for Georgia Legislators* (Inst. of Law and Govt., Univ. of Ga., Athens, 2nd ed., 1960); Gilbert Y. Steiner and Samuel K. Gove, *Legislative Politics in Illinois.* The latter study emphasizes the informal aspects of the legislative process. In addition, legislative agencies in individual states have prepared manuals or handbooks on legislative procedures. As examples, see Illinois Legislative Council, *Lawmaking in the Illinois General Assembly* (Ill. Legis. Council, Springfield, 1960); Louisiana Legislative Council, *A Manual for Louisiana Legislators* (La. Legis. Council, Baton Rouge, rev. 1955); Arthur A. Ohnimus, *The Legislature of California* (Calif. Legis. Assembly, Sacramento, 1959).

[24] Georgia requires that appropriation bills, as well as those for raising revenue, originate in the lower chamber.

siding officer[25] to the appropriate standing committee, which considers the measure and reports its recommendations.[26] Second reading, the next step in the process, is the point at which, in most states, the bill is read in full with opportunity for debate and amendment.[27] Engrossment, which follows second reading, consists in making a new, typed copy of the bill, as amended, before sending it on to third reading. Third reading, like first, is usually by title only, and is followed by a formal vote on the question "Shall the bill pass?" Most state constitutions require that this final vote be taken in each house by roll call and that the "yeas and nays" of the individual members be entered upon the journal.[28] The fact that roll calls normally consume many hours of time during a legislative session has led some states to install electrical voting devices whereby a roll call vote can be recorded in less than a minute. Indeed, by 1962 thirty states employed such devices in one or both legislative chambers.[29] It is usual to require, for final passage of a bill, a favorable vote of a majority of all the *members* of each house—not merely a majority of those present and voting.

After being passed by the house in which it originated, a bill goes through substantially the same procedure in the other chamber. If the second house makes important changes, a conference committee may be appointed to work out an agreement which, it is hoped, will be acceptable to both houses.[30] When the bill has finally passed both houses in the same form, it is "enrolled" for presentation to the governor. Enrollment consists in writing or printing the bill in full, in its final form, upon official paper. At the end of the enrolled bill spaces are provided for the signatures of the speaker of the house and the president of the senate (which officers must certify that the bill was properly passed by their respective houses) as well as that of the governor. The various courses of action which the governor may take upon bills presented for his signature are considered in the following chapter in connection with the veto power.

Of the several steps in the legislative process, those likely to prove most vital in determining the course and contents of legislation are: (1) that reading (usually second) in each house which is in full and accom-

[25] In the Ohio house of representatives bills are referred to standing committees by a "reference committee." Concerning the work of this committee, see Roscoe Baker, "The Reference Committee of the Ohio House of Representatives," *Amer. Polit. Sci. Rev.*, XXXIV, 306-310 (Apr., 1940). In the Illinois senate, bills are first referred to a "committee on assignment of bills."

[26] See below, "Committee Stage."

[27] See below, "The Three Readings."

[28] Other votes are usually taken *viva voce*, unless a rising or roll-call vote is demanded as provided by the rules of the house concerned.

[29] Cf. Herbert L. Wiltsee, "Structure and Procedures" [of State Legislatures], *The Book of the States*, 1962-63, pp. 33-39.

[30] See below, "The Conference Committee."

panied by debate; (2) committee stage in the respective houses; and (3) the conference committee. These steps, which will now be considered in turn, may be looked upon as "obstacles" which a bill must clear to become law. Of course, gubernatorial action, as discussed later, may also be crucial.

The Three Readings. Practically every state requires, usually by constitutional provision and otherwise by rules of the chambers, that every bill be read in each house three times, on as many different days, before passage. Though this rule may ordinarily be suspended by two-thirds vote of the house concerned, several states provide that reading by sections on final passage shall in no case be dispensed with. The reading requirement dates back to a time when bills were not printed for the information of members—indeed to a time when many members could not read—and was designed to provide reasonable assurance that legislators would be correctly advised as to the contents of measures before voting upon them. Nowadays, however, it is common practice, required in some states by constitutional provision, to print all bills at some point prior to final passage. An appropriate provision for printing makes it possible for members to inform themselves of the contents of pending measures, and would seem to obviate any necessity for a requirement of reading in full.[31] Where the requirement of reading in full or by sections is retained, it is widely ignored or circumvented. Indeed, this is almost necessarily so since, in view of the bulk of present-day legislation, it would be practically impossible for the legislature, within the time at its disposal, to give full reading to every measure introduced, or even to all those which ultimately become law. In those states having constitutional provisions requiring reading by sections, various means have been devised for the purpose of saving time. In Kansas, for example, it is common practice to comply with the constitutional requirement by reading each section number and the first few lines of the section, then skipping the remainder down to the beginning of the next section. Since any one member may object to this proceeding and demand complete reading, there is no real danger in the practice.[32] Nevertheless, such proceedings are little short of ludicrous in view of the adequate provision made in that state for the printing of bills, and of the further fact that, when bills *are* read individually and in full by sections, the reading is generally ignored by members. A visitor to the legislature on such an occasion will note that, as the reading clerk drones on in monotonous tones, some members gather in groups for conference or visiting, others sit nonchalantly at their desks reading newspapers, while

---

[31] The Model State Constitution (6th ed., art. IV, sec. 4.15) requires that bills be "printed and upon the desks of the members in final form at least three days prior to final passage."

[32] Guild, *Legislative Procedure in Kansas*, 33.

few if any pay the slightest attention to the reading of the bill. This general inattention is not necessarily to be deprecated, since long before the formal reading takes place most members have informed themselves as fully as they wish concerning the bill's subject matter and have decided how their votes will be cast.

From what has been said it will be clear that usually two, and sometimes all three, of the official "readings" which a bill must undergo in the course of its journey through each house are in practice little if anything more than perfunctory readings of the bill's title. It should also be clear that this *must* be so if the legislature is to have time for the performance of its essential work. But it should not be supposed that all of the bills which become law are enacted without being subjected at any point in the legislative process to a full, careful, and deliberate reading accompanied by opportunity for discussion and debate. Just as it seems clearly unwise to require by constitutional provision that *every* bill be read in full before enactment,[33] so it is necessary, if the legislative process is to function properly, to provide for such reading when circumstances justify. In practice many bills, particularly important measures of a controversial nature, *are* read in full at some stage of legislative procedure. Except in states with constitutional stipulation that third reading shall be in full, the complete reading, which is normally accompanied by opportunity for debate and amendment, usually occurs on second reading. In some states the full reading of bills takes place in "committee of the whole" rather than in regular house or senate sessions. Although composed of the entire membership of the chamber concerned, the committee of the whole differs from a regular session of house or senate in that the regular presiding officer relinquishes the chair to a "chairman of the committee of the whole," and the ordinary rules of procedure are relaxed so as to encourage general debate and expedite action. Any action taken upon a measure in committee of the whole must, like the action of any other committee, be reported to the house or senate for formal approval.

At whatever point in the legislative process it may occur, the full reading of bills is an extremely important step in that process. Here opportunity is provided for the entire membership of the chamber to debate the merits and demerits of a proposed measure and to offer amendments. Where second reading is in full, third reading is usually by title only, with no opportunity for debate and amendment. The vote which follows second reading then becomes vitally important in determining whether the proposed measure is ultimately to pass the house. This vote is commonly

[33] House Bill No. 24 in the 1961 regular session of the Illinois general assembly, as finally enacted and published in the session laws, covers 763 *printed* pages. The person would be bold indeed who would assert that this measure, which codified the statutes of the state relating to cities and villages, should have been read in full in each house before passage.

on the question "Shall the bill be engrossed and read a third time?" An adverse vote on the question, unless reconsidered, kills the bill. On the other hand, a favorable vote at this point gives reasonable assurance of final passage in the chamber concerned.[34]

Committee Stage. Each bill, soon after its introduction, is normally referred to a standing committee for consideration.[35] After a bill has been considered in one or more meetings of the committee, it is reported back to the house concerned unless, as frequently happens, the committee chooses to kill the measure by failing to report it. A committee report usually makes one of four recommendations: (1) that the bill be passed in its original form; (2) that the bill be amended in specified respects and passed in such amended form; (3) that another bill, drafted by the committee, be substituted for the original bill and passed; or (4) that the bill be not passed. The last of these recommendations is uncommon in most states, where, according to general practice, a bill which is opposed by committee is killed, not by reporting it adversely, but by failing to report it at all. Any recommendation made by a committee must, of course, be approved by vote of the chamber to be effective. In most states, however, since the majority party in the chamber ordinarily controls a majority of the members of each committee, rejection of committee recommendations tends to be unusual.[36]

Although committee stage in the legislative process varies in importance from state to state, overall it is one of the significant steps. It is in committee that a bill is considered in detail by a relatively small group of legislators who tend to acquire some degree of expertness in the subject matter with which that committee deals; and it is before the committees that interested citizens and groups are normally afforded an opportunity to present their views relative to pending legislation. Any person desiring it will usually, upon request, be accorded a hearing before a committee. On important measures it is common practice for committees to hold public hearings at which all persons and groups wishing to do so may present their views in person or through counsel. Committee stage is further significant because, for reasons already noted, amendments which are approved in committee are likely to be adopted by the house concerned; and committees are thus influential in determining the final form of legis-

[34] Bills may, of course, be voted down upon third reading even where this order of procedure prevails, but such action is unusual. Illinois is exceptional in this respect. In that state many bills are defeated on a third-reading roll-call vote.

[35] This step *may*, by vote of the house in which a measure is pending, be omitted and the bill advanced to its next reading without reference to committee. Such procedure, however, is not the usual practice.

[36] A recent study in Illinois found this not to be the case in that state. See Steiner and Gove, *op. cit.*, Chap. 3. Jewell also questions the widespread notion of the importance of state legislative committees. Malcolm E. Jewell, *The State Legislature: Politics and Practice,* 93-103.

lation. Finally, committee stage is important in some states because of the fact that committees virtually possess the power of life and death over measures referred to them.

Except in those states which require that all bills be reported, it is usual for committees to kill a substantial portion of the measures received by failing to report them back to the chamber—"pigeonholing," as the practice is commonly called.[37] It is apparently not unusual for as many as a third, or even half, of all bills introduced to meet this fate.[38] Any committee is likely to pigeonhole numerous bills because committee members feel that the subject matter is frivolous to unwise, or perhaps for political reasons. In addition, there is sometimes found in a legislative chamber a carefully selected committee whose specific duty, as generally understood by the legislators, is that of pigeonholing and thereby killing every measure referred to it. This committee is usually dignified in the rules by an innocent and general title which will permit the reference to it of bills on any subject, but may be known familiarly to house members by some such significant name as "graveyard committee," "morgue," or "pickling vat."[39]

The Conference Committee. When a bill passed by one house is amended by the other, it is then returned to the first chamber for further action. The first house may, of course, accept the amendments made by the second, in which case the bill is ready for enrollment and presentation to the governor. It not infrequently happens, however, that the first house refuses to concur in the amendments and requests the appointment of a conference committee for the purpose of adjusting the difference between the houses.[40] In that event, the presiding officers of the respective houses appoint a designated number of "conferees" [41] to serve as members of the conference committee. A separate conference committee is appointed for each bill "sent to conference." In selecting conferees, the presiding officers ordinarily have rather broad discretion, but as a rule choose members who have special knowledge of, or are particularly interested in, the bill concerned. Frequently the chairman of the house and senate committees which have already considered the measure, and sometimes the bill's author, are included. Sometimes, of course, members are chosen for political reasons. It is the purpose of the conference committee to discuss

[37] For a discussion of rules in various states which are designed to curb this practice in one way or another, see Luce, *Legislative Procedure*, 159 ff.

[38] Cf. Dodds, *op. cit.*, 57.

[39] See Luce, *Legislative Procedure*, 167; Walker, *Law Making in the United States*, 207.

[40] The conference committee is less extensively used in state legislatures than in Congress (see Dodds, *op. cit.*, 51; Chamberlain, *op. cit.*, 252-253), but nevertheless is an important agency in some states.

[41] The number is often three from each house, but varies from state to state. Although the two houses are usually equally represented, this is not always the case.

the points of difference between the two houses and, if possible, reach an agreement which will be acceptable to both chambers. The rules of many states limit the conference committee to consideration of matters upon which the houses are in disagreement, although some states permit the making of any change which seems desirable, even to the inclusion of new subject matter.[42] Regardless of what the rules may provide, it is usually possible in practice for the conference committee to go a long way in the direction of rewriting the bill.

When the conference committee reaches an agreement, reports are made to the houses by their respective conferees. As a general rule, reports of conference committees are debatable but not amendable. Both houses, therefore, must accept the recommendations of the conference committee without change if they are to become effective, and in practice conference committee reports are usually accepted by the houses. Rejection of a conference report by either or both houses normally kills the measure. Occasionally, however, a second and even a third conference committee will be appointed in an effort to reach an acceptable agreement.

The conference-committee system has been criticized a good deal by students of legislative procedure. As previously pointed out,[43] the evils of the device have served as one of the strongest arguments for unicameralism. It is said that, since the chambers usually approve whatever the conference committee recommends, too much power rests in the hands of a small group of legislators. Emphasis is placed also upon the fact that the deliberations of the conference committee are not public. It is pointed out that the committee oftentimes does its work so near the end of the session that the chambers have little alternative but to accept whatever recommendations it may make. This fact, coupled with the smallness of the group, makes the conference committee a favorite point of attack by lobbyists. But, for all its weaknesses, the conference committee seems to be a necessity under the bicameral system. As long as there are two houses there will be disagreements between those houses, and some method of resolving such differences must be provided.

Influence of the Rules Committee

What has been said regarding the successive steps in the passage of a bill applies, of course, to the regular, *normal* procedure as prescribed by constitutional provisions and the rules of the respective houses. It should be noted, however, that insofar as procedure is prescribed by rule and not by the constitution, it is subject to variation at the will of the re-

---

[42] Austin F. Macdonald, *American State Government and Administration* (Crowell, New York, 6th ed., 1960), 143-144.
[43] Above, Chap. VII, "Relative Merits of Bicameralism and Unicameralism."

spective chambers. In practice, variations from normal procedure are frequent, particularly for the purpose of advancing more rapidly measures which the majority wishes to push to final enactment. This may be accomplished either by suspending the regular rules for a particular purpose or by adopting a special rule for an individual case. Since suspension ordinarily requires a two-thirds vote whereas a special rule may be adopted by a simple majority, the latter practice often affords the more practicable means of attaining the desired end.

In making variations from the usual order of procedure, the house or senate usually looks for leadership to its committee on rules. This committee, which like other standing committees is controlled by the majority party, is accorded a highly privileged status. It may meet even when the house or senate is in session; report to the chamber at any time, even if that involves the interruption of other business; and secure immediate action upon its recommendations. Suppose, for example, that a particular bill is reported favorably by a standing committee. Under normal procedure the bill is then placed on the calendar[44] at the foot of the list of bills awaiting second reading. Now if the majority leaders wish to expedite action on this measure, instead of waiting for days or weeks until the bill would be reached in the regular course of events, they advise the chairman of the rules committee of their desire for prompt action. The chairman thereupon calls a meeting of the committee, at which a special rule is prepared advancing the designated bill from the foot of the calendar to the top. The special rule is then reported to the chamber and adopted, whereupon the bill in question may be given second reading at once.

It will thus be seen that the rules committee may be much more important than the regular rules in determining the fate of a particular bill. The role of the committee becomes increasingly important near the end of the legislative session when calendars are crowded. At that time, only favorable action by the rules committee may be effective in saving proposed legislation which would otherwise be lost because it was not reached for consideration before the session's end. It is little wonder that membership on the rules committee is a coveted position, normally reserved for the seasoned legislator who has served his party well. Here again, however, state-by-state practices vary greatly. The rules committees in some states are primarily concerned with developing the standing rules at each session and do not play a role in determining the flow of legislation.

[44] A legislative calendar consists of lists of bills awaiting various stages of legislative action. Additions to any list are normally made at the foot of the list, and it is expected that business will be disposed of in regular order, working from the top downward, unless particular measures are advanced by special rule. In Illinois bills are listed in numerical order but there is no assurance that they will be considered in that order.

The Legislative Product

The number of laws enacted by state legislatures in the United States is little short of astounding. A regular legislative session in a typical state will see the introduction of hundreds—frequently thousands—of bills. In the 1960-61 legislative session, for example, more than 110,000 bills were introduced. In approximately half of the states the total number of bills introduced in the two houses was more than 1,000; and in New York, for the two regular sessions, it exceeded 17,000.[45] This multiplicity of proposals is attributable in part to the wide variety of problems which confront state legislatures for solution; but also in some measure, no doubt, to a feeling on the part of many legislators that their activity in sponsoring bills will be taken as an indication of their value to constituents. Although, on the average, only about a third of all bills introduced actually become law, the number of new laws enacted is large. In 1960-61, from the more than 110,000 bills introduced something like 36,000 new enactments, concerning almost every conceivable subject, were placed upon the statute books of the various states.[46] A count of introductions and enactments alone does not, of course, afford a complete picture of the legislative output since some bills have a far-reaching effect while others are of minor importance. Yet a count in itself is of some significance as an indication of the vast amount of grist that is being fed into the legislative mills.[47]

Although the total amount of legislation is enormous, the situation as it affects the individual citizen is actually much less formidable than it appears at first glance. In the first place, the citizen is, for the most part, affected only by the statutes enacted in his own state, having at most but a cursory interest in legislation of the forty-nine other commonwealths. In the second place, there are many enactments in his own state, such as those making minor amendments to earlier laws or effecting changes in the details of governmental organization, which are of little direct and vital concern to the average individual. The number of enactments in which citizens generally have a direct and substantial interest—such, for example, as those making important changes in the laws relating to taxation or elections—is surprisingly small. Consequently, though it would be quite impossible for the average citizen to "know the law" in the sense of being familiar with all state statutes and keeping abreast of detailed changes therein, it is entirely possible for him to keep informed on those major matters of legislation of which knowledge is likely to be useful to him.

---

[45] *The Book of the States,* 1962-63, pp. 56-57.
[46] Cf. *Ibid.*
[47] For a discussion of the number of enactments, but more important, the contents of the new laws, see Institute of Public Affairs, *The Fifty-seventh Texas Legislature: A Review of its Work* (Univ. of Tex., Austin, 1962).

At the close of a legislative session all of the acts passed in that session are usually brought together and published in a printed volume known as the state "session laws." For a regular session this volume is likely to run to several hundred pages, and not infrequently it exceeds a thousand.[48] It contains all acts and resolutions whether new or amendatory and whether of permanent or temporary effect. For each state there is also published, at more or less regular intervals, what is variously known as the "revised statutes," "compiled statutes," "consolidated statutes," or "code of laws" of the state. The revised statutes, to use what is probably the most common name, may be in one or several volumes. They are published in some states officially and in others by private publishers of law books. In either case they contain, under a topical arrangement, all the general laws of the state in effect as of the date of publication. In each successive edition new statutes are added and amendments taken into account, while laws which have expired or been repealed since the last preceding edition are omitted. For the purpose of ascertaining the law upon any particular subject, the revised statutes are normally more useful than the session laws. However, with respect to matters upon which the legislature has acted since the latest edition of the revised statutes was published, recourse must be had to the session laws for pertinent statutes or amendments of more recent date.

Sources of Legislation

It would be a grave error to assume that all measures enacted into law by state legislatures have their actual origin with the legislators themselves. To be sure, every bill must be formally introduced by a member of the legislative body. But, as a matter of fact, many—indeed, apparently, most—of the bills which become law, as well as of those introduced, have their actual origin outside the legislature and are introduced by members at the request of interested persons or organizations. In a study of the 1929 session of the Ohio senate,[49] Professor Harvey Walker found that, of the 267 bills introduced, only 70, or 26 percent of the total number, had their origin within the legislature. Of these, 38 originated with senate or joint committees, leaving only 32 which had their origin in the minds of individual senators. Of the 197 bills (74 percent of all introduced) originating outside the legislature, 78 originated with state and local administrative offices, 20 with individual constitutents, and 99 with citizen organizations. It will therefore be seen that approximately three-fourths of

[48] Occasionally the session laws comprise more than a single volume. This may be due merely to the bulk of the enactments, or, in a few of the states which still permit special legislation, to the fact that "public acts" and "special and private acts" are published separately.

[49] Harvey Walker, "Where Does Legislation Originate?" *Nat. Mun. Rev.*, XVIII, 565-567 (Sept., 1929).

all bills introduced had their actual origin outside the legislative chamber —principally with administrative officials or lobbies of one kind or another. Of further significance is the fact that a higher percentage of the measures originating outside the legislature actually became law than was true of those originating within the legislature.[50] Similar surveys made by Professor Walker, based on the 1939 session in both houses of the Ohio legislature, confirmed, in general, his findings in the earlier study.[51] Particularly noteworthy has been the strong and growing influence of public administrative agencies in the shaping of legislative policy. Thus, a study of the sources of New York state legislation revealed that more than half of the statutes enacted in 1941 had been proposed and sponsored by state and local administrative officers and agencies, and more than a fourth of them by the state departments.[52]

Massachusetts operates an unusual system whereby citizens may, in effect, introduce legislative proposals before the General Court, as the legislature is called in that state, by filing petitions through their senators or representatives.[53] The importance of private individuals and organizations as a source of legislation in that state is attested by the results of an analysis of the 1961 legislative session.[54] Of the 3,227 petitions, reports, and messages filed with the General Court, 1,041, though officially filed by legislators, originated with private citizens or organizations. Of the 755 proposals which emerged as enactments, 33 percent originated from private sources as compared with 40.2 percent from legislators, the remaining enactments originating with the governor, administrative departments and agencies, and combinations of legislators and private individuals or organizations. In evaluation of the Massachusetts system it has been said: "Private petition is plainly an important direct, and probably an equally important indirect, source of legislation. It has served to bring to the lawmaking process both practical legislative proposals and fresh ideas. And it is equally clearly a method, valued and used by the citizens, through which the legislative instrument is operated."[55]

[50] Actually reaching the statute books were 8 percent of the bills originating with individual senators and legislative committees, 49 percent of those originating with administrative offices, and 24 percent of those originating with individual constituents and citizen organizations.

[51] Harvey Walker, "Well Springs of Our Laws," *Nat. Mun. Rev.*, XXVIII, 689-693 (Oct., 1939); Walker, "Who Writes the Laws?" *loc. cit.*

[52] Elisabeth McK. Scott and Belle Zeller, "State Agencies and Lawmaking," *Pub. Admin. Rev.*, II, 205-220 (Summer, 1942).

[53] John E. Powers, "Organization and Procedures of the General Court," in Robert R. Robbins, ed., *State Government and Public Responsibility 1962: The Role of the General Court in Massachusetts* (Lincoln Filene Center for Citizenship and Pub. Affairs, Tufts Univ., Medford, Mass., 1962), 8-20, 12.

[54] Mary B. Newman, "The General Court: An Instrument of the People of Massachusetts," in Robbins, ed., *op. cit.*, 21-60.

[55] *Ibid.*, 44.

The Lobby and Its Regulation[56]

The fact that many laws have their origin outside the legislative chambers brings to attention the practice which is commonly known as "lobbying." In a broad sense, lobbying includes any and all practices by which persons who are not members of the legislature seek to influence members with respect to their attitude toward legislative proposals. In a narrower and more common sense, the term is confined to the activities of those persons[57] who, for hire or otherwise, represent the interests of organized groups before legislative bodies. Lobbying takes its name from the supposition that its practice involves "buttonholing" legislators in the lobbies or corridors of the legislative halls for the purpose of conferring with them and seeking their support. Nowadays, however, this form of lobbying is much less effective than others, such as appearing before committees, circulating literature, and holding conferences in places less public than statehouse corridors. The purpose of the lobbyist may, of course, be either to secure the passage of legislation favorable to the organization which he represents or to bring about the defeat of measures deemed inimical to the interests of that organization.

The number of organizations represented at state capitals by lobbyists is legion. Dr. Dayton McKean, in a study of lobbying in New Jersey, lists 164 statewide organizations or groups appearing before the legislature of that state, to say nothing of numerous local groups and interests. These organizations may be said, in general, to represent eleven interest groups: business, labor, agriculture, the professions, religious groups, public employees, veterans, women, motorists, education, and reform groups. To mention but a single example from each division of this classification, the organizations include the New Jersey State Chamber of Commerce, New Jersey State Federation of Labor, New Jersey Farm Bureau, New Jersey State Bar Association, Catholic Daughters of America, New Jersey State Firemen's Association, American Legion, New Jersey State League of Women Voters, New Jersey Automobile and Motor Club, New Jersey Congress of Parents and Teachers, and Good Government Council.[58] So varied are the lobbying organizations in the states that almost any bill of major importance is likely to find lobbyists arrayed both for and against it. A bill to establish minimum wages for schoolteachers may be fostered by teacher organizations and opposed by "economy leagues" or taxpayers'

[56] On the subject generally, see Edward B. Logan, *Lobbying;* Belle Zeller, ed., *American State Legislatures,* 214-239. For studies relating to individual states, see Belle Zeller, *Pressure Politics in New York;* Dayton David McKean, *Pressures on the Legislature of New Jersey.*

[57] Lobbyists themselves usually prefer to be called "legislative agents," "legislative counsel," or "legislative representatives." Cf. Logan, *op. cit.,* 1.

[58] McKean, *op. cit.* Chap. 3.

federations. A proposal to consolidate counties may be supported by the "good government league" and opposed by organizations of county officials. A bill to permit cities to adopt manager government may have the support of the League of Women Voters and the opposition of organized labor. Thus it will readily be seen that almost every interest, whether selfish or of lofty purpose, is represented before the legislature.

Contrary to widespread belief, lobbying as such is not to be condemned. Under a popular form of government every interest group is entitled to place its views and wishes before the legislature, and it is largely through the medium of the lobbyist that this right is exercised. As one writer has said, "the honest lobbyist properly and with benefit to the public plays the part in the legislature that counsel plays in the court." [59] It is only when the lobbyist resorts to dishonest or disreputable means of gaining his ends that lobbying becomes reprehensible. Such means may be anything from outright bribery to a mere misleading of legislators to believe that the lobbyist is a disinterested and impartial champion of the public welfare. While interest groups are entitled to maintain lobbies, legislative members are equally entitled to know who the lobbyists are and what interests they represent, and to be assured, as far as possible, that the lobbyists will employ only legitimate means of influence.

In an effort to bring lobbying into the open and to curb pernicious practices, more than half of the states have enacted laws regulating lobbyists and their activities.[60] Most of these statutes impose one or more of three types of regulatory provision: (1) requiring the lobbyist or his employer, or both, to register with some state agency, frequently the secretary of state; (2) requiring the lobbyist or his employer, or both, to file at the close of each session verified accounts of their expenditures for legislative purposes; and (3) prohibiting the employment of lobbyists under agreements which make their compensation contingent upon the success of their efforts.[61]

The number of lobbyists registered under the regulatory laws varies from state to state, in part because of differences in registration requirements. Under a new Texas law, 4,534 lobbyists registered in 1959, while in Wisconsin 284 lobbyists registered representing 413 employers. The Texas lobbyists, according to expense statements filed as required by the statute, spent $122,034; while the Wisconsin lobbyists, it has been estimated, spent $400,000. In 1960 the 301 lobbyists registered in Massachusetts reported spending $317,232; in New York 167 lobbyist expense statements totalled

---

[59] Abbot Low Moffat, "The Legislative Process," *Cornell Law Quar.*, XXIV, 223-233, 229 (Feb., 1939).

[60] Belle Zeller, "The State Lobby Laws," *The Book of the States*, 1962-63, pp. 80-86. Professor Zeller's article includes a tabular analysis of the provisions of the regulatory statutes in the various states.

[61] Cf. Walker, *Law Making in the United States*, 294-295; Logan, *op. cit.*, 66-71.

$369,497; and in Alaska, 71 registered lobbyists declared expenditures of $88,302.[62] In the 1961 Illinois session 485 lobbyists were registered—more than twice the number of legislators.[63]

Though the results of the regulatory laws as administered in the various states have not been altogether satisfactory, it would appear that statutes of this nature, if properly enforced, should effect considerable improvement in the general tone of lobbying practices.

The Problem of Technical Assistance: The Legislative Reference Bureau[64]

It was pointed out in the preceding chapter that state legislators are not, and should not be, a group of legislative experts. Yet the process of legislation at certain points requires the use of scientific knowledge and skill; and, in order to provide the members of the legislature with appropriate expert assistance, most states have established some sort of "legislative reference bureau." [65] This bureau is operated in some states as a division of the state library, and in others is under a special governing board.[66] The bureau is usually in the charge of a director, executive secretary, or librarian, who in turn is provided with a staff of trained assistants. Whatever the form of its organization, the legislative reference bureau is usually charged with two principal functions: (1) providing a library of statute law and materials relating to legislative problems, and assisting legislators in its use; and (2) drafting bills for introduction into the respective houses.[67]

The maintenance of a reference library is the older and more uni-

[62] Zeller, "The State Lobby Laws," loc. cit.

[63] Samuel K. Gove, "The Business of the Legislature," Univ. of Ill. Law Forum, Vol. 1963, pp. 52-71 (Spring, 1963).

[64] For a discussion of technical assistance generally, see Edward F. Staniford, Legislative Assistance (Bur. of Pub. Admin., Univ. of Calif., Berkeley, 1957). The most comprehensive work on legislative reference bureaus is J. H. Leek, Legislative Reference Work: A Comparative Study. A briefer but more recent account will be found in Council of State Governments, Legislative Reference Bureaus and Libraries. Although a reference bureau was established in the New York state library as early as 1890, the Wisconsin reference department, created in 1901, is generally regarded as the pioneer in modern legislative reference work. On the early development of the work in Wisconsin, see Charles McCarthy, The Wisconsin Idea (Macmillan, New York, 1912).

[65] Though rather commonly entitled a "bureau," the reference agency in a number of states is designated variously as a "department," "division," "section," "service," "library," or "office." A list of the services in the respective states, indicating their organization and duties, will be found in The Book of the States, 1964-65, pp. 74-83.

[66] The governing board in Illinois consists of the governor and the chairmen of the judiciary and appropriations committees of the house and senate.

[67] A third function in several states is that of preparing periodic revisions of the state statutes. In some states bill-drafting is a function of the attorney general's office rather than of the legislative reference bureau.

versal function of the reference bureau, and is designed to make it possible for members of the legislature to secure adequate and reliable information concerning legislative matters in which they may be interested or upon which they may be called to vote. More spectacular, however, is the function of bill-drafting, a task which the average legislator is quite unprepared to perform for himself. "The framing of a statute," says an eminent authority on legislation, "is among the most difficult tasks that confront the intellect. . . . The task calls for mastery of language, lucidity of style, familiarity with technical significances, command of both constitutional and statutory law, logical capacity, unusual powers of foresight, and a knowledge of the field concerned that cannot be too extensive." [68] To perform for legislators this highly technical task of stating clearly and concisely in legal language the idea which it is desired to enact into law, the typical reference bureau is equipped with a staff of professional bill-drafters. Oftentimes these persons have been trained in the law before specializing in legislative drafting. When an individual legislator desires to introduce a bill on any subject, he may go to the reference bureau and explain to the director or an assistant the purpose which he wishes to accomplish by the proposed legislation. A member of the drafting staff is thereupon assigned the task of drafting the bill which, when completed, is delivered to the legislator for introduction into the chamber of which he is a member. Members of the bureau staff are frequently able to serve legislators in various ways in addition to the actual work of drafting. They may help legislative members to clarify their ideas, show them how their proposals might be correlated with other legislation, existing or proposed, and advise as to the probable constitutionality of proposed measures. Legislators, of course, are under no compulsion to use the official bill-drafting service; and measures are still introduced, more frequently in some states than in others, which have been drawn by legislators themselves, by private lawyers at the request of legislators, or by lobbyists. But the tendency to make use of the drafting agency is strong. In some states, indeed, it is not unusual in a given session to have more than 90 percent of all bills introduced drafted by the staff of the legislative reference bureau.[69]

The Problem of Leadership

If the legislature is to function most effectively as a lawmaking body, it must be provided with some form of responsible leadership. Somewhere responsibility must be lodged for planning a tentative legislative program in advance of legislative sessions and for sponsoring that program in the legislative chambers. This is not to say that the legislature should become a rubber-stamp agency, approving as a matter of course

[68] Robert Luce, *Legislative Procedure* (Houghton, Boston, 1922), 566.
[69] Cf. Walker, *Law Making in the United States*, 224.

whatever program may be presented to it. But it is to say that thinking and planning should be done in anticipation of legislative sessions; that a tentative program, based upon facts rather than guesswork, should be formulated; and that some person or group should be charged with the duty of explaining that program before the legislative body. The legislature itself may then take whatever course of action it deems desirable. Without some such provision for leadership, it is almost inevitable that much of the early part of the session will be devoted to planning which should have been done beforehand; and that the session's end will bring a "last minute rush" in which many measures will be enacted without adequate consideration while others, however meritorious, will be "caught in the jam" and meet their death as unfinished business.

This problem of leadership in the state legislatures has not been satisfactorily solved. To a limited extent, leadership is provided by the party system through the adoption of state platforms and the ability of the majority party, under normal circumstances, to secure the enactment of the measures which it sponsors. But in practice in state legislatures there are relatively few "party measures," in the sense of proposals upon which voting follows fairly straight party lines.[70] Moreover, under the bicameral system, party leadership can mean little if, as sometimes happens, the respective chambers are controlled by different parties. A second source from which some degree of legislative leadership normally flows is the governor. Although the earliest state constitutions placed the governor in a position of subservience to the legislature, the more recent tendency has been to increase the formal powers of the governor with respect to legislation and to look to the executive office more and more for leadership in legislative matters.[71] Naturally, the influence of a particular governor in this direction will depend in no small measure upon the character of his personality and whether or not his party controls the legislative chambers. But at best party leadership is unofficial, and gubernatorial leadership must be exerted from outside the legislative body. A significant recent development in the direction of providing for *official* leadership *within* the legislature is seen in the legislative council movement.[72]

[70] A 1954 survey found that party cohesion was strong in 17 states, moderate in 11, and weak in 20. Zeller, ed., *American State Legislatures*, 190-191. The extent of party voting in various states is reported in Malcolm E. Jewell, "Party Voting in American State Legislatures," *Amer. Polit. Sci. Rev.*, XLIX, 773-791 (Sept., 1955); William J. Keefe, "Comparative Study of the Role of Political Parties in State Legislatures," *Western Polit. Quar.*, IX, 726-742 (Sept., 1956).

[71] The governor's position as a legislative leader is discussed in the following chapter.

[72] A problem affecting the role of leadership is the generally inadequate staff provided for the legislative leaders. In most states, the contrast with the United States Congress is striking. For a description of present staffing patterns, see Council of State Governments, *Professional Assistance for Legislative Standing and Interim Committees and Legislative Leaders* (The Council, Chicago, 1961).

Legislative Councils [73]

A legislative council has been "simply described as a permanent joint committee of the legislature, meeting between regular legislative sessions and giving advance consideration to problems expected to confront the next legislature. Its purpose is to formulate a legislative program for the next session." [74] The first legislative council was established in Kansas in 1933,[75] and by 1964 councils or council-type agencies were in existence in forty-two states.[76] In composition, the council varies from state to state. Its size ranges from five members in South Carolina to twenty-seven in Kansas, except in Nebraska, Oklahoma, Pennsylvania, and South Dakota where all members of the legislature are members of the council. In each of these latter states, however, council activities are actually guided by an executive committee. Though there are a few exceptions, most councils are now composed entirely of legislative members. The trend has been toward eliminating executive officers and private citizens from membership.[77]

Since the Kansas council is oldest and has served to some extent as a prototype for some of those established more recently, its composition and powers may be particularly noted. It consists of ten senators and fifteen representatives appointed by the president of the senate (lieutenant governor) and speaker of the house, subject to approval by majority vote of the respective chambers, with the two presiding officers as additional ex officio members. Representation of the major political parties on the council is to be in proportion to party membership in the respective chambers. The principal duties of the council are: (1) to collect information

[73] The definitive work on legislative councils is William J. Siffin, *The Legislative Council in the American States.* See also Frederic H. Guild, "The Development of the Legislative Council Idea," *Annals of Amer. Acad. of Polit. and Soc. Sci.*, CXCV, 144-150 (Jan., 1938); Roy H. Johnson, "A Review of Legislative Councils," *Univ. of Kansas City Law Rev.*, VIII, 65-72 (Feb., 1940); Charles M. Kneier, "Illinois Legislative Council Completes Its First Year," *Nat. Mun. Rev.*, XXVIII, 640-645 (Sept., 1939); Jack A. Rhodes, "The Legislative Council: A Program for Planning and Research," *Southwestern Soc. Sci. Quar.*, XXVII, 54-61 (June, 1946); Frederic H. Guild, "Legislative Councils: Objectives and Accomplishments," *State Govt.*, XXII, 217-219, 226 (Sept., 1949); Norman Meller, "The Policy Position of Legislative Service Agencies," *Western Polit. Quar.*, V, 109-123 (Mar., 1952); Harold W. Davey, "The Legislative Council Movement in the United States, 1933-1953," *Amer. Polit. Sci. Rev.*, XLVII, 785-797 (Sept., 1953).

[74] Johnson, *op. cit.*, 65.

[75] Michigan also established a council in 1933, but the agency was abolished six years later. A new council was established by the Michigan constitution of 1963.

[76] Though "legislative council" is the most common title for these agencies, several are entitled legislative research commissions and a few are known by still other names. Data concerning the composition and organization of council agencies may be found in *The Book of the States, 1964-65*, pp. 84-85.

[77] Herbert L. Wiltsee, "Legislative Service Agencies," *The Book of the States, 1962-63*, pp. 63-67.

concerning the government and general welfare of the state; (2) to examine the effects of previously-enacted statutes and recommend amendments thereto; (3) to deal with important issues of public policy and questions of statewide interest; and (4) to prepare a legislative program, in the form of bills or otherwise, to be presented at the next session of the legislature. The council is required to meet as often as may be necessary to perform its duties, and in any event at least quarterly. It is required to make periodic reports to all members of the legislature; and its recommendations must be completed and made public at least thirty days prior to the legislative session at which they are to be submitted.

An important adjunct to the council in Kansas and most other council states is a permanent fact-finding agency in the form of a research department directed by a trained researcher and staffed by competent personnel. It is the function of the research department to secure information upon problems submitted to it by the council, and to present its findings in the form of formal reports or otherwise, as the council may direct. Reports of the research department are usually distributed not only to council members but to all members of the legislature. The entire legislative membership is thus supplied, well in advance of a legislative session, with reliable factual data concerning the more important problems which are likely to come before the session for consideration.[78]
rence, 1963).

If, upon the basis of its deliberations and the results of its research activities, the council deems such action wise, it may draft bills for introduction into the respective chambers and recommend these proposals for passage as "council" measures. Indeed, the council idea seems basically to involve the formulation *and recommendation* by the council of a definite legislative program. But there has been some fear that too active support of a definite program by the council may lay that body open to the charge of attempting to set itself up as a "little legislature," thus generating intralegislative friction and jealousy; and this may be the reason why some councils have preferred to limit their activities to discussing legislative problems, conducting research thereon, and laying the results of that research before the legislature without recommendation.[79] In general, however, the experience of the longer-established councils appears to indicate that the fear that the council will become a little legislature and usurp basic legislative functions is largely groundless.[80] Just how far it is

---

[78] For a comprehensive account of the Kansas council covering its first thirty years, see William H. Cape and John Paul Bay, *An Analysis of the Kansas Legislative Council and its Research Department* (Govtl. Research Center, Univ. of Kan., Lawrence, 1963.

[79] Cf. Kneier, *op. cit.* Siffin classifies 21 of the councils existing at the time of his study as recommendation makers and 15 as not. Siffin, *op. cit.*, 123-128.

[80] Guild, "Legislative Councils: Objectives and Accomplishments," *loc. cit.* It has been said that the little-legislature charge is now irrelevant. Wiltsee, "Legislative Service Agencies," *loc. cit.*

practically expedient for a council to go in the active support of a specific program of legislation may well depend, of course, upon political circumstances in the particular state concerned.[81] Even where the council does not attempt to exercise positive leadership through the presentation and support of a definite "council program," its functions in laying the groundwork for legislative discussion and providing reliable facts concerning alternative courses of action seem clearly to justify its existence.

Interim Committees and Commissions

An agency of legislative research and planning which is being used ever more widely, especially in states without legislative councils, is the interim committee or commission established by one session of the legislature with directions to study a designated problem and report to a subsequent session. New York was reported in 1962 as spending some $2 million a year for the research activities of some forty interim legislation committees; California averages half as much for the support of some forty-five to fifty such committees; and use is made of special interim research committees in most of the other noncouncil states.[82] Even in states with legislative councils, interim committees and commissions are created. In Illinois, a state where the council does not make recommendations, twenty-six permanent legislative commissions including the council have been established. During the 1961-63 biennium, fifteen additional interim commissions functioned in that state.[83]

Some interim committees and commissions are composed solely of legislators, while others also include administrative officials or citizen members, or both. Specific topics which have been assigned to various interim committees for investigation and report cover virtually the entire range of governmental organization and operation at the state and local levels. Included in the list are problems of administrative organization and reorganization, legislative procedure, constitutional revision, taxation, educational facilities and financing, state institutions, highways, business and industry, labor, and public health and welfare. The investigatory work of an interim committee is commonly carried on by a research staff employed by the committee to serve under its direction; and in many instances the result is a comprehensive research report accompanied by a

---

[81] Cf. Siffin, op. cit.

[82] Wiltsee, "Legislative Service Agencies," loc. cit. For an indication of the scope of these study groups, see State of New York, Concurrent Resolutions and Laws Creating or Extending Special Joint Legislative Committees and Selected Temporary State Commissions (Secretary of the N.Y. Senate, New York, 1962); California Legislative Analyst, California Interim Legislative Committees and Reports, 1955-57 (Sacramento, 1957).

[83] Illinois Legislative Council, Legislative Commissions, 1961-63 (Ill. Legis. Council, Springfield, 1961).

program of specific committee recommendations for legislative consideration.

Fiscal Services

A recent development among the states is the establishment of permanent legislative fiscal agencies to permit the legislature to play a more important role in developing state fiscal policies. These agencies provide fiscal services for the legislators including budget analysis and review, fiscal analysis, and post-audit. In a few states the post of legislative auditor has been established. Thirty-six states have been said to provide one or more fiscal services for the legislature either through a special agency concerned with such matters or by assigning one or more of these functions to a general service agency, such as a legislative council.[84]

The Task of the Legislator

Having now considered the organization and procedures of state legislatures, it is appropriate to make certain general observations with respect to the task which confronts the individual legislator—he who, with others like him, must actually operate the legislative machine. In final analysis, the lawmaking function, in the sense of formulating and giving expression to public policy, resolves itself into a matter of adjusting and reconciling conflicting interests. From all sides, from persons and groups in all walks of life, the legislature is flooded with requests for new laws and changes in existing statutes. Each interest group solemnly counsels the legislature as to what the public interest—which, naturally, each largely identifies with its own group interest—requires in the way of legislation. Among the various demands for legislative action conflicts inevitably arise —between industry and agriculture, between management and labor, between rural and urban dwellers, and so on. Confronted with these conflicting claims, it is the duty of the legislator to consider carefully all facts and arguments available and then, having reached a conclusion as to what legislation will best serve the public good, to use his influence and vote in an effort to bring about the enactment of that legislation.

The task of the legislator being, then, the adjusting or compromising of conflicting interests, the question naturally arises as to what qualifications best fit an individual to perform the duties of the legislative office. Certainly the average legislator has little need to be an expert in the purely mechanical aspects of lawmaking, for in most states adequate assistance in such matters is now provided through legislative reference services. Nor, since most legislation has its origin outside legislative cham-

[84] Council of State Governments, *Fiscal Services for State Legislatures* (The Council, Chicago, 1961).

bers, must he necessarily be adept at suggesting laws which should be enacted. But the legislator should be a person who is qualified, by temperament and experience, to take a broad view of public questions; to weigh conflicting interests and arguments carefully; and, in arriving at decisions, to place the general good above the good of any individual or group. His task, if it is to be most effectively performed, calls for ability on the part of the legislator to act both as representative and as judge. In the first of these capacities he should be able to present effectively the views of his own constituents, and in the second to weigh judiciously the claims and arguments presented by others. As legislation tends increasingly to originate outside legislative halls, and as varied interests tend more and more to be represented before the legislature by lobbyists, this "judicial" aspect of the legislator's assignment becomes ever more important. And, with this development in the nature of the legislative task, it becomes increasingly essential that we choose as legislators persons who are fitted by judicial temperament to weigh conflicting claims and reach sound conclusions as regards what action the public interest may require.[85]

Legislative Reorganization

In conclusion, it may be pointed out that recent years have witnessed a growing interest, both official and popular, in the improvement of state legislatures. During the 1940's, studies of state legislatures with a view to possible reorganization were made in several states, some by official agencies and others by private organizations, and the recommendations set forth in the reports on those studies covered the entire field of legislative personnel, organization, and procedures.[86] Later, the National Legislative Conference established a Committee on Legislative Processes and Procedures, the report of which, released in 1960, included an eleven-point program for legislative improvement. Specific recommendations of the committee concerned such matters as removing the restrictions upon the length of regular sessions, increasing the pay of legislators, lengthening the legislative term, reducing the number of committees, adequate staffing, and revising procedures with a view to expediting legislative action while at the same time assuring adequate deliberation.[87]

[85] Cf. Walker, "Who Writes the Laws?" *loc. cit.;* Moffat, *op. cit.*

[86] One of the most comprehensive of the reports of an official character is the *Final Report of the New York State Joint Legislative Committee on Legislative Methods, Practices, Procedures and Expenditures* (Legislative Doc. No. 31, Albany, 1946).

[87] See National Legislative Conference, *American State Legislatures in Mid-Twentieth Century.* For further consideration of this subject, see Zeller, ed., *American State Legislatures;* The American Assembly, *The Forty-eight States: Their Tasks as Policy Makers and Administrators* (Columbia Univ., New York, 1955); Jefferson Fordham, *The State Legislative Institution;* John A. Perkins, "State Legislative Reorganiza-

As the result of studies such as these, and of the interest which caused the studies to be undertaken and in turn has been stimulated by them, beginnings in legislative reorganization have been made in several states, some of the steps in this direction having already been noted at earlier points in this chapter and the one preceding. In many instances legislative pay has been increased. Several states have reduced the number of committees in one or both houses. Legislative councils have been established in four-fifths of the states, ever wider use is being made of interim committees and commissions, and serious consideration is being given in various instances to revision of the procedural rules. As aids to new members, several legislatures now hold presession conferences and most provide information booklets or manuals. Presession conferences are designed to familiarize inexperienced members with the physical layout of the capitol building, the reference and bill-drafting services, and the elements of legislative procedure; whereas the informational manuals explain rules of procedure in nontechnical language and provide information concerning reference and research aids and other matters of particular interest to new legislators. If action along these various lines continues and spreads to other states, as it seems likely to do, coming years should find our state legislatures ever better qualified to perform their duties.

REFERENCES

ABERNETHY, Byron R., *Constitutional Limitations on the Legislature* (Govtl. Research Center, Univ. of Kan., Lawrence, 1959).

Advisory Commission on Intergovernmental Relations, *Apportionment of State Legislatures* (U.S. Govt. Printing Office, Washington, 1962).

BAKER, Gordon E., *Rural versus Urban Political Power* (Random, New York, 1955).

——, *State Constitutions: Reapportionment* (Nat. Mun. League, New York, 1960).

BLAIR, George S., *Cumulative Voting: An Effective Electoral Device in Illinois Politics* (Univ. of Ill. Press, Urbana, 1960).

BOYD, William J. D., *Patterns of Apportionment* (Nat. Mun. League, New York, 1962).

BRECKENRIDGE, A. C., *One House for Two: Nebraska's Unicameral Legislature* (Pub. Affairs Press, Washington, 1957).

---

tion," *Amer. Polit. Sci. Rev.*, XL, 510-521 (June, 1946); Lynton K. Caldwell, "Strengthening State Legislatures," *Ibid.*, XLI, 281-289 (Apr., 1947); Lester B. Orfield, "Improving State Legislative Procedure and Processes," *Minn. Law Rev.*, XXXI, 161-189 (Jan., 1947); Richard L. Neuberger, "Toward Restoring States' Rights," *N.Y. Times Mag.*, Oct. 26, 1952, pp. 9, 24, 26-27; Frank E. Horack, Jr., "Can American State Legislatures Keep Pace?" *Rocky Mt. Law Rev.*, XXVI, 468-486 (June, 1954).

Buck, A. E., *Modernizing Our State Legislatures* (Amer. Acad. of Polit. and Soc. Sci., Philadelphia, 1936).

Carroll, Daniel B., *The Unicameral Legislature of Vermont* (Vt. Hist. Soc., Montpelier, 1932).

Chamberlain, Joseph P., *Legislative Processes, National and State* (Appleton-Century-Crofts, New York, 1936).

Colvin, David L., *The Bicameral Principle in the New York Legislature* (Author, New York, 1913).

Council of State Governments, *American Legislatures: Structures and Procedures* (The Council, Chicago, 1959).

———, *Legal Services for State Legislatures* (The Council, Chicago, 1960).

———, *Legislative Reference Bureaus and Library Services* (The Council, Chicago, 1960).

———, *The Offices of Legislative Clerks and Secretaries in the States* (The Council, Chicago, 1957).

David, Paul T., and Eisenberg, Ralph, *Devaluation of the Urban and Suburban Vote* (2 vols., Bur. of Pub. Admin., Univ. of Va., Charlottesville, 1961, 1962).

Dodds, H. W., *Procedure in State Legislatures* (Amer. Acad. of Polit. and Soc. Sci., Philadelphia, 1918).

Fordham, Jefferson B., *The State Legislative Institution* (Univ. of Pa. Press, Philadelphia, 1959).

Griswold, Thelma I., *Bicameralism in Ohio* (Western Reserve Univ. Bookstore, Cleveland, Ohio, 1937).

Jewell, Malcolm E., *The State Legislature: Politics and Practice* (Random, New York, 1962).

———, ed., *The Politics of Reapportionment* (Atherton, New York, 1962).

Lee, Eugene C., *The Presiding Officer and Rules Committee in Legislatures of the United States* (Bur. of Pub. Admin., Univ. of Calif., Berkeley, 1952).

Luce, Robert, *Legislative Assemblies* (Houghton, Boston, 1924).

———, *Legislative Principles* (Houghton, Boston, 1930).

———, *Legislative Problems* (Houghton, Boston, 1935).

———, *Legislative Procedure* (Houghton, Boston, 1922).

McKay, Robert B., *Reapportionment and the Federal Analogy* (Nat. Mun. League, New York, 1962).

McKean, Dayton David, *Pressures on the Legislature of New Jersey* (Columbia Univ. Press, New York, 1938).

National Legislative Conference, *American State Legislatures in Mid-Twentieth Century* (Chicago, 1960).

National Municipal League, *Compendium on Legislative Apportionment* (Nat. Mun. League, New York, 2nd ed., 1962).

Page, Thomas, *Legislative Apportionment in Kansas* (Govtl. Research Center, Univ. of Kan., Lawrence, 1952).

Reed, Alfred Z., *The Territorial Basis of Government under the State Constitutions* (Columbia Univ. Press, New York, 1911), Chaps. 7, 8.

Reinsch, Paul S., *American Legislatures and Legislative Methods* (Century, New York, 1907).

Schaffter, Dorothy, *The Bicameral System in Practice* (State Hist. Soc. of Ia., Iowa City, 1929).

Senning, John P., *The One-House Legislature* (McGraw-Hill, New York, 1937).

SHULL, Charles W., *American Experience with Unicameral Legislatures* (Detroit Bur. of Govtl. Research, Detroit, 1937).

SIFFIN, William J., *The Legislative Council in the American States* (Ind. Univ. Press, Bloomington, 1959).

STEINER, Gilbert Y., and Gove, Samuel K., *Legislative Politics in Illinois* (Univ. of Ill. Press, Urbana, 1960).

WAHLKE, John C., EULAU, Heinz, BUCHANAN, William, and FERGUSON, Leroy C., *The Legislative System: Explorations in Legislative Behavior* (Wiley, New York, 1962).

WALKER, Harvey, *Law Making in the United States* (Ronald, New York, 1934).

————, *The Legislative Process* (Ronald, New York, 1948).

WILLOUGHBY, W. F., *Principles of Legislative Organization and Administration* (Brookings Inst., Washington, 1934).

WINSLOW, C. I., *State Legislative Committees* (Johns Hopkins Press, Baltimore, 1931).

ZELLER, Belle, *Pressure Politics in New York* (Prentice-Hall, Englewood Cliffs, N.J., 1937).

————, ed., *American State Legislatures* (Crowell, New York, 1954). (Report of the Committee on American Legislatures of the American Political Science Association). This study contains an excellent bibliography on state legislatures.

9

The Governor

The Office of Governor

The principal executive officer in each of the fifty states is the governor. Under the earliest state constitutions the governor occupied a relatively weak position. He had little independent appointing power. Many appointments to executive and judicial offices were made by the legislature; and, where appointing power was lodged in the governor, his appointments were usually subject to legislative confirmation. In most of the original states the governor possessed no power of veto over legislative acts; and the fact that he was usually elected by the legislature rather than directly by the people made him largely subservient to the legislative branch.[1] As was suggested in Chapter I, the assignment to the governor of such a secondary role, accompanied by the placing of almost unlimited power in the legislature, was but a natural reaction to unhappy experiences with royal governors during the colonial period.

Further experience was soon to demonstrate, however, that this original division of authority between legislature and state governor was unsatisfactory. Legislatures abused their unbridled power, and governors were in no position to interpose any check upon them. Hence a tendency developed, as new constitutions were framed and older ones amended, to impose restrictions upon legislative authority while increasing correspond-

[1] Of the original states, only Massachusetts and South Carolina gave the governor the veto power, and only in Massachusetts and New York was he popularly elected. Leslie Lipson, *The American Governor: From Figurehead to Leader*, 14.

ingly the powers of the gubernatorial office. Choice of the governor was taken from the legislature and placed directly in the hands of the voters, thus giving the executive a position relatively independent of the legislative will. The governor's appointing powers were increased and he was given the power of veto. Indeed, the history of the gubernatorial office during the past century has been one of constantly increasing power and prestige. To be sure, as we shall see,[2] some states have gone much farther than others in strengthening the governor's position, particularly with respect to his control over administration. But in all states the position of the governor today is much superior to what it was in earlier times. The present-day governor not only is the formal head of the state but is possessed of broad authority with respect to both administration and legislation.[3]

Qualifications, Term, and Compensation

In all but a few states, certain qualifications for the office of governor are prescribed by constitutional provision. These most frequently relate to age, United States citizenship, and length of residence in the state. The minimum-age requirement is commonly thirty years, but in a few instances is twenty-five. In Oklahoma the minimum age is thirty-one, and in Hawaii it is thirty-five. United States citizenship is required of the governor in all states, either specifically or through the requirement that he be a qualified elector. Some states, in addition, specify that he shall have been a citizen for a prescribed length of time, varying from two to twenty years, preceding his election. Most states require a given period of residence within the state preceding election, this requirement ranging from one year to ten with five years most common.

It will readily be seen that the constitutional qualifications are of a purely formal nature, in no way assuring that their possessor will have the ability and experience necessary for success in the office. Indeed, the constitutional requirements are largely superfluous, for rarely would a person not having them be able to secure nomination and election. There have, however, been instances in which persons have been elected to the governorship who did not possess the constitutional qualifications and who for that reason have been barred from assuming office. In 1935, for example, Governor-elect Moodie of North Dakota was held by the state supreme court to be ineligible because he had not, as the constitution re-

---

[2] Below, Chap. X.

[3] The tendency toward strengthening the gubernatorial office is still in evidence. See Leslie Lipson, "The Executive Branch in New State Constitutions," *Pub. Admin. Rev.*, IX, 11-21 (Winter, 1940); William H. Young, "The Development of the Governorship," *State Govt.*, XXXI, 178-183 (Summer, 1958).

quired, been a legal resident of the state for five years immediately preceding his election.[4]

From a practical standpoint, a much more important qualification than those prescribed by the constitution is that of political "availability"—in other words, vote-getting capacity. Ability to secure votes depends upon innumerable factors. A candidate for the governorship should be widely and favorably known throughout the state. His personality should be such as to attract rather than repel voters. He must usually have the support of politically potent organizations. If he is a dynamic speaker and vigorous campaigner, so much the better. Above all, in his past public and private career he must not have offended any group, political or otherwise, which might be able to block his nomination or election. Obviously no one person can possess in the highest degree all attributes of the strong candidate, but the candidate who is to be successful must possess them in some effective combination.

The governor's term of office is four years in thirty-five states and two years in fifteen.[5] There has been a general tendency toward the longer term. The earliest constitutions commonly provided a term of a single year; and the states which now have the four-year term include most of those which have revised their constitutions fairly recently. This tendency seems to be due to a feeling that a minimum of four years is required to enable a governor to become proficient in the exercise of his duties and to demonstrate any powers of leadership that he may have. Furthermore, where the two-year term prevails the incumbent, if he desires to continue in office, must begin to devote attention and effort to his campaign for renomination and reelection when his first term is scarcely well under way. Reelection is quite common in states having the two-year term, but less frequent where the term is four years. Indeed, about half of the states with the four-year term make an incumbent ineligible for a second consecutive term.[6] Provisions prohibiting reelection appear to be founded upon the belief that extended tenure in the gubernatorial office is conducive to the building of a powerful political machine under the governor's domination. In an election contest between an incumbent gover-

[4] State ex rel. Sathre v. Moodie, 65 N.D. 340 (1935). A few months earlier the same court had held that conviction of a federal felony disqualified Governor Langer from continuing in office. The North Dakota constitution requires that the governor be a qualified elector, and the court held that the federal conviction, by disqualifying Mr. Langer as an elector, disqualified him from holding the gubernatorial office. State ex rel. Olson v. Langer, 65 N.D. 68 (1934). An account of these cases, and of the related political background, will be found in Roy L. Miller, "The Gubernatorial Controversy in North Dakota," Amer. Polit. Sci. Rev., XXIX, 418-432 (June, 1935).

[5] Tables showing the term and salary of the governor in each of the states will be found in The Book of the States (Council of State Govts., Chicago), 1964-65, pp. 142, 152.

[6] A few other states, including some with the four-year term and some with the two-year, limit an incumbent to two consecutive terms.

nor and an outside challenger, there can be little doubt that the prestige of office and control of patronage give the incumbent a substantial advantage. On the other hand, it may be contended that ineligibility for reelection removes a potent incentive to efficient administration. Furthermore, a governor who would have sufficient influence to secure his own reelection if he were reeligible will frequently be able to dictate the choice of his successor, and under such circumstances it is scarcely to be expected that machine-building will be seriously impeded.[7]

The salary of the governor varied, in 1964, from $10,000 in Arkansas to $50,000 in New York. Only eight states paid more than $25,000, while four paid less than $15,000.[8] Some states, in addition to the cash salary, provide the governor, at state expense, with an official residence. Notwithstanding that the gubernatorial salary has during recent years been increased in many states, there are still several where, in view of the expenses which a governor is called upon to meet, the compensation is clearly inadequate.

Nomination, Election, and Removal

Although a few states retain the convention method of nomination, gubernatorial candidates are now nominated in most states by primary elections. In every state, election is by direct popular vote.[9] The vote required for election is usually a mere plurality of all votes cast. However, at least two states—Vermont and Georgia—require a majority, and provide that, if no candidate receives such, the legislature shall make a choice from among those persons (two in Georgia and three in Vermont) receiving the largest popular votes.

Except in Oregon, the governor may be removed from office by the

[7] For a comprehensive discussion of tenure limitations, see Joseph E. Kallenbach, "Constitutional Limitations of Reeligibility of National and State Chief Executives," *Amer. Polit. Sci. Rev.*, XLVI, 438-454 (June, 1952).

[8] *The Book of the States*, 1964-65, p. 142.

[9] Mississippi employs a combination of popular vote and electoral votes intended to safeguard white control of the office; and Georgia for many years used a county-unit system of voting in statewide primaries which operated to increase rural influence in the selection of gubernatorial candidates. See Robert B. Highsaw and Charles N. Fortenberry, *The Government and Administration of Mississippi* (Crowell, New York, 1954), 70; Cullen B. Gosnell and C. David Anderson, *The Government and Administration of Georgia* (Crowell, New York, 1956), 41-42. In 1963, the United States Supreme Court declared the Georgia county-unit system unconstitutional as a violation of the equal-protection clause of the Fourteenth Amendment. *Gray v. Sanders*, 372 U.S. 368 (1963). Whether, in view of the decision in the Georgia case, the Mississippi practice would survive a challenge of its constitutionality in the federal courts, seems problematical. Cf. Donald S. Vaughan, "Mississippi's System for Electing a Governor," *Pub. Admin. Survey* (Bur. of Govtl. Research, Univ. of Miss.), Vol. X, No. 6, pp. 1-5 (July, 1963).

process of impeachment. For reasons previously discussed,[10] this is a cumbersome and little-used method of removal. Although impeachment charges have been preferred against many governors,[11] few have been convicted and removed from office. Removals during the present century include those of Governors Sulzer of New York (1913); Ferguson of Texas (1917); and Walton and Johnston of Oklahoma (1923 and 1929, respectively).[12] Unfortunately, political considerations have clearly been involved in many impeachment proceedings. In 12 states, the governor may be removed by the popular recall.[13] However, only one governor— Frazier of North Dakota in 1921[14]—has as yet been removed from office by this means.

Powers of the Governor: Executive Powers: Appointment and Removal

Practically all state constitutions, with slightly varying phraseology, make it the duty of the governor "to see that the laws are faithfully executed." Viewed in its broad aspect, execution of the law involves not only apprehension and prosecution of violators of criminal statutes, but also the carrying out of a multitude of statutes providing for the performance of governmental services. In practice, the actual power of a governor in the execution of state law depends largely upon the degree of his control over the subordinates through whom he must act; and this, in turn, depends in no small measure upon the extent of the governor's power to appoint and remove those subordinates. Although the governor's power in this respect has been substantially increased during the past century, it is not yet commensurate with the constitutional duty of executing the laws of the state. In only a minority of the states do the courts take the view that the powers of appointment and removal are necessarily and exclusively executive in character, and therefore vested in the governor by the constitutional grant of executive power. Consequently, in most states the power of the governor to appoint and remove is dependent entirely upon definite grants of such authority made either by constitutional pro-

---

[10] Above, Chap. VIII.

[11] In Oklahoma, a state in which impeachment has been especially popular, the first twenty-three years of statehood saw no less than thirteen impeachment messages sent from house to senate. Cortez A. M. Ewing, "Impeachment of Oklahoma Governors," *Amer. Polit. Sci. Rev.*, XXIV, 648-652 (Aug., 1930).

[12] For accounts of these cases see Jacob A. Friedman, *The Impeachment of Governor William Sulzer;* "Impeachment of Governor Ferguson," *Amer. Polit. Sci. Rev.*, XII, 111-115 (Feb., 1918); Ewing, "Impeachment of Oklahoma Governors," *loc. cit.*

[13] This method of removal is discussed above, Chap. VI.

[14] See Dorr H. Carroll, "The Recall in North Dakota," *Nat. Mun. Rev.*, XI, 3-5 (Jan., 1922).

vision or by statute.[15] The extent of this authority varies widely from state to state, being in general greater in those states which have effected administrative reorganization.

As compared with the appointing power of the President, that of most state governors is relatively meager. In the first place, various major state officers corresponding roughly to the heads of executive departments in the national government, are, by constitutional requirement, popularly elected. Furthermore, where the appointing power *is* lodged in the governor it is frequently hedged about by important limitations. Thus many states require gubernatorial appointments to have the approval of the senate or, in states having such an agency, of the executive council. Whereas the President's hand is strengthened by the custom according to which his nominations to cabinet positions are usually accorded senatorial confirmation without question, a like practice seems not to have developed generally in the states with regard to gubernatorial appointments. Moreover, with respect to members of state boards and commissions, the governor's appointing power is sometimes further limited by requirements that representation be given to different political parties, professional groups, or geographic regions. And in a growing number of states, as of course is true in the federal government also, executive appointments to subordinate administrative positions are now made under a merit system administered by a civil service agency.[16]

Notwithstanding these exceptions and limitations, however, the governor's appointing power is considerable in all states and of especial consequence in reorganized states. In Illinois, for example, though the constitutional offices of secretary of state, auditor, treasurer, superintendent of public instruction, and attorney general are elective, the governor, with senatorial consent, appoints the directors of the various statutory or "code" departments.[17] Members of numerous state boards and commissions, such as the tax commission and public utilities commission, are in most states appointed by the governor. And the governor quite generally has authority to fill vacancies in state administrative positions, this power extending in some instances even to elective offices.

The governor's removal power, like his power of appointment, is circumscribed by constitutional and statutory limitations.[18] In some states

[15] For a comprehensive discussion of constitutional grants of the powers of appointment and removal, and their interpretation by the courts, see John Murdoch Dawley, "The Governor's Constitutional Powers of Appointment and Removal," *Minn. Law Rev.*, XXII, 451-478 (Mar., 1938).

[16] See below, Chap. X.

[17] These departments, in 1964, numbered seventeen: finance, revenue, agriculture, labor, mines and minerals, public works and buildings, public health, registration and education, conservation, insurance, public safety, aeronautics, personnel, financial institutions, mental health, public aid, and children and family services.

[18] Under the United States Constitution, as interpreted by the Supreme Court, the President possesses full power to remove officers whose duties are strictly execu-

the removal power may be exercised by the governor only on address of the legislature, whereas in others executive removals must be approved by the senate or executive council. Several state constitutions expressly enumerate the causes for which removals may be made, the most common of which are incompetency, neglect of duty, and malfeasance in office. Where, however, as in Illinois, the governor's determination of the existence of these causes is final and conclusive,[19] nominal restrictions of this nature impose little actual restraint.

Though it is true that the governor's powers of appointment and removal are considerably less extensive than those of the President, the governor's position in these respects is being gradually, if slowly, strengthened. Recent constitutional and statutory changes in various states have given the governor additional authority in these directions; and, though the courts in general still interpret such grants of power strictly, they are somewhat more liberal than formerly.[20] This trend with respect to gubernatorial powers is to be commended. If we are to hold the governor responsible for the performance of his constitutional duty to see that the laws of the state are executed, he must, as a practical necessity and in fairness, be endowed with authority through which he can in turn hold his subordinates responsible to him.

Supervision of Administration

The governor is, at least nominally, the general overseer of the state's administrative machinery. He is expected to exercise supervision over the various departments, boards, commissions, and offices of the state government, and to coordinate their work. In actual practice, however, the ability of the governor to direct and supervise administrative officers depends in large measure upon whether he appoints and may remove those officers; and, as we have seen, the governor's power of appointment and removal is in many states quite inadequate. Only in states which have reorganized the administrative branch of government to enlarge the governor's power of appointment and removal is that official in a position to act as a *real* supervisor of administration; and not even in those states is the governor's administrative position as strong as is that of the President in the national field. Yet recent years have witnessed a substantial strengthening of the governor's supervisory powers.[21] Especially

---

tive in character, and that power may not be restricted by Congress. However, with respect to officials charged with duties of a quasi-legislative or quasi-judicial nature, the President's removal power is limited to that which has been conferred by statute. *Myers* v. *United States*, 272 U.S. 52 (1926); *Rathbun* v. *United States*, 295 U.S. 602 (1935); *Weiner* v. *United States*, 357 U.S. 349 (1958).

19 *Wilcox* v. *People*, 90 Ill. 186 (1878).

20 See Dawley, *op. cit.*

21 To this general statement there is an occasional exception. In Florida, for

noteworthy has been the tendency to increase gubernatorial powers in relation to financial supervision. Moreover, a majority of the states have now established formal "managerial" agencies, directly responsible to the governor, to aid the chief executive in matters of supervision. These agencies, in the form of budget commissions, finance departments, departments of administration, and the like, provide the governor with information, see that his decisions are carried out by department heads, and in general assist him in the performance of his supervisory duties.[22]

Military Powers

The governor is the military as well as the civil head of the state. He is commander-in-chief of the militia, or National Guard as it is now officially called, except when the state forces are called into federal service. In practically every state the governor is authorized to call forth the guard to execute the laws, suppress insurrection, and repel invasion, and this power is exercised with surprising frequency. Usually the National Guard, when thus called out, is used only to assist the civil authorities in enforcing the law; but at times the governor goes further and proclaims a state of martial law. Under martial law, or martial rule as it is more appropriately called, the military forces, instead of merely supporting the civil authorities, actually supplant the latter in the control of some or all governmental functions. In extreme cases the civil courts are supplanted by military tribunals.[23]

Circumstances under which, in practice, troops are called forth or martial rule is established vary widely. One of the most common occasions for such action is disorder or threatened disorder arising from labor disputes. In such cases, the strikers are usually treated as insurgents and troops are used to enable employers to continue operation with nonunion labor. Occasionally, however, the troops have been thrown on the workers' side, as when Governor Olson of Minnesota, during a truck strike in 1934, prevented operation by trucking companies which refused to accept

---

example, the governor remains relatively weak in the field of administration, with many important administrative functions being vested in ex officio boards and commissions composed of the governor and some or all of six other elective officers. Because of the important powers possessed by these latter officials, Florida's system of state government is often referred to as the "cabinet system." See Wilson K. Doyle, Angus McKenzie Laird, and S. Sherman Weiss, *The Government and Administration of Florida* (Crowell, New York, 1954), Chap. 6.

[22] Leonard D. White and M. Harvey Sherman, "The Governors March On," *State Govt.*, XIII, 195-197, 206 (Oct., 1940). See also Leonard D. White, *Trends in Public Administration* (McGraw-Hill, New York, 1933), Chap. 14. Cf. below Chap. X, "Departments of Administration."

[23] On martial rule in general, see Charles Fairman, *The Law of Martial Rule* (2nd ed.); Robert S. Rankin, *When Civil Law Fails.*

a compromise recommended by federal conciliators.[24] Troops are also used by governors with some frequency for preservation of order and protection of life and property upon occasions of flood, fire, hurricane, earthquake, or other widespread disaster. In an effort to reduce the number of traffic accidents, the governors of several states during recent years have at times ordered the use of National Guardsmen to assist the state police in patrolling the highways on holiday weekends.[25]

Occasionally military force has been employed for purposes which, if not merely trivial, would seem clearly within the competence of the ordinary law-enforcement agencies. Thus, Governor William H. Murray of Oklahoma is reported to have called forth the militia "to prevent the foreclosure of farm mortgages, to enforce a bank holiday, to deliver from jail one committed for nonpayment of alimony, to take charge of ticket sales at the football game between the state's two institutions of higher learning, and for similar weighty causes." [26] In some instances governors have declared "martial law" as a means of dealing with political rivals, though at times their efforts in this direction have been checked by the judiciary. During the 1930's, for example, a governor of South Carolina "tried to get rid of the highway commissioners by declaring them to be insurgents—only to be restrained by the state supreme court"; and a Georgia governor "proclaimed 'martial law' around the highway department's building as a device for excluding the chairman whom he had already been enjoined from removing, and later expanded his proclamation to protect his military agents from punishment for their contempt—all of which was brought to naught by the state supreme and the federal district courts." [27]

Fortunately, the federal courts have now made it clear that there are constitutional limitations upon the power of state governors to rule by executive decree under the guise of martial law. In the leading case of Sterling v. Constantin, decided in 1932, the United States Supreme Court was called upon to consider the validity of executive orders by which Governor Sterling of Texas sought to limit the output of oil wells in certain areas of the state. The governor had proclaimed that a state of insurrection against the conservation laws existed in the oil-producing counties, declared martial law, issued orders limiting oil production in the counties concerned, and directed the military authorities to enforce the orders. The Supreme Court, however, found that, since there had actually been no in-

---

[24] Charles Fairman, "The Law of Martial Rule and the National Emergency," *Harvard Law Rev.*, LV, 1253-1302 (June, 1942).

[25] A Michigan experiment of this nature is described in John W. Lederle and Robert H. Pealy, " 'Halo' over Michigan Drivers," *State Govt.*, XXVII, 252-254, 259-260 (Dec., 1954).

[26] Fairman, "The Law of Martial Rule and the National Emergency," *loc. cit.*, 1276.

[27] *Ibid.*

surrection or violence, there was no military necessity for the resort to executive decree in the regulation of oil production, and that therefore the governor's action in issuing the regulatory orders was an unjustifiable interference with liberty and property in violation of the Fourteenth Amendment to the United States Constitution.[28] In 1957 a federal district court enjoined Governor Faubus of Arkansas from using the National Guard to prevent eligible Negro pupils from attending Little Rock's Central High School in accordance with an integration plan adopted by the Little Rock school board and approved by the court.[29] And in 1959 a three-judge federal court in Minnesota enjoined Governor Freeman from declaring martial law and using the National Guard to shut down the strike-bound meat-packing plant of Wilson and Company in Albert Lea while local government and the civil courts were still functioning.[30]

During the past decade or so the role of the National Guard has undergone a distinct change.[31] Once confined almost exclusively to law enforcement and patrol duties, the nonfederal activities of the National Guard are today concerned in large measure with rescue and relief. Functions in connection with floods, for example, clearly show the new trend. Originally limited for the most part to prevention of looting, National Guard activities in this field now emphasize such measures as evacuation of flood victims, operation of relief centers, and provision of emergency medical services. "Guardsmen now are called upon principally to help their neighbors, in marked contrast with their former all too frequent duty of being arrayed, in battle garb, against the people of their own communities." [32]

Civil Defense

The governor plays an important part in organization of the state for civil defense—the protection of the civilian population in the event of armed attack. Under the Federal Civil Defense Act, civil defense is envisaged as a joint responsibility of the national, state, and local governments; and provision is made for federal advice and assistance to the

---

[28] *Sterling* v. *Constantin,* 287 U.S. 378 (1932).

[29] *Aaron* v. *Cooper,* 143 F. Supp. 855 (1957). The order of the district court was affirmed by the court of appeals and the United States Supreme Court declined to review the decision.

[30] *Wilson & Co.* v. *Freeman,* 179 F. Supp. 520 (1959). Governor Freeman thereupon rescinded his declaration of martial law but National Guard troops remained in the area for some time to aid local law-enforcement officers in preserving order. See G. Theodore Mitau, "The Governor and the Strike," in Richard T. Frost, ed., *Cases in State and Local Government* (Prentice-Hall, Englewood Cliffs, N.J., 1961), 207-218.

[31] Bennett M. Rich and Philip H. Burch, Jr., "The Changing Role of the National Guard," *Amer. Polit. Sci. Rev.,* L, 702-706 (Sept., 1956).

[32] *Ibid.,* 705.

state and local governments in the establishment and operation of civil-defense programs. Most states have now enacted legislation providing for organization, under the governor, of volunteer civil defense forces, with the local mayors sharing responsibility in their respective communities. Programs planned by the state and local organizations, with federal assistance and coordination, include such measures as preattack evacuation, establishment of emergency welfare centers to care for evacuated populations, and protection against radioactive fallout and biological warfare. The national Governors' Conference has been active in the encouragement of shelter programs and other civil defense activities; and many states have recently adopted "continuity of government" amendments to their constitutions empowering the legislature to provide for temporary relocation of the seat of government and for the temporary filling of vacancies in public offices in the event of enemy attack.[33] In this age of atomic and hydrogen bombs, and with continued uneasiness in the international situation, civil defense functions readily assume a rank of major importance.

Most states now make their civil defense agencies responsible also for dealing with natural disasters at the state level. In the event that state forces are unable to cope with the situation, it is the governor who, under the Federal Disaster Act, requests the President to declare that the disaster is major in character and to authorize the extending of federal assistance.[34]

Legislative Powers

The governor is not only the chief executive of the state, but, in a very real sense, the chief legislator as well.[35] Certain powers and duties in connection with the legislative process are conferred upon him by constitutional provisions; and, quite aside from such provisions, a governor of strong personality, through his personal and political leadership, will inevitably exert a profound influence upon the course of legislative action. As the elected representative of the people of the entire state, the governor is coming to be looked to more and more for leadership in legislative matters as well as in the execution of the law. Indeed, Theodore Roosevelt testified that, as governor of New York, more than half of his work was in the direction of getting needed legislation.[36] Chief among the constitu-

[33] Val Peterson, "The States and Civil Defense," *State Govt.*, XXVIII, 82-85, 95 (Apr., 1955); Vincent J. Browne, "Civil Defense in the States," *The Book of the States*, 1962-63, pp. 441-444.

[34] Peterson, *op. cit.*

[35] On the general subject of the governor's legislative leadership, see Leslie Lipson, "Influence of the Governor upon Legislation," *Annals of Amer. Acad. of Polit. and Soc. Sci.*, CXCV, 72-78 (Jan., 1938). See also Malcolm E. Jewell, *The State Legislature: Politics and Practice* (Random House, New York, 1962), Chap. 5.

[36] Theodore Roosevelt, *An Autobiography*, 282.

tional powers of the governor with respect to legislation are those of (1) recommending, by "message," measures for legislative consideration; (2) calling special legislative sessions and, in some states, determining what measures may be considered in such sessions; and (3) checking legislative action through exercise of the veto.[37]

Messages to the Legislature

Practically every state constitution provides that the governor shall supply the legislature with information concerning the condition of the state, and with recommendations for legislative action. Some constitutions stipulate that such information and recommendations shall be presented at each legislative session; others make the requirement with respect to regular sessions only; while still others merely state that the governor shall give information and make recommendations "from time to time." Whatever the form of constitutional provision, the general practice is for the governor to present a message to the legislature at the beginning of each session, regular or special, and to submit such additional messages as he may see fit during the course of the session. The message delivered at the beginning of the regular legislative session is frequently referred to as the "state of the state" message. In it the chief executive usually discusses current economic and social conditions in their relation to state government, reviews at least briefly the financial condition of the state, and then outlines, more or less specifically, recommendations as to legislation which, in his judgment, should be enacted at the session concerned. Messages to special legislative sessions and special messages during the course of regular sessions are likely to be confined rather closely to specific recommendations. In states having the executive budget system, as all but a few of the states do,[38] a separate "budget message," devoted exclusively to financial matters, is usually presented near the beginning of the regular session.

Gubernatorial messages are sometimes sent in writing to the respective houses of the legislature and read therein by reading clerks; and at other times are delivered in the form of a personal address by the governor before a joint session of the two houses. In determining whether to present a message in writing or by personal address, the governor is likely to be influenced both by the subject matter of the message and by his proficiency as a public speaker. Recently there has been increasing use of the personal address; and it is now quite common for messages to be broad-

[37] A minor legislative power in some states is that of adjourning the legislature in case the two houses disagree as to time of adjournment. In practice, occasion seldom arises for the exercise of this power, though in Illinois it has been invoked three times within the last twenty years.

[38] See below, Chap. XXV, "The Budget-Making Authority."

cast by local radio stations, with portions thereof frequently being televised. Whatever the method of delivery, a message will ordinarily be prepared by the governor with a view to getting his legislative program before the public as well as before the legislature.

The degree to which a governor is actually successful in securing the enactment of his legislative program as outlined in his messages is naturally dependent upon a multitude of factors. Among these may be mentioned the governor's personal popularity; his popularity with other leaders of his political party both within the legislature and outside; the strength of his party in the legislative chambers; and his ability and willingness to make effective use of other powers, such as those of veto and appointment, in persuading or coercing individual legislators to support his recommendations. Still another important factor is the general nature of the times, there being an especially marked tendency to look to the executive for leadership in days of social and economic stress or in times of war or threat of war.[39]

Control Over Special Sessions

The governor of every state is empowered to call special sessions of the legislature, and in most states complete discretion rests with him in determining when such sessions are to be called.[40] In some states a special legislative session, when convened by the governor, may consider and transact any business which might be considered at a regular session. Other states, however, permit the governor to determine what shall be considered at special sessions.[41] Some of the latter states have constitutional provisions stipulating that special legislative sessions shall consider only matters specified by the governor in his proclamation convening the sesssion; while others permit the consideration of subjects specified in such proclamation and, in addition, any other matters which the governor may, during the session, lay before the legislature by message. Provisions thus limiting the business which may be transacted at special sessions are designed to require the legislature to confine its attention to matters pertaining to the emergency which has made the session necessary, leaving all other business for consideration in regular sessions. Of the two types of limitation, that which permits the consideration both of matters specified in the proclamation calling the session and of other matters submitted by the governor is preferable. It may be quite impossible for the governor, at the time of drafting a proclamation calling a special session, to foresee

---

[39] Summaries of trends in state government as reflected in governors' messages appear each year in the magazine *State Government,* usually in the Spring issue.

[40] See above, Chap. VII, "Special Sessions."

[41] For a general discussion of the subject, see M. T. Van Hecke, "Legislative Power at Special Sessions," *Cornell Law Quar.,* IX, 447-462 (June, 1924).

every matter connected with the emergency which will require legislative attention. Moreover, new emergency situations calling for legislative action may arise during the course of the session. In at least one of the states, Illinois, whose constitutions provide that a special session may consider only the business specified in the governor's call it has been found possible to secure the benefits of the more liberal type of provision by permitting the governor, while one special session is in existence, to call another to meet concurrently with the first. Each of these legally distinct sessions may then consider the matters designated in the particular proclamation by which it was convened. At best, however, such a practice is a circuitous means of achieving what the constitution might better permit in express terms.[42]

Constitutional provisions limiting matters to be considered at a special session to those submitted by the governor appear to be subject to one important exception, namely, impeachment proceedings against the governor or other impeachable officers. According to prevailing judicial opinion, impeachment charges may be preferred and tried at a special legislative session even though the matter has not been included in the governor's proclamation or messages. The courts take the view that impeachment is a judicial process and that constitutional limitations upon business which may be transacted at special sessions apply only to matters of a legislative nature. Thus the courts upheld the impeachment and removal of Governors Sulzer of New York and Ferguson of Texas upon conviction on impeachment charges voted at special sessions called for other purposes. Governor Walton of Oklahoma also was impeached and removed at a special session.[43]

The Veto Power [44]

At the final stage of the legislative process, the governor possesses, in every state except North Carolina, an important negative voice in his

---

[42] In a few states special legislative sessions are permitted to consider subjects specified in the governor's call and, in addition, such other matters as the legislature, by a two-thirds vote or some other extraordinary majority, may agree to take up. Under such circumstances, special sessions tend to resemble additional regular sessions, with consideration being given to many matters not included in the gubernatorial call. Coleman B. Ransone, Jr., *The Office of Governor in the United States,* 212; Coleman B. Ransone, Jr., *The Office of Governor in the South,* 87.

[43] See M. T. Van Hecke, "Impeachment of Governor at Special Session," *Wis. Law Rev.,* III, 155-169 (Apr., 1925); Frank M. Stewart, "Impeachment in Texas," *Amer. Polit. Sci. Rev.,* XXIV, 652-658 (Aug., 1930).

[44] For general discussions of the gubernatorial veto, see John A. Fairlie, "The Veto Power of the State Governor," *Amer. Polit. Sci. Rev.,* XI, 473-493 (Aug., 1917); Frank W. Prescott, "The Executive Veto in American States," *Western Polit. Quar.,* III, 98-112 (Mar., 1950). Studies pertaining to individual states or groups of states are Niels H. Debel, *The Veto Power of the Governor of Illinois;* Knute E. Carlson, *The Exercise of the Veto Power in Nebraska;* Glenn R. Negley, "The Executive Veto

power to disapprove or "veto" legislative measures.[45] The veto power is in some states applicable only to bills, whereas in others it applies also to certain forms of resolution which require action by both legislative houses. In every instance the veto is of the qualified or suspensive type, subject to being overridden by subsequent legislative action. The vote necessary to override the veto varies from state to state. A few states require only the same vote as that necessary to pass the measure in the first instance. Generally, however, there is a higher requirement, the most common being a two-thirds affirmative vote of the members of each house.[46] Even in those states where a vetoed bill may be repassed by a vote no larger than that required for original passage, the gubernatorial negative may not be ineffective. Under such circumstances, especially if the governor is personally popular, the legislature may hesitate to take action which is directly contrary to his wishes as evidenced by the veto. It is usual to require that the governor return a vetoed bill to the house in which it originated, together with a statement of his reasons for disapproval—a statement commonly referred to as a "veto message."

While the legislature is in session, the governor is allowed a specified length of time for the consideration of bills presented to him. If he does not act upon a bill within this period, by signing or vetoing it, the measure becomes law without his signature. The period thus allowed for considering bills varies among the states from three days to fifteen, with a five-day period most common. Some states allow the governor a fixed number of days, varying from three to forty-five, after adjournment of the legislature, within which to consider and act upon bills presented to him during the last few days of the session or after adjournment. Since the governor usually receives large numbers of bills from the legislature at the very end of the session, a provision of this nature, with a liberal time allowance, is not only desirable but essential if the governor is to be able to give careful consideration to all measures presented to him.

It has been noted that, when the governor takes no action upon a bill, the measure becomes law without his signature at the end of a fixed

---

in Illinois," *Amer. Polit. Sci. Rev.*, XXXIII, 1049-1057 (Dec., 1939); M. Nelson Mc-Geary, "The Governor's Veto in Pennsylvania," *Ibid.*, XLI, 941-946 (Oct., 1947); Harold M. Dorr, "Judicial Interpretation of the Executive Veto in Michigan," *Ibid.*, XXVIII, 1056-1063 (Dec., 1934); Harold M. Dorr, "The Executive Veto in Michigan," *Mich. Hist. Mag.*, XX, 91-110 (Winter, 1936); Jacob A. Swisher, "The Executive Veto in Iowa," *Ia. Jour. of Hist. and Politics*, XV, 155-213 (Apr., 1917); Frank W. Prescott, "The Executive Veto in Southern States," *Jour. of Politics*, X, 659-675 (Nov., 1948); Samuel R. Solomon, "The Governor as Legislator [in New York]," *Nat. Mun. Rev.*, XL, 515-520 (Nov., 1951).

[45] Cf. John A. Fairlie, "The Executive Power in the State Constitution," *Annals of Amer. Acad. of Polit. and Soc. Sci.*, CLXXXI, 59-73 (Sept., 1935).

[46] In Alaska, vetoes are considered by the two legislative houses in joint session. In the case of revenue or appropriation bills or items, a three-fourths vote of the legislative membership is required to override a veto; while other vetoes may be overridden by a two-thirds vote of the members.

number of days if the legislature is still in session.[47] Where the legislature adjourns before a particular bill has been before the governor for the full number of days allotted him by the constitution for its consideration, the effect of gubernatorial inaction differs as between two groups of states. In one group, a bill under such circumstances does not become law, this being what is commonly called the "pocket veto" or veto by inaction. In states of the other group, the bill becomes law unless formally vetoed within the time allowed for the consideration of such measures. It is usual to require that a bill vetoed after adjournment of the legislature be filed, together with the governor's veto message, with the secretary of state. Vetoes after adjournment, like pocket vetoes, usually effect absolute defeat of the bills concerned, the legislature having no opportunity to override them. In a few states, however, the constitution requires that a bill vetoed after adjournment may be returned to the next session of the legislature, which may reconsider the measure and, if the necessary vote can be secured, override the veto. New Jersey and Hawaii provide for reconsideration of bills vetoed after adjournment at a special legislative session meeting for that purpose without executive call.

With respect to appropriation measures, all but eight of the states empower the governor to veto particular items of a bill while approving the remainder.[48] This power of "item veto" makes it unnecessary for the governor to choose between accepting every item of an elaborate appropriation bill or vetoing the measure in its entirety. On the other hand, existence of the power may encourage legislators to approve for political reasons items of appropriation which they know the governor will veto, thereby diverting from themselves and to the governor the displeasure of persons who would have stood to benefit from the appropriations concerned. As an alternative to vetoing an appropriation item, the governors of a few states may reduce the item and approve the reduced amount. Washington does not confine the principle of the item veto to appropriation measures, but permits the governor to veto individual sections of any bill.

In summary, it appears that any of three courses may be taken by the governor with respect to a bill presented for his approval:[49] he may

[47] In Missouri, the passage of a joint resolution is required to make effective as law a bill which the governor has not returned within the fifteen days allowed him for its consideration.

[48] States without the item veto are Indiana, Iowa, Maine, Nevada, New Hampshire, North Carolina (which has no veto provision whatsoever), Rhode Island, and Vermont. Vetoes of items may be overridden in the same manner as vetoes of entire bills. In West Virginia the regular budget bill does not require executive action, and therefore the item veto applies only to supplementary appropriations. Cf. Prescott, "The Executive Veto in Southern States," *loc. cit.*, 672. On the item veto generally, see V. L. W., "The Item Veto in the American Constitutional System," *Georgetown Law Jour.*, XXV, 106-133 (Nov., 1936).

[49] In North Carolina, where no veto power exists, bills are not presented to the governor.

(1) sign it, (2) veto it, or (3) take no action on it. A fourth alternative—that of approval in part and veto in part—is, as we have seen, applicable in most states to appropriation bills and in one state to all bills.[50] Signature of a bill by the governor within the period allowed him by the constitution results in its becoming a law. A bill vetoed while the legislature is still in session is returned to that body for reconsideration and may, by the prescribed vote, be passed over the governor's veto. In most states a bill vetoed after legislative adjournment is thereby finally killed, but in a few states such a measure is returned to a subsequent session of the legislature for reconsideration. Where the governor takes no action whatever upon a bill, the measure becomes law without his signature at the end of a certain number of days, provided that the legislature is still in session. If the legislature adjourns before the expiration of the time allotted the governor for its consideration, the bill becomes law in some states, while in others gubernatorial inaction operates as a pocket veto.

The veto power appears originally to have been conferred upon the governor to enable the chief executive to prevent, or at least check, the enactment of unconstitutional legislation. Nowadays, however, the power is freely used upon grounds of policy or expediency, with a view to preventing the passage of measures which the governor believes to be unwise.[51] The frequency and effect of vetoes naturally vary from state to state and from time to time, depending to some extent, though by no means solely, upon the personal and political relationships between the governor and the legislature. A further factor in determining the effectiveness of the veto in a particular state is the size of the vote necessary to override the governor's negative.[52] It is also to be noted that the effectiveness of the power in some states has been increased, especially during recent years, by the fact that a large percentage of all vetoes occur after adjournment of the legislature.[53] In most instances, as suggested above, such vetoes, though suspensive in form, are in practice absolute since the legislature has no opportunity to override them.

On the whole, the executive veto has proved an effective means of defeating legislative measures opposed by the governor. Of the 24,928 bills enacted in 1947 in the various states, 1,253, or 5 percent, were

[50] Yet a fifth course, known as executive amendment, is open to the governor in four states—Alabama, Massachusetts, New Jersey, and Virginia. Under this plan, the chief executive is empowered to return a bill to the house of its origin with the suggestion of changes which would make the measure acceptable to him. See Ransone, *The Office of Governor in the United States,* 182-184; Ransone, *The Office of Governor in the South,* 83-85.

[51] It appears that approximately three-fourths of all recent vetoes in New York have been based on policy, and only one-fourth on unconstitutionality, drafting defects, and other grounds. Solomon, "The Governor as Legislator," *loc. cit.*

[52] Cf. Fairlie, "The Veto Power of the State Governor," *loc. cit.*

[53] In New York, more than 92 percent of the governor's vetoes during the years 1927-1951 were accomplished after adjournment. Solomon, "The Governor as Legislator," *loc. cit.*

vetoed; and of the vetoes only 22, or less than 2 percent, were overridden.[54] Indeed, the percentage of vetoed bills which are overridden "has declined almost to the vanishing point." [55]

The Pardoning Power[56]

In contrast with the governor's executive and legislative powers, the pardoning power is essentially judicial in nature.[57] This power is placed in the hands of the chief executive to enable him, in unusual cases, to correct injustices resulting from judicial action or to "temper justice with mercy." An executive pardon may be either conditional[58] or absolute. A full or absolute pardon absolves the recipient from further punishment and from any other legal consequences of his conviction. Thus, if the conviction resulted in his disfranchisement or ineligibility to public office, the pardon operates to restore those privileges.

In slightly more than half of the states the pardoning power is vested solely in the governor. However, many of the states in this group provide an advisory pardon board to hold hearings on applications and make recommendations to the governor; and certain others provide a pardon attorney or other official to perform clerical duties connected with pardon applications and to assist the governor in making investigations. In about a dozen states the power is vested in the governor but may be exercised only with the concurrence of the executive council, the senate, or a pardon board. In the remaining states, some ten in number, the pardoning power is vested, not in the governor, but in a pardon board of which the governor is usually a member. It will thus be seen that, al-

[54] Prescott, "The Executive Veto in American States," *loc. cit.* In addition to the 1,253 full vetoes, there were 53 measures of which certain parts were disapproved.

[55] *Ibid.*, 112. In New York, during the years 1927-1951, more than 26 percent of all bills submitted to the governor were vetoed and not a single veto was overridden. Solomon, "The Governor as Legislator," *loc. cit.* In Illinois no veto has been overridden in the last twenty years, notwithstanding that about 10 percent of all bills passed by the legislature during that period encountered executive disapproval.

[56] The following discussion of the pardoning power draws heavily upon data presented in United States Department of Justice, *Attorney General's Survey of Release Procedures,* Volume III: *Pardon.* A general account may also be found in Christen Jensen, *The Pardoning Power in the American States.* For a discussion of the power as applied to capital cases, see Austin W. Scott, Jr., "The Pardoning Power," *Annals of Amer. Acad. of Polit. and Soc. Sci.,* CCLXXXIV, 95-100 (Nov., 1952).

[57] Another instance in which the governor acts judicially is in holding hearings on requests for the rendition of fugitives from justice. On the rendition process generally, see above, Chap. IV, "Interstate Rendition."

[58] Pardons have been granted, for instance, upon condition that the recipient leave the state; that he abstain from the use of intoxicating liquor; or that he be and remain a law-abiding citizen. If the stipulated conditions are violated, the pardon becomes void. See Jensen, *op. cit.,* 127-130.

though the governor participates in the exercise of the pardoning power in almost every state,[59] his power is not always plenary.

The governor's power of pardon extends, of course, only to violations of state law and not to federal offenses. Moreover, certain state offenses are specifically excepted from the pardoning power. Thus, all but some 6 states except impeachment cases, and a majority of the states except cases of treason as well. Whereas the President may pardon for federal offenses either before or after conviction, most governors are permitted to pardon only after conviction.

The pardoning power is, from the governor's standpoint, perhaps the most troublesome of gubernatorial powers. Relatives and friends of convicted persons are forever imploring the chief executive to exercise the power; and the consideration of these requests consumes much time and entails no little responsibility.[60] Although the pardoning power should be exercised in appropriate cases, its excessive use may impede the administration of justice. In practice, the extent to which the power has actually been employed has varied widely. Some governors have granted many pardons and others few. Mrs. Miriam Ferguson, as governor of Texas, pardoned 3,500 persons in two years, whereas her predecessor had granted only 17 pardons in four years.[61] The number of pardons granted in different states and at different times will naturally vary with changing conditions. Yet it seems clear that in some instances of numerous pardons the reason therefor is to be found in the mere inability of the incumbent governor to say "no" in appropriate cases. Thus one governor is said to have given as his reason for pardoning criminals that "he could deny Carrie [his wife] nothing and she could refuse nothing to anyone else." [62] Not every pardon, it should be noted, has as its purpose the release of the recipient from punishment. Some pardons are granted, after full sentence has been served, for the purpose of restoring political privileges to convicted citizens or making convicted aliens eligible for citizenship.

In addition to the power to grant pardons, the governor usually possesses power to dispense the lesser forms of clemency known as commutation and reprieve. A commutation is a substitution of a lesser for a greater penalty. Thus a death sentence may be commuted to life imprisonment, or a twenty-year prison sentence to ten years. A reprieve, on the other hand, is a mere postponement or suspension of the execution of sentence, and is most commonly used to stay, for a designated number of days, the execution of the death penalty. Most state constitutions expressly stipulate that the governor may grant reprieves and commutations;

[59] Georgia's constitution of 1945 provides for an appointive board of pardons and paroles of which the governor is not a member.

[60] Cf. Alfred E. Smith, *Up to Now: An Autobiography*, 306 ff.

[61] United States Department of Justice, *op. cit.*, 148.

[62] Quoted in Edwin H. Sutherland, *Principles of Criminology* (Lippincott, Philadelphia, 4th ed., 1947), 511.

and, where the power to grant these lesser forms of clemency is not provided for in express terms, the courts hold that it is included in the greater power of granting pardons.

The Governor and Public Relations

Closely intertwined with the governor's activities as chief executive and legislative leader are his efforts to explain his program to the public, both before and after its enactment by the legislature, and to secure support for it. This role in public relations is constantly increasing in significance. Indeed, Professor Coleman B. Ransone, in his excellent book on the American governorship, concludes that it is today the governor's most time-consuming function.[63] The governor must grant personal interviews to as many as he reasonably can of the persons who wish to see him. Some governors have adopted the practice of setting aside a designated time—perhaps an afternoon each week—at which they will hold "open house" and talk with anyone who desires to see them for any reason. A governor's official correspondence tends to be voluminous; and there are numerous telephone calls, public speeches, radio addresses, and personal appearances. Finally, since the governor is a prime source of news, there is the problem of handling his relations with the press. Though the governors of some states hold no formal press conferences, preferring to deal with press representatives individually, many of the chief executives schedule regular conferences, typically two each day, in the morning and afternoon.[64] In view of the growing burden of such activities, it is not surprising that many governors have added public relations men to their official staffs.[65]

The Job of Being Governor

The governorship of an American state, especially one of the more populous states, is today a job of no mean proportions. The governor is chief executive, legislative leader, and in many instances the leader of his political party. In those states which have most fully centralized administrative responsibility in the governor's hands the chief executive is virtually manager of a huge business—a business the cost of which, in some states, now exceeds a billion dollars a year. The governor represents his state in the Governors' Conference[66] and other interstate activities, and is the state's official spokesman in its dealings with the national government.

[63] Ransone, *The Office of Governor in the United States,* 116-117.
[64] *Ibid.,* 116-117, 126-128.
[65] Homer E. Scace, "The Governor Needs Staff," *Nat. Mun. Rev.,* XL, 462-467, 479 (Oct., 1951). Cf. Bernard Rubin, *Public Relations and the Empire State* (Rutgers Univ. Press, New Brunswick, N. J., 1958).
[66] See above, Chap. IV, "The Governors' Conference."

In addition, the governor in a real sense is the elected "representative-at-large" of the entire population of the state, and as such must be prepared to receive and handle requests of all sorts, including some which he has no conceivable power to grant.

The actual activities of a particular governor at a particular time depend, as Professor Ransone has pointed out, upon many factors. Among these are the constitutional grant of gubernatorial powers, the attitude of the legislature, the governor's position in his party, prevalent customs and traditions, and the governor's own conception of his powers and duties. Every governor has considerable leeway in determining what functions he will emphasize, and decisions in this matter vary widely.[67] The amount of time ordinarily devoted to particular activities tends to vary also with the population of the state. In the less populous states, for example, the gubernatorial staff is small and the chief executive conducts more official business personally through interviews and telephone calls. In more populous states, on the other hand, the governor's staff is larger and his office more highly organized, with the work of telephoning and seeing people delegated in greater degree to staff members.[68]

Some days of course are spent by the governor away from his office, traveling about the state or elsewhere to make speeches and attend meetings and conferences of various kinds.[69] On the days spent in his office, the governor of a typical state is likely to follow a busy routine approximating the one suggested in the accompanying table. Bulking large in this schedule, though interspersed with other activities, are conferences with department heads, legislators, the public, and the press. By any reasonable standard, the governor in most states has today achieved a central position of leadership in both legislation and administration, and in public relations as well.[70]

THE GOVERNOR'S DAY

TIME	ACTIVITIES
8:30 to 9:30 a.m.	Reading and answering previously screened correspondence.
9:30 to 10:30 a.m.	Conferences with department heads or legislators.
10:30 to 11:00 a.m.	Press conference.
11:00 to 12:30 p.m.	Interviews or conferences with public, legislators, and department heads.

[67] Ransone, *The Office of Governor in the United States,* 118-119.
[68] *Ibid.,* 123-124.
[69] Cf. *Ibid.,* 125.
[70] Cf. George W. Spicer, "Gubernatorial Leadership in Virginia," *Pub. Admin. Rev.,* I, 441-457 (Autumn, 1941). For a recent evaluation based on personal work with many governors, see Frank Bane, "The Job of Being a Governor," *State Govt.,* XXXI, 184-189 (Summer, 1958).

12:30 to 2:00 p.m.	Lunch, during which the governor welcomes some group meeting in the city or has a luncheon conference.
2:00 to 4:00 p.m.	Additional conferences with public, legislators, and department heads.
4:00 to 4:30 p.m.	Press conference.
4:30 to 6:00 p.m. or later	Clears up additional correspondence, makes phone calls, plans work with staff, etc.
7:00 p.m.	Frequently attends a banquet or similar gathering where he is either the principal speaker or must "put in an appearance."

SOURCE: Coleman B. Ransone, Jr., *The Office of Governor in the United States* (University of Alabama Press, University, Alabama, 1956), p. 124. Reproduced with permission. As Professor Ransone points out, the schedule here presented "will not be valid for all states, particularly for the larger states such as New York, California, and Illinois, where the governor spends much less of his time seeing people than he does in the average state." *Ibid.*, p. 123.

The Executive Council

Three New England states—Maine, Massachusetts, and New Hampshire—have, as a carry-over from early days,[71] executive councils "for advising the governor in the executive part of government." [72] In addition to having general advisory authority, these councils, by constitutional provision, share with the governor the exercise of certain specific executive powers. Thus council consent is necessary in all three states to the appointment of certain officers and to the issuance of pardons; and in Massachusetts and New Hampshire to convening special sessions of the legislature. The council consists of five members in New Hampshire, seven in Maine, and eight in Massachusetts. Members are chosen by popular election in Massachusetts and New Hampshire, and by the legislature in Maine. The North Carolina constitution provides for a "council of state" of four ex officio members (secretary of state, auditor, treasurer, and superintendent of public instruction) to "advise the governor in the execution of his office." As in Massachusetts and New Hampshire, this council shares with the governor the power of calling special legislative sessions. Certain other states have agencies, usually constituted on an ex officio basis, which are known as executive councils but which, though charged with various executive and administrative responsibilities, are not general advisory bodies to the governor.

[71] In colonial times the governor's council was an appointive body which advised the governor on executive matters, acted as the upper house of the legislature, and, with the governor, served as the highest court. Present-day councils, however, have been stripped of all but executive functions.

[72] Cf. A. N. Holcombe, "The Executive Council, with Special Reference to Massachusetts," *Amer. Polit. Sci. Rev.*, IX, 304-308 (May, 1915); Clement E. Vose, *The Executive Council of Maine in Decline.*

Who Are Our Governors?

What can be said, in general, of the background and ability of the men[73] who have occupied the governor's chair in the various states in recent years? Survey studies of American governors since 1900[74] indicate that our state executives have, in general, been persons of substantial ability and experience drawn from the business and professional classes. A large majority of the recent governors have attended college, and the percentage of college men continues to increase. Indeed, during the 1940's nearly 88 percent of the governors were college graduates or had attended college for some period of time. With respect to occupational background, lawyers predominate, approximately half of the chief executives being drawn from the legal profession. The other vocations represented are many and varied, with merchandising, farming, manufacturing, banking, and journalism relatively prominent. Several recent governors have been professional educators.

Most of the governors have had previous experience in public office, some having held several different offices before reaching the governorship. Many have been members of the state legislature or held other state or local offices, and some have held federal offices.[75] During the early years of the present century, relatively few incumbents of the gubernatorial office returned to the public service in other capacities after the expiration of their terms. Lately, however, there has been a tendency for ex-governors to reenter governmental service in some capacity, a substantial number being elected to Congress—especially the Senate[76]—or appointed to federal administrative posts. Though there have been some exceptions, it would appear that during recent decades there has been a general trend upward in the caliber of our governors. That trend may be attributable, at least in part, to the fact that the gubernatorial office itself has been steadily growing in power and prestige.

[73] There have been two woman governors—Nellie T. Ross of Wyoming, and Miriam A. Ferguson of Texas—each of whom was elected to the governorship after that office had been held by her husband. Mr. Ross died during his term as chief executive, and Mr. Ferguson was impeached and removed from office. Cf. Solomon, "American Governors Since 1915," *loc. cit.* below.

[74] Austin F. Macdonald, "American Governors" [1900-1910], *Nat. Mun. Rev.*, XVI, 715-719 (Nov., 1927); Samuel R. Solomon, "American Governors Since 1915," *Ibid.*, XX, 152-158 (Mar., 1931); John A. Perkins, "American Governors, 1930 to 1940," *Ibid.*, XXIX, 178-184 (Mar., 1940); Samuel R. Solomon, "U.S. Governors 1940-1950," *Ibid.*, XLI, 190-197 (Apr., 1952); John K. Gurwell, "Governors of the States," *State Govt.*, XIV, 157-158, 172 (July, 1941); Cortez A. M. Ewing, "Southern Governors," *Jour. of Politics*, X, 385-409 (May, 1948).

[75] A detailed analysis of governors' office careers is available in Joseph A. Schlesinger, *How They Became Governor.*

[76] In the early 1950's it was reported that at least a fourth of the current membership of the United States Senate consisted of former governors. Solomon, "U. S. Governors 1940-1950," *loc. cit.*

Succession to the Governorship

Every state constitution makes provision for succession to the office of governor in certain contingencies. Most states provide that a designated officer shall succeed to the gubernatorial office, or assume the duties thereof, in event of the governor's death, removal from office, or resignation; or of his "disability" or "inability" to perform his official duties. Somewhat more than half of the states also provide that the designated successor shall act if the governor is absent from the state. In the thirty-eight states having the office of lieutenant governor, that official is first in the line of succession to the governor's office.[77] Among the twelve states which have no lieutenant governor, the president of the senate is the governor's successor in eight,[78] and the secretary of state in four.[79]

The Lieutenant Governor

The lieutenant governor is elected at the same time and in the same manner as the governor, serves for the same term, and must have the same qualifications. His two primary functions are those of (1) succeeding to the governor's duties under prescribed circumstances and (2) presiding over the state senate.[80] In several states the lieutenant governor is a member of certain boards, but in only a few instances is he assigned administrative duties on anything approaching a full-time basis. Perhaps the broadest assignment of such duties is in Indiana, where the office is a full-time job with the incumbent serving as director of one of the administrative departments and as chairman or a member of several boards and commissions.[81] Since in most states the lieutenant governor has few if any duties except when the legislature is in session, his compensation is usually in the form of a relatively small salary, or a per diem during legislative sessions. Some states provide, however, that when the lieutenant governor

[77] A few constitutions designate only the immediate successor to the governorship, leaving to the legislature the regulation of succession beyond that point. In most states, however, the constitution itself, after designating the first successor, lists from one to six other officers who shall succeed to the governorship, in a specified order, if necessity arises. A common provision is that, after the lieutenant governor, the president *pro tempore* of the senate, and after him the speaker of the house, shall be next in line.

[78] Florida, Maine, Maryland, New Hampshire, New Jersey, Oregon, Tennessee, and West Virginia. Tennessee provided by statute in 1951 that the speaker (president) of the senate shall have the title of lieutenant governor.

[79] Alaska, Arizona, Utah, and Wyoming.

[80] The lieutenant governor's position as president of the senate has been discussed at a previous point. See above, Chap. VII, "Officers and Employees."

[81] Richard I. Hofferbert, "The Lieutenant Governorship in Indiana," *Indiana Pub. Affairs Notes* (Bur. of Govt. Research, Ind. Univ.), Vol. IV, No. 1 (Jan.-Feb., 1962).

serves as governor he shall receive the same rate of compensation as that provided for the governor himself.

When the governor and lieutenant governor are elected separately, as they ordinarily are, it is not unusual for the two officers to be of different political parties. Where this is the case and the lieutenant governor succeeds to the governorship by reason of the governor's death, resignation, or removal, there may be an abrupt change in party control of the administrative branch between elections. Furthermore, on some occasions lieutenant governors, upon assuming the duties of the governorship temporarily because of the governor's disability or absence from the state, have made appointments to or removals from office, or taken other forms of action which have embarrassed the governor upon his resumption of duties. In an effort to lessen the likelihood of such occurrences, New York, Michigan, and several other states have recently made provision that, in electing the governor and lieutenant governor, a single vote shall be cast jointly for candidates for both offices nominated by the same party. Under this plan, which should virtually assure that the governor and lieutenant governor will be of the same party, incidents of the kinds mentioned, although still possible, would be less likely to occur. Insofar as the plan may foster cordial relations between the two officers, it should be additionally advantageous in those states where the lieutenant governor is assigned some regular administrative duties.

Most students of government agree that the lieutenant governorship is an unnecessary office. Almost a fourth of the states now get along very well without it. A president of the senate chosen from that body's membership is in general preferable to an independently-elected "outsider" as a presiding officer; and almost any other elective officer would be quite as likely as the lieutenant governor to serve as a satisfactory successor to the governorship. The limited administrative duties which are imposed upon the lieutenant governor could readily be performed by other officers. Since the lieutenant governorship is a constitutional office, its elimination would, of course, require constitutional amendment. Abolition of the office, however, in addition to effecting a modest saving in expense, would appear to be a desirable step in the direction of shortening the ballot.[82]

The Problem of Disability

It is a relatively simple matter to determine when, because of the governor's death, removal, resignation, or absence from the state, the

[82] Concerning the office generally and proposals for its reform, see Benjamin Nispel, *Reform of the Office of Lieutenant Governor;* Charles Kettleborough, "Powers of the Lieutenant-Governor," *Amer. Polit. Sci. Rev.,* XI, 88-92 (Feb., 1917); Warren Rex Isom, "The Office of Lieutenant-Governor in the States," *Ibid.,* XXXII, 921-926 (Oct., 1938); Robert F. Patterson, "The Lieutenant-Governor in 1944," *State Govt.,* XVII, 348-349, 356-357 (June, 1944).

gubernatorial office legally devolves upon the designated successor. The provision for succession to the office in case of the governor's disability, however, is the source of some difficulty, due to the fact that most constitutions neither define disability nor provide any definite means of determining its existence or nonexistence. It is sometimes alleged by the lieutenant governor or other officer who is first in line of succession that the governor is actually unable, because of illness or otherwise, to perform his duties properly, while the governor himself claims that he is not disabled and insists upon retaining his office. In some instances the lieutenant governor has gone so far as to attempt to take over the governor's duties; and in such cases serious questions are likely to arise concerning the legality of the acts performed by the governor and lieutenant governor respectively. In Illinois, for example, during a period of nearly two years in 1939 and 1940, there was considerable question as to whether or not the illness of Governor Horner was so serious as to constitute disability within the meaning of the state constitution. During much of this time the governor's office was conducted from the executive mansion; and for a brief period the lieutenant governor claimed to have taken over the gubernatorial office and to be acting as governor.[83] Such an unfortunate situation might be prevented by providing in the constitution some specific means of determining when disability does and does not exist. As matters now stand, only five states make constitutional provision for determining whether the governor is disabled. In four of these—Alaska, Michigan, Mississippi, and New Jersey—the provisions are sufficiently broad to cover either physical or mental disability, while Alabama's provision applies to mental disability only. The provisions in Alabama, Michigan, Mississippi, and New Jersey empower the state supreme court to settle the disability question, while Alaska provides that the procedure for determining disability shall be prescribed by statute.[84] Other states would do well to follow the lead of these pioneers by conferring upon the supreme court, an ex officio board of state officials, or some other agency, authority to decide the troublesome question of gubernatorial disability.

REFERENCES

ABERNETHY, Byron R., *Some Persisting Questions Concerning the Constitutional State Executive* (Govtl. Research Center, Univ. of Kan., Lawrence, 1960).

[83] Clyde F. Snider, "Gubernatorial Disability," *Univ. of Chicago Law Rev.*, VIII, 521-529 (Apr., 1941).

[84] An Oregon statute, enacted in 1959, provides for determination of the governor's disability by unanimous vote of a "conference" consisting of the chief justice of the state supreme court, the superintendent of the state hospital, and the dean of the medical school of the University of Oregon. *Oregon Laws*, 1959, Chap. 672.

BECKWITH, Edmund R., and others, *Lawful Action of State Military Forces* (Random House, New York, 1944).

BLACK, Henry C., *The Relation of the Executive Power to Legislation* (Princeton Univ. Press, Princeton, N. J., 1919), Chaps. 5, 7.

CARLSON, Knute E., *The Exercise of the Veto Power in Nebraska* (Neb. State Hist. Soc. and Neb. Legis. Ref. Bur., Lincoln, 1917).

DEBEL, Niels H., *The Veto Power of the Governor of Illinois* (Univ. of Ill., Urbana, 1917).

FAIRMAN, Charles, *The Law of Martial Rule* (Callaghan, Chicago, 2nd ed., 1943).

FANNIN, Paul, and others, *The Office of Governor in Arizona* (Bur. of Govt. Research, Ariz. State Univ., Tempe, 1964).

FINLEY, John H., and SANDERSON, John F., *The American Executive and Executive Methods* (Century, New York, 1908).

FRIEDMAN, Jacob Alexis, *The Impeachment of Governor William Sulzer* (Columbia Univ. Press, New York, 1939).

Institute of Government and Public Affairs, University of Illinois, *The Office of Governor* (The Institute, Urbana, 1963).

JENSEN, Christen, *The Pardoning Power in the American States* (Univ. of Chicago Press, Chicago, 1922).

LAFOLLETTE, Robert M., *LaFollette's Autobiography: A Personal Narrative of Political Experiences* (Robert M. LaFollette Co., Madison, Wis., 1913), especially Chaps. 6-8.

LIPSON, Leslie, *The American Governor: From Figurehead to Leader* (Univ. of Chicago Press, Chicago, 1939).

New York State Constitutional Convention Committee, *Problems Relating to Executive Administration and Powers* (Report of the Committee, Vol. VIII, Albany, 1938).

NISPEL, Benjamin, *Reform of the Office of Lieutenant Governor* (Pub. Affairs Press, Washington, 1958).

RANKIN, Robert S., *When Civil Law Fails* (Duke Univ. Press, Durham, N. C., 1939).

RANSONE, Coleman B., Jr., *The Office of Governor in the South* (Bur. of Pub. Admin., Univ. of Ala., University, Ala., 1951).

————, *The Office of Governor in the United States* (Univ. of Ala. Press, University, Ala., 1956).

RICH, Bennett M., *State Constitutions: The Governor* (Nat. Mun. League, New York, 1960).

RIKER, William H., *Soldiers of the States: The Role of the National Guard in American Democracy* (Pub. Affairs Press, Washington, 1957).

ROHR, Charles J., *The Governor of Maryland: A Constitutional Study* (Johns Hopkins Press, Baltimore, 1932).

ROOSEVELT, Theodore, *An Autobiography* (Scribner, New York, 1913), Chap. 8.

SCACE, Homer E., *The Organization of the Executive Office of the Governor* (Inst. of Pub. Admin., New York, 1950).

SCHLESINGER, Joseph A., *How They Became Governor* (Govtl. Research Bur., Mich. State Univ., East Lansing, 1957).

SMITH, Alfred E., *Up to Now: An Autobiography* (Viking, New York, 1929), especially Chaps. 11-22.

United States Department of Justice, *Attorney General's Survey of Release Procedures,* Volume III: *Pardon* (U.S. Govt. Printing Office, Washington, 1939).

VOSE, Clement E., *The Executive Council of Maine in Decline* (Bur. for Research in Mun. Govt., Bowdoin Coll., Brunswick, Me., 1959).

WILLIAMS, G. Mennen, *A Governor's Notes* (Inst. of Pub. Admin., Univ. of Mich., Ann Arbor, 1961).

10

Administrative Organization and the Civil Service

Nature of Administration

Administration, as the term will be used in this chapter, may be defined as the application and execution, in detail and day by day, of the laws and other regulations which government imposes upon the people, and the performance of the various public services which government provides. The term *administrative organization* will be used to denote the structure and interrelationships of those governmental agencies which are engaged primarily in administrative work. In introducing our discussion of state legislatures,[1] it was suggested that the governmental process consists basically of two steps—the determination of public policy and the execution of that policy. Administration is concerned with the latter of these steps. When the legislative branch of government has decided what activities and services are to be undertaken by the state, it becomes the task of the various administrative agencies to see that this program of activities and services is carried out in accordance with the legislative intent. Administration is concerned with the actual work of protecting life and property, providing educational facilities, regulating business enterprise, building highways, caring for the needy, and performing the numerous other functions of the modern state. Though governmental administration, in a broad sense, includes the work of the courts, judicial organization and administration are reserved for consideration in subse-

[1] See above, Chap. VII, "The Legislative Function."

quent chapters[2] and attention is here confined to the executive branch.[3]

Importance of Good Administrative Organization

Efficiency or inefficiency in government results from the interplay of many and varied forces. Two important factors in determining the relative efficiency of administration are (1) the qualifications of the officers and employees engaged in administrative activities, and (2) the nature of the organizational setup through which those persons must work. At one time, little attention was given by students of government to forms of organization, it apparently being assumed that able officials would get good results from any type of organization. Nowadays, however, more attention is given to matters of organization. There seems, indeed, to be an unfortunate tendency in some quarters to overemphasize matters of mere form, to the neglect of the personal element. As a matter of fact, both personnel and organization are important. It is true, of course, that the best of governmental machinery will not produce good results if operated by incompetent personnel. But, given capable and honest officials, efficient administration will be promoted by suitable forms of organization and impeded by inappropriate forms.

The importance of proper administrative organization is further enhanced by the very nature of the administrative function. Whereas the legislative function normally comes into play only periodically, during sessions of the legislative body, administration is a continuous process. Most governmental services are provided the year round, many of them being available twenty-four hours a day. Moreover, it is through the various administrative agencies that the average person experiences his daily contacts with government, and by the standards of these agencies that he judges the character of government as a whole. Many persons go through life without ever visiting a session of the state legislature; yet practically all, at one time or another, have direct contact with the state or local officials who administer schools, elections, licenses, highways, tax assessments, and the like. When we add to these considerations the further fact that most of the money which we pay in taxes, notwithstanding that its expenditure must be authorized in broad terms by the legislature, is actually spent under the immediate supervision of administrative officers, it becomes clear that the organization of our public administrative agencies is a matter of genuine concern to all of us.

[2] Below, Chaps. XI, XVII.

[3] This major division of governmental organization was originally termed the *executive* but is now, because of the nature of its principal duties, frequently referred to as the *administrative* branch. The latter term will be more generally used in this chapter, though the two terms might with propriety be employed interchangeably. A distinction of a general nature is sometimes made as between executive and administrative *officers* on the ground that the duties of the former involve greater discretion than those of the latter. The branch of government with which we are here concerned includes officers of both classes.

Traditional Administrative Organization

As we have seen in earlier chapters, the legislative function in the states is vested primarily in the state legislature, although the governor is assigned a definite and important part. The function of administration, on the other hand, falls to the executive or administrative branch of government. Though the composition of this branch varies widely in detail from state to state, it usually includes (1) the governor as nominal head; (2) a group of elective administrative offices established by the constitution; (3) various offices, boards, and commissions[4] created by statute; and (4) the numerous employees who constitute the staffs of these different agencies. Prior to the reorganization movement, which will be discussed presently, little provision was made for systematic coordination of the work of these varied instrumentalities, over many of which the governor was powerless to exercise control. This state of affairs, in which administrative "organization" is virtually *dis*organization and the administrative branch, though nominally headed by the governor, is in reality headless, still prevails in states that have not been substantially reorganized.

The office of governor has already been discussed[5] and will be considered in this chapter principally in its relation to problems of administrative organization and reorganization. Subordinate administrative personnel will be treated later in the present chapter. It will be well at this point to note the general characteristics of the other two groups of instrumentalities mentioned above, namely, the constitutional elective offices and the statutory administrative agencies.

The Constitutional Offices

Most state constitutions, in addition to providing for a governor and lieutenant governor,[6] establish several other administrative offices. Though in some instances the incumbents of these offices are appointed by the governor and senate or elected by the legislature, they are most commonly chosen by popular vote. As a general rule they are nominated and elected in the same manner, and serve for the same term, as the governor. The number of constitutional officers varies considerably from state

---

[4] Though a technical distinction is sometimes drawn between boards and commissions, that distinction is not essential to our purpose. State legislatures, in giving offical titles to administrative agencies, seem quite as likely to use one name as the other. The board and the commission are alike in being plural agencies, usually consisting of three or more members, in contrast to the single-headed administrative office.

[5] Above, Chap. IX.

[6] The office of lieutenant governor is considered above, Chap. IX.

to state, but is most commonly in the neighborhood of 6.[7] Quite generally included in the group are the secretary of state, attorney general, treasurer, and auditor.[8] The functions of each of these officers will be considered briefly at this point. Notwithstanding that the offices are established by constitutional provision, their powers and duties, for the most part, are prescribed by statute.[9]

The Secretary of State. The secretary of state is generally the official custodian of state records and archives. He is keeper of the state seal, by use of which he is required to authenticate gubernatorial proclamations, commissions of appointment, and certain other public documents. He is charged with the publication and distribution of the state session laws. He usually has important duties in connection with election administration; issues certificates of incorporation; and registers trademarks. In many states he is charged with the compilation and publication of a state manual or register, and of election statistics. In some states he issues automobile licenses and administers state laws regulating the issuance and sale of corporate securities. Other duties of a miscellaneous nature are imposed upon him in different states.[10]

The Attorney General. The functions of the attorney general fall into three principal categories. In the first place, he is the legal adviser, with respect to their official powers and duties, of the governor, of other administrative officers, boards, and commissions, and of the state legislature. Frequently it is his duty to give advice also to certain local officials, especially prosecuting attorneys. If, for instance, the governor wishes advice as to the constitutionality of a bill which is awaiting his signature, or if the state tax commission desires assistance in interpreting a provision in the tax laws, the question may be submitted to the attorney general. The latter official, either personally or through a designated member of his staff, studies the matter concerned and prepares a formal opinion which is transmitted to the official requesting it. These opinions of the attorney general are published from time to time in book form; but it is to be noted that they do not, like judicial decisions, have the force of law.

[7] Cf. John A. Fairlie, "The Executive Power in the State Constitution," *Annals of Amer. Acad. of Polit. and Soc. Sci.*, CLXXXI, 59-73 (Sept., 1935).

[8] There are a few states in which one or more of these offices exist by statutory rather than constitutional provision. Another office commonly established by constitutional provision is that of superintendent of public instruction. The superintendent's office is considered below, Chap. XX, in the discussion of the role of the states in public school administration.

[9] For further general discussion, see Kirk H. Porter, *State Administration*, Chaps. 3, 4, 5; John M. Mathews, *Principles of American State Administration*, Chap. 6.

[10] A tabular analysis of functions of the respective secretaries of state will be found in *The Book of the States* (Council of State Govts., Chicago), 1945-46, p. 565.

They are, in fact as in name, opinions only, and may, if litigation subsequently arises, be overturned by the courts. In practice, however, the great majority of the questions upon which opinions are given are never raised in actual litigation; and, where they are so raised, if the opinions have been competently prepared, the courts are likely in most instances to arrive at the same conclusion as has the attorney general. In any event, the attorney general's interpretation of a law stands as authoritative unless overturned by judicial decision.

Secondly, it is the duty of the attorney general, in cases to which the state is a party or in which some state officer or agency sues or is sued in an official capacity, to appear in court as the representative of the state or its officer or agency. And, finally, as the principal law-enforcement officer of the state below the governor, the attorney general is charged with certain powers and duties relative to the prosecution of persons accused of crime. In that connection, he is generally authorized to advise and assist local prosecuting attorneys; and in some states he may, under certain circumstances, supersede the local prosecutor. This phase of the attorney general's work will be given further consideration in the chapter relating to law enforcement.[11]

The Treasurer. The treasurer is the official custodian of state funds. It is his duty to receive state revenues, keep them safely, and make disbursements therefrom as authorized by law. Many forms of revenue are collected in the first instance by other governmental agencies and by them turned over to the treasurer. Thus state property taxes are usually collected by local treasurers; state sales and gasoline taxes are in some states collected by separate departments of revenue or finance; and fees of varied nature are collected by numerous state agencies. Ultimately, however, most state moneys are required to be paid into the treasury for safe-keeping and disbursement.

The duties of the state treasurer are largely formal and ministerial in nature, rather than discretionary. Treasurers are placed under official bond to protect the public against loss of funds through their carelessness or dishonesty. At one time treasurers were required to account only for

[11] Below, Chap. XVII. Various aspects of the office of attorney general are considered in Council of State Governments, *The Office of Attorney General: Personnel and Financing;* John A. Fairlie, "Law Departments and Law Officers in American Government," *Mich. Law Rev.,* XXXVI, 906-934 (Apr., 1938); John A. Fairlie and Donald F. Simpson, "Law Departments and Law Officers in the States," *State Govt.,* XIV, 237-238, 251-254 (Oct., 1941); John A. Fairlie and Donald Simpson, "Law Officers in Illinois," *John Marshall Law Quar.,* VIII, 65-79 (Sept., 1942); Nathaniel L. Goldstein, "The Office of the Attorney General of the State" [of New York], *N.Y. State Bar Assn. Bull.,* XVI, 183-190 (Dec., 1944); Dee Ashley Akers, "The Advisory Opinion Function of the Attorney General" [in Kentucky], *Ky. Law Jour.,* XXXVIII, 561-598 (May, 1950); "The Office of Attorney General in Kentucky" (Report of the Department of Law to the Committee on the Administration of Justice in the Commonwealth of Kentucky), *Ibid.,* Vol. LI, No. 5 (Special Issue, 1963).

the principal amount of funds placed in their custody, and enjoyed complete discretion in determining how and where the funds should be kept. Under those circumstances, treasurers frequently used inactive funds in their custody in their personal business or deposited them in favored banks, and looked upon any earnings as a perquisite of their offices. Nowadays, however, most states have public-depository laws requiring that state funds be deposited in banks designated by a state board of finance (of which the treasurer is frequently a member), and providing that interest shall be the property of the state.[12] Bank deposits payable on demand draw interest only at a low rate, if at all. Funds not required for immediate use are therefore often placed on "time" deposit. Time deposits, evidenced by the issuance of "certificates of deposit," are not subject to withdrawal until the expiration of a specified number of months and draw a higher rate of interest than do demand deposits. Some states now follow the practice of investing a portion of their inactive funds in short-term securities of the United States Government, or in their own securities or those of their political subdivisions. Since treasurers frequently have millions of dollars on hand which will not be disbursed for some weeks or months, the wise investment of idle funds may constitute a significant source of state revenue.[13]

The Auditor. The two principal functions of the auditor are those of (1) authorizing disbursements from the state treasury, and (2) making periodic audits of the accounts of the treasurer and other officers who handle state funds. In performing the first of these functions, the auditor acts as a check upon the treasurer as well as the various governmental agencies to which appropriations of money are made. When the legislature has passed an appropriation act, the auditor sets up an account for each individual appropriation. Before any expenditure can actually be made pursuant to an appropriation, the auditor must be convinced that the purpose of the expenditure is the one for which the appropriation was made, and that there is an unexpended balance sufficient to cover the proposed payment. When he is satisfied that these requirements have been met, the auditor signs an order or warrant upon the treasury, and only then can the treasurer make the necessary disbursement. This function of the auditor, which is called the *pre*audit because it occurs before

[12] Provisions of state depository laws are discussed in Martin L. Faust, *The Custody of State Funds* (Nat. Inst. of Pub. Admin., New York, 1925). See also, by the same author, *The Security of Public Deposits* (Pub. Admin. Service, Chicago, 1936).

[13] Advisory Commission on Intergovernmental Relations, *Investment of Idle Cash Balances by State and Local Governments* (U.S. Govt. Printing Office, Washington, 1961); R. Joseph Monsen and Garth L. Mangum, "Alternative Investment Outlets for Idle State Operating Funds," *State Govt.*, XXXVI, 189-197 (Summer, 1963).

expenditure, has recently been shifted in some states, and quite properly, from the elective auditor to an appointive comptroller. In performing the second or *post*audit function, the auditor examines the accounts and records of state officers to determine whether financial transactions already made have been regular and in conformity to law. If he finds the accounts of an officer in proper order, he so certifies. In the event that his examination reveals a default or unlawful acts of any kind, it is his duty to see that appropriate legal proceedings are instituted to protect the public interest. Some states have now shifted the postaudit function from the elective auditor to a legislative auditor whose office is somewhat similar to the General Accounting Office in the federal government.[14]

Statutory Agencies

In earlier times, when state functions were few and simple, the activities of the state government could, for the most part, be carried on by the usual constitutional officers and their staffs. But, as traditional functions of government were expanded and new functions undertaken,[15] the establishment of additional administrative agencies became necessary. These new agencies were created in some instances by constitutional provision, but more often by statute. Though at times newly assumed functions were assigned to existing agencies, there was a tendency to create a new agency for the administration of each new activity undertaken. In doing this, no standard pattern was followed. Individual officers were provided in some instances, and boards or commissions in others. Some of the officers and boards were popularly elected, others were appointed by the governor (usually with senatorial consent), while still others were constituted on an ex officio basis. Thus there grew up a heterogeneous mass of state administrative agencies, differing widely in form and composition, and operating, for the most part, quite independently of each other. The list of these agencies naturally varied considerably from state to state. To mention only a few of the more common, there were boards of charities, tax equalization boards, election canvassing boards, public utilities commissions, prison boards, insurance commissioners, boards of health, and banking commissioners. In some states the total number of administrative agencies was well over a hundred. The work of many of these statutory agencies, in their present-day forms, will be discussed later in appropriate chapters dealing with governmental functions.

[14] On the auditor and other auditing officials in the respective states, see James W. Martin and others, *The State Auditor* (Bur. of Bus. Research, Univ. of Ky., Lexington, 1942). See also below, Chap. XXV, "Execution of the Budget."

[15] See Carroll H. Wooddy, "The Growth of Governmental Functions," Chap. 25 of *Recent Social Trends in the United States* (McGraw-Hill, New York, 1934). Pp. 1292-1307 treat especially of state functions.

The Problem of Correlation and Control

From what has been said one would surmise, and correctly, that state administrative machinery, having grown in piecemeal fashion and without planning, eventually reached a sad state of disorganization. Each of the multitudinous agencies carried on its work with little knowledge or thought of what other agencies were doing. Overlapping of functions and conflicts of jurisdiction were inevitable. The governor, though nominal head of the administrative branch, actually had little authority through which he could correlate the work of the various agencies. Elective officers and boards were quite independent of the chief executive; and, with respect to appointive agencies, the governor's power of control was usually circumscribed by the requirement that he obtain senatorial approval of his appointments, and by serious limitations upon his removal power. Even if the governor *had* possessed adequate powers over the individual officers and boards, their very number would have made proper supervision practically impossible. As a result of the inefficiency and extravagance flowing from this thoroughly unsatisfactory situation, it was ultimately realized that, if state government was to function properly, the administrative branch would have to be reorganized with a view to reducing the number of separate administrative agencies and strengthening the governor's supervisory powers.

Purposes and Principles of Reorganization

The basic purposes or aims of state administrative reorganization have been two: (1) economy and (2) efficiency. These two objectives are, of course, closely interrelated. Taken together, they may imply either a reduction in public expenditures or the provision of more and better governmental services for the same amount of money. With a view to promoting economy and efficiency in government, reorganization projects have usually proceeded along two principal lines, namely, those of *integration* and *centralization*. Indeed, integration and centralization may be said to constitute the central principles of administrative reform.

Integration is the term applied to the grouping together in a single department of various related activities which, prior to reorganization, were administered by a number of independent agencies.[16] The integration process involves the replacement of a large number of independent and uncorrelated agencies by a small number of major departments. Thus all activities related to agriculture may be placed in one department, those concerning public works in another, and those related to public welfare in a third. By this process it is sought to correlate all activities in

---

[16] *Departmentalization* is another term sometimes used to describe this process.

a given field, eliminate duplication of effort, and reduce to manageable size the number of administrative units over which the governor is expected to exercise supervision. By centralization is meant the strengthening of the governor's power of control over the administrative machinery.[17] This is usually achieved by placing at the head of each of the newly created departments a commissioner or director appointed by the governor[18] and serving at his pleasure. Only when the administrative setup has been made manageable through integration, and the governor has been placed in direct control through his power of appointment and removal, is it reasonable to hold the chief executive politically responsible to the electorate for the effective conduct of the administrative branch.[19]

Though integration and centralization form the core of the reorganization process, certain ancillary principles of importance have been applied in various states. On the theory that a single head facilitates promptness of action and centralizes administrative responsibility, there has been a rather general tendency to substitute single officials (commissioners or directors) for boards and commissions as heads of administrative agencies, though, even when single heads are provided, boards are sometimes retained within departments for the performance of quasi-legislative or quasi-judicial functions.[20] In many states the governor's

[17] Some writers prefer to apply to this process the term *concentration,* reserving the term *centralization* to describe an increase of control by the federal government over the states or by the states over their subdivisions. Cf. Porter, *State Administration,* Chap. 9.

[18] Sometimes with the consent of the senate.

[19] Professor Phillip Monypenny has pointed out that reducing or limiting the number of state administrative departments, in an effort to keep within reasonable limits the number of subordinates reporting directly to the governor, has effected an intrinsic change in the position of the department head. As state activities have multiplied, the functions performed by each department have tended to become more and more varied and to be apportioned among a larger number of administrative subdivisions *within* the department. In these circumstances, the qualifications required of a successful department head are no longer confined to professional skill in a single field of specialization but include that broader competence in general administrative management so essential to the governor himself at a higher level. Phillip Monypenny, "The Changing Position of the Department Head in State Government," *State Govt.,* XXIV, 112-114 (Apr., 1951).

[20] Many administrative agencies, in addition to their duties of a strictly administrative character, are charged with the performance of various functions quite similar in their nature to those performed by legislatures or courts. Thus a state department of health, in promulgating rules regulating the holding of public meetings during epidemics, is engaged in what is virtually legislative work; and a state tax commission, in reviewing local assessments, performs work essentially judicial in nature. Though as a practical matter it is necessary to delegate many such functions to administrative agencies, state constitutions, expressly or by implication, usually prohibit the delegation of *legislative* or *judicial* powers to executive or administrative agencies. Hence the courts, in order to sustain necessary delegations of authority, commonly make a distinction between functions truly legislative or judicial and those which, on the other hand, are only *quasi*-legislative or *quasi*-judicial in nature, thereby permitting delegation of functions of the latter type to administrative bodies. The distinction is a vague one at best, being based principally upon the *amount* of dis-

position has been substantially strengthened by including in the reorganization plan provision for an executive budget.[21] And finally, in order to expedite gubernatorial supervision of administration, many states have provided the governor with managerial or "staff" agencies designed specifically to advise and assist him in the exercise of his supervisory duties.[22]

The Reorganization Movement

Although there had been earlier attempts in several states to improve particular phases of administrative organization, the first state to adopt a reasonably thorough plan of reorganization was Illinois, in 1917. In enacting its Civil Administrative Code of that year, the Illinois legislature consolidated numerous administrative agencies into nine major departments,[23] each headed by a director appointed by the governor with the consent of the senate. Other states followed suit, and by 1938 more than half of the states had adopted reorganization plans of one kind or another.[24] During the ensuing decade only a few additional states reorganized; but the late 1940's and the 1950's witnessed a sharp revival of the reorganization movement evidenced by the establishment of the Little Hoover Commissions to be considered presently. As a result of this renewed interest, many of the states which had reorganized earlier acted to effect further changes and some additional states took initial action. All told, some three-fourths of the states have now effected a substantial degree of reorganization, and most of the others have taken *some* steps in that direction at one time or another. It seems appropriate, however, to speak of those states which have taken only minimal action as being still unreorganized.[25]

---

cretion involved in the function concerned. Students of public administration rather generally agree that, though responsibility for functions of a strictly administrative nature should be centralized in individual officers, quasi-legislative and quasi-judicial functions are more appropriately performed by plural agencies. An occasional scholar has voiced the opinion that, in the case of agencies charged with quasi-legislative or quasi-judicial functions of major importance, the most appropriate form of organization is a plural head—board or commission—to perform those functions, with the strictly administrative functions of the agency vested in a single administrator appointed by and responsible to the plural head. See, for example, Kirk H. Porter, "The Administrative Process and the Quasi-Legislative Function," *Ia. Law Rev.*, XXXVII, 21-35 (Fall, 1951).

[21] For a discussion of the executive budget and its advantages, see below, Chap. XXV, "The Budget-Making Authority."

[22] See below, "Departments of Administration."

[23] The number of departments has since been changed from time to time and is now (1964) seventeen.

[24] Reorganization plans adopted and proposed in the various states down to 1938 are summarized in A. E. Buck, *The Reorganization of State Governments in the United States.*

[25] See James R. Bell and Earl L. Darrah, *State Executive Reorganization;* John C. Bollens, *Administrative Reorganization in the States Since 1939;* Council of

In most states, as we have seen, various elective offices are established by constitutional provision, and ordinarily it is not within the competence of the legislature to place the departments headed by these constitutional officers under the governor's direction. However, some degree of centralization with respect to the work of these departments has been achieved by transferring functions from such agencies to statutory departments which are under the governor's control. This has been possible because state constitutions, when they establish administrative offices, usually do not prescribe their powers and duties. A few states—notably Massachusetts, New York, and Virginia—have amended their constitutions to reduce the number of constitutional offices and thereby give the legislature a freer hand in reorganization. Generally, however, in view of the difficulty of securing constitutional amendments, legislatures have confined their reorganization efforts to such changes as could be accomplished by statute. As a result, there are to be found in many of the so-called reorganized states two distinct groups of administrative departments. In one group, the departments are established by statute and controlled by the governor through his power to appoint and remove department heads. Departments of the other group are headed by elective constitutional officers and are largely independent both of the governor and of each other. If the constitutional officers are of the same political party as the governor, there is likely to be at least some degree of cooperation between their departments and the chief executive. Yet even this element of coordination may be lacking if these department heads and the governor are allied with different factions within the party. Such a situation is not unusual since party leaders, in seeking to present a "balanced" ticket to the voters, frequently deem it expedient to nominate candidates for at least some of the constitutional administrative offices from a different party faction than that represented by the gubernatorial nominee.

The number of statutory departments operating under the governor's direction[26] in reorganized states varies rather widely, but in many

State Governments, *Reorganizing State Government;* Council of State Governments, *A Progress Report on State Reorganization in 1950;* Lynton K. Caldwell, "Perfecting State Administration, 1940-46," *Pub. Admin. Rev.,* VII, 25-36 (Winter, 1947); Leslie Lipson, "The Executive Branch in New State Constitutions," *Ibid.,* IX, 11-21 (Winter, 1949); John A. Perkins, "Reflections on State Reorganizations," *Amer. Polit. Sci. Rev.,* XLV, 507-516 (June, 1951); W. Brooke Graves, "Some New Approaches to State Administrative Reorganization," *Western Polit. Quar.,* IX, 743-754 (Sept., 1956). Numerous articles concerning reorganization in individual states are to be found in the *National Municipal Review* (now the *National Civic Review*), *State Government, Public Administration Review,* various law journals, and other periodicals; and current developments are summarized in each issue of the Council of State Governments' biennial *Book of the States.*

[26] In states, such as Illinois and Nebraska, where the reorganization law is known as the civil administrative code, these departments are sometimes referred to as "code" departments.

instances there are now a dozen or more. Though departmental titles are by no means standardized, the departments most generally found are those of finance, public works, public welfare, labor, agriculture, and education. Departments of public health and conservation are common, though health activities are sometimes assigned to the welfare department and conservation functions to the department of agriculture. Some states have recently established separate departments of mental health. Other departments of varied titles and character are found in individual states. In an effort to keep the governor's supervisory task within bounds, several states limit by constitutional provision the number of principal administrative departments which may be established. The recently-adopted constitutions of Alaska, Hawaii, and Michigan, for example, fix the maximum number at twenty.

Some states require that the governor's appointments to department headships have the approval of the senate, whereas others do not. Though the necessity of securing senatorial confirmation limits somewhat the governor's control over department heads, and hence his responsibility for their acts, such requirement has in some instances been necessary to allay the fear that, without a check of this nature, governors would use the appointing power to build personal political machines. In some states department heads serve at the governor's pleasure, while in others they are appointed for definite terms. Even where appointed for fixed terms, however, they may, in some instances, be removed by the governor at any time. Such a power of removal strengthens substantially the governor's power of direction over the departments concerned.

State Surveys as Basis for Reorganization

Reorganization of the administrative setup in the various states has usually been preceded by a survey study designed to analyze existing organization, discover weaknesses therein, and formulate recommendations for improvement. In some states these surveys have been made under the direction of the governor and financed from funds placed at his disposal by the legislature, while in other instances studies have been made by special committees or commissions established by the legislature for that particular purpose. Whether under executive or legislative sponsorship, the actual work of making the surveys has usually been delegated to trained research workers. Some states for this purpose have used "home talent," drawing frequently upon the political science faculties of their state universities, while others have employed professional survey organizations.[27]

[27] Cf. Buck, *op. cit.*, 38-40. The better known survey organizations include the Institute of Public Administration, New York City; Griffenhagen and Associates, Chicago; and the Public Administration Service, Chicago.

Findings and recommendations resulting from these surveys have been fairly uniform. The studies have revealed large numbers of uncorrelated administrative agencies operating inefficiently and expensively; and the recommendations of the surveying agencies and their sponsors have usually centered around integration, centralization, and improved budgetary procedure. There has, however, been much variation in the extent to which these recommendations have actually borne fruit. Some state legislatures have enacted reorganization laws by which the recommendations have been made effective almost in their entirety; others have put into effect some, but by no means all, of the recommendations; while in still other states the recommendations have not resulted in any reorganization of major consequence. In practically every state there has now been at least one administrative survey of some kind, yet a considerable number of states have enacted no reorganizing legislation worthy of the name. Whether or not they have produced tangible results, the reports of the various state surveys have usually been published, and these reports serve as valuable sources for the comparative study of state governments.

Several states have made it the continuing responsibility of the state budget officer or some other executive agency to investigate administrative organization and recommend changes therein. In practice, however, investigations and recommendations made under provisions such as these, by agencies concerned primarily with regular administrative duties, appear generally to have been of a fragmentary nature. Under normal circumstances, a comprehensive overall study of administrative machinery can probably be made most effectively by a special investigatory agency established for that specific task.

The Little Hoover Commissions

In 1947 Congress established at the national level a Commission on Organization of the Executive Branch of the Government to investigate the organization and operation of the departments and other agencies of the executive branch and recommend changes which would promote economy, efficiency, and improved service. This bipartisan commission was composed in part of members of Congress and federal administrators and in part of private citizens. Under the chairmanship of ex-President Herbert Hoover and popularly known as the Hoover Commission, it conducted the most thorough overall study yet made of the executive branch of the federal government and published its findings and recommendations in a monumental report, one of the early results of which was enactment by Congress of the Administrative Reorganization Act of 1949.

Stimulated by this federal activity, a number of state legislatures in their 1949 sessions created study commissions patterned more or less after the federal survey agency and popularly known as "Little Hoover Commissions." Several additional states established similar agencies in their 1951 legislative sessions; and still others provided for a study of their administrative machinery by interim legislative committees or legislative councils. Altogether, more than 30 states in this new wave of enthusiasm for administrative reorganization provided for surveys to be conducted in one way or another.[28] Of the special commissions established for study purposes, some were composed entirely of state legislators and some entirely of private citizens; others included both private citizens and legislators, while yet others combined legislative, administrative, and citizen membership.[29]

Within a few months, most of the survey agencies filed reports of their findings and recommendations.[30] Some of the agencies limited their recommendations to measures which could be accomplished by administrative order or statutory action, while others recommended constitutional changes. As would be expected, the degree to which commission recommendations have been approved and implemented, by legislative action or otherwise, has varied widely among the states. In general, it appears that most has actually been accomplished where constitutional amendment was not attempted but where only such recommendations were made as were achievable through statutory change. Professor Karl Bosworth, in a study of legislative implementation of reorganization proposals as of 1952, found that, of 24 states where there was basis for judgment at that time, legislative response to commission recommendations had been "pronouncedly positive"—in the sense of accepting all or nearly all of the major proposals—only in New Hampshire and New Jersey. In nine states, on the other hand, response had been distinctly "negative," with few if any recommendations approved; while in 13 states legislative response was characterized as "ambivalent," with approval being accorded

[28] John W. Lederle and Dorothee E. Strauss, "The Little Hoover Commissions," *Mich. Govtl. Digest*, No. 4 (Bur. of Govt., Univ. of Mich., Nov. 4, 1949); Hubert R. Gallagher, "State Reorganization Surveys," *Pub. Admin. Rev.*, IX, 252-256 (Autumn, 1949); Ferrel Heady, "States Try Reorganization," *Nat. Mun. Rev.*, XLI, 334-338, 345 (July, 1952).

[29] "State Reorganization Studies," *State Govt.*, XXIII, 200-203, 209-211 (Sept., 1950).

[30] For examples, see *Report of the Commission on State Government Organization to the General Assembly and Governor of Connecticut* (Hartford, 1950); *Organization and Functioning of the State Government* (Report of the Illinois Commission to Study State Government, Springfield, 1950); *Report of the Iowa Governmental Reorganization Commission* to Governor William S. Beardsley for submission to the Fifty-fourth General Assembly (Des Moines, 1950); *How to Achieve Greater Efficiency and Economy in Minnesota's Government* (Recommendations of the Minnesota Efficiency in Government Commission, St. Paul, 1950); *Report of the Commission on Reorganization of State Government of the State of Montana to the Thirty-third Legislative Assembly* (Helena, 1953); *Report of the New Hampshire Reorganization Commission to Governor Sherman Adams on the Reorganization of State Administrative Agencies* (Concord, 1950).

a substantial portion, but by no means all, of the commission proposals.[31]

Reorganization by Executive Order

While most of the reorganizational measures which have been adopted have been effected by legislative enactment, some have required constitutional amendment and some changes of lesser nature have been brought about by order of the governor or department heads under rule-making authority granted by statute. As yet, however, little use has been made at the state level of executive orders as a means of effecting changes of major importance such as the establishment, consolidation, or abolition of administrative agencies. At the national level, on the other hand, Congress since 1939 has authorized the President to make substantial organizational changes by executive order subject to legislative disapproval or veto. Under this method of procedure, the President drafts proposals or "plans" for reorganization, incorporates them in executive orders, and submits them to the houses of Congress. These orders become effective as law *unless* disapproved by the legislative body within a specified number of days. At times the reorganization law has provided that disapproval by a *single* house shall constitute a veto, while at other times disapproval by *both* houses has been necessary to prevent the orders from taking effect.

Recently a few state legislatures, following federal precedent, have authorized reorganization by executive order. Pennsylvania's reorganization act of 1955 empowers the governor to prepare and transmit to the legislature plans which shall be effective after thirty days unless disapproved by either legislative chamber.[32] A Michigan law of 1958 established procedures quite similar to the federal plan; and the new Michigan constitution of 1963 provides for reorganization by executive order subject to legislative veto. Under the constitutional provision the period allowed the legislature for consideration of the governor's proposals is sixty days during a regular session, or a full session if of shorter duration. While the earlier statute provided for a one-house veto, the constitutional provision further strengthens the hand of the chief executive by providing a two-house veto under which both legislative chambers must disapprove executive orders to render them ineffective.[33] Alaska's constitution provides that the governor may make changes in the organization of the executive branch by executive orders to become effective unless disapproved by a majority of all legislative members in joint session, the period allowed the legislature for exercise of its veto power being the same as in Michigan.[34]

---

[31] Karl A. Bosworth, "The Politics of Management Improvement in the States," *Amer. Polit. Sci. Rev.*, XLVII, 84-99 (Mar., 1953). This article presents an excellent analysis of the factors affecting the likelihood of favorable legislative response to reorganization proposals.

[32] *Laws of Pa.*, 1955, No. 8.

[33] *Pub. Acts of Mich.*, 1958, No. 125; *Const. of Mich.* (1963), art. V, sec. 2.

[34] *Const. of Alaska* (1959), art. III, sec. 23.

In New Hampshire, on the other hand, a provision in reorganization legislation of 1949 for reorganization by executive order subject to legislative veto was rendered inoperative when a majority of the state's supreme court justices, in an advisory opinion to the governor and council, expressed the view that it was unconstitutional.[35]

Arguments in favor of administrative reorganization by executive order center around the proposition that the governor, who is charged with responsibility for the day-by-day operation of the administrative branch, is in a better position than are members of the legislature to know what organizational changes would be beneficial. It is not contended that the governor should possess reorganization power without legislative check, but reservation to the legislature of the power of disapproval is believed to provide an adequate safeguard of the legislative prerogative. Authorization of reorganization by executive order does not, of course, preclude the legislature from making directly, through statutory enactments, organizational changes which the members may desire. All in all, provision for reorganization by executive order would seem to be advantageous, and it appears not unlikely that additional states in the future will authorize this form of reorganizational action. It may be of significance that two of the states which have recently framed constitutions— Alaska and Michigan—have given constitutional status to the plan.

Departments of Administration

A significant feature of many reorganizations, as previously noted, has been the providing of a general managerial agency to assist the governor in the performance of his supervisory activities; and in some instances agencies of this nature have been established apart from more general reorganization. Although some such agencies are designated as departments of finance or by other titles, many are called departments of administration and that title is employed here in a generic sense. A state department of administration has been characterized as "an over-all management organization through which the Governor can effectively and efficiently exercise his responsibilities." [36] Among the older departments of administration are those established in Minnesota in 1939 and in Michigan in 1948.

The Minnesota department, under a commissioner of administration appointed by the governor, exercises broad supervisory authority over state administrative activities of an internal or "housekeeping" character.

[35] *Laws of N.H.*, 1949, Chap. 43; *Opinion of the Justices*, 96 N.H. 517 (1950). South Carolina's reorganization act of 1948 provides for formulation of reorganization plans by a state reorganization commission and for the governor's transmission of such plans, with his approval or disapproval, to the legislature. However, the legislature is required to take *positive* action on the plans, in the form of a concurrent resolution of approval, to make them effective. *Acts of S.C.*, 1948, No. 621.

[36] Council of State Governments, *A State Department of Administration*, 1.

The commissioner of administration is in many respects the equivalent of a state business manager, as indeed he is sometimes called. He prepares the biennial budget; approves the establishment of bureaus or other subdivisions within departments; has charge of the state capitol and other state-owned buildings; purchases supplies, materials, and equipment for all states agencies; and, with approval of the governor and the director of civil service, may transfer employees from one department or agency to another. In most respects the decisions of the commissioner are final, subject only to review by the governor on request of the head of the administrative agency affected.[37] The Minnesota plan has now been in operation for more than two decades, and appears to have enjoyed a substantial degree of success in enhancing the governor's effectiveness as chief executive.

Michigan's department of administration, like that of Minnesota, engages in a wide variety of managerial activities. Under the headship of an appointive controller who serves at the pleasure of the governor, the Michigan department is charged with the functions, among others, of preparing the state budget, supervising state accounting systems, serving as a central purchasing agency, maintaining the state capitol and office buildings, supervising the operation and maintenance of state-owned motor vehicles, and operating a central duplicating and mailing service. The effective functioning of the Michigan department has been hampered in some measure by the existence of a State Administrative Board consisting of elective state officers and having approval authority over many forms of departmental action. Nevertheless, a recent study concludes that the department "has demonstrated the gains in state administrative practices which can be made, even under exceptionally trying conditions, by such a central management agency. . . . The record of the Michigan department can be taken as an encouraging sign by other states which have created similar agencies or contemplate doing so."[38]

By the early 1960's more than thirty states had established departments of administration or equivalent agencies. All but a few of these were charged with the functions of budgeting and purchasing; and a substantial majority of them were responsible for central accounting. Many of the departments provide central data processing services, and a considerable number of them are responsible for various functions in the field of personnel management. Included among the states having depart-

---

[37] T. G. Driscoll, "The Commissioner of Administration in Minnesota," *The Book of the States*, 1945-46, pp. 145-150; Harold L. Henderson, "How a State Can Be Managed," *Nat. Mun. Rev.*, XXXV, 508-513, 524 (Nov., 1946); Leslie M. Gravlin, "An Effective Chief Executive," *Ibid.*, XXXVI, 137-141 (Mar., 1947).

[38] Ferrel Heady and Robert H. Pealy, *The Michigan Department of Administration*, 132. See also Ferrel Heady and Robert H. Pealy, "The Michigan Department of Administration: A Case Study in the Politics of Administration," *Pub. Admin. Rev.*, XVI, 82-89 (Spring, 1956).

ments charged with a broad range of functions are Indiana, Kansas, Maryland, Pennsylvania, Rhode Island, Vermont, and Wisconsin.[39]

Partial versus Comprehensive Reorganization

From the discussion to this point, it will be apparent that even among the so-called reorganized states there is much variation in the thoroughness with which administrative reorganization has been effected.[40] Upon the basis of their relative thoroughness, state reorganizations are sometimes classified as "partial" or "comprehensive"; though obviously the distinction is by no means an exact one and, even under the more comprehensive plans, there is usually no attempt to consolidate *all* nonconstitutional agencies into departments.

An especially troublesome problem in reorganization, and one to which no completely satisfactory solution has yet been found, is presented by certain agencies—such as tax commissions, public utilities commissions, and industrial commissions—which are charged with the performance of quasi-legislative and quasi-judicial duties as well as functions strictly administrative in nature. Stated in its simplest terms, the problem is that of preserving the independence of these agencies with respect to their quasi-legislative and quasi-judical work, while at the same time making them accountable to the governor in administrative matters. Though in some instances agencies of this character have themselves been designated as departments, more often they have been allowed to remain as "independent establishments" or, as an alternative, placed nominally within related departments but accorded a largely autonomous status.[41]

Finally, it should be pointed out that administrative organization, if it is to be efficient, cannot be static. The best of reorganization plans, unless subjected to occasional revision, will in time become obsolete. As new functions are undertaken by the state, additional administrative agencies often become necessary, and these should be fitted properly into the existing organizational setup. Some states, unfortunately, have done a

---

[39] Joe E. Nusbaum, "State Departments of Administration: Their Role and Trends of Development," *State Govt.,* XXXV, 124-129 (Spring, 1962).

[40] For a summary of the number of departments created and the number of agencies abolished in the first fifteen states to reorganize, see William H. Edwards, "A Factual Summary of State Administrative Reorganization," *Southwestern Soc. Sci. Quar.,* XIX, 53-67 (June, 1938). Professor Edwards' data suggest that actual reduction in the number of administrative agencies effected through reorganization has been considerably less than commonly supposed.

[41] For comprehensive discussions of the problem, see James W. Fesler, *The Independence of State Regulatory Agencies;* Robert E. Cushman, *The Independent Regulatory Commissions.* Though Professor Cushman's treatise is concerned primarily with the federal government, he gives some attention to state experience and suggests certain differences in the "commission" problem as it relates to the federal and state governments, respectively. See especially his Chaps. 2, 7.

good job of reorganization and then proceeded to dissipate many of its benefits by creating, within a few years, numerous new agencies outside the established administrative departments. In order to keep administrative organization up to date, not only must changes be made from time to time to take into account new functions and improved procedures; but there may well be also, every few years, a new survey study of the administrative branch, with a view to determining whether a more comprehensive overhauling is again desirable.[42] The fact that many of the states recently providing for Little Hoover Commissions were among those which had already effected reorganization in various degrees in previous years emphasizes the fact that administrative reorganization is by its very nature a continuing problem, calling for periodic reexamination and action if governmental organization is to be kept abreast of current needs.

Results of Reorganization

To what degree has state administrative reorganization actually been successful in achieving its objectives of economy and efficiency in government? Unfortunately, the results of reorganization do not lend themselves to statistical measurement.[43] The preponderant opinion among political scientists has certainly been that reorganization is sound in principle and that accomplishments in reorganized states have been substantial. Yet there have been some who have questioned the generally accepted doctrines of reorganization.[44] That reorganization has strengthened the administrative position of the governor, there can be no doubt. But as a basic postulate of reorganization it is assumed that strengthening the gubernatorial office will increase the chief executive's feeling of responsibility and at the same time lead the voters to be more discriminating in their choice of governors; and the extent to which such results have actually flowed from reorganization is not clear. Factors responsible for the presence or absence of economy and efficiency in government are so varied and complex that, even where improvement follows reorganization, it may be difficult or impossible to establish a definite relationship of cause and effect. It is of interest that some of the strongest claims of benefits flowing from reorganization have been made with reference to the administrations of governors who themselves initiated and sponsored reorganization movements. May it not be possible, in such cases, that those gov-

[42] Cf. Buck, *op. cit.*, 38.

[43] J. Mark Jacobson, "Evaluating State Administrative Structure—The Fallacy of the Statistical Approach," *Amer. Polit. Sci. Rev.*, XXII, 928-935 (Nov., 1928).

[44] See, for instance, F. W. Coker, "Dogmas of Administrative Reform," *Ibid.*, XVI, 399-411 (Aug., 1922); Harvey Walker, "Theory and Practice in State Administrative Organization," *Nat. Mun. Rev.*, XIX, 249-254 (Apr., 1930); Charles S. Hyneman, "Administrative Reorganization—an Adventure into Science and Theology," *Jour. of Politics*, I, 62-75 (Feb., 1939). Other articles and books expressing skepticism are discussed in Professor Hyneman's article.

ernors were such strong and able executives that they would have achieved much the same results without reorganization?[45] There is little doubt that proper organization facilitates the work of able public officials in their efforts to provide honest and efficient government. Yet one is led to wonder whether, in recent years, the proponents of administrative reorganization may not have placed undue emphasis upon mere organizational forms.

In general, the principles of integration and centralization appear to be basically sound. But that is not to say that complete reorganization on those principles is the wisest course of action in every state and under all circumstances. It is unfortunate that, as the present writer believes, proponents of reorganization have devised a reorganization formula of which they have virtually made a fetish and which they tend to prescribe for every state regardless of local differences.[46] As a matter of fact, what is best in an individual state at a given time will depend largely upon local conditions. A particular administrative agency which is operating economically and efficiently may well be let alone, even though its organization violates theoretical principles dear to the hearts of efficiency experts. On the other hand, when investigation reveals improper functioning, the principles of integration and centralization are useful as indicating the general lines along which reorganization should, under most circumstances, proceed. This being the case, certain states which have effected only "partial" reorganization may actually have exercised more discrimination than some of their sister states which have adopted "comprehensive" plans.[47]

Control over Administration

At this point it should be made clear that, though popular election does not commend itself as a method of choosing administrative officials, means must be provided, in a democracy, for making the administrative branch of government ultimately responsible to the public. In those states which have gone farthest in centralizing administrative power in the hands of the governor, it may be possible, through proper controls over the chief executive, to enforce responsibility on the part of administrative officers and employees all down the line. But where, as in many states, the administrative branch is still largely decentralized, it is necessary to pro-

[45] Cf. Hyneman, "Administrative Reorganization—an Adventure into Science and Theology," *loc. cit.*, 71.

[46] Mention has already been made of the substantial degree of uniformity in reorganization recommendations emanating from survey organizations and other groups. See above, "State Surveys as Basis for Reorganization."

[47] Charts of the organization of the executive branch in each of the fifty states are to be found in Earl L. Darrah and Orville F. Poland, *The Fifty State Governments: A Compilation of Executive Organization Charts.*

vide for the exertion of control directly upon administrative personnel at all levels of authority. Elective administrative officers are of course responsible to the voters, in the sense that they must stand for reelection periodically if they are to retain their positions. At best, however, this form of responsibility can be enforced only at recurring intervals. Direct popular control in some measure may be exerted over administrative officials, both elective and appointive, by public opinion and, in certain states, by the power to remove such officials by the popular recall.[48] Some control over administration is exercised by the judicial branch of government. Thus the courts, in appropriate cases, will issue writs of mandamus to compel administrative officials to perform legal duties; prevent illegal action by writ of injunction; and declare invalid unlawful administrative acts already committed.[49]

In the final analysis, however, the most effective control over the governor and his administrative subordinates is that exercised by the state legislature. It is the legislature which, in most cases, creates and may abolish administrative agencies, and defines their power and duties. Appointments to administrative posts must, in many instances, be approved by the senate; and legislatures quite generally possess the power of removing administrative officers by impeachment. The investigatory powers of the legislature may be used to good advantage both in stimulating individual administrative officers to put forth their best efforts and in revealing weaknesses in administrative organization and procedure. Finally, it is the legislature which must provide the funds to permit administrative agencies to operate; and, in determining the purposes for which funds may be spent, the legislature may effectively control administrative action. That popular control over administration should thus be exercised in large part through the legislature as an intermediary is a practical necessity. Legislative bodies are concerned primarily with determining public policy and expressing that policy in the form of law. But for actual

[48] See above, Chap. VI, "The Popular Recall."

[49] In an effort to afford additional protection against arbitrary action by administrative agencies in matters of rule-making and adjudication, a number of states during recent years have enacted administrative procedure laws patterned in some measure after a Model State Administrative Procedure Act sponsored by the National Conference of Commissioners on Uniform State Laws. These acts, as they relate to rule-making, are concerned with such matters as requirements for notice to interested persons, and opportunity for such persons to express their views, before rules are adopted; and appropriate publication of the rules after adoption. With respect to administrative adjudication, the acts seek to codify procedural practices with respect to such matters as the giving of notice, use of the subpoena power to compel testimony at hearings, and rules as to the admissibility of evidence. Some of the statutes also broaden the grounds for judicial review of administrative action. Ferrel Heady, *Administrative Procedure Legislation in the States;* Ferrel Heady, "State Administrative Procedure Laws: An Appraisal," *Pub. Admin. Rev.,* XII, 10-20 (Winter, 1952). Though there is some difference of opinion as to the overall merits of this legislation, Professor Heady concludes, on the basis of a study made in the early 1950's, that in general its effect has been "mildly beneficial." Heady, *Administrative Procedure Legislation in the States,* 130.

execution of public policy the legislature must rely upon the administrative branch; and the legislative process may be rendered a nullity unless the legislature possesses effective means of assuring that its policies will be faithfully carried out.[50]

The Civil Service

Thus far in our discussion of the administrative branch of government we have been concerned principally with matters relating to the governor, as chief administrator, and to department heads. But most of the actual work of administration must, of necessity, be done by subordinate officers and employees in the various administrative agencies. These officers and employees constitute the civil service,[51] and the quality of government depends in no small measure upon the competence of the members of this service and the conditions under which they work. The importance of the state civil service is indicated in some measure by the mere number of employees in the fifty states, which stood, at mid-1964, at nearly 2 million.[52]

For many years, and especially during the middle decades of the 19th century, the spoils system was rampant in American government, both national and state. Positions in the civil service were looked upon as "spoils" belonging to the party in power, by virtue of its having been victor at the polls. The positions went to "deserving" party workers, with all too little regard for fitness; and a change in party ascendancy usually brought a "clean sweep," in which incumbents were discharged in wholesale fashion so that their places might be filled by members of the newly victorious party. Under such conditions, it is not surprising that the public service was frequently characterized by waste and inefficiency.[53]

The Merit System in the States

It was the federal government which finally led the way in civil service reform by the enactment, in 1883, of the Pendleton Civil Service Act. Following the federal example, state civil service laws were enacted

---

[50] Concerning the role of Kentucky's Legislative Research Commission in providing legislative surveillance of administration, see Gladys M. Kammerer, "Legislative Oversight of Administration in Kentucky," *Pub. Admin. Rev.*, X, 169-175 (Summer, 1950).

[51] Strictly speaking, the civil service includes all nonmilitary officers and employees of the governmental unit concerned. However, the term is more generally used, as here, in a narrower sense which excludes officers and employees of the legislative and judicial branches and, within the administrative branch itself, excludes the chief executive and other high administrative officers. The term *civil service law* will be used herein, in its now generally-accepted sense, as meaning a statute designed to establish the merit system in civil service.

[52] Monthly data published by United States Bureau of Labor Statistics.

[53] For a discussion of the continued operation of the spoils system in one state, see H. O. Waldby, *The Patronage System in Oklahoma.*

in New York in 1883 and Massachusetts in 1884, but no other state took similar action for more than twenty years. In 1905, however, the movement was renewed with the enactment of legislation in Illinois and Wisconsin, and thereafter other states gradually fell into line. Today, more than half of the states have laws designed to apply the merit system, as distinguished from the old spoils system, to the selection and management of employees in many or all state departments, and several others have systems of more limited application.[54] Since 1939, moreover, as a result of an amendment to the Social Security Act requiring that federal-aid funds granted thereunder be administered by merit-system employees, states without general civil service systems have established special merit systems for state and local employees engaged in the administration of unemployment compensation or any form of public assistance financed in part from federal funds.[55] Such systems have also been established for local employees engaged in these functions in states which have general civil service systems for state but not for local employees. These special merit systems are administered in many states by "merit system councils," which are in reality civil service commissions of limited jurisdiction. As a result of the federal requirement, state and local employees engaged in these particular social security activities are now under the merit system in every state.

Personnel Agencies

The typical state civil service law[56] provides for administration of the merit system by a civil service commission or department of personnel.[57] Early laws regularly provided for the commission type of organiza-

---

[54] See O. Glenn Stahl, *Public Personnel Administration* (5th ed.), 44-46; Keith Ocheltree, "Developments in State Personnel Systems," *The Book of the States*, 1964-65, pp. 174-177. *The Book of the States* (pp. 178-181) lists the following states as having merit systems of broad though not necessarily complete, coverage in 1963: Alabama, Alaska, California, Colorado, Connecticut, Georgia, Hawaii, Illinois, Kansas, Kentucky, Louisiana, Maine, Maryland, Massachusetts, Michigan, Minnesota, Nevada, New Hampshire, New Jersey, New Mexico, New York, North Carolina, Ohio, Oklahoma, Oregon, Rhode Island, Utah, Vermont, Virginia, Washington, Wisconsin, and Wyoming. In a few additional states civil service laws have been enacted but have subsequently been repealed or declared unconstitutional.

[55] See Albert H. Aronson, "Merit Systems under the Social Security Act," *Pub. Personnel Rev.*, I, 24-28 (Apr., 1940). The principal forms of public assistance so financed are old-age assistance, aid to the needy blind, aid to dependent children, aid to the permanently and totally disabled, and medical assistance for the aged.

[56] The merit system in most instances rests entirely upon statute. Several states, however, have constitutional provisions requiring the legislature to establish such a system.

[57] In some instances the official title of the personnel agency is something other than civil service commission or personnel department. In Maryland, personnel functions are performed by a single personnel commissioner; while Alaska, Kansas, and Rhode Island vest such functions in personnel divisions within their departments of administration. A table showing the titles and composition of the personnel agencies of the various states appears in *The Book of the States*, 1964-65, pp. 178-181.

tion. The most prevalent provision was for a commission of three members appointed by the governor and senate for six-year overlapping terms, with the stipulation that not more than two of the three commissioners should be members of the same political party. The provisions for staggered terms and representation of different parties were designed, of course, to provide some degree of protection against domination of the commission by a particular governor or party. Yet there remained the incongruous situation, under this setup, of a *bi*partisan agency administering what was designed to be a *non*partisan personnel system. Recognizing this inconsistency, several states provided that there should be appointed by the commission or the governor, on the basis of merit, a personnel director to serve as the commission's executive officer charged with immediate supervision of the agency's administrative activities.[58] More recently some states have placed responsibility for personnel management in a department of personnel under a commissioner or director appointed by and responsible to the governor. In some instances the commissioner or director is required to meet specified professional qualifications with regard to training or experience in personnel work. Where the departmental system of organization is used the civil service commission is sometimes retained for the performance of quasi-legislative and quasi-judicial functions such as rule-making and the holding of removal hearings. In other instances functions of this nature are performed by special boards constituted for the purpose.

Functions of Personnel Agencies

Early civil service commissions confined their efforts for the most part to the preparation and administering of examinations for entry into the service, and the compilation of "eligible registers" from which appointments might be made. Their primary objective was the negative one of keeping incompetents out of the public service. But, as the science of personnel administration advanced, it became clear that, though proper recruitment is essential, it is only the first step in a comprehensive personnel program. If morale and proper standards of performance are to be maintained within the service, promotion as well as appointment must be on the basis of merit; salaries must be provided which are commensurate with those paid in private employment; there must be like pay for like work throughout the service; facilities must be made available for "in-service" training through which employees, while on the job, may increase their efficiency and keep abreast of new developments; appropriate provision must be made for dealing with disciplinary matters, and for re-

[58] Concerning this and other forms of commission organization, see William Seal Carpenter, *The Unfinished Business of Civil Service Reform*, 36-42; William Seal Carpenter, "Reformer's Task Never Done," *Nat. Mun. Rev.*, XLI, 339-345 (July, 1952).

moving from the service such incompetents as have secured positions notwithstanding the examining procedure; definite policies must be established with respect to vacations and sick leave; and provision must be made for a retirement system. Hence the modern personnel agency, in addition to the original function of administering entrance examinations, finds itself charged with such duties as preparing position classifications and salary schedules; keeping efficiency ratings of employees; giving promotional examinations; organizing and administering training programs; and formulating and promulgating rules concerning such matters as transfers, layoffs, suspension and reinstatement, vacations and leaves of absence, and retirement.[59] Obviously, the agency must be provided with an adequate staff of professional and clerical employees if it is to perform these varied functions in an effective manner.

Jurisdiction of Personnel Agencies

In conclusion, it should be pointed out that the mere fact that a particular state has a civil service law gives little indication of the extent to which the merit principle actually prevails in the selection and management of the state's employees.[60] To obtain a true picture of the situation, two further factors must be taken into consideration: (1) the extent of the jurisdiction of the civil service commission; and (2) the relative efficiency with which the provisions of the law are, in practice, administered.

Some of the earlier civil service statutes applied to only a few of the state departments or institutions, though most of these were ultimately amended to extend their provisions to other agencies. But it is not unusual, even today, for legislatures in civil service states, when establishing new administrative agencies, to exempt their employees from civil service provisions. Moreover, all laws exempt certain classes of officers and employees —notably elective officers, department heads, and secretaries and clerks whose duties are supposed to be of a confidential nature—from the commission's jurisdiction; and in some instances this list of exemptions is so extensive as to constitute a serious limitation upon the application of merit principles.

Merit System Not a Matter of Legislation Alone

Finally, it must be recognized that the best of civil service laws will accomplish little if administered inefficiently or dishonestly. Personnel of-

---

[59] Cf. Stahl, *op. cit.*, 429-430; Winston W. Crouch and Judith Norvell Jamison, *The Work of Civil Service Commissioners*, Chap. 4. See also National Civil Service League and National Municipal League, *A Model State Civil Service Law*.

[60] The Kansas law, for example, was rendered ineffective for many years by failure of the legislature to appropriate funds for the commission's work.

ficers who, while rendering lip service to the merit principle, are spoils-
men at heart, can find innumerable ways of circumventing statutory requirements. The letter of the law may be observed while its spirit is
flagrantly violated. Thus, the customary provision that an appointing officer may select any one of the three persons who stand highest on the appropriate register of eligibles[61] opens the way, if misused, for personal or
partisan favoritism. Another means of corrupting civil service laws is
through abuse of the provision relating to temporary appointments. To
the end that governmental services may not be interrupted, civil service
statutes generally provide that if, when a vacancy occurs, there is currently in existence no register of eligibles for positions of the class involved, the personnel agency may authorize the head of the agency in
which the vacancy exists to make a temporary appointment to fill the
vacancy until such time as an examination can be held and a register
of eligibles established. Some personnel officers seem deliberately to have
allowed registers of eligibles to expire or become exhausted in order to
permit the making of temporary appointments of a partisan nature.[62] Persons given such "temporary" appointments have sometimes retained their
positions for months or even years. Though the statutes usually impose a
limit—frequently of ninety days—on the duration of temporary appointments, in the absence of a prohibition of renewals a favored person may
be retained by renewing his appointment again and again. And even if an
examination is given and a register established soon after a temporary appointment is made, if the temporary appointee is a candidate for the regular appointment his temporary tenure may still have served his purpose
by familiarizing him with the duties of the job and thereby giving him an
advantage over other competitors in the examination.

All in all, it is clear that a civil service system will be no better than
the men who administer it. Furthermore, personnel officers are not likely
to be more favorable toward the merit system than are the officials who
appoint them. If, therefore, we are to have a real merit system in the
states, it is essential not only that we secure the enactment of sound personnel legislation, but also that we elect governors who will appoint to
personnel agencies persons who actually believe in, and will work for, the
merit principle in government.

[61] Though some laws provide that only the highest name on the register shall
be certified to the appointing officer, the "rule of three" is more common.

[62] Of a very different nature were the temporary "war-duration" appointments
made in various states, some with examination and some without, during World
War II while most persons of the age and qualifications of those normally seeking civil
service positions were serving in the armed forces or engaged in war-production
work. These appointments served the dual purpose of keeping civil service positions
open for regular state employees on leave for war service, and of preventing the
civil service rolls from becoming loaded with older and less qualified workers.

REFERENCES

BELL, James R., and DARRAH, Earl L., *State Executive Reorganization* (Bur. of Pub. Admin., Univ. of Calif., Berkeley, 1961).

BOLLENS, John C., *Administrative Reorganization in the States Since 1939* (Bur. of Pub. Admin., Univ. of Calif., Berkeley, 1947).

BUCK, A. E., *The Reorganization of State Governments in the United States* (Columbia Univ. Press, New York, 1938).

CAPE, William H., and STENE, Edwin O., *State Civil Service in Kansas* (Govtl. Research Center, Univ. of Kan., Lawrence, 1954).

CARPENTER, William Seal, *The Unfinished Business of Civil Service Reform* (Princeton Univ. Press, Princeton, N. J., 1952).

COUNCIL of State Governments, *A Progress Report on State Reorganization in 1950* (The Council, Chicago, 1950).

———, *A State Department of Administration* (The Council, Chicago, 1957).

———, *Reorganizing State Government* (The Council, Chicago, 1950).

———, *The Office of Attorney General: Personnel and Financing* (The Council, Chicago, 1955).

CROUCH, Winston W., and JAMISON, Judith Norvell, *The Work of Civil Service Commissions* (Civil Service Assembly, Chicago, circa 1956).

CUSHMAN, Robert E., *The Independent Regulatory Commissions* (Oxford Univ. Press, New York, 1941), Chaps. 2, 7.

DARRAH, Earl L., and POLAND, Orville F., *The Fifty State Governments: A Compilation of Executive Organization Charts* (Bur. of Pub. Admin., Univ. of Calif., Berkeley, 1961).

FESLER, James W., *The Independence of State Regulatory Agencies* (Pub. Admin. Service, Chicago, 1942).

HEADY, Ferrel, *Administrative Procedure Legislation in the States* (Univ. of Mich. Press, Ann Arbor, 1952).

———, *State Constitutions: The Structure of Administration* (Nat. Mun. League, New York, 1961).

———, and PEALY, Robert H., *The Michigan Department of Administration* (Bur. of Govt., Inst. of Pub. Admin., Univ. of Mich., Ann Arbor, 1956).

KAPLAN, H. Eliot, *The Law of Civil Service* (Matthew Bender, Albany, N.Y., 1958).

LIPSON, Leslie, *The American Governor: From Figurehead to Leader* (Univ. of Chicago Press, Chicago, 1939), especially Chaps. 5, 6.

MATHEWS, John M., *Principles of American State Administration* (Appleton, New York, 1917).

National Civil Service League and National Municipal League, *A Model State Civil Service Law* (New York, 1953).

PFIFFNER, John M., and PRESTHUS, R. Vance, *Public Administration* (Ronald, New York, 3rd ed., 1953).

PORTER, Kirk H., *State Administration* (Crofts, New York, 1938).

POWELL, Norman J., *Personnel Administration in Government* (Prentice-Hall, New York, 1956).

STAHL, O. Glenn, *Public Personnel Administration* (Harper & Row, New York, 5th ed., 1962).

TORPEY, William G., *Public Personnel Management* (Van Nostrand, New York, 1953).

UHL, Raymond, *State Personnel Administration in South Carolina* (Bur. of Pub. Admin., Univ. of S. C., Columbia, 1950).

WALDBY, H. O., *The Patronage System in Oklahoma* (The Transcript Co., Norman, Okla., 1950).

WEAVER, Robert H., *Administrative Reorganization in Louisiana* (Bur. of Govt. Research, La. State Univ., Baton Rouge, 1951).

WHITE, Leonard D., *Introduction to the Study of Public Administration* (Macmillan, New York, 4th ed., 1955).

11

The State Judiciary

The Judicial Function

The judicial function consists essentially in hearing and deciding legal controversies. A basic function of any government is that of providing tribunals for the peaceful settlement, according to legal principles, of disputes arising among individuals or groups, or between individuals or groups and the government. The controversies or "cases" which the courts are called upon to adjudicate in the course of their work are of two general classes: civil and criminal.

Civil Cases

A civil case is usually concerned with a dispute between private parties regarding their respective legal rights and duties. The party who institutes the suit is known as the plaintiff, and the party against whom the action is brought as the defendant. Civil suits, like civil law, are concerned with such matters as property rights, contracts, torts,[1] and domestic relations. Frequently they are instituted in an effort to recover damages arising from breach of contract or for unlawful injury to the plaintiff's person or property. Thus, a person who has been struck by an automobile and injured, one who believes that his reputation has been impaired by slanderous statements, or one whose property has been subjected to trespass, may institute a civil suit for damages. The fact that the plaintiff in such a case is successful in securing a damage judgment does not in itself make certain that he will actually obtain his money from the defendant, since the government in no way guarantees the payment of a civil judgment.

[1] Tort is a legal term used to denote civil wrongs (as distinguished from crimes) arising otherwise than from breach of contract.

However, certain law-enforcement officers attached to the courts—marshals, sheriffs, and constables—will give a successful plaintiff all possible assistance in his efforts to collect by such means as "levy of execution" upon the defendant's property or garnishment of his salary or wages.

It is to be noted that, in most instances, the government is not itself a party to civil cases, but is concerned only with providing the judicial machinery through which persons who have suffered wrongs may secure appropriate redress. This is not to say, however, that governmental units are never parties to civil suits. Though the states themselves, as an attribute to their "sovereignty," may not be made defendants in their own courts except by their own consent, they may, as plaintiffs, institute civil actions; and provision is now quite generally made by law for permitting suits against them under some circumstances. More than a third of the states have enacted general laws making themselves subject to suit in certain types of cases, most commonly on claims arising out of contract but in many instances on tort claims as well. For the most part such suits are brought in the regular trial courts though a few states have established special "courts of claims." Some of the states having no general legislation on the subject give their consent to suit in particular cases, from time to time, by special legislation acts.[2] Certain units of local government—notably counties—are considered to be mere administrative subdivisions of the state and therefore as partaking of the state's immunity from suit. However, most states have enacted general laws authorizing such units to sue in the regular courts and making them liable to suit. Cities, as municipal corporations, may sue and be sued in the same manner as natural persons and private corporations. In any event, as will be seen in a moment, the government as a party to a civil suit plays a role distinctly different from its function in a criminal case.

Criminal Cases

Criminal cases involve alleged infractions of the criminal law—that body of law which defines crimes and penalizes their commission. A crime, in turn, is any antisocial act which the legislative body has considered sufficiently dangerous to the public peace and safety to justify its prohibition and punishment. Crimes range all the way from minor misdemeanors (such as violations of city traffic ordinances),[3] through serious felonies

[2] Cf. Roger V. Shumate, "Tort Claims Against State Governments," *Law and Contemp. Probs.*, IX, 242-261 (Spring, 1942). An excellent summary of the extent of state liability and agencies for the settlement of claims against the various states is to be found in Frederick C. Spiegel, *The Illinois Court of Claims: A Study of State Liability* (Univ. of Ill. Press, Urbana, 1962), 40-59.

[3] Traffic violations, together with certain other "petty offenses," are sometimes considered noncriminal in nature, or at most as only *quasi* crimes. Cf. Lewis Mayers, *The American Legal System*, 70. For our purposes, however, it seems best to include all such minor offenses in the misdemeanor category.

(such as robbery or homicide), to treason, which is the most serious offense against the state. It is the function of the court, in a criminal case,
to determine whether the accused person actually committed the crime
with which he is charged and, if his guilt is established, to impose an appropriate penalty as provided by law. In criminal cases, in contrast to
those of a civil nature, the government not only provides judicial tribunals
for their determination but is itself the prosecuting party corresponding to
the plaintiff in civil suits. All criminal actions, even those in the minor
courts, are instituted in the name of the state or the people against the
alleged offender as defendant. Such actions are usually instituted by the local prosecuting attorney, though occasionally they are begun by the attorney general or, when involving violations of municipal ordinances, by
the city attorney. The work of the courts in trying criminal cases, and
some of the special problems involved, are considered at greater length in
the chapter on law enforcement.[4]

Judicial Review of Legislation

An extremely important function of courts in America, though incidental to the exercise of their primary function of deciding cases, is that
of passing upon the validity of legislative acts.[5] This power of "judicial
review," as it is called, arises from the fact that the courts, in considering
controversies brought before them, must, as we shall see presently, determine the provisions of law which are applicable to the facts of the respective cases. Now it sometimes happens that the courts find, or believe
they find, two provisions that are contradictory. If both provisions are in
enactments of equal rank—for example, if both are in state statutes—and
it is found that one was enacted at a later date than the other, the court
merely gives effect to the more recent expression of the legislative will and
holds that the earlier provision has been repealed by implication. But
what if the conflict is between laws of different grade or rank—for example, between a state statute and a provision of the state constitution? In
that event, the courts consider it their duty to give effect to the constitution, as the higher form of law, and to disregard and refuse to enforce the
conflicting statutory provision. This exercise by a court of its power to
"declare a statute unconstitutional" does not operate to remove the act
from the statute books. The court merely holds that the act is not, and
never was, valid, because it is in conflict with a higher form of law. Acts
declared unconstitutional remain on the statute books unless repealed by
the legislative body by which they were enacted. But it is assumed, and
usually with justification, that if another case should arise under such a

---

[4] Below, Chap. XVII.
[5] It should be understood, of course, that the courts, in appropriate cases, will
pass upon the validity of action by executive and administrative agencies, as well as
upon that of legislative bodies.

measure, the courts would again refuse to recognize it as law. Thus the act, though remaining on the statute books, becomes a dead letter and unenforceable.

The courts of most states,[6] like those of the federal government, will pass upon the constitutionality of a legislative act only when necessary to do so in deciding an actual controversy which has been brought before them in the usual manner. The courts will not, for example, advise the legislature in advance concerning the constitutionality of a proposed law for the regulation of business enterprises. If, however, the act is passed and a company being prosecuted for violation of it claims that the measure is unconstitutional, the courts must then decide the question, since punishment cannot lawfully be inflicted for violating a statute which is itself invalid.[7]

Advisory Opinions[8]

In contrast to the general practice, the constitutions of Massachusetts, Maine, New Hampshire, Rhode Island, Michigan, and Colorado provide that the justices of the highest court shall, or may, give their opinions upon important questions of law when requested to do so by the governor or either branch of the legislature. Two other constitutions—those of Florida and South Dakota—require the giving of such opinions to the governor only. In addition, Alabama and Delaware make statutory provision for advisory opinions; and the North Carolina court renders such opinions under long-established custom, though without either constitutional or statutory provision therefor.[9] Opinions are rendered in Delaware to the governor, and in Alabama and North Carolina to the governor or either legislative chamber. All told, therefore, advisory opinions are available in eleven states to the governor, and in eight of those states to either house of the legislature as well.[10]

[6] For exceptions see below, "Advisory Opinions."

[7] Two excellent studies of the operation of judicial review are Oliver P. Field, *Judicial Review of Legislation in Ten Selected States;* Franklin A. Smith, *Judicial Review of Legislation in New York, 1906-1938.*

[8] The most comprehensive general work on advisory opinions is Albert R. Ellingwood, *Departmental Cooperation in State Government* (Macmillan, New York, 1918). For briefer accounts, see Paul C. Clovis and Clarence M. Updegraff, "Advisory Opinions," *Ia. Law Rev.,* XIII, 188-198 (Feb., 1928); W. F. Willoughby, *Principles of Judicial Administration* (Brookings Inst., Washington, 1929), Chap. 7; "Advisory Opinions on the Constitutionality of Statutes," *Harvard Law Rev.,* LXIX, 1302-1313 (May, 1956).

[9] Preston W. Edsall, "The Advisory Opinion in North Carolina," *N.C. Law Rev.,* XXVII, 297-344 (Apr., 1949).

[10] In several other states advisory opinions have been rendered during various periods in the past, in some instances under statutory authority and in others merely as a matter of practice, but it appears that in each case, with the exceptions mentioned in the text, the statutory authorization has been repealed or declared unconstitutional or the practice discontinued. Cf. F. R. Aumann, "The Supreme Court and the Advisory Opinion," *Ohio State Univ. Law Jour.,* IV, 21-55 (Dec., 1937).

Availability of advisory opinions makes it possible for the legislature, before enacting proposed legislation, or for the governor, before signing a bill, to secure the opinion of the justices with respect to its constitutionality.[11] It is true that such opinions are usually considered to be opinions of the individual justices rather than opinions of the court;[12] and, furthermore, that they are advisory only and not final adjudications. Indeed, if actual litigation subsequently arises, the court is free to construe a statute quite differently from the manner in which it was construed by the justices in an advisory opinion. Nevertheless, advisory opinions serve as significant indications of the manner in which a measure is likely to be construed by the court. If properly used, they should reduce the amount of unconstitutional legislation placed upon the statute books and prevent much unnecessary litigation.[13]

Declaratory Judgments

In addition to deciding civil and criminal cases and, in some jurisdictions, rendering advisory opinions, the courts in most states now perform another service in the rendering of declaratory judgments. By means of the declaratory judgment the courts "decide such issues as the proper construction of a statute, ordinance, or written instrument, such as a will, deed, or contract immediately upon the issue arising and without waiting for one of the interested parties to take the action that will lead to [sic] the other interested party or parties to seek redress for injuries believed to have been done them." [14] The declaratory judgment is designed to provide a means of determining the respective rights of the parties to a legal controversy before one of those parties actually takes action which would lead the other, believing he has suffered a wrong, to institute a suit for redress. It is to be noted that, in order to provide a proper cause for a declaratory judgment, though no actual or alleged wrong need yet have been committed, there must be an actual controversy between a plaintiff and a defendant regarding their respective legal rights under the statute or instrument concerned. Indeed, in the words of the foremost authority on the subject, "an action for a declaratory judgment must exhibit all the usual conditions of an ordinary action, except that accomplished physical injury need not necessarily be alleged." [15]

11 The Michigan provision authorizes the requesting of opinions as to the constitutionality of legislation *after it has been enacted into law but before its effective date.*

12 Only in Colorado and Michigan are advisory opinions given by the *court* rather than the justices thereof.

13 For a detailed analysis of actual experience with advisory opinions in five states, see Oliver P. Field, "The Advisory Opinion—An Analysis," *Ind. Law Jour.*, XXIV, 203-230 (Winter, 1949).

14 Willoughby, *op. cit.*, 80.

15 Edwin Borchard, *Declaratory Judgments* (Banks-Baldwin Law Pub. Co., Cleveland, 2nd ed., 1941), 29.

The declaratory judgment should be clearly distinguished from the advisory opinion, with which, unfortunately, it is sometimes confused. An advisory opinion is not rendered between parties to a controversy, but is given upon request to the governor or legislature, and is often rendered without the hearing of argument. Furthermore, an advisory opinion is binding upon no one, not even the judges who render it,[16] whereas a declaratory judgment is of binding effect as between the parties involved.[17]

More than forty states have now enacted statutes authorizing the courts to render declaratory judgments, most of them having adopted the uniform act recommended by the Conference of Commissioners on Uniform State Laws.[18]

The Judicial Process

The judicial process consists in the application of general rules of law to the facts of particular cases. But since the typical legal controversy involves a dispute between the parties concerned as to the facts, or the rules of law applicable, or both, a court must first make a determination of what the facts actually are, and of the law to be applied, before it can make the necessary application of that law to the facts. The parties to a case state their respective versions of the facts, presenting testimony of witnesses, and perhaps other evidence, in support of those versions. Between the two versions, however, there may be serious disagreement, and it is the task of the court to ascertain the *true* facts. For the purpose of determining questions of fact, trial courts commonly make use of the jury;[19] but, where a jury is not employed, questions of fact as well as those of law are decided by the judge. In determining what legal rules are applicable to a particular set of facts, the courts draw on various sources of law, and these will be noted in the following section. Only after judicial determination has been made of the facts and the law, is a court prepared to proceed to the final step in adjudication, namely, the application of law to facts. It will thus be seen that the hearing and determination of a typical civil or criminal case involves three fundamental steps: (1) deter-

[16] *Ibid.*, 73. Indeed, as Professor Borchard points out, the rendering of an advisory opinion is not, strictly speaking, a judicial function at all, but is a function of an attorney general or law officer which, in certain states, has been conferred upon the judges of the highest court.

[17] As to the effect of a declaratory judgment and the means of enforcing rights declared, see 16 *Amer. Jurisprudence*, "Declaratory Judgments," secs. 16, 78.

[18] Borchard, *Declaratory Judgments* (2nd ed.), 133; Edwin Borchard, "The Next Step Beyond Equity—the Declaratory Action," *Univ. of Chicago Law Rev.*, XIII, 145-179 (Feb., 1946); *The Book of the States* (Council of State Govts., Chicago), 1964-65, p. 103.

[19] For a discussion of the jury system in criminal cases, see below, Chap. XVII. "The Trial Jury."

mination of the facts, (2) determination of the law, and (3) application of the law to the facts to arrive at a decision or judgment.

In the actual handling of cases, the courts follow rules of procedure of a technical and complicated nature. At common law the power of determining rules of judicial procedure rested with the courts themselves. In the American states, however, procedural matters are now regulated in considerable detail by constitutional and statutory provisions, though the courts may still determine their own procedure in matters not covered by the constitution or statutes. The widespread assumption by constitutional conventions and state legislatures of the function of regulating the details of judicial procedure has been unfortunate, since those bodies have neither the time nor the technical knowledge requisite to the task. As a result of general dissatisfaction with the existing situation, there is now a substantial movement, widely supported by the organized bar and students of judicial administration, to restore to the courts the power to determine their own rules of procedure;[20] and constitutional or legislative action in this direction has now been taken in some states.

Law Applied by State Courts

State courts, in deciding the cases brought before them, apply various forms of law—national, state, and local. In the first place, there are the United States Constitution, the state constitution, and, in some instances, city and county charters. Secondly, there are legislative enactments, including acts of Congress, state statutes, and ordinances enacted by city councils and county boards. In the third place, there are executive orders, promulgated under constitutional or statutory authority by administrative agencies of the national, state, and local governments. And, finally, there is the common law of the state.

The United States Constitution requires[21] that state judges give effect to the provisions of that document and of federal statutes and treaties; and many cases, especially in the minor courts, have to do with enactments of local governmental units. However, the bulk of important litigation in the state courts concerns rights and duties under *state* law—constitutional, statutory, or common.[22] State constitutions and statute-

---

[20] See Willoughby, *op. cit.*, Chap. 32.

[21] Art. VI.

[22] Still another system of rules, known as *equity*, is also administered by the state courts. Equity developed in England, and later in America, as a body of jurisprudence supplementary to the common law; and had as its purpose the providing of remedies for wrongs with respect to which the common law provided no adequate remedy. One of the most important differences between equity and the common law is that, while the latter is only *remedial* in nature, equity provides a system of *preventive* justice. Whereas the common law not only attempts to provide reparation for a wrong after it has been committed, equity, by use of the injunction, seeks to prevent the commission of threatened wrongs. Equity and common law were originally admin-

making have been discussed in earlier chapters.[23] The nature of the common law and its relation to statutory law will be examined briefly at this point.

As contrasted with statutory law, which is the product of legislative enactment, common law is *judge-made* law based upon precedent. Developed by English courts over a period of several centuries, the common law was brought to American shores by the early English settlers; and, continuing its development here, ultimately became the basis of the legal system of each of our fifty states, with the single exception of Louisiana.[24] Whereas enacted laws of legislatures are written within the comparatively brief compass of statute books, the common law is to be found in written form only in the multitudinous reports of past decisions and opinions of English and American courts.

The common law has evolved through operation of the legal principle of *stare decisis*. According to this principle, when a particular point of law has once been decided by a court of competent jurisdiction, that decision stands as a precedent to be followed in future cases involving similar circumstances. Common law is sometimes said to be customary law, but that is true only in the sense that early judges, when confronted with questions upon which they could find no precedents in reported court decisions, sometimes applied accepted customs in making their decisions and thereby incorporated those customs into the law. Since a custom could become law only through being applied by a court in the settlement of a legal controversy, what the judges actually did in such instances was to indulge in judicial law*making*. Courts may, and occasionally do, overrule past decisions, but such action is infrequent. If a court believes that injustice would result in a particular case from following an authoritative precedent, instead of overruling the earlier decision the court is likely to find grounds for distinguishing between the earlier and immediate cases.[25] The manifold cases decided present so many shades of similarity and difference that judges frequently are able to find weighty precedent for reaching alternative decisions in a given case. Under such

---

istered by two separate and distinct sets of courts, and this practice still continues in some half-dozen states. About a dozen other states administer the two forms of jurisprudence through a single set of courts, but preserve the distinction between law cases and equity cases. In a majority of the American states today, however, even the distinction between law and equity cases has been abandoned, and both legal and equitable rules are administered by the same courts under uniform procedure. It will thus be seen that the distinction between common law and equity is largely disappearing. Concerning the nature of equity and its administration, see Clarence N. Callender, *American Courts: Their Organization and Procedure*, Chap. 10; Mayers, *op. cit.*, 61-64.

[23] Above, Chaps. I, VII, VIII.

[24] As a result of early French influence, Louisiana's legal system is based upon the Continental "civil law" system rather than upon the English common law.

[25] Cf. John M. Mathews, *The American Constitutional System* (McGraw-Hill, New York, 2nd ed., 1940), 12.

circumstances it is inevitable that judges, in deciding cases, should, incidentally to the determination and application of law, share in the molding of that law.

Adherence to judicial precedent, while making for certainty in the law, may, if practiced too slavishly, impede proper adaptation of legal principles to changed conditions. However, since the common law of the state is inferior in rank to the state constitution and statutes, any common-law rule which is not kept abreast of the times by judicial mutation may be changed by statutory provision or by constitutional amendment. Constitutional and statutory law thus taking precedence over common law, the courts, in determining the law to be applied in a given case, look first to the constitution and legislative enactments. Only when those sources fail to supply a rule covering the point at issue do the judges turn to judicial precedent and apply the common law.

Jurisdiction of State Courts

Under the United States Constitution, just as Congress possesses only delegated powers of legislation, so the federal courts have only such jurisdiction as is conferred upon them by constitutional provision; and, just as all legislative power not delegated to Congress is reserved to the state legislatures, so all judicial power not delegated to the federal courts rests with the courts of the respective states. By constitutional provision, the federal courts are given jurisdiction over cases arising under the United States Constitution, federal laws or treaties, or admiralty law—in other words, cases in which a "federal question" is involved. Federal jurisdiction is likewise extended to cases, regardless of their subject matter, to which certain enumerated classes of persons or governmental units are parties. Cases in the latter category include, among others, those affecting foreign ambassadors or consuls, those to which the United States is a party, those between two or more states, and those between citizens of different states.[26] Every legal controversy which does not concern such subject matter or parties as to place it within the jurisdiction of the federal courts can be tried and determined only by state tribunals. Moreover, many types of cases within federal jurisdiction *may* be tried also by state courts. The mere conferring of jurisdiction over controversies of a particular nature upon the federal courts does not of itself deny to the state courts concurrent jurisdiction in such cases. Only in those instances where Congress by statute has made federal jurisdiction exclusive [27] are the state courts barred from acting. Consequently, many kinds of cases, such as

---

[26] *Const. of U.S.*, art. III, sec 2.

[27] Cases with respect to which federal jurisdiction has thus been made exclusive include, among others, cases under the patent or copyright laws, bankruptcy proceedings, suits against ambassadors or consuls, and federal criminal prosecutions.

those between citizens of different states,[28] may be brought in *either* federal or state courts at the option of the plaintiff. If the plaintiff elects to bring such an action in a state court, however, the case may, upon request by the defendant and before actual trial of the controversy, be "removed" to a federal court. Once a case has been decided by the highest court of a state, it may be "appealed" to the United States Supreme Court only if some federal question is involved. If, for example, the validity of a state statute has been challenged on the ground that it violates the *state* constitution, the decision of the state supreme court is final and conclusive; but if, on the other hand, the state statute is alleged to violate the *federal* constitution, it may be possible to secure a review of the state court's decision by the highest court of the land.

Structure of the State Judicial System

The composition and jurisdiction of the various courts comprising the state judiciary are determined in part by constitutional provision and in part by statute. In general, it may be said that such matters as the different grades of courts, the number of judges, and how judges shall be chosen, are dealt with in considerable detail by most state constitutions, though some discretion is left with the legislature, particularly with respect to minor courts. In the matter of jurisdiction the legislature usually enjoys a somewhat broader power of regulation, but even here there are often important constitutional provisions governing the kinds of cases that may be tried by the different classes of courts. Though the judicial hierarchy varies somewhat from state to state, the courts of which it is composed fall rather naturally into five classes or grades: (1) justice-of-the-peace courts and other tribunals of petty jurisdiction; (2) courts of intermediate grade; (3) courts of general trial jurisdiction; (4) appellate courts; and (5) the state supreme court.[29] Making due allowance for some variations in title, courts of the first, third, and fifth of these classes exist in every state, while tribunals of the second and fourth categories are found in some states but not all. Each of the five grades of courts will now be considered.[30]

[28] By statutory provision, Congress has limited the cases that may be taken into the federal courts on the basis of such "diverse citizenship" of the parties to those in which the amount in controversy exceeds $10,000.

[29] Cf. Willoughby, *op. cit.*, 243-247.

[30] Notwithstanding that judges of courts of the lower grades are frequently selected and paid by local governmental units, these tribunals are, from the legal standpoint, integral parts of the state judicial system. For this reason these "local" courts, except for brief attention to municipal courts in connection with the discussion of city government, are considered at this point rather than in the chapters dealing with local-government organization.

Justices of the Peace

The lowest rung in the judicial ladder is the court presided over by the justice of the peace.[31] Though appointed by the governor in a few states, justices of the peace are in most instances chosen by popular election. The election district is usually the township or some other subdivision of the county; and the term of office is in most cases either two or four years. Justices are not required to have, and ordinarily do not have, any legal training. Indeed, many of them have only a minimum amount of formal education of any kind. A 1956 study in North Carolina revealed that, of the justices then in office in that state, not one had a law degree, 75 percent had not attended college, and 40 percent had not attended high school.[32] Notwithstanding that justices are ordinarily elected from smaller areas, their courts usually possess jurisdiction throughout the county.

The judicial functions of the justice of the peace fall into three categories. In the first place, he tries civil cases wherein the amount involved does not exceed a fixed sum. This maximum varies considerably from state to state but is usually not more than a few hundred dollars. Though some of the civil actions in justice-of-the-peace courts arise out of torts, the majority of such suits are based upon contracts, express or implied. Common examples are actions seeking to collect unpaid bills or rents, or to secure judgment on promissory notes.[33] In the second place, the justice tries minor criminal cases. The fines and jail sentences which he may impose are strictly limited by the constitution or by statute; and it is not within his competence to impose a penitentiary sentence. The criminal offenses most commonly tried by justices' courts are breaches of the peace, traffic-law violations, infractions of health regulations, and violations of municipal ordinances.[34] Finally, as a "committing magistrate," the justice may hold preliminary hearings in cases involving more serious crimes. The purpose of such a hearing is not to determine the guilt or innocence of the suspected person, but merely to decide whether there is sufficient evidence against him to justify his being held for further action.

[31] Urban areas in some states are provided with petty courts presided over by "police magistrates," with jurisdiction similar to that of justices of the peace. These magistrates' courts in some instances supplement, and in others supplant, the justice-of-the-peace courts.

[32] Isham Newton, *The Minor Judiciary in North Carolina* (Unpublished Ph.D. Thesis, University of Pennsylvania, 1956); cited in Henry J. Abraham, *The Judicial Process*, 130.

[33] See Callender, *op. cit.*, 52-55.

[34] *Ibid.*, 50-51. Juries are used only occasionally in justice-of-the-peace courts. The decision of a justice of the peace, in either a civil or a criminal case, may usually be appealed to a court of intermediate or general trial jurisdiction. When such appeal is taken, however, the higher tribunal does not act, strictly speaking, as an appellate court, but tries the case *de novo*, that is, without reference to the earlier proceeding before the justice.

If the justice, as a result of the preliminary hearing, finds that the evidence against the suspected person is substantial, it is his duty to hold the suspect pending action by the grand jury or the filing of an information by the prosecuting attorney. This he may do by requiring the suspected person to give bond for his appearance or, if the required bond cannot be given or the offense is nonbailable, by committing him to jail.[35] Justices of the peace, in addition to their judicial functions, are usually vested with certain powers or duties of a nonjudicial nature. Thus they are quite generally authorized to perform marriage ceremonies and, in a few states, serve as members of county or town governing boards.[36]

During recent years, the institution of the justice of the peace has been widely criticized. Of English origin, the office was established in the American colonies and early states in a rural society, at a time when laws were relatively few and simple, and when primitive facilities for transportation and communication made it desirable that some means of administering homespun justice be made available within a few miles of every citizen. As the country developed, the office came to be regarded as a normal part of the judicial system, being required in many states by constitutional provision. With the passing of time, however, an agricultural society was changed into one which at many points was highly industrialized; social relations and the laws governing those relations became numerous and complex; and transportation progressed to a point where the county courthouse was more readily accessible to the average litigant than had been the residence of a neighboring justice a few decades earlier. Because of these facts, it is now widely believed that the justice-of-the-peace court has outlived its usefulness and should be supplanted by a court of minor jurisdiction organized along more modern lines.[37]

For one thing, it is clear that our present-day law, with its manifold technicalities, cannot be properly administered by laymen. But even more serious are the evils arising from the fee system of compensation. Although there are some exceptions, particularly in urban areas, the large majority of justices in most states are paid no salary, but receive as their compensation fees assessed as a part of the "costs" in the cases brought before them. It is therefore incumbent upon a justice, if he desires to derive any income from his "judgeship," to conduct his office in a manner that will attract business to his court. In a civil case, the plaintiff is usually free to bring his action before any of several justices within the county. The justice who is fortunate enough to be the one chosen, in gratitude for this piece of business and in the hope of securing other cases in the future, will likely be disposed to decide the case in the plaintiff's favor. Indeed, civil

[35] Cf. *Ibid.* Grand jury indictment and the prosecutor's information are discussed below, Chap. XVII.
[36] See below, Chap. XV, "Justices of the Peace."
[37] See below, "Abolition of Justice-of-the-Peace Courts."

cases in justices' courts are so generally decided in the plaintiff's favor that it has been said facetiously that J. P. (the common abbreviation for justice of the peace) means "judgment for the plaintiff."

A study of justice-of-the-peace courts in six Michigan counties revealed that, of 933 civil cases disposed of, 926, or 99.2 percent of the total, resulted in judgments for the plaintiff.[38] According to a survey in Tennessee, of 25,088 civil cases tried by sixty-seven justices, judgment was given for the plaintiff in 24,663 cases, or 98.3 percent of the total.[39] While the very nature of civil cases brought before justices' courts would lead one to expect that a large proportion of such cases would be decided in the plaintiff's favor even by the most impartial tribunal, the percentages of plaintiff judgments revealed by such studies as these seem clearly to be excessive. Enlightening on this point are the results of a study in Indiana, where at the time of the survey several of the more populous counties had salaried justices operating in urban areas. A survey of civil cases revealed that in those counties which had some salaried justices, only 53.6 percent of all such cases resulted in judgment for the plaintiff, whereas in counties having all justices on a fee basis judgment given for the plaintiff in more than 79 percent of the cases.[40]

With respect to criminal cases, one of the most widespread evils of the justice-of-the-peace system is that of the "speed trap." A justice desiring to make his office profitable establishes himself along a main highway in or near a small village that imposes an absurdly low speed limit. He then allies himself with one or more constables having ambitions similar to his own. The constable makes wholesale arrests of unwary motorists and prefers charges against them in the justice's court. The justice imposes a small fine, and assesses costs sufficient to cover his own fee and that of the arresting constable. If the motorist appears to be a person of modest means, or if he protests vigorously enough, the "court" may remit the fine and require only the payment of costs, which will generally run to several dollars. In any event, the victim, with some grumbling, will usually pay the amount demanded and be on his way rather than attempt to present a defense. Thus the justice and the constable, through cooperative effort,

---

[38] Edson R. Sunderland, "The Efficiency of Justices' Courts," in Arthur W. Bromage and Thomas H. Reed, *Organization and Cost of County and Township Government* (Mich. Comsn. of Inquiry into County, Township and School Dist. Govt., Detroit, 1933), 142-146.

[39] T. L. Howard, "The Justice of the Peace System in Tennessee," *Tenn. Law Rev.*, XIII, 19-38 (Dec., 1934).

[40] Gail M. Morris, *Justice of the Peace Courts in Indiana* (Bur. of Govt. Research, Ind. Univ., Bloomington, 1942), 25-26. Like the percentage of plaintiff judgments in civil cases, the percentage of convictions in criminal cases in justice courts is extremely high. Insofar as it has been possible to determine from official records and local investigations, it appears that, on the average, some 98 percent of all traffic-violation cases tried before justices of the peace result in convictions. George Warren, *Traffic Courts*, 217-219.

are able to build up a lucrative business. Fortunate indeed is the motorist who travels widely and has not, at some time, fallen prey to the nefarious speed trap.[41]

Another evil growing out of the fee system of compensation is that of "fee splitting." According to this practice, justices competing for criminal cases may seek to attract business to their respective courts by offering to divide their own fees with constables or other arresting officers who will bring cases before them. Though it is impossible to ascertain the extent of this pernicious and illegal practice, it certainly has existed in numerous instances and there is reason to believe that it is relatively widespread.[42]

Some states, in regulating the fees of justices in criminal cases, go so far as to provide that the justice shall receive a fee only if he finds the defendant guilty. In the celebrated Tumey case,[43] the United States Supreme Court held such a provision with respect to a mayor's court invalid as endangering judicial impartiality in violation of the "due process of law" clause of the Fourteenth Amendment; and the courts of some states, on the basis of this decision, have voided convictions in justice-of-the-peace courts where the justice has clearly had a pecuniary interest in the outcome. In other states, however, the courts have upheld fee provisions of the kind mentioned, taking the view that the circumstances involved are different from those which prevailed in the Tumey case. Thus it has been held in some instances that the right to demand a jury trial, or the right to a *de novo* trial on appeal, preserves due process of law notwithstanding the justice's pecuniary interest.[44]

After examining the weaknesses of the justice-of-the-peace system, one writer declares: "The justices of the peace as a class are wholly unqualified for the positions they occupy. The pernicious fee system and local politics break down their integrity and lead to corruption. They are often ignorant and wholly uncontrolled by statute or constitution. Their decisions are purely personal. The administration of justice by these lay magistrates is uncertain, unequal and unstable, and in truth, the system as such, is a denial of justice according to our highest conception of that term." [45]

[41] With regard to the speed-trap evil in Indiana, see Morris, *Justice of the Peace Courts in Indiana,* 17-18.

[42] For a discussion of alleged fee-splitting in one Tennessee county, see J. W. Manning, "In-Justices of the Peace," *Nat. Mun. Rev.,* XVIII, 225-227 (Apr., 1929).

[43] *Tumey* v. *Ohio,* 273 U.S. 510 (1927).

[44] See Kenneth Vanlandingham, "Pecuniary Interest of Justices of the Peace in Kentucky: The Aftermath of Tumey v. Ohio," *Ky. Law Jour.,* XLV, 607-625 (Summer, 1957), and cases there cited; *In re Borchert,* 57 Wash. 2d 719 (1961).

[45] Chester H. Smith, "The Justice of the Peace System in the United States," *Calif. Law Rev.,* XV, 118-141, at 140 (Jan., 1927).

Courts of Intermediate Grade

In some states there are to be found, between the justice-of-the-peace courts and the courts of general trial jurisdiction to be discussed presently, courts possessing jurisdiction broader than that of the justices, but which nevertheless falls short of general trial jurisdiction. These intermediate tribunals are sometimes organized on a county basis and known as county courts. Some of the so-called municipal courts within cities also belong to this class. Intermediate courts, while empowered to try civil and criminal cases which would be beyond the jurisdiction of justices of the peace, usually have concurrent jurisdiction with the courts of the justices over matters falling within the competence of the latter. That is to say, the plaintiff in a minor case may elect to sue either before a justice of the peace or in the court of intermediate jurisdiction. The intermediate courts, moreover, frequently have authority to hear appeals from justice-of-the-peace courts; and, where special probate courts are not provided, probate matters are often included within their jurisdiction.[46] Judges of the intermediate courts are usually elected by the voters of the county or municipality.

General Trial Courts

The general trial courts are those authorized to try civil cases without limitation as to the amount involved, and criminal cases regardless of the seriousness of the offense charged.[47] These tribunals are usually called county,[48] district, or circuit courts, though still other names are used in some states. Their judges are chosen in most states by popular election, each judge ordinarily serving either a single county or a district or circuit comprising two or more counties. Where several counties are grouped together in a judicial district or circuit, it is usual for the judge to hold court in each county in turn.

It is in the courts of this class that major civil actions and criminal prosecutions for felony are usually instituted. Some minor cases also are brought in these courts, for, the most petty cases sometimes excepted, the general trial courts commonly have concurrent jurisdiction with justices of the peace in lesser civil and criminal matters. In addition to their broad original jurisdiction, these courts generally have authority, sometimes concurrent with that of intermediate courts, to hear appeals from justices of

---

[46] See Willoughby, *op. cit.*, 245-246.

[47] Probate jurisdiction is also exercised by the general trial courts in some instances.

[48] In some states the county court is a court of intermediate jurisdiction, ranking below the general trial courts. See above, "Courts of Intermediate Grade."

the peace. Though they try many cases without juries, it is the general trial courts which make most extensive use of the petit jury in both civil and criminal cases.[49]

Appellate Courts

About 12 states, in order to reduce the volume of appeals to the supreme court, have created one or more appellate courts between the general trial courts and the state's highest tribunal. Appellate-court judges most commonly are elected, but in a few states are appointed by the governor or consist of trial-court judges assigned to appellate-court duty. Their jurisdiction is in most cases exclusively appellate, their work consisting principally in hearing and determining appeals from the general trial courts. In many classes of cases the decision of an appellate court is final, but in various important matters further appeal may be taken to the supreme court. Whereas a court of petty, intermediate, or general trial grade is presided over by a single judge, an appellate court, like a supreme court, consists of a "bench" of three or more judges and renders decisions by majority vote. Since appellate courts, in reviewing the decisions of lower tribunals, pass in most instances only upon matters of law, and not upon questions of fact, they do not ordinarily make use of the jury.[50]

The State Supreme Court

At the apex of the state judicial system is a single high court with jurisdiction throughout the state. This tribunal is usually, though not always, called the supreme court,[51] and that title will be used here in a generic sense to designate the highest court in any state. In every state except New Hampshire, the supreme court is established by constitutional provision rather than by statute.[52] The number of members of the tribunal varies among the states from three to nine, with courts of five or seven members most common. Supreme court judges are popularly elected in most states, though in some they are appointed by the governor or elected by the legislature.[53]

One member of the court is designated as "chief justice," and the other members are known as "associate justices." The method by which

[49] A comprehensive description of the general trial courts will be found in Council of State Governments, *Trial Courts of General Jurisdiction in the Forty-eight States.*

[50] Regarding the structure and jurisdiction of appellate courts in the respective states where they are found, and the advantages and disadvantages of courts of this nature, see Kentucky Legislative Research Commission, *Intermediate Appellate Courts.*

[51] In New York, for instance, the highest tribunal is entitled the "court of appeals," whereas the tribunal bearing the title of "supreme court" is of lower rank.

[52] Council of State Governments, *The Courts of Last Resort of The Forty-eight States,* 3.

[53] See below, "Selection of State Judges: Election versus Appointment."

the chief justice is chosen displays considerable variation. In some states he is appointed or elected as such; in others, he is the senior justice in point of service; in still others, he is the justice whose term will first expire; and, in yet another group of states, he is designated as chief justice by the members of the court.[54] The chief justice presides over the court's sessions and usually enjoys some supervisory authority over court business, but has only the same voting power as the associate justices.

The jurisdiction of the supreme court is principally appellate, and in some states is exclusively so. In deciding appealed cases, the purpose of the high court is to correct the errors of lower tribunals and to unify the interpretation of the law.[55] Where there is an appellate court below the supreme court, some cases reaching the latter do so on appeal from the appellate tribunal. Elsewhere appeals go directly from the general trial courts to the supreme court, as indeed do many appeals even in states having appellate courts. In some states the supreme court has a limited amount of original jurisdiction, which often includes authority to issue writs of mandamus, quo warranto, and habeas corpus. Since it functions principally as an appellate tribunal, the supreme court ordinarily makes no use of the jury.

In deciding cases, the supreme court acts by majority vote. When a particular case has been heard and decided, one of the judges who voted with the majority is designated, usually by the chief justice, to write the "opinion" of the court. This opinion is an explanation of the reasoning whereby the court arrived at its decision, and usually includes numerous citations to earlier cases in which points of law similar to those involved in the case at hand have been decided. Any member of the court who voted with the majority, and therefore concurs in the result of the decision, but who reached that result by a line of reasoning different from that stated in the opinion as prepared by his colleague, may, if he wishes, file a "concurring" opinion setting forth his own line of reasoning. Furthermore, when the court is divided, any judge who voted with the minority may file a "dissenting" opinion in which he explains why he believes the case should have been decided differently. All of these opinions are published in the *National Reporter System* issued by the West Publishing Company, and for all but a few states they are officially published in volumes known as the state's *Supreme Court Reports*.[56] Majority opinions become "precedents" [57] to be followed in subsequent cases. Though a state supreme court decision stands as "controlling" only in the courts of that

---

[54] See Roscoe Pound, *Organization of Courts*, 169-170.

[55] Cf. Willoughby, *op. cit.*, 247.

[56] Appellate-court opinions customarily are published in the same manner as those of the state supreme court. Opinions of general trial and inferior courts are rarely published.

[57] See above, "Law Applied by State Courts."

particular state, the decisions of a given state are frequently cited in other jurisdictions as "persuasive" precedents.

Selection of State Judges: Election versus Appointment

Methods of selecting judges vary considerably among the states, and even within a single state it is not uncommon to find different methods in use for the members of different tribunals. In some ten eastern and southern states, the judges of most courts are appointed by the governor (usually with the consent of the senate or executive council) or elected by the legislature; and the new state of Hawaii provides for appointment by the governor with senatorial consent. Approximately three-fourths of the states, however, choose all or most of their judges by popular election.[58] This is unfortunate inasmuch as the two qualifications which, apart from personal integrity, are most to be desired in judges—namely, legal learning and judicial temperament—are not best secured by the elective process. Under popular election, political strength and personal popularity are likely to be the determining factors in the choice of judges, rather than the fitness of the various candidates to fill the offices sought. Moreover, the elective system as it normally operates requires that judges, if they are to retain their positions, forsake periodically the dignity of judicial office and enter actively into political campaigns.[59]

Recognizing these weaknesses of the prevailing system, some states have taken steps designed to lessen the evils of partisan election. Thus, more than a dozen states, though retaining popular election, now choose their judges on nonpartisan ballots;[60] and some states which continue to use party designations provide for the holding of judicial elections at different times from elections for filling legislative and executive offices. Although these practices may be steps in the right direction, they by no means overcome the basic objections to popular election. "Nonpartisan" elections are frequently less nonpartisan in practice than in name; and separate judicial elections, though perhaps increasing the attention given to the qualifications of judicial candidates, retain the partisan factor.[61]

---

[58] Methods of selecting judges in the various states are summarized in Council of State Governments, *State Court Systems* (1956 revsn.), Table II. See also Evan Haynes, *The Selection and Tenure of Judges*, Chap. 2; Kansas Legislative Council, *Selection of Judges;* Abraham, *op. cit.*, 26-39; Thomas R. Robinson, "Selection of Judges," *Conn. Bar Jour.*, XV, 291-305 (Oct., 1941); Paul Brosman, "Judicial Selection in the United States," *Tulane Law Rev.*, XXIII, 491-498 (June, 1949).

[59] See Stuart H. Perry, "Shall We Appoint Our Judges?" *Annals of Amer. Acad. of Polit. and Soc. Sci.*, CLXXXI, 97-108 (Sept., 1935).

[60] Louden L. Bomberger, "Non-Partisan Selection of Judges," *Ind. Law Jour.*, XVI, 57-65 (Oct., 1940).

[61] Separate judicial elections have the additional disadvantage of increasing the frequency with which the voter is expected to go to the polls.

Several states, led by California and Missouri, have gone further than merely to provide for election of judges on nonpartisan ballots or at special judicial elections, and have adopted systems for the selection of judges which represent a compromise between appointment and popular election. The purpose of these plans, in general, is to retain some degree of popular control over judicial personnel while at the same time eliminating the most serious defects of popular election.

The California Plan

A constitutional amendment adopted in California in 1934 provides that any judge of the supreme court or of a district court of appeal who desires to be a candidate to succeed himself may, shortly before the expiration of his term, declare his desire to retain his judgeship. His name is then placed on the ballot, without the name of any opposing candidate, and the electors vote upon the sole question of whether he shall be retained in office for another term. By this means the incumbent judge stands for reelection entirely upon his own record and does not have to compete with the personal popularity of an opposing candidate. If a majority of those voting on the question vote in favor of his retention, the incumbent remains in office; but, if the vote goes against him, a vacancy occurs. All vacancies are filled by appointment by the governor with the approval of a commission on qualifications. This commission consists of the chief justice of the supreme court, the presiding justice of one of the courts of appeal, and the attorney general, and it acts by majority vote. The name of any person appointed to fill a vacancy is placed upon the ballot at the next general election, and the voters decide whether he shall serve out the term for which he was appointed. Should the vote go against the appointee, a vacancy again occurs, and is filled by the method of appointment just described.[62]

The Missouri Plan[63]

Under the Missouri plan, adopted by constitutional amendment in 1940 and continued in its essential features by the new constitution of

---

[62] Charles Aikin, "A New Method of Selecting Judges in California," *Amer. Polit. Sci. Rev.*, XXIX, 472-474 (June, 1935). The California plan may also be applied to superior courts by adoption by popular vote in the respective counties. Concerning the operation of the plan under successive governors, see Malcolm Smith, "The California Method of Selecting Judges," *Stanford Law Rev.*, III, 571-600 (July, 1951).

[63] Although first adopted by Missouri and popularly known as the Missouri plan, the essential features of this scheme for nonpartisan selection and merit reelection of judges have been advocated by the American Judicature Society since 1913 and by the American Bar Association since 1937. Cf. *Jour. of Amer. Judic. Soc.*, XLVI, 1 (June, 1962); W. St. John Garwood, "Judicial Selection and Tenure—the Model Article Provisions," *Ibid.*, XLVII, 21-29 (June, 1963). The text of the Society's model article is reproduced in *Ibid.*, 8-12.

1945, a judge of the supreme court or of a court of appeals [64] may, near the end of his term, file with the secretary of state a declaration of candidacy for reelection. When such declaration is filed, there is submitted to the voters in the general election, on a separate judicial ballot, the question of whether the judge shall be retained in office. The winning of this election returns the judge to his office for another term. If, however, a majority of those voting on the question vote against the judge's retention, or if he fails to file a declaration of candidacy, a vacancy is created. All vacancies are filled by gubernatorial appointment, but in making an appointment the governor is required to select one of three persons nominated by a nonpartisan judicial commission. This commission consists of seven members: the chief justice of the supreme court as chairman, three lawyers designated by the organized bar, and three laymen appointed by the governor. The term of a judge serving by virtue of appointment extends only to the end of the calendar year within which is held the first general election after he has been twelve months in office; but a popular vote in favor of his retention in office operates to return the incumbent for a full twelve-year term.[65]

The Missouri plan of judicial selection, like that of California, is designed to combine the best features of the ordinary systems of appointment and election, while at the same time providing safeguards available under neither. "Missouri's experience," wrote the chief justice of that state's supreme court at the close of the first decade under the new system, "has demonstrated the plan's effectiveness in bringing about a gradual and continuing improvement of the judiciary. It has taken the courts out of politics. Political parties have respected it and have made no effort to influence elections under it. Judicial qualities have been substituted for party affiliations as the principal basis for selecting and retaining judges. Court dockets have been brought up to date, delays lessened and expense

[64] Also under the plan are circuit and probate judges within the city of St. Louis and Jackson county (Kansas City); judges of the St. Louis courts of criminal correction; and judges of courts of record in such judicial circuits outside St. Louis and Jackson county as may adopt the system by popular vote.

[65] Nominations to lower-court judgeships are made by a five-member circuit judicial commission established in each judicial circuit where there are courts operating under the plan. For a comprehensive discussion of the origins and operation of the Missouri plan, see Jack W. Peltason, *The Missouri Plan for the Selection of Judges*. See also Thomas F. McDonald, "Missouri's Ideal Judicial Selection Law," *Jour. of Amer. Judic. Soc.*, XXIV, 194-198 (Apr., 1941); Forrest M. Hemker, "Experience under the Missouri Non-Partisan Court Plan," *Ibid.*, XLIII, 159-161 (Feb., 1960); William W. Crowdus, "The Operation of the Missouri Non-Partisan Court Plan," *Neb. Law Rev.*, XXIII, 177-186 (Oct., 1944); Henry A. Bundschu, "The Missouri Non-Partisan Court Plan—Selection and Tenure of Judges," *Univ. of Kansas City Law Rev.*, XVI, 55-67 (Apr.-June, 1948); Laurance M. Hyde, "Choosing Judges in Missouri," *Nat. Mun. Rev.*, XXXVIII, 491-493, 503 (Nov., 1949); Laurance M. Hyde, "Missouri Provides New Methods in Improving the Administration of Justice," *State Govt.*, XXIII, 28-31, 39 (Feb., 1950); Charles P. Blackmore, "Court Plan Matures," *Nat. Civic Rev.*, XLVIII, 62-67 (Feb., 1959).

of litigation reduced because judges spend no time campaigning for re-election but are free for court work." [66]

In 1958 the neighboring state of Kansas provided for the selection of supreme-court judges by a plan closely paralleling that of Missouri; and the basic features of the Missouri plan have now been applied to some or all state courts in Alabama, Alaska, Iowa, and Nebraska. Illinois, under the terms of a constitutional amendment effective at the beginning of 1964, retains partisan election for the initial choice of judges but follows Missouri in providing for reelection without competition.

Judicial Tenure

Whereas federal judges serve during good behavior, state judges are usually elected or appointed for fixed terms.[67] In the general trial courts, terms of four or six years, though by no means universal, are most common. Except in Vermont, where it is two years, the term of supreme court judges ranges from six years in seventeen states to twenty-one years in Pennsylvania. A few states do not prescribe a fixed judicial term. These include Massachusetts and Rhode Island, in which tenure is during good behavior; New Hampshire, where judges serve to the age of seventy; and New Jersey, where initial appointments to the supreme and superior courts are for seven years but reappointments are for good behavior subject to compulsory retirement at the age of seventy.

In order that judges may perform their work fearlessly and impartially, it is desirable that their tenure of office be secure and that they be protected against arbitrary removal. For that reason the judicial term is, in most states, longer than the terms provided for legislative and executive officers. If a satisfactory method of removing incompetent judges were provided, much could be said for judicial service during good behavior. However, since adequate provisions for removal are at present wanting, a definite term, though a relatively long one, seems preferable.[68]

Removal of Judges

Four principal methods of removing judges from office are employed in the states: (1) by impeachment, (2) by concurrent resolution of the legislature, (3) by popular recall, and (4) by action of higher courts. Impeachment is available as a method of removal in practically every state. It is unsatisfactory, however, in that the impeachment process may

---

[66] Hyde, "Choosing Judges in Missouri," *loc. cit.*, 503.

[67] For tabulations of judicial terms in the respective states, see Council of State Governments, *State Court Systems* (1956 revsn.), Table IV; *The Book of the States*, 1964-65, p. 125.

[68] Cf. Willoughby, *op. cit.*, Chap. 28. See below, "Removal of Judges."

usually be invoked only on the ground that the judge is guilty of criminal conduct, and does not permit removal for mere incompetency or for physical or mental disability.[69] About half of the states empower the legislature to remove judges by concurrent resolution of the two houses, this method differing from the impeachment process principally in that a formal trial is not required.[70] In practice, neither impeachment nor removal by resolution is frequently used. A few states permit the popular recall of judges,[71] though this method of judicial removal is usually not favored among students of government, even by those who believe that the principles of the recall are sound as applied to legislative and executive officers. It is the function of the courts to apply the law, as it exists, with an even hand, and in so doing to protect minority rights against infraction by majorities. To subject judges to the threat of recall in the event that they render decisions which, though sound in law, are unpopular, is not only unfair to the judges themselves but is likely to interfere with judicial independence. Only some 6 states provide that judges of lower courts may be removed by higher judicial tribunals, though, in view of the unsatisfactory nature of the other methods discussed, it would seem that the feasibility of adopting this means of removal might well be considered by other states.[72]

Notwithstanding formal removal provisions of the types noted, and the fact that an occasional judge is removed for commission of a criminal offense or other serious misconduct, there exist in most states no practical means of removing a judge for mere incompetency, neglect of judicial duty, or unethical conduct. A few states, however, have taken steps designed to remedy this situation in some measure. Illinois now provides that judges may be removed for cause by a commission composed of supreme, appellate, and circuit court judges. New York for some years has had a Court on the Judiciary comprised of judges of the higher courts of the state and empowered to order the removal of judges for cause. Members of the court on the judiciary are the chief judge of the court of appeals (the state's highest tribunal), the senior associate judge of the court of appeals, and one justice of the appellate division of the supreme court in each judicial department. The chief judge of the court of appeals is the presiding officer of the court on the judiciary. In this capacity the chief judge may convene the court on his own motion, and is required to con-

[69] Impeachment as a method of removing public officers was considered at an earlier point in connection with the powers of the legislature. See above, Chap. VIII, "Judicial Power: Impeachment."

[70] In a few instances the removal power rests with the governor after the necessary resolution has been adopted by the legislature.

[71] Concerning recall procedures generally, see above, Chap. VI, "The Popular Recall."

[72] The recent removal of a Texas district judge by the state supreme court is described by H. Malcolm McDonald in "Texas Removes and Replaces a Judge," *Jour. of Amer. Judic. Soc.*, XXXVIII, 47-50 (Aug., 1954).

vene it upon written request of the governor, a presiding justice of the appellate division of the supreme court, or a majority of the executive committee of the state bar association. California, in 1960, embarked upon a novel experiment in judicial removal. By constitutional amendment there was created a Commission on Judicial Qualifications composed of five judges appointed by the state supreme court, two lawyers selected by the state bar, and two citizens appointed by the governor. The commission is empowered to investigate complaints against judges and recommend their removal for cause by the supreme court. During the first two years of its existence the commission received 163 complaints concerning such matters as absenteeism, drunkenness, and emotional disturbance. Many of these proved, on initial examination, to be trivial in nature, but 46 were thought by the commission to deserve further investigation. Several judges resigned or retired as a result of the commission's inquiry; and in 1961 a judge resigned when advised by the commission that his removal would be recommended for habitual intemperance. This early experience appears to indicate that the commission has exercised a wholesome influence. It has been reported, for example, that the mere existence of the commission has caused many "short-day" judges to lengthen their court sessions.[73] These various measures seem to suggest some of the approaches to the problem of removing unfit judges which might well be explored by other states.

Compensation of Judges

The fee system of compensating justices of the peace, and the evils flowing from this, have already been discussed. Judges of the general trial and higher courts are usually paid a regular salary, the amount of which is fixed by statute. Twenty-six states were recently reported as paying their supreme court judges annual salaries of $20,000 or more.[74] Other states do not pay as much, and judges of the trial courts are usually paid considerably less than supreme court judges; yet it may be said that, in general, judicial salaries are reasonably adequate. Salaries of supreme and appellate court judges are paid from the state treasury. Judges of general trial and intermediate courts are paid in some instances by the state, in others by the counties or other local government units, and in still others in part by the state and in part by local units. Some state constitutions, as one means of preserving judicial independence, provide that the compensation of judges may not be reduced during their term of office.

[73] Murray Teigh Bloom, "Unseating Unfit Judges," *Nat. Civic Rev.*, LII, 70-72, 119 (Feb., 1963).
[74] *The Book of the States*, 1964-65, p. 128.

Judicial Reorganization

Recent decades have witnessed growing interest in the improvement and modernization of state judicial systems, and many states have taken significant steps in that direction. Measures designed to improve provisions regarding the selection, tenure, and removal of judges have already been discussed. States in substantial number have sought to remedy some of the weaknesses of the obsolescent justice-of-the-peace system or have abolished the system altogether. Another, though related, approach has been through simplification of court structure with the object of reducing jurisdictional conflict and overlap and expediting the handling of cases. Still other reorganization features in a number of states have had to do with procedural and management matters such as modernization of court rules, the conduct of judicial research, and the overall supervision of court business. In many instances, improvements in these latter categories have been effected through the establishment of judicial councils or conferences and court administrative offices. Some of these programs of judicial reorganization will now be considered.[75]

Abolition of Justice-of-the-Peace Courts

As pointed out earlier in this chapter, the justice-of-the-peace system is today thoroughly unsatisfactory as the foundational unit of state judicial organization. Many civic groups, crime commissions, and students of judicial administration have called for abolition of the system and its replacement by courts of minor jurisdiction organized along more modern lines.[76] What is needed is a system of minor courts having countywide jurisdiction and presided over by salaried magistrates. Preferably, these magistrates should be appointed rather than elected and should be chosen from the legal profession. The number of magistrates should be small enough, and they should be so distributed geographically, that each would have sufficient business to justify his service on a full-time basis, the provision of a suitable courtroom and necessary law books, and the employment of a clerk to keep the court records. Fortunately, progress in the directions indicated is now well under way, several states having provided or authorized, in some or all counties, local tribunals embodying at least some of the features suggested as desirable.

Virginia led the way in the early 1930's with the establishment of

---

[75] On reorganization problems generally, see Arthur T. Vanderbilt, ed., *Minimum Standards of Judicial Administration;* Arthur T. Vanderbilt, "The Essentials of a Sound Judicial System," *Northwestern Univ. Law Rev.,* XLVIII, 1-15 (Mar.-Apr., 1953).

[76] Cf. Willoughby, *op. cit.,* Chap. 22.

a system of "trial justices" appointed by the judges of the circuit court and paid a regular salary. The jurisdiction to try civil and criminal cases formerly possessed by justices of the peace was transferred to the trial justices, justices of the peace being limited henceforth to the issuance of certain forms of process such as warrants and subpoenas. The trial justice system appears to have resulted in a higher grade of court personnel than under the old justice-of-the-peace system, and in more efficient judicial administration at lower cost. In 1956, after serving the state for more than 20 years, the trial justice system was absorbed into a new system of county and municipal courts.[77]

Beginning in 1937, the Tennessee legislature enacted a number of special laws abolishing justice-of-the-peace courts in particular counties and creating in their stead "general sessions" courts consisting of salaried judges with countywide jurisdiction; and in 1959 the system of general-sessions courts was made statewide except for six counties.[78] A Maryland law of 1939 authorized the establishment in the counties of that state of trial magistrates' courts presided over by appointive, salaried judges. Missouri's new constitution, adopted in 1945, abolished the justice-of-the-peace system and established in each county one or more magistrate courts with countywide jurisdiction. In the less populous counties the probate judge serves ex officio as a magistrate, any additional magistrates in such counties, and all of those in larger counties, being elected. Reports on the operation of the new courts indicate that they are being found distinctly superior to the old justice-of-the-peace tribunals.[79]

In New Jersey, pursuant to the state's new constitution of 1947, elective justices of the peace have been supplanted by district and municipal courts under appointive magistrates. California's constitution was amended in 1950 to reorganize the minor judiciary in that state. Under the new provision and implementing legislation, judges of justice courts, who are elected for six-year terms, are required either to have been admitted to the practice of law or to have passed a qualifying examination, and are paid a regular salary.[80] Justice-of-the-peace tribunals in Ohio were

[77] Acts of Va., 1956, Chap. 555. Concerning the operation of the earlier system, see Arthur F. Kingdon, "The Trial Justice System of Virginia," Jour. of Amer. Judic. Soc., XXIII, 216-221 (Apr., 1940).

[78] Henry N. Williams, "General Sessions Courts in Tennessee," Ibid., XXXI, 101-104 (Dec., 1947); Kenneth E. Vanlandingham, "The Decline of the Justice of the Peace," Kan. Law Rev., XII, 389-403 (Mar., 1964). Where general-sessions courts have been established, justices of the peace, though deprived of jurisdiction over civil and criminal cases, retain their powers to perform marriages and serve as members of the quarterly court (county board).

[79] Forest E. Abbuhl, "Maryland Modernizes Its Justice of the Peace System," The County Officer, XVI, 77-78, 81 (Mar., 1951); Martin L. Faust, Five Years Under the New Missouri Constitution (Mo. Pub. Expediture Survey, Jefferson City, 1950), 16-17.

[80] Joseph Harrison, "Judicial Reform in New Jersey," State Govt., XXII, 232-236, 247-248 (Oct., 1949); Jour. of Amer. Judic. Soc., XXXIV, 58 (Aug., 1950); Ibid., 120 (Dec., 1950).

replaced in 1957 by a system of county courts under salaried judges. Another state to take action in 1957 was Indiana, which provided that the number of justices shall not exceed two (in some instances one) in any township; that in the more populous townships justices shall be compensated on a salary basis; that suitable courtrooms for justices shall be maintained at township expense; and that in the future all justices, save for those with specified previous service, shall either be attorneys or pass an examination approved by the state supreme court.[81]

In Connecticut, justices of the peace and municipal courts were replaced in 1961 by a new state-operated circuit court. Illinois, as part of a general program of court reorganization effective in 1964, replaced justices of the peace with state-salaried magistrates appointed by circuit judges and operating within the framework of the circuit courts. Other states which have recently abolished justice-of-the-peace courts include Colorado, Michigan, and North Dakota. In North Carolina, as a result of a constitutional amendment adopted in 1962, justice-of-the-peace courts are to be abolished by 1971. Finally to be noted is the fact that the traditional justice of the peace has been supplanted by municipal courts in several of the country's larger cities.

The constitutional and statutory provisions of the various states just mentioned are suggestive of the kind of action that might well be taken elsewhere. In states where the office of justice of the peace is established by the constitution, it can, of course, be completely abolished only by constitutional amendment. But, even in many of these states, the legislature has broad powers over jurisdiction and may render the justice-of-the-peace court largely innocuous by transferring most or all of its criminal and civil jurisdiction to county courts presided over by salaried judges. Experience suggests, however, that remedial legislation, if it is to be generally effective, must be of compulsory rather than optional character. Justices of the peace and other local officers are usually so well organized and so influential with the local electorate that they can successfully block the adoption by local vote of any proposal designed to curtail their powers.

Court Unification

With respect to the judicial system as a whole, perhaps the most serious weaknesses growing out of traditional forms of organization are (1) lack of specialization, (2) inequalities in the distribution of work, and (3) lack of uniformity in interpretation and administration of the law. By and large, the organization of our courts on a geographic rather than a functional basis prevents any substantial degree of specialization. Each court usually serves a city, county, district, circuit, or some other geo-

[81] *Laws of Ohio,* Vol. 127 (1957), p. 978; *Laws of Ind.,* 1957, Chap. 322.

graphic area, and handles all types of cases therein. Hence it is practically impossible for a judge to become a specialist in any particular kind of cases, such as criminal, equity, or domestic relations. Moreover, under the geographic basis of organization the dockets of some courts are crowded while those of others are light, and no adequate provision is made for transferring judges temporarily from courts having little to do to those that are overworked. Some courts with congested dockets are so far behind in their work that several years may elapse between the filing of a suit and its coming to trial, with the result, at times, that justice delayed is virtually justice denied. Finally, in the absence of central supervision, judicial administration is far from uniform, especially in the field of criminal law. Considerable discretion is commonly vested in the courts with respect to criminal penalties to be imposed, with the result that a given offense is likely to draw widely different penalties at different places in the same state, depending upon the attitude of the particular judge before whom the case is tried.

One of the most comprehensive proposals advanced for the remedy of these and other weaknesses of existing judicial organization is the plan for a "unified" state court, the principles of which have had the support of various bar associations and have been incorporated into the Model State Constitution prepared by the National Municipal League. Under this plan, which is patterned after the English system, all existing courts of the various grades, or at least those having civil jurisdiction, would be organized into a single unified state court, which would be divided, in turn, into a number of branches and divisions. For example, there might be a supreme-court branch, an appellate branch, a general-trial branch, and lesser tribunals of limited jurisdiction. To permit specialization, the trial branch might be organized in three divisions for the handling of jury cases, equity cases, and probate matters, respectively. All state judges would be judges of the unified court, and would be assigned to hold sessions at various points in the state as judicial business might require. Either the chief justice of the court or a judicial council under his chairmanship would exercise broad supervisory powers over the judges and their work. These powers would include those of assigning judges to the various branches and divisions, transferring judges temporarily from light to heavy dockets, and prescribing rules of procedure designed to expedite and secure uniformity in judicial administration.[82] The merits of the unified court plan have long been recognized by students of judicial administration, and for many years its principles have been applied to municipal tribunals in several large cities.[83] During the last two decades some or all features of the plan have been adopted by a number of states with respect to their overall court systems, in some instances by constitu-

[82] Willoughby, *op. cit.*, Chap. 19.
[83] *Ibid.*, Chap. 21. See also below, Chap. XIV, "Municipal Courts."

tional amendment and in others through the adoption of new constitutions.

Missouri's new constitution of 1945 provided for a substantial degree of unification by empowering the supreme court to establish rules of practice and procedure for all courts, and to make temporary transfers of judicial personnel from one court to another.[84] In 1948 New Jersey, in thoroughly reorganizing an antiquated judicial system under the terms of her new constitution of 1947, adopted the unified plan in many of its essential features. The New Jersey judiciary, under the new plan, consists of a supreme court, a superior court in three divisions (law, chancery, and appellate), county courts, and local district and municipal courts, all presided over by appointive judges. The chief justice of the supreme court is the administrative head of the entire court system, with broad authority to assign judges to particular divisions of the superior court and to transfer judges temporarily from one court to another; and power to prescribe rules for all tribunals in the system is vested in the supreme court.[85]

A constitutional amendment approved in North Carolina in 1962 provides for combining the courts of that state into a general court of justice with appellate, superior court, and district court divisions. Illinois, by constitutional amendment effective in 1964, reorganized five regular grades of courts and numerous special tribunals into courts of three levels —supreme, appellate, and circuit—and vested in the supreme court administrative authority over all courts in the state, including the power to make temporary reassignment of judges. Alaska's constitution stipulates that the courts of that state "shall constitute a unified judicial system for operation and administration," and makes the chief justice of the supreme court the administrative head of all courts. And Michigan's new constitution of 1963 vests the judicial power of that state exclusively in one court of justice divided into a supreme court, a court of appeals, a trial court of general jurisdiction known as the circuit court, a probate court, and other courts of limited jurisdiction which the legislature may establish by a two-thirds vote of each house. The supreme court is given general superintending control over, and power to prescribe procedural rules for, all courts of the state.[86]

[84] *Const. of Mo.* (1945), art. V, secs. 5, 6.

[85] *Const. of N.J.* (1947), art. VI; Joseph Harrison, "Judicial Reform in New Jersey," *State Govt.*, XXII, 232-236, 247-248 (Oct., 1949). For summaries of accomplishments under the new system, see Willard G. Woelper, "Jersey Justice Streamlined," *Nat. Mun. Rev.*, XLI, 283-287, 315 (June, 1952); Arthur T. Vanderbilt, "The First Five Years of the New Jersey Courts under the Constitution of 1947," *Rutgers Law Rev.*, VIII, 289-310 (Spring, 1954); William J. Brennan, Jr., "After Eight Years: New Jersey Judicial Reform," *Amer. Bar Assn. Jour.*, XLIII, 499-502, 564-566 (June, 1957).

[86] *Const. of N.C.* (1868 as amended), art. IV, secs. 1, 2; *Const. of Ill.* (1870 as amended), art. VI, secs. 1, 2; *Const. of Alaska* (1959), art. IV, secs. 1, 16; *Const. of Mich.* (1963), art. VI, secs. 1, 4, 5.

In view of the advances accomplished under these recently-adopted constitutional provisions, and of the widespread current interest in judicial reorganization, it is to be expected that additional states will take steps toward court unification in the years ahead.

Judicial Councils and Conferences

Although court unification has only recently begun to gain momentum, widespread recognition of the need for improving judicial administration is seen in the creation in most states, in some instances by constitutional provision but more often by statute, of judicial councils or judicial conferences or both. Judicial councils are usually composed of judges representing the different grades of state courts and of representatives of designated nonjudicial groups or agencies. These latter include, in various states, the bar association, the attorney general's office, the general citizenry, the judiciary committees of the state legislature, and the law school of the state university. The council's presiding officer is usually the chief justice of the supreme court. Council members not serving ex officio are generally designated by the governor or the chief justice.

The principal functions of the council ordinarily consist in compiling judicial statistics, conducting research in judicial adminstration, and recommending for legislative action desirable changes in judicial organization and rules of procedure. Although most councils possess only investigatory and advisory powers, that of California is authorized actually to adopt rules of procedure and to transfer judges from court to court to facilitate the clearing of congested dockets. Several other councils have rule-making authority. The councils are commonly required to file annual reports, and these documents, when published, serve as a useful source of information concerning the work of the state courts. A National Conference of Judicial Councils coordinates the work of the councils in the respective states.[87]

During the last few years a number of states have established judicial conferences either to replace or supplement their judicial councils.[88] The conferences most commonly meet annually and are considerably larger in their membership than the councils. Ordinarily the judges of all courts of record in the state are conference members and in several instances there are nonjudicial members as well. Illustrative of the broad membership found in some states is that of the New Jersey con-

[87] An excellent account of the organization and work of judicial councils is Glenn R. Winters, "Silver Anniversary of the Judicial Council Movement," *Jour. of Amer. Judic. Soc.,* XXXIII, 43-49, 79-84 (Aug., Oct., 1949). See also Willoughby, *op. cit.,* Chap. 20; Pressly S. Sikes, "The Work of Judicial Councils," *Amer. Polit. Sci. Rev.,* XXIX, 456-472 (June, 1935); Charles S. Coffey, "The Judicial Council Movement," *Tenn. Law Rev.,* XVI, 960-967 (June, 1941).

[88] See recent issues of *The Book of the States.*

ference, where, to the trial and appellate judges, are added delegates representative of the municipal magistrates. Nonjudicial members include the attorney general and county prosecutors, members of the board of bar examiners, the majority and minority leaders of each of the legislative houses, representatives of the various law schools in the state, officers and trustees of the state bar association, the president and representatives of each county bar association, and ten laymen appointed by the chief justice.[89] Judicial conferences are concerned with such matters as court organization, rules and procedures, and with the preservation of court records. They study all aspects of judicial administration and make recommendations to the legislature for improvements therein. Where the judicial council is retained it may, as in Virginia, serve as a working committee for the conference.[90] "Judicial councils and conferences in many states have contributed significantly to the improvement of the administration of justice through studies of problems of judicial organization and operation. They also help to bring together judges of various types of courts within a state, to mutual advantage. If, in addition to judges, they include lawyers and laymen in their membership, they help to unite bench, bar and the general public in the common cause of judicial reform." [91]

Court Administrative Offices

Still another recent development in the way of instrumentalities for improving judicial administration is the court administrative office, usually headed by a court-appointed director or administrator and charged with performing a variety of housekeeping and business functions for the judicial tribunals. The administrative office at the state level is patterned in some measure after the Administrative Office of the United States Courts established by Congress in 1939. Among the duties assigned to the administrative office in various states are those of collecting and compiling statistical data pertaining to judicial business, keeping a current inventory of the condition of court dockets, determining the needs of the respective courts for assistance, making recommendations concerning the assignment of judges for the relief of congested dockets, preparing budget estimates for the courts, and making recommendations for improvement of the judicial system. The Conference of Chief Justices has recommended the establishment of a court administrative office, together with a judicial

[89] Francis R. Aumann, *The Instrumentalities of Justice: Their Forms, Functions, and Limitations,* 59.

[90] *The Book of the States,* 1952-53, p. 460. See also Edward W. Hudgins, "The Judicial Council and Judicial Conference in Virginia," *State Govt.,* XXVII, 17-19 (Jan., 1954).

[91] *The Book of the States,* 1954-55, p. 431.

council or conference, in every state, and by the early 1960's such an office had been created in approximately half of the states. In 1955 the heads of these offices were organized as the National Conference of Court Administrators (now the National Conference of Court Administrative Officers) which meets annually with the Conference of Chief Justices and has as its aim the improvement of administrative procedures and practices in the state courts.[92]

REFERENCES

ABRAHAM, Henry J., *The Judicial Process* (Oxford Univ. Press, New York, 1962).

American Bar Association, *The Improvement of the Administration of Justice* (Amer. Bar. Assn., 3rd ed., 1952).

AUMANN, Francis R., *The Instrumentalities of Justice: Their Forms, Functions, and Limitations* (Ohio State Univ. Press, Columbus, 1956).

BALDWIN, Simeon E., *The American Judiciary* (Century, New York, 1905).

BRUCE, Andrew A., *The American Judge* (Macmillan, New York, 1924).

CALLENDER, Clarence N., *American Courts: Their Organization and Procedure* (McGraw-Hill, New York, 1927).

Council of State Governments, *State Court Systems* (The Council, Chicago, 1956 revsn.).

———, *The Courts of Last Resort of the Forty-eight States* (The Council, Chicago, 1950).

———, *Trial Courts of General Jurisdiction in the Forty-eight States* (The Council, Chicago, 1951).

FIELD Oliver P., *Judicial Review of Legislation in Ten Selected States* (Bur. of Govt. Research, Ind. Univ., Bloomington, 1943).

FRANK, Jerome, *Courts on Trial: Myth and Reality in American Justice* (Princeton Univ. Press, Princeton, N. J., 1949).

HAYNES, Evan, *The Selection and Tenure of Judges* (Nat. Conf. of Judicial Councils, 1944).

Kansas Legislative Council, *Selection of Judges* (Kan. Legis. Council, Topeka, 1956).

KAPLAN, Benjamin, and HALL, Livingston, eds., "Judicial Administration and the Common Man," *Annals of Amer. Acad. of Polit, and Soc. Sci.*, CCLXXXVII, Philadelphia, May, 1953.

Kentucky Legislative Research Commission, *Intermediate Appellate Courts* (Ky. Legis. Research Comsn., Frankfort, 1956).

[92] *Ibid.*, 1956-57, pp. 194-95; William L. Frederick, "State Judicial Systems," *Ibid.*, 1962-63, pp. 117-122; Willard G. Woelper, "Work of the Modern Administrator of Courts," *Annals of Amer. Acad. of Polit. and Soc. Sci.*, CCLXXXVII, 147-153 (May, 1953); Meredith H. Doyle, "The Administrative Officer of the Courts: His Role in Government," *State Govt.*, XXX, 262-263, 279-280 (Dec., 1957); Frederick W. Invernizzi, "The Office and Work of the Court Administrator," *Jour. of Amer. Judic. Soc.*, XLIII, 186-189 (Apr., 1960). Various data concerning court administrative offices are set forth in *The Book of the States*, 1964-65, p. 133.

LUMMUS, Henry T., *The Trial Judge* (Found. Press, Chicago, 1937).

MAYERS, Lewis, *The American Legal System* (Harper, New York, 1955).

PELTASON, Jack W., *The Missouri Plan for the Selection of Judges* (Univ. of Mo., Columbia, 1945).

POUND, Roscoe, *Organization of Courts* (Little, Boston, 1940).

SMITH, Franklin A., *Judicial Review of Legislation in New York, 1906-1938* (Columbia Univ. Press, New York, 1952).

VANDERBILT, Arthur T., *Judges and Jurors: Their Functions, Qualifications and Selection* (Boston Univ. Press, Boston, 1956).

————, ed., *Minimum Standards of Judicial Administration* (Nat. Conf. of Judicial Councils, 1949).

WARREN, George, *Traffic Courts* (Little, Brown, Boston, 1942).

WETMORE, Ruth Y., *The Justice of the Peace in Kansas* (Govtl. Research Center, Univ. of Kan., Lawrence, 1960).

WILLOUGHBY, W. F., *Principles of Judicial Administration* (Brookings Inst., Washington, 1929).

V

Local Organization and Powers

12

Units of Local Government

Number of Units

The number of local governmental units existing in the United States at a given time cannot be determined with exactness. Any attempt to take a "census" or make an enumeration of units meets with serious obstacles. Since organization and dissolution of units are going on continually, any enumeration is likely to be somewhat out of date before it is finished. This difficulty, however, can be at least partially overcome by making the enumeration as of a designated past date. But the result of an enumeration will depend also upon the definition of "governmental unit" which the enumerator adopts. Different definitions will include different geographic areas as units of government and, in the application of a single definition, the question will frequently arise as to whether a given area, in view of its organization and powers, is entitled, under the definition, to be classed as a governmental unit.[1]

In spite of these difficulties, the efforts of certain persons and organizations during the past three decades have provided us with nationwide data concerning local governmental units which are as accurate as

[1] Some of the subdivisional *areas* of the various states which, though used for governmental purposes, have no governmental organization of their own and hence are not entitled to be classed as *units* of government, include voting precincts, wards for electing members of city councils, tax assessment districts, districts for the election of state legislators, congressional districts, districts for the election of judges, and commissioner districts for election of members of the county board.

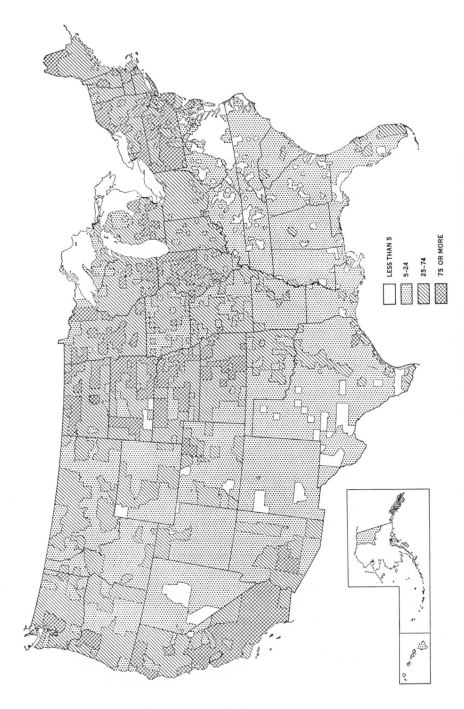

NUMBER OF LOCAL GOVERNMENTS PER COUNTY: 1962

LESS THAN 5

5-24

25-74

75 OR MORE

U.S. Department of Commerce. Bureau of the Census.

could reasonably be expected. The pioneer in the work of enumerating local units was Professor William Anderson of the University of Minnesota, whose first enumeration was made during the early 1930's. His original data were subsequently revised as of January, 1941; and during the early 1940's, the Governments Division of the United States Bureau of the Census, aided by Professor Anderson's valuable files, made an enumeration as of 1942.[2] Since the latter date there have been three Census Bureau enumerations, as of the respective years 1952, 1957, and, most recently, 1962.[3]

In conducting its 1962 survey, the Census Bureau counted as a unit of government any "organized entity which, in addition to having governmental character, has sufficient discretion in the management of its own affairs to distinguish it as separate from the administrative structure of any other governmental unit." It will thus be seen that, to be considered as a governmental unit, an entity must possess three distinct attributes: organized existence, governmental character, and substantial autonomy. Applying this definition, the Bureau found the total number of local governmental units in the United States in 1962 to be 91,185. The total number in each state, and the number belonging to each of the major types or categories of units, are indicated in the following table. It will be noted that, as among the individual states, the number of local units ranged from 20 in Hawaii to 6,452 in Illinois. The average number per

UNITS OF LOCAL GOVERNMENT IN THE UNITED STATES: 1962

STATE	ALL LOCAL UNITS	COUN-TIES	MUNICI-PALITIES	TOWNS AND TOWN-SHIPS	SCHOOL DISTRICTS	SPECIAL DISTRICTS
Alabama	732	67	349		114	202
Alaska	56		40		10	6
Arizona	378	14	61		251	52
Arkansas	1,208	75	417		417	299
California	4,022	57	373		1,630	1,962
Colorado	1,193	62	253		312	566
Connecticut	398		34	152	8	204
Delaware	207	3	51		90	63
District of Columbia	2		1			1
Florida	764	67	366		67	264

[2] William Anderson, *The Units of Government in the United States* (1942 ed.); United States Bureau of the Census, *Governmental Units in the United States: 1942.*

[3] United States Bureau of the Census, *Governments in the United States in 1952;* United States Bureau of the Census, *1957 Census of Governments,* Vol. I, No. 1: *Governments in the United States;* United States Bureau of the Census, *Census of Governments: 1962,* Vol. I: *Governmental Organization.* Most of the statistical data presented in this chapter are from the 1962 report.

UNITS OF LOCAL GOVERNMENT IN THE UNITED STATES:
1962 (Cont.)

STATE	ALL LOCAL UNITS	COUN- TIES	MUNICI- PALITIES	TOWNS AND TOWN- SHIPS	SCHOOL DISTRICTS	SPECIAL DISTRICTS
Georgia	1,218	159	561		197	301
Hawaii	20	3	1			16
Idaho	834	44	200		121	469
Illinois	6,452	102	1,251	1,433	1,540	2,126
Indiana	3,091	92	546	1,009	884	560
Iowa	2,642	99	944		1,336	263
Kansas	5,410	105	618	1,546	2,261	880
Kentucky	872	120	365		208	179
Louisiana	628	62	258		67	241
Maine	658	16	21	470	26	125
Maryland	351	23	152			176
Massachusetts	586	12	39	312	29	194
Michigan	3,816	83	509	1,259	1,866	99
Minnesota	5,212	87	845	1,822	2,343	115
Mississippi	772	82	266		158	266
Missouri	3,726	114	892	329	1,649	742
Montana	1,387	56	124		1,015	192
Nebraska	5,124	93	537	478	3,264	752
Nevada	136	17	17		17	85
New Hampshire	550	10	13	221	221	85
New Jersey	1,395	21	334	233	512	295
New Mexico	305	32	80		91	102
New York	3,802	57	612	932	1,231	970
North Carolina	675	100	449			126
North Dakota	3,028	53	356	1,387	986	246
Ohio	3,358	88	932	1,328	833	177
Oklahoma	1,959	77	533		1,225	124
Oregon	1,469	36	222		484	727
Pennsylvania	6,201	66	1,003	1,555	2,179	1,398
Rhode Island	97		8	31	2	56
South Carolina	552	46	255		109	142
South Dakota	4,463	64	307	1,072	2,940	80
Tennessee	657	95	280		14	268
Texas	3,327	254	866		1,474	733
Utah	423	29	212		40	142
Vermont	424	14	68	238	32	72
Virginia	380	98	236			46
Washington	1,646	39	263	66	411	867
West Virginia	389	55	224		55	55
Wisconsin	3,726	72	563	1,271	1,752	68
Wyoming	464	23	90		207	144
United States Total	91,185	3,043	17,997	17,144	34,678	18,323

SOURCE: United States Bureau of the Census, *Census of Governments: 1962*, Vol. 1: *Governmental Organization*, 29.

state for the entire country exceeded 1,800, although half of the states had less than 1,000 units each. With appropriate allowance for exceptions (see the above map), it may be said that local units tend to be fewest in the South, the Rocky Mountain West, and Alaska, and most numerous in the Northeast and Midwest and on the West Coast. Seven states with more than 4,000 units each account for two-fifths of the total number.

Trends in Numbers

Notwithstanding the present superabundance of local governments in the United States, their total number has been substantially reduced during recent years. According to the Census Bureau's data, the number decreased from 155,067 in 1942 to 91,185 in 1962—a reduction of more than 40 percent in the 20-year period. For the most part the curtailment has been the result of widespread consolidation of school districts. Indeed, during the period under consideration the number of school districts was reduced by 68 percent—from more than 108,000 to fewer than 35,000, though in the overall net picture this reduction was offset in some measure by modest increases in the numbers of units of certain other types. Except for school districts, the principal trend toward reduction is found in the case of townships, although here it is much less pronounced. The number of towns and townships reported was some 1,800 less in 1962 than in 1942; but this is explained mainly by the fact that Iowa's townships, counted in the 1942 census, have been considered in subsequent enumerations to have reached a state of such negligible importance that they no longer deserve inclusion in a listing of separate governmental units. The most striking increase is in special districts for nonschool purposes, those units increasing in number from 8,299 in 1942 to 18,323 in 1962—an increase of 120 percent. Municipalities showed a net gain in number for the period of some 11 percent. Of all local units, counties remain the most nearly constant in number. Between 1942 and 1962 two new counties were organized—one in New Mexico and the other in Wisconsin; and Hawaii was admitted as a state with three counties. On the other hand, one Louisiana county (parish) included in the 1942 count merged its government with that of an overlying city; one Massachusetts county merged with an overlying town; two Virginia counties were eliminated—one by becoming a part of an independent city and the other by converting itself into such a city; and Connecticut's eight counties were deorganized.[4] As a result of these changes, the number of counties reported was seven less in 1962 than in 1942. The specific increase or decrease in number of local units in each category is indicated in the accompanying table.

[4] As of January, 1963, two additional Virginia counties were eliminated by merger with cities.

UNITS OF LOCAL GOVERNMENT IN THE UNITED STATES:
CHANGES IN NUMBERS, 1942-1962

	1942	1962	INCREASE OR DECREASE
Counties	3,050	3,043	−7
Municipalities	16,220	17,997	+1,777
Towns and Townships	18,919	17,144	−1,775
School Districts	108,579	34,678	−73,901
Special Districts	8,299	18,323	+10,024
Total	155,067	91,185	−63,882

Source: United States Bureau of the Census.

Classes of Units

Units of local government differ widely, both as among different states and within a single state, with respect to such matters as area, legal nature, form of governmental organization, and functions. However, if we ignore countless variations in detail, it is possible to group local units into a relatively small number of classes on any one of several bases. On the basis of their legal nature, for example, units may be divided into two groups or classes, namely, municipal corporations and quasi-municipal corporations.[5] Again, depending upon whether they are empowered to perform numerous governmental services or a single function, local units may be classified as being either agencies of *general* government or *special* governmental districts. The former class would include counties, cities and villages, towns, and townships; while the latter would embrace school districts, sanitary districts, irrigation districts, and any other district established for the performance of a single function.[6] Convenience in our present discussion will best be served, however, by dividing all units of local government into four principal classes: (1) counties; (2) municipalities; (3) towns and townships; and (4) special districts.[7] The number and chief characteristics of units in each of these classes will be considered briefly in the following sections, and the governmental organization of the units of each class will be described in succeeding chapters.

Counties. The county is the most nearly universal of all units of local government. Geographic subdivisions known as counties are found in every state except Alaska and Louisiana; and the parishes of Louisiana

[5] See below, "Legal Nature of Local Units."

[6] Occasionally, a district created to provide a single service is subsequently empowered to provide one or more additional services. In such a case, however, the unit would continue to be classed as a special district unless given governmental powers of a broad and general nature such as those possessed by counties, cities, and townships.

[7] Cf. Anderson, *op. cit.*, 15, 16.

occupy a legal and political position so similar to that of counties else-where that they are considered as counties in this and subsequent chapters. There are, however, a few counties which do not maintain independently-organized county governments, as well as some areas—principally those within certain cities—which are not legally within any county. In all, 88 areas were reported in the Census Bureau's 1962 enumeration as lacking distinct county governments. Included in the list of such areas were the following 30 "geographic" counties: (1) Rhode Island's five counties and Connecticut's eight which, though existing as geographic entities, do not have county governing bodies for performing the usual county functions. (2) Three "unorganized" counties in western South Dakota, which do not have their own governmental organization but are attached to adjoining counties for judicial and administrative purposes. (3) The five counties within New York City, the Louisiana parishes of Orleans (city of New Orleans) and East Baton Rouge (city of Baton Rouge), the Massachusetts counties of Suffolk (city of Boston) and Nantucket (township of Nantucket), the Hawaiian county of Kalawao (state of Hawaii), and Philadelphia county (city of Philadelphia) in Pennsylvania—each of which retains certain county offices but has become so completely merged with its city, township, or state government that it may be considered to have lost, for all practical purposes, its separate corporate existence. (4) The city and county of Denver, city and county of San Francisco, and city and county of Honolulu, which have consolidated city-county governments but operate primarily as cities. The remaining 58 areas also lacking county government, in this instance because they are not located within any county, were as follows: (1) St. Louis, Missouri; Baltimore, Maryland; and 33 "independent" Virginia cities. Each of these municipalities has been legally separated from county territory, and county functions are performed within its boundaries by the city government. (2) The District of Columbia. (3) Yellowstone Park areas within the states of Idaho, Montana, and Wyoming, respectively. (4) Nineteen election districts in Alaska.[8]

Excluding the nonfunctioning counties and the areas outside counties enumerated in the preceding paragraph, the Census Bureau found 3,043 counties operating with organized county governments in 1962. The number of counties per state ranged from three in Delaware and Hawaii to 254 in Texas. In area, organized counties vary from 20,131 square miles in the case of San Bernardino county, California, to 25 square miles in the case of Arlington county, Virginia. The population of individual counties varied, according to the 1960 census, from more than 6,000,000 in

[8] United States Bureau of the Census, *Census of Governments: 1962*, Vol. I; *Governmental Organization*, 16, 17. Cf. Anderson, *op. cit.*, 19-25. Concerning the independent cities of Virginia, see Raymond B. Pinchbeck, "City-County Separation in Virginia," *Nat. Mun. Rev.*, XXIX, 467-472 (July, 1940).

Los Angeles county, California, to less than 1,000 in several of the most sparsely populated western counties.

Counties are primarily units for *rural* government. However, with the exceptions previously noted, incorporated municipalities remain parts of the respective counties in which they are located, and property within their limits is subject to taxation for county purposes. In the larger municipalities, some of the services supplied in rural areas by county government, such as law enforcement and highway maintenance, often become municipal functions, and the municipality comes to overshadow the county in everyday importance to the average citizen. On the other hand, the governments of some highly urbanized counties find themselves providing, for the residents of unincorporated areas, more and more services, such as fire protection and garbage disposal, which would ordinarily be considered as municipal in character.

The traditional functions of county government are law enforcement, judicial administration, construction and maintenance of roads and bridges, recording of legal documents, and relief of the poor through the maintenance of county almshouses. These basic functions, in some instances in modernized forms, have maintained first-rate importance in most states to the present day; but during recent decades many new functions have been added. The newer fields of service opened to counties by the legislatures of various states include health protection and hospitals, agricultural aid, weed control, predatory animal control, fire protection, libraries, park and recreational facilities, planning and zoning, public utility services, airports, harbors, and public markets.[9] It is to be noted that, concurrently with the conferring of new functions upon counties, there has been a tendency to transfer certain other functions from the counties to the state. Thus county highways have been transferred to the state in North Carolina, West Virginia, Delaware, and most counties of Virginia. And, under the Federal Social Security Act, old-age assistance and certain other federally aided assistance programs have been largely taken over by the state and federal governments, though in some instances the counties are permitted to participate in the administration of those programs. During recent years, therefore, counties have been gaining some new functions and at the same time losing others to the state and federal governments. All told, it cannot be said that county functions have suffered any net diminution. On the contrary, it would appear that counties are of greater functional importance today than they were a generation ago, and that further expansion of the services provided by their governments is likely to continue in the future.

County boundaries may be changed by the state legislature subject

---

[9] Charles M. Kneier, "Development of Newer County Functions," *Amer. Polit. Sci. Rev.*, XXIV, 134-140 (Feb., 1930); M. H. Satterfield, "The Growth of County Functions Since 1930," *Jour. of Politics*, III, 76-88 (Feb., 1941); Clyde F. Snider, "American County Government: A Mid-Century Review," *Amer. Polit. Sci. Rev.*, XLVI, 66-80(Mar., 1952).

to any restrictions that may be imposed upon the legislative power by the state constitution. Typical of such restrictions are those requiring approval of changes by the voters of the counties or territory concerned, and those which provide that the legislature shall exercise its power through general laws and not by special act. Many states now have general laws establishing a procedure whereby county boundaries may be changed by local action, such procedure usually involving petition followed by popular vote. In practice, however, county boundary changes are infrequent.

Municipalities. Whereas counties are principally units for rural government, municipalities are primarily for *urban* government. When a particular area ceases to be strictly rural in nature through the settlement of families in proximity to each other, this more densely populated region has need for various governmental services, such as fire protection and sewage disposal, the need for which is lacking, or at least not acute, under purely rural conditions. When this situation arises, it frequently happens that the governments already existing within the territory—county, township, or both—are without legal authority to provide the services required by the urban or semiurban area; or that, if the necessary authority does exist, the rural dwellers are unwilling to be taxed to provide these additional services for their urban neighbors.[10] It then becomes desirable to create an additional governmental unit, in the form of a municipal corporation, through which the urban inhabitants may provide for themselves those services which their needs require.

At one time it was quite common to incorporate each individual municipality by a special act of the state legislature, and this practice is still followed in several eastern and southern states. Elsewhere, however, municipalities are now established under the terms of general statutes which permit any community having a specified minimum population, within a stated maximum area, to organize as a municipal corporation by following a prescribed procedure. This procedure usually involves a petition followed by vote of the local inhabitants on the question of incorporation.

In every state the larger municipalities are legally designated as "cities," and this designation is used in some states for all municipalities regardless of size. In Kansas, for instance, the smallest municipal corporations are "cities of the third class." Many states, however, though in some instances providing for several classes of "cities," apply a different designation to their smallest municipalities. The designations most commonly used in this way are those of "village" and "town," [11] though that of "borough" is employed in a few states. In states employing these different

[10] Cf. Lane W. Lancaster, *Government in Rural America* (Van Nostrand, New York, 2nd ed., 1952), 25-27.

[11] These small municipalities are not to be confused with the subdivisions of the county which are called towns in New England and in a few other states. See below, "Towns and Townships."

designations, it is usual for a municipality to incorporate first as a village, town, or borough, as the case may be, and later, when it has acquired the necessary population, to change by popular vote to *city* organization. Since, however, mere increase in population may not operate to change automatically the legal status of a municipality, it being necessary that the change be made by popular vote, it is not unusual to find in a given state communities still operating as villages, towns, or boroughs notwithstanding that they have more than enough inhabitants for city status. Conversely, a city may lose in population until it has less than that required for initial incorporation as a city without reverting to village status. Apart from the matter of population, the principal differences between cities on the one hand, and villages, towns, and boroughs on the other, lie in the fact that the "lesser" municipalities are usually provided with somewhat simpler governmental organization and endowed with less extensive powers than are cities.

Incorporated municipalities range in area from Oklahoma City, whose more than 600 square miles give it the greatest extent of any city in the United States and probably in the world, down to tiny incorporated places of less than one square mile. In population, New York City of course takes first place, with its 7,781,984 inhabitants as of 1960. The smallest municipality, from the standpoint of population, which actually carries on a government is not known, but it appears that there are many with less than 25 inhabitants.[12] Of the 17,997 municipalities reported by the Census Bureau in 1962, only 130 had populations exceeding 100,000, while a majority of the entire number (54 percent) had fewer than 1,000 inhabitants each.[13]

The functions performed by municipalities, though duplicating in some measure those of counties and townships, are for the most part new or expanded ones made necessary by urbanization. Among the most essential are police protection, fire protection, sewage disposal, water supply, health service, and park and recreation facilities. In general, the number of functions performed is in direct proportion to the population of the municipality, and in metropolitan cities it is astoundingly large. In Detroit, for example, a survey by Dr. Lent Upson revealed that the city government, as of 1942, was performing no less than 396 distinct services or activities for its citizens.[14] The functions of our large cities are, indeed, more numerous and varied than those of any other units of local government except perhaps a few of the most populous metropolitan counties.

Towns and Townships. Governmental subdivisions of the county, known as towns or townships, exist in twenty-one states. Save for certain

---

[12] Anderson, *op. cit.*, 29.

[13] United States Bureau of the Census, *Census of Governments: 1962*, Vol. I: *Governmental Organization*, 3.

[14] Lent D. Upson, *The Growth of a City Government* (Detroit Bur. of Govtl. Research, Detroit, 1942).

"wildland" tracts in Maine, New Hampshire, and Vermont, and a relatively small number of incorporated cities, all of the territory of the six New England states is divided into towns,[15] which constitute the principal units of local government in that region. Though some New England villages are incorporated separately from the towns in which they are located and carry on their own governments, most so-called "villages" are merely semiurban portions of the town and are under the jurisdiction of the town government.[16] New England towns are usually irregular in shape and contain from twenty to forty square miles. Towns vary widely in population. Several exceed 25,000, while many have less than 500 inhabitants. The typical town includes considerable rural territory, but also one or more "village" settlements or trading centers. However, some towns are completely rural and others are more thoroughly urbanized. Town functions vary with the type of town. In purely rural areas, they are confined for the most part to supplying those basic governmental services that are essential even in sparsely settled communities, such as highways, education, and aid to the needy. Towns with semiurban settlements are likely to provide various additional services, such as fire protection, sewers, lights, water, parks, and libraries.[17] And the most highly urbanized towns may supply practically all governmental services which elsewhere are provided by cities. New England towns are created, their boundaries are established, and they are on occasion deorganized, by their respective state legislatures, usually by special acts. In 1962, New England towns totaled 1,424, the number in individual states ranging from 31 in Rhode Island to 470 in Maine.

Outside New England there are fifteen states, principally in the northeast and north central regions, in which civil townships exist for governmental purposes.[18] The civil township is to be distinguished from the so-called "congressional" or "survey" township. The congressional

---

[15] Cf. Lancaster, *op. cit.*, 34. The unorganized or wildland tracts in Vermont and New Hampshire are small, but in Maine they comprise some 40 percent of the state's total area, principally in the northwest. Cf. John W. Fleming, "Maine's Unorganized Territory Creates Few Problems," *Nat. Mun. Rev.*, XXVIII, 228-233, 237 (Mar., 1939); below, Chap. XVI, "Deorganization."

[16] The separate incorporation of villages has made most headway in Vermont, where 65 incorporated villages were reported in existence in the 1950's. See Frank G. Bates, "Village Government in New England," *Amer. Polit. Sci. Rev.*, VI, 367-385 (Aug., 1912); John P. Wheeler, "Towns in Transition," *Nat. Civic Rev.*, XLVIII, 68-72, 105 (Feb., 1959). An interesting development in another New England state is discussed in Lashley G. Harvey, "The Village District in New Hampshire," *Amer. Polit. Sci. Rev.*, XL, 962-965 (Oct., 1946).

[17] Cf. Bates, *op. cit.*

[18] These "township states" are Illinois, Indiana, Kansas, Michigan, Minnesota, Missouri, Nebraska, New Jersey, New York, North Dakota, Ohio, Pennsylvania, South Dakota, Washington, and Wisconsin. In New York and Wisconsin, following New England terminology, the subdivisions here under discussion are officially designated as towns, but because their nature and functions are more like those of townships outside New England they are considered here as townships. In the statutes of some other township states the term *town* is used interchangeably with *township*.

township, six miles square and with each of its thirty-six one-mile-square "sections" bearing a distinctive number, was first established by the famous Survey Ordinance of 1785 enacted by the Congress of the Confederation for the survey and disposal of public lands in the Northwest Territory. Subsequently this land-survey system, devised to facilitate the description and location of land in documents and records pertaining thereto, was extended by the United States Congress to other federal territories, with the result that congressional townships exist today in many states both within and without the group having civil townships. In states having both civil and congressional townships, the boundaries of the two types are in some instances coterminous and in others not. In any event, the congressional township, though useful for purposes of land description, is without governmental organization or authority, and hence is *not* to be considered as a unit of local government.[19] Where used in this book, therefore, the term *township*, unless otherwise indicated, is to be considered as referring to the civil township.

In about half of the township states, township organization covers the entire state area. Illinois, Missouri, Nebraska, and Washington, however, make township government optional with the respective counties, and as a result there are townships in some counties only. A few other states, notably Minnesota and the Dakotas, contain some sparsely settled areas in which organized township government does not exist.

In 1962 there were 15,720 townships in the fifteen township states, the number in individual states varying from 66 in Washington, where townships exist in only one county and part of another, to 1,822 in Minnesota. Most townships are rectangular in shape and, though there is some variation in size, the typical civil township is of approximately the same extent as the congressional township, namely, thirty-six square miles, whether or not the boundaries of the two coincide.[20] Though there are some populous townships, the great majority have only small populations and are essentially rural in character.[21]

Except where urbanized townships have been empowered to perform certain services usually provided by municipalities, township functions are of a distinctly rural nature. The most prevalent major functions are those of maintaining country roads and providing aid to the needy. In some states the township is an important unit for school administration. Local law enforcement in rural areas is carried on in part by constables

19 In some instances congressional townships are, or at one time have been, incorporated as "school townships," but only for very limited purposes which do not justify their classification as distinct governmental units.

20 Indiana's civil townships, for example, have an average area of 35.48 square miles, yet less than one-fifth of them have boundaries coterminous with those of congressional townships.

21 City and village areas are included within the townships in some states and not in others. In a few states, village areas are included but not city areas.

and justices of the peace elected in the respective townships. Other township functions in various states include the assessment of property for taxation, issuance of public health regulations, maintenance of cemeteries and drains, control of noxious weeds, and provision of parks and libraries.

Township boundaries are usually established, and may be changed, by the county governing board. However, the discretion of the board in exercising this power is frequently limited by statutory stipulations that boundary changes may be made only upon petition by the local residents concerned or with their approval at a referendum election.

Special Districts. The fourth class of local-government units consists of special-purpose districts established for the performance of a single governmental function or, occasionally, of a few related functions. Of these districts, the type best known and by far the most prevalent is, of course, the school district. In 1962, 34,678 school districts were reported in existence in forty-six states.[22] The system of small districts for school administration had its origin, in the early days of our country, in the desire to provide educational facilities within reasonable walking distance of every family. It owes its perpetuation, in large measure, to the mere strength of tradition, though another contributing factor has doubtless been the desire to keep the schools "out of politics" by keeping their government independent of the units charged with providing civil government in general. Though some school districts serve large city populations, and the average population of rural districts has increased substantially during recent years as a result of widespread consolidation, there are still many small rural districts each of which has but a handful of pupils and maintains only a one-teacher elementary school.[23]

Special districts for nonschool purposes numbered more than 18,000 in 1962, with every state reporting some such units and the number in individual states ranging from 6 in Alaska to 2,126 in Illinois. These districts are extremely varied in nature.[24] To mention but a few types, there

[22] In the four states having no districts, all local schools were operated by general-purpose governments—principally by counties in Maryland, North Carolina, and Virginia, and in Hawaii by the state. Several states in which the towns, townships, or counties administer most schools nevertheless have some districts; and about half of the states employ the district system as the predominant form of school organization. See below, Chap. XX.

[23] Several types of school districts are sometimes found in a single state. In Illinois, for example, there are elementary districts, twelve-grade districts, high school districts, and districts of various special types.

[24] See John C. Bollens, *Special District Governments in the United States* (Univ. of Calif. Press, Berkeley, 1957); United States Bureau of the Census, *Special District Governments in the United States* (U.S. Bur. of the Census, Washington, 1954); Charles Kettleborough, "Special Municipal Corporations," *Amer. Polit. Sci. Rev.*, VIII, 614-621 (Nov., 1914); Frederic H. Guild, "Special Municipal Corporations," *Ibid.*, XIV, 286-291 (May, 1920); F. H. Guild, "Special Municipal Corporations," *Nat. Mun. Rev.*, XVIII, 319-323 (May, 1929); Kirk H. Porter, "A Plague of Special Districts," *Ibid.*, XXII, 544-547, 574 (Nov., 1933).

are park districts, sanitary districts, health districts, road districts, fire protection districts, flood prevention districts, soil conservation districts, drainage districts, utility districts, water supply districts, cemetery districts, and even mosquito abatement districts. As previously indicated, the present tendency is toward a decrease in the number of school districts and an increase in the number of special districts for other purposes.[25]

Most special districts are endowed, subject to statutory or constitutional limitations, with either the taxing power or the power to levy special assessments, and with borrowing authority. On the other hand, soil conservation districts of the type mentioned above have no power to tax or issue bonds, but rely for their support upon contributions, in money or otherwise, from cooperating farmers and from the local, state, and federal governments.

The reasons for creating special-purpose districts are many and varied. Probably the most important single reason lies in the facts that many present-day governmental problems concern areas not coterminous with the traditional units of government—county, township, and municipality; and that the special district affords a means of establishing governmental units with boundaries coincident, or more nearly so, with problem areas. Thus a group of counties may be formed into a soil conservation district to carry on a soil building program adapted to a particular region; two or more contiguous townships may join in establishing a public health district that will enable their community, because of the larger area to be served and the broader tax base, to employ full-time, qualified health personnel and provide modern health services; or several neighboring municipalities may form a sanitary district to deal with the common problem of sewage disposal.[26] On the other hand, rural portions of a single township or county may establish a fire protection district; or a flood prevention district may be established comprising portions of several counties.

Another reason for the establishment of special districts is the desire to enlarge local borrowing power. Many state constitutions place strict limitations upon the power of local governments to borrow money, such limitations ordinarily being expressed in terms of a certain percentage of the assessed valuation of taxable property. Usually, however, *each* separate local entity is permitted, if authorized by the state legislature, to borrow up to the specified limit, notwithstanding that several units may serve the same area and therefore derive their revenue from taxation of the same property. Take, for example, a state whose constitution provides that no local government may become indebted to an amount exceeding 5 percent of its assessed valution. Now suppose that a city of this state desires to establish a park system which would necessitate the issuance of bonds, but finds that it has already exhausted its constitutional borrowing power.

[25] See above, "Trends in Numbers."
[26] See below, Chap. XVI, "Functional Consolidation."

Under these circumstances, and provided that the state statutes permit such action, the inhabitants may establish a special park district. The boundaries of this district may be substantially, or even exactly, coterminous with those of the city, yet the district has its own governing body and possesses, independently of the city, its own taxing and borrowing powers. Thus the park district, though embracing the same territory as the city, may proceed to issue the park bonds which the city government was unable to issue, and to provide for retirement of the indebtedness from a tax levy imposed by the district.[27]

Special districts, of whatever type, are ordinarily established under authority of state statutes.[28] Some districts owe their existence to special legislative enactments; but the large majority have been organized under statutes which are, at least in form, of general application. However, in states with constitutions prohibiting special legislation, it is not uncommon to find that a statute which on its face applies throughout the state, or to all places within a stipulated classification, has in reality been enacted at the request of a single community wishing to establish a district of the type concerned, and has been phrased in general terms so as not to violate the constitutional prohibition.

As indicated at an earlier point, the number of nonschool special districts in the United States is growing apace, more than doubling during the twenty-year period from 1942 to 1962. Although most districts serve a useful purpose, their creation further complicates a local-government setup which is already too complex. For this reason, some students of government believe that the establishment of new districts should be checked and that many existing districts should be abolished. Were this done, present district functions would be transferred to general-purpose governmental units such as counties and cities, which might then be empowered to provide service and tax differentials of the kind described in a later chapter.[29]

Pyramiding and Overlapping of Units

On the basis of this brief survey of the various types of local governmental units, a bit of reflection will disclose that practically every American lives under, and contributes directly or indirectly to the support of, several "layers" of local government. Even in the most strictly rural areas, residents usually live under county and school district, and often township, governments. For urban dwellers there must be added the

[27] Additional reasons for the creation of special districts are discussed in Clyde F. Snider, *Local Government in Rural America* (Appleton-Century-Crofts, New York, 1957), 243-245.

[28] In some instances, however, special districts are established or authorized by constitutional provision rather than by statute.

[29] Cf. Bollens, *op. cit.*, 259. See below, Chap. XVI, "Tax Differentials."

municipal government, and often one or more special districts. The complexity of local government reaches its maximum in the metropolitan areas in and surrounding our larger cities. Every Chicagoan, for example, lives under six major local governments—those of Cook County, the City of Chicago, the Chicago School District, and Chicago Park District, the Chicago Sanitary District, and the Cook County Forest Preserve District; and in the area surrounding Chicago are municipalities, counties, townships, and special districts in profusion. In 1957 the nation's 174 metropolitan areas, as defined by the Census Bureau, were served by 15,658 local governments. The New York City-New Jersey area alone had 1,074 units, the Chicago area 954, and the Philadelphia area 705.[30] At the time of the 1960 census, 171 municipalities, in addition to Chicago, were situated in Cook County. Here, as elsewhere in Illinois, the local-government picture is further complicated by the fact that some municipalities are located in two or more counties.

Legal Nature of Local Units: Quasi-Municipal Corporations versus Municipal Corporations Proper

All of the governmental units considered are public corporations, created by or under authority of state law, for the purpose of performing for the people who comprise them one or more services—services which, in the judgment of those establishing the units, can be better performed cooperatively through governmental organization than individually through private effort. As corporate entities, local governmental units are endowed with perpetual succession, notwithstanding changes in the body of inhabitants; they may sue and be sued, hold property, and exercise whatever other powers have been conferred upon them by the state.

The law recognizes two classes or grades of public corporation, namely, the quasi-municipal corporation and the municipal corporation proper. Cities and their lesser counterparts—villages, boroughs, and incorporated towns—have the status of true municipal corporations. In most states all other local governmental units—counties, towns, townships, school districts, and other special districts—are classed as quasi-municipal corporations. Quasi-municipal corporations are said to be created by the state, without reference to the wishes of the local inhabitants, as administrative subdivisions for the better execution of certain governmental activities of statewide interest and importance. Such activities would include, for example, the assessment and collection of taxes, provision of educational facilities and health services, and the enforcement of state

---

[30] United States Bureau of the Census, *Local Government in Standard Metropolitan Areas*, 2. Concerning governmental problems in metropolitan areas, see below, Chap. XVI, "Metropolitan Adjustments."

law. Municipal corporations proper, on the other hand, are established at the request, or at least with the acquiescence, of the local inhabitants, and have as their foremost purpose the carrying on of activities and the provision of services which are primarily of local interest—as, for example, the provision of local utility service and the enactment and enforcement of regulatory ordinances. Only secondarily does the true municipal corporation function as an administrative area for state governmental purposes.

Although the distinction between quasi and true municipal corporations is important for legal purposes, it is not always clear in actual application. Corporations of both types may serve at the same time as state administrative areas and as organs of local self-government. The difference is merely one of degree—the quasi-municipal corporation being *primarily* an administrative subdivision of the state and the true municipal corporation *primarily* an instrumentality of local government. Moreover, the attributes noted above as characteristic of quasi-municipal corporations apply more fully to some units ordinarily placed in that category (notably counties) than to others. And, with the tendency to increase the powers of counties and other quasi-municipal corporations in local matters, the distinction is gradually becoming of less practical significance.[31]

Powers of Local Units

Local governments in the United States have strictly limited powers. As the various local units are created by the state, so they derive from the state, either by express grant or by necessary implication, all the powers they possess. They have no inherent powers whatsoever, and even their delegated powers are strictly construed by the courts.

The principle of delegation and strict construction of powers, with respect to municipal corporations proper, has been given its classic statement by Judge John F. Dillon in the following form, frequently referred to as "Dillon's Rule":[32]

It is a general and undisputed proposition of law that *a municipal corporation possesses and can exercise the following powers, and no others:* First, those granted in *express words;* second, those *necessarily or fairly implied* in or *incident* to the powers expressly granted; third, those *essential* to the accom-

[31] Cf. Jefferson B. Fordham, *Local Government Law,* 15-17; George S. Blair, "The Changing Legal Status of Counties," *The County Officer,* XXI, 92-94 (May, 1956). Leading cases on the distinction between quasi-municipal and municipal corporations are *Commissioners of Hamilton County* v. *Mighels,* 7 Ohio St. 109 (1857); *County of Cook* v. *City of Chicago,* 311 Ill. 234 (1924). On the subject generally, see Roger W. Cooley, *Handbook of the Law of Municipal Corporations,* especially Chaps. 1, 16-18.

[32] John F. Dillon, *Commentaries on the Law of Municipal Corporations* (Little, Brown, Boston, 5th ed., 1911), Vol. I, sec. 237.

plishment of the declared objects and purposes of the corporation,—not simply convenient, but indispensable. Any fair, reasonable, substantial doubt concerning the existence of power is resolved by the courts against the corporation, and the power is denied.

Substantially the same rule applies to quasi-municipal corporations, which the courts have held again and again to possess only those powers delegated to them in express words or by reasonable implication.[33] Except for the home-rule powers conferred upon certain municipalities and counties by constitutional provision in some states,[34] all powers possessed by the various units of local government are conferred by the state legislature through statutory enactments, and may be modified or revoked in like manner.

Although the rule of strict construction as set forth by Judge Dillon is still widely applied by the courts in determining the powers of local governments, there seems to be a growing tendency to question its present-day appropriateness. The rule was formulated in the 1870's during an era when municipal scandals were notorious, and it was apparently designed to serve as a safeguard against local misgovernment.[35] But today, it is argued, local governments are no less likely than the states themselves to be honest and efficient. The belief is expressed that the rule is no longer needed as a means of protecting the states against local waste and inefficiency and that, in practice, it actually affords little or no such protection. There have always been some courts more liberal than most in interpreting the implied powers of local governments and less strict in determining what local powers are indispensable;[36] and it appears that the number of tribunals taking this attitude is increasing. Furthermore, constitution-makers and legislators of late have given evidence in several instances of a disposition to relax, or depart from, the rule of strict construction. Thus the new constitutions of New Jersey and Michigan explicitly declare that constitutional and statutory provisions concerning local governments shall be liberally construed in their favor; and that of Alaska stipulates that a liberal construction shall be given to the powers of local-government units.[37] In 1963 the Iowa legislature enacted a statute provid-

[33] See, for example, *Barber* v. *County Court of Mercer County,* 85 W. Va. 359 (1920); *King* v. *Maries County,* 297 Mo. 488 (1923); *Dodge County* v. *Kaiser,* 243 Wis. 551 (1943).

[34] See above, Chap. III.

[35] Cf. Advisory Commission on Intergovernmental Relations, *State Constitutional and Statutory Restrictions upon the Structural, Functional, and Personnel Powers of Local Government* (U.S. Govt. Printing Office, Washington, 1962), 24.

[36] Cf. Charles M. Kneier, *City Government in the United States* (Harper, New York, 3rd ed., 1957), 163-165; Jewell Cass Phillips, *Municipal Government and Administration in America* (Macmillan, New York, 1960), 78-83.

[37] *Const. of N.J.* (1947), art. IV, sec. 7, par. 11; *Const. of Mich.* (1963), art. VII, sec. 34; *Const. of Alaska* (1959), art. X, sec. 1. Also of interest is Alaska's extraordinarily broad grant of power to home-rule boroughs and cities to "exercise all legislative powers not prohibited by law or by charter." *Ibid.,* sec. 11.

ing that statutes shall be interpreted as conferring broad powers upon cities and towns, and that powers of municipalities in local matters are not limited to those expressly granted by the legislature.[38] All in all, though there is little likelihood that the traditional rule of strict construction will soon be abandoned, there is reason to believe that the rule is destined in the years ahead to undergo further erosion through judicial decisions and constitutional and statutory provisions.

Legal Liability of Local Governments

A final question concerning local governments is that as to whether the local units are legally liable for personal or property damage sustained by individuals or private corporations as the result of negligence or other wrongful acts on the part of local officers and employees. This problem resolves itself into two principal aspects—those, respectively, of (1) tort [39] liability and (2) contractual liability.

In the tort field,[40] questions frequently arise as to whether damages may be recovered from the governmental unit concerned for injuries sustained from such causes as a defective county bridge, the negligent operation of a city fire truck, or negligence in connection with a municipally-operated utility. In the exercise of their broad powers of control over local governments, state legislatures are free to impose tort liability upon local units if they see fit to do so. Some such legislation of a piecemeal nature has been enacted, providing for liability in connection with particular functions, but apparently nothing approximating a *comprehensive* regulation of tort liability by statute has been attempted in any state. Hence our inquiry becomes limited, for the most part, to the common-law rules of liability which the courts will enforce in the absence of regulatory legislation.

In the case of municipal corporations proper, the courts emphasize the fact that their governments act in a dual role: As agencies of the state, and acting in a *governmental* capacity, they perform on behalf of the state at large various public services of statewide interest; and at the same time, as agencies of the local inhabitants, and acting in a *corporate* capacity, they perform other services of a more strictly local nature and carry on activities similar to business enterprises conducted by private corporations. Projecting this distinction into the field of tort liability, the courts hold that a municipality, when acting in a governmental capacity,

---

[38] *Nat. Civic Rev.*, LII, 441 (Sept., 1963).

[39] On the meaning of the term *tort*, see above, Chap. XI, footnote 1.

[40] On the subject of tort liability in general, see Dillon, *op. cit.*, Vol. IV, Chap. 32; Eugene McQuillin, *The Law of Municipal Corporations*, Vol. VI (2nd ed. as revised to 1936), Chap. 53; Fordham, *op. cit.*, Chap. 11; Edwin M. Borchard, "Government Liability in Tort," *Yale Law Jour.*, XXXIV, 1-45, 129-143, 229-258 (Nov., Dec., 1924, Jan., 1925).

356 Local Organization and Powers

partakes of the state's immunity and is therefore not liable for its torts unless expressly made so by statute. When, on the other hand, the municipal corporation acts in its corporate capacity, it assumes the same degree of liability as would attach to a private corporation under similar circumstances.

Though this distinction between governmental and corporate functions is easily stated, its application in practice involves some difficulty. With respect to certain municipal functions, the courts of the various states are in substantial agreement concerning the category to which they belong; but other functions are considered as governmental in some states and corporate in others. Police and fire protection, education, and health activities, for instance, are almost universally held to be of a governmental nature, and hence municipalities are not liable for injuries arising from the performance of these functions. On the other hand, municipally-owned utilities and markets are quite generally held to be corporate. But there is yet a third or "border-line" group of functions, including, for example, parks, street maintenance, sewers, and swimming pools, with respect to which the courts are in disagreement as to their classification and the matter of liability depends, therefore, upon the state in which the alleged wrongful act is committed.[41]

With respect to quasi-municipal corporations the rule has long been that, since these units are exclusively, or at least primarily, mere subdivisions of the state for the performance of governmental functions, they share in the state's immunity and hence are not liable for torts in connection with any of their activities unless made so by statutory provision. While nonliability continues to be the general rule with respect to counties and other quasi-municipal corporations, there has been a tendency in some states during recent decades to depart from the rule on occasion;[42] and it seems not unlikely that further extension of the liability of such corporations may be expected to accompany their gradual assumption, under statutory authority, of various functions which, when performed by municipalities, have been classed as of corporate character.[43]

In the matter of contractual liability, quasi and true municipal corporations alike are, in most states, held fully responsible for the performance of contracts into which they have lawfully entered, and must respond

[41] Cf. Kneier, *City Government in the United States* (3rd ed.), Chap. 10.

[42] Cf. Charles M. Kneier, "The Legal Nature and Status of the American County," *Minn. Law Rev.*, XIV, 141-156 (Jan., 1930). The Illinois supreme court recently refused to apply the doctrine of immunity to school districts on the ground that the rule has no rightful place in present-day society. *Molitor v. Kaneland Community Dist. No. 302*, 18 Ill. 2d 11 (1959).

[43] Our concern here is of course only with the liability of local governmental units as incorporated entities, as distinguished from the individual liability of their officers and employees. In the absence of statutory provision to the contrary, public officers and employees are ordinarily personally liable for their wrongful acts whether or not there is liability on the part of the governmental unit concerned.

in damages for the breach of such contracts.[44] The distinction between governmental and corporate functions has no application in the matter of contractual liability, nor does the state's immunity extend in this field even to quasi-municipal corporations.

REFERENCES

ANDERSON, William, *The Units of Government in the United States* (Pub. Admin. Service, Chicago, 1942 ed.). This bulletin was reprinted with a brief appendix in 1945, and again with an additional appendix in 1949.

Bureau of Municipal Research, University of Texas, *Units of Local Government in Texas* (Univ. of Tex. Press, Austin, 1941).

Bureau of Municipal Research and Service, University of Oregon, *The Units of Local Government in Oregon* (Bur. of Mun. Research and Service, Univ. of Ore., Eugene, 1962).

COOLEY, Roger W., *Handbook of the Law of Municipal Corporations* (West Pub. Co., St. Paul, 1914).

DILLON, John F., *Commentaries on the Law of Municipal Corporations* (5 vols., Little, Boston, 5th ed., 1911), especially Chaps. 2, 7, 32.

FORDHAM, Jefferson B., *Local Government Law* (Found. Press, Brooklyn, 1949).

HIGHSAW, Robert B., and MULLICAN, Carl D., Jr., *The Units of Government in Mississippi* (Bur. of Pub. Admin., Univ. of Miss., University, Miss., 1949).

Illinois Tax Commission in Cooperation with Works Progress Administration, *Atlas of Taxing Units* [in Illinois] (Survey of Local Finance in Ill., Vol. I, Ill. Tax Commission, Springfield and Chicago, 1939).

LANDERS, Frank M., *Units of Government in Michigan* (Bur. of Govt., Univ. of Mich., Ann Arbor, 1941).

McQUILLIN, Euguene, *The Law of Municipal Corporations* (7 vols., Callaghan, Chicago, 2nd ed., 1928, as currently revised), especially Chaps. 2, 10, 53.

REID, Joseph W., Jr., *The Units of Government in Alabama* (Bur. of Pub. Admin., Univ. of Ala., University, Ala., 1946).

RHYNE, Charles S., *Municipal Law* (Nat. Inst. of Mun. Law Officers, Washington, 1957).

SNIDER, Clyde F., STEINER, Gilbert Y., and LANGDON, Lois, *Local Taxing Units: The Illinois Experience* (Inst. of Govt. and Pub. Affairs, Univ. of Ill., Urbana, 1954).

United States Bureau of the Census, *Census of Governments: 1962, Vol. I: Governmental Organization* (U.S. Govt. Printing Office, Washington, 1963).

————, *Governmental Units in the United States: 1942* (U.S. Govt. Printing Office, Washington, 1944).

————, *Governments in the United States in 1952* (U.S. Govt. Printing Office, Washington, 1953).

————, *1957 Census of Governments*, Vol. I, No. 1: *Governments in the United States* (U.S. Govt. Printing Office, Washington, 1957).

[44] Dillon, *op. cit.*, Vol. IV, sec. 1610; Kneier, "The Legal Nature and Status of the American County," *loc. cit.*

————, *1957 Census of Governments*, Vol. I, No. 2: *Local Government in Standard Metropolitan Areas* (U.S. Govt. Printing Office, Washington, 1957).

————, *1957 Census of Governments*, Vol. I, No. 3: *Local Government Structure* (U.S. Govt. Printing Office, Washington, 1957).

WHITE, Max R., *Units of Local Government in Connecticut* (Inst. of Pub. Service, Univ. of Conn., Storrs, rev. by Patricia Stuart, 1959).

13

County Government

The government of the typical American county is so complicated and disorganized as to make logical analysis and description extremely difficult. Its structure varies from state to state, and often among counties of the same state. It consists of numerous officers, boards, and commissions, the titles of which are far from standardized. Some of these agencies are established by constitutional provision and others by statute; some are elected by the voters, others appointed, and still others constituted on an ex officio basis. In addition to the county officers and members of county boards and commissions, the personnel of county government includes an imposing array of deputies, assistants, and employees. Though fairly definite relationships between the various agencies have in some cases been worked out, there are many instances in which a particular county agency so lacks proper supervision, as well as coordination with related agencies, as to operate virtually as a "little government" in and of itself. One writer, indeed, has gone so far as to suggest that, if American county government is established upon any principle, it is that of confusion.[1]

Yet, notwithstanding this unfortunate situation, the governments of most counties throughout the country are to a considerable extent organized along the same broad lines, and may be said to consist of (1) a general governing body, usually known in everyday parlance as the "county board," which controls the fiscal affairs of the county, performs some administrative functions, and exercises at least a modicum of supervisory

[1] Roger H. Wells, *American Local Government*, 80.

359

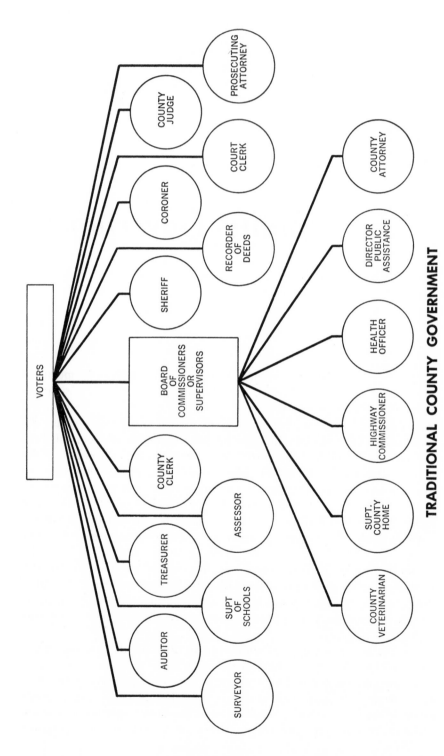

TRADITIONAL COUNTY GOVERNMENT

VOTERS

BOARD
OF
COMMISSIONERS
OR
SUPERVISORS

PROSECUTING
ATTORNEY

COUNTY
JUDGE

COURT
CLERK

CORONER

RECORDER
OF
DEEDS

SHERIFF

COUNTY
CLERK

TREASURER

ASSESSOR

AUDITOR

SUPT
OF
SCHOOLS

SURVEYOR

COUNTY
ATTORNEY

DIRECTOR
PUBLIC
ASSISTANCE

HEALTH
OFFICER

HIGHWAY
COMMISSIONER

SUPT.
COUNTY
HOME

COUNTY
VETERINARIAN

authority over county affairs in general, and (2) a considerable and varied list of officers, boards, and commissions charged with more specific tasks. The most widely prevalent major county officers, other than members of the county board, are the sheriff, coroner, clerk, treasurer, recorder or register of deeds, and superintendent of schools. The county board and each of these officers will be considered in turn, after which brief attention will be given to some of the other county agencies.

The County Board: Composition and Organization

The county governing body in various states is officially entitled the board of commissioners, board of supervisors, county court, fiscal court, levy court, board of revenue, and the like, but the common name of county board will be used in a generic sense in this chapter.[2] With an occasional exception, the board is popularly elected. In most instances the agency takes one of two forms—a relatively small "board of county commissioners" or a somewhat larger "county board of supervisors." The board of commissioners is the more prevalent type, being almost universal in the South and West and common in other sections as well. It consists most often of three members, though sometimes of five, seven, or even a larger number. Election of members is usually by and from the voters of the county at large. However, a number of states either require that members reside in different commissioner districts or actually elect by districts. Members of the larger boards of supervisors, such as are found in New York, Michigan, and Wisconsin, are usually elected by and from the various townships of the county. It is common for each township to elect at least one supervisor, and for additional board members to be elected from the more populous communities either as township representatives or as representatives of the cities and villages. Such provisions often result, in populous counties or those having numerous townships, in boards of huge size. In 1955, for example, nine Illinois counties had boards of supervisors of more than forty members each; and the board of Wayne county (Detroit), Michigan, was reported in 1952 as having no less than ninety-seven members.[3] In some states the small board of commissioners is found in all counties; in others the board of supervisors is used exclusively; while

---

[2] In Arkansas, and in certain counties of Georgia and South Carolina, the principal county governing agency is a single official rather than a board. Detailed data concerning the composition of county governing bodies in the respective states are to be found in United States Bureau of the Census, *County Boards and Commissions*. For a summarization of these data, see Edward W. Weidner, "The Confused County Picture," *Nat. Mun. Rev.*, XXXV, 166-171 (Apr., 1946).

[3] John P. Keith, "County Home Rule for Michigan," *The County Officer*, XVII, 234-240, 245, 252 (Aug., 1952). Prior to a reduction in its size under the terms of a statute of 1943, the membership of the Wayne county board had numbered 162. Claude R. Tharp, *A Manual of County Administrative Organization in Michigan* (Univ. of Mich. Press, Ann Arbor, 1944), 4.

Illinois and a few other states give to some or all counties a choice between the two forms. Most Tennessee counties have a relatively large governing agency in the form of a "quarterly court" composed of the justices of the peace of the county; and the Louisiana police jury (governing authority of the parish), consisting of members elected by wards, is in some instances a fairly large body.

Regular sessions of the county board, usually quarterly or monthly, are provided for by the state constitution or by statute. Provision is also commonly made for the calling of special sessions, either at the discretion of some designated officer, such as the county clerk, or at the request of a given number of board members. There is a tendency for the smaller boards to meet more frequently than the larger ones. Most boards choose annually one of their members to serve as president or chairman. However, some states provide that the county judge or some other designated officer shall serve as chairman of the governing body; and an occasional county, such as that of Cook in Illinois, has a popularly-elected president of the board. The larger boards ordinarily set up a system of committees, and matters of county business are given committee consideration before being considered by the entire board. Members of county boards are usually compensated on a per diem basis, though in some instances regular salaries are provided.

Powers of County Boards

County government ordinarily centers, insofar as it may be said to have a center, in the county board. The board is sometimes referred to as the legislative body of the county, but scarcely deserves that title. It is true that such powers of a legislative nature as the county possesses are vested in the board, but those powers are not numerous. The foremost legislative power of the board is its control over county finance. It is the county board which, under authority conferred by the state and subject to state-imposed limitations, levies county taxes, makes appropriations, and incurs indebtedness.[4] Another class of legislative powers, now more com-

---

[4] There are several exceptions to this general rule. In Maine, New Hampshire, and Massachusetts, and in South Carolina counties other than Charleston, county finances are for the most part managed directly by the state legislature or the county delegation in the legislature. In Arkansas, county taxes are levied and appropriations made by a quorum court consisting of the county judge and a majority of the justices of the peace of the county. Fiscal affairs of Indiana counties are controlled by an elective council of seven members; and occasional counties in a few other states are provided with special fiscal-control bodies apart from their general governing boards. United States Bureau of the Census, *County Boards and Commissions,* 8-9; Harold C. Grinnell, *Studies in Local Government and Taxation in Rural New Hampshire* (Agricultural Experiment Station, Univ. of N. H., Durham, 1943), 29; Clyde F. Snider, "The Organization and Functions of County Boards in Indiana," *Ind. Law Jour.,* XII, 281-315 (Apr., 1937); Ralph Eisenberg, "The Logroll, South Carolina Style," in Richard T. Frost, ed., *Cases in State and Local Government* (Prentice-Hall, Englewood Cliffs, N.J., 1961), 155-163.

monly conferred upon county boards than formerly, consists of those of a "regulatory" nature, such as the power to enact zoning regulations for rural and suburban areas and the power to regulate amusement places and the sale of liquor outside municipalities. Nevertheless, most of the powers of the county board are of an executive or administrative character, and the courts usually look upon the board as an administrative body.[5]

The administrative powers and duties of the county board are numerous and varied. The board has control of county buildings and other county property. It makes contracts on behalf of the county, and examines and settles claims against the county. The board usually appoints some county officers, assistants and deputies to certain other officers, and a considerable number of county employees. It may also have the power of filling vacancies in elective offices. In some states the board fixes, usually within statutory limits, the compensation of county officers and employees. Some county boards exercise important functions in connection with the holding of elections, such as laying out election precincts, providing polling places, and appointing precinct election officials. Where the township system prevails, it is frequently the county board which is vested with authority to divide the county into townships and to make subsequent alterations in township boundaries.

The powers enumerated in the preceding paragraph, together with the fiscal and regulatory powers previously mentioned, do not by any means constitute a complete list of the powers of county boards. The list here given is intended to include only the most important powers of the board, and some of the lesser ones most commonly conferred. Since the powers of county officers are prescribed by state law, those belonging to the county board naturally vary somewhat from state to state, but in any case they are numerous and relate to almost every aspect of county government. Indeed, all powers conferred upon the county, and the exercise of which is not specifically delegated by law to other county officers, are exercised by the county board.

Relative Merits of Large and Small Boards

A question which naturally arises is that as to whether large or small county boards are better adapted to serving the county as a general governing body. In reality, each type of board possesses some advantages over the other, yet neither is completely satisfactory. The large board, while permitting broader representation, is likely in populous counties to reach a size unwieldy for administrative purposes. Because of its numerous membership, the board must rely largely upon the work of com-

[5] For a comprehensive discussion of the authority of state legislatures to confer local legislative powers upon counties, see Herman Walker, Jr., "The Delegation of Police Power to Counties," *La. Law Rev.*, III, 522-558 (Mar., 1941). County boards in some instances also perform functions of a judicial nature.

mittees; and, although committee action is nominally subject to control
by the entire board, the system is likely to result in practice in a high degree of decentralization in administrative responsibility. With respect to
legislative activities, the election of board members by townships or other
districts tends to emphasize local as against county-wide interests and to
encourage logrolling tactics. The small board, on the other hand, is better
adapted to the performance of administrative functions, but is believed by
some to provide inadequate representation for legislative purposes. As
regards relative cost, comparative studies in Illinois, where some counties
have the small board of commissioners and others the larger board of
supervisors, indicate that, between counties of similar size and population
in that state, the large-board system makes for higher overhead costs in
county government.[6] Similarly, studies which have compared costs between different states, some having large and others small county boards,
lead to the conclusion that the cost of maintaining the larger boards is
distinctly greater than in the case of the smaller.[7]

By and large, it appears that most of the difficulties arising from
either type of board result from the fact that both administrative and
legislative duties are imposed upon the same agency. If county administrative functions were centered in a single official,[8] the county board might
be limited to policy-determining functions, and a membership somewhat
larger than our smallest boards of commissioners but considerably smaller
than our largest boards of supervisors would probably be most satisfactory.[9] As matters stand today, the small board seems clearly preferable in
the great majority of American counties. In most counties social and economic interests are sufficiently homogeneous to enable a board of three to
five members, whether elected by districts or at large, to be adequately
representative for performance of its limited legislative functions; and
the small board is distinctly advantageous for administrative purposes.
The desirability of a manageable board for administration is emphasized
by the fact that the county governing body serves *primarily* as an administrative agency and only secondarily as a local legislative organ. Fortunately, two-thirds of the nation's counties are now provided with relatively small boards, and a number of others have governing bodies of
moderate size. But there still remain many counties, particularly among

[6] M. H. Hunter, *Costs of Township and County Government in Illinois* (Bur. of
Bus. Research, Univ. of Ill., Urbana, 1933); H. K. Allen, *Costs and Services of Local
Government in Selected Illinois Counties* (Bur. of Bus. Research, Univ. of Ill., Urbana,
1936).

[7] Cf. M. Slade Kendrick, *Comparison of the Cost of Maintenance of Large and
of Small County Boards in the United States* (Agricultural Experiment Station, Cornell Univ., Ithaca, N.Y., 1929).

[8] See below, "The Problem of a County Executive."

[9] Cf. John A. Fairlie, *Town and County Government in Illinois* (Report of the
Joint Legislative Committee, 47th General Assembly of Ill., Vol. II, Springfield, 1913),
85-86.

those of a rural or semirural character, where a reduction in board size would facilitate administration without impairing the effectiveness of the body as a minor legislative agency.

The Sheriff

The office of sheriff is one of the oldest known to the English common law, and it exists today in every state but Alaska. Except in Rhode Island, where sheriffs for the respective counties are appointed by the governor, and in Hawaii, where the sheriff is a state officer appointed by the attorney general, the office is filled by popular election. The term of office is usually either two or four years. Choice by popular election makes it unlikely that a sheriff will be especially fitted by past experience for the duties of his office; and, in some states, constitutional provisions to the effect that a sheriff may not succeed himself, or may not serve more than two consecutive terms, make it all but impossible for him to improve his qualifications by experience in office.[10] Thus most incumbents of the sheriff's office are in no sense law-enforcement officers of the trained, professional type. The sheriff receives compensation for his services in the form of fees, a salary, or both; the modern tendency being to provide a fixed salary and to require the sheriff to turn into the county treasury such fees as he collects. In the performance of his duties the sheriff is assisted by deputies whom he appoints and for whose official acts he is responsible.

The duties of the sheriff fall into three principal categories: (1) he is conservator of the peace within his county; (2) he is an officer of the court or courts of record in the county; and (3) he is keeper of the county jail.[11]

As a peace officer, it is the duty of the sheriff to maintain the peace, to seek out and arrest lawbreakers, to quell disorders, and to suppress riots. Since cities and villages are usually provided with their own organized police forces, the law-enforcement activities of the sheriff are largely confined to rural areas. If a situation arises which cannot be adequately dealt with by him and his deputies, the sheriff is authorized to summon to

[10] Some degree of experience in the office of sheriff in certain communities within states having the constitutional prohibition of a second consecutive term is an incidental result of "working agreements" according to which each of two prominent members of the dominant party organization of a county runs for every other term as sheriff and, upon being elected, appoints the other as his chief deputy. Thus each of the two persons concerned is continuously active in the work of the sheriff's office, alternately as sheriff and as deputy. A similar practice appears to exist in some counties in relation to offices other than that of sheriff, with respect to which there is a constitutional bar to immediate reelection—especially the office of treasurer.

[11] In Kentucky, except in Jefferson county (Louisville), jail administration is in the hands of a county jailer, who is a separate and distinct officer popularly elected as such. In a few states, a fourth duty of the sheriff in all or some counties is that of collecting taxes.

his aid the *posse comitatus* or "power of the county." The posse on any given occasion consists of such able-bodied men of the county as the sheriff has called upon to assist him in enforcing the law; and state statutes provide penalties for failure to serve at the sheriff's call. In extreme emergencies, the sheriff may ask the governor of the state for assistance from the National Guard.[12]

In his capacity as a court officer, it is the sheriff's duty, personally or by deputy, to attend sessions of courts of record and to serve legal process issuing therefrom. Such process includes, for example, various writs, warrants of arrest, summonses to jurors, and subpoenas to witnesses. It is also a duty of the sheriff to execute court judgments. In criminal cases this may involve keeping in the county jail persons given short sentences for misdemeanors, or conveying felons to state penal institutions. It may even fall to the sheriff to execute death sentences, by hanging or otherwise, though in most states such sentences are now executed in state prisons. On the civil side, a common task of the sheriff is that of seizing and selling property to satisfy judgments.

As keeper of the jail, the sheriff is charged with supervision of the jail building, and with the custody and feeding of prisoners. Where he is allowed a fixed sum per meal or per day for prisoners' board, he frequently finds it possible to make a substantial profit from this transaction.[13] It is the sheriff's legal duty to protect the life and health of his prisoners, and in some states he may be removed from office for permitting a prisoner to be taken from his custody and lynched.

During recent years, there has been a tendency for the sheriff's duties as court officer and jail keeper to overshadow his law-enforcement activities. One reason for this, undoubtedly, is the fact that the typical sheriff's office is provided with neither the equipment nor the personnel essential to a modern countywide police system, while municipalities have their own police forces and rural law enforcement is being placed more and more in the hands of state police systems.[14] Another reason, of perhaps even more significance, is the fact that the fees provided for service of court process and the execution of judgments, and the opportunity to make a profit from the boarding of prisoners, make those aspects of the sheriff's work more lucrative than the tracking down of criminals.

In view of these circumstances some students of law enforcement have come to believe that the office of sheriff, in its present form, should be abolished.[15] Were this done, the sheriff's duties as a peace officer might

---

[12] The governor may, of course, order National Guard units to duty in any community without request from the local sheriff. On the governor's use of the guard in law enforcement, see above, Chap. IX, "Military Powers."

[13] See below, Chap. XVII, "The County Jail."

[14] See below, Chap. XVII, "The State Police."

[15] See, for example, R. E. Heiges, "Goodbye to the Sheriff," *Social Science,* XI, 137-141 (Apr., 1936).

be transferred to the state police, or to professionalized county constabularies such as have already been established in a few counties. Other duties of the office, i.e., the service of court process and keeping of the jail, being ancillary to the work of the courts, might be transferred to the clerk or clerks of the courts of record, or imposed upon a newly-created functionary appointed by the courts.

But the office of sheriff is of such antiquity, and so intrenched in our political system and our state constitutions, that its abolition or substantial curtailment in the near future is extremely unlikely.[16] A possible alternative to abolition which may merit consideration under some circumstances is that of making the office a more effective part of our law-enforcement machinery by establishing organized county police systems or highway patrols directly under the sheriff's control and supervision. Where such a plan is adopted, as it has been in a few urban counties,[17] it would seem well to relieve the sheriff of his civil duties so that he may be free to devote his undivided attention to law enforcement.

The Coroner

Another county officer with a long common-law history is the coroner. The office of coroner is not as universal as that of sheriff, but is found in about three-fourths of the states.[18] Though appointed by the governor or the courts in a few states, coroners are in most instances chosen by popular election. The term is ordinarily two years or four and, as in the case of the sheriff, state constitutions sometimes provide that a coroner may not succeed himself or that he may not serve more than two consecutive terms. A few states require that the coroner be a practicing physician, and in any event the voters in filling the office seem to prefer physicians. Next after physicians, undertakers constitute the occupational group most heavily represented among coroners, but there is scarcely any

[16] The charter of St. Louis county, Missouri, was amended in 1954 to establish a county police department under a bipartisan board of police commissioners and to limit the duties of the sheriff to those of keeping the jail and serving court process. See *Nat. Mun. Rev.*, XLIII, 487 (Oct., 1954); *Ibid.*, XLIV, 479 (Oct., 1955).

[17] Bruce Smith, *Rural Crime Control*, Chap. 4.

[18] In several states the coroner's office has been abolished and the duty of holding inquests transferred to justices of the peace; and in some other jurisdictions, as will appear later in this section, coroners have been supplanted by medical examiners. Cf. Smith, *op. cit.*, 199-217. Studies of the coroner's office in individual states include George S. Blair, *The Office of County Coroner in Kansas* (Kan. State Teachers Coll., Emporia, 1953); Minnesota Legislative Research Committee, *The Coroner System in Minnesota* (Minn. Legis. Research Committee, St. Paul, 1954); Richard A. Myren, *Coroners in North Carolina: A Discussion of their Problems* (Inst. of Govt., Univ., of N.C., Chapel Hill, 1953); Coleman B. Ransone, Jr., *The Office of Coroner in Alabama* (Bur. of Pub. Admin., Univ. of Ala., University, Ala., 1957); Charles H. Johnson, "The Wisconsin Coroner System," *Wis. Law Rev.*, May, 1951, pp. 529-547. On the office generally, see National Municipal League, *Coroners in 1953: A Symposium of Legal Bases and Actual Practices* (Nat. Mun. League, New York, 1953).

calling without some representation.[19] Regardless of his vocation in private life, the coroner is all too often a petty politician and a cog in the local political machine.[20] In most instances his compensation is in the form of fees.

The single principal function of the present-day American coroner is that of holding inquests to determine the cause of deaths occurring by violence or under suspicious circumstances or, in some states, by accident.[21] An inquest involves an examination of the body and a study of all circumstances relating to the death. If there is evidence of crime, an autopsy by a physician may be ordered. The purpose of the inquest is to secure and preserve all available information and evidence which might be helpful to the prosecuting authorities if a criminal offense has been committed.

In conducting an inquest, the coroner in some states may, and in others must, make use of a coroner's jury. This agency consists of a small number of members—frequently six—chosen by the coroner, often from among bystanders or from residents of the neighborhood. The coroner presides over the jury and in large measure dominates its proceedings. When presiding at an inquest, he plays a dual role: (1) as a medical examiner, he is supposed to be able to determine the effects of wounds, bruises, fractures, poisons, and the like, in causing death; and, (2) as a magistrate, he must conduct the hearing, examine witnesses, and instruct the jurors with respect to their legal duties. Few coroners combine the qualifications of lawyer and physician needed for the proper performance of these duties.[22]

At the conclusion of an inquest, the coroner's jury deliberates briefly and returns its verdict. Coroners' verdicts are of four principal types.[23] (1) When the jury believes that the victim came to his death under circumstances for which no one is criminally liable, it returns a verdict of natural death, accidental death, or suicide, as the case may be. A verdict of this nature ordinarily ends the case, though it does not preclude further investigation if such is desired by the prosecuting officials. (2) If the jury believes that the deceased met death by violence or by any other means involving criminal liability, but is unable to discover the perpetrator of the crime, it may return a verdict stating its opinion that the victim met death at the hands of some person or persons unknown to

[19] Smith, *op. cit.*, 190-191.

[20] Cf. Lane W. Lancaster, *Government in Rural America* (2nd ed.), 170-173.

[21] Smith, *op. cit.*, 189. A contingent function of the coroner in most states is that of performing the duties of sheriff in the event of a vacancy in the sheriff's office or in any case in which the sheriff is disqualified. Likewise, if it should become necessary to arrest the sheriff, the warrant of arrest is directed to the coroner for service.

[22] Cf. *Ibid.*, 193.

[23] The first three of these are distinguished and discussed by Kirk H. Porter in his *County and Township Government in the United States*, 184-185.

the jury. When a verdict of this type is returned, it becomes the duty of the police and prosecuting attorney, if they are not already doing so, to attempt to find and apprehend the criminal. (3) If the jury believes that it is justified in fixing responsibility for the death upon some specific person or persons, it renders a verdict naming the person or persons believed to be responsible. On the basis of such a verdict, the coroner has authority to issue a warrant for the arrest of the person or persons named. (4) Finally, there is the open verdict, wherein the jury, though perhaps assigning a medical cause of death, makes no finding with respect to the existence or nonexistence of criminal liability. An example would be a verdict, in a case of death from injuries received in an automobile accident, stating merely that death was "due to a cerebral hemorrhage caused by a skull fracture received in an auto collision." [24] Such a verdict leaves entirely to police and prosecuting officers the task of deciding whether liability apparently exists and, in the event of an affirmative decision, instituting appropriate action.

In practice, coroners' verdicts, whether rendered by a coroner or a coroner's jury, are sometimes so vague or meaningless as to be of no assistance whatever to the prosecuting authorities. Some are even written in an illiterate manner. Actual examinations of coroners' records have, for example, revealed the following "verdicts": "Found dead"; "Head severed from body"; "Diabetes, tuberculosis, or nervous indigestion"; "Could be diabetes or poison"; "Died suddenly after taking medicine";[25] "So far as I could ascertain I found She came to her death from A natur cause comenly caled hart failure and I found no cause to Suspect Eny foul play"; "I lerned the man while Under the Enfluence of Whiskey or white mule Just willfully drowned himself"; and "the deceased came to her death by Natural Causes Unknown." [26]

The coroner's office has for some years been the subject of considerable criticism.[27] Students of the problem seem rather generally to agree that the office, in its traditional form, has no place in a modern law-enforcement system. As an alternative, it is recommended by many that the medical-examiner system, now operating on a statewide basis in several states and in a number of individual counties elsewhere, be extended

---

[24] Cf. *Champaign-Urbana [Ill.] News-Gazette*, Mar. 17, 1948, p. 3.

[25] Herman M. Adler, "Medical Science and Criminal Justice," *Criminal Justice in Cleveland* (Cleveland Found., Cleveland, 1922), Part V, p. 467.

[26] Raymond Moley, "The Sheriff and the Coroner," *Missouri Crime Survey* (Macmillan, New York, 1926), Part II, pp. 95-96.

[27] Cf. Richard S. Childs, "Rubbing Out the Coroners," *Nat. Mun. Rev.*, XXXIX, 494-496 (Nov., 1950); LeMoyne Snyder, "Justice and Sudden Death," *Jour. of Amer. Judic. Soc.*, XXXVI, 142-147 (Feb., 1953); Glenn W. Ferguson, "It's Time for the Coroner's Post-Mortem," *Ibid.*, XXXIX, 40-46 (Aug., 1955). For an account generally favorable to the coroner system in California counties, see Henry W. Turkel, "Merits of the Present Coroner System," *Jour. of Amer. Med. Assn.*, CLIII, 1086-1092 (Nov., 21, 1953).

to other jurisdictions.[28] Under this system, the work of a medical nature elsewhere performed by coroners is in the hands of medical examiners who are required to be physicians and some of whom, in addition, are trained pathologists. Examiners are appointed in Maine, Massachusetts, and New Hampshire by the governor and council; in Maryland and Virginia by ex officio state commissions on post mortem examinations; in Rhode Island by a chief medical examiner who, in turn, is appointed by the attorney general; and in New York City by the mayor, from civil service lists.[29] Nonmedical phases of the coroner's work are vested in the prosecuting attorney,[30] thereby conferring upon that official, who must ultimately present to the court such evidence of crime as may be discovered, power to supervise the collection of that evidence from the beginning.

The medical-examiner system is commendable in that it separates the medical and legal aspects of the coroner's work, places them in different hands, and attempts to secure higher standards in the performance of both. In practice, however, the system appears to work more satisfactorily in urban counties where medical examiners are trained pathologists serving on a full-time, salaried basis, than in rural counties where the examiners are general practitioners paid by fees.[31] This may well suggest the establishment in rural areas of medical-examiner districts large enough to support the services of trained pathologists. A noteworthy step in this direction has been taken in Kansas where, under the terms of a 1963 law, 105 elective county coroners will be replaced by 38 district coroners who are appointed by judges of the respective judicial districts from nominees designated by local medical societies, and are required to be physicians.[32]

The County Clerk

The office of county clerk exists in about half of the states, and is usually filled by popular election. One of the clerk's principal duties in

[28] On the system generally, see Oscar T. Schultz and E. M. Morgan, *The Coroner and the Medical Examiner* (Nat. Research Council Bull. No. 64, July, 1928); George H. Weinmann, *A Compendium of the Statute Law of Coroners and Medical Examiners in the United States* (Nat. Research Council Bull. No. 83, Aug., 1931); American Academy of Forensic Sciences and others, *A Model State Medico-Legal Investigative System* (Nat. Mun. League, New York, 1954); National Conference of Commissioners on Uniform State Laws, *Model Post-Mortem Examinations Act* (Nat. Conf. of Commissioners on Uniform State Laws, Chicago, 1954).

[29] Cf. Smith, *op. cit.*, 205-211. In New Hampshire the medical examiner is officially entitled the medical referee.

[30] In certain instances some of these functions are imposed upon judicial officers.

[31] Cf. Smith, *op. cit.*, 207-209.

[32] Cf. James T. McDonald, *Decisions of the 1963 Kansas Legislature* (Govtl. Research Center, Univ. of Kan., Lawrence, 1963), 130. For further discussion of the coroner and the medical-examiner system, see Clyde F. Snider, *Local Government in Rural America*, 328-336.

most of the states having the office is that of serving as secretary to the county board.[33] In this capacity he prepares the agenda for board meetings, attends the meetings, and keeps the minutes. Where there is no auditor or comptroller, claims against the county are filed with the clerk for examination and allowance by the county board; and, when claims have been allowed, warrants are drawn upon the county treasury by the clerk for countersignature and payment by the treasurer. Though the clerk does not share with the county board the legal power of allowing claims, any recommendations that he may make are likely to carry a great deal of weight, since he ordinarily will have gone over the claims prior to the board meeting, and will have sought to determine whether the goods concerned have been delivered or the services performed. The clerk makes formal record of ordinances, resolutions, and other forms of action taken by the board. In some states, in addition to serving as secretary to the county board, he acts as clerk of one or more of the county's courts of record.

Other duties, varying from state to state, are frequently imposed upon the county clerk. In some states he performs important functions in connection with elections, such as receiving nominating petitions, supervising the preparation of ballots, and acting as county registrar of voters. It is not unusual for the clerk to be charged with the issuance of various licenses, such as those for hunting and fishing, marriage licenses, and permits to operate dance halls and other amusement establishments outside municipal corporations. Because of his relation to the county board and his various miscellaneous duties, the clerk's office tends to become a sort of clearing house for county business in general.

The County Treasurer

County treasurers, usually elective, are found in some or all counties in most states. The primary duties of the county treasurer are those of (1) receiving county revenues, (2) acting as custodian of county funds, and (3) disbursing county moneys according to law. As collector of the property tax, in which capacity he serves in most states,[34] the treasurer ordinarily collects not only the tax due the county itself, but also the amounts due the various governmental subdivisions within the county as well as that, if any, due the state. After thus collecting the total tax, he remits to the various other local governments and to the state their respective shares.

[33] Where the clerk is primarily the servant of the county board, it would be more logical if he were appointed by that body. In states where the office of county clerk does not exist, the auditor or some other designated official serves as the board's secretary.

[34] In some states the property tax is collected by the sheriff, and a few other states provide for a county collector other than the treasurer.

To protect the public against loss of funds through dishonesty, negligence, or mistake on the part of the county treasurer, that official is usually required to provide an indemnity bond in an amount sufficient to cover any such losses. At one time it was a common practice for treasurers to keep as their own property any interest paid by banks on county deposits. More recently, however, many states have enacted "county-depository" laws which (1) provide for designation by the county board or a special finance board of banks which may serve as depositories for county funds, (2) require the county treasurer to deposit in those banks public funds in his custody, and (3) stipulate that interest paid on the funds shall be public property.

Some states, by constitutional provision, either prohibit the county treasurer from succeeding himself or provide that he shall not serve more than two successive terms. These provisions were apparently inserted in state constitutions for the purpose of insuring a careful audit of the treasurer's books at frequent intervals, when there is a change of incumbent of the office. Today, however, more and more states are adopting the practice of requiring a thorough audit at regular intervals regardless of whether there is a change of incumbent. When this is done the provisions limiting reeligibility are quite unnecessary as far as proper auditing is concerned, and in practice serve only to insure that the treasurer will be, at any given time, a person relatively inexperienced in the duties of his office.[35]

The treasurer's duties, it will be observed, are essentially of a ministerial and bookkeeping nature. He is vested with little or no discretion, being merely required to receive revenues, keep public funds safely, and make payments therefrom upon proper warrant. Moreover, the treasurer's records are often duplicated, to a large extent, by those of some other county officer, particularly the clerk or auditor. When these facts are considered, it is difficult to justify retention of the office of county treasurer in many of the counties where it now exists. A few states have merged the treasurer's office with some other county office; and, in some counties in Georgia and elsewhere, the office has been entirely abolished and provision made for the designation of banks to serve as county depositories and disbursing agents.[36] Both of these plans deserve more widespread consideration, particularly as applied to small rural counties. Where the office is retained the treasurer should, because of the nonpolicy-forming character of his duties, be appointed by the county board rather than elected as at present.

[35] But see above, footnote 10.
[36] See, for example, Melvin Clyde Hughes, *County Government in Georgia*, 25-26.

The Recorder or Register of Deeds

About half of the states provide for an elective county recorder or register of deeds [37] whose duty consists in making and preserving public records of various kinds of legal documents. The documents for which recording facilities are almost always provided are those relating to real estate titles. These include deeds, mortgages, leases, and instruments showing the satisfaction of mortgages and leases. Records of this nature are designed to protect landowners by providing them with a complete history of the title to their respective properties; and also to protect would-be purchasers or mortgagees by making it more readily possible for them to detect flaws in land titles.

Some states provide also for recording documents concerning title to personal property. These include chattel mortgages; releases, extensions, and assignments of such mortgages; and bills of sale. Other instruments, the recording of which is provided for in some states, include liens of various kinds, articles of incorporation, marks and brands of livestock, and city street plans and real estate subdivisions.

It was long customary to record documents by handwriting in heavy bound volumes, and this practice is still widely followed. Today, however, some states authorize use of loose-leaf books and typewriting. And more and more states are now providing that recorders may employ photostatic or microfilming processes. The microfilming process, in particular, seems to offer distinct promise in the field of recording.[38] Records photographed on microfilm require relatively little storage space and, by the use of appropriate projection apparatus, are made readily available for examination. Laws authorizing the microfilming of records ordinarily permit destruction of the originals after a designated number of years. It is also usually stipulated that the microfilm reproduction shall be deemed to be an original record, and that it may be so introduced as evidence before courts or administrative agencies.[39]

The County Superintendent of Schools

The office of county school superintendent exists in some three-fourths of the states, and in a majority of these is filled by popular election. Next to election, the most prevalent method of selection is appoint-

[37] In other states the recording function is devolved upon other specified county or town officers.

[38] See Margaret C. Norton "Microphotography and County Records," *Illinois Libraries*, XXVI, 505-509 (Dec., 1944). For a discussion of the shortcomings of the process, see Jerry McDonald, "The Case Against Microfilming," *Amer. Archivist*, XX, 345-356 (Oct., 1957).

[39] For further discussion of the office of recorder, see Snider, *op. cit.*, 156-159.

ment by a county board of education, though still other methods are used in a few states.[40]

In fifteen states, for the most part in the South, the county is the principal unit for school administration, and it is here that the county superintendent has the greatest power. Most of these county-unit states provide that the county superintendent shall serve as the executive officer of a county board of education by which he is appointed, and clothe him with much the same administrative authority as that commonly possessed by city school superintendents.[41]

In other states, however, the position of the county superintendent is much weaker. Ordinarily city schools are not under his jurisdiction, and his function consists merely in exercising some degree of supervisory authority over the rural schools of his county. The foremost duty of the superintendent is that of visiting and inspecting the schools under his jurisdiction. He is the official adviser of teachers and school officers and, through his visits and advice, he attempts to raise the general standards of the schools and to improve instruction therein. The superintendent usually serves as a sort of liaison officer between the state department of education and the local schools, being charged with carrying out the rules and regulations of the state agency. Local claims for state-aid funds are in many states presented and paid through the county superintendent's office. The superintendent in some instances appoints a county attendance officer to enforce state compulsory attendance laws, and in other states himself serves ex officio as attendance officer. Other duties commonly imposed upon county superintendents include the conducting of teachers' institutes and the examining of candidates for certain classes of teachers' certificates.

Other County Officers and Boards

A county office of long standing, but of very minor importance today, is that of the *surveyor*. This office exists in most states outside New England. The surveyor is usually popularly elected and compensated by fees. His primary duty is that of making land surveys and determining boundary lines and corners, when ordered to do so by the courts or upon the request of individual landowners.[42] Since, however, the boundaries of

---

[40] N. William Newsom, *The Legal Status of the County Superintendent* (U.S. Office of Educ., Washington, 1932). For further discussion of the office, see Julian E. Butterworth, *The County Superintendent in the United States* (U.S. Office of Educ., Washington, 1932); Robert B. Highsaw and Harold S. Thames, *A Guidebook of the County Superintendent of Education* (Bur. of Pub. Admin., Univ. of Miss., University, Miss., 1951); Minnesota Legislative Research Committee, *The Office of Superintendent of Schools* (Minn. Legis. Research Committee, St. Paul, 1952).

[41] See below, Chap. XX, "Units for Public-School Administration," "The County."

[42] In some instances the surveyor also serves ex officio as county highway engineer or supervisor.

landholdings have now become relatively stabilized, there is little call for his services. The office might well be abolished and such surveys as are required made by licensed private surveyors.

A *county highway superintendent,* charged with supervising the construction and maintenance of roads and bridges under county jurisdiction, is found in many states. This official usually is appointed by the county board and works under the board's direction.

The office of *county auditor,* usually filled by election, is provided for some or all counties in approximately a third of the states. The principal duty of the auditor is that of examining claims against the county, before their presentation to the county board, and making recommendations to the board with respect to their allowance or disallowance. When a claim has been allowed, the auditor issues a warrant upon the treasury for its payment. In some instances the auditor is also empowered to examine the accounts of other county officers, either annually or at his discretion. More often, however, this function is performed by accountants employed by the county board or, as is coming to be more and more common, by state examiners. In Indiana and some other states where the office of county clerk does not exist, the auditor serves as clerk to the county board.

A *county assessor,* usually popularly elected, is found in some or all counties in a majority of the states. Where the county is the basic geographic unit for assessment purposes, the county assessor is directly responsible for assessing real and personal property within his county for purposes of the property tax. On the other hand, when the office of county assessor exists in states employing the township or some other subdivision of the county as the basic assessment unit, the duties of the county assessor ordinarily consist in advising and instructing township or district assessors and supervising their work. In some instances, the county assessor is also charged with reviewing the original assessment lists of these officers and assessing omitted property. Some states have recently provided for appointive, rather than elective, county assessment officials.

Although not, strictly speaking, a county officer, the *county agricultural agent* is of such importance as to deserve mention.[43] Typically the county agent serves, and his office is financed by, three levels of government—federal, state, and county.[44] The agencies which supervise the

[43] On the office generally, see Gladys Baker, *The County Agent* (Univ. of Chicago Press, Chicago, 1939).

[44] At one time the county farm bureau served in several states, either in place of the county government or in conjunction therewith, as local sponsor for the county-agent program. However, this relationship of the program to the farm bureau encountered a great deal of criticism, particularly at the hands of rival farm organizations; and in the late 1950's the promulgation of restrictive rules by the United States Department of Agriculture served to bring about the dissolution of the formal tie to the bureau. Nevertheless, individual members of the farm bureau are frequently active

county-agent program, on behalf of the various governments concerned, are the United States Department of Agriculture, the extension service of the state agricultural college, and the county board. The functions performed by the county agent are numerous and varied, and differ somewhat from state to state. As illustrative of the duties with which he is commonly charged may be mentioned those of promoting improved agricultural methods; conducting farm demonstrations; assisting in the organization of cooperative marketing associations; promoting 4-H club work and cooperating in the work of other farm clubs and organizations; and giving advice to farmers on practical farm problems. County agents at times have been called upon to play an important role in the local administration of the agricultural and soil-conservation programs of the federal government.

Other officers and agencies found in some or all counties of various states include the county *health officer* or board, county *welfare superintendent*, county *board of* (tax assessment) *review*, county *attorney*, county *board of education*, county *library board*, county *election board*, county *voters' registration officer*, county *purchasing officer*, county *planning commission*, county *veterinarian*, and—the farm women's counterpart of the agricultural agent—the county *home demonstration agent*. Several of these agencies will be considered, in connection with the work they perform, in subsequent chapters dealing with governmental functions.[45]

County Employees

Carrying on the work of county government requires, in addition to the various county officers and their deputies, county employees the number of which will depend, at least in some measure, upon the size and population of the county. Some of these employees perform duties of a clerical nature in the various courthouse offices, while others, as for example certain highway and welfare employees, engage in work which may take them to all parts of the county. The total number of county officers and employees in the United States, as of October, 1962, has been estimated by the United States Bureau of the Census at 884,000.[46]

---

in the county-agent program, and in some instances bureau participation continues on an informal basis. For a comprehensive discussion of the subject, see William J. Block, *The Separation of the Farm Bureau and the Extension Service* (Univ. of Ill. Press, Urbana, 1960).

[45] See also United States Bureau of the Census, *County Boards and Commissions;* Edward W. Weidner, "Confused County Picture II," *Nat. Mun. Rev.,* XXXV, 228-232, 239 (May, 1946).

[46] United States Bureau of the Census, *State Distribution of Public Employment in 1962* (U.S. Bur. of the Census, Washington, Apr., 1963). Concerning the extent to which counties employ the merit system in the selection of employee personnel, see below, Chap. XVI, "Problems of Organization."

Lack of Integration

Little has been done at the county level in the direction of integrating or departmentalizing governmental activities on a functional basis.[47] That is to say, county administrative organization consists of a large number of relatively independent agencies, instead of a small number of major departments each performing all county services within a given field. In a particular county, for example, the county home, assistance to the needy in their own homes, old-age assistance, and the like, may each be administered by a different agency instead of all through a single county welfare department.[48] Instead of having a single department of public works, engineering and related activities may be scattered among various agencies such as a highway superintendent, surveyor, drainage commissioner, park board, and airport commission. Provision for a small number of major administrative departments to displace more numerous smaller agencies should reduce overlapping and foster coordination of all activities in a given field, and is particularly desirable in a county having a principal executive officer.[49]

The number of administrative departments which it is desirable to have is not likely to be uniform for all counties of the same state. In general, more populous counties will require more departments because their governments engage in a greater variety of activities. This being the case, it would seem wise, if integration is attempted, to establish by statute, for all counties, only a few basic departments which every county, regardless of its character and population, will need. These should probably include departments of finance, public welfare, public works, and law enforcement; and, in those states where the county is the principal unit for school administration, a department of education. The county board should then be empowered to establish such additional departments as the needs of each individual county may require.[50]

The Problem of a County Executive

From the foregoing discussion it will be apparent that there is not, in the typical American county, any single official charged with the over-

<hr>

[47] Administrative integration at the state level is discussed above, Chap. X, "Purposes and Principles of Reorganization."

[48] Under the stimulus of federal-aid requirements, many states have now integrated the administration of some or all of the local welfare activities that are supported in part by the federal government. See below, Chap. XVIII, "Local Organization."

[49] See below.

[50] Cf. R. C. Atkinson, "Principles of a Model County Government," *Nat. Mun. Rev.*, XXII, 469-486 (Sept., 1933, Supp.).

sight of county administration in general. The national government has its president, each of the fifty states its governor, and every city (save those operating under the commission form of government) its mayor or manager as a principal executive or administrative officer whose duty it is to coordinate, at least in some measure, the multifarious administrative activities of the governmental unit he serves. But in county government there is no counterpart of these executive officers. Insofar as there is any centralization at all of administrative powers and duties at the county level, such powers and duties are placed, as we have seen, in the hands of the county board—a body which in many instances is much too large for administrative work and which is charged also with the exercise of such legislative authority as is vested in the county. The need for a genuine county executive, at least in the more populous counties, has long been recognized by students of county government as well as by some county administrators, and in a growing number of counties an executive officer of one kind or another, with varying powers and responsibilities, has now been established. Provision for such an officer is usually accompanied, in some measure, by the establishment of major administrative departments to replace some of the traditional county officers. The heads of the new departments ordinarily are appointed by the executive officer, either alone or with the approval of the county board.[51]

Elective County Executives

Several counties have been provided with elective executives, somewhat similar in powers and duties to the mayors of cities. Since the 1890's Cook county (Chicago), Illinois, has had an elective "president of the county board" possessing substantially the powers of a mayor, including those of appointment and veto. Since 1900 Hudson and Essex counties in New Jersey have had elective executives with the title of county supervisor. Though possessing the veto power, this official actually has only nominal supervisory authority over subordinate personnel inasmuch as he lacks the power of appointment.[52] During the 1930's the New York counties of Nassau and Westchester adopted charters providing for elective county executives.[53] In those counties the elective executive is the chief administrative officer of the county and the official head of the county gov-

[51] Snider, op. cit., Chap. 7. For a discussion of literature on the subject, see Edward W. Weidner, "A Review of the Controversy over County Executives," Pub. Admin. Rev., VIII, 18-28 (Winter, 1948).

[52] James M. Collier, County Government in New Jersey, 16-17; James M. Collier, "Elected County Chief Executives in New Jersey," The County Officer, XX, 47-48 (Feb., 1955).

[53] For an evaluation of the Westchester charter in operation, see Hugh W. Robertson, "Westchester Likes Executive," Nat. Mun. Rev., XXXVIII, 219-223 (May, 1949).

ernment. He is vested with powers of appointment, supervision, and removal similar to those of a fairly strong mayor;[54] he may also veto acts and resolutions of the county board, subject to the power of the board to override the veto by a two-thirds vote. Home-rule charters adopted by St. Louis county, Missouri, in 1950, and Baltimore county, Maryland, in 1956, provide for elective executives. The St. Louis county functionary has relatively broad powers of appointment and supervision as well as veto authority. In Baltimore county the official is vested with the veto power and is declared to be "the chief executive officer of the county and the official head of the county government." With approval of the county governing body the elective executive appoints a county administrative officer who, in turn, appoints department heads with the approval of the executive.[55] A charter adopted in 1957 by Jefferson parish, Louisiana, provides for an elective parish president. Other counties which have recently been provided with elective executives include Milwaukee county, Wisconsin, De-Kalb county, Georgia, and the New York counties of Suffolk, Erie, Oneida, and Onondaga—the latter two by provision of home-rule charters adopted in 1961. Altogether, therefore, some 12 counties, all of them relatively populous,[56] now have elective executives endowed with some or all of the powers normally possessed by mayors. Appointments made by elective executives must usually have the approval of the county board.

In counties having no formal provision for a chief executive officer there is frequently a disposition to vest in one of the traditional elective officers some of the duties normally falling to a principal administrator. Where the office of county clerk exists, the clerk is often the official by whom such duties can most readily be performed. His position as secretary to the governing body, and the fact that he keeps a record of county financial transactions and in some instances prepares the preliminary budget, place the clerk at the center of county administration. A Wisconsin study of 1942 revealed that, through exploitation of their secretarial and fiscal duties, the clerks in thirty of that state's counties, "approximated, unofficially but none the less effectively, the position of county executive."[57]

Where there is no county clerk, or occasionally even where there is, another elective officer sometimes serves as a limited executive. In Arkansas counties the administrative powers assigned in most states to a

[54] See below, Chap. XIV, "Weak-Mayor versus Strong-Mayor Government."

[55] The arrangement in Baltimore county is similar to a plan now in operation in several large cities, whereby a professional chief administrative officer is appointed by and responsible to the mayor rather than the council. It is sometimes referred to as the *mayor*-manager plan to distinguish it from the more common *council*-manager plan. See below, Chap. XIV, "A Chief Administrative Officer."

[56] Of the counties mentioned in the text, none had a 1960 population of less than 200,000 and several had populations exceeding a million.

[57] L. H. Adolfson, "The County Clerk as 'Manager,'" *Nat. Mun. Rev.*, XXXIV, 125-128 (Mar., 1945).

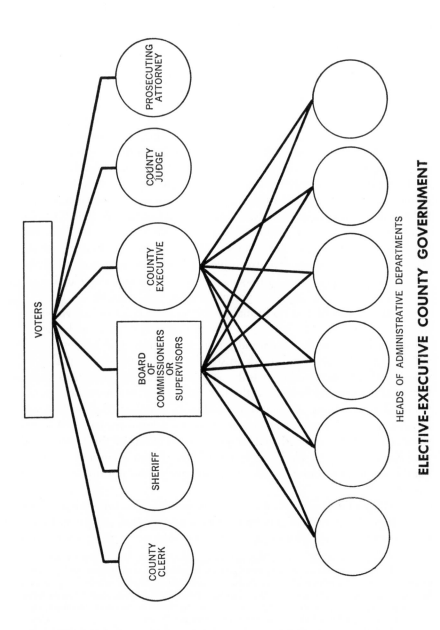

HEADS OF ADMINISTRATIVE DEPARTMENTS

ELECTIVE-EXECUTIVE COUNTY GOVERNMENT

county governing board are exercised by the county judge, whose role in certain respects approaches that of a chief administrator.[58] In the forty or so Georgia counties having either the county "ordinary" or a single commissioner of roads and revenues as their principal governing authority, those officers serve, in a measure, as elected county executives.[59] The probate judge in some Alabama counties assumes, at times, a position substantially similar to that of a county chief executive;[60] and a few North Carolina counties have conferred the powers and duties of a chief executive upon a full-time chairman of the county governing board.[61]

Appointive Executives: Managers and Quasi Managers[62]

During recent decades more than a score of counties have adopted the manager form of government, now in operation in many American cities,[63] and a somewhat larger number have adopted schemes partaking of certain features of the manager plan. Under *orthodox* manager government, as applied to counties, legislative or policy-determining powers are vested in a small county board, usually elected at large. This body controls county finances, enacts ordinances, and determines, insofar as such determination is a matter of county discretion, the nature and extent of county services and the amount of money to be expended for each. The board also appoints a county manager, solely on the basis of his personal qualifications for the post and without any reference to political affiliation

[58] Cf. Edward W. Reed and Henry M. Alexander, *The Government and Finance of Counties in Arkansas* (Bur. of Bus. and Econ. Research, Univ. of Ark., Fayetteville, 1953), 24.

[59] Hughes, *op. cit.*, 20-23.

[60] Karl A. Bosworth, *Black Belt County: Rural Government in the Cotton Country of Alabama* (Bur. of Pub. Admin., Univ of Ala., University, Ala., 1941), 33-39, 110-111; Karl A. Bosworth, *Tennessee Valley County: Rural Government in the Hill Country of Alabama* (Bur. of Pub. Admin., Univ. of Ala., University, Ala., 1941), 21-22.

[61] Paul W. Wager, ed., *County Government Across the Nation*, 410.

[62] See National Municipal League, *The County Manager Plan* (new ed., 1950); George W. Spicer, *Fifteen Years of County Manager Government in Virginia* (Univ. of Va. Extension, Charlottesville, 1951); John C. Bollens, *Appointed Executive Local Government: The California Experience* (Haynes Found., Los Angeles, 1952); National Municipal League, *Digest of County Manager Charters and Laws* (7th ed., 1963); Charles M. Kneier, "The County Manager Plan," *Pub. Management*, XII, 45-49 (Feb., 1930); Paul W. Wager, "The Case for the County Manager Plan," *Ibid.*, 78-82 (Mar., 1930); Robert B. Highsaw, "City and County Manager Plans in the South," *Jour. of Politics*, XI, 497-517 (Aug., 1949); Margaret Rohrer, "County Manager Government in California," *The County Officer*, Vol. XV, No. 6, pp. 25-31 (Sept., 1950); W. Earl Weller and Craig M. Smith, "Sixteen Years of Progress," *Nat. Mun. Rev.*, XLII, 393-397 (Sept., 1953); George W. Spicer, "Manager Counties Evaluated," *Ibid.*, 331-337 (July, 1953).

[63] The manager plan is given further consideration in the chapter relating to city government. See below, Chap. XIV.

or requirement of local residence. It is the duty of the manager, as the executive officer of the county, to direct and coordinate the administration of county affairs in accordance with the policies established by the board. To enable him to do this, he is empowered to appoint and remove his principal administrative subordinates without the necessity of securing approval by the county board. The manager serves at the pleasure of the board, which may remove him at any time if it believes that he is not performing his task efficiently. While he remains in office, however, the manager is to be free from interference by the county board in administrative matters; and he, in turn, is to leave matters of policy determination to the board.

At the beginning of 1963 manager government was in operation in twenty-six American counties in ten states: ten counties in North Carolina, four in Virginia, three in California, two each in Georgia and Maryland, and one each in Florida, Nevada, Montana, New York, and Tennessee.[64] Some of these counties had adopted the manager plan through home-rule charter provisions, in others the system had been established by special legislative act, and in still others adoption had taken place under optional statutes. For the most part the manager counties are of an urban or semi-urban nature. Five of the twenty-six have populations exceeding a half-million; only nine have less than 100,000 inhabitants; and the sole sparsely populated rural county in the group is Petroleum county, Montana, with a 1960 population of 894 in an area of more than 1,600 square miles. It will be noted that, for a variety of reasons, the manager plan as applied to counties has not spread rapidly. The strength of tradition in local institutions, the opposition of political machines, and apathy on the part of the general citizenry, are deterrents to the rapid spread of anything new in governmental organization. Furthermore, constitutional barriers must in many states be removed before an appointive office of manager can be established. In Nebraska, for example, an optional county-manager act was declared unconstitutional by the state supreme court as violating a constitutional requirement that all county officers be elected.[65]

In those counties where it now operates, the manager plan seems to be giving satisfactory results. In general, the present governments of such counties appear to be more efficient than those which the manager plan supplanted. This by no means indicates, however, that all counties

[64] The Municipal Year Book, 1963, pp. 522-553. The Year Book, published by the International City Managers' Association, Chicago, lists in each issue, along with manager cities, the counties currently operating under manager government. It is to be noted that this list includes only counties wherein the manager's powers are sufficiently broad, and the legal relations between the manager and the county board are of such nature, as to meet the Association's standards for manager government. Counties with governmental systems which, though called "manager" plans, do not meet those standards, are not included.

[65] State v. Tusa, 130 Neb. 528 (1936).

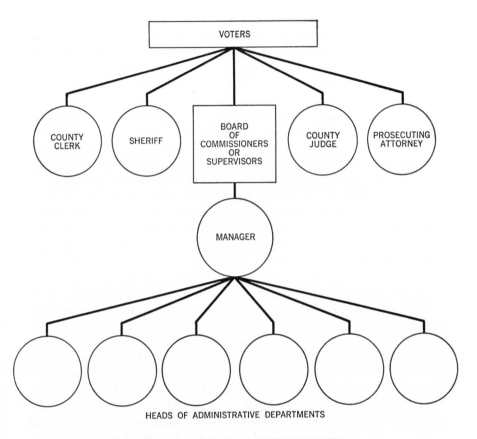

VOTERS

COUNTY CLERK

SHERIFF

BOARD OF COMMISSIONERS OR SUPERVISORS

COUNTY JUDGE

PROSECUTING ATTORNEY

MANAGER

HEADS OF ADMINISTRATIVE DEPARTMENTS

COUNTY-MANAGER GOVERNMENT

should adopt the manager system. As yet the plan has been tried in relatively few counties, and in several of those for only brief periods. Moreover, as previously pointed out, the counties that have tried the plan are for the most part of an urban or semiurban nature; and it is in such counties that manager government appears likely to produce best results. Whether a particular county would be wise in adopting the manager plan will depend upon local conditions and the relative efficiency of the existing government. Some critics of the plan maintain that, particularly in sparsely populated rural counties, major county functions are so few, and these few regulated in such detail by state statutes and administrative agencies, that there is really no function for a manager to perform.[66] Furthermore, in many counties of small population the cost of the manager's office might prove an undue burden upon the taxpayers unless it were made possible to eliminate certain other offices by transferring their duties to the manager. One student of the problem, indeed, believes that the manager plan would probably be financially impracticable in from half to three-fourths of the counties of the country.[67] Yet, though a single instance provides little basis for generalization, it may be of some significance that experience with the plan in the one strictly rural county where it has been tried (Petroleum county in Montana) appears to have been most gratifying.[68]

A substantial number of counties in various states are operating under what might be called "quasi-manager" plans. These have some of the features of manager government, and indeed are sometimes called manager plans, but in one or more respects (usually in the scope of authority granted to the manager and the degree of his freedom from interference by the county board in administrative matters) they fall short of the standards ordinarily accepted as essential to orthodox manager government. Hamilton county (Chattanooga), Tennessee, and Charleston county, South Carolina, have operated under such modified manager plans since 1941 and 1949, respectively.[69] In Cuyahoga county (Cleveland), Ohio, the board of county commissioners in 1952 created the position of county administrative officer to be filled by board appointment. The new

[66] For statements of the case against the manager plan for rural counties, see Kirk H. Porter, "A Wet Blanket on the County Manager Plan," *Nat. Mun. Rev.*, XVIII, 5-8 (Jan., 1929); Howard M. Kline, "No Job for a County Manager [in rural Maryland counties], *Ibid.*, XXVIII, 358-364 (May, 1939).

[67] Arthur C. Millspaugh, *Local Democracy and Crime Control* (Brookings Inst., Washington, 1936), 170.

[68] Harold G. Halcrow, *County Manager Government in Montana: Presenting a Case Study of Petroleum County* (Agricultural Experiment Station, Mont. State Coll., Bozeman, 1949); R. R. Renne, "Too Small to be Efficient?" *Nat. Mun. Rev.*, XXXVI, 78-82 (Feb., 1947); R. R. Renne, "Montana Pace Setter," *Ibid.*, XLVII, 115-118, 131 (Mar., 1958).

[69] Concerning the Charleston plan, see William F. Larsen, "Tradition Bows to Efficiency," *Nat. Mun. Rev.*, XXXIX, 497-500 (Nov., 1950).

official functions as an administrative assistant to the board, aiding the county commissioners in the performance of their managerial and administrative duties.[70] The home-rule charter adopted in 1962 by Washington county, Oregon, provides that the county board shall appoint an administrative officer who "shall administer those county affairs placed in his charge by the board."

Particularly outstanding among quasi managers are the appointed executives found in more than half of California's counties. Only three of that state's counties, as previously noted, have orthodox managers; but a much larger number have executive officers failing in some measure to meet the prescribed standards for inclusion in that category. Officers of the latter type are commonly referred to, officially or otherwise, as "chief administrative officers." The first California county to provide for an officer of this nature was Los Angeles, where the plan was inaugurated in 1938. So successful was the plan in this instance that many other counties subsequently adopted some or all of its features.[71] As of 1961, it was reported that no less than 32 of the state's 57 counties had appointed administrators of the quasi-manager type.[72]

The authority granted to California's chief administrative officers is not the same in all counties. Professor John Bollens suggests, however, that there are, generally speaking, only two important formal differences between county managers and chief administrative officers in that state. In the first place, managers usually have specific authority to appoint and remove department heads and certain other personnel, whereas most chief administrative officers can only make recommendations to the county governing board concerning appointments and removals. Secondly, managers ordinarily are authorized to prepare the annual budget for submission to the county board, while chief administrative officers usually are limited to collecting departmental estimates and transmitting these to the board along with their own suggestions. In practice, however, as Bollens points out, even these legal distinctions sometimes become blurred, with chief administrative officers reviewing and revising budgetary estimates and having their personnel recommendations approved as a matter of course.

[70] "The New County Administrative Officer," *Greater Cleveland,* Vol. XXVII, No. 5 (Jan. 29, 1952). For an appraisal of early experience under the plan, see Cleveland Bureau of Governmental Research, *Development of the Administrative Officer in Cuyahoga County: A Report to the Board of County Commissioners of Cuyahoga County, Ohio* (Cleveland, 1955).

[71] Abraham Holtzman, *Los Angeles County Chief Administrative Officer: Ten Years' Experience* (Bur. of Govtl. Research, Univ. of Calif., Los Angeles, 1948); Earl R. Strathman, "They Like Los Angeles Plan," *Nat. Mun. Rev.,* XXXVII, 428-432 (Sept., 1948).

[72] International City Managers' Association, *Recent Council-Manager Developments and Directory of Council-Manager Cities with Supplement: Noncouncil-Manager Communities with Council-Appointed Administrators* (Int. City Mgrs'. Assn., Chicago, 1961), 39-40.

Actually, therefore, in the day-by-day performance of their duties, chief administrative officers may approximate managers more closely than their formal authority would indicate.[73]

Quasi managers of one kind or another have been provided in certain counties in still other states. As regards the range of their authority, officers of this nature vary all the way from executive secretaries vested by the county board with only a few managerial duties to some of California's chief administrative officers who, save for formal authority to appoint and remove department heads and prepare the budget, have practically all powers ordinarily conferred upon a manager. Though plans such as those here described do not meet all the standards of authentic manager government, they seem nevertheless, in most of the counties where they operate, to be producing at least some of the beneficial results expected of the orthodox manager system.[74]

REFERENCES

BOLLENS, John C., and SCOTT, Stanley, *Local Government in California* (Univ. of Calif. Press, Berkeley, 1951).

BRADSHAW, William L., *County Government Manual for the Missouri Constitutional Convention of 1943* (Aug., 1943).

BROMAGE, Arthur W., *American County Government* (Sears Pub. Co., New York, 1933).

COLLIER, James M., *County Government in New Jersey* (Rutgers Univ. Press, New Brunswick, N.J., 1952).

FAIRLIE, John A., and KNEIER, Charles M., *County Government and Administration* (Century, New York, 1930).

GILBERTSON, H. S., *The County: The "Dark Continent" of American Politics* (Nat. Short Ballot Org., New York, 1917).

HODGSON, James G., *The Official Publications of American Counties* (bibliography) (Author, Colo. State Coll., Fort Collins, 1937).

HUGHES, Melvin Clyde, *County Government in Georgia* (Univ. of Ga. Press, Athens, 1944).

LANCASTER, Lane W., *Government in Rural America* (Van Nostrand, New York, 2nd ed., 1952).

National Municipal League, *Digest of County Manager Charters and Laws* (Nat. Mun. League, New York, 7th ed., 1963).

———, *Model County Charter* (Nat. Mun. League, New York, 1956).

———, *The County Manager Plan* (Nat. Mun. League, New York, new ed., 1950).

[73] Bollens, *Appointed Executive Local Government*, 119-123. See also John C. Bollens, "Administrative Integration in California Counties," *Pub. Admin. Rev.*, XI, 26-34 (Winter, 1951).

[74] For an analysis of the positions and powers of representative county managers, quasi managers, and elective executives, see "A Profile of Fifty County Administrators and their Counties," *The County Officer*, XXIX. 373-380 (Oct., 1963).

New York State Office for Local Government, *County Charters in New York State: A Comparative Guide to Leading Charter Provisions* (N.Y. State Office for Local Govt., Albany, 1963).

PORTER, Kirk H., *County and Township Government in the United States* (Macmillan, New York, 1922).

SMITH, Bruce, *Rural Crime Control* (Inst. of Pub. Admin., Columbia Univ., New York, 1933), Chaps. 2, 4, 6.

SNIDER, Clyde F., *Local Government in Rural America* (Appleton-Century-Crofts, New York, 1957).

——, and Howards, Irving, *County Government in Illinois* (Southern Ill. Univ., Carbondale, 1960).

United States Bureau of the Census, *County Boards and Commissions* (U.S. Govt. Printing Office, Washington, 1947).

——, *Elective Offices of State and County Governments* (U.S. Bur. of the Census, Washington, 1946).

WAGER, Paul W., ed., *County Government Across the Nation* (Univ. of N.C. Press, Chapel Hill, 1950).

WELLS, Roger H., *American Local Government* (McGraw-Hill, New York, 1939), 77-83.

Studies of county government in particular states, only a few of which have been cited in this chapter, are available for many states.

The issues of the *National Municipal Review* for August, 1932 (with a supplement entitled "Constitutional Barriers to Improvement in County Government"), October, 1934, and February, 1939, are symposia on county government.

From 1937 to 1949, the *American Political Science Review* carried annual articles summarizing developments in the field of county and township government. These articles appear variously in the October, December, and February issues. For a more general summary, see Clyde F. Snider, "American County Government: A Mid-Century Review," in the issue of the *Review* for March, 1952.

The *National Civic Review* now carries in several of its issues for each year, a department entitled "County Government" in which selected current developments are reported.

14

City Government

Forms of American City Government and Their Relative Prevalence

Three principal forms of city government exist in the United States at the present time: (1) mayor-council; (2) commission; and (3) council-manager. Of these, the mayor-council, adapted from English origins, is the traditional and still the predominant form. More than half of all cities of over 5,000 population have mayor-council government.[1] Most smaller municipalities classed as cities are governed also under the mayor-council system; and, in addition, many villages and incorporated towns, though their legislative and executive organs may have titles other than those of council and mayor, respectively, have governments that are essentially of the mayor-council variety.[2]

Both the commission and council-manager forms are products of the present century. Though governments resembling in some respects what has come to be known as the commission plan had previously operated for brief periods in a few cities,[3] commission government is generally considered as having had its beginning in the Galveston charter of 1901. This charter was granted by special act of the Texas legislature, at the request of a committee of Galveston citizens, after the mayor-council government of the city had revealed itself inadequate to deal with problems resulting from a disastrous flood occurring in September of 1900. The new government was outstandingly successful in Galveston, and in 1905 the

---

[1] *The Municipal Year Book* (Int. City Mgrs'. Assn., Chicago), 1963, p. 160.

[2] See below, "Government of Villages, Boroughs, and Incorporated Towns."

[3] For example, in Sacramento, New Orleans, Memphis, and Mobile. See T. S. Chang, *History and Analysis of the Commission and City Manager Plans of Municipal Government in the United States*, 49-54.

neighboring city of Houston asked for and was granted a somewhat similar charter. During the next decade, the commission plan attracted much public interest. State after state enacted legislation authorizing cities to adopt the system, frequently with various deviations from the Galveston prototype which experience or logic seemed to suggest as desirable. In still other states, commission charters were adopted under home-rule provisions or granted by special act of the state legislature, so that within a few years the plan was in operation in cities of more than forty states.[4] The peak of commission government's popularity was reached about 1917, at which time some five hundred cities were operating under the plan. Since then there have been relatively few new adoptions, and some cities have abandoned the plan, often in favor of the newer manager system. Most of the cities adopting commission government have been of medium or smaller size, the plan having enjoyed its greatest popularity and success in places of less than 50,000 population.[5] Only 251 cities of over 5,000 population were reported in 1963 to be operating under commission government,[6] and it is probable that the total number of commission-governed cities of all sizes is now less than five hundred. The largest cities operating under the plan at the end of 1963—all with populations between 250,-000 and 500,000—were Memphis, Portland (Oregon), St. Paul, and Tulsa.[7] Buffalo, which adopted commission government in 1916 but abandoned it in 1927, is the only city of over 500,000 to have tried the plan. Des Moines, whose adoption of the plan in 1908 did much to popularize commission government during the early period, abandoned it for the council-manager system in 1949.

The first American city to employ a city manager was Staunton, Virginia, in 1908. However, active interest in, and spread of, the manager plan really dates from its adoption by Dayton, Ohio, in a home-rule charter which became effective in January, 1914. Since that date, a substantial number of municipalities have adopted manager government each year and the number of abandonments has been surprisingly small. Most of the adoptions have been effected either under home-rule charter provisions or under optional manager laws enacted by state legislatures; but some have been by special legislative act, and others by ordinance of the city council under statutory authority to establish necessary offices. In 1963 council-manager government was reported to be operating in some 1,800 cities and towns in forty-eight states.[8] Like commission government, the man-

[4] Cf. *Ibid.*, Chap. 5.

[5] Cf. Thomas H. Reed, *Municipal Government in the United States* (rev. ed.), 196.

[6] *The Municipal Year Book*, 1963, p. 160.

[7] Cf. *Ibid.*, 168. Birmingham had abandoned the plan during the year in favor of mayor-council government.

[8] See "City Manager Profession and Directory," *The Municipal Year Book*, 1963, pp. 519-553; "Council-Manager Government," *Ibid.*, 307-310. The two states having no manager municipalities were Hawaii and Indiana.

ager plan has been most popular among cities of medium or smaller size. The largest city yet to experiment with the plan is Cleveland, which abandoned it after seven years. Of all council-manager cities in 1963, only 55 had 1960 populations exceeding 100,000, and only four—Cincinnati, Dallas, San Antonio, and San Diego—exceeded 500,000.

Mayor-Council Government

Under the mayor-council system, the principal governing agencies of the city are an elective council and an elective mayor. The council is the local legislative or policy-determining body, while the mayor is, at least nominally, the local chief executive. Thus there is observed, under the mayor-council plan, the separation of legislative and executive powers which constitutes one of the fundamental principles of our state and national governments.

The Council: Its Composition and Organization

At one time, and especially among the larger eastern cities, bicameral councils were common in the United States. Today, however, virtually all city councils, if not all, are unicameral.[9] The size of individual councils varies greatly. In most cities the number of members is somewhere between five and twenty.[10] However, in very small municipalities the number is occasionally as small as three; and in some larger cities it exceeds twenty. For example, the number of members is twenty-nine in St. Louis, thirty-three in Cleveland, thirty-six in New York, and fifty in Chicago. Though some states provide for councils varying in size with the population of the municipality, in the country as a whole there is no standard relationship between city size and the number of council members. Some relatively small cities have large councils and some large cities small councils.[11] In the old bicameral councils, it was usual for members of upper chambers to be called aldermen and members of the lower chambers councilmen. Members of the unicameral councils of today are known as aldermen in some cities and as councilmen in others.

Council members are chosen by popular vote, usually for terms of two or four years. In some instances the terms of members are staggered, only a part of the membership being elected at any one time. Nomination is most commonly by primary election, but in some cases it is by petition or, especially in very small municipalities, by caucus. Members are nominated and elected in some municipalities on a partisan basis and in others under the nonpartisan plan.

[9] Cf. *Nat. Civic Rev.*, LII, 548 (Nov., 1963).
[10] Cf. Edwin A. Cottrell, "City Council Organization," *Pub. Management*, XVII, 95-98 (Apr., 1935).
[11] *Ibid.*

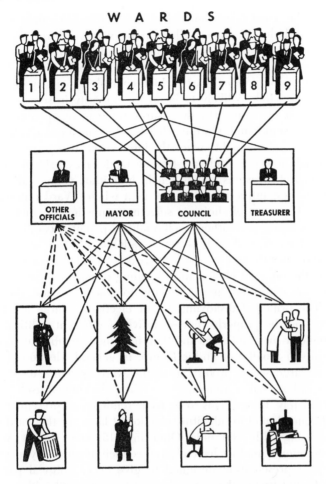

MAYOR-COUNCIL GOVERNMENT

Courtesy of National Municipal League. Reproduced with permission.

Some cities elect all members of the council from the city at large, whereas others are divided into wards or districts with one or more councilmen chosen from each such area. In some instances a part of the members are elected at large and a part by wards. Though the ward or district system is common among municipalities of all sizes, it is most prevalent among the larger cities. Several cities follow the plan of electing the council president at large while all other councilmen are chosen by wards or districts.

Both the ward system and election at large have their respective advantages and disadvantages. Election by wards assures that council membership will be spread geographically, and thus makes possible the representation of any special interests peculiar to particular localities. Moreover, since the political party which controls a majority of the votes in the city as a whole is likely to be in the minority in some wards, the ward system of election virtually assures some minority representation from the party standpoint. On the other hand, councilmen elected on the ward basis may be inclined to place the interests of their respective wards above citywide interests, and vote-trading tactics may lead to enactment by the council of measures which benefit individual communities but do not serve the best interests of the city as a whole. Ward representation also narrows the range of choice in selecting councilmen, which is unfortunate if some wards are without well qualified potential candidates while other wards have several such persons available. Election of councilmen at large overcomes the more important weaknesses of the ward system by broadening the range of choice and impelling councilmen, since they are elected by the voters of the entire city, to place citywide above local interests. The principal disadvantages of election at large are that the council may not be properly representative of different political parties and economic or social interests and that, if council membership is numerous, it results in a ballot of undue length. In general, election of council members at large seems preferable to the ward system, except in very large cities and in smaller municipalities where the council itself is unduly large. Fortunately, there seems to be some tendency at present to reduce the size of councils and to substitute election at large for the ward system.

Beginning with Ashtabula, Ohio, in 1915, some twenty American cities at one time or another have elected council members by a system of proportional representation designed to give every political party, and every substantial group of voters who are in agreement with respect to candidates or policies, representation in the council, as nearly as possible, in proportion to its voting strength. In order to achieve its purpose, this plan requires either that the entire council be elected at large or that election districts be used returning three or more numbers each. Under the Hare system of the single transferable vote, which is the plan of proportional representation used in this country, each voter has an opportunity to indicate on his ballot his first choice, second choice, and so on, being entitled to indicate, in order, as many choices as he wishes. In the counting process, if a voter's ballot cannot help elect the candidate of his first choice, either because that candidate has already been elected by other ballots or because he has received so few votes that his candidacy is hopeless, the ballot is transferred to the voter's second-choice candidate or, if it cannot be of help to him, to the voter's third- or highest-choice candidate whom it can help elect. The system thus strives to make each voter's ballot as effective as possible, and to give representation to each party or group in proportion to the number of votes cast by its members. The city having the longest experience with proportional representation is Cincinnati, where the plan was in effect from 1926 to 1958. Most of the other cities which have experimented with the plan have been smaller, though it was used by Cleveland from 1921 to 1931 and by New York from 1938 to 1949. Whatever its merits, proportional representation never gained widespread popularity. In several instances the plan was declared unconstitutional and it has now been abandoned by virtually every municipality that adopted it.[12]

Regular meetings of the council are usually held weekly or monthly, and provision is made for the convening of special meetings when necessary. As a rule, meetings are more frequent in larger than in smaller municipalities. In some cities the mayor is the council's presiding officer, in others the council elects a president from its own membership, and in still others a president of the council is elected as such by the city's voters. All but the very small councils make considerable use of the committee system, most proposals being referred to committees for study and report prior to their consideration by the council as a whole.

Council Powers and Procedure[13]

All powers granted to a city by charter or statute, and not expressly delegated to the mayor or some other municipal officer, vest in the council. Though the council is primarily a legislative body, its powers include some of an administrative nature as well. On the legislative side, the principal phases of the council's authority are (1) financial and (2) regulatory. Subject to such limitations as are imposed by charter or by the state constitution or statutes, it is the council that levies city taxes, makes appropriations of city funds, and borrows money on the credit of the municipality. In the regulatory field, the council usually has power to enact local legislation dealing with a wide variety of matters, such as health, traffic, building standards, and zoning. Council authority in administrative matters includes such powers as those of letting contracts and ordering the construction of

[12] For further explanation of proportional representation and its operation in American municipal government, see Charles M. Kneier, *City Government in the United States* (3rd ed.), 226-236; Jewell Cass Phillips, *Municipal Government and Administration in America*, 275-280. For a summary and evaluation of New York's experience, see Belle Zeller and Hugh A. Bone, "The Repeal of P. R. in New York City—Ten Years in Retrospect," *Amer. Polit. Sci. Rev.*, XLII, 1127-1148 (Dec., 1948). Cincinnati's experience is recounted and appraised in Ralph A. Straetz, *P. R. Politics in Cincinnati: Thirty-two Years of City Government through Proportional Representation* (N.Y. Univ. Press, New York, 1958).

[13] See Harvey Walker, "Legislative Powers of City Councils," *Pub. Management*, XVII, 130-133 (May, 1935); Emmett L. Bennett, "Legislative Procedure of City Councils," *Ibid.*, 199-205 (July, 1935).

public improvements. In general, the extent of the council's powers over administration depends upon the degree of administrative authority vested in the mayor.[14]

Council action normally takes one of two forms—that of an ordinance or a resolution. The ordinance is the highest and most authoritative form of action that it is possible for the council to take. If within the council's power and passed by appropriate procedure, an ordinance operates within the city as a local law.[15] Charter provisions or council rules usually require that ordinances be given three readings before the council and be passed with most of the formalities attending the enactment of state statutes. Council action of a permanent character and general application can ordinarily be taken only by ordinance. Action by ordinance is thus required in most legislative matters, and especially those of a regulatory nature. The procedure for adopting resolutions is generally less elaborate and formal than the ordinance procedure. Resolutions are commonly employed by the council in taking action of an administrative character.

The Mayor[16]

Under the mayor-council system the mayor is popularly elected, usually from nominees designated by primary election or by petition. In most instances election is by simple plurality vote, though a few cities employ systems of preferential voting designed to secure majority elections.[17] The mayoral term in most cities is either two years or four. The two-year term is the more common at present, but the longer term seems to be growing in favor, especially among larger cities. In some instances, particularly in New England, the term is but a single year.

The powers of the mayor fall into two principal categories, namely, those of an executive or administrative nature and those which are legislative in character.[18] Most important among his administrative powers are

[14] See below, "Weak-Mayor versus Strong-Mayor Government."

[15] Cf. William Anderson and Edward W. Weidner, American City Government (rev. ed.), 424-425.

[16] On the office of mayor, see Russell M. Story, The American Municipal Executive. For enlightening observations by outstanding mayors as related in works of autobiographical character, see Tom L. Johnson, My Story (Huebsch, New York, 1911); Brand Whitlock, Forty Years of It (Appleton, New York, 1914); Daniel W. Hoan, City Government: The Record of the Milwaukee Experiment (Harcourt, New York, 1936). A series of eighteen articles descriptive of as many individual mayors will be found in various issues of the National Municipal Review for the years 1926-1929. See also Webb Waldron, "The Mayor Gets Things Done," Nat. Mun. Rev., XXXIII, 7-10, 13 (Jan., 1944).

[17] For explanations of preferential voting, see Charles M. Kneier, City Government in the United States (3rd ed.), 365-370; Austin F. Macdonald, American City Government and Administration (6th ed.), 261-263.

[18] In some instances the mayor is vested also with judicial authority. See below, "Municipal Courts."

those of appointment and removal, together with the incidental power of direction which stems from those primary powers. The mayor is ordinarily vested with the power to appoint at least some, and sometimes all, of his principal administrative subordinates.[19] In some cities mayoral appointments must have the approval of the council, while in others such approval is not required. Many mayors appoint, in addition to the higher administrative officers, large numbers of minor officers and employees, though these lesser appointments in some cities are now subject to civil service regulations. Officers appointed by the mayor are usually subject to removal by him. However, in many cities the removal power may be exercised by the mayor for specified causes only; and, where appointments are subject to council approval, such approval is often required for removals also. Another administrative power frequently vested in the mayor is that of preparing the annual budget for submission to the council.[20]

Of the mayor's legislative powers, the most important are the veto power and the power to make recommendations to the council. Charters and statutes commonly make it the duty of the mayor to recommend to the council such measures as he may deem expedient, and this he does by formal message or otherwise. The actual influence of the mayor's recommendations upon council action will naturally depend to a large extent upon the political and personal relationships between the chief executive and council members. Ordinances and resolutions adopted by the council must ordinarily be submitted to the mayor for his signature or veto. In almost every city, however, the mayoral veto may be overridden by an extraordinary vote—commonly two-thirds—of the council. A minor legislative power often possessed by the mayor is that of calling special sessions of the council and, in some instances, of determining what business may be considered in such sessions. Where the mayor is the council's presiding officer, he usually has the right to vote in case of a tie.

Department Heads

To facilitate the carrying on of municipal activities, the administrative branch of government in all cities of any considerable size is organized into departments, each charged with the performance of a particular phase of the city's work. Thus, even in a relatively small city, there will likely be found a police department, a fire department (though sometimes the police and fire-protection functions are combined in a single department of public safety), a department of public works, and perhaps a finance department and department of public health. In general, there is some relation between the size of the city and the number of administrative departments, the number sometimes reaching twenty or more in larger

---

[19] See below, "Department Heads."
[20] See below, Chap. XXV, "The Budget-Making Authority."

cities. At the head of each department is either an individual officer, usually called a commissioner, or some sort of board. Though the board system of heading departments was once widely used and is still employed to some extent, the commissioner system is now generally preferred for most departments. At one time it was common practice to choose department heads by popular election. Today, however, the power to appoint these major administrative officers is usually vested in the mayor, either with or without the requirement of council approval. The present tendency, moreover, is away from the requirement of council approval and in favor of giving the mayor a free hand in the matter. Vesting the mayor with an unfettered power of selection is only proper, since the department heads are the officers upon whom he must rely for assistance and cooperation in the performance of his duties to see that laws are properly executed and that municipal services are properly performed.

Other Administrative Officers

Other offices of a general administrative nature found in most cities regardless of size are those of city clerk, city treasurer, and city attorney.[21] In small municipalities the incumbents of these offices sometimes serve on a part-time basis, while in the largest cities they not only are full-time officers, but have numerous subordinates within their departments.

The *city clerk* is popularly elected in some cities, but is more often chosen by the council. The clerk is secretary to the council and custodian of city records. He attends council meetings, keeps a journal of council proceedings, and makes a record of ordinances and resolutions adopted. He usually issues licenses and permits of various kinds, and in some cities he is charged with the management of municipal elections. In addition to performing the specific duties imposed upon it, the clerk's office commonly serves as a general clearing house for information concerning the city government. The office is therefore significant not only because of the importance of complete and accurate records, but because of its numerous contacts with the public.

The *treasurer* is usually chosen either by popular election or by mayoral appointment, and the primary functions of his office are the collection, custody, and disbursement of municipal funds. City property taxes are sometimes collected directly by the city treasurer, but in other

---

[21] On the office of city clerk, see William B. Munro, *Municipal Administration* (Macmillan, New York, 1934), Chap. 7; John M. Pfiffner, *Municipal Administration* (Ronald, New York, 1940), 52-54. The office of city treasurer is discussed in Lent D. Upson, *Practice of Municipal Administration* (Century, New York, 1926), Chap. 7. For discussions of the city attorney's office, see Henry Hodges, *City Management* (Crofts, New York, 1939), Chap. 13; Munro, *op. cit.*, Chap. 6; Pfiffner, *op. cit.*, 54-58; Thomas H. Reed, *Municipal Management* (McGraw, New York, 1941), Chap. 13; Upson, *op. cit.*, Chap. 11.

instances are collected by the county treasurer, along with other local and state levies, and subsequently remitted to the city. Other forms of municipal taxes, as well as special assessments, are collected by the city treasurer, and revenues of other city departments are turned over to the treasurer at regular intervals. Funds in the treasurer's custody are frequently required by law to be kept on deposit in banks designated by the city council or a finance board. Payments from municipal funds are made by the treasurer upon order of the proper finance officer of the city, pursuant to council appropriation.

The *city attorney*, city solicitor, or corporation counsel, as he is variously called, is the city's chief law officer. His duties are numerous and varied. He gives opinions concerning their legal powers and duties to councilmen, the mayor, department heads, and other city officers; represents the city in the courts in civil suits to which it is a party, either as plaintiff or as defendant; attempts to adjust damage claims against the city to avoid litigation; prepares ordinances for submission to the council, and sometimes bills, which the city is interested in having enacted into law, for presentation to the state legislature; draws, or approves from the legal standpoint, most municipal contracts; approves the fiduciary bonds of municipal officers and employees; and, in some cities, prosecutes violators of city ordinances.[22] In many larger cities the city attorney is appointed by the mayor, but in smaller municipalities he is usually either popularly elected or chosen by the council. Mayoral appointment, with the requirement of council confirmation, would seem to be the most logical method of selection, since the duties of the office pertain to both the legislative and administrative branches of the city government and the incumbent should therefore have the confidence of both branches.

Weak-Mayor versus Strong-Mayor Government

It is usual to distinguish between two types of mayor-council government: the weak-mayor type and the strong-mayor type.[23] The general basis of distinction is the extent of the mayor's power as compared with that of the council, particularly in administrative matters. More specifically, the powers mainly involved are those of appointment, removal, and budget-making. Under the weak-mayor plan, most of the department heads are popularly elected or, if they are appointed by the mayor, his

[22] Elsewhere persons charged with criminal violations of city ordinances are prosecuted either by a special city prosecutor or by the regular prosecuting attorney of the district. Concerning the work of the latter officer, see below, Chap. XVII, "The Prosecuting Attorney."

[23] Although this differentiation is useful, the distinction between the two types is by no means exact. Some cities fall clearly within one category or the other, but some have governments which partake of the characteristics of both types to such an extent that classification on this basis is difficult if not impossible.

appointments are subject to council approval. Council approval is also prerequisite to the exercise by the mayor of whatever removal power may be vested in him. The budget is prepared by a council committee, or by a board of which the mayor may be a member but which in any event he does not control. Under such a system, it will readily be seen, the council is in a position to exercise a dominant hand in controlling administrative matters, and the mayor may easily be relegated to the background where he is chief executive in name only. The weak-mayor variety of the mayor-council plan is the original form of American municipal government and exists even today in the large majority of mayor-council cities. Though most widely prevalent among smaller municipalities, some of the larger cities still have governments of this type.

Under the strong-mayor plan, the mayor has unrestricted authority to appoint and remove department heads, and therefore to supervise and direct their work. The budget is prepared either directly by the mayor or by a budget director appointed by and responsible to him. In a few cities in which the financial powers of the mayor are strongest, the council is prohibited from increasing items in the mayor's budget or inserting new items, being limited to making reductions or deletions. The strong-mayor plan thus assures to that officer powers commensurate with his duty of executing the laws and supervising the administration, and makes him the city's chief executive in fact as well as in name. The council has its administrative powers reduced to a minimum and becomes almost exclusively a legislative body for the enactment of ordinances. Thus the separation of legislative and administrative powers is carried out more fully than under the weak-mayor plan. Strong-mayor government has now been established in many mayor-council municipalities, its most widespread adoption being among the larger cities.[24]

A Chief Administrative Officer

During recent decades the administrative position of the mayor in several large cities, including some from both the strong-mayor and weak-mayor groups, has been substantially strengthened by provision for mayoral appointment of a professional managerial officer to serve more or less as a "second in command" in matters of city administration. Founded on the proposition that the mayor, especially in a large city, needs administrative help, the new official is variously entitled chief administrative officer, managing director, business administrator, and the like. His powers and duties, though varying from city to city, fall into three principal

[24] The distinction here made between weak-mayor and strong-mayor government is based, of course, upon the *legal powers* of the mayor and council, respectively. In practice, the actual influence of a particular mayor may depend quite as much upon his personality and qualities of leadership as upon the legal authority vested in his office by charter or statute.

categories: appointment and removal of certain department heads, supervision of various administrative activities, and the provision of advice and
assistance to the mayor. Because the functions of such an administrative
officer are in many respects similar to those of a city manager, the new
plan is sometimes called the mayor-manager plan. It differs essentially,
however, from the council-manager plan, which is discussed below, in
that the managerial officer is appointed by and responsible to the mayor
rather than the council. Proponents of the new scheme believe that it
adapts the manager plan, which in its usual form has not been well received by large cities, to the needs of such municipalities; and that, in so
doing, it secures the advantages of manager government without sacri-
ficing the leadership which may be provided by an elective chief executive. In providing the mayor with professional assistance in the performance of his administrative duties, the new arrangement releases more
mayoral time for attention to matters of policy formation. New York City,
Chicago, Philadelphia, San Francisco, and New Orleans are among the
mayor-council cities which now provide for a managerial officer under
the mayor.[25]

Commission Government[26]

Commission government varies in detail from city to city, but its
essential features are everywhere much the same. Where the plan exists
in its purest form, the only elective officers of the city are the commissioners, usually numbering five but sometimes three or seven. Commissioners are ordinarily elected from the city at large, nomination and election by nonpartisan ballot being the general rule. The commissioners
function in a dual capacity. Collectively, they form the commission or
council, as it is variously called, which is the legislative and policy-determining body of the municipality. Individually, each commissioner serves
as head of one of the administrative departments, the number of departments in a given city equaling the number of commissioners. It will thus
be seen that under this form of government the principle of separation of
powers is abandoned, both legislative and administrative authority being
vested in and exercised by the same officers. Commissioners are usually

25 Wallace S. Sayre, "The General Manager Idea for Large Cities," *Pub.
Admin. Rev.*, XIV, 253-258 (Autumn, 1954). A rejoinder to the Sayre article will be
found in John E. Bebout, "Management for Large Cities," *Ibid.*, XV, 188-195 (Summer, 1955). See also Charles M. Kneier, *City Government in the United States* (3rd
ed.), 211-216.

26 On the subject of commission government, see Ernest S. Bradford, *Commission Government in American Cities*; Henry Bruere, *The New City Government*;
T. S. Chang, *History and Analysis of the Commission and City Manager Plans of Municipal Government in the United States*; Clinton R. Woodruff, ed., *City Government
by Commission*. More recent accounts of the plan will be found in the municipal-
government textbooks included in the list of references at the end of this chapter.

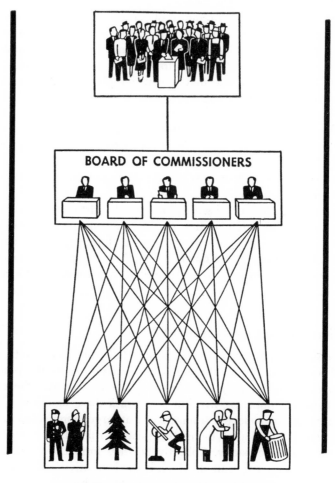

COMMISSION GOVERNMENT

Courtesy of National Municipal League. Reproduced with permission.

paid a regular salary. The office is a full-time position in larger cities, while in smaller municipalities commissioners are sometimes required to devote a specified number of hours per day to their public duties. Most commission laws and charters provide for the initiative, referendum, and recall.[27]

In some cities, individual commissioners are elected to the headship

[27] These devices for direct popular control of government are discussed above, Chap. VI.

of specific departments. Under this plan, each aspirant to a seat on the commission must seek election to a designated administrative post such as that of finance commissioner or commissioner of public works. In other instances, election is merely to membership on the commission, assignment of individual commissioners to particular departments being made by the commission itself by majority vote. One member of the commission, in addition to heading an administrative department, serves as mayor. In some cities the mayor is elected to that post by the voters; in others, he is designated by the commission from its membership: and in still others, it is provided that the commissioner receiving the largest number of votes shall be mayor. However chosen, the mayor is merely the titular head of the city. He presides over council meetings, and performs such social duties as receiving distinguished visitors and representing the city on ceremonial occasions. But otherwise his powers are the same as those of the other commissioners. He has no veto power and in most instances no independent appointing authority.

General administrative officers such as the city clerk, city treasurer, and city attorney are usually appointed by the commission.[28] The power of appointing subordinate personnel in the various departments is likewise vested, in most instances, in the commission as a whole, though in some cities this power rests with the individual commissioners for their respective departments, or with the mayor, to be exercised with commission approval. Even where the commission as a whole is the formal appointing agency, it is not uncommon to find, in practice, a system of reciprocal "courtesy" by which the commission defers to the wishes of each individual commissioner with respect to the selection of personnel for his own department.

Commission government has certain advantages, among the more important of which are a simple and understandable framework of government and the short ballot. On the other hand, serious weaknesses are inherent in the plan. In the larger cities operating under commission government, the system has required the allocation among three, five, or at most seven departments, of functions so numerous as to make quite impossible anything even approximating unifunctional departments. Each department must deal with such a varied list of activities that specialization is impossible and some activities are almost certain to be neglected. Moreover, in a city of considerable size the commission may be too small to be properly representative for legislative purposes. But the most serious weaknesses of commission government, whatever the size of the city, are two: (1) administration by amateurs and (2) decentralization of administrative responsibility.

Students of government have long recognized that, while members

[28] In some instances these officers are popularly elected, but such practice is not in strict accord with the principles of commission government.

of legislative bodies should be elective, competent administrators can best be secured by appointment. Yet, under the commission plan, the heads of administrative departments are chosen by election, and hence their requisite qualification becomes vote-getting ability rather than administrative knowledge or skill. Under such circumstances, it is not only possible but probable that the elected commissioners will be amateurs at the administrative tasks assigned them. Moreover, commission government lacks centralized responsibility for administrative supervision. In theory, to be sure, the individual commissioners as department heads are subject to control by the commission as a whole, which in turn is responsible to the voters for the conduct of administrative matters. But what is envisaged is merely responsibility of the group rather than of a single supervisory official, and even this group responsibility is likely to mean little in practice. So common is the custom on the part of commissions of deferring to the wishes of each individual commissioner with respect to administrative, and even legislative, matters concerning his department, that it is scarcely an overstatement to say that under commission government there are three, five, or seven chief executives, each virtually a petty potentate within his own domain.[29]

Council-Manager Government[30]

The council-manager plan is designed to overcome the principal weaknesses of commission government, namely, administration by amateurs and decentralization of administrative responsibility. The plan emphasizes the professional element in administration, while at the same time placing responsibility for supervising the entire administrative branch upon a single individual—the city manager. The council in manager cities is, on the average, somewhat larger than under the commission plan. Councils of nine or more members are common, and it is not unusual for at least a part of the councilmen to be elected by wards or districts. The nonpartisan form of election is used in many manager cities. As under the commission plan, there is no separation of legislative and administrative powers, both being vested in the council. But although no separation of *powers* exists, there is a separation of *functions*. The council itself exer-

[29] Cf. Howard G. Fishack, "Commission Government Has Not Redeemed Newark," *Annals of Amer. Acad. of Polit. and Soc. Sci.*, CXCIX, 71-77 (Sept., 1938).

[30] On the council-manager system, see Chang, *op. cit.;* Leonard D. White, *The City Manager;* Clarence E. Ridley and Orin F. Nolting, *The City-Manager Profession;* Charles P. Taft, *City Management: The Cincinnati Experiment;* Harold A. Stone, Don K. Price, and Kathryn H. Stone, *City Manager Government in the United States;* National Municipal League, *The Story of the Council-Manager Plan* (28th ed.); Stuart A. MacCorkle, "Small Manager Cities Thrive," *Nat. Mun. Rev.*, XXXIX, 130-135 (Mar., 1950); Charles M. Kneier, "The City Manager and the Courts," *Pub. Management*, XXXIII, 148-154 (July, 1951); William A. Sommers, "Council-Manager Government: A Review," *Western Polit. Quar.*, XI, 137-148 (Mar., 1958).

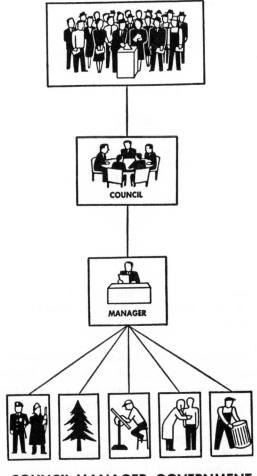

COUNCIL-MANAGER GOVERNMENT

Courtesy of National Municipal League. Reproduced with permission.

cises the legislative function; but, instead of the councilmen also carrying on the administrative work of the city, the council appoints a manager who in turn selects the department heads and supervises administrative activities.[31]

[31] There are some manager charters and laws which require that managerial appointments have council approval. Such provisions, however, are in violation of one of the basic principles of the manager system, namely, that the manager's administrative authority should be made commensurate with his responsibility by giving him a completely free hand in the selection of his subordinates.

It will thus be seen that, under the council-manager plan, the council has two primary functions: (1) to serve as the city's legislative body, enacting ordinances and resolutions expressive of municipal public policy; and (2) to appoint the city manager. The principal duties of the manager ordinarily include the following:[32]

1. To see that all laws and ordinances are enforced.

2. To exercise control over all departments and appoint, supervise, and remove department heads and subordinate employees subject to personnel regulations.

3. To make such recommendations to the council concerning the affairs of the city as may seem to him desirable.

4. To keep the council advised of the financial condition and future needs of the city.

5. To prepare and submit to the council the annual budget.

6. To prepare and submit to the council such reports as may be required by that body.

7. To keep the public informed, through reports to the council, regarding the operations of the city government.

In addition, manager charters and laws usually state that the manager shall perform such other duties as may be prescribed by charter or statutory provision or required of him by ordinance or resolution of the council.[33]

The office of mayor is generally retained under the council-manager system but, as under the commission plan, the mayor is merely the titular head of the city government. Though popularly elected in some instances, he is usually chosen by the council from its own members. He presides over council meetings and is the city's ceremonial head, but possesses neither appointing nor veto power.

The essence of council-manager government lies in the relationship between the elective council and the appointive manager.[34] As the policy-determining body, the council decides what services are to be provided by the city government, how much money shall be spent for those services, and how that money shall be raised. It is the duty of the manager, as the city's principal administrative officer, to carry out the policies and plans of the council as efficiently and economically as possible. Having established general policies, the council is expected to give the manager a free hand in making administrative decisions and in executing council policies through subordinates of his own choosing. Neither the council as a whole

[32] Clarence E. Ridley and Orin F. Nolting, *The City-Manager Profession* (Univ. of Chicago Press, Chicago, 1934), 17-18.

[33] Cf. *Ibid.*

[34] The council-manager plan of city government has sometimes been compared to the corporate form of organization in private enterprise, with the voters representing the stockholders, the council the board of directors, and the city manager the superintendent or general manager of the corporation.

nor any individual councilman should attempt to control the manager in his administrative action. The task of the manager, stated in general terms, is that of producing satisfactory results in the administration of the city's work program, and for the production of such results he is directly responsible to the council. If the manager's administration becomes unsatisfactory, he may be dismissed at any time by the council, since he is appointed to serve at the council's pleasure and not for a definite term.[35]

Just as the council must not dictate to the manager in administrative matters, so the manager, on his part, must refrain from attempting to control the council in matters of policy. This is not to imply, however, that the manager exercises no influence in policy-making. In the words of Clarence E. Ridley, who was for many years Executive Director of the International City Managers' Association, "The city manager by the very nature of his job acts as a policy formulator." Policy-formulation and administration inevitably overlap, and best results require teamwork between councilmen and manager.[36] It is the duty of the manager to make recommendations, to supply the council with information, and to advise the council upon request; and, to facilitate the carrying out of these aspects of the managerial function, it is usually made the duty of the manager to attend council meetings. But the manager must remember at all times that he is primarily the executor, and not the determiner, of municipal policy, and must never urge, in policy matters, the acceptance of his judgment as opposed to that of the council. When, as has unfortunately occurred in some instances, either council or manager invades the province and usurps the functions of the other, the entire theory of the manager system breaks down.

Council-manager charters and laws usually provide that the manager shall be appointed without reference to political affiliation and that he need not be, when appointed, a resident of the city.[37] The purpose of the latter provision is to enable the council, in selecting a manager, to canvass the entire country for the best qualified person obtainable for the salary that it is felt the city can afford to pay. The ideal manager should be a versatile person, since he will be called upon to deal with matters relating to engineering, law, finance, social welfare, and many other fields. Since so much of the city's work is of an engineering nature, it is not surprising that many managers have been drawn from the en-

---

[35] An occasional charter or law makes the manager removable by popular recall. This, however, is not in accordance with the theory of manager government that the manager's direct responsibility is solely to the council, and that he is responsible to the voters only indirectly through the council. In a few instances the manager is appointed for a fixed term, but this is undesirable as weakening the council's ultimate control over administration.

[36] Clarence E. Ridley, *The Role of the City Manager in Policy Formulation*, 1-2.

[37] Notwithstanding these legal provisions, politics sometimes enters into the selection of managers, and many councils in practice tend to prefer local men.

gineering profession. This may be justifiable in smaller municipalities. But in large cities, with their manifold activities, it is more essential that the manager be a person with general executive ability, skilled in the selection and supervision of subordinates and having a well-rounded social viewpoint, than that he be especially skilled in engineering or any other single field of knowledge. In such cities the "expert" element in administration can readily be provided by the department heads or their subordinates. A sizable number of present-day managers have bachelor's degrees, and some of them master's degrees, in public administration. The salaries paid to managers vary, in a general way, with the size of the city served. In 1963, in manager cities of more than 10,000 population, the range was from $6,000 to $30,000.[38]

Like other forms of city government, the council-manager plan has its advantages and disadvantages, real and alleged. Perhaps the two outstanding advantages of the plan are (1) the centralization in a single official of responsibility for administrative supervision, and (2) the emphasis of the professional element in the selection of this chief administrator. Manager government is superior to the weak-mayor and commission plans with respect to both of these factors, and with respect to the second is preferable to the strong-mayor system also. Whereas political availability is usually an important factor in the selection of an elective mayor, the appointive manager, where the plan operates properly, is chosen solely on the basis of his training, experience, and other qualifications for administrative work.

Two objections commonly offered to the council-manager plan are (1) that it is undemocratic, and (2) that it fails to make adequate provision for the political leadership desirable in matters of policy-formulation. To the first of these objections there is actually no substance. It is based upon the assumption that, since the manager is appointed rather than elected, the result will be a chief executive irresponsive to the public will and beyond popular control. To this contention it may be replied that the manager is appointed by a council chosen directly by, and subject to the control of, the voters. Moreover, a small council is in a much better position than the general public to observe and evaluate the work of a chief executive, and an unsatisfactory manager may be dismissed by the council at any time by simple majority vote. An elective mayor, on the other hand, is chosen for a definite term and, in many instances, is removable from office prior to the expiration of that term only by extraordinary vote of the council, or sometimes by popular recall or other special proceeding. The argument with respect to lack of political leadership has somewhat more validity, but by no means condemns the plan. The theory of the manager system is that leadership in political, as distinguished from administrative, matters will be supplied by the mayor; but it must be

[38] *The Municipal Year Book*, 1963, pp. 222-224.

admitted that experience has failed to demonstrate that this is usually the case. Indeed, the weak position of the mayor under the manager plan may discourage persons with qualities of leadership from seeking that office. On the other hand, it should be remembered that many mayors under the mayor-council system fail to provide strong and wholesome leadership. And finally, it may well be that the predominant position of the council under the manager plan will tend to encourage the development of political leadership within that elective body.[39]

Some Observations on Governmental Forms

In contrast with the situation in Europe, where practically all cities of a particular country have the same general form of governmental organization, substantial variety exists in American municipal government. Here we have developed three major forms of city government—four if we choose to regard as distinct forms the weak-mayor and strong-mayor types of the mayor-council system. Moreover, there are, even among cities having governments of the same general type, numerous variations in detail. This being the case, it is not surprising that there has been considerable controversy concerning the relative merits of the respective forms of city government.

Some of the advantages and weaknesses of the different forms have been noted in the previous discussion. From the original weak-mayor system, strong-mayor government developed, as we have seen, with a view to centralizing administrative responsibility and stressing the separation of legislative and administrative powers. This development was doubtless due in no small measure to a disposition, conscious or otherwise, to imitate, in the municipal field, the institutions of our federal government. Strong-mayor government is constantly gaining in favor, especially among the larger cities, and seems destined to spread in the future. It is likely, however, that the weak-mayor system will be continued in the large majority of smaller municipalities for many years to come.

The commission plan, during its heyday, seemed to give most cities adopting it better government than they had experienced under the older forms which the commission system supplanted. This may have been due in part to the fact that any substantial change in the form of government is likely to be accompanied by a temporary awakening of public interest in governmental affairs. But the new plan was naturally most often adopted by cities that were dissatisfied with their existing governments; and resulting improvements probably flowed in no small measure from

[39] Various aspects of the problem of political leadership in manager cities are considered, under the general topic "Leadership and Decision-Making in Manager Cities," in articles by Charles R. Adrian, Dorothee Strauss, and Karl A. Bosworth, respectively, in *Pub. Admin. Rev.*, XVIII, 208-222 (Summer, 1958).

the fact that the reduction in the size of the council (commission), elected at large, served to eliminate from public office many of the persons who had been responsible for the unsatisfactory conditions prevailing under the preexisting system. Although commission government has continued to give reasonable satisfaction in many of the cities where it operates, it was early revealed to have certain inherent weaknesses, especially as compared with the newer council-manager plan; and these have operated to check its spread and in some instances have caused its abandonment. With respect to the number of cities operating under it, the commission plan during recent decades has certainly made no net gain and probably has actually lost ground. Though the plan will doubtless be retained in many of the cities where it now exists, its adoption by any large number of additional cities is highly improbable.

The council-manager plan, with its emphasis upon a professional, business-like method of conducting municipal administration, is the latest and most promising major development in city-government forms. This is by no means to say that manager government is a panacea for all municipal ills, nor is it to suggest that all cities should adopt the plan. But the facts that manager government has spread steadily since its inception more than fifty years ago, and that the number of abandonments of the plan has been extremely small,[40] indicate that it has given satisfaction in a large majority of the municipalities where it has been tried. The plan is seemingly best adapted to cities of moderate size, rather than to either the very largest or the smallest. It presupposes the responsibility of the manager to a council small enough to exercise vigilant surveillance over his work, and in very large cities so small a council may not afford adequate representation for legislative purposes. In very small cities municipal activities may be too meager and the tax base too narrow to make the employment of a full-time manager financially feasible.[41] Nevertheless, present manager municipalities vary in population from less than a thousand to more than a half-million. The record of manager government to date is, on the whole, outstandingly good, and its prospects for the future are bright. There seems to be little doubt that the plan is destined to spread steadily; but that it will become the predominant form of American city government in the foreseeable future is extremely unlikely.

From what has been said, it will be apparent that the present-day trend is away from the weak-mayor and commission forms of government

[40] From 1908 to 1963 only 97 local units abandoned manager government by popular vote, and 22 of these subsequently readopted the plan. See *The Municipal Year Book*, 1963, p. 309. Concerning reasons for abandonment, see Arthur W. Bromage, *Manager Plan Abandonments* (Nat. Mun. League, New York, 6th ed., 1964). Cf. Edwin O. Stene and George K. Floro, *Abandonments of the Manager Plan: A Study of Four Small Cities* (Govtl. Research Center, Univ. of Kan., Lawrence, 1953).

[41] It is possible, of course, for a single manager to serve more than one small municipality, as is now being done in a few instances.

and toward the strong-mayor and council-manager plans. Though the two latter forms, as we have seen, differ in some fundamental respects, they are similar in that both provide for centralizing administrative responsibility in the hands of a single chief administrator; and it is this factor no doubt, more than any other, that accounts for the increasing popularity of these plans as compared with the more decentralized forms. Extreme administrative decentralization, in municipal government as elsewhere, is falling into disrepute.

In concluding these observations, the question may well be raised as to whether there is not a tendency today to attach too much importance to mere *forms* of government. It has long been recognized that the relative efficiency of government is determined by the interaction of two factors: (1) the forms of governmental organization, and (2) the character of the public officials and employees who operate that organization. That the matter of governmental form is important there can be no doubt, for proper organization will aid honest and competent officials in providing public services efficiently and economically. But the best form of organization will mean little if the machinery of government falls into the hands of corrupt or incompetent officials, or of officials who refuse to observe the spirit as well as the letter of the form of organization they operate.

Too often public-spirited citizens' organizations have fought valiantly and successfully for the adoption of some improvement in governmental form, only then to let down, draw a sigh of relief at a task sup· posedly done, and permit control of the new organization to slip into the hands of politicians. The manager plan, for example, offers splendid possibilities as a form of government. But if, as has been the case at times in Kansas City, the voters elect a machine-dominated council which appoints a politician as manager, government may be as thoroughly boss-ridden under a manager charter as under the mayor-council system. And if, as occurred in Cleveland, the manager insists upon being a political leader and the council submits to his domination, the spirit of manager government completely ceases to function.[42] On the other hand, that competent and high-minded officials often achieve good results under less modern governmental forms has been amply demonstrated. An outstanding example of this fact is afforded by the government of Milwaukee, usually

[42] See Leonard White, *The City Manager*, Chaps. 1, 3. On the Kansas City situation, see also Walter Matscheck, "Kansas City: Where the Manager Plan has Failed," *Annals of Amer. Acad. of Polit. and Soc. Sci.*, CXCIX, 57-63 (Sept., 1938). At other times the manager plan has operated effectively in Kansas City. See Stanley High, "Kansas City Has Its Chin Up," *Nat. Mun. Rev.*, XXX, 561-564 (Oct., 1941); Kenneth E. Midgley, "Kansas City Citizens Rally to Whip Machine," *Ibid.*, XXXI, 282-284 (May, 1942); Richard B. Fowler, "Kansas City Voters Score Again," *Ibid.*, XXXIII,, 258 (May, 1944); Karl Detzer, "Everything's Changed Now," *Ibid.*, XXXVIII, 320-323, 338 (July, 1949).

classed as a weak-mayor city, under the mayoralty of Daniel W. Hoan which extended over nearly a quarter-century.[43]

Finally, the character of the personnel which will operate our city governments, whatever their form, depends ultimately upon the voters. Democratic government can function at its best only when the general citizenry is informed upon, and takes an active interest in, public affairs. An apathetic electorate invites perversion of the best of government forms. Citizen interest, moreover, must extend continuously to the day-by-day administration of government, and not be limited to periods of reform. One of the best examples of intelligent and influential citizen action is afforded by the City Charter Committee of Cincinnati. This is a citizens' organization which, having campaigned successfully for the adoption of manager government, was given a permanent basis with a view to stimulating public interest in good government, nominating and electing members of the city council, and bringing to bear upon those members the pressure of an interested and informed public opinion.[44]

Government of Villages, Boroughs, and Incorporated Towns

Lesser municipalities, variously known as villages, boroughs, or incorporated towns,[45] generally have as their principal governing agency a board of from three to seven, or occasionally as many as nine, members elected at large. Board members are usually known as trustees or councilmen. Whatever its official title, the governing board is the policy-determining organ of the municipality, controlling municipal finances and exercising such ordinance-making authority as has been conferred upon it by statute. Each village, borough, or town ordinarily has an elective chief officer who is the titular head of the municipality. This official is most commonly entitled mayor or president. Other officers commonly found in these minor municipalities, elected in some cases and appointed in others, are the clerk, treasurer, marshal, and street commissioner. The chief municipal officer usually presides over sessions of the governing body. In some instances his executive powers are not of great importance. In others he is vested with most of the powers possessed by the mayors of larger municipalities, the form of village government in such cases being, in fact if not in name, the mayor-council system. Some states permit villages,

---

[43] Cf. Jewell C. Phillips, "Good Government under the Old Forms," *Annals of Amer. Acad. of Polit. and Soc. Sci.*, CXCIX, 91-98 (Sept., 1938).

[44] The organization, activities, and financing of the City Charter Committee are described in *Citizen Organization for Political Activity: The Cincinnati Plan* (Nat. Mun. League, New York, rev. ed., 1941). The story of the Committee in its earlier years is also related in some detail by Charles P. Taft in his book *City Management: The Cincinnati Experiment.*

[45] See above, Chap. XII, "Municipalities."

boroughs, or towns, like cities, to adopt commission or manager government under optional statutes or to determine their own governmental forms under constitutional home-rule provisions.[46]

Municipal Courts[47]

Municipal courts, whatever their nature, are in reality units of the state judicial system, which has been discussed in a preceding chapter,[48] and have little or no relationship to city-government forms. "City court" or "police court" in smaller municipalities is usually presided over by an elective magistrate known variously by such titles as city judge, police judge, and police magistrate. In some instances the mayor is city magistrate, in which case the court is often referred to as the "mayor's court." These minor courts, whatever their names, ordinarily have jurisdiction over violations of city ordinances, other misdemeanor cases, and civil suits involving not more than a specified amount. They are also empowered to hold preliminary hearings in felony cases. In some instances their jurisdiction is the same as that of justices of the peace, and in others it is somewhat broader.

Some metropolitan cities have been provided with "unified municipal courts"[49] of rather broad jurisdiction, designed to permit some degree of specialization in judicial work. Under this plan, instead of having each judge try cases of all kinds arising anywhere within the city or within a judicial district, all municipal judges are members of a single court which, however, is organized into a number of "divisions," each handling only cases of a particular type. Each member of the court is assigned, usually by a chief justice, to one of the court's divisions, and thus has an opportunity to specialize in cases of a given kind.

The first unified judicial tribunal in a major American city was the Municipal Court of Chicago, which was organized in 1906 to supersede justice-of-the-peace courts and has served in some measure as a pattern for several other municipalities. The Chicago court consisted of thirty-seven elective members—a chief justice and thirty-six associate justices. It had jurisdiction throughout the city over misdemeanor cases and civil controversies of various kinds, and was authorized to hold preliminary hearings in felony cases. In addition to about 12 district police branches, wherein specialization was not practiced, the court was organized into

[46] Further discussion of the government of small municipalities may be found in Charles M. Kneier, *City Government in the United States* (3rd ed.), Chap. 15.

[47] For discussions of judicial administration in cities, see Charles M. Kneier, *City Government in the United States* (3rd ed.), Chap. 27; Benjamin Baker, *Urban Government*, Chaps. 11, 12; Austin F. Macdonald, *American City Government and Administration* (6th ed.), Chap. 13; Jewell Cass Phillips, *Municipal Government and Administration in America*, Chap. 13; Henry Hodges, *City Management*, Chap. 25.

[48] Above, Chap. XI.

[49] On the unified-court concept, see also above, Chap. XI, "Court Unification."

some 24 specialized civil and criminal branches. Civil branches included an attachments and garnishments branch, a rent branch, and a small-claims branch. Among the branches handling criminal matters were a felony court, a traffic court, a boys' court, a domestic relations court, and a morals court.[50] The Chicago court served the city until 1964 when, as part of a statewide program of judicial reorganization, it was absorbed into a new system of circuit courts. Among the cities which now have municipal courts somewhat similar to the Chicago tribunal are Detroit, Cleveland, Philadelphia, Milwaukee, and Atlanta.

Government of Washington, D.C.

No discussion of American municipal government, however brief, should close without some attention to the government of the nation's capital city. The city of Washington, or more properly the District of Columbia (for that is the official title of the municipal corporation),[51] is governed as provided by Congress under its express constitutional authority "to exercise exclusive legislation . . . over such district . . . as may . . . become the seat of the Government of the United States."[52] Under the present system of government, established by a law of 1878, the principal local authority is a commission consisting of two residents of the District, appointed by the President with Senatorial consent for three-year terms, and an officer of the engineer corps of the Army detailed by the President to serve for an indefinite term as engineer commissioner.[53] This

---

[50] Albert Lepawsky *The Judicial System of Metropolitan Chicago* (Univ. of Chicago Press, Chicago, 1932), 25-28.

[51] The city of Washington has been coextensive with the District of Columbia since 1895. The District has a land area of 61 square miles, and had a 1960 population of 763,956. This made it the country's ninth city in number of inhabitants, its population exceeding that of eleven of the fifty states.

[52] *Const. of U.S.*, art. I, sec. 8.

[53] Concerning the District's government, see Laurence F. Schmeckebier, *The District of Columbia: Its Government and Administration;* Laurence F. Schmeckebier and W. F. Willoughby, *The Government and Administration of the District of Columbia: Proposals for Change* (Brookings Inst., Washington, 1929); Griffenhagen and Associates, *The Organization of Government for the District of Columbia* (U.S. Govt. Printing Office, Washington, 1939); Lewis B. Sims, "Intergovernmental Fiscal Relations in the Nation's Capital," *Nat. Mun. Rev.*, XXVI, 223-229, 240 (May, 1937); Cedric Larson, "The Manager Plan for the Nation's Capital?" *Ibid.*, XXVIII, 371-373, 406 (May, 1939); James C. Auchincloss, "City Manager for Washington?" *Ibid.*, XXXVI, 618-624 (Dec., 1947); Alfred Steinberg, "Let's Set Washington Free," *Ibid.*, XLII, 270-275 (June, 1953); Richard M. Scammon, "Washington Votes Again," *Ibid.*, XLV, 328-333 (July, 1956); Geddes W. Rutherford, "Reorganization of the Government of the District of Columbia," *Amer. Polit. Sci. Rev.*, XXXIII, 653-655 (Aug., 1939); Katherine A. Markwell, "Home Rule for the District of Columbia Without Constitutional Amendment," *Geo. Washington Law Rev.*, III, 205-218 (Jan., 1935); Lucy Somerville Howorth, "The Griffenhagen Report," *Fed. Bar Assn. Jour.*, III, 305-308 (Apr., 1939); Merlo J. Pusey, "Washington: A National Disgrace," *Forum*, CII, 241-248 (Dec., 1939); Alden Stevens, "Washington: Blight on Democracy," *Harper's Mag.*, CLXXXIV, 50-58 (Dec., 1941).

three-member commission functions as a plural executive, being charged with law enforcement and the supervision of administrative activities. It has also been vested by Congress with limited legislative powers of a local nature concerning such matters as police, building regulation, and health. Principal legislative authority over the District, however, including financial control, is exercised directly by Congress. Many administrative agencies of the federal government are charged with District functions; and the courts of the District are federal courts.[54]

Since a large proportion of the property within the District is owned by the federal government and is therefore exempt from local taxation, Congress makes an annual contribution toward the support of the District government. The amount of the federal contribution was fixed in 1878 at 50 percent of District expenditures, but was subsequently reduced to 40 percent. In 1925 Congress began the practice of making its contribution in the form of a lump sum rather than a percentage of District expenditures, and the tendency has been for the federal contribution to constitute an ever decreasing portion of the District budget.[55] Indeed, the federal contribution for at least one fairly recent year amounted to less than 9 percent of the District's total expenditures.[56]

There has long been widespread dissatisfaction with the present system of District government. Several survey studies have been conducted and various proposals for modification have been made, but as yet no major change has been effected. In the matter of administration, it will be noted that the District government is somewhat analogous to the commission form discussed earlier in this chapter, and, like that form, fails to centralize administrative responsibility. The fact that District functions are divided between the federal and local governments makes for confusion, and the allocation of costs between the two governments is a difficult problem. In 1939, in reporting the results of a study made under congressional authority, the firm of Griffenhagen and Associates characterized the District government as "unbelievably complex, confused, illogical, and cumbersome." They recommended abolition of the present commission and the creation of a governing body of five or seven members (the method of selecting the governing body was excluded from the study). This body would be vested with full ordinance-making power in local matters, thus relieving Congress of responsibility for looking after detailed local affairs. All administrative authority would be centralized in a District Administrator, appointed for an indefinite term either by the governing body or by the President on the body's recommendation and having many of the attributes of a city manager. Seventeen administrative departments would be provided, the heads of which would be appointed

[54] Cf. Howorth, *op. cit.;* Auchincloss, *op. cit.*
[55] Sims, *op. cit.*
[56] Steinberg, *op. cit.*

by the Administrator.[57] More recently a congressional committee, on the basis of exhaustive study, recommended an outright manager plan with a locally-elected council and eleven administrative departments.[58]

From what has been said, it will doubtless have occurred to the reader that the District government includes no locally-elected officers. District residents have, to be sure, means of expressing their views on local matters, as, for example, in hearings before congressional committees and through a citizens' advisory council.[59] Nevertheless, they have no direct participation, through the electoral process, in their local government, which in reality performs the combined functions of state, county, and municipality. Moreover, though many persons who live more or less permanently in Washington retain a legal residence in some state and may vote there by absentee ballot or otherwise, those whose legal residence is within the District were until recently completely disfranchised in national elections as well. In 1955 Congress passed an act permitting District residents, through party elections called primaries, to choose District members of the national party committees, delegates and alternates to national nominating conventions, and members of local party committees.[60] And the Twenty-third Amendment to the United States Constitution, adopted in 1961, authorizes the District to choose presidential electors equal in number to the number of Representatives and Senators in Congress to which the District would be entitled if it were a state, provided that the District shall in no event have more electors than the least populous state. Accordingly, District residents at present choose their party officials and participate in the election of the President and Vice President. Even now, however, they elect no local officers and no members of Congress. It is to be hoped that the recent measures in the direction of conferring suffrage upon District residents will prove to be but early steps in a broader program of enfranchisement.

REFERENCES

ADRIAN, Charles R., *Governing Urban America* (McGraw-Hill, New York, 1955).

ANDERSON, William, and WEIDNER, Edward W., *American City Government* (Holt, New York, rev. ed., 1950).

BAKER, Benjamin, *Urban Government* (Van Nostrand, Princeton, N.J.: 1957).

[57] Griffenhagen and Associates, *op. cit.*

[58] Auchincloss, *op. cit.*

[59] William H. Young, *Ogg and Ray's Introduction to American Government* (Appleton-Century-Crofts, New York, 11th ed., 1956), 655.

[60] "Party Primaries for Washington, D.C.," *Nat. Mun. Rev.*, XLIV, 527 (Nov., 1955); Scammon, *op. cit.*

BRADFORD, Ernest S., *Commission Government in American Cities* (Macmillan, New York, 1911).

BROMAGE, Arthur W., *Introduction to Municipal Government and Administration* (Appleton-Century-Crofts, New York, 2nd ed., 1957).

———, *On the City Council* (Geo. Wahr Pub. Co., Ann Arbor, Mich., 1950).

BRUERE, Henry, *The New City Government: A Discussion of Municipal Administration Based on a Survey of Ten Commission Governed Cities* (Appleton, New York, 1913).

CHANG, T. S., *History and Analysis of the Commission and City Manager Plans of Municipal Government in the United States* (Univ. of Ia., Iowa City, 1918).

HOAN, Daniel W., *City Government: The Record of the Milwaukee Experiment* (Harcourt, New York, 1936).

International City Managers' Association, *The Municipal Year Book* (Int. City Mgrs'. Assn., Chicago, annually).

KNEIER, Charles M., *City Government in the United States* (Harper, New York, 3rd ed., 1957).

MacCORKLE, Stuart A., *American Municipal Government and Administration* (Heath, Boston, 1948).

MACDONALD, Austin F., *American City Government and Administration* (Crowell, New York, 6th ed., 1956), Part I.

MUNRO, William B., *The Government of American Cities* (Macmillan, New York, 4th ed., 1926).

National Municipal League, *Forms of Municipal Government: How Have They Worked?* (Nat. Mun. League, New York, 1951).

———, *The Story of the Council-Manager Plan* (Nat. Mun. League, New York, 28th ed., 1962).

PEEL, Roy V., ed., "Better City Government," *Annals of Amer. Acad. of Polit. and Soc. Sci.*, CXCIX, Philadelphia, Sept., 1938.

PHILLIPS, Jewell Cass, *Municipal Government and Administration in America* (Macmillan, New York, 1960).

REED, Thomas H., *Municipal Government in the United States* (Appleton-Century, New York, rev. ed., 1934).

RIDLEY, Clarence E., *The Role of the City Manager in Policy Formulation* (Int. City Mgrs'. Assn., Chicago, 1958).

———, and Nolting, Orin F., *The City-Manager Profession* (Univ. of Chicago Press, Chicago, 1934).

SCHMECKEBIER, Laurence F., *The District of Columbia: Its Government and Administration* (Johns Hopkins Press, Baltimore, 1928).

STONE, Harold A., PRICE, Don K., and STONE, Kathryn H., *City Manager Government in the United States: A Review After Twenty-Five Years* (Pub. Admin. Service, Chicago, 1940).

STORY, Russell M., *The American Municipal Executive* (Univ. of Ill., Urbana, 1918).

TAFT, Charles P., *City Management: The Cincinnati Experiment* (Holt, New York, 1933).

WHITE, Leonard D., *The City Manager* (Univ. of Chicago Press, Chicago, 1927).

WOODRUFF, Clinton R., ed., *City Government by Commission* (Appleton, New York, 1911).

ZINK, Harold, *Government of Cities in the United States* (Macmillan, New York, rev. ed., 1948).

15

Towns, Townships, and Special Districts

NEW ENGLAND TOWN GOVERNMENT

The Town Meeting

The New England town affords the outstanding example in the United States today of a governmental unit which operates as a direct democracy instead of employing a representative body for purposes of policy-determination.[1] The principal governing authority of the town is the town meeting.[2] Every qualified voter of the town is eligible to attend this primary assembly, and in many instances, particularly in the rural towns, a considerable proportion of those entitled to attend actually do so. A regular "annual" meeting is held in each town during

---

[1] Township meetings, frequently in a somewhat degenerate form, are held in certain other states; and annual school meetings serve as the policy-determining organs of school districts in some states both within and outside New England. See below, "Township Government," "School District Government."

[2] See Clyde F. Snider, *Local Government in Rural America*, 195-199; Max R. White, *The Connecticut Town Meeting* (rev. ed.); Samuel T. Williamson, "Town Meeting at Salt Harbor," *N.Y. Times Mag.*, Mar. 21, 1948, pp. 16, 29-31; John W. Alexander and Morroe Berger, "Is the Town Meeting Finished?" *Amer. Mercury*, LXIX, 144-151 (Aug., 1949); Lincoln Smith, "Town Meeting Government," *Soc. Science*, XXX, 174-185 (June, 1955); Kendall Banning, "Is the Town Meeting Democratic?" *Nat. Mun. Rev.*, XXIV, 152-155 (Mar., 1935); Ernest G. Miller, "Farewell Town Meeting," *Ibid.*, XLVII, 162-165, 170 (Apr., 1958).

the spring months (except in Connecticut, where the meeting is usually in October); and there are such special meetings during the year as are found necessary for the transaction of town business. Special meetings may be called at the discretion of the board of selectmen, and in some states must be called upon application of a specified number or percentage of the town's voters. Each meeting, whether annual or special, is held in response to a warrant or "warning" issued by the selectmen, designating the exact time and place of the meeting and setting forth an agendum of the business to be transacted. In early times the townsmen were notified of meetings by constables calling at each house, but nowadays notification is by publication and posting. Town meetings are usually held in a town hall. If a town has but a single village (as a trading center or hamlet is commonly called even though unincorporated), the town hall is frequently located there; but if there are several such settlements the hall may be erected near the town's geographical center, which may not be within any village. If the town hall is too small to accommodate the number of voters likely to attend, the meeting may be held in a school auditorium or some other more commodious building.

The principal functions of the annual town meeting are (1) to receive the reports of town officers, (2) to levy taxes, (3) to vote appropriations for the ensuing year, (4) to authorize necessary borrowing, (5) to elect town officers, and (6) to enact bylaws for the government of the town. The presiding officer of the meeting is the moderator. Originally, each meeting was called to order by the town clerk, and the group selected a moderator from its membership. This plan of selecting a citizen-moderator for each individual meeting was believed to lessen the possibility that the town officers might tend to dominate the meeting should one of their number preside, and the plan is still in widespread use. In some cases today, however, the moderator is elected for a definite term and presides over all meetings during that term. Vermont towns, for example, elect their moderators in an annual town meeting for a one-year term; while in New Hampshire the moderator is elected at the regular biennial election for a term of two years. Whatever the tenure and method of selection, it is a common practice for the same person to be chosen as moderator again and again over a period of years.[3] The town clerk serves as secretary of the meeting.

As soon as the meeting has been organized, polls are opened for election of the principal town officers by secret ballot.[4] Voting continues throughout the day, even while the business session, which ordinarily does

---

[3] Recent trends in the office are considered by Lincoln Smith in his article "The Moderator in Eclipse," *Amer. Quar.*, XI, 166-177 (Summer, 1959).

[4] Though this is the traditional method of choosing town officers and is still followed in many places, officers are now chosen in some instances in separate town elections—sometimes occurring on a different date from that of the town meeting.

not begin until after noon, is in progress.[5] Some voters, more interested in personalities than in issues, vote for officers but do not attend the business session. It frequently happens that the business included in the warrant for the annual meeting is so heavy that one or more adjourned sessions are necessary to dispose of it.

The New England town meeting has had an illustrious history, and it seems still to function satisfactorily in many rural communities. In many other communities, however, meeting attendance has declined markedly, with the same small group of persons, in some instances, dominating meeting proceedings year after year.[6] Populous towns, on the other hand, face problems of a somewhat different nature.[7] The mere fact of a large population is likely to result in a large and unwieldy meeting, and may well mean that the town hall will not accommodate all of the voters who wish to attend. Operation of the town meeting in the more populous towns has been further complicated by European immigration, which has introduced population elements unaccustomed to democratic institutions and, especially in industrial communities, has fostered factionalism. These factors have caused many of the larger towns to consider how traditional town government might be modified to meet changed conditions. It has indeed been said by a careful student that there is scarcely a New England town of over 5,000 population which has not, since the turn of the century, debated the question of reform or abolition of the town meeting.[8] In some instances the weaknesses of the town meeting in its original form have been overcome, at least in part, by adoption of the representative town meeting, which will be discussed presently.

A special problem is presented by those rural towns of a resort character in which much of the taxable property is owned by nonresidents who have purchased homes for occupation during the summer months only. Many of these owners of summer homes maintain their legal residence elsewhere and therefore do not qualify as town voters, and in any event they are usually absent from the town when the regular town meeting is held. Under these circumstances, a relatively small number of permanent residents are in a position, in the town meeting, to levy taxes and make appropriations from which they may stand to benefit, but the burden of which must be borne by taxpayers who are not represented in the meeting. A possible remedy for this undesirable situation, though necessitating statutory and perhaps constitutional changes, has been sug-

---

[5] In some instances caucuses are held prior to the town meeting to nominate candidates for office.

[6] Duane Lockard, *The Politics of State and Local Government* (Macmillan, New York, 1963), 327-328; James Wilson and Robert W. Crowe, *Managers in Maine,* 10; Andrew E. Nuquist, "March Meeting," *Vermont Life,* Vol. I, No. 3, pp. 9-11, 39 (Spring, 1947).

[7] Cf. Lane W. Lancaster, *Government in Rural America* (2nd ed.), 41-42.

[8] Orren C. Hormell, *Maine Towns,* 17.

gested in the form of a referendum by mail in which nonresident tax-payers would be afforded an opportunity to vote for or against proposed appropriations of substantial amount.[9]

The Board of Selectmen

The principal administrative agency of the town is the board of selectmen (called the town council in Rhode Island). This board ordinarily consists of three, five, or seven members, with the three-member board most common. Selectmen are elected at the town meeting or at a separate town election where such is held. In some instances their term is a single year, but in others a longer term is provided. The towns of Vermont and New Hampshire, and some of those in Massachusetts, choose their selectmen for three-year staggered terms; some Connecticut towns elect their selectmen biennially; and in Maine terms of longer than one year are permissible. Whatever the term of office, reelection tends to be the custom. The compensation of selectmen, like that of most other town officers, is usually regulated by town bylaws and, except in the more populous communities, is relatively small.[10]

The selectmen carry on the business of the town between town meetings. Their specific duties, which are numerous and varied, are prescribed by state statutes and town bylaws. The function of the selectmen in issuing warrants for calling town meetings has already been noted. They have charge of town property, lay out highways, and conduct elections. They examine claims against the town and issue orders for their payment. Authority is usually vested in the selectmen to grant numerous kinds of licenses; and, in the larger towns, the granting of licenses and permits for building and construction purposes, and for regulating hawkers, peddlers, lodging houses, gasoline stations, and various kinds of amusements, is a time-consuming function. In some smaller towns the selectmen act as assessors, overseers of the poor, and health officers, though elsewhere individual officials are provided for the performance of those duties. The selectmen are also charged with the appointment of various minor town officers. In Massachusetts, for instance, the statutes provide for some forty separate officers who are appointed, under specified circumstances, by the selectmen.[11]

The Town Clerk

Apart from the board of selectmen, the most important town officer is the clerk. Indeed, from the standpoint of general services performed,

---

[9] Banning, *op. cit.*
[10] See John F. Sly, *Town Government in Massachusetts*, 158, footnote 3.
[11] *Ibid.*, 156-157.

the clerk may well be considered to outrank the selectmen. The clerk in most instances is elected annually, though in Connecticut his term of office is two years. In any case, reelection is common. It is not unusual for the same person to be retained in the office for twenty to forty years, and occasionally the office remains in the same family for successive generations.[12]

The clerk keeps a record of the proceedings of town meetings, and is custodian of the town archives in general. He registers births, marriages, and deaths; in Connecticut, Vermont, and Rhode Island is recorder of deeds; and in Rhode Island is clerk of the probate court. Not only is he charged by statute with a great variety of duties, but he is the person to whom other town officers and townsmen alike appeal for all sorts of information. In a very real sense, he is the general factotum of the town.[13]

Other Town Officers

An elective town treasurer receives town revenues, is responsible for their custody, and pays claims against the town on order of the selectmen.

Assessors and overseers of the poor are elected in the larger towns and some of the smaller ones as well. Town assessors are charged with the assessment of real estate and personal property for purposes of state and local taxation. Overseers of the poor (now known in some instances as overseers or directors of public welfare) care for town paupers and, where such an institution is maintained, supervise the town almshouse.

The elective peace officer of the town is the constable,[14] with duties corresponding in general to those of the sheriff in the county. As in the case of the typical sheriff, the constable of the present day gives relatively little time to the enforcement of criminal law. He is chiefly a process-server for the selectmen and justices of the peace, sometimes acting also as a tax collector. Though considered as state rather than town officers, justices of the peace are in some instances elected by towns.[15]

An elective school board or committee has control of the town schools.[16] Highway officers with various titles are elected, or appointed by the selectmen.

[12] Ibid., 157.

[13] Cf. Roger H. Wells, American Local Government, 84.

[14] In Rhode Island there is also a town sergeant, with duties similar in some respects to those of the constable.

[15] Justice-of-the-peace courts are discussed above, Chap. XI.

[16] In general, the town is the unit for local school administration in New England, functioning either through the regular town government or as a legally distinct school corporation. However, there are some instances of smaller school districts organized within the towns and independent of the town school units. See below, footnote 26.

The statutes provide, for some or all towns, a lengthy list of minor officers, some of them elected, but most of them now appointed by the selectmen. These include, among others, sealers of weights and measures, poundkeepers, fence-viewers, surveyors of lumber, forest-fire wards, fish wardens, and inspectors of various kinds.[17]

Recent Developments in Town Organization: The Representative Town Meeting

Pure democracy, under which governmental authority is exercised directly by the voters in primary assemblies, is practicable only within limited areas having comparatively small populations. In extensive regions, or in smaller areas with large populations, direct democracy must give way to democratic institutions of the representative type. This has been the experience of New England, where several of the more populous towns of Massachusetts, and a few towns in other states, have found it expedient to abandon the town meeting in its traditional form for the representative or "limited" meeting.

As this newer plan operates in Massachusetts, the town is divided by the selectmen into precincts, with the voters of each precinct electing an equal number of delegates to serve as "town meeting members." These elected members, together with various town officers designated as members ex officio, make up the town meeting. This representative meeting possesses substantially the same powers as the plenary meeting which it supplants. Any elector of the town is entitled to speak at meetings of the representative assembly, but voting is restricted to members.[18] Representative meetings were recently reported as varying in size, in most instances, from 50 to 150 members.[19]

The first Massachusetts town to adopt the representative town meeting was Brookline, which did so in 1915 in pursuance of a special enabling act passed by the Massachusetts general court (legislature) earlier in the same year. By 1928 fourteen other Massachusetts towns had followed Brookline's example and adopted the plan, in each instance by popular vote pursuant to legislative authorization. All of these fifteen towns had relatively large populations—the smallest around 9,000. Prior to 1926 the state constitution as interpreted by the courts prevented the legislature from authorizing the adoption of the representative town meeting by towns of less than 12,000 population, but a constitutional amendment of that year provided that the plan might be authorized in any town of more than 6,000 inhabitants.[20] The fact that the legislature, between

---

[17] Cf. Snider, *Local Government in Rural America*, 203 and footnote 37.
[18] Sly, *op. cit.*, Chap. 7.
[19] Lockard, *op. cit.*, 329.
[20] Sly, *op. cit.*, Chap. 7.

1928 and 1940, authorized adoption of the representative meeting in some eighteen additional towns would seem to indicate that the plan was giving general satisfaction in those communities which had adopted it earlier.[21] In 1931 a law was enacted providing a standard form of representative town meeting government that may be adopted by any Massachusetts town in which a representative town meeting has been established by special statute. The standard act, when adopted by any such town, replaces the special legislative act under which the town previously operated.[22]

Outside Massachusetts, little use has been made of the representative town meeting. However, ten Connecticut towns were reported in 1963 to be operating under the plan;[23] and it is used by at least one town each in Maine and Vermont.

Finance Committees

As an agency for determining fiscal policy, the town meeting has suffered from the need for a consideration of the town's financial problems, and the formulation of a tentative financial program, by some smaller body prior to the annual meeting. This need, which exists in all towns but is more acute in the larger communities, has been met in a measure in some instances by requiring the board of selectmen to prepare a budget for submission to the meeting. Another approach to the problem is through the establishment of a special budget-making agency. Known variously by such titles as finance committee, finance board, and budget committee, agencies of this nature are now employed in many towns, including a substantial number in each of four states: Connecticut, New Hampshire, Maine, and Massachuetts.

The Connecticut statutes provide that any town may, at any annual or special town meeting, vote to establish a six-member board of finance. Members of the board are elected for overlapping terms of three years in towns having annual elections and six years in those where elections are biennial. It is the duty of the board, after a public hearing, to prepare the town budget for presentation to the town meeting. The finance board is in a particularly strong position since, though the town meeting may reduce or strike out items from the budget as prepared by the board, it may not increase items or insert additional ones.[24]

Under the terms of a municipal budget law originally enacted in

[21] See Alexander Lincoln, "Some Notes on Representative Town Meetings," *Mass. Law Quar.*, Vol. XXXIII, No. 1, pp. 30-46 (Apr., 1948).

[22] *Ann. Laws of Mass.*, 1952, Chap. 43a.

[23] *Nat. Civic Rev.*, LII, 104 (Feb., 1963).

[24] *Gen. Stats. of Conn.*, 1958, secs. 7-340, 7-344, 9-202; John E. Dever and Joseph M. Loughlin, "Financial Control through Boards of Finance," *Mun. Finance*, XXIV, 97-100 (Nov., 1951).

1935, any New Hampshire town may, by vote of the annual town meeting, establish a budget committee.[25] This committee consists of three, six, nine, or twelve members at large, who may either be appointed by the moderator or elected by the town meeting; one member chosen by the school board of each school district in the town;[26] one member of the board of commissioners of each village district;[27] and one member of the town board of selectmen. The number of members at large and the method of their choice are to be determined, within the statutory alternatives, by the town meeting; while the selectmen and village-district commissioners are designated by their respective boards for service on the committee. It is the duty of the budget committee, after consultation with local officers and after public hearings, to prepare the annual budget of town, school, and village-district expenditures for submission to the annual meetings of the respective units. The law provides that no appropriation may be made for any purpose not included in the budget and that the total amount appropriated by the town, school district, or village district shall not exceed by more than 10 percent the amount allocated to it in the budget. However, the budget committee may submit, without approval, items which its members do not wish to recommend but which they believe the voters should be allowed to act upon; and appropriations may be made for such items as long as total appropriations for each unit (town, school, or village district) do not exceed budgetary recommendations by more than the 10 percent allowed.

In Maine and Massachusetts town finance committees, under various names, are established by town bylaws. In the latter state, however, establishment of a committee is required in every town with an assessed valuation of more than a million dollars; and it appears that committees have actually been established in practically all Massachusetts towns of over 6,000 inhabitants and Maine towns of over 3,000. These committees vary in size, with a membership of nine or fifteen being most common. Members are ordinarily appointed by the moderator for overlapping terms. The committees are nonpolitical, their membership usually consisting of business and professional men who hold no public office. The principal duty of the finance committee consists in studying the town's finances and making recommendations to the town meeting with respect

25 *N.H. Rev. Stat. Ann.*, 1955 and 1961 supp., Chap. 32. For a recent account of the law and its operation, see Ernest G. Miller, *The Municipal Budget Law of New Hampshire*.

26 Each New Hampshire town is constituted by law a school district, with a school meeting corresponding to the town meeting in town government and with its own school board. However, school districts organized under special acts retain their organization and are not included in the town district, unless they vote to dissolve their corporate existence and unite with the town district. *N.H. Rev. Stat. Ann.*, 1955, secs. 194:1, 194:37.

27 The New Hampshire village district is a special-purpose district established to provide one or more municipal services for its inhabitants.

to appropriations and borrowing. Such a function, properly performed, introduces the rudiments of modern budgetary procedure into town government. Though legally the powers of the committee are almost solely advisory, in practice its recommendations are ordinarily followed. All in all, it appears that finance committees in both Maine and Massachusetts have exercised a distinctly wholesome influence in the formulation of town policies.[28]

Town Managers

In small rural towns, where administrative services are few and simple, the board of selectmen functions fairly satisfactorily in the supervision of administration. But in the more populous places there is genuine need for a single qualified person to supervise and coordinate administrative activities. This has led some New England towns to adopt the manager plan of government now operating in many American cities and a few counties. Under this plan the selectmen, instead of themselves supervising highway maintenance, public assistance, and other administrative functions, appoint a qualified manager to supervise those activities. The manager serves at the pleasure of the board of selectmen, and usually devotes his full time to the management of town affairs.[29] He appoints his principal administrative subordinates, prepares the town budget, and serves as advisor to the selectmen. In this way, more centralization of administrative responsibility is achieved, as well as a greater degree of professional skill in matters of administration, than is possible where administrative supervision is exercised directly by the selectmen.[30]

Connecticut, Maine, Vermont, and New Hampshire have general permissive statutes authorizing the adoption of the town manager plan. The laws of Maine, Vermont, and New Hampshire permit any town to provide for a manager by vote of the town meeting; and the same privilege is extended by Connecticut to any town having a board of finance.

[28] Sly, *op. cit.*, 208-212; Hormell, *op. cit.*, 17-19; Danforth W. Comins, "Powers, Duties, and Procedure of Town Finance Committees," in Charles J. Rohr, Alfred A. Brown, and Vernon P. Helming, eds., *Local Government in Massachusetts* (Bur. of Pub. Admin., Mass. State Coll., Amherst, 1941), 7-12; Richard A. Atkins and Lyman H. Ziegler, "Citizen Budgeting in Massachusetts," *Nat. Mun. Rev.*, XXX, 568-573 (Oct., 1941).

[29] In several Vermont communities a manager is employed jointly by two towns or by a town and an incorporated village therein; and a few Maine managers serve more than a single town.

[30] In some instances, the manager is appointed and controlled by an elective town council or board other than the board of selectmen. The manager plan of government is described more fully in relation to its operation in cities and counties. See above, Chaps. XIII, XIV. In several Massachusetts towns the board of selectmen appoints an executive secretary as a full-time administrator to assist the board in the performance of its duties. See Edward T. Dowling, *Administrative Organization in Massachusetts Towns,* Chap. 4.

Massachusetts has no optional town-manager law, but has granted manager government to a few towns by special legislative enactments. The usual procedure in that state, in the case of a town desiring to adopt the manager plan, has been for the town meeting first to set up a local committee to draft a manager charter. Such a charter having been drafted and approved at a town meeting, it is submitted to the state legislature with the request that it be enacted into law; and, in enacting such a special charter, the legislative body makes its effectiveness contingent upon a final approval by the town meeting. Some of the present manager towns in Connecticut and Maine are also operating under special legislative charters, rather than under the general permissive statutes of their respective states. Rhode Island towns may adopt manager charters under constitutional home-rule provisions.[31]

In 1963, according to the International City Managers' Association, nearly 200 New England towns were operating under the manager plan. Approximately two-thirds of the total number were in Maine, with the remaining third scattered among the other five states of the region.[32]

TOWNSHIP GOVERNMENT

Township Meetings

Of the fifteen states which employ the township as a unit of local government,[33] eight make statutory provision for a township meeting modeled after the town meeting of New England. These township-meeting states are Illinois, Michigan, Minnesota, Nebraska, North Dakota, South Dakota, Washington, and Wisconsin.[34] All qualified voters of the township are potential members of the township meeting. The usual practice is for the meeting, like its New England prototype, to elect a moderator to preside over its deliberations, though in Michigan the township

[31] National Municipal League, *Town Management in New England;* Dowling, *op. cit.*, Chap. 3; Orren C. Hormell and Lawrence L. Pelletier, *The Manager Plan for Maine Municipalities;* Wilson and Crowe, *op. cit.;* Massachusetts Federation of Taxpayers Associations, *The Town Manager Plan in Massachusetts* (Mass. Federation of Taxpayers Assns., Boston, rev. ed., 1951); Lashley G. Harvey, "First Break in New Hampshire," *Nat. Mun. Rev.*, XXXV, 521-524 (Nov., 1946); Lawrence Pelletier, "New England Pioneers Again," *Ibid.*, XXXVIII, 79-84 (Feb., 1949); Lincoln Smith, "Town Manager Government—A Case Study," *Soc. Science*, XXXIII, 27-35 (Jan., 1958); Lincoln Smith, "Town Manager Government—An Evaluation," *Ibid.*, XXXIV, 27-34 (Jan., 1959). See also Sly, *op. cit.*, 194-205.

[32] See the directory of manager municipalities in *The Municipal Year Book*, 1963, pp. 522-553.

[33] See above, Chap. XII, footnote 18. County subdivisions called townships exist also in several other states but only as administrative areas for the assessment and collection of taxes or for judicial purposes, and not as corporate governmental units.

[34] The township meeting was used in New York down to the early 1930's.

supervisor serves as moderator and in Wisconsin the chairman of the township board is chairman of the meeting. Provision is made for an annual meeting on a specified date in the spring, and for calling such special meetings as the business of the township may require.

The principal powers of the township meeting are those of (1) electing township officers, (2) levying taxes and making appropriations, (3) authorizing the borrowing of money, and (4) enacting bylaws for the government of the township. In general, the powers of the township meeting are less extensive than those of the New England town meeting, and even one or more of the basic powers just mentioned may be lacking in a particular state. In some instances, for example, township officers are elected, not in the township meeting, but in a regular township election.[35]

But though the township meeting in this group of states, for the most part in the Midwest, bears a close resemblance to the New England town meeting with respect to statutory composition and powers, it does not possess the vitality of its New England counterpart, being, in practice, considerably less important as a governmental agency than the statutory provisions would suggest. Such survey studies as have been made of attendance at township meetings indicate that, while there are certain localities and individual townships where the meeting is well attended, this is the exception rather than the rule. In townships having several hundred voters it is not unusual for as few as a dozen to attend the annual meeting. Each year sees meetings in many Illinois townships with attendance of five persons or less. When, as is often the case, the number of other voters in attendance is less than the number of township officers present, the latter are in a position to dominate the meeting and control its action. And if, as sometimes happens, only the township officers attend, they constitute the meeting. Under such circumstances, township affairs are actually controlled by the elective township officers, though legal responsibility therefor rests by statute with the voters. All in all, it may be said that the spirit of town-meeting government has failed to "take root" in most of the midwestern townships in which the meeting system has been established by law. In view of the widespread failure of the township meeting to function as an effective agency for the management of local affairs, it has frequently been recommended that the system be completely abolished, with the powers now exercised by the meeting being transferred to the

[35] It is also to be remembered that the township itself is less important as a governmental unit than the town. As the principal unit of local government in New England, the town has jurisdiction over a wide range of local functions, including even the schools in some instances; whereas the position of the mid-western township is distinctly secondary to that of the county and its functions are meager. This may well account in part for the fact, as noted in the succeeding paragraph, that township meetings usually attract less attendance and interest than do town meetings in New England.

township board. A less drastic, and perhaps preferable, course of action might be directed toward preserving the meeting in communities, even though they be relatively few, where the system actually functions as intended, while abolishing it elsewhere.

Township Boards

Every township state, including those with and those without township meetings, provides by statute for some sort of township governing board. The official title of this agency varies from state to state. In some instances it is designated merely as the town or township board. Several states use the title of board of supervisors or board of trustees. The title is township committee in New Jersey, advisory board in Indiana, board of directors in Missouri, and board of auditors in Illinois. For purposes of the present discussion the term *township board* will be used in a generic sense to designate any such agency, whatever its official title.

Most commonly, though by no means always, the township board consists of three members. In approximately half of the township states the board is strictly an elective body, composed of persons elected as board members; elsewhere, however, the composition of the board is wholly or in part ex officio. Thus the board consists in Illinois of the supervisor, the clerk, and three elective members; in Nebraska of the clerk, the treasurer, and a justice of the peace; and in Missouri of the trustee and two elective members.

The powers of the township board vary from state to state, and particularly as between those states having the township meeting and those that do not. In states having no meeting, the board is the general governing authority of the township, usually possessing the taxing power and other financial powers vested elsewhere in the meeting. In such states the board generally has some licensing and regulatory authority. A power of the board in practically all states, whether or not there is a township meeting, is that of auditing and allowing claims against the township. The board frequently is vested with some appointing power, the officers most commonly appointed being commissioners of highways. In addition to granting authority over specific matters, the statutes of several states provide that the board shall have charge of all township affairs not committed by law to other officers. The township board frequently serves ex officio as a township board of health, and sometimes also as a board of tax review or equalization. Sometimes individual board members serve ex officio in various capacities, such as those of fence-viewer and overseer of the poor.[36]

36 The title of the latter officer has recently been changed in some states to su- pervisor of public assistance.

A Chief Township Officer

Approximately half of the township states, including some with and some without the township meeting, confer upon a single official powers sufficiently broad to justify his being considered the head officer of the township. In such states the management of township affairs may be said to vest in this officer, assisted and checked in some matters by the township board, rather than in the board itself. The chief officer is known in Illinois, Michigan, and New York as the supervisor; in Indiana, Kansas, and Missouri as the trustee; and in Wisconsin as the town chairman.[37] Except in Indiana, the chief officer is a member of the township board; and in Illinois, Michigan, New York, and Wisconsin he is a member of the county board also. He usually serves in various ex officio capacities, such as those of township treasurer, assessor, and overseer of the poor. In Kansas even the township taxing power is vested in the trustee, to be exercised, however, with the concurrence of the county board.

Perhaps the authority of the chief township officer is greatest in the case of the township trustee in Indiana. That official serves his township ex officio as clerk, treasurer, overseer of the poor, inspector of elections, fence viewer, and, in the less populous townships, assessor. He is also trustee, clerk, and treasurer of the school township, which serves as the principal local unit for school administration. In these various legal capacities the trustee serves as the chief administrative officer of his township for both civil and school purposes. He has charge of township property, prepares civil and school budgets, examines and settles claims against the township, administers public assistance, and manages the rural schools of his township. Until 1932, when township roads in Indiana were transferred to the county, the trustee also performed important functions in the field of highway construction and maintenance. The taxing, appropriating, and borowing powers of the township, however, are in the hands of the township advisory board.[38]

Other Township Officers

Two other officers elected in the townships of most states are the clerk and the treasurer, though, as we have seen, the supervisor or trustee in some instances serves ex officio in one or both of these capacities. The

---

[37] Cf. Kirk H. Porter, *County and Township Government in the United States*, 312-313.

[38] See Clyde F. Snider, *Township Government in Indiana*, Chaps. 1, 2; Frank G. Bates, "The Indiana Township—An Anachronism," *Nat. Mun. Rev.*, XXI, 502-504 (Aug., 1932).

clerk is custodian of the township records. He is clerk to the township board; and in Illinois, Kansas, Michigan, and Nebraska he is a member of the board. In states having township meetings the clerk is secretary of the meeting. The treasurer receives township taxes and other revenues, has custody of these, and pays out the same upon order of the township board. In some instances he is required to keep the funds in his custody on deposit in a bank or banks designated by the township board as township depositories.

Yet another elective township officer in some states is the assessor, whose duty it is to assess, usually under some degree of county or state supervision, real and personal property within his township for purposes of taxation. Occasionally there is also an elective township collector who collects taxes and pays over the money to the treasurer. There is a tendency at the present time, however, to abolish the township offices of assessor and collector and to make the county the primary unit for tax assessment and collection.

The office of overseer of the poor or supervisor of public assistance is filled in a number of states by the township supervisor or trustee ex officio, but in some instances is elective. It is ordinarily the duty of this official to dispense outdoor assistance—principally in the form of food, clothing, rent money, and medical care—to indigent persons residing within his township, and to determine what persons from the township are entitled to admission to the county home or almshouse.

A township officer who is more commonly appointed by the township board than elected is the highway commissioner. This officer is charged with the construction and maintenance of minor roads and bridges. Miscellaneous township officers, generally appointive, for which provision is made in some states, include pound-masters, weed commissioners, and fence-viewers.

Justices of the Peace

Townships serve in several states as districts for the election of justices of the peace. The number of justices to be chosen in each township is fixed by state constitutional or statutory provision, or by the county board under statutory authority. In general, it may be said that this number, which may be uniform for all townships of a given state or may vary with the population of the respective townships, is from two to five. It frequently happens, however, that there are actually fewer justices in a particular township than the number provided for by law. This may result either from a dearth of candidates for the office or from the failure of persons elected to qualify by taking the necessary oath.

The judicial functions of justices of the peace, and the general dissatisfaction with justice-of-the-peace courts, have been considered in the chapter dealing with the state judiciary.[39] Justices also possess certain non-judicial powers. One of these is the performance of the marriage cere-mony, and the term *marrying justice* bears witness to the well-known fact that some justices specialize in this function. They may also administer oaths and take acknowledgments, and in some instances are members of the township board. Where election as justice of the peace carries with it membership on the township board, the office is sometimes sought for that reason by persons who have no intention of serving in a judicial capacity.[40]

Constables

It is usual for each township to elect as many constables as justices of the peace.[41] The constable is charged with two principal duties: (1) as a conservator of the peace, it is his duty to preserve order within his town-ship and to arrest law violators; and (2) as an officer of the justice-of-the-peace court, he serves summonses, warrants, and subpoenas, and executes judgments of the court. As in the case of sheriffs,[42] most constables give more attention to their court duties than to their duties as peace officers.[43] This is especially understandable in the case of the constable, inasmuch as he usually derives his sole compensation from the fees of his office and no fees are provided for patrol duty or other merely protective services. The replies of sixty-one Illinois sheriffs to a questionnaire some years ago indicated that in fifty-six of the sixty-one counties the constables were entirely inactive in police work.[44] Surveys in other states[45] lead to the conclusion that the utter ineffectiveness of the constable as a peace officer is not peculiar to Illinois, but is generally prevalent throughout the coun-try. Students of law enforcement and judicial administration seem in gen-eral to agree that the office of constable, like that of justice of the peace, has outlived its usefulness and should be abolished.

[39] Above, Chap. XI. See also Bruce Smith, *Rural Crime Control*, Chap. 7.

[40] In the nontownship states of Kentucky and Tennessee, justices of the peace in most counties are members of the county governing body; and in Arkansas, also a nontownship state, they are members of the county fiscal body (quorum court).

[41] In a few nontownship states constables are appointed rather than elected. See Smith, *op. cit.*, 82.

[42] See above, Chap. XIII, "The Sheriff."

[43] Among the exceptions are those constables who team up with justices of the peace in operating speed traps. Concerning the speed-trap evil, see above, Chap. XI, "Justices of the Peace."

[44] *Illinois Crime Survey* (Ill. Assn. for Criminal Justice, Chicago, 1929), 340. It is expected that the office of constable will be abolished in Illinois when a recent constitutional amendment reorganizing the state's judiciary has been fully imple-mented.

[45] See Smith, *op. cit.*, 84-92.

SCHOOL DISTRICT GOVERNMENT

The school district is the principal unit of local school administration in twenty-four of the fifty states.[46] In these "district states" the relatively small school district, rather than any larger governmental area, is the basic unit, both financial and administrative, for providing elementary and secondary education. Though school districts exist in some places or for certain purposes in some states employing the township or county as the principal school unit,[47] it is the government of school districts in the "district states" with which we are here concerned.

District Meetings

Some states make provision, at least in rural districts, for an annual school meeting somewhat comparable to the town and township meetings previously discussed. The district meeting consists of all resident voters of the district who choose to attend. It is in most cases held in the spring and presided over by the chairman of the district board. The usual powers of the district meeting are those of: (1) electing members of the district board; (2) making the tax levy; (3) authorizing the acquisition or sale of real estate; (4) fixing the length of the school term, subject to a minimum length prescribed by statute; and (5) determining district policies in general, insofar as local discretion is allowed under state law.

District Boards

Every school district, whether having a school meeting or not, is provided with a governing board. Referred to in everyday parlance as the "school board," the official title of this agency is usually board of directors, board of trustees, or board of education. In rural districts the board most commonly consists of three members. In urban places, on the other hand, the usual number of members is five, seven, or nine, with a few districts having boards of fifteen members or more. Board members as a rule are elected by the voters of the district, at the district meeting if such is provided and otherwise in a regular school election. Nominations are variously made by primary election, petition, caucus, and self-announcement.

[46] Of the remaining twenty-six states, nine employ the town or township as the principal unit, fifteen the county, and two (Delaware and Hawaii) the state. See below, Chap. XX, "Units for Public-School Administration."

[47] In Indiana, for example, though the township is the basic unit for school administration and finance, the "district" is recognized by law as the area served by a particular school.

Exceptions to the elective method of choosing board members are most commonly found in the larger city districts, a substantial number of which have appointive boards. Where appointment is used, the appointing power is usually vested in the mayor (sometimes to be exercised with the approval of the city council), but occasionally it rests with the council or the courts.[48] The term of board members varies, the three-year staggered term being most common. Indeed, where the board consists of three members the three-year term is almost universal, one member being chosen annually. The usual officers of the district board are a chairman (sometimes officially entitled president or moderator), a clerk, and a treasurer. In some states these officers are elected to their respective positions by the voters, while in others they are chosen by the board itself. The chairman is always a member of the board, and the other officers are usually members. Some states, however, permit district boards to select the clerk and treasurer from outside their membership. In a few instances the county treasurer serves as treasurer of the various school districts within his county, and the office of district treasurer is dispensed with.

The school board exercises broad authority over district affairs. It is charged with the care and maintenance of school property; purchases necessary supplies; hires teachers; provides transportation for pupils; determines the curriculum within statutory limitations; examines and allows claims against the district; and, in general, sees that the provisions of the state school law are complied with. In districts where the school meeting exists, the board, in theory at least, functions primarily as an administrative agency charged with carrying out district policy as determined by the meeting. Where there is no school meeting, most functions ordinarily performed by this group, where it exists, devolve upon the board, which thus becomes both the determiner and the administrator of district policy. In such instances it is the board that levies the district tax, authorizes expenditures, and borrows money on behalf of the district. In most cases, however, the issuance of bonds requires approval by the district voters. In populous urban districts it is usual for the board to appoint a superintendent to administer the schools on its behalf, confining its own activities principally to matters of policy-formulation and finance.

The City-School District Financial Relationship

A special problem in urban areas, where a school district and a municipality often have boundaries which are approximately or even exactly coterminous, concerns the proper financial relationship between the

[48] Cf. Fred Engelhardt, *Public School Organization and Administration* (Ginn, Boston, 1931), 59-62; Madaline Kintner Remmlein, *The Law of Local Public School Administration* (McGraw-Hill, New York, 1953), Chap. 1.

two corporations. Should the city school district, like districts in rural areas, have its own taxing, spending, and borrowing powers, independent of any control by the city council, or should school expenditures, like expenditures for streets and police protection, be subject to council control? According to whether the school district does or does not depend upon the city council for its funds, the school-city relationship is sometimes characterized as *dependent* or *independent,* respectively.

Professional schoolmen and students of government generally hold different views as to which of the two plans is preferable, though the members of neither group are fully agreed among themselves.[49] A majority of the schoolmen favor the independent plan. They look upon education as the most essential of all governmental functions and reason that, because of this supreme importance, the school authorities should be free to raise whatever funds they feel are needed, subject to no veto by the city council. Furthermore, they believe that, by and large, school boards attract a higher type of personnel than do city councils, and that the independent school board tends to keep education out of "city-hall politics." Most political scientists, on the other hand, believe that the dependent plan is to be preferred. They readily acknowledge the importance of education, but insist that the financial needs of the schools should be considered in relation to the needs of other municipal agencies, such as the departments of police, health, and fire protection, which also perform essential public services. A properly balanced program of expenditures, in their estimation, can be achieved only if the finances of the school board, like those of other municipal spending agencies, are subject to ultimate control by a common authority—the city council. Nor are political scientists as fully convinced as most schoolmen seem to be of the general absence of personal and partisan politics from school-board activities.

Whatever the theoretical merits of the respective relationships, neither can be said to be preferable to the other under any and all circumstances. In selecting a plan for a particular community, much consideration should be given to local conditions—especially to the general competence and efficiency of the city government, past and present. And in any event the independent plan, now followed in a large majority of American cities, has the weight of tradition behind it and seems destined to be the prevalent form of school-city relationship for many years to come.

[49] See, for various views, Ellwood P. Cubberley, *Public School Administration* (Houghton, Boston, 1929 ed.), 78-80; Henry G. Hodges, *City Management* (Appleton-Century-Crofts, New York, 1939), 682-683; John M. Pfiffner, *Municipal Administration* (Ronald, New York, 1940), 522-523; Charles M. Kneier, *City Government in the United States* (Harper, New York, 3rd ed., 1957), 314-316; Charles H. Judd, "Abolish the School Boards," *Pub. Management,* XV, 321 (Nov., 1933); Ernest A. Engelbert, "Education—A Thing Apart?" *Nat. Mun. Rev.,* XLII, 78-82 (Feb., 1953). An excellent study of school-city relationships in cities of 50,000 population or more, made jointly by a professor of education and a professor of political science, is Nelson B. Henry and Jerome G. Kerwin, *Schools and City Government.*

GOVERNMENT OF SPECIAL DISTRICTS

Special-purpose districts, of whatever variety, almost invariably have some sort of board as their central governing agency. The members of these boards are variously known as trustees, directors, or commissioners. The number of members is most commonly three or five, though larger boards are not unusual. Some boards are elective, but in numerous instances a part or all of the membership is appointive or ex officio. In the case of certain types of districts, such as those for drainage or local improvement purposes, voting for the members of elective governing boards is sometimes limited to landowners. Where appointment is used, the appointing power is vested ordinarily in some local officer or body, such as the mayor, county board, or county judge, but occasionally in the governor or some other state agency.

Special-district governing boards are vested by statute with those powers which the state legislature has believed necessary for carrying out the purposes of the respective districts. These usually include the power to acquire property, by eminent domain if necessary; to levy taxes or special assessments, or both; and to borrow on the credit of the district. However, there is ordinarily a statutory limit upon the tax rate; and it is commonly provided that the borrowing power may be exercised only with the approval of the district voters in an election. The board authorizes district expenditures, and lets contracts for materials and services. It frequently appoints a chief executive officer to superintend the work of the district under the board's general direction. Other necessary personnel may be appointed either directly by the board or by the executive officer with the board's approval.

REFERENCES

ASSEFF, Emmett, *Special Districts in Louisiana* (Bur. of Govt. Research, La. State Univ., Baton Rouge, 1951).

BIRD, Frederick L., *Local Special Districts and Authorities in Rhode Island* (Bur. of Govt. Research, Univ. of R.I., Kingston, 1962).

BLAWIE, James and Marilyn, *The Michigan Township Board: Its Powers and Duties* (Govtl. Research Bur., Mich. State Univ., East Lansing, 1957).

BOLLENS, John C., *Special District Governments in the United States* (Univ. of Calif. Press, Berkeley, 1957).

BRADSHAW, William L., and GARRISON, Milton, *Township Organization in Missouri* (Univ. of Mo., Columbia, 1936).

BROMAGE, Arthur W., and REED, Thomas H., *Organization and Cost of County and Township Government* (Mich. Comsn. of Inquiry into County, Township, and School Dist. Govt., Detroit, 1933).

CANTOR, Gilbert, *The New Hampshire Town Clerk* (Univ. of N.H. Bookstore, Durham, 1954).

DOWLING, Edward T., *Administrative Organization in Massachusetts Towns* (Bur. of Govt. Research, Univ. of Mass., Amherst, 1960).

DRURY, James W., *Township Government in Kansas* (Govtl. Research Center, Univ. of Kan., Lawrence, 1954).

FAIRLIE, John A., and KNEIER, Charles M., *County Government and Administration* (Century, New York, 1930), Chaps. 20-22.

GOULD, John, *New England Town Meeting: Safeguard of Democracy* (Stephen Daye Press, Brattleboro, Vt., 1940).

GUITTEAU, William B., *Ohio's Townships: The Grassroots of Democracy* (Toledo Printing Co., Toledo, 1949).

HENRY, Nelson B., and KERWIN, Jerome G., *Schools and City Government* (Univ. of Chicago Press, Chicago, 1938).

HORMELL, Orren C., *Maine Towns* (Bowdoin Coll., Brunswick, Me., 1932).

———, and Pelletier, Lawrence L., *The Manager Plan for Maine Municipalities* (Bowdoin Coll., Brunswick, Me., 1949).

LANCASTER, Lane W., *Government in Rural America* (Van Nostrand, New York, 2nd ed., 1952), pp. 34-46, 61-70, 227-240.

MILLER, Ernest G., *The Municipal Budget Law of New Hampshire* (Univ. of N.H. Bookstore, Durham, 1959).

National Municipal League, *Town Management in New England* (Nat. Mun. League, New York, 1940). A collection of articles from the *National Municipal Review*.

NUQUIST, Andrew E., *Town Government in Vermont* (Govt. Research Center, Univ. of Vt., Burlington, 1964).

PARKS, Robert W., *Soil Conservation Districts in Action* (Ia. State Coll. Press, Ames, 1952).

PORTER, Kirk H., *County and Township Government in the United States* (Macmillan, New York, 1922), Chaps. 2, 13, 16.

SCOTT, Stanley, and BOLLENS, John C., *Special Districts in California Local Government* (Bur. of Pub. Admin., Univ. of Calif., Berkeley, 1949).

SLY, John F., *Town Government in Massachusetts* (Harvard Univ. Press, Cambridge, 1930).

SMITH, Bruce, *Rural Crime Control* (Inst. of Pub. Admin., Columbia Univ., New York, 1933), Chaps. 3, 7.

SNIDER, Clyde F., *Local Government in Rural America* (Appleton-Century-Crofts, New York, 1957), Chaps. 8-10.

———, *Township Government in Indiana* (Bur. of Bus. Research, Ind. Univ., Bloomington, 1932).

THARP, Claude R., *A Manual of Township Government in Michigan* (Bur. of Govt., Univ. of Mich., Ann Arbor, 1948).

United States Bureau of the Census, *Special District Governments in the United States* (U.S. Bur. of the Census, Washington, 1954).

WELLS, Roger H., *American Local Government* (McGraw-Hill, New York, 1939), pp. 83-87, 89-93.

WHITE, Max R., *The Connecticut Town Meeting: A Handbook for Moderators and Other Town Meeting Officials* (Inst. of Pub. Service, Univ. of Conn., Storrs, rev. ed., 1951).

———, and Raissi, Shirley, *Forms of Town Government in Connecticut* (Inst. of Pub. Service, Univ. of Conn., Storrs, 1952).

WILSON, James, and Crowe, Robert W., *Managers in Maine* (Bur. for Research in Mun. Govt., Bowdoin Coll., Brunswick, Me., 1962).

16

Reorganization of Local Government

Preceding chapters have described the nature and organization of the various types of local governmental units and indicated certain shortcomings of the existing system. In the light of this background, we may now examine some of the measures which have been proposed, and to some extent are being adopted, with a view to improvement. Problems of local reorganization are extremely varied and complex. Our present discussion will be concerned, for the most part, with problems relating primarily to the need for areal readjustments, though attention will also be called briefly to certain problems of internal organization, most of which are considered more fully in other connections.[1]

PROBLEMS OF AREA

The number and variety of local governmental units in the United States have been described in a previous chapter.[2] The existence of more than 90,000 such units inevitably results in many units of small area and

[1] Reconstruction problems of still other categories are considered elsewhere in this book. Thus, problems of local functions are discussed in the section devoted to state and local functions (Chaps. XVII-XXIII); problems of local finance are treated in the section relating to finance (Chaps. XXIV and XXV); and the relations of local units to the state and federal governments and to each other are considered in Chapters III and IV.

[2] Above, Chap. XII.

in much overlapping. These small, overlapping areas have, in turn, produced widespread confusion, waste, and inefficiency.

In the first place, our complicated system of local areas is confusing to the citizen and voter. As was pointed out in Chapter XII, the typical citizen lives under several layers of local government. In Illinois, for example, everyone lives under at least three local governments and some persons live under as many as nine. Under such circumstances, the maze of overlapping units frequently becomes so complicated that it is virtually impossible for the average citizen to obtain a clear mental picture of his local government and to take an intelligent interest in local public affairs. In the second place, the multiplicity of local governments in uneconomical. With few exceptions, each unit of government has its own set of officials and, though the pay of many individual officers may be small, their compensation in the aggregate constitutes a considerable burden upon the taxpayer.

Finally, many small units are today administering functions which could be handled more efficiently by larger areas. As units for the construction and maintenance of roads, for example, most townships and many counties find it financially impossible, or at least unduly burdensome, to employ qualified engineering personnel and provide modern mechanical equipment. If up-to-date machinery is purchased, it is idle much of the time. Since townships and counties vary widely in assessed valuation, some will be able to provide better systems of roads than others; and, unless there is some coordination of the activities of the different units, no assurance exists that their respective highway systems will serve as parts of an integrated whole. In suppressing disease and carrying on health-promotion activities, fairly large units are necessary in order to provide trained, full-time personnel and modern equipment; yet the township continues in some states to be the unit charged with primary responsibility for public-health work in rural areas. Provision of relief or public assistance cannot satisfactorily be made the responsibility of small local units, since communities containing relatively large numbers of dependents are often the very ones which do not have the taxable property necessary to support them. And, in the field of education, it is becoming increasingly clear that the small district must give way to larger administrative and financial units if educational opportunity is to be equalized and effective instruction provided.

Geographic Consolidation

If, as seems apparent, the smallness of existing areas is in part responsible for present-day governmental ills, a possible remedy which immediately suggests itself is that of geographic consolidation. Should it not be possible, by establishing fewer and larger units through a program of consolidation, to make our system of local government more understandable, economical, and efficient? While the principle of consolidation is applicable to local units generally, it has been most frequently urged with respect to counties and school districts.[3]

County Consolidation

For many years, county consolidation has been widely advocated by political scientists and others as a desirable step in the direction of local reorganization. County-consolidation studies have been made in many states, and in several instances specific plans for consolidation have been suggested.[4] Present-day counties were laid out in "horse and buggy" days, apparently on the assumption that it was desirable to have counties of such size that the county-seat city would be reasonably accessible to all citizens. This assumption was probably valid at that time, and would seem to be equally so today; but, with the automobile and improved roads, the county seat of a much larger county is now even more accessible to citizens than was that of the small county a few decades ago.

Many states have constitutional or statutory provisions authorizing contiguous counties to consolidate voluntarily, yet since the beginning of the present century the more than 3,000 counties in the country have been reduced in number by only three through voluntary consolidation.[5] In 1919, rural James county in Tennessee consolidated with the neighboring county of Hamilton, which contains the city of Chattanooga; and in 1932 the two rural Georgia counties of Campbell and Milton were merged with Fulton county, containing the city of Atlanta.[6] The extremely slow

[3] For an account of an unsuccessful attempt to consolidate adjacent cities, see Phillip Monypenny and Gilbert Y. Steiner, "Merger? The Illinois Consolidation Case," in Richard T. Frost, ed., *Cases in State and Local Government* (Prentice-Hall, Englewood Cliffs, N.J., 1961), 267-279.

[4] For illustrative proposals for individual states, see Scoville R. Heckart and G. S. Klemmedson, *County Consolidation in Colorado* (Colo. Experiment Station, Colo. Agr. Coll., Fort Collins, 1933); Vernon G. Sorrell and J. Raymond Stuart, *County Consolidation in New Mexico* (Univ. of New Mex., Albuquerque, 1934); Shelden C. Menefee, *A Plan for Regional Administrative Districts in the State of Washington* (Univ. of Wash., Seattle, 1935); C. E. Allred and B. H. Luebke, *Areal and Functional Consolidation of Tennessee Counties* (Univ. of Tenn., Knoxville, 1943); Nevada Legislative Counsel Bureau, *County Consolidation and Reorganization in Nevada* (Nev. Legis. Counsel Bur., Carson City, 1948); Melvin Clyde Hughes, *County Government in Georgia* (Univ. of Ga. Press, Athens, 1944), Chap. 11. On County consolidation in general see Arthur C. Millspaugh, *Local Democracy and Crime Control*, 104-122; J. W. Manning, "The Progress of County Consolidation," *Nat. Mun. Rev.*, XXI, 510-514 (Aug., 1932); Richard L. Neuberger, "Economy Begins at Home," *Ibid.*, XLI, 501-503, 530 (Nov., 1952).

[5] In addition, two of South Dakota's "unorganized" counties have been eliminated—one by consolidation with another unorganized county and a second by annexation to an organized county. See below, footnote 25.

[6] Both of these consolidations were effected under special legislative enabling acts. In the case of the Tennessee merger, the proposal to consolidate was submitted to popular vote in James county only, consolidation being made compulsory upon Hamilton county when ratified by James.

progress of county consolidation by voluntary means is not difficult to understand. A proposal to consolidate one county with another is likely to meet with bitter opposition on the part of various elements in the county, since the legal identity of the county would be lost by the merger. Officials and politicians will usually be found in opposition, and many ordinary citizens will, from a sense of local pride or patriotism, oppose the abolition of their county. Tradesmen and residents of the municipality which, by the merger, would lose its status as a county seat, are usually prepared to fight consolidation—a disposition that is only natural inasmuch as the very economic life of many county-seat cities is largely dependent upon the location there of the county offices. Moreover, opposition may be encountered also in the county *with* which it is proposed to consolidate one or more other counties, even though the loss on its part of legal identity or of the county seat is not involved. This is especially true if the county or counties to be merged with the continuing county are relatively "poor" from the standpoint of taxable property, since merger may then result in an increased tax rate in the continuing county in order to provide proper services in the areas consolidated therewith.

Together, these various elements of opposition will usually be strong enough to defeat proposals for the voluntary merger of counties; and state legislatures, even where they have the power, are reluctant to force consolidation in the face of widespread popular opposition. Barring the remote possibility of a program of compulsory consolidation, the only method of securing county mergers would seem to be through a program of popular education which would convince the average voter that it is good business to place economy and efficiency in local government above local pride and politics. Such a program, even if feasible, will require much time, and it therefore seems fairly clear that no substantial reduction in the number of governmental units may be expected in the near future through the physical consolidation of counties.

The costs of county government which would most likely be substantially reduced by consolidation are those of an overhead nature—especially expenditures for officers' salaries, office expenses, and courthouse maintenance. A study of the probable results of consolidation in selected Nebraska counties indicates that other costs, constituting from two-thirds to three-fourths of total expenditures, would not be influenced appreciably by merger.[7] Moreover, as the Nebraska study suggests, a distinction should be made between *reducing* county governmental costs and merely *redistributing* those costs. When, for example, a rural county merges with an urban county, the tax rate in the former is almost certain to decrease. But, if high standards of service are inaugurated within the rural area, the tax rate in the urban territory may remain the same or may

[7] Edward B. Schmidt, *County Consolidation: Relation of Size of Counties to the Cost of County Government in Nebraska* (Univ. of Neb., Lincoln, 1934), 4.

actually increase. This results from the fact that there is shifted to the urban taxpayers a part of the cost of supplying services to the rural area—a shift which may be desirable in the interest of better government, but which should be recognized as a transfer of, rather than a reduction in, governmental costs. It is significant that both of the consolidations actually effected—the one in Tennessee and the other in Georgia—have involved the merger of rural counties with urban. In each case it appears that the taxpayers of the rural areas have benefited both through lower taxes and through better roads, schools, and other local services, but that much of this benefit has been at the expense of the urban taxpayers.[8] Indeed, during the five years following the Georgia merger, expenditures within the area embraced within the former rural counties exceeded tax revenues therefrom by about $100,000 annually.[9]

School Consolidation

Consolidation of school districts for many years proceeded slowly. The earlier laws providing for consolidation were almost entirely optional in nature, with the result that local pride and politics operated, as in the case of county-consolidation statutes, though not quite so effectively, to retard action. The slow pace of consolidation prior to the 1940's is vividly illustrated by the experience of Illinois where, notwithstanding the existence of more than 12,000 districts and the availability of permissive legislation, only 227 districts were eliminated by consolidation during the 32 years from 1905 to 1937.[10] More recently, the inauguration of new consolidation programs in a number of states has given the movement added impetus. Though some mergers have continued to take place through local action of a strictly voluntary character, the most extensive consolidations have generally been achieved where, as in Illinois, state aid has been denied to districts with few pupils,[11] or where, as in Kansas, outright compulsion has been employed. During the twenty years from 1942 to 1962, as noted in an earlier chapter,[12] the total number of school districts in the United States was reduced from more than 108,000 to fewer than 35,000—and some consolidation programs are still under way.[13] Illinois

[8] *Ibid.*, 51-52; Arthur W. Bromage and Thomas H. Reed, *Organization and Cost of County and Township Government* (Mich. Comsn. of Inquiry into County, Township, and School Dist. Govt., Detroit, 1933), 73-74.

[9] E. H. Bradley, "An Appraisal of County Consolidation in Georgia," *Nat. Mun. Rev.*, XXVI, 366-367 (July, 1937).

[10] Illinois Legislative Council, *Some Aspects of School Administration in Illinois* (Ill. Legis. Council, Springfield, 1938), 22-23.

[11] Under current Illinois provisions, state aid is not available, where transportation of pupils is feasible, to any elementary district with fewer than 15 pupils in average daily attendance or to any high school with an average daily attendance of less than 60 pupils.

[12] Above, Chap. XII.

[13] For the number of districts, by states, as of 1962, see above, Chap. XII, "Number of Units" and accompanying table.

has eliminated more than 10,000 districts, and Kansas and Missouri more than 6,000 each. Michigan, Minnesota, New York, Texas, and Wisconsin have eliminated more than 4,000 districts each, and smaller reductions, though substantial, have been made elsewhere. Indeed, some reduction in the number of districts has been made in every "district" state.

The procedures provided for achieving consolidation under recent and current programs show considerable variation. Several states have followed the plan of providing by law for the establishment of county "school survey committees" or "school reorganization committees" to examine existing districts and district boundaries and prepare plans for reorganization and consolidation. Usually the plans thus prepared are considered merely as recommendations which the local voters may adopt or reject in referendum elections, though some states have empowered the reorganization committees to put their plans into effect, after public hearings thereon, by compulsory order.[14]

The need for consolidating school districts is even more urgent than that for county consolidation, and it is therefore gratifying that the school-reorganization program has made so much headway. Experience indicates that no consolidation program purely voluntary in character is likely to effect the optimum degree of merger within any reasonable period of time and, therefore, that some element of compulsion, direct or indirect, is necessary if satisfactory results are to be expected. This fact doubtless explains why a considerable number of states have turned to compulsory programs of consolidation or to the "encouragement" of consolidation by providing special forms of state aid to consolidated districts or by denying aid to districts with small enrollments which refuse to consolidate.[15]

Township Abolition

One possible means of simplifying American local government would be the complete abolition of governmental units of a particular class or type and the transfer of their function to other units. The type of unit the elimination of which has been most widely advocated is the township as it exists in fifteen states, principally in the northeastern and

[14] The Kansas statute empowering county committees to effect compulsory consolidation was ultimately held unconstitutional by the state supreme court as an attempt to delegate legislative power to the committees. However, measures were enacted by the state legislature to validate the numerous consolidations that had already been effected under the enabling statute, and this validating legislation was sustained by the court. State v. Hines, 163 Kan. 300 (1947); State v. Common School District No. 87, 163 Kan. 650 (1947). Cf. Kansas Legislative Council, School District Reorganization: Kansas Experience, 1945-1947 (Kan. Legis. Council, Topeka, 1947).

[15] An excellent brief analysis of the school-consolidation movement and of various approaches to the problem followed in different states will be found in John C. Bollens, Special District Governments in the United States (Univ. of Calif. Press, Berkeley, 1957), 197-227. For a more extensive account, including case reports of sixteen state programs, see C. O. Fitzwater, School District Reorganization: Policies and Procedures.

north central regions.[16] Townships in these states usually have an area of some thirty-six square miles—too small for the economical financing or efficient administration of governmental activities. The principal functions ordinarily performed fall in the fields of law enforcement, public assistance, and highway maintenance, and in each of these the county will usually be found carrying on similar or related work. Thus, the township constable is the counterpart in miniature of the county sheriff; where townships administer outdoor assistance, public aid of an institutional nature is usually provided by a county home or almshouse; and, while the least-traveled roads may be maintained by the township, those more generally traveled are likely to be under county jurisdiction. Studies in various states have strongly indicated that township government is unnecessarily wasteful and costly, and that the taxpayers could obtain the same or better services for less money if townships were abolished and their functions transferred to the county.[17] In considering the necessity for township government, it should be borne in mind that in more than half of the states townships as governmental units have never existed. Moreover, in one state—Oklahoma—townships were actually abolished, for all practical purposes, by a constitutional amendment of 1933 depriving them of the power to levy taxes. The Oklahoma legislature then transferred to the county those functions which had been performed by the township, the most important being that of highway construction and maintenance. Experience under the new setup seems to have demonstrated that the counties have provided as good services as had the townships and at considerably less cost.[18] In another state—Iowa—township government has degenerated to such an extent that the Census Bureau no longer includes the state's townships in its counts of governmental units.[19]

The principal argument for retention of the township is that it keeps government "close to the people" and provides a "training school of democracy." This argument, however, loses much of its effectiveness when one considers the widespread lack of interest in township government and elections, and the small attendance at township meetings in the states whose laws provide for such assemblies.[20] On the basis of experience, and

[16] See above, Chap. XII, "Towns and Townships"; Chap. XV, "Township Government." The New England town has retained much of its original vigor as a local governmental unit, and there seems to be little or no sentiment in favor of its abolition.

[17] See, for example, M. H. Hunter, *Costs of Township and County Government In Illinois* (Bur. of Bus. Research, Univ. of Ill., Urbana, 1933); H. K. Allen, *Costs and Services of Local Government in Selected Illinois Counties* (Bur. of Bus. Research, Univ. of Ill., Urbana, 1936); Bromage and Reed, *Organization and Cost of County and Township Government;* William L. Bradshaw and Milton Garrison, *Township Organization in Missouri* (Univ. of Mo., Columbia, 1936).

[18] L. D. Melton, "The Elimination of Township Government in Oklahoma," *Nat. Mun. Rev.*, XXVII, 405-407 (Aug., 1938).

[19] Cf. Richard C. Spencer, "Iowa Townships Still Here?" *Ibid.*, XLI, 397-399 (Sept., 1952).

[20] See above, Chap. XV, "Township Meetings."

in view of modernized methods of travel and communication, the conclusion seems inescapable that the functions of present-day townships could be more efficiently and economically performed by counties, and that townships should therefore be abolished.[21] A committee on county government of the National Municipal League, after careful study, has recommended that townships be gradually eliminated by transferring township functions to the county, city, or state; permitting individual townships to deorganize or consolidate; and providing that townships may be abolished by county option.[22] Township abolition would, of course, require considerable time. Tradition is strong, and the township is a traditional institution. Its elimination would be opposed by well-organized township officials in the name of democracy. Moreover, in some states constitutional changes would be required. Notwithstanding these difficulties, however, there is strong evidence that abolition of the township would promote efficiency and economy in government at the local level.[23]

Deorganization

An alternative to state-wide abolition of local units of a particular class is the provision for deorganization, on either a voluntary or a compulsory basis, of individual units. Under this plan the particular unit concerned may or may not retain its identity as a geographic and taxing area, but in any event its governmental organization is dissolved and local governmental services are provided within its borders by some neighboring or overlying unit.[24]

[21] For a statement of the contrary view, see William B. Guitteau, *Ohio's Townships: The Grassroots of Democracy* (Toledo Printing Co., Toledo, 1949).

[22] Arthur W. Bromage, "Recommendations on Township Government" (Report No. 3 of the Committee on County Govt. of the Nat. Mun. League), *Nat. Mun. Rev.*, XXIII, 139-145 (Feb., 1934, Supp.).

[23] Cf. Arthur W. Bromage, "Shall We Save the Township?" *Nat. Mun. Rev.*, XXV, 585-588 (Oct., 1936); Clyde F. Snider, "The Twilight of the Township," *Ibid.*, XLI, 390-396 (Sept., 1952); James W. Drury, "Townships Lose Ground," *Ibid.*, XLIV, 10-13 (Jan., 1955); Paul W. Wager, "Townships on Way Out," *Ibid.*, XLVI, 456-460, 475 (Oct., 1957). For a proposal of a new type of "rural municipality" to replace the traditional township, see Theodore B. Manny, *Rural Municipalities*. The boundaries of the rural municipality, according to its proponents, would be so drawn that the unit would consist not of "standardized 'blocks' of the earth's surface such as townships," but rather of "real groups of living human beings as nearly homogeneous in their common interests as it is possible to obtain." *Ibid.*, 221. Occasionally the view is expressed that working for improvement of the township is a more practicable alternative than seeking its abolition. Cf. Irving Howards, "Rural Progress Step [in Illinois]," *Nat. Civic Rev.*, XLIX, 286-292 (June, 1960).

[24] For a comprehensive discussion of deorganization, see William S. Carpenter, *Problems in Service Levels*, Chap. 4. According to Professor Carpenter, at least 36 states have provided by general law for the deorganization of counties, townships, municipalities, or special districts; while in some other states, especially those of New England, local governmental units may be deorganized by special legislative act. Relatively little use, however, has thus far been made of deorganization statutes. *Ibid.*, 96-97.

Three of South Dakota's counties are "unorganized," [25] each being attached to an adjacent organized county for judicial purposes and the performance of essential governmental services; and both of the Dakotas have enacted legislation authorizing the voluntary deorganization of counties.[26] The North Dakota law applies only to counties of less than 4,000 population, while that of South Dakota is applicable to any organized county. Deorganization under either law is to be accomplished by petition and popular vote within the county to be deorganized. In South Dakota the state legislature is to designate by joint resolution the organized county to which a deorganizing county is to be attached for judicial and other governmental purposes. North Dakota provides that a deorganizing county may make an agreement with an adjoining county for attachment thereto, and that if this is not done the governor shall by proclamation designate the county to which the deorganized county is to be attached. Both states provide that taxes shall be levied upon the property within a deorganized county to pay any outstanding indebtedness incurred prior to deorganization. Apparently no county has thus far been deorganized under either of these laws, though at least one North Dakota county—that of Billings, in 1940—voted upon and defeated a proposal for deorganization.

Of the township states, Minnesota seems to have accomplished most in the way of township deorganization. Under the laws of that state, county governing boards may by resolution dissolve any township within their respective borders (1) when the township has failed to exercise its powers for a period of ten years; (2) when the assessed valuation of the township falls below $40,000; (3) when the tax delinquency of the township, exclusive of taxes delinquent by reason of being legally contested, amounts to 50 percent of the assessed valuation; or (4) when the state or federal government has acquired title to 50 percent of the real estate of the township.[27] A few townships have been dissolved by county boards under this permissive authority. Dissolutions in greater number, however, were effected between 1933 and 1937, during which period the statutes made it *mandatory* upon county boards to dissolve any township where township government had failed to function for ten years, or where there existed certain specified conditions of low assessed valuation, high tax de-

[25] There were five such counties in the state prior to 1943, when the legislature, by special act, consolidated the unorganized county of Washington with that of Shannon. Subsequently, the unorganized county of Armstrong was annexed to the organized county of Dewey under enabling legislation of 1951. *Laws of S.D.*, 1943, Chap. 23; *Ibid.*, 1951, Chap. 37.

[26] *Laws of N.D.*, 1939, Chap. 122; *Laws of S.D.*, 1943, Chap. 45. The North Dakota statute as subsequently amended appears in *N.D. Century Code*, 1960, secs. 11-30-01 to 11-30-21. See also Kenneth Wernimont, "County Disorganization for North Dakota," *Nat. Mun. Rev.*, XXVIII, 769-772 (Nov., 1939).

[27] *Minn. Stat. Ann.*, 1957, sec. 368.47. In certain counties the question of dissolution is subject to popular referendum upon petition therefor.

linquency, or widespread government ownership of real estate.[28] In all, some 150 Minnesota townships appear to have been deorganized under these various statutes. Though this number is not insignificant, it represents a reduction of less than 8 percent in the total number of townships in the state.[29] Most or all of the deorganizations have occurred in the northern cut-over region of the state, and the total number includes all or some townships in each of some ten or a dozen counties. When Minnesota townships are deorganized their functions—chief among which are road construction and maintenance, assessment of property, and supervision of elections—are transferred to their respective counties.[30] Another state which has had a number of township deorganizations under permissive legislation, with functions transferred to the counties, is North Dakota.[31] Under North Dakota law, deorganization is effected by voter petition therefor, followed by favorable vote at the annual township meeting.[32]

In Maine, approximately 40 percent of the state's area, principally in the northwestern portion, has never been organized into towns, but is administered directly by the state; and, during recent decades, additions have been made to this "unorganized" territory through the deorganization of individual towns by special legislative acts. Towns thus deorganized have usually been so sparsely settled and had assessed valuations so low that they have found the maintenance of organized local government unduly burdensome. They have therefore sought and received from the state legislature permission to surrender their corporate charters and revert to unorganized status. Essential governmental services in the areas thus deorganized are provided by state and county officials, and in a few instances by officers of adjacent towns. Public assistance and education become state charges, except that in deorganized towns having more than 200 inhabitants the schools are supported by local taxation. In providing school facilities, the state commissioner of education may maintain schools within the deorganized areas, transport pupils to neighboring towns, or board pupils near some school. Local roads are under the jurisdiction of the county commissioners. Assessment of property for taxation falls to the state tax assessor. Residents of deorganized areas vote in neighboring towns for national, state, and county officers. It will be noted that, when

[28] Cf. *Session Laws of Minn.*, 1933, Chap. 377; *Ibid.*, 1935, Chap. 342; Carpenter, *Problems in Service Levels*, 100-102, 116. Apparently, however, this statutory mandate was not obeyed by the county boards in all cases. See William Anderson, "Minnesota—Dissolution of Townships," *Nat. Mun. Rev.*, XXIV, 229 (Apr., 1935).

[29] There were 1,822 townships in Minnesota in 1962 as compared with 1,973 in the early 1930's. William Anderson, *The Units of Government in the United States* (1934 ed.), 11; United States Bureau of the Census, *Census of Governments: 1962*, Vol. I, *Governmental Organization* (U.S. Govt. Printing Office, Washington, 1963), 29.

[30] Cf. Carpenter, *Problems in Service Levels*, 116-120.

[31] *Ibid.*, 104-105.

[32] *N.D. Century Code*, 1960, secs. 58-02-25 to 58-02-32.

deorganization occurs in Maine, most town functions are transferred to the state rather than to the counties. This is not surprising, since the New England county exists primarily as a judicial area and is relatively unimportant as a unit of local government.[33]

Deorganization affords a means whereby the inhabitants of sparsely settled areas may be provided with essential governmental services without being subjected to the exorbitant taxation which would be necessary to support local governmental organization therein. Where, as in the county-deorganization laws of the Dakotas, it is provided that governmental services shall be performed and taxes levied in deorganized units by the governments of adjacent units at the same level, the criticism may arise that the inhabitants of deorganized areas are left without a voice in their local government. Criticism of this nature is less valid where provision is made for government of the deorganized area by a larger overlying unit. This, as has been noted, is the plan followed in the case of deorganized townships in Minnesota and North Dakota, wherein government is provided by the county, and in that of deorganized Maine towns, which are governed by the state.

Transfer of Functions

Yet another means of reducing the waste and inefficiency flowing from unduly small governmental areas is the transfer of specific functions from smaller to larger units. The function thus far most frequently transferred is that of road construction and maintenance. Within relatively recent years, for example, county highways have been transferred to the state in North Carolina, Delaware, West Virginia, and most Virginia counties. Indiana, Iowa, and Michigan have transferred township roads to the county; and in Arkansas the county has supplanted subdivisional road districts for highway purposes. Various counties in Kansas, Washington, and Texas, have adopted the county-unit plan of highway administration under optional statutes, thereby transferring to county jurisdiction local roads previously maintained by townships or road districts. Assessment of property for taxation is another function which has been transferred in several states from township to county jurisdiction.

Generally speaking, transfer of highway and assessment administration to larger governmental units appears to have produced results sufficiently gratifying to recommend more widespread use of larger units in these and other fields. Proposals for transfer of functions are likely to

[33] O. J. Scoville, "Liquidating Town Government in Decadent Rural Areas of Maine," *Jour. of Land and Pub. Util. Econ.*, XIII, 285-291 (Aug., 1937); William S. Carpenter, "Decentralization in Maine," *Amer. Polit. Sci. Rev.*, XXXII, 1139-1142 (Dec., 1938); John W. Fleming, "Maine's Unorganized Territory Creates Few Problems," *Nat. Mun. Rev.*, XXVIII, 228-233, 237 (Mar., 1939). Two Vermont towns were deorganized in 1937. *Acts and Resolves of Vermont*, 1937, Nos. 269, 292.

encounter opposition from officials of units from which the transfer is to be made, and also from other persons who believe they see in any degree of centralization a danger to local self-government. This opposition, however, is rarely as vocal or effective as it is where complete abolition or deorganization of the smaller units is sought.[34]

Functional Consolidation

One of the most promising developments in the field of local government during recent years has been the growing use of what has come to be known as functional consolidation. As distinguished from physical or geographic consolidation, functional consolidation involves the cooperation of two or more governmental units in the performance of particular functions. This cooperation may be effected either by establishing a special district or through contractual agreement.[35] Although sometimes the result of a mandatory law, functional consolidation more often takes place voluntarily under permissive authority conferred upon the local units by constitutional or statutory provision. It is to be found in both urban and rural areas. In urban areas, an important element in bringing about functional consolidation is the fact that certain governmental problems, such as health protection, water supply, and sewerage, can be met most effectively only by a governmental unit having jurisdiction throughout the region. In rural areas, though a similar motive may be influential in many cases, a special reason for functional consolidation lies in the need for a unit large enough to make economically feasible the employment of qualified technical personnel and the provision of modern equipment in the field concerned.

Where the special-district plan is used, there is ordinarily established a district including within its boundaries two or more "general" governmental units of a given type—i.e., counties, townships, or municipalities. This district then performs for the inhabitants within its limits, through its own agencies, a specific governmental function previously performed by the various general-government units individually. Districts created for this purpose may be full-fledged governmental units, with their separate corporate identity and their own taxing power,[36] or they may be mere administrative areas financed by the component general-government units. The multicounty health districts found in New Mexico and several other states, and Virginia's four district homes (almshouses)

---

[34] Cf. Clyde F. Snider, "State-Rural Relations," *The Book of the States* (Council of State Govts., Chicago), 1945-46, pp. 54-60.

[35] The "district" and "contract" methods of functional consolidation are not mutually exclusive, since special administrative districts are sometimes established by general-government units through contractual agreement.

[36] See above, Chap. XII, "Special Districts"; Chap. XV, "Government of Special Districts."

serving twenty-seven counties and cities, afford examples of functional consolidation of the special-district variety.[37]

The contract variety of functional consolidation, though newer than the special-district type, is spreading more rapidly.[38] Under the contract method, two or more local units of the same or different types enter into an agreement providing either for the establishment of a joint department or agency to perform the service concerned for all units that are parties to the agreement, or that one of the units involved will provide the service for one or more others in return for a money payment. Many states have enacted legislation enabling local governmental units to enter into contracts for the cooperative performance of specifically-named functions. Thus several states authorize the establishment by this means of multi-county welfare departments and health departments. Other services that may be provided through intergovernmental contract in various states include libraries, recreational facilities, airports, fire protection, water supply, and sewage disposal. Of even more significance has been the adoption by a growing number of states, since 1930, of constitutional or statutory provisions conferring broad authority upon local governmental units to enter into contracts for the performance of a wide range of local functions. Indeed, some states have now gone so far as to authorize the contractual performance of *any* governmental function common to the contracting units. Some of these constitutional provisions and statutes apply only to intercounty cooperation, whereas others authorize counties to contract also with any governmental units within their borders, and still others permit contracts between or among units of the same or different types in almost any combination. In most instances a local unit is empowered to enter into a contract by action of its governing board, though in some cases there must be popular approval of the agreement in a referendum election.

Two of the broadest enabling statutes are those of Louisiana and Minnesota, enacted in 1942 and 1943, respectively. The Louisiana law empowers parishes to act jointly with each other, or with municipalities or special districts, in any undertaking within the power of the cooperating units. Such joint arrangements may include, but are not limited to, activities concerning: (1) police, fire, and health protection; (2) public utility services; (3) collection and disposal of garbage and other refuse;

---

[37] For other examples of functional consolidation in Virginia, see Virginia State Chamber of Commerce, *Opportunities for Economy in County Government in Virginia* (Va. State Chamber of Commerce, Richmond, 1947), 22-32; Robert H. Tucker, "Progress in Virginia County Government," *The Commonwealth* (Va. State Chamber of Commerce), XVI, 7-9, 26-27 (Jan., 1949).

[38] A discussion of functional consolidation of this type will be found in Carpenter, *Problems in Service Levels,* Chap. 2. Professor Carpenter designates contracts effecting functional consolidation by the term *interjurisdictional agreements.* See also below, "Intergovernmental Agreements."

(4) construction and maintenance of public improvements; (5) recreational and educational facilities; (6) flood control, drainage, and reclamation projects; and (7) the purchase of materials, supplies, and equipment. Agreements for joint undertakings must be in writing; must be approved by ordinance or resolution of the governing bodies of the units concerned; and may provide for a joint committee or other administrative agency to administer their terms.[39] The Minnesota statute provides that two or more governmental units may, by agreement entered into through action of their governing bodies, jointly exercise any power common to the contracting parties. The term "governmental units" was originally defined as including cities, villages, boroughs, counties, towns, and school districts; but a 1949 amendment extended the provisions of the act to other subdivisions as well.[40]

Especially significant is the fact that four state constitutions of recent adoption—those of Missouri, Georgia, Alaska, and Michigan—include broad provisions relating to functional consolidation. Missouri provides that contiguous counties, not exceeding ten in number, may, by popular vote in each county concerned, join in performing any common function or service, or in the employment of any county officer or employee common to the counties. Furthermore, any municipality or political subdivision of the state may, in the manner provided by law, contract with other municipalities or subdivisions, or with other states or their municipalities or subdivisions, or with the United States, for the construction or operation of any public improvement, or for a common service.[41] The Georgia provision is as follows:[42]

> The State, state institutions, any city, town, municipality or county of this State may contract for any period not exceeding fifty years, with each other or with any public agency, public corporation or authority now or hereafter created for the use by such subdivisions or the residents thereof of any facilities or services of the State, state institutions, any city, town, municipality, county, public agency, public corporation or authority, provided such contracts shall deal with such activities and transactions as such subdivisions are by law authorized to undertake.

Alaska declares that "Agreements, including those for cooperative or joint administration of any functions or powers, may be made by any local government with any other local government, with the State, or with the United States, unless otherwise provided by law or charter." [43] And Michigan provides that the legislature by general law shall authorize local governments to enter into contractual understandings or agreements with one

---

[39] Acts of La., 1942 (reg. sess.), No. 246.
[40] Session Laws of Minn., 1943, Chap. 557; Ibid., 1949, Chap. 488.
[41] Const. of Mo. (1945), art. VI, secs. 14, 16.
[42] Const. of Ga. (1945), art. VII, sec. 6.
[43] Const. of Alaska (1959), art. X, sec. 13.

another or with the state for the joint administration of any function which each would have the power to perform separately.[44] Other states having constitutional or statutory provisions conferring broad authority for functional consolidation of the contractual variety include California, Nevada, Ohio, Pennsylvania, and Wisconsin. Though the scheme is frequently employed in rural areas, it is most widely used in populous urban communities and examples are mentioned in the discussion of metropolitan problems at a subsequent point in this chapter.[45]

METROPOLITAN ADJUSTMENTS [46]

As indicated in an earlier chapter, local government reaches its greatest complexity in highly urbanized areas.[47] It is in the large cities and their surrounding territory that the multiplicity and overlapping of governmental units are likely to be most pronounced. Long-standing problems of large cities have been vastly complicated by the phenomenal growth of suburban populations. Most of the country's principal cities are now growing relatively slowly, and indeed some of them are actually declining in population. Suburban populations, on the other hand, are increasing at a rapid rate—the result of migration from both the large cities and rural territory. The Census Bureau considers as a metropolitan area any county or group of contiguous counties containing at least one city or "twin cities" with a population of 50,000 or more, together with any contiguous county or counties which are essentially metropolitan in character and are socially and economically integrated with the central city or cities. In early 1962 there were 212 such areas in the United States, embracing nearly two-thirds of the nation's population and more than 18,000 local governments. The term "metropolitan area" is employed in this discussion in a more general sense to mean any considerable area of relatively high urbanization.

The typical metropolitan county will include a central city, a number of smaller "satellite" municipalities, unincorporated suburban communities, and rural territory. Many metropolitan areas extend into two or more counties, and some into more than a single state. Police and fire protection, health, schools, public transportation, traffic control, water

---

[44] *Const. of Mich.* (1963), art. VII, sec. 28.

[45] Below, "Intergovernmental Agreements."

[46] On the subject generally, see Paul Studenski, *The Government of Metropolitan Areas in the United States;* Victor Jones, *Metropolitan Government;* Betty Tableman, *Governmental Organization in Metropolitan Areas;* Robert C. Wood, *Suburbia;* Scott Greer, *Governing the Metropolis;* Scott Greer, *Metropolitics;* Council of State Governments, *The States and the Metropolitan Problem.*

[47] See above, Chap. XII, "Pyramiding and Overlapping of Units."

supply, sewerage, building regulation, planning, and zoning are only some of the fields in which the needs and interests of various governmental units and types of units may be closely interrelated. Within a given metropolitan area, for example, there are likely to be found several governments providing a specific service for their respective residents, while other residents of the area are entirely without the service. Thus a dozen or more municipalities may be providing fire protection for their inhabitants, perhaps less efficiently and at higher cost than would be the case if a single government provided such protection for all, while at the same time residents of unincorporated places must establish special districts for the purpose or go without public fire protection of any kind. In an effort to provide some measure of solution for such problems, various programs of action have been suggested and some of them have been placed in operation in at least a few communities.[48] Five of these will be considered briefly in this discussion: (1) city-county consolidation, (2) local "federalism," (3) metropolitan special districts, (4) intergovernmental agreements, and (5) tax differentials.

City-County Consolidation [49]

City-county consolidation involves the merger, within a given area, of city and county governments. The purpose of such consolidation is to lessen duplication and overlapping by having a single set of officials perform functions that otherwise would be performed by two governments— city and county. Consolidation of city and county governments has ordinarily been preceded by a separation of the city concerned, usually after extension of its boundaries to take in some additional territory, from the county in which it has been located.[50] Metropolitan cities which have been thus separated from their counties and provided with governments for the performance of both city and county functions are San Francisco, Denver, Baltimore, and St. Louis. The first two of these are legally designated, respectively, as the city and county of San Francisco and the city and county of Denver. Baltimore and St. Louis, on the other hand, are des-

---

[48] Cf. Advisory Commission on Intergovernmental Relations, *Alternative Approaches to Governmental Reorganization in Metropolitan Areas;* Gladys M. Kammerer, *The Changing Urban County* (Pub. Admin. Clearing Service, Univ. of Fla., Gainesville, 1963); C. J. Hein, *The Stake of Rural People in Metropolitan Government* (U. S. Dept. of Agriculture, U. S. Govt. Printing Office, Washington, 1961).

[49] See John A. Rush, *The City-County Consolidated;* Paul Studenski, *The Government of Metropolitan Areas in the United States*, Chaps. 10, 11; Thomas H. Reed, "City-County Consolidation," *Nat. Mun. Rev.*, XXIII, 523-525 (Oct., 1934); Frederick P. Gruenberg, "Philadelphia's City-County Dilemma," *Ibid.*, XXIX, 385-387, 395 (June, 1940); Richard A. Atkins, "The First Hundred Years" [of consolidation in Boston and Suffolk county], *Ibid.*, XXX, 90-95 (Feb., 1941); Alfred F. Smith, "San Francisco: A Pioneer in the Consolidation Movement," *Ibid.*, 152-156 (Mar., 1941).

[50] Cf. Victor Jones, *Metropolitan Government*, 130.

ignated merely as cities, though their governments perform county as well as city functions.[51]

Another variety of city-county consolidation, somewhat different from the city-county separation just noted, is that in which the city's boundaries are extended to embrace the entire county wherein it is situated.[52] An example of this form of consolidation is to be found in Philadelphia, where city boundaries have been made coterminous with those of Philadelphia county, though the merger of city and county offices is not complete. Partial consolidation of city and county governments exists also in the cases of Boston and the county of Suffolk, New Orleans and Orleans parish, Baton Rouge (Louisiana) and the parish of East Baton Rouge,[53] and New York City and the five counties within its borders.

The most recent consolidation of a city with a county occurred in 1962 when the local voters approved a plan for merger of the governments of Davidson county, Tennessee, and the city of Nashville. Under this plan, the existing city and county governments were abolished and replaced by a single new government known as the Metropolitan Government of Nashville and Davidson County. A half-dozen suburban cities within the county retain their separate incorporation but are placed under the jurisdiction of the metropolitan government for area-wide services.[54]

City-county consolidation appears, in practice, to have been beneficial in some measure in the communities where the plan has been employed. However, such consolidation has serious limitations as a general approach to the metropolitan problem,[55] and indeed raises problems of its own. Where a metropolitan area, as is frequently the case, extends beyond the boundaries of a single county, city-county consolidation cannot provide a single areawide government.[56] And even where a single large city within a single county is involved, there remains the problem of determining the proper amount of territory to be included within the consolidated city-county. If the separation plan is followed and only such territory surrounding the central city is included as appears to be needed for population expansion in the immediate future, it is likely that the urban popula-

[51] Virginia cities (but not the state's less populous municipalities known as towns) are also separated from their respective counties, their governments performing both city and county services. See Raymond B. Pinchbeck, "City-County Separation in Virginia," *Nat. Mun. Rev.*, XXIX, 467-472 (July, 1940).

[52] Cf. Reed, *op. cit.*

[53] Charles G. Whitwell, "The New Parish-City Government of Baton Rouge," *Southwestern Soc. Sci. Quar.*, XXIX, 227-231 (Dec., 1948); R. Gordon Kean, Jr., "Consolidation That Works," *Nat. Mun. Rev.*, XLV, 478-485, 493 (Nov., 1956).

[54] Daniel R. Grant, "Consolidations Compared," *Nat. Civic Rev.*, LII, 10-13, 29 (Jan., 1963); Kammerer, *op. cit.*, 5-8. For a comprehensive account, see David A. Booth, *Metropolitics: The Nashville Consolidation* (Inst. for Community Development and Services, Mich. State Univ., East Lansing, 1963).

[55] Cf. Council of State Governments, *The States and the Metropolitan Problem: A Report to the Governors' Conference*, 74-75, 84-85.

[56] Tableman, *op. cit.*, 16.

tion will ultimately overflow the boundaries of the city-county. Unless those boundaries are then extended, the neighboring county or counties will be faced with the task of providing services for unincorporated urban areas, and there may be lacking adequate cooperation between the city-county and its neighbors in the solution of problems common to the metropolitan area. When, on the other hand, city boundaries are made county-wide, except in the case of a small urbanized county such as Philadelphia, there is likely to be a considerable amount of rural territory which will be required, at least for some years and perhaps indefinitely, to pay taxes for providing services to urban residents.[57] These considerations make clear the desirability of providing in city-county consolidation plans means for periodic boundary adjustments to take account of population trends.

Local "Federalism"

Another possible approach to metropolitan problems is through application of some of the features of federalism to interlocal relationships. As usually envisaged, local federalism would apply to county-city relations and would involve conferring authority upon the county in matters of countywide concern, while vesting in the cities within the county jurisdiction over matters of a local nature. Although similar in some respects to a genuine federal system, the plan falls short of true federalism in that the constituent cities as such would have no part in amending the law or charter which established the division of authority between county and cities.[58]

Plans involving some elements of federalism have been suggested over the years for various metropolitan communities but have in most instances failed of adoption. Ordinarily an amendment to the state constitution is required, followed by the drafting of a charter and its subsequent approval by the local voters, and these hurdles it has usually been impossible to surmount.[59] Probably the nearest approximation to local federalism now in existence is provided under the charter approved by the voters of Dade county (Miami), Florida, in 1957. The charter, according to a declaration in its preamble, establishes a "metropolitan government"; and the new government is popularly known as Metro. Power over various matters of countywide concern are conferred upon the central county government. That government, for example, is authorized to provide arterial highways, public transportation systems, parks, and playgrounds; to regulate or operate public utilities; to adopt and enforce building codes;

---

[57] Cf. L. R. Chubb, "The Financial Aspects of City-County Consolidation," *Nat. Mun. Rev.*, XXVIII, 101-104 (Feb., 1939); Reed, *op. cit.*

[58] The nature of genuine federalism, as seen in the national-state relationship in this country, is considered above, Chap. II, "Nature of the Federal System."

[59] Cf. Advisory Commission on Intergovernmental Relations, *op. cit.*, 76.

and to engage in planning and zoning. Each of the county's 26 cities, all of which retain their separate incorporation, is authorized "to exercise all powers relating to its local affairs not inconsistent" with the charter. Thus the county government is the sole local government for unincorporated areas, but shares functions with the municipalities within their borders.[60] By and large, initial experience under the plan appears to have been gratifying. City officials seem rather generally to have felt that the charter's grant of powers to the county government is too broad; but the local voters have twice rejected proposed amendments which would have weakened the central government and strengthened the municipalities. On the basis of a comprehensive study of the background and adoption of the charter, and of the new government's operation during its first five years, Professor Edward Sofen concludes that, "Despite a great many obstacles, Metro has made significant progress." [61]

Metropolitan Special Districts

More easily achieved than city-county consolidation or local federalism, as a means of promoting local-government integration, is the creation of metropolitan special districts. Such districts ordinarily may be established by statutory authority without the need for constitutional amendment, and are less likely than the other plans to encounter strong opposition from incumbent local officials, since the jobs of those officials are not directly imperiled. The special district as an instrument for effecting functional consolidation in general has already been considered. It is appropriate here to note the significant role of such districts in metropolitan reorganization.

A metropolitan special district is a district which covers all or substantial parts of one or more metropolitan areas, and the use of such districts is increasing. Although most districts of this nature are limited to the performance of a single service, a few are multifunctional. In some instances the districts have been created primarily with a view to circumventing constitutional limitations on the taxing and borrowing powers of counties and cities; but in substantial measure the development has been a response to the need for performance of various local-government functions on an area-wide basis. Water supply, sewerage, public transportation, and the supplying of electric power are some of the services now performed for various communities through metropolitan districts. Examples of such districts are the Cleveland Metropolitan Park District; the Metropolitan Sanitary District of Greater Chicago, which provides sewerage facilities for Chicago and more than 100 neighboring municipalities;

---

[60] Edward Sofen, *The Miami Metropolitan Experiment* (Ind. Univ. Press, Bloomington, 1963), Chap. 5.
[61] *Ibid.*, 219.

and the Metropolitan Water District of Southern California, which supplies water to portions of three metropolitan areas.[62]

Intergovernmental Agreements

Intergovernmental contracts or agreements of the kind described in the discussion of functional consolidation are especially well-adapted to use in metropolitan areas and are rapidly increasing in number. Through arrangements of this nature the residents of a small governmental unit may be able to purchase various public services from a larger neighboring unit more economically than if they were to provide these services for themselves. Or several individual units, by pooling their needs and resources, may foster efficiency and economy through the joint performance of functions.

Two of the most extensive programs of cooperative agreements are to be found in the Los Angeles and Philadelphia areas. In the 1940's some 200 intergovernmental contracts were reported as currently in effect in the Los Angeles area of California, many of these being agreements under which the government of Los Angeles county performed property assessment, health protection, and other services for various cities within its borders.[63] More recent years have witnessed the incorporation in Los Angeles county of a considerable number of new municipalities which have never intended to establish full-fledged administrative machinery for the performance of municipal services but have expected to secure desired services from county-government departments through contractual arrangements. This unusual development has resulted in a further increase in the number of intergovernmental contracts in the area.[64] As of 1959 more than 800 contracts were in effect between cities and the Los Angeles county government;[65] and in 1962 it was reported that the county was providing to 73 cities, under some 1,300 individual agreements, services ranging from microfilm record storage to construction of city streets and the provision of police and fire protection.[66] More than 700 interjurisdictional

---

[62] Bollens, *Special District Governments in the United States*, Chap. 6; Advisory Commission on Intergovernmental Relations, *op. cit.*, 49-58. Professor Bollens' chapter is devoted in its entirety to metropolitan districts and constitutes an excellent treatment of the subject.

[63] Frank M. Sewart and Ronald M. Ketcham, "Intergovernmental Contracts in California," *Pub. Admin. Rev.*, I, 242-248 (Spring, 1941); Judith Norvell Jamison, "Neighboring Areas Join Hands," *Nat. Mun. Rev.*, XXXV, 111-114 (Mar., 1946).

[64] The principal reasons underlying this development are analyzed by Evan A. Iverson in "The Incorporation Movement in Los Angeles County," *BGR Observer* (Bur. of Govtl. Research, Univ. of Calif., Los Angeles), June, 1957.

[65] Samuel K. Gove, *The Lakewood Plan* (Inst. of Govt. and Pub. Affairs, Univ. of Ill., Urbana, 1961), 11.

[66] Address by Arthur G. Will, County-City Coordinator of Los Angeles County, before the Annual Conference of the National Association of County Officials, New York City, July 11, 1962.

agreements, dealing with road construction and maintenance, education, and a variety of other matters, were reported in the 1950's as existing in the Philadelphia metropolitan region—an area embracing five counties in Pennsylvania and three in New Jersey.[67]

Tax Differentials

Lastly, mention may be made of tax differentials as a possible means of mitigating some of the difficulties encountered in metropolitan areas. At present it is usual to require that any property tax levied by a local governmental unit be imposed uniformly throughout its jurisdiction. Under the tax-differential plan, a unit would be empowered to provide for portions of its territory services in addition to those provided on a unit-wide basis, and to levy taxes for their support only upon property within the area served. Thus a broad grant of power might be conferred upon counties to provide in unincorporated urban areas, and to finance from special taxes levied therein, services of a municipal nature needed in such communities but not in rural portions of the county. Such a plan, it would seem, should go far toward eliminating objections by rural taxpayers to the extending of special services to urban areas, since those services would no longer be supported by countywide taxation.

Although tax differentials have been endorsed by some scholars and included in several recent proposals for metropolitan reorganization, they seem as yet to have been authorized by state law or charter provision in only a few instances. Something approaching the usual conception of tax differentials is to be found in the city-parish of Baton Rouge, Louisiana, where rural and urban areas pay different tax rates, and in the new metropolitan government of Nashville and Davidson county, Tennessee, under which the Nashville area constitutes an Urban Services District empowered to levy additional taxes for the support of services required within the district but not in outlying rural areas.[68] Several consolidated city-town and borough-town governments in Connecticut use a system of separate taxing districts whereby the taxpayers of the entire area pay for governmental services of general benefit while only the taxpayers of the urban area pay for special urban services.[69] And an Oregon statute of 1957 permits cities to annex fringe areas with property taxes being imposed, for a limited period of time, at less than the full city rate.[70] On the whole, tax differentials appear to deserve more widespread consideration

[67] Jeptha J. Carrell, "Learning to Work Together," *Nat. Mun. Rev.*, XLIII, 526-533 (Nov., 1954).

[68] Kenneth C. Tollenaar, "Taxation Differentials," *Nat. Civic Rev.*, XLVIII, 118-122 (Mar., 1959); Kammerer, *op. cit.*, 6-7.

[69] See Max R. White, "Town and City Consolidation in Connecticut," *Amer. Polit. Sci. Rev.*, XXXVI, 492-502 (June, 1942).

[70] *Oregon Laws*, 1957, Chap. 613; cited in Tollenaar, *op. cit.*

than has thus far been accorded them as a means of introducing a greater degree of flexibility into local tax and service programs and discouraging the undue proliferation of special districts.

PROBLEMS OF INTERNAL ORGANIZATION

Determination of the most desirable area, or combination of areas, for carrying on the functions of local government, is but one aspect of the general problem of local reorganization. Having determined, insofar as it is possible, what areas should exist for governmental purposes, there still remain other equally important problems, one of which is the task of providing those areas with efficient internal organization for carrying on their work. Various problems of internal organization and reorganization at the local level are discussed at some length in other chapters. At this point, however, brief mention will be made of some of the more important of these in an endeavor to present a more adequate overall picture of the reorganization problem.

The need for internal reorganization in local government is most acute in the case of the county. The county is the most nearly universal of all local-government units in the United States, performs a large variety of functions, and spends a great deal of tax money. Moreover, it is with respect to the county that tradition has operated most effectively to prevent the abandonment of ancient and outmoded forms. Probably the most pressing need of county government today is for a single chief executive, elective or appointive, to exercise overall supervision of county administrative agencies. Closely related to the need for a county executive is that for establishing a small number of major administrative departments to perform functions now scattered among many uncorrelated agencies. Another need in many instances is for reorganization of the county governing board. That body should be large enough to serve satisfactorily as the policy-determining body of the county, yet not so large as to be unwieldy, and its members should be elected from the county at large. If a county executive is established, the board should be relieved of its administrative duties and its function limited to the determination of county policy. The archaic office of coroner should be replaced by the medical-examiner system; and the county clerk should be chosen by the county board instead of by popular election.[71]

A form of county reorganization which might well be more widely adopted is that of office consolidation. It has long been recognized that many counties, and especially those in sparsely populated areas, have excessive numbers of offices, and that in numerous instances a single officer might well perform the duties now devolved upon two or more. Office

[71] See above, Chap. XIII.

consolidation would shorten the ballot, should reduce overhead costs, and perhaps might also result in the attraction of better qualified personnel to the more important consolidated offices. A number of states have constitutional or statutory provisions authorizing consolidation of county offices, and some consolidations have actually taken place. Michigan's constitution, for example, has long provided that the offices of county clerk and register of deeds may be consolidated at the discretion of the board of supervisors, and several of the state's rural counties have made such consolidations.[72] The county clerk is ex officio register of deeds in some three-fourths of the counties of Nebraska, and in more than a third of the state's counties he serves also as clerk of the district court.[73] Montana's legislature, pursuant to a constitutional amendment of 1934, has authorized the consolidation of any two or more of eight constitutional offices in any county by order of the board of county commissioners.[74] Several counties have consolidated some of their offices under this legislation, though in some instances the consolidation orders have subsequently been rescinded.[75] In California counties operating under general state law,[76] county offices may be consolidated into various combinations by ordinance of the board of supervisors.[77] As of 1950, according to Professor John Bollens, 96 consolidations were in effect in 47 of the state's 48 general-law counties. For example, 34 counties had consolidated the offices of coroner and public administrator; 11 the offices of treasurer and tax collector; eight the offices of sheriff and coroner; and six the offices of auditor, clerk, and recorder. Most of the consolidations had been effected in rural counties and apparently were designed to combine two or three part-time elective offices into a single full-time position.[78]

Improvement in governmental organization has made more progress in municipalities than in any other class of local unit. This is perhaps best illustrated by the spread, during recent decades, of the strong-mayor and council-manager forms of municipal government.[79] Yet many American municipalities today continue to operate under antiquated and inefficient governmental forms. Recent innovations in New England town government are serving to improve town organization and to adapt traditional forms to modern conditions. These developments include the representa-

[72] Const. of Mich. (1908), art. VIII, sec. 3; Ibid., (1963), art. VII, sec. 4.

[73] Nebraska Legislative Council, Report of the Committee on Reorganization of County Government (Neb. Legis. Council, Lincoln, 1950), 17.

[74] Const. of Mont. (1889 as amended), art. XVI, sec. 5; Rev. Codes of Mont., 1947, secs. 16-2501 to 16-2507. The offices concerned are those of clerk, sheriff, treasurer, superintendent of schools, surveyor, assessor, coroner, and public administrator.

[75] Roland R. Renne, "County Office Consolidations in Montana," Nat. Mun. Rev., XXVIII, 143-148 (Feb., 1939).

[76] As distinguished from those under home-rule charters.

[77] Deering's Calif. Govt. Code Ann., 1951, sec. 24300.

[78] John C. Bollens, "Administrative Integration in California Counties," Pub. Admin. Rev., XI, 26-34 (Winter, 1951).

[79] See above, Chap. XIV.

tive town meeting, finance committees, and town managers.[80] It has previously been suggested in this chapter that the township as it exists in a group of northeastern and north central states should be abolished. If the township is retained, its governmental organization should be overhauled. Desirable steps in this direction would be abolition of the township meeting where it exists by law but does not function properly; establishment, where such does not now exist, of a principal township administrative officer; and abandonment of township justices of the peace in favor of a system of salaried trial justices with countywide jurisdiction.[81] In the township, as in the county, tradition has been a strong force in preventing the modernization of governmental machinery. This fact, however, has been relatively less serious in the case of the township, which performs fewer functions and exists in less than a third of the states.

A need in local governmental units of all types, and especially those serving rural areas, is for extension of the merit system of personnel administration. Only New York State requires that the merit system be used by all local units. Most of the larger American municipalities now employ the system to some extent, but a large majority of the smaller cities and villages are without it. Most cities operating under the merit system have their own civil service commissions, though some are served by state or county personnel agencies.[82] Outside the larger cities, the spoils system is, by and large, still deeply entrenched in local government. Perhaps as many as 300 counties are today provided in some manner with civil service machinery. Most New York counties have their own civil service commissions or personnel officers, as do some counties—for the most part from among the more populous ones—in other states.[83] Another group of counties, drawn principally from Ohio and New Jersey, have their personnel functions performed by state agencies—a plan which is particularly well adapted to counties and other local units of relatively small population. Nevertheless, approximately 90 percent of the counties continue to be unserved by civil service agencies of general jurisdiction, and a large majority of county employees are subject to appointment and dismissal on a patronage basis.[84] As regards townships and special districts, only a few such units are provided with merit systems.

[80] See above, Chap. XV.

[81] See above, Chap. XI, "Abolition of Justice-of-the-Peace Courts;" Chap. XV, "Township Government."

[82] For a discussion of personnel problems in municipalities, see Municipal Manpower Commission, *Governmental Manpower for Tomorrow's Cities* (Report of the Commission, McGraw-Hill, New York, 1962).

[83] For an account of the New York system, see Henry J. McFarland, "Personnel Services for Local Government: The New York Program," *Pub. Personnel Rev.*, XVI, 148-152 (July, 1955).

[84] Cf. O. Glenn Stahl, *Public Personnel Administration* (Harper, New York, 5th ed., 1962), 46-47. As indicated in Chapter X above, special merit systems are provided, where general civil service provisions do not exist, for local welfare employees engaged in the administration of public assistance programs financed in part by federal funds under the Social Security Act.

FUTURE OF REORGANIZATION

Past developments and present trends suggest certain general directions in which reorganization is likely to proceed in the years to come. In the first place, it seems reasonable to expect that efforts to improve the internal organization of local governmental units along lines similar to those discussed in the preceding section will continue, and that, over a period of time, many of these will meet with success. Tradition, constitutional obstacles,[85] and the reluctance of state legislators to impose changes of a compulsory nature will combine to make the process of modernizing local-government machinery a slow one, but that further progress will take place there can be little doubt.

With respect to areal adjustments the future is more uncertain. Changes of this nature are, in practice, even more difficult to effect than changes in organization. Yet it seems justifiable to expect that some progress will be made, especially in the direction of reducing the number of local governmental units. That the number of counties will be substantially reduced through consolidation in the foreseeable future is not at all probable. On the other hand, consolidation of school districts is already far advanced in a number of states and is likely to be given further impetus by additional laws making compulsory the consolidation of schools with small attendance or providing for the allocation of state aid in such a manner as to encourage mergers. Though consolidation of city and county governments has as yet been effected in only a few instances, the recent merger of Nashville and Davidson county in Tennessee may indicate a renewal of interest in the plan, and it is quite possible that the future may see its adoption in other metropolitan communities. Adoption of the new charter of Dade county, Florida, may well give some encouragement to proponents of local federalism. In any event, the growing seriousness of metropolitan problems and the increasing attention which is being accorded them suggest that highly-urbanized areas will constitute the principal focus of reorganizational activities in the years immediately ahead.

Deorganization of individual counties, towns, and townships is not likely to proceed rapidly; but, where legislation permitting such action is available, some units in sparsely-settled areas will doubtless deorganize their governments to lessen their tax burden. Voluntary deorganization seems to offer greatest possibilities in those states, such as Maine and

---

[85] Cf. Howard P. Jones, "Constitutional Barriers to Improvement in County Government" (Report No. 1 of the Committee on County Govt. of the Nat. Mun. League), *Nat. Mun. Rev.*, XXI, 525-542 (Aug., 1932, Supp.); M. H. Satterfield, "Counties in a Straitjacket," *Ibid.*, XXXVII, 81-85, 124 (Feb., 1948).

South Dakota, which have traditionally had some unorganized territory.[86] Statewide abolition of townships, however desirable, will be difficult to achieve in most states and cannot be expected to take place on anything approaching a nationwide scale in the near future. Though many special-purpose districts should be abolished and their functions transferred to appropriate general-government units, dissolutions of special districts during recent years have been more than offset by the creation of new units of the same category.

Gradual transfer of specific functions from smaller to larger units seems certain to continue, and progressively more use will be made of functional consolidation, particularly of the contract variety. Functional consolidation is in a sense an alternative to geographic merger, offering the advantages of the larger unit in the provision of certain services in instances where complete consolidation is for various reasons impracticable. Though the district form of functional consolidation is advantageous in some instances, it is subject to the objection that it further increases the number of local units. The contractual form, on the other hand, obviates this disadvantage and provides a flexible and practicable means of cooperation between any number of local units of the same or different types.

Finally, it must be recognized that reorganization can be effected only by a laborious process at best, and that perfection is not to be expected. All that can be hoped for is a constant striving in the direction of improvement. In the opinion of the present writer, any practicable plan for reconstructing local areas must have among its primary objectives both a substantial reduction in the total number of local governmental units and the reduction to a minimum of the number of layers of government under which the individual citizen lives. We must abandon the notion that the degree of popular control over local government is directly proportional to the number of local units. Quite to the contrary, a simplification of local government, including the elimination as far as possible of overlapping areas, should actually foster democratic control and stimulate vigorous participation in local affairs.

REFERENCES

Advisory Commission on Intergovernmental Relations, *Alternative Approaches to Governmental Reorganization in Metropolitan Areas* (U.S. Govt. Printing Office, Washington, 1962).

ANDERSON, William, *The Reorganization of Local Government in Minnesota* (League of Minn. Municipalities, Minneapolis, 1933).

[86] Cf. Carpenter, *Problems in Service Levels*, 123.

————, *The Units of Government in the United States* (Pub. Admin. Service, Chicago, 1942 ed., reprinted with appendixes in 1945 and 1949).

BROMAGE, Arthur W., *American County Government* (Sears Pub. Co., New York, 1933), Chap. 10.

CARPENTER, William S., *Problems in Service Levels: The Readjustment of Services and Areas in Local Government* (Princeton Univ. Press, Princeton, N.J., 1940).

Council of State Governments, *The States and the Metropolitan Problem: A Report to the Governor's Conference* (The Council, Chicago, 1956).

FESLER, James W., *Area and Administration* (Univ. of Ala. Press, University, Ala., 1949).

FITZWATER, C. O., *School District Reorganization: Policies and Procedures* (U.S. Office of Education, Washington, 1957).

GREER, Scott, *Governing the Metropolis* (Wiley, New York, 1962).

————, *Metropolitics: A Study of Political Culture* (Wiley, New York, 1963).

JONES, Victor, *Metropolitan Government* (Univ. of Chicago Press, Chicago, 1942).

KETCHAM, Ronald M., *Intergovernmental Cooperation in the Los Angeles Area* (Bur. of Govtl. Research, Univ. of Calif., Los Angeles, 1940).

LANCASTER, Lane W., *Government in Rural America* (Van Nostrand, New York, 2nd ed., 1952), Chap. 15.

MANNY, Theodore B., *Rural Municipalities: A Sociological Study of Local Government in the United States* (Century, New York, 1930).

MERRIAM, Charles E., PARRATT, Spencer D., and LEPAWSKY, Albert, *The Government of the Metropolitan Region of Chicago* (Univ. of Chicago Press, Chicago, 1933).

MILLSPAUGH, Arthur C., *Local Democracy and Crime Control* (Brookings Inst., Washington, 1936), especially Chaps. 4-7.

Reorganization of Local Government in New York State (Sixth Report of the N.Y. State Comsn. for the Revsn. of the Tax Laws, Albany, 1935).

RUSH, John A., *The City-County Consolidated* (Author, Los Angeles, 1941).

STUDENSKI, Paul, *The Government of Metropolitan Areas in the United States* (Nat. Mun. League, New York, 1930).

TABLEMAN, Betty, *Governmental Orgnization in Metropolitan Areas* (Univ. of Mich. Press, Ann Arbor, 1951).

WOOD, Robert G., *Suburbia: Its People and their Politics* (Houghton, Boston, 1958).

VI____

State and Local Functions

17

Law Enforcement

Thus far our concern has been with the legal nature of state and local governmental units, the fundamental laws through which they are established, their relations to each other and to the federal government, the means of popular control over them, and their internal organization and powers. But governments exist for the performance of services, and to that important aspect of the subject we now turn. A description of all the multifarious activities carried on by the state and local governments is quite beyond the scope of this general work. However, in this next group of chapters, consideration will be given to various selected functions of major significance.

One of the most fundamental of these is the enforcement of criminal law. In the field of civil law, as we have previously seen,[1] the function of government consists merely in laying down the rules that are to govern individuals in their relations with each other and in providing judicial tribunals in which controversies may be adjudicated. With respect to the criminal law, however, government assumes the additional responsibility of preventing, insofar as possible, violations of the law, and of punishing such infractions as do occur. Though there is now a considerable body of federal criminal law enforced by federal officers through the federal courts, American criminal law is for the most part state law and its enforcement is primarily a function of state government.[2] In actual prac-

[1] Above, Chap. XI.
[2] Whereas common law constitutes an important part of the civil law of the states, the criminal law is now largely statutory. In some states, indeed, no act is treated as criminal unless made so by statute.

tice, however, basic responsibility for law enforcement has now been delegated in large measure to the various units of local government, with the states themselves maintaining only a general and somewhat attenuated supervision over the local authorities.

Organization for Law Enforcement

For the purpose of carrying on the function of law enforcement the states and local governments are provided with a variety of administrative officers and agencies whose duties consist in preserving the peace, arresting violators of the law, and prosecuting such offenders in the criminal courts. Although many of these agencies have already been discussed in other connections,[3] their respective roles in the law-enforcement process will be further considered in this chapter; and particular attention will be directed to certain important agencies, such as the state police, prosecuting attorney, and grand and petit juries, which are not given extended consideration elsewhere.

State Law-Enforcement Agencies

At the state level, the principal agencies for the enforcement of criminal law are the governor, the attorney general, the National Guard, and the state police. The governor stands at the head of the state's law-enforcement machinery, and is charged by the constitution with the duty of seeing that the laws are "faithfully executed." Notwithstanding the explicit nature of this constitutional mandate, the chief executive in most states has no adequate means of control over those officers—principally the attorney general and prosecuting attorneys—upon whom he must rely for assistance in its performance. Being in most instances popularly elected, these officials are quite independent of the governor. In striking contrast to this situation is the federal organization, under which the President as principal law-enforcement officer is assisted by an attorney general, district attorneys, and United States marshals, all of whom he appoints and may remove. It seems certain that the organization of a state department of justice along the lines of the federal system, under which the governor would have the power to appoint and remove the state attorney general, prosecuting attorneys, and perhaps also sheriffs, would go far toward making the enforcement of state law more efficient.[4]

---

[3] See above, Chaps. IX (governor and National Guard), X (attorney general), XIII (sheriff), XV (constable).

[4] Several states have "state departments of justice" of one kind or another, but none of these approaches the federal pattern. See W. L. Gosslin, "Streamlined Law Enforcement; a State Department of Justice for Oregon," *Commonwealth Rev.*, XXII, 253-265 (Jan., 1941).

Though the attorney general ranks next to the governor in the law-enforcement hierarchy, his actual participation in criminal law enforcement is not extensive. He does, however, have some functions in connection with the prosecution of accused persons before the courts, and these will be considered at a subsequent point in this chapter.[5] As we have seen,[6] the National Guard is not infrequently employed by the governor to maintain order in situations with which the ordinary law-enforcement agencies are unable to cope.

The State Police. Every state has a state police force of some kind. In some instances the force is a special highway patrol charged only with enforcement of motor-vehicle regulations, while in others the force is vested with general jurisdiction to enforce all state laws. The police system in some states constitutes a separate department of the state government, and in others is merely a subdivision of a department. The commissioner or superintendent of police usually is appointed by the governor and is responsible to the chief executive either directly or indirectly.[7] Some states maintain a state bureau of criminal identification and investigation either as a part of the state police department or independent thereof.

The state police force is primarily an agency for the enforcement of law in rural areas. Some states specifically prohibit the state police from acting within the limits of municipalities except at the request of the local authorities;[8] and in most other states, as a matter of practice, the state authorities act within municipalities only upon local request. A common limitation upon the powers of the state police, even in those states where they enjoy general law-enforcement jurisdiction, is the prohibition of their employment in connection with strikes, lockouts, and other labor disputes —a limitation ordinarily owing its existence to the influence of organized labor.[9]

Applicants for appointment to state police forces are usually required to pass examinations designed to test their physical, mental, and moral fitness. These examinations tend to eliminate candidates who are totally unfit, but do not always result in selection of those best qualified. In some states the police force has been placed under the jurisdiction of a state personnel agency, and there is an encouraging trend toward the selection of state police officers on a merit basis.[10]

---

[5] See below, "The Attorney-General and Criminal Prosecution."

[6] Above, Chap. IX.

[7] Cf. *The Book of the States* (Council of State Govts., Chicago), 1948-49, pp. 663-664; Frank D. Day, "State Police and Highway Patrols," *Ibid.*, 1964-65, pp. 461-466.

[8] David G. Monroe, *State and Provincial Police*, 20-21.

[9] *Ibid.*; Bruce Smith, *Police Systems in the United States* (rev. ed.), 179.

[10] Monroe, *State and Provincial Police*, Chap. 5; David G. Monroe, "State Police and State Highway Patrols," *The Book of States*, 1948-49, pp. 481-488; Day, *op. cit.*

Local Law-Enforcement Agencies

The principal local officers concerned with maintenance of the peace and the apprehension of lawbreakers are the sheriff in the county, the constable in the township, and the town marshal and city police within incorporated municipalities. Two other law-enforcement agencies at the local level, namely, the grand jury and the prosecuting attorney, will be given special consideration at this point.

The Grand Jury. The primary function of the grand jury is to consider cases of law violation laid before it by the prosecuting attorney for the purpose of determining whether the evidence against suspected persons is sufficient to warrant bringing them to trial. It does not determine the question of whether a suspected person is guilty of the offense concerned. Since the grand-jury proceeding is not a trial, the suspected person has no right to appear before the jury, which is concerned only with weighing the evidence *against* him. If the jury, after due deliberation, concludes that the evidence is sufficient to justify bringing the suspect to trial, it returns an *indictment,* which is a formal charge or accusation, in the name of the state, that the suspected person committed the crime concerned. If, on the other hand, the jury deems the evidence insufficient for indictment, the suspected person is not brought to trial unless charged with the crime in a subsequent proceeding.[11]

Another power of the grand jury is that of acting as a general investigatory body. In such a capacity, it sometimes conducts investigations of matters of public concern, such as alleged election frauds and the conduct of public offices. Such investigations usually result in special reports, and sometimes also in the return of indictments.[12]

Members of the grand jury are usually chosen by lot, often in the same manner as members of the petit jury.[13] The body varies in size in the different states from five to twenty-three members.[14] At common law

[11] See below, "The Prosecuting Attorney," "Preferring of Charges."

[12] Cf. W. F. Willoughby, *Principles of Judicial Administration,* 193-194. Grand juries occasionally are charged with duties in connection with certain noncriminal proceedings such as recommending the issuance of liquor licenses, passing on the location of highways, and participating in the removal of public officials. "The Grand Jury—Its Investigatory Powers and Limitations," *Minn. Law Rev.,* XXXVII, 586-607 (June, 1953).

[13] See below, "The Trial Jury."

[14] Michigan employs a system, commonly known as a "one-man grand jury," under which a single official, and he a judge, performs investigatory functions in connection with alleged crimes similar in many respects to functions vested in grand juries in other states. A comprehensive account of the history and operation of the Michigan system is to be found in Robert G. Scigliano, *The Michigan One-Man Grand Jury* (Govtl. Research Bur., Mich. State Univ., East Lansing, 1957). Several other states now have, or in the past have had, statutes authorizing judicial inquiry into the com-

there were twenty-three members, the vote of twelve being necessary for returning an indictment, and the common-law rule is still followed in some states. In several states the grand jury consists of twelve members, nine of whom must concur in an indictment. In no instance does indictment require a unanimous vote.

The Prosecuting Attorney.[15] So important is the work of the prosecuting attorney that his office may well be termed the keystone in the arch of law enforcement. The official title of this officer varies from state to state—being in different instances prosecuting attorney, state's attorney, commonwealth attorney, county attorney, etc.—but that of prosecuting attorney is most indicative of his principal duties and will be used in a generic sense in this discussion. Strictly speaking, the prosecuting attorney is an officer of the state, but since he is usually chosen locally and serves a particular community he may for practical purposes be considered a local official. In some states there is a prosecutor for each county, whereas in others a single official serves a district embracing two or more counties. Though appointed in a few states by the governor, the attorney general, or the courts,[16] the prosecuting attorney is in most states popularly elected, the usual term of office being two, four, or six years. His principal powers and duties are concerned with two phases of law enforcement: the preferring of formal charges against persons suspected of having committed crimes; and the prosecution in the courts of persons against whom charges have been filed.[17] In sparsely populated rural counties the prosecutor's office is manned by the prosecuting attorney, sometimes with a deputy and a stenographer. In metropolitan counties, on the other hand, the work of the office requires an extensive staff, including assistant prosecutors, numerous clerical employees, and sometimes special police and investigators.[18]

---

mission of crime by procedures resembling those of Michigan. See Glenn R. Winters, "The Michigan One-Man Grand Jury," *Jour. of Amer. Judic. Soc.*, XXVIII, 137-151 (Feb., 1945).

[15] An excellent series of articles on the office of prosecuting attorney by Newman F. Baker and Earl H. DeLong will be found in sundry issues of the *Journal of Criminal Law and Criminology* for the years 1933-1935. See also Newman F. Baker, "The Prosecuting Attorney: Legal Aspects of the Office," *Ibid.*, XXVI, 647-678 (Jan.-Feb., 1936).

[16] "The Office of Attorney General in Kentucky," *Ky. Law Jour.*, Vol. LI, No. 5 (Special Issue, 1963), pp. 90S-91S.

[17] In some states the prosecuting attorney has, in addition to his duties of criminal law enforcement, various duties of a civil nature such as giving legal advice to the county board and other county officers, conducting civil cases to which the county is a party, and instituting court action for the collection of delinquent taxes. In other states these civil functions are performed by another law officer, sometimes known as the "county attorney."

[18] Cf. Newman F. Baker and Earl H. DeLong, "The Prosecuting Attorney: The Process of Prosecution," I, *Jour. of Crim. Law and Criminol.*, XXVI, 3-21 (May, 1935).

The prosecutor, as previously noted, lays before the grand jury cases of law violation that have come to his attention and submits to the jury such evidence against suspected persons as he has been able to obtain. Prior to presenting a case to the grand jury for action, the prosecuting attorney usually drafts an indictment document, which he transmits to the jury with the evidence. If the jury votes to indict, this document is validated by the jury foreman's endorsing it with the words "a true bill" and signing his name. If the decision is against indicting, the endorsement is that of "no true bill" or "bill not found." Finally, the prosecuting attorney is the official adviser of the grand jury with respect to its powers and procedure. From these relationships, it will readily be seen that the prosecutor is in a position to exert a powerful influence—indeed, in most instances, a determining influence—upon grand-jury action. The jury normally considers only matters submitted to it by the prosecuting attorney, and whether or not an indictment is returned depends almost entirely upon the prosecutor's diligence and skill in collecting and presenting evidence in the case.[19]

The grand jury is an ancient institution of the English law, and its use, especially in felony cases, is still widely required in the American states by constitutional or statutory provision. However, a majority of the states now permit at least some use of the *information* as an alternative to grand-jury indictment in the preferring of criminal charges, particularly in cases of lesser crimes.[20] In many states prosecution of practically all cases may now be by information;[21] and in some it has become the practice to use this device almost exclusively.[22]

An information is a formal accusation or charge of crime filed against a suspected person by the prosecuting attorney. Its effect, in bringing the accused to trial, is the same as that of an indictment, and it differs from the latter only in that it is filed by the prosecutor, on his own initiative and responsibility, without grand-jury action. Whether or not an information will be filed in a particular case is wholly within the discretion of the prosecuting attorney. In view of what was said above concerning his relationship to the grand jury, it will now be seen that the prosecuting attorney exercises a momentous power in determining who shall and who shall not be charged with crime. Where the information is used,

[19] The grand jury may, to be sure, return indictments on its own initiative and authority in matters not laid before it by the prosecuting attorney, but in practice this is seldom done. When the jury does thus act on its own responsibility, the instrument through which charges are preferred is sometimes called a "presentment" to distinguish it from the usual indictment found upon recommendation of the prosecutor.

[20] For a comprehensive analysis of the requirement and use of the grand jury, see Wayne L. Morse, "A Survey of the Grand Jury System," *Ore. Law Rev.*, X, 101-160, 217-257, 295-365 (Feb., Apr., June, 1931).

[21] Raymond Moley, "The Initiation of Criminal Prosecutions by Indictment or Information," *Mich. Law Rev.*, XXIX, 403-431 (Feb., 1931).

[22] Justin Miller, "Informations or Indictments in Felony Cases," *Minn. Law Rev.*, VIII, 379-408 (Apr., 1924).

the decision as to whether it shall issue is solely his; and in the case of grand-jury action it is largely within his power to determine whether an indictment shall be found.

When a suspected person has been charged, either by indictment or by information, with the commission of a crime, it becomes the duty of the prosecuting attorney to prepare the case against the accused and to conduct the prosecution, in the name of the state, before the proper court. In performing this duty, it is the prosecutor who, personally or by deputy, participates in selection of the trial jury; gathers, organizes, and presents evidence against the accused; examines the state's witnesses; cross-examines defense witnesses; and makes the state's final plea to the jury. These functions require, for their effective performance, a high degree of legal knowledge and oratorical skill. Given a reasonable amount of evidence against the accused, the likelihood of securing a conviction depends almost entirely upon the ability and energy of the prosecuting attorney. A special power of the prosecutor of much potential importance is that of asking the court to enter a *nolle prosequi* or dismissal of the case. Motion for a *nolle prosequi* is usually made on the ground that the state has insufficient evidence to secure a conviction, and that it would therefore be a waste of time and money to proceed with the prosecution. Though the motion has perfectly legitimate uses, as for example in a case where the state's key witness has died, it may also be used by a prosecuting attorney who wishes to bring about the dismissal of cases for personal or political reasons.

The paramount importance of the prosecuting attorney in law enforcement serves to indicate that the office should be filled by one of the most able and experienced members of the local bar. Unfortunately, in many instances it is not so filled. The salary of the prosecutor is usually insufficient to attract the best legal talent,[23] and popular election is scarcely a method whereby the services of the most able lawyers can be secured. The office, particularly in rural areas, is often held either by a young lawyer fresh from school, who seeks by this means to widen his acquaintance and at the same time gain some experience, or, less frequently, by an older attorney whose career in private practice has not been outstanding. In either case, the incumbent is likely to prove a poor match for experienced criminal lawyers of the class often retained by persons accused of major crimes.

The Attorney General and Criminal Prosecution

In three states—Alaska, Delaware, and Rhode Island—responsibility for conducting criminal prosecutions is imposed upon the state attorney

---

[23] In some rural counties the prosecutor finds it necessary to supplement his public salary by engaging in part-time private practice. This results in a division of his interest and efforts, often to the detriment of his public work.

general rather than upon locally-elected prosecuting attorneys. Some other states give the attorney general nominal power of supervision over local prosecutors and provide that he shall render assistance to the local officials; but these provisions do not operate to clothe the attorney general with any real power of control. In most states the attorney general possesses the *power*, either under the common law or by statute, to conduct criminal prosecutions generally or those involving specified offenses. This power of prosecution is ordinarily concurrent with that of the local prosecutor, though in some states the attorney general's authority is broad enough to enable him to assume control of a prosecution which has been instituted by the local officer. In any event, the power of the attorney general to conduct prosecutions are of a permissive nature only, and in practice are rarely exercised. This is natural in view of the fact that both the attorney general and the local prosecutor are elective officials. Since the local prosecutor is charged with the *duty* of prosecution, whereas the attorney general is only vested with the *power* to take action in his discretion, the state official is likely to take the position that it is up to the local electorate to choose a prosecutor who will give them efficient law enforcement. Moreover, action taken against the wishes of locally-elected officials could easily offend local voters whose support the attorney general might need in a campaign for reelection. Many states make it the duty of the attorney general to conduct before the state supreme court criminal proceedings which have been appealed to that tribunal. This duty, however, seems often to be performed in a perfunctory manner. All in all, it appears that, notwithstanding rather broad legal *powers* with respect to prosecution, the actual participation of the attorney general in this aspect of law enforcement is, in most states, virtually negligible.[24]

The Law-Enforcement Process

For convenience, the normal process by which the criminal laws of the state are enforced may be considered as falling into seven successive steps: (1) maintenance of the peace; (2) arrest of law violators; (3) preliminary hearing; (4) preferring of charges; (5) arraignment; (6) prosecution and trial; and (7) punishment of convicted persons.

Maintenance of the Peace. The first duty in law enforcement is that of preserving the peace and preventing, insofar as possible, infractions of the law. To this end, state police, sheriffs, constables, city police, and town marshals patrol streets and highways and visit establishments and

[24] For a comprehensive discussion of the subject, see Earl H. DeLong, "Powers and Duties of the State Attorney-General in Criminal Prosecution," *Jour. of Crim. Law and Criminol.*, XXV, 358-400 (Sept.-Oct., 1934). Cf. also "The Office of Attorney General in Kentucky," *loc. cit.*

gatherings where disorder is likely to arise or law violations occur. Thus police officers seek, by their very presence, to encourage law observance.

Arrest of Law Violators. When, notwithstanding these precautions, an infraction of the criminal law takes place, it is the duty of the police officers to seek out and arrest the perpetrator of the criminal act. In their searching for criminals, the police are assisted by the state bureau of identification, where such exists, as well as by access to the files of fingerprints and other identification aids maintained by the larger municipal police departments. The extensive fingerprint files of the Federal Bureau of Investigation are also available for use by state and local law-enforcement officers.

Arrest has been defined as "the taking of a person into custody in order that he may be forthcoming to answer for the commission of an offense,"[25] and is made sometimes with and sometimes without a warrant.[26] A warrant of arrest is a court order directing the arrest of a designated person or persons, issued upon complaint of a private citizen—usually some person who has been injured by the crime complained of—or of a law-enforcement officer. As a general rule, a police officer may arrest without a warrant any person who commits a crime, either misdemeanor or felony, in his presence. For offenses not committed in the officer's presence a warrant is usually necessary except that, in the case of a felony, arrest may be made without warrant if the officer has *reasonable cause* to believe that the person arrested has committed the crime. Private citizens possess much the same legal authority as do police officers to make arrests for offenses committed in their presence, but in practice this authority is seldom exercised.[27] Few persons wish to incur either the personal danger or the legal responsibility that the making of an arrest might involve. And, in a civil damage suit for false arrest, a jury is likely to be less lenient toward a private individual than towards a public officer who believed himself to be acting in the course of duty.

Preliminary Hearing. An arrest having been made, the next step, which ordinarily follows within a few hours, is to take the arrested person before a court for a preliminary hearing. This proceeding usually takes place before a justice of the peace or the judge of some other minor court, and its purpose is to determine whether the evidence against the sus-

[25] American Law Institute, *Code of Criminal Procedure* (1930), sec. 18. For a scholarly analysis of the law of arrest, see Rollin M. Perkins, "The Law of Arrest," *Ia. Law Rev.*, XXV, 201-289 (Jan., 1940).

[26] Cf. Rocco Tresolini, Richard W. Taylor, and Elliott B. Barnett, "Arrest Without Warrant: Extent and Social Implications," *Jour. of Crim. Law, Criminol., and Police Sci.*, XLVI, 187-198 (July-Aug., 1955).

[27] In a very few states private persons, like police officers, may arrest in the case of felonies on reasonable suspicion. David Fellman, *The Defendant's Rights*, 13.

pected person is sufficient to justify holding him for action by the grand jury or prosecuting attorney. It is a common practice at preliminary hearings to hear only evidence against the suspect, although the latter must be permitted to make a statement if he wishes to do so. To justify holding the suspect, the court must be convinced by the evidence submitted that the crime charged has been committed and that there is reasonable ground to believe that the defendant is guilty. If the magistrate is so convinced, he "binds over" the suspect to the grand jury or to await the filing of an information by the prosecutor. On the other hand, if the magistrate decides that the evidence does not show a case, he discharges the prisoner. Although a discharge at this point usually terminates the proceeding against the suspected person, it is no constitutional bar to his subsequent rearrest on the same charge.[28]

Bail. When a suspected person, on the basis of the preliminary hearing, is ordered held for further action, the committing magistrate who issues the order must, unless the offense is nonbailable (this is frequently true of capital offenses), permit the release of the suspect on bail pending such action. In doing this, the magistrate fixes the amount of the bail bond which the suspect must post as security for his future appearance at the prescribed time. The amount of the bond may be posted in cash or negotiable securities or, as is more commonly the case, bond is supplied by a friend or a professional bondsman. In most instances, the security offered is in the form of real estate. Adequacy of the security must be approved by the magistrate, who in this connection usually has the assistance of the prosecuting attorney's office in an investigatory and advisory capacity. If the suspect is unable to supply the required bail, or if his offense is nonbailable, he is placed in jail to await further disposition of his case.

The supplying of bail bonds has at times, and especially in metropolitan communities, been pervaded by corrupt politics, professional bondsmen together with politically-minded magistrates and prosecuting attorneys having developed what has become known as a "bail-bond racket." Magistrates and prosecutors may decline to approve bonds other than those offered by favored bondsmen, and the latter, assured of a virtual monopoly, are free to charge the highest fees that the law allows. Security may be approved which is wholly inadequate. The same real estate may be accepted as security on numerous bonds, to a total amount far in excess of its value, and, in case of default, the prosecutor may take no action to collect from the bondsman. The Missouri Crime Survey reports a St. Louis bondsman who owned real estate assessed at $24,100 and mortgaged for $31,500. In a single year, this man was permitted to be-

---

[28] Cf. Clarence N. Callender, *American Courts: Their Organization and Procedure* (McGraw, New York, 1927), 171-173.

come surety on bonds aggregating $670,295. And, when the survey was made, he was surety on outstanding bonds totaling $90,000, and was subject to suit on $30,000 in forfeitures.[29]

Preferring of Charges. The next step in the law-enforcement process is the preferring of formal charges against the suspected person. This is done either by grand-jury indictment or by information filed by the prosecuting attorney.[30] These respective procedures have been explained earlier in this chapter,[31] and it has been pointed out that the information has now supplanted the indictment, in greater or less degree, in many states. Originating in England as a device to extract from the people of a locality knowledge concerning matters of interest to the crown, the grand jury gradually developed into an instrument for protecting the people against arbitrary accusation and prosecution by the crown; and it was this latter purpose that the framers of American state constitutions had in mind when they incorporated in those documents the provision that felony prosecutions might be commenced only by grand-jury indictment.[32] At the present time, however, with the office of public prosecutor what it is, the grand jury seems to be in large measure superfluous. It tends to be dominated by the prosecutor and to become a mere "rubber stamp" for his wishes. Yet, while the prosecutor may be able to control the grand jury in its determination of whether an indictment shall be returned, he cannot be held responsible for the jury's action. When, on the other hand, the information is employed, it is impossible for the prosecutor to shift responsibility in the matter of preferring charges to shoulders other than his own. Comparative studies seem to indicate that, in general, the information possesses the following advantages over the indictment: (1) it saves time; (2) it is cheaper; (3) it results in fewer unsuccessful prosecutions; and (4) it properly centers in the prosecutor responsibility for action which, in any event, he is likely to control.[33] Because of these advantages, it is coming to be widely believed that states which have not yet done so would do well to follow the example of those that have largely abandoned use of the grand jury. Perhaps the agency should be retained for general investigations, and for action in cases where, for special reasons, the court may see fit to summon a grand jury. But constitutional

[29] Missouri Association for Criminal Justice, *The Missouri Crime Survey*, 211-212.

[30] Indictment may, and sometimes does, precede arrest. This is likely to be true, for example, where indictments are returned as the result of investigations of such matters as election frauds, and may occur in the case of any individual suspect who has not yet been apprehended. In such instances, "bench warrants" for arrest of the accused are issued by the trial court on the basis of the indictments.

[31] See above, "The Grand Jury," "The Prosecuting Attorney."

[32] H. L. McClintock, "Indictment by Grand Jury," *Minn. Law Rev.*, XXVI, 153-176, 156 (Jan., 1942).

[33] Cf. Moley, *op. cit.*

insistence upon use of the grand jury in all felony cases seems clearly to constitute a hindrance rather than an aid to effective law enforcement.[34]

Arraignment and Plea. Formal charges having been preferred, the accused is next arraigned before the trial court. At this point, the indictment or information is read to the accused and he is given opportunity to plead "guilty" or "not guilty" to the charges contained therein. Should he decline to plead, a plea of "not guilty" is entered by the court. When a plea of guilty is made, trial is in most instances dispensed with and the court proceeds to pronounce judgment and sentence. Some states, however, have statutes relating to capital offenses which either prohibit the entry of a plea of guilty or provide that, notwithstanding such plea, the court shall proceed with trial by jury.[35] A plea of not guilty brings the case to trial.

Prosecution and Trial. Though misdemeanors are often tried, in the first instance, in minor tribunals, prosecutions for felony are ordinarily instituted in the general trial courts.[36] In the trial court it is the prosecuting attorney who, as we have seen, conducts the state's case against the defendant. The defendant is represented by private counsel, counsel appointed by the court, or a public defender.[37] The right to be tried by jury is generally guaranteed to defendants in criminal actions by constitutional provision; and, although jury trial may be waived in some jurisdictions and under some circumstances, waiver in felony cases is rare.

The Trial Jury. The jury here involved is the petit or trial jury, as distinguished from the grand jury which has been previously discussed. It is the trial jury which, on the basis of the evidence presented, the arguments of counsel, and the instructions of the court concerning the law involved, decides whether or not the accused is guilty of the offense charged, and returns its verdict accordingly.[38] At common law the trial jury consisted of twelve persons. Today, many states provide for the trial of misdemeanors by juries of less than twelve members,[39] though the jury

[34] The United States Constitution, in a provision (Fifth Amendment) applying to the federal government but not to the states, stipulates that "No person shall be held to answer for a capital or otherwise infamous crime, unless on a presentment or indictment of a grand jury. . . ." In view of this requirement, all major criminal offenses against the federal government are prosecuted on grand-jury charges. Misdemeanors, however, may be prosecuted in the federal courts on information.

[35] See 22 *Corpus Juris Secundum,* "Criminal Law," sec. 422.

[36] See above, Chap. XI.

[37] See below.

[38] The petit jury is also frequently used in civil cases.

[39] Francis X. Busch, *Law and Tactics in Jury Trials,* 29.

of twelve is still almost universally required in the trial of major crimes.[40]

Constitutions or statutes in the various states prescribe qualifications for jury service. There is usually a lower age limit of twenty-one or twenty-five, and sometimes also an upper limit of sixty-five or seventy. Citizenship or eligibility to vote is frequently required, residence qualifications are common, and there is sometimes a property-ownership or taxpaying test.[41] With respect to other qualifications, the Illinois law may be taken as fairly typical. It prescribes that jurors shall be "In the possession of their natural faculties and not infirm or decrepit. . . . Free from all legal exceptions, of fair character, of approved integrity, of sound judgment, well informed, and who understand the English language." There is usually a lengthy list of statutory exemptions covering especially professional people and public officers. Among the classes thus commonly exempted are clergymen, lawyers, physicians, school teachers, state and local officers, policemen, and firemen. Formerly, juries were composed exclusively of men. During recent decades, however, most states have modified their constitutional and statutory provisions to permit jury service by women, some merely making women *eligible* for jury duty but providing that they shall be excused upon request, and others imposing the same *liability* for service upon women as upon men.

The first step in the selection of a jury is the preparation of a list of names from which a panel may be drawn. The duty of preparing this list is placed, in different states, upon the county board, certain town officers, jury commissioners appointed by the court, or other designated officers. In most states names for the jury list are taken from either the local assessment rolls or voters' registration lists, though some jurisdictions make use of city directories, telephone directories, and census reports. From the list so prepared, names to the number prescribed by law are chosen, usually more or less at random, and placed in the jury box. When a new panel of jurors is needed, the court clerk draws a designated number of names from the box, and the persons so chosen are summoned to appear for service. The summoning of jurors has traditionally been a function of the sheriff, and is such today in most states. In a few jurisdictions, however, summons is now made by registered mail, a practice which seems to be more efficient than the older method and also, since

[40] Most states now permit the drawing of one or more "alternate" jurors in addition to the regular panel. Alternate jurors hear the evidence and arguments along with the regular jurors and are available to replace any of the latter who may die, or become disabled or otherwise disqualified, during the course of the trial. The use of alternate jurors is desirable, particularly in long-protracted cases, as a means of avoiding mistrials and the expense and inconvenience which new trials involve. Cf. *Ibid.*, 30-31.

[41] An analysis of jurors' qualifications in the respective states will be found in *Ibid.*, 86-88.

sheriff's fees are eliminated, more economical. When a particular case is called, the plan usually followed is to place in a box the names of all jurors present and not engaged, and to draw twelve names for presentation to the parties for examination and challenge. Each party ordinarily is entitled to a specified number of *peremptory* challenges—i.e., challenges without cause stated—and an unlimited number of challenges *for cause*, such as bias or relationship to parties involved. In a criminal case, examination and challenges are made for the state by the prosecuting attorney and for the defendant by his counsel. When a prospective juror is dismissed on challenge another name is drawn, and this process continues until a jury has been obtained which is acceptable to both the prosecution and the defense.[42]

Most states require that, in criminal cases, jury verdicts be returned by unanimous vote. From a strictly numerical standpoint, this makes it twelve times as difficult to secure as to prevent a conviction. In order to secure a verdict of guilty, the prosecutor must convince *every* member of the jury, beyond reasonable doubt, of the defendant's guilt; whereas the defense attorney may "hang" the jury by convincing a *single* member that there is reasonable doubt of guilt. Few would disagree with the principle of Anglo-American law that an accused person is to be presumed innocent until his guilt has been demonstrated, and that the burden of proving guilt is upon the state. Nevertheless, the question may well be raised as to whether the unanimity requirement does not place the prosecution under an *undue* handicap. Many students of criminal law enforcement are coming to believe that all reasonable rights of a defendant might be adequately safeguarded, and at the same time the interests of society more fully protected, by permitting the return of a verdict, except perhaps in the case of capital offenses, by something less than a unanimous vote. This, it may be pointed out, is now permitted by slightly more than half of the states in civil cases, and by a few states in the trial of lesser crimes. Where the rule of unanimity has thus been abandoned, the vote required is most commonly five-sixths or three-fourths of the jurors, although a few states permit verdicts by smaller majorities.[43]

[42] This paragraph is based principally upon J. A. C. Grant, "Methods of Jury Selection," *Amer. Polit. Sci. Rev.*, XXIV, 117-133 (1930).

[43] Illinois Legislative Council, *Majority Jury Verdicts in Civil Cases* (Ill. Legis. Council, Springfield, 1962); "Five-Sixths Jury Verdicts: New York Legislation of 1937," *Columbia Law Rev.*, XXXVII, 1235-1238 (Nov., 1937); Glenn R. Winters, "Majority Verdicts in the United States," *Law Society Jour.*, X, 380-387 (Nov., 1942); Busch, *op. cit.*, 34-35. The model Code of Criminal Procedure drafted by the American Law Institute would retain the unanimity requirement in capital cases, but permit a verdict by a five-sixths vote in other felony cases and a two-thirds vote in misdemeanor cases. For evaluations of the jury system and suggestions for its improvement, see Jerome Frank, *Courts on Trial: Myth and Reality in American Justice* (Princeton Univ. Press, Princeton, N.J., 1949), Chaps. 8, 9; Julius H. Miner, "The Jury Problem," *Jour. of Crim. Law and Criminol.*, XXXVII, 1-15 (May-June 1946); Curtis Bok, "The Jury

Punishment of Convicted Persons. When a verdict of guilty has been returned by the trial jury, the defendant may move to "arrest the judgment" or to be granted a new trial. If such motions are not made, or are made and denied, the court pronounces sentence as provided by the statutes for the offense concerned.[44] The sentence may take the form of a fine, a term of imprisonment,[45] or both. At one time the punishment of criminals was looked upon as a matter of retribution or the wreaking of vengeance. Modern ideals demand, however, that reformation rather than vengeance constitute the principal consideration in the treatment of convicted persons. Imprisonment of criminals finds its justification today in (1) the protection of society against persons who would be dangerous if at large, and (2) the attempted reform or rehabilitation of those persons.

The County Jail

A well-nigh universal institution of rural government is the county jail, controlled by the county board but under the direct care and management of the sheriff.[46] The jail is used for the detention of two classes of prisoners: (1) persons awaiting action by the grand jury or the trial court, and held because they are unable to provide bail or are accused of nonbailable offenses, and (2) persons serving short sentences (normally of less than a year) for offenses of which they have been duly convicted.

System in America," *Annals of Amer. Acad. of Polit. and Soc. Sci.*, CCLXXXVII, 92-96 (May, 1953).

[44] Cf. Callender, *op. cit.*, 195-198. A convicted defendant will usually be able to find statutory grounds upon which appeal may be taken to a higher court. If the higher court consents to review the case, this operates to stay the imposition or execution of sentence until the appeal is disposed of. *Ibid.*

[45] Imprisonment was originally used only for the temporary detention of persons awaiting trial or execution of sentence. Not until the latter half of the 18th century was the practice adopted of incarcerating prisoners for the purpose of punishment. Sanford Bates, *Prisons and Beyond*, 31.

[46] Kentucky counties other than Jefferson (Louisville) have elective jailers separate and distinct from the office of sheriff. For general discussion of jails and jail problems, see Louis N. Robinson, *Jails: Care and Treatment of Misdemeanant Prisoners in the United States;* Myrl E. Alexander, *Jail Administration;* Joseph F. Fishman (in collaboration with Vee Perlman), *Crucibles of Crime: The Shocking Story of the American Jail;* Bates, *op. cit.*, Chap. 3; James V. Bennett, "The Medieval County Jail," *Forum,* C, 260-264 (Nov., 1938); Joseph F. Fishman and Vee Terrys Perlman, "Let's Abolish the County Jail," *Survey Graphic,* XXVIII, 26-27, 39-41 (Jan., 1939); Louis N. Robinson, "The Perennial Jail Problem," *Jour. of Crim. Law and Criminol.,* XXXV, 369-374 (Mar.-Apr., 1945). Representative reports on jail surveys in individual states are New Jersey Department of Institutions and Agencies, *New Jersey Jail and Workhouse Survey* (N.J. Dept. of Institutions and Agencies, Trenton, 1936); W. T. Hammack, *Survey of County Jails in West Virginia* (U.S. Bur. of Prisons, Washington, 1946); Roy Casey, "Missouri Jail Survey," *Proceedings of the Seventieth Annual Congress of the American Prison Association* (New York, 1940), 402-410. Many cities and villages have jails or lockups in connection with their police departments for the temporary detention of prisoners. Results of a survey of Chicago's police lockups are reported in Eugene S. Zemans, *Held Without Bail* (John Howard Assn., Chicago, 1949).

County jails have long been the subject of widespread criticism. For one thing, it is said that most jails are unsanitary, and many downright filthy. Another criticism stems from the lack of any means of classifying and segregating prisoners. Convicted persons and those awaiting trial, first offenders and habitual criminals, juveniles and adults—all are herded together in close quarters. Again, it is pointed out that most jail inmates are kept in absolute idleness, to their physical and mental detriment. A fourth criticism is directed against the prevalent fee system of feeding prisoners, whereby the sheriff is allowed a fixed sum for each meal supplied, regardless of the amount or quality of food served. The result of this plan almost inevitably is substandard meals served at a relatively high cost to the county.[47]

It appears that these criticisms are, on the whole, justified. Yet present-day conditions show some improvement over those of a few decades ago. Better sanitary facilities have been installed in some jails. Many counties now maintain juvenile detention homes in which youthful prisoners are kept, rather than in the jail. Some states provide for employment of county prisoners on highway projects or for leasing their services to private contractors. However, for the most part these schemes, and particularly those of the leasing variety, have not worked satisfactorily.[48] Finally, some states have abandoned the fee system of feeding prisoners in favor of a system by which the county board merely allows and pays bills incurred by the sheriff for the purchase of food and its preparation for the prisoners. The latter plan, if proper care is taken in examining and allowing claims, is considerably superior to the old fee system.

The deficiencies of the county jail flow in no small measure from the fact that the average county, in view of its limited need for jail facilities, is too small to support a modern, sanitary institution. In some instances, where state laws permit, individual counties have sought a solution to the problem by closing their jails and arranging with neighboring counties or with cities to house their prisoners in return for a stipulated compensation. Forty counties and thirteen cities in Virginia have been reported to be cooperating in the use of twenty-one jails.[49] While such schemes might well be used more widely, a still more thorough solution would be possible through abandonment of all or most county jails and the establishment instead of a system of regional jails maintained by the state. In North Carolina, short penal sentences are served in state-operated

[47] A deplorable institution found in some jails is the "kangaroo court" by means of which, under the guise of self-government, some of the inmates—often those of the lowest type—dominate and persecute their fellow prisoners. See Robinson, *op. cit.*, 21-22, 27; Fishman, *Crucibles of Crime*, 73-75; Bennett, *op. cit.*

[48] Wisconsin's plan of permitting prisoners, under appropriate circumstances, to be gainfully employed outside the jail during working hours, appears to have resulted in benefits to both the prisoners and the public. See Wilbur J. Schmidt, "Wisconsin's Jails and the Huber Law," *State Govt.*, XXX, 243-245, 250-251 (Nov., 1957).

[49] Virginia State Chamber of Commerce, *Opportunities for Economy in County Government in Virginia* (Va. State Chamber of Commerce, Richmond, 1947), 27.

prison camps, though county jails are retained for the detention of persons awaiting trial; and Virginia has established two state jail farms for misdemeanants.[50]

State Penal Institutions

Prison sentences for felonies are served in state penal institutions. Practically every state supports at least one penitentiary, as well as various reformatories, houses of correction, or "training schools" for women and juvenile offenders.[51] Unlike county jails, the state institutions generally attempt to provide some system of employment for prisoners. Such provision has three principal merits: (1) in employing the hands and minds of prisoners it promotes their physical and mental well-being, at the same time allowing them less time to plot escape or plan future crimes; (2) it permits inmates to learn useful trades by which to support themselves after release; and (3) it helps pay the cost of maintaining the institutions. Nevertheless, a substantial percentage of the inmates of state penitentiaries and reformatories still remain idle. One obstacle to the establishment of prison-labor systems has been the opposition of organized labor to competition, in the open market, of prison-made goods with goods made by free labor. This objection has now been largely overcome in many states by adoption of the "state-use" system under which prison factories produce only goods which the state itself would otherwise have to buy, such as automobile license tags and clothing for inmates of state charitable and penal institutions.

Probation and Parole

It was suggested above that modern penology emphasizes the reformative, as distinguished from the punitive, purpose of imprisonment. Two administrative devices designed to promote the reformation of persons convicted of crime are probation and parole.[52]

[50] *Ibid.*, 28; Paul W. Wager, "Effects of North Carolina's Centralization," *Nat Mun. Rev.*, XXVI, 572-577 (Dec., 1937).

[51] Organization for prison administration in the respective states is analyzed in Milton Chernin, *Probation—Prisons—Parole*, 1-10. Concerning recently-effected and needed improvements in prison policy and management, see Austin H. MacCormick, "Progress in American State Prisons," *State Govt.*, XXII, 112-115 (Apr., 1949); Richard A. McGee, "California Builds a New Prison System," *Ibid.*, XXV, 143-146, 159-161 (July, 1952); H. O. Teets and Walter Dunbar, "Standards for Prisons," *Ibid.*, XXVII, 61-63 (Mar., 1954); Allan Shivers, "The Texas Prison System: A Record of Progress," *Ibid.*, 114-115, 128 (June, 1954); John Bartlow Martin, "Prison: The Enemy of Society," *Harper's Mag.*, Vol. CCVIII, No. 1247, pp. 29-38 (Apr., 1954).

[52] On the subjects generally, see David Dressler, *Probation and Parole;* Chernin, *op. cit.;* John W. Tramburg, "Probation and Parole—The Pay-Off," *State Govt.*, XXVIII, 125-127, 140 (June, 1955); James V. Bennett, "Probation and Parole Among the States," *Ibid.*, XXX, 130-133, 136 (June, 1957); Fred Finsley, "Parole and Probation," *Ibid.*, XXXVI, 198-203 (Summer, 1963).

Probation is the conditional suspension, by a trial court, of the imposition or execution of a prison sentence. Such suspension is granted for the most part to juveniles or first offenders. The scheme finds its justification in the assumption that, whereas association with hardened criminals in penal institutions might be detrimental to the persons concerned, their supervision outside such institutions is likely to have a reformative effect. Probationers are required to conduct themselves properly and to abide by all terms of their probation as set by the court. They are under the supervision of, and must report regularly to, probation officers working under the court's jurisdiction. If a probationer violates the terms of his probation in any way, he may be immediately arrested and required to serve his sentence without further ado.

Parole is the conditional release, by a parole board or other administrative agency, of a person who has served part but not all of a prison sentence.[53] It will be seen that parole differs from probation in two respects: (1) it is granted by an administrative agency rather than by the courts, and (2) it is granted only after part of the sentence has been served. Though applicable to a definite sentence as well, the parole system is most commonly employed in conjunction with the "indeterminate sentence." An indeterminate sentence is one which specifies a minimum and a maximum term of imprisonment rather than fixing the period of imprisonment at a definite number of years. Under the indeterminate-sentence laws of some states the minimum and maximum periods of imprisonment for each offense are prescribed by statute; while in other states the court or jury is empowered to fix minimum and maximum terms, on each conviction, within a statutory range.[54] The theory underlying the indeterminate sentence is that an administrative agency, after a prisoner has served a part of his sentence and on the basis of his conduct record during incarceration, is more competent to determine when, in the interest of himself and of society, he should be released, than is the trial judge or jury at the time of conviction. Parolees are supervised by parole officers until the parole agency believes that discharge is warranted, or for such other period as may be prescribed by law. A parolee who violates the terms of his parole may be taken into custody and recommitted to the penal institution for the remainder of the maximum term.

The degree to which probation and parole are actually used varies greatly from state to state. The success of the schemes would seem to depend basically upon two factors: (1) the degree of care exercised in

[53] The parole-granting agency in most states is a central parole board serving all state penal institutions. In some states, however, separate boards serve individual institutions; while in still others the governor is the sole parole-granting authority, though sometimes acting only on the recommendation of a parole board or another agency. Illinois Legislative Council, *Indeterminate Sentence and Parole Laws* (1950), 10.

[54] *Ibid.*, 2 ff.

the selection of probationers and parolees, and (2) the effectiveness of the supervision over them. With respect to neither of these factors does there seem to be any substantial uniformity among the states.

Defense of the Indigent

It is a cardinal principle of American justice that a person accused of crime shall have the right to be represented in court by a lawyer; and almost without exception state constitutions, in their bills of rights or elsewhere, contain provisions guaranteeing that right. In most states, however, the constitutional provision is interpreted as meaning merely that a defendant shall not be denied the privilege of employing his own counsel. National statistics indicate that more than half of those accused of crime in this country are without funds to employ a lawyer.[55] In the interest of substantial justice, therefore, it becomes the duty of government to provide counsel for a large number of defendants who are unable to provide their own.

Some state constitutional provisions, it is true, require that the trial court appoint counsel for indigent defendants in all or certain kinds of criminal cases. Furthermore, the Fourteenth Amendment to the United States Constitution has been interpreted to require appointment of counsel, unless competently waived, for indigent persons being prosecuted for serious crimes in state courts.[56] In a large majority of the states, however, except for the federal requirement just noted, the decision as to whether provision shall be made for appointment is largely a matter of legislative policy. Statutes on the subject vary widely as to the types of cases in which free counsel will be supplied. Where such counsel is required or permitted it is usually provided in one or the other of two ways: by the system of assigned counsel or by that of the public defender.[57]

Assigned Counsel. The traditional method of providing counsel for indigent defendants is that known as assigned counsel. Under this plan the trial judge, usually at the time of arraignment, appoints some lawyer to represent the defendant. Since lawyers are considered to be officers or agents of the courts, it is their duty to accept assignments whether or not any provision is made for their compensation. Some states formerly provided for assignment of counsel in capital cases only, but most now require or permit

[55] Orison S. Marden, "A Modern Defender Program," *Jour of Amer. Judic. Soc.,* XLI, 107-110 (Dec., 1957).

[56] William M. Beaney, *The Right to Counsel in American Courts,* Chap. 5; Fellman, *op. cit.,* 115-119; *Gideon* v. *Wainwright,* 372 U.S. 335 (1963).

[57] The two systems are discussed and compared in Emery A. Brownell, *Legal Aid in the United States,* Chap. 6; Junius L. Allison and John F. Hassett, "Counsel for the Indigent Defendant," *Jour. of Amer. Judic. Soc.,* XLI, 102-106 (Dec., 1957). In a few communities there are "voluntary defender" programs financed from private funds with contributions, in occasional instances, from public sources.

assignment in all felony cases. Many states make statutory provision for assignment in misdemeanor cases as well, though it appears that in practice assignment in such cases is seldom made. Payment of assigned counsel from public funds is authorized, with respect to some or all cases, in a majority of the states. The amount of compensation is in some instances left to the discretion of the court, and in others fixed at a definite lump sum or per diem.[58]

The system of assigned counsel appears to have worked fairly satisfactorily in capital cases for two reasons. In the first place, at least some compensation is usually paid in such cases; and, probably of more importance, the publicity attendant upon a capital case is frequently of considerable advertising value to the lawyer.[59] In other than capital cases, unfortunately, the plan has been rather generally a failure. Compensation in such cases is either nonexistent or inadequate, and there is usually no compensating factor in the form of desirable publicity. The lawyers assigned to defendants are often young and inexperienced. Moreover, unscrupulous lawyers sometimes use defense assignments as a means of extorting money from relatives of the accused, ostensibly to pay expenses involved in locating witnesses and otherwise preparing an adequate defense. If the amount demanded for such alleged purposes cannot be raised, by those concerned, in a lump sum, the lawyer may accept payment in installments, care being taken, by securing from the court a series of continuances, that the case does not come to trial, and that therefore the defendant remains in jail, until the final installment has been paid.[60]

The Public Defender. In an effort to overcome the weaknesses of assigned counsel, the office of public defender has now been established in some communities. The public defender is an elective or appointive [61] public officer who is paid a salary from the public (usually the county) treasury, and whose duty it is to defend all persons accused of crime who are unable to employ their own counsel and request the trial court to provide counsel for them.[62] The office finds justification in the principle

[58] Reginald H. Smith and John S. Bradway, *Growth of Legal-Aid Work in the United States* (rev. ed.), 75-77; Allison and Hassett, *op. cit.*

[59] Smith and Bradway, *op. cit.*, 77.

[60] See Philip J. Finnegan, "The Work of the Public Defender of Cook County," *Jour. of Crim. Law and Criminol.*, XXVI, 709-718 (Jan.-Feb., 1936). Under an unusual plan which has operated in New Jersey for several years, and apparently with beneficial results, all lawyers of the county are assigned in alphabetical rotation as counsel for indigent defendants in noncapital cases. Richard Hartshorne, " 'Equal Justice for All': The Bar and the Indigent Criminal Defendant," *Amer. Bar Assn. Jour.*, XXXVII, 104-106 (Feb., 1951).

[61] Appointment, where that method of selection is employed, is frequently by the judges of the courts of criminal jurisdiction.

[62] The court may, under special circumstances, make assignment of counsel other than the public defender. A few public-defender offices render limited assistance to indigent persons involved in civil litigation.

that it is as much the duty of government to see that innocent persons are acquitted as to see that the guilty are convicted. Therefore, just as a public prosecutor is provided to conduct judicial proceedings against accused persons, so a regular public defender should be provided to represent the interests of the indigent accused.[63] Statistics compiled by the National Legal Aid and Defender Association indicate that, in 1962, approximately 90 American communities were provided with public defenders. Thirty-one defenders were found in Illinois and twenty-three in California, with the remainder scattered among some dozen states. Chicago, Los Angeles, Minneapolis, and Miami were among the more populous communities served. During the year the various defenders provided defense in some 150,000 criminal cases.[64]

The most important advantage of the public-defender system over that of assigned counsel lies in the more effective defense secured by indigent persons from full-time, salaried government lawyers who specialize in defense work. But there are other incidental advantages. Many public defenders, while putting forth every effort on behalf of accused persons for whom any substantial defense can be offered, encourage clients whose cases are clearly hopeless to plead guilty. This saves not only the time of the court but also the cost of juries in such cases. There is also a saving, in states which provide compensation for assigned counsel, of the money that would otherwise be spent for that purpose. Indeed, it appears that in some instances these various savings have more than offset the cost of the defender's office, thus resulting in a net cash saving to the taxpayers.[65]

Since strictly rural counties seldom have enough criminal-court business to require the services of a full-time defense lawyer for the indigent, it is not surprising that the public-defender movement has made most progress in urban communities. Though progress even there has not been rapid, the results of the system where tried have in general been gratifying, and it may reasonably be expected that the office of public defender will become more common in the future.[66]

[63] In theory, it is the duty of the prosecuting attorney to protect the innocent as well as to see that the guilty are punished. The very nature of the prosecutor's office, however, makes it inevitable that he will be concerned almost exclusively with preparing and presenting cases against accused persons. Indeed, a prosecutor's success as a public servant is judged in large measure by the percentage of convictions that he obtains.

[64] National Legal Aid and Defender Association, *Statistics of Legal Aid Work in the United States and Canada: 1962* (Nat. Legal Aid and Defender Assn., Chicago, 1963). Several additional defender organizations were reported as being supported wholly or partly from private funds.

[65] Cf., for example, Finnegan, *op. cit.*, 717-718.

[66] On the office generally, see Mayer C. Goldman, *The Public Defender;* Smith and Bradway, *op. cit.*, Chap. 11; Samuel Rubin, "Justice for the Indigent: The Need for Public Defenders," *Amer. Bar. Assn. Jour.*, XXXIX, 893-896, 931 (Oct., 1953); David Mars, "Public Defenders," *Jour. of Crim. Law, Criminol., and Police Sci.*, XLVI, 199-210 (July-Aug., 1955). The literature on the subject is, for the most part,

REFERENCES

ALEXANDER, Myrl E., *Jail Administration* (Charles C. Thomas, Springfield, Ill., 1957).

BATES, Sanford, *Prisons and Beyond* (Macmillan, New York, 1936).

BEANEY, William M., *The Right to Counsel in American Courts* (Univ. of Mich. Press, Ann Arbor, 1955).

BROWNELL, Emery A., *Legal Aid in the United States* (Lawyers Co-op. Pub. Co., Rochester, N.Y., 1951).

BUSCH, Francis X., *Law and Tactics in Jury Trials* (Bobbs, Indianapolis, 1949).

CHERNIN, Milton, *Probation—Prisons—Parole* (Bur. of Pub. Admin., Univ. of Calif., Berkeley, 1941).

DRESSLER, David, *Probation and Parole* (Columbia Univ. Press, New York, 1951).

FELLMAN, David, *The Defendant's Rights* (Holt, New York, 1958).

FISHMAN, Joseph F. (in collaboration with Vee Perlman), *Crucibles of Crime: The Shocking Story of the American Jail* (Cosmopolis Press, New York, 1923).

GOLDMAN, Mayer C., *The Public Defender* (Putnam, New York, 1917).

HAYNES, Fred E., *The American Prison System* (McGraw-Hill, New York, 1939).

Illinois Association for Criminal Justice, *Illinois Crime Survey* (Ill. Assn. for Crim. Justice, Chicago, 1929).

Illinois Legislative Council, *Indeterminate Sentence and Parole Laws* (Ill. Legis. Council, Springfield, 1950).

―――, *Some Aspects of Indeterminate Sentence and Parole Laws* (Ill. Legis. Council, Springfield, 1957).

"Law Enforcement in Kentucky" (Report to the Committee on the Administration of Justice in the Commonwealth of Kentucky by the Department of Law), *Ky. Law Jour.*, Vol. LII, No. 1 (1963-1964).

LEONARD, V. A., *Police Organization and Management* (Found. Press, Brooklyn, 1951).

McCLEERY, Richard H., *Policy Change in Prison Management* (Govtl. Research Bur., Mich. State Univ., East Lansing, 1957).

MILES, Arnold, *How Criminals Are Caught* (Macmillan, New York, 1939).

Missouri Association for Criminal Justice, *Missouri Crime Survey* (Macmillan, New York, 1926).

---

favorable concerning the establishment of the defender's office. For presentations of the contrary point of view, see William Scott Stewart, "The Public Defender System is Unsound in Principle," *Jour. of Amer. Judic. Soc.*, XXXII, 115-118 (Dec., 1948); Edward J. Dimock, "The Public Defender: A Step towards a Police State?" *Amer. Bar Assn. Jour.*, XLII, 219-221 (Mar., 1956). A reply to the latter article is presented in Cornelius J. Harrington and Gerald W. Getty, "The Public Defender: A Progressive Step towards Justice," *Ibid.*, 1139-1142 (Dec., 1956). A Model Defender Act was approved by the National Conference of Commissioners on Uniform State Laws in 1959. The text of the model act, together with comment, appears in *Jour. of Amer. Judic. Soc.*, XLIII, 96 (Oct., 1959). Legal counsel for the poor in civil cases is considered in the chapter on public welfare. See below, Chap. XVIII, "Legal Aid."

MOLEY, Raymond, *Politics and Criminal Prosecution* (Minton, New York, 1929).

MONROE, David G., *State and Provincial Police: A Study in Police Functioning in the United States and Canada* (Int. Assn. of Chiefs of Police and Northwestern Univ. Traffic Inst., Evanston, Ill., 1941).

ORFIELD, Lester B., *Criminal Procedure from Arrest to Trial* (N.Y. Univ. Press, New York, 1947).

ROBINSON, Louis N., *Jails: Care and Treatment of Misdemeanant Prisoners in the United States* (Winston, Philadelphia, 1944).

SMITH, Bruce, *Police Systems in the United States* (Harper, New York, rev. ed., 1949).

———, *Rural Crime Control* (Inst. of Pub. Admin., New York, 1933).

———, *The State Police* (Macmillan, New York, 1925).

———, ed., "New Goals in Police Management," *Annals of Amer. Acad. of Polit. and Soc. Sci.*, CCXCI, Philadelphia, Jan., 1954.

SMITH, Reginald H., and BRADWAY, John S., *Growth of Legal-Aid Work in the United States* (U.S. Bur. of Labor Statistics, Washington, rev. ed., 1936), Chap. 11.

VOLLMER, August, *The Police and Modern Society* (Univ. of Calif. Press, Berkeley, 1936).

———, and PARKER, Alfred E., *Crime and the State Police* (Univ. of Calif. Press, Berkeley, 1935).

WILLOUGHBY, W. F., *Principles of Judicial Administration* (Brookings Inst., Washington, 1929), Parts II, V, VI.

WILSON, O. W., *Police Administration* (McGraw-Hill, New York, 1950).

18

Public Welfare

The Welfare Function

As used by different persons and in different situations, the term *public welfare* has a variety of meanings. In its broadest sense of public activities carried on in the interest of the general well-being, it includes virtually all governmental functions. In a narrower and more usual sense, it denotes those tax-supported services provided for the benefit of certain disadvantaged groups in society, particularly the dependent, delinquent, and criminal classes, and those persons who suffer from physical or mental handicaps. As thus employed the term embraces sundry forms of public assistance (traditionally known as poor relief); institutional care for criminal, delinquent, and defective persons; and special services to various groups such as underprivileged children, the handicapped classes, and veterans.[1] It is with this more restricted meaning that the term is used in this chapter. Institutions for the care of criminals have already been considered in the discussion of law enforcement.[2] Attention will be given here to various forms of public assistance, institutional care for the defective and delinquent classes, and certain special welfare programs.

The national government has for many years engaged in various activities of a welfare nature, such as those for the protection and advancement of Indians on reservations, for the care of disabled soldiers and sailors, and for the promotion of child welfare, but prior to 1933 consist-

[1] Cf. Marietta Stevenson, *Public Welfare Administration*, 1-2; E. C. Lindeman, "Public Welfare," *Encyclopaedia of the Social Sciences*, Vol. XII (Macmillan, New York, 1934), 687-689.

[2] Above, Chap. XVII, "The County Jail," "State Penal Institutions."

ently denied responsibility for the relief of persons in need.[3] In the year
mentioned, Congress for the first time made federal funds available to the
states, and through the states to the local governmental units, for relief
purposes. Although these grants were relatively small in amount and were
soon discontinued, the Social Security Act of 1935 launched the national
government upon a permanent program of grants-in-aid to the states for
assistance to three specific classes of needy persons—the aged, the blind,
and dependent children. In 1950, the grant-in-aid program was enlarged
to include needy persons 18 years of age or over who are permanently
or totally disabled; and in 1960 a further enlargement authorized grants
for medical assistance to elderly persons. The growing importance of welfare activities of the national government is reflected in the establishment,
in 1939, of a Federal Security Agency charged with administration of the
social-security program and other welfare services, and the subsequent
merger of that agency, in 1953, into a new Department of Health, Education, and Welfare at the cabinet level.

The states from early times have maintained institutions for the
care of certain defective, delinquent, and criminal classes, but for many
years most other welfare activities, among which support of the poor was
the most important, were made the responsibility of local governmental
units. Eventually, however, the state governments began to assume a more
important role in the welfare field, and during the depression years of the
1930's, in part as a result of federal stimulus, this trend was greatly accelerated. In some instances the states have undertaken the actual performance of additional welfare services. More generally, however, increased state participation in welfare programs has taken the form of
state financial aid to the local governments for welfare purposes and, as
a corollary of this, an expansion of central supervision and control over
local welfare activities. Quite generally the requirement of meeting state-
prescribed standards accompanies such financial assistance, and state welfare agencies are vested with supervisory authority to see that these standards are met.

Welfare Organization: State Organization

When the earliest institutions were established by the states for
the care of criminal and defective classes, it was customary to place each
such institution under the management of a separate board of trustees.
However, beginning with Massachusetts in 1863, most states established
either state *boards of charities* with advisory or supervisory powers over
the different institutions, or state *boards of control* charged with actual
management of the various institutions and supplanting the individual

[3] Josephine C. Brown, *Public Relief, 1929-1939*, p. 37.

institutional boards.[4] Later these boards were generally superseded by *departments of public welfare;* and during the early decades of the present century there was a trend in the direction of placing all welfare activities in these departments. This movement, however, made more progress in some states than in others, and apparently complete integration was not attained in any state. More recently, with welfare functions increasing rapidly in scope and the departments growing to huge proportions, a number of states have again decentralized welfare administration in some measure. Thus, some have transferred correctional institutions to separate departments, some have provided separate agencies for administering public-assistance programs, and several have placed mental institutions in separate departments of mental health. Nevertheless, the welfare department remains in most states the most important single agency for welfare administration.[5]

State welfare departments differ widely both in organization and in powers. Responsibility for administration of the department is in most instances divided in some manner between a welfare board or commission and a principal executive officer. Members of the board are usually appointed by the governor for overlapping terms, and in many cases receive no remuneration other than necessary expenses. The board either formulates departmental policy and regulations for administering the department, or advises with the executive officer in their formulation. The executive officer, usually given the title of commissioner or director, is in most instances appointed either by the governor or by the welfare board. Where, as is frequently the case, the welfare department either administers federally-aided public-assistance programs or supervises their local administration, departmental organization must comply with standards established under the Federal Social Security Act if the state is to share in federal funds for those purposes. This fact has played an important part in raising organizational standards in state welfare departments and reducing political influence in welfare administration.[6]

Local Organization

At the local level the principal agency for welfare administration in most states is the county welfare department. Prior to the inception of the social security program, county government generally included no agency for the administration of an integrated welfare program. Poor re-

[4] Frederic H. Guild, *State Supervision and Administration of Charities* (Ind. Univ., Bloomington, 1916).

[5] Several states use the title "department of social welfare," and other titles occasionally employed include those of "department of public assistance" and "department of social security."

[6] Cf. Marietta Stevenson and Alice MacDonald, *State and Local Public Welfare Agencies.*

lief, where a county function, was frequently administered directly by the county governing board or by overseers of the poor appointed by the board. Other welfare activities, where such existed, were managed in some instances by the county board and in others by some other county agency. Thus, systems of "mothers' pensions," the forerunner of aid to dependent children, were administered in some states by the county court; children's homes were frequently administered either by the court or by a special board; and the county almshouse was, as it still is in many instances, managed directly by the county board. Nevertheless, there were some early attempts at partial integration. By 1933 about a third of the states had made provision, on either a mandatory or a permissive basis, for the establishment of agencies charged with administering two or more welfare services on a countywide basis.[7]

The Social Security Act stipulated, as a prerequisite to federal grants-in-aid, that programs of old-age assistance, aid to the blind, and aid to dependent children be either administered directly by a state agency or locally administered under state supervision. A considerable majority of the states adopted the latter plan and established county welfare departments or similar county agencies in conformity with federal standards.[8] These county departments vary greatly in the details of their organization, but usually include a welfare board and a director who is the department's executive officer. Members of the welfare board are most commonly appointed by the county governing body, but in a number of states some or all members are appointed by the state welfare department, by the governor, or in still some other manner. The director in most states is appointed by the county welfare board, subject to qualifications and procedures prescribed by the state department, though in some instances the state department makes the appointment. Staff members of the county department are appointed according to merit-system rules, usually as the result of competitive examination. The principal duty of the county welfare department ordinarily consists of administering, under state supervision, the federal-aid programs of public assistance. These are now five in number: old-age assistance, aid to the blind, aid to dependent children, aid to the permanently and totally disabled, and medical assistance for the aged. The county department receives applications for these forms of aid, investigates the applicants, and determines, subject to appeal to the state welfare agency, whether aid should be granted and if so in what amount. After an award of assistance has been made, the county department keeps in touch with the recipient in order to be advised if and when a change in his circumstances warrants discontinuance of the assistance

[7] Mary Ruth Colby, *The County as an Administrative Unit for Social Work* (Children's Bur., U.S. Dept. of Labor, Washington, 1933), 23-36.

[8] In a few states, cities or (in New England) towns participate in administering the federal-aid programs.

or a modification of its amount. Reports are made regularly by the county department to the state supervising agency. In many states, the county welfare department is charged with various functions in addition to administration of the five programs mentioned. Examples of such additional duties are the administration of general poor relief, supervision of probationers, and provision of child-welfare services. Some states have sought to place virtually all local public-welfare activities, or at least those in rural areas, under the department's jurisdiction.

The larger cities of the country commonly have their own public-welfare departments under commissioners appointed by the mayor or manager.[9] Some of these departments are elaborately organized and provide a wide variety of social services. Townships rarely have anything even approximating a welfare department, such welfare functions as are devolved upon those units usually being performed by the general township officers. The welfare function most frequently conferred upon townships is the administration of general assistance, a function which is performed in many states by the township trustee or supervisor, sometimes in an ex officio capacity as overseer of the poor or supervisor of assistance. In New England towns this form of assistance is usually administered through the town selectmen or by elected or appointed overseers of the poor.[10]

Public Assistance

Care of the needy was for many centuries left to private philanthropy and ecclesiastical organizations, but was recognized in England as a public duty prior to the establishment of the earliest English settlements in America. From colonial days it has been generally acknowledged in this country that the taxpayers must provide the necessities of life for those who are unable to support themselves. At first the support of the poor in each community was considered to be a duty of local government.[11] Recent years, however, have witnessed two significant developments in support of the needy as a public function. In the first place, the state and national governments have accepted a large share of responsibility for programs in this field. Secondly, there has been growing recognition of the fact that poverty is in large measure the result of social rather than individual causes; and with this has come a noticeable change in the public attitude toward recipients of aid. This change in attitude is nowhere seen more clearly than in the changes in terminology which are being adopted by welfare workers and officially incorporated into state

[9] In some instances the commissioner is appointed by a welfare board.

[10] For further discussion of state and local welfare organization, see Arthur C. Millspaugh, *Public Welfare Organization*, Chaps. 6-9; Stevenson, *Public Welfare Administration*, Part II, Chaps. 2, 3; R. Clyde White, *Administration of Public Welfare* (2nd ed.), Chaps. 4, 5; Wayne Vasey, *Government and Social Welfare*, Chaps. 9, 10.

[11] Cf. Edith Abbott, *Public Assistance*, Vol. I, p. 3; Brown, *op. cit.*, 3.

statutes through amendments to, or codifications of, the welfare laws. In various states, for example, in an effort to remove any stigma from recipients of public aid, "pauper laws" have become "public-assistance codes," "paupers" have become "needy persons," "poor relief" has become "public assistance," "overseers of the poor" have become "supervisors of public assistance," the "poorhouse" has become the "county home," and the "inmates" of that institution have become "residents" or "patients." Though this newer terminology is clearly indicative of a pronounced trend and seems generally preferable to the old, its adoption as yet is far from universal. Since the older nomenclature is still retained in some states, the old and the new will be used interchangeably in the discussion which follows.

Kinds of Assistance

Public-assistance measures are classified in two principal ways. The first of these distinguishes between *indoor* and *outdoor* assistance. Indoor assistance is that provided to poor persons within the doors of public institutions, whereas outdoor aid is given outside such institutions, usually within the homes of the recipients. Each of the two forms has its peculiar advantages and disadvantages. The indoor variety is almost essential for needy persons who because of sickness or other physical or mental handicaps require constant attention and care. It is less difficult to provide proper care for such persons in an institution equipped for that purpose than elsewhere, and less expensive to care for several in a common institution than in their respective homes. Outdoor assistance has the advantage of greater flexibility. In the case of an able-bodied poor person who has some income but not enough for his entire support, the simplest and often the most economical course is to supply him with such supplementary funds as will enable him to maintain his home. Another alleged advantage of outdoor assistance is the fact that the social stigma of pauperism is less pronounced than in the indoor type. Accepting public funds or grocery orders for use in one's own home is a very different thing from going "over the hill to the poorhouse." Yet it must be admitted that this very absence of social stigma may encourage some persons to apply for outdoor assistance while they would make further effort to support themselves before seeking admission to an institution. When this occurs on a large scale, only the most vigilant administration will prevent the public-assistance rolls from being "padded" with the names of persons who are not actually entitled to public support.

At one time, indoor assistance was looked upon as the normal means of supporting persons who are permanent public charges, while outdoor assistance was considered as intended primarily for those who require help only temporarily. Today, however, there is a tendency to confine indoor assistance to the sick and handicapped classes and to prefer the outdoor variety in other cases. One of the principal reasons for this trend is doubtless the fact that outdoor assistance permits recipients to lead more normal lives than is possible for inmates of institutions. Regardless of the respective merits of indoor and outdoor assistance, it is necessarily the latter which must be expanded in times of economic depression and widespread unemployment, if for no other reason than the physical inadequacy of public institutions to provide care for the large numbers of needy persons.[12]

A second classification of public-assistance programs distinguishes between *general* and *categorical* assistance. According to this distinction, general assistance is that available to all whose support is a public responsibility and who are not eligible for aid under any of the special or categorical programs. Categorical assistance is designed to aid poor persons of special classes or categories. At the present time, four major outdoor-assistance programs are found in all of the states. One of these, the general-assistance program, is administered and financed wholly by the state and local governments. The other three are the categorical programs of old-age assistance, aid to the blind, and aid to dependent children. Two additional categorical programs were in operation in 1962 in some states but not all—that of aid to the permanently and totally disabled in 46 states and that of medical assistance for the aged in 25.[13] All of the categorical programs are administered by the states or by local agencies under state supervision, and are financed in part by federal aid. In mid-1962 about 7.3 million persons were receiving aid under the six outdoor-assistance programs, general and categorical.[14]

The county almshouse, which is the principal institution for public assistance of the indoor variety, has traditionally been a general-assistance agency, though in some states these institutions have now been converted into nursing homes for the infirm and chronically ill. The public assistance provided by state institutions for the defective and handicapped classes is of a categorical nature, but many of these establishments provide care for defective and handicapped persons without regard to their pecuniary status, and are therefore not to be considered as primarily relief agencies.

General Outdoor Assistance

Outdoor assistance of a general nature usually takes the form of food, clothing, shelter, fuel, utility service, and medical supplies, or of

[12] Unemployment compensation as a means of alleviating need on the part of the unemployed is discussed in the chapter on labor regulation. Below, Chap. XXIII.

[13] Cf. United States Department of Health, Education, and Welfare, *Annual Report: 1962*. Data in this report are for the federal fiscal year ending June 30, 1962. The four states not providing disability assistance were Alaska, Arizona, Indiana, and Nevada. Arizona inaugurated a program at the beginning of fiscal 1963.

[14] *Ibid.*, p. 64.

money grants for the purchase of these and other necessities. In a majority of the states this form of assistance is primarily a county responsibility. Elsewhere the unit most commonly charged with the function is the township or, in New England, the town. A few states provide for county administration in some counties and township administration in others; and in several instances assistance is administered by municipalities.[15]

The demand for outdoor assistance fluctuates widely with changes in economic conditions and the extent of unemployment, and also varies somewhat with the seasons, being heavier during the winter months. Because of variations in eligibility requirements and available funds, assistance programs are quite uneven as among the different states; and frequently there are also variations in adequacy as between different localities within the same state.[16] In early 1935, at the depth of an economic depression and before the categorical-assistance features of the social-security program had become operative, more than 5 million cases—families and single individuals—were receiving general assistance from the state and local governments.[17] Subsequently, as cases were transferred from general assistance to the categorical programs, and as employment opportunities were afforded in defense and war industries, drastic curtailment of the general-assistance programs became possible. More recently the categorical programs have increased still further in relative importance; and in 1962 the number of persons receiving general assistance was well under a million.

Generally speaking, it seems unwise to administer outdoor assistance through any governmental unit smaller than the county. The average township is too small to maintain a welfare department with trained case workers and other personnel. Moreover, under township administration assistance standards are likely to vary considerably, with the amounts provided being adequate in some units and inadequate in others. Ordinarily the townships with heavy assistance loads are the very ones which, because of low property valuations, are least able to support their needy residents from local taxes. This financial inequality is counterbalanced in some measure by state grants-in-aid to the poorer townships, but the inadequacy of the township as an administrative unit, even with state supervision, remains. Because of this fact there has been some tendency during recent years, in states where township administration has prevailed in the past, to transfer responsibility for general assistance to the county, which in many instances is already administering the categorical programs.

[15] Cf. Millspaugh, *op. cit.*, 278-282.

[16] Rose J. McHugh, "Public Assistance," *Social Work Year Book: 1947* (Russell Sage Found., New York), 371-387.

[17] *The Book of the States* (Council of State Govts., Chicago), 1945-46, p. 327.

Categorical Assistance: The Federal-State Programs

As previously noted, five programs of categorical assistance are now administered by the states with federal financial assistance under the terms of the Social Security Act. This act prescribes various standards with which a state plan for administering any one or more of these programs must comply in order to qualify for federal aid. It is required that the program be made effective in all political subdivisions of the state and that, if administered by local governmental units, it be made mandatory upon them. A single state agency must either administer the program or supervise its administration by local agencies. Provision must be made for granting to any applicant whose claim for assistance is denied, an opportunity for a hearing before the state agency. Methods of administering the program must be established, including merit-system principles of personnel management, that will meet the approval of the Social Security Administration. The state administrative agency must be required to make such reports to the Social Security Administration as the latter may prescribe. It is required that, in determining the need of applicants for assistance, consideration be taken of any other income or resources they may have, except for certain earned-income exemptions in the case of aid to the blind. Concurrent receipt of more than one form of public assistance must be prohibited. The Social Security Act does not require the states to impose any citizenship or residence requirement as a condition of eligibility for assistance payments, but does provide that a state may not impose, for old-age assistance, any age requirement of more than sixty-five years. The act also sets maximum residence requirements for each program which may not be exceeded in case the state sees fit to prescribe a residence qualification. In the case of medical assistance for the aged, no durational residence requirement is permitted.

The state government itself is required by the Social Security Act to participate in the financing of the categorical programs. In practice some states pay all of the nonfederal portion from the state treasury, while others require counties or other local units to bear a part of the cost. Federal contributions are determined by statutory formulas which have been changed from time to time, generally in the direction of greater liberality. In 1962, the federal share of the total cost of the five programs was approximately 60 percent, the state share 32 percent, and the local share 8 percent.[18] Federal aid originally was denied for any assistance payments to inmates of public institutions, though some states provided for payments to such persons from state or state and local funds. Amendments to the provisions of the Social Security Act relating to old-age assistance, aid

[18] United States Department of Health, Education, and Welfare, *Annual Report: 1962*, p. 68.

to the blind, and disability aid now permit federal sharing in assistance payments to patients in public medical institutions other than mental or tuberculosis hospitals, provided that such persons are otherwise qualified for aid under those programs.

Each of the federal-state programs of categorical assistance will now be given individual consideration.[19]

Old-Age Assistance. In 1960 there were more than 16 million persons sixty-five years of age or over in the United States, constituting 9 percent of the entire population; and, with increasing longevity, the proportion of elderly people is constantly rising.[20] Dependency is inevitably more prevalent among persons in the higher age group than throughout the general population. A surprisingly large number of such persons are without either savings or income and have no relatives to support them. Many suffer from some chronic disease, and those who are able-bodied frequently find it difficult to secure employment because of their advanced age. For these reasons, the provision of assistance to the aged has come to be recognized as a major problem in the welfare field. Even before passage of the Social Security Act, about half of the states had enacted old-age pension laws or other statutes designed to foster old-age security, though in some instances actual provision of the aid envisaged was made optional with the respective counties.[21]

The Social Security Act, in its original form, sought to provide security for the aged through two distinct programs.[22] One of these was a system of nationally-administered old-age insurance in which the state and local governments have no part. Financed by a payroll tax falling equally on employer and employee,[23] this system was designed to provide monthly retirement benefits for workers upon their reaching the age of sixty-five. Under the terms of recent amendments retirement is now permissible at age sixty-two, though, in the case of men, with reduced benefits. Amendments have also broadened the plan to include benefits to the widows and other dependent survivors of retired workers, as well as benefits for long-term disability; and the program is now known as old-age, survivors, and

[19] For a summary of conditions for the granting of federal aid to the states, and a tabular analysis of the various state laws governing the categorical programs (except that of medical assistance for the aged), see Social Security Administration, *Characteristics of State Public Assistance Plans under the Social Security Act* (U.S. Govt. Printing Office, Washington, 1962). See also Social Security Administration, *Public Assistance under the Social Security Act* (U.S. Govt. Printing Office, Washington, 1961).

[20] On the general problems of aging and care for the aged, see Council of State Governments, *The States and their Older Citizens.*

[21] Colby, *op. cit.,* 4.

[22] A third program for the aged—that of medical aid—was added by amendment in 1960. See below, "Medical Assistance for the Aged."

[23] Self-employed persons who are under the plan pay three-fourths of the combined rate for employer and employee.

disability insurance. Though coverage under the program has now been extended to several classes of workers who were originally exempt, some workers are still excluded—principally those who are irregularly employed or whose earnings do not meet the minimum requirements for coverage. Furthermore, in some cases the benefits paid to retired workers under the plan are not sufficient to provide for their basic needs. As a means of aiding aged persons who have no coverage or inadequate coverage under the system of old-age insurance, the second program under the Social Security Act provides for federal grants-in-aid to the states for assistance to the needy aged. It should be emphasized that, unlike retirement benefits under the national system of old-age insurance, which are received by retired persons as a matter of right and without regard to their financial status,[24] old-age assistance benefits from state and federal funds constitute a form of poor relief or public assistance, being paid as a gratuity and only to aged persons who are needy.

State laws providing for old-age assistance vary somewhat in detail, but since federal standards must be met if aid is to be forthcoming from the national treasury, there is a strong tendency toward uniformity of the state legislation in its major aspects. The age requirement for receiving assistance is almost universally sixty-five years.[25] A few states require United States citizenship, but most do not. There is usually a residence requirement, but the states vary considerably with respect to length of state residence required. In many instances the minimum requirement is fixed at the maximum permitted under federal-aid standards. This, for old-age assistance as well as for aid to the blind and disability aid, is five years of the last nine preceding application and including continuous residence during the year immediately preceding. Nearly half of the states, however, require less than the federal maximum. Several require but a single year, and in a few instances the only requirement is residence within the state at the time of application. Some states make assistance payments a lien upon any property owned by the recipient and provide that, upon his death, the amount of the payments shall constitute a claim against his estate.

The statutory definition of need, as a qualification for old-age assistance, also shows some variation, but its general purport is much the same everywhere. In about half of the states, a needy person is defined as one who does not have sufficient income or other resources to provide a reasonable subsistence compatible with decency and health, and in most

---

[24] In providing benefits for dependents and survivors, as distinguished from the primary benefits paid to retired workers themselves, the element of need does enter in some measure into the program.

[25] Colorado provides, in addition, for assistance payments to needy persons sixty to sixty-five years of age who meet prescribed conditions of long residence in the state or are maintained in public mental institutions. Such payments, however, do not qualify for federal aid.

other states substantially the same idea is expressed in slightly different language. The amount of assistance granted to a qualified applicant depends upon his individual circumstances and is intended, together with his private income or resources, if any, to enable him to live in a decent and healthful manner. Many states, however, provide that the award may in no case exceed a specified maximum amount, though with additional sums being allowed for medical care.

In 1962 the recipients of old-age assistance throughout the country numbered 2.2 million. This represented a slight decrease from the number a year earlier, due largely to liberalization of eligibility requirements for federal old-age and survivors insurance and the transfer of some aged persons in medical institutions or nursing homes to the new program of medical assistance for the aged. Total payments to recipients in 1962 totaled nearly $2 billion, with an average monthly payment per recipient of $72.[26]

Aid to the Blind. Aid to the blind is designed to provide financial assistance to needy persons who are completely blind or whose vision is so impaired as to prevent them from carrying on activities for which eyesight is essential. The definition of blindness that must be met by applicants in order to qualify for assistance payments differs to some degree in the various states. Though in some instances stated in more general language, it is usually expressed in technical terms. A typical provision requires that central visual acuity in the better eye be 20/200 or less with correcting glasses or that there be a disqualifying field defect. The standard of need required of applicants is comparable in general to that for old-age assistance, except that in the case of aid to the blind certain amounts of earned income are disregarded. Residence requirements also are much the same as for old-age assistance, though many states waive any requirement of a specific length of residence in the case of applicants who were residents of the state when they became blind. Only a few states require recipients to be United States citizens, and fewer than half impose minimum-age qualifications. Where a minimum age is required it is usually sixteen, eighteen, or twenty-one years. As in the case of old-age assistance, some states impose a maximum limit upon the amount of individual awards while others do not.

In terms of the number of recipients, aid to the blind is a small program as compared with old-age assistance and aid to dependent children. In 1962, however, more than 100,000 persons benefited from the program. Total assistance payments amounted to some $93 million, with an average monthly payment per recipient of $77.[27]

[26] United States Department of Health, Education, and Welfare, *Annual Report: 1962*, pp. 65, 130.
[27] *Ibid.*, p. 131.

Aid to Dependent Children. At one time it was customary to care for dependent and neglected children either in the county almshouse along with adult paupers or in orphans' homes maintained by religious, social, or fraternal organizations or, less commonly, by county or state governments.[28] Today, though children in considerable number are still provided for in children's homes of various kinds, institutional care is less widely used than formerly. It has long been recognized that even the best of institutions cannot provide the normal home environment desirable for the rearing of children, and during recent decades there has been a strong tendency to make constantly increasing use both of foster-home care and of financial assistance designed to enable mothers of dependent children to maintain their own homes.[29] The latter method of care is especially advantageous where a mother can demonstrate that she is a suitable person to retain custody of her dependent children. Not only does it enable the children concerned to grow up in their mother's home rather than in a public or private institution, but in many cases it is more economical from the standpoint of public or private charity. Often a mother will have some income of her own that will need merely to be supplemented from the public treasury to enable her to maintain her home, whereas if the home is broken up and the children placed in institutions the cost of their entire support becomes a charge on public or private charity. Prior to the Social Security Act, many states had enacted legislation providing for mothers' pensions, or mothers' aid as a means of caring for dependent children, though most of these laws were inadequate in various respects and some made the payment of benefits optional with the county governments. The Social Security Act offered federal grants-in-aid toward the support of federally-approved statewide systems of this type of public assistance in an amplified form called aid to dependent children.

The Social Security Act defines a dependent child as a needy child under the age of eighteen who has been deprived of parental support or care by reason of the death, continued absence from the home, or physical or mental incapacity of a parent, and who is living with his father or mother, or with any other of a specified list of relatives, in a place of residence maintained by one or more such relatives as his or their own home. State definitions tend to be substantially similar to that of the federal law. Under the federal law, payments may also be made for the support of children in approved foster homes, and some states authorize such payments. To qualify for federal aid, a state may not impose any residence requirement in excess of a single year. Though a few states do not require any

[28] Martha P. Falconer, "Institutions for the Care of Children," *Encyclopaedia of the Social Sciences,* Vol. III (Macmillan, New York, 1930), 410-412. The term *orphanage* or *orphans' home* has been widely applied to institutions for child care notwithstanding that only a small percentage of the children cared for there are actually orphans.
[29] *Ibid.*

specified period of residence, most of them have the one-year requirement. Rarely is there a citizenship qualification. The general purport of the "need" requirement in the various states is that the private resources available for the support of the child must be insufficient to provide a reasonable subsistence compatible with health and well-being. Some states limit individual payments to a specified amount but others impose no limit. Federal law now permits payments for support of needy adult caretakers as well as for needy children themselves, and the program is currently known as aid to *families with* dependent children. In 1961, through provisions now scheduled to expire in 1967, Congress temporarily broadened provisions for federal grants-in-aid to include assistance to needy children of *unemployed* parents, and some states have broadened their aid programs correspondingly. In 1962, aid-to-dependent-children payments were made to nearly a million families throughout the nation for the support of 3.6 million children and caretakers. Total expenditures for the year exceeded $1.3 billion, with an average monthly payment per recipient of $31.[30]

In addition to administering aid to dependent children under the federal-state system, or supervising the administration of that program by local agencies, state welfare departments usually perform various other child-welfare services. Among the most important of these are the supervision of children's institutions and child-placement agencies operated by private organizations or local governments, and the licensing and inspection of foster homes.[31]

Aid to the Permanently and Totally Disabled. A fourth categorical program, inaugurated as a result of 1950 amendments to the Social Security Act, provides aid to needy persons eighteen years of age or over who are permanently and totally disabled. The definition of need varies among the states but in many instances is the same as for old-age assistance. Definition of qualifying disability is not prescribed by federal law but is left to the respective states. Some states have adopted comprehensive statutory definitions while others have preferred to leave definition in large measure to administrative determination. A few states have adopted definitions so narrow as to confine assistance to persons who are bedridden or housebound. More common, however, are definitions sufficiently liberal to permit the granting of assistance to needy persons who, though not housebound, are permanently prevented by disease or other disability from engaging in useful occupations, including home-making. Many of those receiving disability aid are suffering from heart disease, paralysis, or arthritis. Amputees comprise another substantial group. Other recipients suffer from a variety of impairments or diseases, such as mental deficien-

[30] United States Department of Health, Education, and Welfare, *Annual Report: 1962*, pp. 55, 61, 64-66, 130-131.
[31] Cf. Millspaugh, *op. cit.*, 351.

cies, tuberculosis, or cancer.[32] State provisions concerning residence requirements and amount of assistance payments tend to be similar to, and in many instances are identical with, those applicable to old-age assistance. Some states discontinue disability aid at age sixty-five, relying on old-age assistance for the support of older disabled persons. In 1962, expenditures for disability aid in the 46 states operating programs amounted to more than $300 million. Recipients numbered more than 400,000, with an average monthly payment per recipient of $72.[33]

Medical Assistance for the Aged. The newest of the categorical programs, inaugurated under amendments to the Social Security Act effected by the Kerr-Mills Act of 1960, provides assistance to persons over 65 who, though not recipients of old-age assistance, are "medically indigent" in the sense of having income and resources insufficient to meet all the costs of needed medical care. Under this program states may make available a broad range of medical services, including, among others, inpatient hospital services, nursing-home services, physicians' services, outpatient hospital or clinic services, physical therapy, dental services, drugs, eyeglasses, and dentures. State programs must include both institutional and noninstitutional care but need not include all of the services authorized under the federal law. Most of the programs established thus far offer less comprehensive coverage than that authorized under the federal law. Generally, a person with annual income in excess of a specified amount is ineligible for assistance, this amount most commonly being $1,500. Federal contributions to assistance payments range from 50 percent to 80 percent of expenditures, the highest percentages going to states having lowest per capita income. In 1962, though programs were then in operation in only half of the states, medical assistance was provided to more than 100,000 persons with total expenditures of almost $200 million.[34]

The Almshouse

The basic institution in the United States for providing indoor care for the needy is the public almshouse. State homes in the nature of almshouses are to be found in a few instances; in several New England states the conduct of local almshouses is a town function; and some cities maintain

[32] Margaret Greenfield, *Permanent and Total Disability Aid* (Bur. of Pub. Admin., Univ. of Calif., Berkeley, 1953); United States Department of Health, Education, and Welfare, *Characteristics of Recipients of Aid to the Permanently and Totally Disabled: Mid-1951* (Washington, 1953).

[33] United States Department of Health, Education, and Welfare, *Annual Report: 1962*, p. 131.

[34] *Ibid.*, pp. 69-72, 131. At that time it appeared that the medical-assistance program would soon spread to cover most or all of the states.

almshouses. Throughout the nation at large, however, the almshouse is most commonly a county institution. It is known in some states by other names, such as poor-house, poor farm, infirmary, or county home; and the latter title, in view of the changing character of the institution and because of a desire to lessen any social stigma that may attach to inmates, is currently gaining in favor. Although, as will be pointed out presently, many almshouses have been closed during recent decades, it appears that more than 1,000 counties still operate institutions of this nature.[35]

The traditional almshouse has consisted of a single building, commonly of antiquated construction, unsanitary, and lacking in modern conveniences. In many instances a farm is operated in connection with the almshouse, on which is raised some of the food consumed at the institution and occasionally some additional produce for sale. The almshouse superintendent is usually appointed by the county board, and frequently the superintendent's wife serves as matron. All too often these managers have neither any social-service training nor a social outlook. Until comparatively recently, the heterogeneous character of the almshouse population has made practically impossible the provision of proper care for the inmates of any class. The able-bodied and the sick, the old and the young, the mentally competent and incompetent, have been herded together in the one institution. Happily this situation, as we shall see, has now been remedied to some extent, though even today many almshouses make inadequate provision for segregating the different classes of inmates.

Another factor contributing in a large measure to the unsatisfactory nature of almshouse operation has been the small number of inmates for which, in many instances, an institution has been operated. There have always been some governmental units which, though empowered to maintain almshouses, have provided otherwise for their poor requiring indoor care. The general tendency, however, has been for each county or other local unit to maintain its own institution whether or not the number of needy persons within its jurisdiction was large enough to justify such maintenance from an economic standpoint. A survey conducted in the 1920's revealed that, of 2,183 almshouses for which data were available, 137 had no inmates, 787 others had ten or less, and fewer than a third of the total number had as many as twenty-five.[36] As recently as 1950, 32 of Tennessee's 70 almshouses had fewer than ten inmates and 26 others fewer than twenty.[37] An institutional population as small as that existing in many almshouses is clearly insufficient to permit economic operation. High per-inmate costs are almost inevitable, and even then the facilities and care

[35] Clyde F. Snider, "The Fading Almshouse," *Nat. Mun. Rev.*, XLV, 60-65 (Feb., 1956). Cf. Millspaugh, *op. cit.*, 282-283.

[36] Estelle M. Stewart, *The Cost of American Almshouses* (Bur. of Labor Statistics, U.S. Dept. of Labor, Washington, 1925).

[37] William E. Cole and Russell R. Dynes, *Homes for the Homeless in Tennessee* (Division of Univ. Extension, Univ. of Tenn., Knoxville, 1951), 11.

provided are often substandard. In normal times, and especially in rural areas, the number of needy persons requiring institutional care in the typical county is usually insufficient to justify the maintenance of an almshouse, and in times of widespread unemployment and need the present tendency is to meet the extraordinary situation by expanding the various programs of outdoor assistance. In view of these circumstances, it seems clear that the public interest is served in many instances by closing small almshouses and arranging for the care of such institutional cases as exist in almshouses of neighboring conuties, in district institutions, or in private homes at public expense.

Effect of Social Security Program. With the inauguration of the social security program, there was widespread belief that old-age assistance and aid to the blind would sound the death knell of the county almshouse. The Social Security Act, it will be remembered, originally denied federal aid for the payment of benefits to persons who were inmates of public institutions. Because of this fact, it was assumed that the aged and blind in almshouses would leave those institutions and qualify for benefit payments under the new programs, and that, since so large a proportion of almshouse inmates are sixty-five years of age or over, this exodus would permit the closing of many or most of the county institutions.

As a matter of fact, the new programs of categorical assistance did effect a considerable reduction in almshouse populations throughout the country, and substantial numbers of institutions were closed in various states.[38] The effect of the new programs in this direction, however, was less pronounced than had commonly been anticipated, because of the high frequency among almshouse inmates of chronic diseases necessitating institutional care. The National Health Survey of the 1930's indicates that one-half of all persons in the United States aged sixty-five or over suffer from some chronic disease, and the proportion is considerably higher among almshouse inmates than in the general population.[39] It has been estimated, for example, that 80 percent of the inmates of county almshouses in Illinois in 1945 were in need of continuing nursing service.[40] Until more appropriate facilities for care of this nature are made available in

[38] See "Effect of Social-Security Program on Almshouses," *Monthly Labor Rev.*, XLVII, 518-524 (Sept., 1938); T. C. Pihlblad, "A Study of Missouri Almshouses," *Southwestern Soc. Sci. Quar.*, XIX, 201-210 (Sept., 1938); Loula Dunn, "Status of County Almshouses in Alabama," *Pub. Welfare News*, Vol. VI, No. 3 (Mar., 1938), 2-4; Violet M. Fischer, "Kansas County Homes After the Social Security Act," *Soc. Service Rev.*, XVII, 442-465 (Dec., 1943); Raymond M. Hilliard, "The Emerging Function of Public Institutions in our Social Security Structure," *Ibid.*, XX, 479-493 (Dec., 1946).

[39] Cf. Ellen C. Potter, "State Responsibility for the Care of the Chronically Ill," *State Govt.*, XIX, 39-42, 61 (Feb., 1946).

[40] *Interim Report of the [Illinois] Committee to Investigate Chronic Diseases among Indigents* (Springfield, Ill., 1945), 9.

the various states, it is likely to be provided in large measure through the continued operation of almshouses.

Recent Improvements. Although conditions in many almshouses are still far from satisfactory, the general situation with respect to such institutions throughout the country has during recent decades improved in several directions. Certain classes of inmates have rather generally been removed from the almshouse population and provided with more appropriate forms of care. It has become common policy, for example, to provide care for dependent children, to the extent that such care is still institutional, in special children's homes, and to care for needy persons who are insane or feebleminded in appropriate state institutions. This policy has not only resulted in better care for the children and mentally handicapped, but by leaving a less heterogeneous population in the almshouses has simplified the task of providing proper care for persons remaining therein. With the removal of children and defectives from the almshouse, that institution becomes principally, though not solely, a home for the aged.

Gradual improvement is being made in physical plants. Some almshouse buildings have been replaced and others modernized. In both cases more attention is being given than formerly to proper lighting, heating, ventilation, and sanitary facilities, and to kitchen and medical equipment. In some instances there have been substantial improvements in structural plan. To lessen somewhat the "institutional" environment of the almshouse and to promote proper classification of inmates, some local governments have modified the traditional structure by providing, instead of a single large building, either a central building with several detached wings or a number of smaller separate buildings. Under this scheme, known as the "cottage" system, the sick may be placed in separate quarters for special care, old couples may be given quarters together, and other desirable segregation measures may be carried out.[41]

During recent decades, as we have seen, a substantial number of smaller almshouses have been closed. When a county or other local unit discontinues its almshouse, it must ordinarily make some other arrangement for the care of its needy residents, as has been necessary in the past in the case of those units which have never operated almshouses. Many states provide that one local governmental unit may contract with another for the care of its needy, and under this authority some of the counties which have closed their almshouses have arranged to purchase such institutional care as may be required in almshouses of neighboring counties. In other instances the county "boards out" its needy in private homes.[42] Still another approach to the problem of the small almshouse is afforded by the district institution. Under this plan several counties or other local

[41] John L. Gillin, *Poverty and Dependency: Their Relief and Prevention* (3rd ed.), 183-184.
[42] Millspaugh, *op. cit.*, 284; Gillin, *op. cit.*, 186.

units are combined into a special district for operating a single institution for indoor assistance, and the smaller establishments of the individual units can then be discontinued. The underlying purpose of the district system is to provide an administrative unit of sufficient area that its indigent population requiring indoor care will be large enough to make the operation of an institution economically feasible. A good example of the system is provided in Virginia, where in several instances old-style county and city almshouses have been replaced by modern district homes.[43] Joint institutions reported to be operating in other states in the mid-1950's included two bicounty homes and one four-county home in Minnesota; a bicounty home in Pennsylvania; a tricounty home in West Virginia; and two homes in Vermont, one serving three towns and the other five.[44] Joint operation, by enlarging both the territory supporting a single institution and the population served thereby, promotes the economic feasibility of replacing numerous old-style almshouses with a smaller number of modern, well-managed homes.

County Nursing Homes

One of the most significant recent developments has been the conversion of many old-style almshouses into modern nursing homes for care of the aged and chronically ill. As the life span lengthens with the progress of medical science and sanitation, older people constitute an ever-larger proportion of our population, and their care looms constantly larger as a governmental problem. Since the incidence of chronic diseases—cancer, arthritis, rheumatism, heart disease, and the like—is higher among older people than among the younger, the problem of providing institutional care for the needy aged becomes largely one of supplying proper medical and nursing facilities.

As previously indicated, many almshouses were closed during the late 1930's and the following decade as a result of the outdoor assistance programs for the aged and the blind provided under the Social Security Act. Many others, however, notwithstanding their general inadequacy, found it necessary to continue in operation to provide a home for disabled inmates who required nursing care and who were unable to obtain this care, even with the aid of public subsidy, in the homes of relatives or friends or in private institutions. To encourage local governmental units to improve and modernize their facilities, some states provided that old-age assistance and aid to the blind might be paid to the inmates of local institutions who were otherwise qualified to receive such aid, provided the institutions met certain standards prescribed by a specified state agency, usually the welfare department. Since federal grants-in-aid were not at

---

[43] Robert H. Kirkwood, *Fit Surroundings: District Homes Replace County Almshouses in Virginia* (Va. Dept. of Pub. Welfare, Richmond, 1948).
[44] Snider, *op. cit.*

this time available for benefits for such inmates, assistance payments were made wholly from nonfederal funds. The state standards which a county home or other public institution was required to meet in order to qualify its inmates for old-age assistance or aid to the blind, concerned such matters as structural safety and convenience, sanitation, heating and lighting, ventilation, proper fire escapes, equipment, medical facilities, and staff. Inmates of approved institutions receiving old-age assistance or aid to the blind used the money to pay for their institutional care, and thus a considerable portion of the cost of their support was shifted from the local taxpayers to the state. The opportunity to effect this transfer of the tax burden provided a strong incentive for county boards and other local authorities to make the necessary capital outlay to modernize their almshouses.

Some local units modernized their almshouses even in the absence of state legislation of the kind noted in the preceding paragraph, but such legislation served as a potent stimulus to modernization. Many counties converted their old almshouses into adequately equipped and well-managed nursing homes. Further impetus was given to the nursing-home movement when, in 1950, the Social Security Act was amended to inaugurate a program of federal grants for aid to the permanently and totally disabled and to provide that henceforth the federal government would share in assistance payments to needy aged, blind, or disabled persons who were patients in public medical institutions other than tuberculosis or mental institutions. Today, the states are at liberty to make old-age assistance, aid to the blind, disability aid, and medical assistance for the aged, including federal contributions, available to persons otherwise qualified who are patients in county or other publicly operated homes approved as public medical institutions.

The number of nursing homes operated by counties and other local governments has increased appreciably during recent years. Among the states having such homes in largest number are California (where the homes are operated as parts of county hospitals), Illinois, Michigan, New York, and Wisconsin. In a few states, all remaining county institutions are of nursing-home character, old-style almshouses having been completely eliminated.[45] In addition to patients receiving assistance under the federal-aid programs, most nursing homes also serve needy persons whose care is paid for from the general-assistance funds of the town or county of their residence; and some homes admit patients of private means who pay for their own care. With the outdating of the old-style almshouse, the growing seriousness of the problem of chronic illness, and the shortage of private nursing homes offering suitable care at reasonable cost, the development of county nursing homes is one of the most encouraging present-day features of local welfare administration.

[45] *Ibid.*

State Welfare Institutions

Each state maintains several institutions for the care of persons suffering from physical or mental handicaps or otherwise disadvantaged. The classes of persons for whom institutional care is most commonly provided are the mentally ill, the deaf, and the blind. In some states each such institution has its own governing board, though there is usually provision for some supervision by a central state agency. In other states several or all of the institutions are governed by a single board of control, a department of institutions, or the department of public welfare.[46] At one time the function of these institutions for the handicapped classes was considered as being primarily custodial, but more recently there has been increased emphasis upon the medical treatment, education, and rehabilitation of their inmates. Training schools and reformatories for juvenile delinquents are coming to be looked upon as welfare rather than penal institutions, and in some states are under common management with institutions for the handicapped. Institutions of a more strictly penal nature, such as the state penitentiaries, are in some instances managed by the same agency as the institutions for handicapped and delinquent classes, but there is a growing disposition to provide separate management for welfare and penal establishments, respectively. Many states maintain institutions for the care of certain dependent classes other than the handicapped groups. State soldiers' homes for needy veterans are quite common, and some states maintain homes for widows and orphans of soldiers and sailors. As previously noted, a few states maintain almshouses of a general nature.

Mental Health

It has been estimated that mental illness affects 17 million Americans and that mental patients occupy half of the nation's hospital beds.[47] One of the most significant current trends in the public-welfare field is seen in the increasing attention being accorded to this problem. The old "insane asylum" was little more than a prison-type institution for the confinement of persons committed thereto by court order on a finding of insanity. Often housed in an antiquated and unsanitary building, the asylum was likely to be overcrowded, understaffed, and provided with only the most primitive medical facilities.[48] Though condi-

[46] Cf. above, "Welfare Organization: State Organization."

[47] Berwyn F. Mattison and T. Lefoy Richman, *Community Health Services: The Case of the Missing Mileposts* (Pub. Affairs Pamphlets, New York, 1962), 9.

[48] For a graphic description of the deplorable conditions existing in many state mental hospitals, see Albert Deutsch, *The Shame of the States* (Harcourt, New York, 1948).

tions such as these remain widespread, substantial improvement has been made during recent years in many states and improvement is continuing.

Mental-health budgets are increasing rapidly. Modern mental hospitals are supplementing and gradually supplanting the traditional asylums. Overcrowding is being reduced as hospital capacity is expanded and provision is made for outpatient care in less serious cases. Staffs are being enlarged and an effort is being made to recruit qualified psychiatrists, nurses, and administrative personnel. Provision is now made in most states for the voluntary commitment of patients, and commitment procedures have been improved. As previously noted with respect to welfare institutions generally, there is increased emphasis upon treatment and rehabilitation. Some states now make financial aid available for the operation of local mental-health clinics, and many such clinics have been established to provide outpatient treatment as well as "aftercare" for patients who have been released from hospitalization. Increased attention is being given to the needs of younger persons, with special schools, hospitals, or treatment centers being established in some instances for mentally-retarded or emotionally-disturbed children. The growing importance of mental-health activities is amply evidenced by the fact that several states have recently established separate departments of mental health as major administrative units of state government.[49]

Veterans' Service

Welfare services in aid of veterans are important after every war and have been especially so since World War II. Veterans of service in the armed forces now constitute some 15 percent of the nation's population.[50] Though broad responsibilities for the care and readjustment of veterans have been assumed by the national government, state and local services for the benefit of veterans are also of considerable importance. During the later war years and the early post-war period, the states enacted a vast amount of veterans' legislation. Some of these acts merely amended earlier statutes to extend their benefits to veterans of World War II, while others provided for new or expanded services. Eventually many of the benefits offered by this legislation were extended also to veterans of the Korean conflict. State and local veterans' services both supplement the federal program and provide additional and independent benefits.

Needy veterans are of course entitled to public assistance equally

[49] Council of State Governments, *The Mental Health Programs of the Forty-Eight States;* Council of State Governments, *State Action in Mental Health, 1956-57;* Joint Commission on Mental Illness and Health, *Action for Mental Health;* Ruth Turk, "State Mental Health Programs, 1962-1963," *The Book of the States,* 1964-65, pp. 394-401.

[50] Claribel H. Moncure, "Veterans' Benefits and Services," *Social Work Year Book: 1960* (Nat. Assn. of Soc. Workers, New York), 591-600.

with other needy persons, but most of the states have enacted laws providing for additional special assistance to veterans.[51] Many states, as we have seen, maintain soldiers' homes for needy veterans, and some provide veterans' rehabilitation hospitals. Veterans are commonly given preference in civil service appointments, and frequently in other state or local employment as well. Other benefits provided in various states include cash bonuses, free tuition in educational institutions, assistance in securing employment, exemption from certain taxes and license fees, and loans for the establishment of businesses or the acquisition of homes.[52]

Some veterans' services are carried on by state welfare departments, but most states have separate agencies charged with administering various activities in the veterans' interests. These agencies are known by different titles, such as veterans' services office, veterans' commission, or department of veterans' affairs.[53] Whatever its title, the duties of the veterans' agency usually include, in addition to the administration of certain specific programs of the types mentioned above, the providing of information to veterans and their dependents and beneficiaries concerning compensation, insurance, medical, educational, or other benefits to which they may be entitled under federal or state law, and the assisting of those persons in preparing and presenting claims for such benefits. It is commonly made the duty of the state agency to cooperate with all other agencies affording information and services to veterans, whether operated by the national, state, or local government, or by private organizations. Some states provide for the maintenance of district offices of the state veterans' agency at various points throughout the state. In many communities city or county service offices have been established by the local governments to assist veterans and their families in cooperation with national, state, and other local agencies.

Special Programs for the Aged

With elderly people constituting an increasing proportion of the nation's population, there is a growing concern for the special problems of this age group. Efforts are being made not only to see that the physical needs of elderly citizens are met but to assure them of normal places as members of the social and economic communities. The programs of old-age assistance and medical assistance for the aged, and the improvement of nursing-home facilities, have already been discussed. In addition, many state and local governments have inaugurated special programs of various kinds. Some

[51] McHugh, *op. cit.*, 381-382.

[52] State veterans' legislation is analyzed in Council of State Governments, *State Veterans' Programs*. See also Dorthea Pye Simon, "State and Federal Programs for Veterans," *The Book of the States*, 1945-46, pp. 411- 420; "State Veterans' Programs," *Ibid.*, 1948-49, pp. 473-480.

[53] Cf. *The Book of the States*, 1956-57, p. 591.

states have prohibited discrimination in employment on account of age; and some have provided for the training or retraining of older workers as a means of improving their employment opportunities. In some instances retirement systems for public employees have been modified to permit employees who retain their health and competence to work beyond the normal retirement age. Some states provide tax exemptions of one kind or another for older people; and some public housing authorities have constructed projects especially designed and equipped to meet the needs of elderly tenants. Special recreation programs for the elderly are provided in some instances. As of the mid-1960's, some 27 states were reported as having established governmental agencies concerned with problems of aging and the aged.[54]

Legal Aid

Yet another special form of public-welfare service is the provision of legal counsel for poor persons in connection with controversies and litigation of a civil nature.[55] American ideals require "equal justice to all"— to rich and poor alike. Yet it cannot be denied that a litigant with adequate financial means enjoys a distinct advantage over a less fortunate adversary, since he is able to employ the best of counsel, finance new trials and appeals, and, through sheer protraction of litigation if nothing else, wear down the opposition. Recognizing this situation, various steps have been taken, some from early days and others more recently, to assist the poor in overcoming this handicap. Some of these measures have been taken by government and others by private agencies.

Most states have so-called *in forma pauperis* statutes which provide that a poor person, upon taking oath that he is unable to pay the costs and convincing the court that he has a meritorious case, may bring a civil action without charge for court process and have counsel assigned to him without fee. These statutory provisions seem, however, to be rarely used. According to an eminent authority, although the system of assigned counsel in civil cases "looms large in the books," it "has amounted to very little in practice." Indeed, "The large majority of attorneys do not realize that there is any authority which can require them as a matter of duty to give their services without charge to poor persons" in civil litigation.[56]

Of genuine significance, on the other hand, are the legal aid bureaus established in many of the larger cities and some less populous communities for the purpose of providing legal advice and assistance to poor

[54] "State Programs for the Aging," *Ibid.*, 1962-63, pp. 399-404; *Ibid.*, 1964-65, pp. 421-427.

[55] Legal counsel for the poor in criminal cases has been considered in the discussion of law enforcement. See above, Chap. XVII.

[56] Reginald H. Smith, *Justice and the Poor* (Scribner, New York, 1919), 100, 101.

persons in civil matters.[57] Some of these organizations are operated and financed by the city government, but most of them are supported by private philanthropy. Dallas, New Haven, Kansas City (Missouri), and St. Louis are among the cities maintaining municipal bureaus. Among the privately-supported agencies there is much variation with respect to title, form of organization, sponsorship, and method of financing. Many are known as "societies" or "clinics" rather than as bureaus. The more common sponsors include local bar associations, colleges of law, and local "community chests" or "united charities." Some organizations perform their work through full-time, paid attorney employees, while others rely largely upon lawyers who volunteer to give a specified number of hours per week or month, without charge, to this form of public service. Regardless of these variations, the basic purpose of all such organizations, whether private or municipal, is that of making legal services in civil matters [58] available to poor persons either free of cost or at a nominal fee. Some of the larger organizations handle several thousand cases annually, and legal-aid work is coming to be recognized more and more as a significant form of social service.[59] In 1962, according to data compiled by the National Legal Aid and Defender Association, some 240 legal aid offices in the United States handled nearly 400,000 cases.[60]

REFERENCES

ABBOTT, Edith, *Public Assistance*, Vol. I (Univ. of Chicago Press, Chicago, 1940).

ABBOTT, Grace, *From Relief to Social Security* (Univ. of Chicago Press, Chicago, 1941).

BRADWAY, John S., *Legal Aid Bureaus: Their Organization and Administration* (Pub. Admin. Service, Chicago, 1935).

[57] Cf. John S. Bradway, *Legal Aid Bureaus: Their Organization and Administration.*

[58] A few of the organizations handle some criminal cases also.

[59] On the subject generally, see Emery A. Brownell, *Legal Aid in the United States;* Bradway, *Legal Aid Bureaus: Their Organization and Administration;* John S. Bradway and Reginald H. Smith, eds., *Legal Aid Work;* Reginald H. Smith and John S. Bradway, *Growth of Legal-Aid Work in the United States;* John S. Bradway, ed., *Frontiers of Legal Aid Work;* George Scott Stewart, Jr., and Robert D. Abrahams, "Legal Aid in Civil Cases," *Georgetown Law Jour.,* XXVI, 32-59 (Nov., 1937); Sidney B. Jacoby, "Legal Aid to the Poor," *Harvard Law Rev.,* LIII, 940-976 (Apr., 1940); Reginald H. Smith, "Legal Service Offices for Persons of Moderate Means," *Wis. Law Rev.,* Vol. 1949, No. 3 (May, 1949), 416-461; "Legal Aid and Democracy," *Fortune,* Oct., 1952, pp. 142-143, 178, 180; Gertrude Samuels, "Clinic for Legal Aid," *N.Y. Times Mag.,* Mar. 27, 1955, pp. 30, 58.

[60] National Legal Aid and Defender Association, *Statistics of Legal Aid Work in the United States and Canada: 1962* (Nat. Legal Aid and Defender Assn., Chicago, 1963).

————, ed., "Frontiers of Legal Aid Work," *Annals of Amer. Acad. of Polit. and Soc. Sci.*, CCV, Philadelphia, Sept., 1939.

————, and Smith, Reginald H., eds., "Legal Aid Work," *Annals of Amer. Acad. of Polit. and Soc. Sci.*, CXXIV, Philadelphia, Mar., 1926.

BRECKINRIDGE, Sophonisba P., *Public Welfare Administration in the United States: Select Documents* (Univ. of Chicago Press, Chicago, 2nd ed., 1938).

BROWN, Josephine C., *Public Relief, 1929-1939* (Holt, New York, 1940).

BROWNELL, Emery A., *Legal Aid in the United States* (Lawyers Co-op. Pub. Co., Rochester, N.Y., 1951).

BROWNING, Grace, *Rural Public Welfare: Selected Records* (Univ. of Chicago Press, Chicago, 1941), especially the introductory notes to the respective sections of the book.

BURNS, Eveline M., *The American Social Security System* (Houghton, Boston, 1949).

————, *Toward Social Security* (Whittlesey House, New York, 1936).

CARTER, Isabel G., ed., "Appraising the Social Security Program," *Annals of Amer. Acad. of Polit. and Soc. Sci.*, CCII, Philadelphia, Mar., 1939.

COUNCIL of State Governments, *State Action in Mental Health, 1956-57* (The Council, Chicago, 1958).

————, *The Mental Health Programs of the Forty-Eight States* (The Council, Chicago, 1950).

————, *State Veterans' Programs* (The Council, Chicago, rev. ed., 1945).

————, *The States and their Older Citizens* (The Council, Chicago, 1955).

DOUGLAS, Paul H., *Social Security in the United States* (Whittlesey House, New York, 1936).

GILLIN, John L., *Poverty and Dependency: Their Relief and Prevention* (Appleton-Century-Crofts, New York, 3rd. ed., 1937).

JOHNSON, Alexander, *The Almshouse* (Russell Sage Found., New York, 1911).

Joint Commission on Mental Illness and Health, *Action for Mental Health* (Basic Books, New York, 1961).

LANDIS, Benson Y., *Rural Welfare Services* (Columbia Univ. Press, New York, 1949).

MILES, Arthur P., *An Introduction to Public Welfare* (Heath, Boston, 1949).

MILLSPAUGH, Arthur C., *Public Welfare Organization* (Brookings Inst., Washington, 1935).

SMITH, Reginald H., and BRADWAY, John S., *Growth of Legal-Aid Work in the United States* (U.S. Bur. of Labor Statistics, Washington, rev. ed., 1936).

STEVENSON, Marietta, *Public Welfare Administration* (Macmillan, New York, 1938).

————, and MacDonald, Alice, *State and Local Public Welfare Agencies* (Amer. Pub. Welfare Assn., Chicago, 1939).

United States Department of Health, Education, and Welfare, *Annual Report: 1962* (U.S. Govt. Printing Office, Washington).

VASEY, Wayne, *Government and Social Welfare* (Holt, New York, 1958).

WARNER, Amos G., QUEEN, Stuart A., and HARPER, Ernest B., *American Charities and Social Work* (Crowell, New York, 4th ed., 1930).

WHITE, R. Clyde, *Administration of Public Welfare* (American Book, New York, 2nd ed., 1950).

19 ⸻⸻⸻

Health and Housing

HEALTH

Sickness and Medical Care

Notwithstanding marked improvement in the nation's health during recent decades, sickness remains a major problem. Recent data from the National Health Survey indicate that in a single year Americans outside resident institutions experienced 359 million acute illnesses and injuries. During the same year, the average American's activity was restricted some 16 days by illness or injury. An estimated 74 million persons—42 percent of the nation's population—were reported as having one or more chronic ailments of varying severity. More than 14 million persons were limited in their major activity by chronic disease or impairment, and nearly a million were housebound continually by chronic conditions.[1] It is estimated that chronic diseases result in one-half to three-fourths of a billion man-days being lost from production annually.[2] Expenditures for health and medical care in the United States in 1960 amounted to more than $26 billion or nearly $150 per capita—approximately three-fourths of the total deriving from private, and one-fourth from public funds.[3]

Despite these large expenditures, millions of Americans still have only inadequate medical service or none at all. This unfortunate situation

[1] United States Department of Health, Education, and Welfare, *Annual Report: 1962*, p. 143.

[2] United States Department of Health, Education, and Welfare, *Handbook on Programs of the U.S. Department of Health, Education, and Welfare: 1962 edition*, p. 54.

[3] United States Department of Health, Education, and Welfare, *Health, Education, and Welfare Trends: 1962 edition*, p. 26.

is the result of several factors. For one thing, there is in the country as a whole a shortage of physicians, hospitals, and other medical personnel and facilities. Again, existing personnel and facilities are not equably distributed. In general, the states with relatively high per capita wealth or income have better medical care than those less favorably situated, and urban areas are better served than rural.[4] Most of the larger cities now have municipal health departments and one or more hospitals for public use, even though in some instances the services so provided are sadly inadequate. In rural areas, on the other hand, there are many entire counties without either a full-time health department or a hospital of any kind; and it is a well-known fact that the growing tendency for physicians, especially those of the younger group, to prefer either specialization or practice in the cities, is leaving more and more rural communities without a local doctor. But the most important cause of inadequate medical care among the American people is the fact that many low-income families are financially unable to meet the costs of proper care. Private expenditures for medical service tend to vary directly with economic status. Families comprising that half of the nation's population with lowest incomes spend far less than the national average and in many instances less than enough to secure adequate care.[5]

Health as a Public Responsibility

Government exists to promote the public welfare, and an important factor in the well-being of any group of citizens is the state of their physical and mental health. Sickness results in physical suffering, economic loss, and dependency. Government is therefore justified in seeking, by appropriate and lawful means, to prevent sickness and raise the general health level of the community.

Since the United States Constitution does not mention the subject of health, public powers and duties with respect to health protection fall primarily to the respective states. The national government, nevertheless, through the United States Public Health Service and other federal agencies, carries on a variety of activities in the health field. For many years these activities were concerned principally with health research, providing advice and assistance to state and local health officers, and preventing the introduction of diseases from abroad and their spread from one state to another. More recently there has developed a growing program of federal grants-in-aid to the state and local governments for health purposes such as maternal and child health, industrial hygiene, control of

[4] Cf. Committee on the Costs of Medical Care, *Medical Care for the American People*, 5.

[5] Cf. C. E. A. Winslow, "Medical Care for the Nation," *Yale Rev.*, XXVIII, 501-520 (Spring, 1939).

venereal diseases, heart disease, tuberculosis, and cancer, and assistance of state and local units in maintaining full-time general health services. Another major activity of the national government in the health field is, of course, the program of medical care for veterans administered by the Veterans Administration.

Within the states, early health-protection activities were devolved for the most part upon the local governmental units and, apart from provision of some sort of medical care for the indigent, were concerned principally with the combating of epidemics and the abatement of local nuisances.[6] With the passing of time, however, it became increasingly clear that health matters are of state-wide concern, and the state governments gradually assumed more responsibility. Though the checking of epidemics continued to be of first-rate importance, more and more emphasis came to be placed on disease prevention and health education. A relatively recent development in the public health field is the interest which state and local governments are beginning to show in chronic diseases such as rheumatism and arthritis in their various forms, heart disease, high blood pressure, cancer, diabetes, and nephritis.[7] As the acute epidemic diseases, thanks to advances in medical science, decline in frequency and severity, and as the life span lengthens, these chronic diseases of adult life and advanced age bulk ever larger in the problem of medical care. If the problem is to be solved satisfactorily, public health work must become ever more concerned with the care and treatment of patients suffering from such chronic illnesses.[8]

Increased state responsibility in the public health field has taken three main forms: (1) direct performance by the state governments of additional health services; (2) further extension of state supervision and control over local health activities; and (3) subsidization and encouragement of local health services through state grants-in-aid.[9] However, notwithstanding expanded state activity in these various directions, primary responsibility for the initiation and administration of most public health programs still remains with the local-government units.

Public Health Organization: Local Organization

Local boards of health appear to have been established in Massachusetts as early as 1797.[10] During the century that followed, health

[6] Cf. Harry S. Mustard, *Government in Public Health*, 91.

[7] Ellen C. Potter, "State Responsibility for the Care of the Chronically Ill," *State Govt.*, XIX, 39-42, 61 (Feb., 1946).

[8] Joseph W. Mountin, "Participation by State and Local Health Departments in Current Medical Care Programs," *Amer. Jour. of Pub. Health*, XXXVI, 1387-1393 (Dec., 1946). County nursing homes for the chronically ill are discussed above, Chap. XVIII.

[9] Cf. Bernhard J. Stern, *Medical Services by Government*, 59.

[10] Wilson G. Smillie, *Public Health Administration in the United States* (2nd. ed., 1940), 369.

boards and health officers were introduced quite generally throughout the country. Nearly every city and village was provided with some sort of health organization. To serve rural areas, provision was made for township or county boards of health, and sometimes for both in a single state. These early health boards were frequently constituted on an ex officio basis, and in any event possessed very restricted authority. Their powers were limited for the most part to the establishment of quarantine and other regulations to check the spread of communicable disease, the appointment of a health officer to enforce such regulations, and the abatement of nuisances. Early health officers usually served on a part-time basis and, though sometimes physicians, were frequently laymen without any professional qualifications in health work.[11]

From these primitive beginnings, local public health services have developed along three principal lines: (1) expansion of the powers and activities of local health authorities; (2) replacement, in substantial measure, of part-time, nonprofessional personnel by full-time, trained officers and employees; and (3) substitution of larger for smaller geographic areas for the organization of local health services. These various phases of development are of course closely interrelated, since only professional personnel is qualified to perform modern health functions and larger areas are frequently necessary to make feasible the provision of such personnel on a full-time basis.

The first local health department to provide full-time service on a countywide basis appears to have been that of Jefferson county, Kentucky, which contains the city of Louisville. That county in 1908 placed its health officer on a full-time basis and provided him with a staff of sanitary inspectors. Three years later, full-time countywide departments were established in Guilford county, North Carolina, and Yakima county, Washington. All of these three counties contained cities of considerable size, and it remained for Robeson county, South Carolina, to become, in 1912, the first rural county to establish a full-time health department.[12] From this time on, state legislation permitting counties to establish full-time health departments spread rapidly. Such departments usually seek to provide as their minimum full-time staff a medical director, nurses and sanitary engineers sufficient in number to meet the county's needs, and adequate clerical personnel. Inasmuch as many rural counties have neither the financial resources to support a department of this nature, nor a population large enough to require its full-time services, many state laws also authorize the establishment of multicounty departments, the merging of city and county departments, or the organization of two or more counties, townships, or other local units into special public health districts for the

[11] Cf. Allen W. Freeman, ed., *A Study of Rural Public Health Service*, 1; Carl E. McCombs, *City Health Administration*, 50.
[12] Haven Emerson and Martha Luginbuhl, *Local Health Units for the Nation*, 12.

pooling of their resources and needs. By the mid-1940's two-thirds of the states had enacted legislation permitting the organization of local health administration on a county, multicounty, city-county, or district basis.[13] Actual establishment of full-time health departments under state enabling acts proceeded rather slowly at first, but was greatly accelerated as a result of federal grants-in-aid provided by the Social Security Act of 1935. By 1942 somewhat more than 1,800 counties—60 percent of all counties in the country—were served by local health units under the direction of full-time health officers,[14] and more recently the number of counties so served has continued to increase. The officers heading these modern local departments are usually appointed by the mayor in the case of city departments, the county governing board in the case of county departments, and a district governing board in the case of district departments. A local board of health commonly serves the department in an advisory capacity, and in some instances the old plan of having the health officer appointed by the board has been retained.[15]

The importance of the local organization in public health work can scarcely be overemphasized. The national government may grant subsidies and the states may control in matters of policy, but most routine public health services are performed by local agencies.[16] When this is considered, it is clear that present organization at the local level leaves much to be desired. Local health administration still suffers from extreme decentralization. Notwithstanding the elimination over the years of local health units and boards in considerable number, a committee of the American Public Health Association reported in 1945, on the basis of a nationwide study, that 18,000 or more local-government jurisdictions—counties, cities, townships, villages, and special districts—were still responsible for local health service.[17] It was found also that, despite the recent establishment of many new full-time departments, some 40 million Americans—more than a fourth of the nation's entire population—still lived in communities having only part-time local health service or none at all. As the type of reorganization needed to remedy the existing situation, the committee recommended the establishment of a comprehensive system of local health units covering the entire nation and having in each instance sufficient population and resources to support a basic minimum full-time health program. The specific suggestions submitted by the committee

[13] *Ibid.*, 332.

[14] Mustard, *Government in Public Health*, 116.

[15] Harry S. Mustard and Ernest L. Stebbins, *An Introduction to Public Health* (4th ed.), 56.

[16] Mustard, *Government in Public Health*, 114.

[17] Haven Emerson and Martha Luginbuhl, *Local Health Units for the Nation* (Commonwealth Fund, New York, 1945) is the published report of this committee. For a summary of the principal findings and recommendations of the committee, see Martha Luginbuhl, "Local Responsibility for Health Service," *Pub. Admin. Rev.*, VI, 30-41 (Winter, 1946).

called for a total of 1,197 local units—318 single-county units, 821 multi-county units, 36 "county-district" units including *parts* of one or more counties, and 22 city units. Seventy-eight percent of these proposed units would have populations of at least 50,000, the minimum considered desirable for the support of a full-time department. The less populous districts would serve sparsely populated rural communities where districts of 50,000 persons would require unduly large areas. A system of units such as the one suggested should, in the opinion of the committee, make it possible to provide the entire population of the country with minimum full-time health service at reasonable cost. The committee, of course, had no thought of offering a definitive program, but sought merely to outline sound *principles* of reorganization which might be of help to the respective states and localities as they seek improvements in health administration. As such a statement of principles, the committee's recommendations deserve careful study.

State Organization

The first state board of health in the United States was established in Louisiana in 1855, but later became inactive for many years. Massachusetts, in 1869, established the first health board to remain actively in existence from the time of its creation, and in the years that followed such agencies were organized in most other states. As public health activities increased and state governments were reorganized, state boards of health were rather generally replaced by state health departments under single administrative heads, though in most instances a board of some sort was retained within the department in either an administrative or an advisory capacity.[18] Today every state has an agency of some kind, ordinarily termed the department of health, which is charged with administering an overall health program. The chief executive officer of the health department is usually required to be a physician and is appointed in most instances by the governor or the state board of health, or by concurrent action of the governor and board. The official title of this principal officer varies from state to state, the most common titles being those of state health officer, superintendent of health, director of public health, and state health commissioner. To facilitate administration, the health department is organized into various bureaus or divisions, each under a chief or director responsible for a particular phase of the department's work. Divisions commonly found include those of vital statistics, general communicable-disease control, sanitation, maternal and child health, laboratory services, venereal-disease control, and public health nursing. Most departments have a division of general administration, and more than half have divisions of local health administration charged with the as-

[18] Mustard, *Government in Public Health*, 91-92, 101.

sistance and supervision of local health agencies. Employees of state health departments include physicians, dentists, nurses, sanitary engineers, technicians, and health educators, as well as administrative and clerical personnel.[19]

It should not be supposed, however, that all state activities in the field of public health are centralized in the health department. As a matter of fact, health services in most states are dispersed among several state agencies. Thus, registration of vital statistics may be handled by the secretary of state, school health services by the department of education, and water sanitation by the department of public works or public utilities. Other state agencies performing health functions in various states include departments of welfare, agriculture, labor, mining, conservation, and public safety, and a variety of boards and commissions.[20]

Public Health Functions

The health functions of state and local governments are numerous and varied, ranging all the way from control of acute communicable diseases to insect and rodent control and the regulation of garbage disposal. A study by the United States Public Health Service enumerates 36 health services performed by state-government agencies in some or all states, and the list does not purport to be exclusive.[21] Another study lists no less than 19 activities of local health departments,[22] and, as previously indicated, some health functions are administered by other agencies. In this brief discussion attention will necessarily be confined to some of the more common and basic health services.

Disease Control

Many public health activities have to do with the control of communicable and preventable diseases. Physicians are required by law to report cases of communicable disease to the local health authorities, who then investigate and take appropriate control measures. Isolation and quarantine, once the core of public health programs, are still important, but modern preventive medicine makes ever greater use of immunization. Most state health departments supply physicians with free vaccines and sera of various kinds for use in their private practice, while local health

[19] Joseph W. Mountin and Evelyn Flook, *Guide to Health Organization in the United States: 1951*, pp. 42-56; Joseph W. Mountin and others, *Distribution of Health Services in the Structure of State Government: 1950*, pp. 5-36.

[20] Cf. Mountin and Flook, *Guide to Health Organization in the United States: 1951*, pp. 45-52.

[21] *Ibid.*, 45-46.

[22] Mustard and Stebbins, *An Introduction to Public Health* (4th ed.), 57-58.

departments administer vaccines to the indigent and sometimes to the general public.[23]

During recent decades, special control programs have been inaugurated in various fields. Most of the states have developed special programs, financed in part through federal aid, for the control of tuberculosis and venereal diseases. Since early diagnosis plays so important a part in the control of tuberculosis, the programs in that field give much attention to case-finding. Extensive use is made of both skin tests and x-ray examinations. Persons found to be suffering from tuberculosis are advised with respect to hygiene, nutrition, and nursing and medical care, and, to the extent that facilities are available, are provided with care in tuberculosis hospitals. Practically every local health department operates a clinic for venereal-disease control, necessary drugs sometimes being supplied by the state departments.[24] Significant as control measures in this field are the premarital examination laws, now in effect in many states, which require persons applying for a marriage license to present a physician's certification that they are free from venereal disease.[25]

Rising death rates from cancer are causing government at all levels to take an increasing interest in that disease. The federal government has established the National Cancer Institute to engage in research, some cities have established cancer clinics, and most of the states have inaugurated programs, now supported in part through federal grants-in-aid, to facilitate the diagnosis and treatment of cancer.[26] Other diseases that are the subjects of special programs in some states include pneumonia, trachoma, malaria, and poliomyelitis.[27] Increasing attention is being devoted to heart disease, and to chronic diseases such as rheumatism and arthritis which are particularly prevalent among older people.

Sanitation

Sanitation measures of various sorts comprise another major phase of public health work. Health officers inspect public water supplies, and facilities for the disposal of sewage and other wastes. If unsanitary conditions are found, orders are issued for their correction, which orders, if they are reasonable and meet procedural requirements, are ultimately enforceable in the courts. Changes in local water and sewerage systems usually require the approval of state health authorities. Sanitary inspection is provided also for certain other community facilities such as swimming pools and tourist and trailer camps.

[23] Mustard, *Government in Public Health*, 146-151.

[24] *Ibid.*, 157-162.

[25] Cf. Joanne Bolger, "Public Health in the 48 States," *State Govt.*, XIII, 243-245, 254-255 (Dec., 1940).

[26] Cf. Mustard, *Government in Public Health*, 179-180.

[27] Bolger, *op. cit.*

Protection of the community's food supply is an important function of the local health department. Hotels, restaurants, and food markets are inspected by sanitation officers, and unsanitary conditions in such an establishment, if not corrected, may be grounds for revocation of its license to operate. Many cities now require that food handlers submit to medical examination and present health certificates as a condition of employment in such work. Surveys have revealed, in the absence of protective measures, a surprising prevalence among food handlers and domestic servants of diseases such as tuberculosis, syphilis, and gonorrhea. For maximum effectiveness, regulations of the kind under consideration should provide for examinations by the local health department rather than by private physicians, for periodic reexamination, and for revoking the work permit of any food handler found to be infected with, or a potential carrier of, a communicable disease. A special aspect of food control is that of protecting the meat supply. Meat and meat products shipped in interstate commerce are subject to federal inspection, but a substantial quantity of meat is slaughtered locally and never enters interstate trade. To safeguard this source of supply, many cities provide for the licensing and inspection of local slaughterhouses and of animals at the time of slaughter. As an alternative means of protection, some cities have established municipal abattoirs and required that all local slaughtering be done there.[28]

Perhaps the most important of all food protection activities are those concerned with the milk supply. Because milk constitutes a basic food of almost universal use, and because it is so easily contaminated, its protection becomes one of the foremost responsibilities of public health agencies. State laws prohibit the adulteration of milk and milk products, and the sale of substandard products. Eradication of tuberculosis and brucellosis (Bang's disease) from dairy herds is sought through quarantine measures, testing requirements, and provisions for the destruction of infected animals. Beginning in the 1930's, about a third of the states have established milk control boards empowered to regulate prices at which milk is sold.[29] Reasonable price regulation in this field, including the fixing of minimum retail prices, has been upheld on the ground that unrestricted competition and low prices may imperil the quantity and safety of the supply.[30] Local ordinances regulating the production and distribution of milk are concerned with sanitary conditions of dairy farms, barns,

[28] "Municipal Abattoirs in the United States," *Pub. Management*, XX, 46-48 (Feb., 1938).

[29] American Municipal Association, *Milk Control* (Pub. Admin. Service, Chicago, 1937), 3-8; Illinois Legislative Council, *State Regulation of the Sale of Milk* (Ill. Legis. Council, Springfield, 1941); Milton Weisner, comp., *A Summary of the Milk Contol Laws of the Several States* (Pa. Legis. Ref. Bur., Harrisburg, 1950); Earl Warner, *The State Milk Control Agencies in New England* (Agricultural Experiment Station, Univ. of Vt., Burlington, 1951).

[30] *Nebbia* v. *New York*, 291 U.S. 502 (1934).

and milk rooms, and with the cleanliness of cows and their handlers and of milk containers and distributing facilities. To enforce the standards prescribed, local health departments license producers and distributors, inspect farms and plants, and test milk samples for bacterial count.[31] Because of the difficulties and expense involved in protecting raw-milk supplies, especially in populous communities drawing their supplies from widespread areas, more and more cities are requiring pasteurization of all milk and milk products sold within their boundaries. The licensing and inspection of pasteurization plants is ordinarily a responsibility of the state health department.

Vital Statistics

The collecting and recording of vital statistics may be considered as the "bookkeeping" of public health. Just as the collection and analysis of basic economic data are indispensable elements in sound business management, so the recording and analysis of facts pertaining to human life and death are essential to good public health administration.[32] Government can effectively protect the health of its citizens only if it has knowledge of the location, extent, and severity of disease. Vital statistics, in providing this information, reveal sources of danger and aid in determining the effectiveness of control measures.[33]

Vital statistics of significance to public health programs are of three principal types: (1) birth statistics, (2) morbidity (sickness) statistics covering a large variety of "notifiable" diseases, and (3) mortality statistics relating to deaths and their causes. All three types of data are usually required to be reported by physicians, while births are reportable also by midwives, and deaths by coroners and undertakers. Of the various types, mortality statistics are most complete, since it is usually necessary that a death certificate be filed before a burial permit may be issued. Though the persons required by law to report births, sickness, and deaths are subject to penalty for failing to do so, such penalties are seldom imposed. As a result, there is in practice much laxity in reporting, though less now than in earlier times. The inadequacy of existing birth records in many states was forcefully impressed upon the public mind during World War II when birth certificates were widely required of persons seeking employment in government service or defense industries. In many instances it was found, especially with respect to persons in the more advanced age groups, that births had never been recorded or that original records had been lost. To meet this situation, a number of states which

[31] American Municipal Association, *op. cit.*, 10-26.
[32] McCombs, *op. cit.*, 75.
[33] Cf. Schuyler C. Wallace, *State Administrative Supervision over Cities in the United States* (Columbia Univ. Press, New York, 1928), 136.

had not previously done so enacted laws providing for "delayed birth registration." Under such laws, a person for whom no birth record can be found is permitted to establish the date and place of his birth by documentary evidence and affidavits of persons having knowledge of the facts concerned. This having been done, a "certificate of delayed birth registration" is issued and recorded, which thereafter has the same standing in law as an original birth record.

State laws concerning vital statistics commonly provide that physicians and other persons required to do so shall file their reports with local "registrars," who enter the data on local records and then relay the reports to the state health department. Local registrars are frequently county, township, or city clerks serving ex officio as vital statistics officers. In the reporting and recording of vital statistics, widespread use is now made of standard forms recommended by the United States Public Health Service.

Other Public Health Activities

Certainly other major phases of public health work may be mentioned briefly. Every state conducts a program of maternal and child hygiene, and most local health departments provide services in this field. Most states and many cities have industrial hygiene programs designed to foster healthful working conditions in industry and the provision of proper medical care for persons suffering from occupational disease. Both industrial hygiene and maternal and child hygiene are financed in part by federal aid. A standard function of state health departments, ancillary to disease control and sanitation, is the provision of diagnostic laboratory service. State, and sometimes regional, laboratories make examination of all sorts of materials arising from cases and situations having public health significance, such as milk and water samples and specimens and cultures relating to communicable diseases. Examinations are made both for local health departments and for private physicians and hospitals. Many of the larger local departments, however, have their own laboratory facilities.[34] Many states now operate mental-hygiene clinics for the diagnosis and treatment of certain types of psychiatric disorders,[35] and some local health departments have added psychiatrists to their staffs. Alcoholism is now generally considered to be an illness, and during the past two decades a majority of the states have inaugurated programs for the treatment and rehabilitation of alcoholics. Some of these programs are administered by special commissions, but the trend is toward administration through alcoholism units within a state department of health or mental health.[36]

[34] Mustard, *Government in Public Health*, 162-164.

[35] Stern, *op. cit.*, 57. See above, Chap. XVIII, "Mental Health."

[36] John R. Philp, "Government Programs on Alcoholism: Their Scope in North America," *State Govt.*, XXXV, 49-52 (Winter, 1962).

A regular function of both state and local health departments, and one constantly growing in importance, is that of health education. Through newspaper publicity, pamphlets, lectures, films, the radio and television—indeed, through all possible channels of communication—efforts are made to make health knowledge available to the general public in simple and understandable form.[37] One of the most widespread of all health activities is public health nursing. This service is important both in itself and for its contribution to various other health programs, such as that of maternal and child hygiene. Visiting nurses are employed locally by both public and private agencies. Those serving local health departments devote much of their time to health education, particularly among low-income families, but also render maternity service and, to some extent, bedside care for the sick. School nursing in some communities is a function of the health department and in others is provided by nurses employed by the school district.[38] State health departments seek by various means, such as consultant and supervisory services and training programs for local nurses, to assist local communities in maintaining adequate nursing programs.

Government Hospitals

State and local governments are assuming an ever-larger responsibility for providing public hospitals. In 1962, of 7,028 hospitals registered with the American Hospital Association, 4,613 were operated by nongovernmental agencies, 447 by the federal government, and 1,968 by state and local governments. Of the latter, 558 were operated by the states, 794 by counties, 354 by cities, 76 on a city-county basis, and 186 by hospital districts. In addition to general hospitals, these state and local institutions included 320 psychiatric or mental hospitals, 178 tuberculosis hospitals, and some institutions of other specialized types. State and local institutions, while comprising only slightly more than one-fourth of all hospitals, provided well over half of the nation's 1.7 million hospitals beds.[39] Hospital institutions of all types are maintained by governments at both state and local levels, but it is most common for general and tuberculosis hospitals to be administered by local units and mental institutions by the states. General hospitals supported by the states, and some of those operated by larger cities, are designed primarily for indigents, whereas mental and other specialized hospitals, as well as local general hospitals in less populous communities, usually admit both indigent patients and those who pay for their care. In communities having no government hospitals,

[37] Cf. Mustard, *Government in Public Health*, 131.
[38] Committee on the Costs of Medical Care, *op. cit.*, 86-87.
[39] *Hospitals* (*Jour. of Amer. Hosp. Assn.*, Vol. XXXVII, No. 15, Part 2, Guide Issue, Aug. 1, 1963), 450-455.

indigents are ordinarily cared for in private hospitals at public expense.[40]

Notwithstanding the fact that each year sees considerable new construction, population growth has retarded the overcoming of a long-standing deficit in accommodations, and America's hospitals remain far from adequate. Although many cities have inadequate facilities, it is in rural areas that inadequacies are most acute, a third or more of the nation's rural counties having no registered hospitals whatsoever. To provide properly for these rural areas alone would require the construction of several hundred new institutions. As a means of stimulating needed construction, Congress in 1946 passed the Hospital Survey and Construction (Hill-Burton) Act affording federal financial assistance to the states and localities. This law provided $3 million to aid the states in surveying their hospital needs, and authorized grants-in-aid of $75 million a year for five years to help build or improve state, county, city, and private nonprofit hospitals and health centers. Each dollar of federal funds was to be matched by two dollars of state or local money for both survey and building costs. In recognition of the fact that some states are better able than others to provide their own facilities, the law specified that federal funds should be apportioned on the dual basis of population and per capita annual income, thus making the poorer states eligible for more federal money per person than the wealthier. Amendments to the act have subsequently extended its duration from time to time, liberalized the construction grants, and provided that the federal share of construction costs, instead of continuing at the uniform one-third fixed in the original measure, shall vary from one-third to two-thirds depending upon the per capita income of the recipient state. By 1962, federal funds amounting to $1.8 billion dollars had been channeled into the Hill-Burton program. A total of 6,236 projects had been approved under the program, of which 4,728 were completed and in operation.[41]

Health Insurance

From what has been said in the preceding pages, it will be evident that a large portion of the nation's population is today without adequate medical care. In some communities, rich and poor alike are in that situation because of inadequacy of medical personnel and facilities, but to a much larger degree lack of appropriate care is a result of the inability of persons of low income to meet its costs. Amplification of traditional public health services would be an important step in the direction of improvement. It seems apparent, however, that nothing short of a program of pre-

[40] Stern, *op. cit.*, Chap. 6.
[41] United States Public Health Service, *The Hospital Act and Your Community* (U.S. Govt. Printing Office, Washington, 1947); United States Department of Health, Education, and Welfare, *Annual Report: 1962*, p. 192.

paid or tax-supported medical care, sometimes referred to as "health insurance," can make adequate care available to low-income groups. Such a program might be administered by private organizations and financed through voluntary payments from the persons covered, or administered by government and financed either by such voluntary payments or by taxation. College students, whether attending public or private institutions, will in many instances be familiar with the principle of prepaid care in the form of "hospital insurance" financed from a required student fee. Apart from operating plans of this nature in public educational institutions, government in the United States has as yet done little in this direction, though a few other programs of limited extent have been undertaken in cooperation with state or local medical associations.[42] Of far more potential significance than these programs in indicating current interests and trends is the far-reaching "medicare" proposal now under consideration by Congress as a possible addition to the social security program. Although the federal-state program of aid to the medically-indigent aged is essentially one of public assistance rather than of insurance, it also is deserving of mention in this connection.[43]

Privately-administered plans of prepaid medical care are now both numerous and extensive. In 1962 it was reported that no less than 135 million Americans—seven persons out of every ten in the country's entire population—were covered by private hospital insurance. Ninety percent of these had surgical insurance also, and 70 percent had coverage for other physicians' services as well. The largest and best known of these voluntary insurance plans are the Blue Cross for providing prepaid hospital care and the Blue Shield for prepayment of doctors' bills, these plans alone covering some 60 million people. Extensive coverage is also provided through commercial insurance companies, frequently through group-insurance or family-insurance policies. It has been estimated that private health insurance in 1960 paid approximately 60 percent of the public's hospital bills and 30 percent of its doctor bills.[44]

Those who prefer private to public medicine should derive considerable satisfaction from the phenomenal growth of the private programs and the increasing cooperation of the medical profession in their operation. To the extent that such voluntary programs are successful in solving the nation's problem of medical care, the establishment of governmental programs should be unnecessary. In whatever measure voluntary programs prove inadequate, it seems certain that government will ultimately step in to bridge the gap. Through either private or public pro-

[42] Cf. Joseph W. Mountin, "Participation by State and Local Health Departments in Current Medical Care Programs," *loc. cit.;* Stern, *op. cit.,* 154-158.

[43] See above, Chap. XVIII, "Medical Assistance for the Aged."

[44] "What Private Health Insurance Now Offers," *U.S. News and World Report,* Vol. LIII, No. 14 (Oct. 1, 1962), 89-92.

grams, means must be found of providing needed medical care for the large group of low-income but self-supporting citizens who at present, in many instances, receive care inferior to that provided at government expense for indigent persons who are public charges.

HOUSING

The Housing Shortage

Closely related to health is the problem of housing. Under ideal conditions, adequate and decent living quarters should be available to every family and individual at a reasonable purchase price or rental. Present-day housing in America falls considerably short of this standard.

The housing shortage is both qualitative and quantitative. A substantial portion of existing housing is of substandard quality because it is in need of major repairs or lacking in basic sanitary facilities; but, even if all existing housing were repaired and modernized, the quantity still would fall short of that required to house the country's population without overcrowding. The first comprehensive housing survey in the United States was made in connection with the 1940 population census. Of the 27 million nonfarm dwelling units reported in this survey, nearly 4 million needed major repairs and over 6.5 million more lacked running water or private indoor sanitary and bathing facilities. This made a total qualitative shortage in nonfarm areas of 10.5 million dwelling units, or approximately 40 percent of the total number. On the farms, housing conditions were even worse. Of the 7.6 million farm dwellings reported, nearly 2.5 million were in need of major repairs and over 3.7 million more lacked any sort of indoor water supply. This qualitative shortage of 6.2 million represented more than 80 percent of all farm dwellings.[45] The two decades following 1940 witnessed substantial improvement in American housing, and improvement is still continuing. Since the end of World War II, rising incomes and governmental assistance have brought about extensive construction of new units and the repair and modernization of many existing units. Yet, of the 58 million units reported in the 1960 Census of Housing, 27 million or 47 percent, were more than 30 years old. Of the total of units reported, nearly 3 million were classified as dilapidated, an additional 8 million were deteriorating, and still another 4 million, though of sound construction, lacked plumbing facilities. Rural housing continued to be of poorer quality than urban, approximately one-third of all rural units (farm and nonfarm) being dilapidated or lacking plumbing facilities.[46]

[45] *Postwar Housing* (Report by the Subcommittee on Housing and Urban Redevelopment to the Senate Special Committee on Postwar Economic Policy and Planning, 79th Cong., 1st Sess., Aug. 1, 1945.)

[46] United States Bureau of the Census, *U.S. Census of Housing: 1960,* Vol. I: *States and Small Areas, United States Summary,* xxxiv, xlii.

On the quantitative side, it was concluded by a congressional committee in 1945 that, to provide for the expected increase in the number of families during the next decade and to eliminate overcrowding, as many as 6 million new dwellings would probably be required.[47] Overcrowding may result from the use of dwellings too small for the size of the families occupying them, or from the "doubling up" of families, and its extent depends in large measure upon economic conditions. Widespread during the depression years of the 1930's, overcrowding has declined more recently with greater employment opportunities and higher income levels. It remains, however, a serious housing problem, particularly for families of minority groups.[48]

Government and Housing

Government is interested in housing for several reasons. Housing conditions constitute an important factor in the general well-being of a people which it is a duty of government to foster. Good housing makes for a healthy and happy population equipped to participate in the economic and civic life of the community. But government interest in housing may flow from strictly business considerations as well as from altruistic motives. Poor housing generates crime, delinquency, disease, and fire hazard, each of which in turn requires public expenditures for its suppression. Slum districts consistently require relatively higher expenditures than do other areas for police and fire protection, courts, penal institutions, and public health work. From a financial standpoint alone and without reference to social benefits, wise increases in expenditures for governmental housing activities may make possible substantial reductions in public budgetary items for these other services. Thus governmental promotion of good housing may be justified on economic as well as on philanthropic grounds.[49]

The housing problem may be attacked by government in one or more of three principal ways: (1) by the regulation of private housing; (2) by the promotion and encouragement of private housing; and (3) by the actual construction, at public expense, of housing facilities for sale or rent to private families and individuals. Regulatory programs are concerned for the most part with structural safety and rental charges. Structural regulations usually take the form of local building codes, while rent regulation has been undertaken at various times by government at all levels—national, state, and local. Governmental measures for the promotion of private housing have taken several different forms, but have been

[47] *Postwar Housing*, cited above.
[48] Glenn H. Beyer, *Housing: A Factual Analysis*, 75-76.
[49] Cf. Donald Robinson, "Slum Clearance Pays Off," *Nat. Mun. Rev.*, XLIV, 461-465 (Oct., 1955).

designed for the most part to make credit available to private individuals for housing purposes on a long-term basis and at low interest rates. Some programs have provided public credit for housing, while others have sought to encourage private financial institutions to make housing loans on liberal terms. The most comprehensive programs of this character have been undertaken by the national government. Thus the Federal Home Loan Banks provide a credit reserve for savings and loan associations which make loans to individuals for home-financing purposes; and the Home Owners' Loan Corporation in the 1930's made loans directly to individuals for refinancing defaulted home mortgages. The most important program for encouraging private capital to enter the housing field has been that of the Federal Housing Administration. This agency provides government insurance for long-term housing loans made by banks, insurance companies, building and loan associations, and other private financial institutions. Though the states have not done a great deal in the direction of providing credit for private housing, a few have made provision for state loans to veterans for housing purposes. Moreover, several states, as we shall see, have sought to stimulate private housing by granting limited tax exemptions for newly-constructed dwellings or by chartering urban redevelopment corporations designed to build housing projects with private capital. Apart from the war-housing activities of the national government during World War II, the most extensive program of public housing yet undertaken in this country is that carried on by public housing authorities established under state law and assisted by federal loans and subsidies under the United States Housing Act of 1937.[50]

From what has been said, it will be evident that American government at all levels has shown an interest in the housing problem and taken some measures in an effort to alleviate the housing shortage. Though the national and local governments have been most active, state activities have also been significant, especially since it is the state governments which must provide the local units with legal organization and powers in the housing field. Many housing activities involve cooperation on the part of governments on two levels or all three.[51]

Consideration will now be given in further detail to the principal housing activities of the state and local governments. In their efforts to deal with the housing problem, three main powers are available to those governments: (1) the regulatory police power, (2) the taxing power, and

[50] Various phases of the national government's housing activities are described in the annual reports of the Housing and Home Finance Agency.

[51] Notwithstanding the relatively minor role of state government in housing, the 1961-1962 issue of the *Housing and Urban Renewal Directory* published by the National Association of Housing and Redevelopment Officials lists 22 states as having one or more official agencies concerned with housing. Issues of this publication regularly carry a current listing of both official and unofficial housing agencies at all levels of government.

(3) the power of eminent domain. The police power serves as the legal basis of local building codes and zoning regulations, and of rent-regulation measures. The taxing power is employed to raise funds to finance government housing activities of all kinds and sometimes, in a negative manner through tax-exemptions, to encourage residential building. Eminent domain—the power of government to take private property for public use upon payment of just compensation—is used both for the condemnation and demolition of slum dwellings and for obtaining sites for new construction.

Building Codes and Zoning Regulations

All large cities, and many smaller ones as well, have enacted ordinances establishing minimum standards with respect to the structural stability, safety, and healthfulness of residential and other buildings; and county boards are authorized in some states to adopt similar regulations for areas outside of municipalities. These ordinances, commonly known as building codes, deal with such matters as materials of construction; fire escapes; standards of lighting, ventilation, and sanitation; and the safety of electrical and plumbing installations. Building codes must be revised from time to time to take into account new developments in materials and construction techniques, or else some of their provisions, instead of promoting good housing, may actually become a bar to housing progress. Unfortunately, pressures from vested interests sometimes make it difficult to secure desirable changes. An example of this is the vigorous opposition offered by carpenters and other labor groups in many communities to the legalization of prefabricated construction. In times of acute housing shortage, moreover, it is sometimes necessary to relax temporarily some of the building standards desirable in normal times. One of the most difficult problems in connection with building codes is that of prescribing regulations which will provide adequately for structural safety, fire prevention, and health protection, and still not unduly enhance building costs. If the standards prescribed are higher than is necessary to insure reasonable protection of the types sought, the higher rentals resulting from increased construction costs tend to defeat one of the fundamental purposes of public regulation in the housing field.

Closely related to building-code regulations are the provisions of local zoning ordinances. Height limitations imposed by zoning ordinances are designed not only to promote the structural safety of buildings, but also to insure adequate light and air for their occupants; regulations limiting the percentage of lot area that may be occupied by buildings have a similar purpose; and use regulations seek, among other things, to bar manufacturing and commercial enterprises, many of which are noisy or otherwise offensive, from residential districts.

Building codes and zoning regulations are enforced by a system of licensing and inspection. Before new construction or extensive alterations or repairs may be undertaken, a permit must usually be secured from a designated city or county official, and periodic inspection of the work is made during its progress to make certain that all legal requirements are met. Permits for projects that do not conform to building-code or zoning standards are issued only under exceptional circumstances and for good reasons. The requirements of building codes and zoning ordinances usually apply only to buildings constructed or subjected to substantial repair or alteration after their enactment. Unless they become actual nuisances, nonconforming buildings previously constructed are permitted to remain until they are replaced or until major alterations or repairs become necessary.[52]

Rent Control

For those who rent their living quarters, the mere existence of adequate housing facilities means little if the rental charges are beyond their means. In normal times, the law of supply and demand tends to keep rents within reasonable bounds. But when there is a serious housing shortage, some unscrupulous landlords are certain to extort unreasonable rents unless government intervenes to prevent such overcharging. To provide the necessary protection for tenants, the national government and various states and local units have in emergency situations imposed limitations on rental charges. Though these regulations have on various occasions been attacked in the courts, they have generally been sustained when found to be reasonable in character.[53]

Two principal types of rent control have been employed: (1) judicial control and (2) administrative control. The judicial form is best illustrated by a series of statutes enacted by the New York legislature in 1920. Applying to New York City and certain neighboring municipalities, this legislation, which remained in effect for almost a decade, declared that a public emergency existed in the field of housing; that unjust, unreasonable, and oppressive rents were being exacted from tenants under the stress of prevailing conditions; and that congested housing conditions re-

[52] A good discussion of building codes will be found in William B. Munro, *Municipal Administration* (Macmillan, New York, 1934), Chap. 28. See also George N. Thompson, "The Problem of Building Code Improvement," *Law and Contemp. Probs.*, XII, 95-110 (Winter, 1947). On the subject of zoning, see Edward M. Bassett, *Zoning* (Russell Sage Found., New York, 1936, reprinted with additions 1940); Symposium, "Zoning in Illinois," *Univ. of Ill. Law Forum*, Vol. 1954, pp. 167-306 (Summer, 1954).

[53] For general discussions, see Edith Berger Drellich and Andree Emery, *Rent Control in War and Peace* (Nat. Mun. League, New York, 1939); Margaret Rohrer and Douglas M. Frame, *Rent Control* (Bur. of Pub. Admin., Univ., of Calif., Berkeley, 1947); "Emergency Rent Control," *Ill. Law Rev.*, XXXVI, 648-661 (Feb., 1942).

sulting from such rents were endangering the public welfare, health, and morals. It was provided that, in an action by an owner to recover rent for property occupied as a dwelling, a valid defense would be that the rent was unjust and unreasonable and that the agreement under which it was demanded was oppressive. Thus, if a tenant felt that the rent demanded of him was unreasonable, he could refuse to pay it and the owner would then have to bring suit for collecting it. The owner would be required to show his income from the property and his expenses thereon, and on the basis of the evidence submitted the court would pass upon the reasonableness of the rent demanded. If the tenant was ready and willing to pay the amount of rental determined by the court to be reasonable, he could be evicted only if he was alleged by the owner and found by the court to be objectionable, or if the owner desired to occupy the building himself for dwelling purposes, to demolish the building and construct a new one, or to sell the building to a cooperative housing company.[54] Legislation of the same general nature as that of New York was also in effect in Massachusetts during the greater part of the 1920's, and several other states at about this time enacted laws designed, during the housing emergency which followed the First World War, to impose judicial restrictions upon rent increases and evictions.[55]

Rent control by administrative agencies was provided in emergency laws enacted by Congress for the District of Columbia following the First World War and during the Second. The first of these statutes was the Ball Rent Law, which was in effect from 1919 to 1924. Under this law, a three-member commission was empowered to fix fair and reasonable rental rates upon petition of either landlord or tenant, and to prescribe service standards to be maintained by the owner. Tenants whose leases expired were permitted to continue in possession, subject to regulation by the commission, unless the owner desired the premises for his own occupancy. In fixing the charges to be allowed, the commission first determined the value of the property concerned and then, after making allowances for operating costs and depreciation, fixed a rental rate which would provide a return of from 6 to 10 percent on the valuation.[56] In December, 1941, the District of Columbia Emergency Rent Act was passed. Instead of a rent commission as a regulatory agency, this law provided for a single administrator of rent control. Whereas the Ball law had provided for fixing rents on the basis of property valuation, the new measure adopted the rents prevailing on January 1, 1941, as maximum rents, and established minimum service standards for housing accommodations. The administrator was empowered to make adjustments in maximum rents or minimum serv-

---

[54] *Laws of N.Y.*, 1920, Chaps. 942, 944, 951.

[55] Drellich and Emery, *op. cit.*, 38-41.

[56] *Ibid.*, 23-25; Rohrer and Frame, *op. cit.*, 3-4; Clara Sears Taylor, "Do We Need Rent Control Laws Permanently?" *Nat. Mun. Rev.*, XIII, 283-288 (May, 1924).

ice standards or both, whenever in his judgment such charges were justified because of increases or decreases in taxes or other operating expenses.
Either landlords or tenants might petition for adjustments of rents or services. Orders of the administrator, like those of the earlier rent commission,
were made subject to review by the courts. Another example of administrative control is afforded by Denver's municipal rent commission, established by ordinance in 1921 and operated successfully for many months. A
Wisconsin statute of 1920 conferring rent regulatory powers upon the state
railroad commission was declared by the state supreme court to be discriminatory, and therefore unconstitutional, since it applied only to Milwaukee county.[57]

An extensive rent-control program was inaugurated by the national
government, under its defense and war powers, in the Emergency Price
Control Act of 1942. This law provided for the administrative control of
rents in areas including defense industries and military establishments. At
the height of the program, federal rent control was in operation in several
hundred defense-rental areas which together contained well over half of
the nation's population.[58] Subsequent legislation included "local option"
provisions under which state and local governments were empowered to
vote their areas in or out of the federal control program.[59]

Tax Exemption and Graded Taxation

State and local governments have sought, in a few instances, to encourage housing construction by means of tax concessions. In 1920, for
example, the New York legislature authorized counties, cities, towns, and
villages to exempt newly-constructed dwellings from local taxes for a period of ten years. Though New York City was the only local government
to make use of this authority, the exemptions in that city appear to have
stimulated residential building. A few other states, including Vermont and
Wisconsin, have experimented with limited tax exemption of new dwellings.[60]

Another variety of tax concession involves the separate assessment
of land and buildings and the taxation of buildings at a lower rate than
that applied to land. In this manner it is sought to encourage owners of

[57] Rohrer and Frame, op. cit., 4, 26-28; Drellich and Emery, op. cit., 26.

[58] Rohrer and Frame, op. cit., 5-10; "Emergency Rent Control," Ill. Law Rev.,
loc. cit. For further discussion of the federal program, see James C. Downs, Jr., "Rent
Control," Jour. of Land and Pub. Util. Econ., XVII, 406-409 (Nov., 1941); Karl Borders, "Emergency Rent Control," Law and Contemp. Probs., IX, 107-121 (Winter,
1942); James Simsarian, "Rent Control in 1943," Nat. Mun. Rev., XXXII, 17-20, 25
(Jan., 1943); Dorothy Rosenman, "Rent Control Stands Test," Ibid., 128-132 (Mar.,
1943).

[59] Cf. Tighe E. Woods, "Rent Control—The Role of the States," State Govt.,
XXIV, 251, 257 (Oct., 1951).

[60] Mabel L. Walker, Urban Blight and Slums, 279-280.

building lots to build on them or to sell them to persons who will build. The outstanding example of such differential treatment of land and buildings is Pittsburgh's "graded-tax" plan inaugurated in 1914. Over a ten-year period, the city tax rate in Pittsburgh was gradually reduced on buildings and increased on land, and since 1924 the rate on buildings has been one-half that on land.[61] There seems to be little doubt that the Pittsburgh plan has actually stimulated residential and other construction. Building assessments in the city have increased much more rapidly than land assessments. Thus, between 1914 and 1938, while land-value assessments increased only about 15 percent, building-value assessments increased more than 93 percent.[62] It has been suggested also that the plan has played an important role in promoting the city's extensive redevelopment program which was initiated in the 1950's and is still in progress. Overall, a recent appraisal concludes, "it appears clear from the evidence that Pittsburgh's unique tax scheme has indeed made a significant contribution toward producing a better and more prosperous city."[63] In many states, of course, existing constitutional provisions requiring uniformity in taxation would have to be amended before either tax exemption or graded taxation could be employed as a means of encouraging building operations.

Urban Redevelopment Corporations

Yet another instrumentality for the promotion of housing construction is the urban redevelopment corporation. This is a privately owned corporation organized under state law for the purpose of undertaking slum-clearance and housing projects, and is intended as a means of attracting private capital, especially that of insurance companies and other financial institutions, into the housing field. Laws authorizing the establishment of such corporations were enacted in 1941 in New York, Illinois, and Michigan, and within a few years several other states had enacted similar legislation.

The different state laws vary somewhat in their provisions, but all confer certain special privileges upon redevelopment corporations as an inducement to the investment of capital in housing enterprise. The privileges most commonly conferred are partial tax exemption for a limited number of years and use of the power of eminent domain. The latter power is essential as a means of preventing minority property owners from blocking desirable redevelopment projects. In several states it is therefore provided that, when a redevelopment corporation has obtained

[61] *Ibid.*, 266-267; Walter Fairchild, "How the Graded Tax Plan Works in Pittsburgh," *Amer. City*, Vol. LIII, No. 11 (Nov., 1938), 75-76.

[62] Fairchild, *op. cit.*

[63] Percy R. Williams, "The Graded Tax in the Redevelopment of Pittsburgh," *Amer. Jour. of Econ. and Sociol.*, XXII, 251-261, at 261 (Apr., 1963).

title to, or options on, a specified majority percentage of the property constituting the site of a proposed project, it may then secure the remainder through eminent domain proceedings. Some laws, instead of conferring the power of eminent domain directly upon redevelopment corporations, provide that the city may, at the request of such a corporation, exercise the power on its behalf. In an effort to assure that housing projects undertaken by redevelopment corporations are such as to promote the public interest, the sites and plans of proposed projects require the approval of designated state or local authorities. Most of the laws also limit the dividends that redevelopment corporations may pay to their stockholders, at least during the period of tax exemption.[64]

Public Housing

Notwithstanding these various measures for the public regulation and encouragement of private housing, the housing shortage over the country continues to be serious. In a further effort to alleviate the situation, there has been some direct construction of housing facilities by the national and local governments. As yet, however, public housing in the United States has been quite limited. Such projects as have been undertaken have consisted in part of emergency wartime housing for defense workers and military personnel, and in part of low-rent housing for families of meager income.

During the war years of 1917-18 the national government, through the United States Housing Corporation and the United States Shipping Board, built some sixty-six projects for housing workers in war industry;[65] and during the Second World War public construction of war housing was much more extensive. In the latter period more than 850,000 dwelling units, a large proportion of which were of a temporary character, were built by the Federal Public Housing Authority and other federal agencies in more than 700 war-production areas. After the end of the war, much surplus war housing of a movable nature was made available by the national government to municipalities for housing returning veterans and to educational institutions for the use of student veterans and their families.[66] This post-war program of public housing for veterans was a co-

[64] Della Richman, "State Urban Redevelopment Legislation," *The Municipal Year Book* (Int. City Mgrs'. Assn., Chicago), 1946, pp. 311-315; Thomas C. Desmond, "Blighted Areas Get a New Chance," *Nat. Mun. Rev.*, XXX, 629-632, 640 (Nov., 1941); Paul Windels, "Private Enterprise Plan in Housing Faces First Test," *Ibid.*, XXXII, 284-288 (June, 1943); Ruth G. Weintraub and Rosalind Tough, "Redevelopment Without Plan," *Ibid.*, XXXVII, 364-370 (July, 1948); Arthur C. Holden, "Urban Redevelopment Corporations," *Jour. of Land and Pub. Util. Econ.*, XVIII, 412-422 (Nov., 1942); Seward H. Mott, "Urban Redevelopment Legislation Analyzed," *Amer. City*, Vol. LX, No. 8 (Aug., 1945), 83-84.

[65] Margaret H. Schoenfeld, "Progress of Public Housing in the United States," *Monthly Labor Rev.*, LI, 267-282 (Aug., 1940).

[66] Federal Public Housing Authority, *Public Housing: The Work of the Federal Public Housing Authority* (U.S. Govt. Printing Office, Washington, 1946), 1-22.

operative national-state-local affair. The national government supplied the housing facilities concerned, and in most cases also defrayed the cost of moving the structures. On the other hand, the city or college provided necessary land and utilities at the new site and was given title to the housing in its new location. Any rental income collected from the facilities in excess of operating costs and reserves for disposition was to be turned over to the national government, and it was required that the structures be disposed of within two years after the end of the housing emergency. The states also had a share in the financing of these projects. Many of the sponsoring college and universities were state institutions, and several states made grants of funds to sponsoring cities for the payment of all or some part of the local costs.[67]

Prior to 1937, the most extensive peacetime program of government housing construction consisted of fifty projects, located in some forty cities and including approximately 22,000 dwelling units, which were built during the 1930's by the Housing Division of the Public Works Administration. These projects were undertaken primarily to provide employment, but when completed they afforded good housing for low-income families. Though built directly by the national agency and entirely at federal expense, most of these projects were subsequently leased to local housing authorities for operation.[68]

The most significant public-housing program of a peacetime nature yet undertaken in this country had its inception in the United States Housing Act of 1937. This law made no provision whatever for further federal construction, but offered generous financial assistance for slum-clearance and low-rent housing projects built and operated by local public housing authorities organized under state law.[69] To qualify for federal aid, local projects must meet prescribed standards with respect to such matters as maximum construction cost per room and per dwelling unit, acceptance of only low-income tenants, and local financial participation. It is also generally required that for each new dwelling unit constructed a slum unit be eliminated, though in times of acute housing shortage deferment of such elimination may be authorized by the federal administering agency. To administer the program at the federal level, the 1937 law established the United States Housing Authority. This agency subsequently was merged with the Federal Public Housing Authority, which in turn was superseded, in 1947, by the Public Housing Administration—a major unit in the newly-established Housing and Home Finance Agency.

Federal financial assistance to local housing authorities under the United States Housing Act takes two forms—the construction loan and

[67] Dorothy Gazzolo, "Housing Developments in 1946," *The Municipal Year Book,* 1947, pp. 278-287.

[68] Federal Public Housing Authority, *op. cit.,* 45.

[69] Under the federal statute either state or local housing authorities may be granted assistance, but the local type of authority has in practice been used almost exclusively.

the annual contribution. A long-term construction loan at a low rate of interest may be granted in an amount up to 90 percent of the cost of an approved project. The remaining 10 percent of the cost must be obtained from nonfederal sources and may be provided either by the government of the city or county within which the local authority operates, or by private investors through purchase of the authority's bonds. When provided by local government, it may be in the form of cash, land, or services. After a project has been built, the national government will subsidize its operation by means of annual contributions designed to assure low rental charges. This federal subsidy, when combined with annual contributions required of local governments, is intended to be in the amount necessary to keep rentals within the reach of tenants who need the facilities. Local contributions may be in the form of either cash or tax exemption, the latter being the form more commonly used.

Local Housing Authorities

With the passage of the United States Housing Act, state legislatures hastened to enact enabling legislation to permit the organization of local housing authorities which could qualify for financial assistance under the federal program. Most of the states enacted laws under which public housing authorities might be organized by cities or counties, or by both, some also permitting the establishment of regional authorities serving two or more counties. These local housing authorities are governmental corporations empowered to build and operate low-rent housing projects and to enter into contracts with the national government and with local governments for financial assistance. They usually are vested with borrowing power and the power of eminent domain. However, they ordinarily have no taxing power, but rely for funds upon borrowings, income from rentals, and government subsidies. The governing body of the housing authority is a board of directors, the composition of which varies from state to state. A fairly typical provision is for a board of five members, appointed by the mayor in the case of a city authority and by the county board in the case of a county authority. The board of directors usually appoints an executive director to supervise the authority's staff and execute board policies. In some instances there is a state housing agency which exercises supervisory powers over the organization and operation of local housing authorities, sometimes also participating in the appointment of the local boards of directors.[70]

By the end of 1962, there were 1,371 local housing authorities in

[70] Cf. B. J. Hovde, "The Local Housing Authority," *Pub. Admin. Rev.*, I, 167-175 (Winter, 1941); Annette Baker Fox, "The Local Housing Authority and the Municipal Government," *Jour. of Land and Pub. Util. Econ.*, XVII, 280-290 (Aug., 1941).

existence, 140 of these having been established during the preceding twelve months. As of that date, public housing constructed under the 1937 federal legislation as amended was providing dwellings for more than 2 million persons. More than a half-million low-rent dwellings were located in 45 states, the District of Columbia, Puerto Rico, and the Virgin Islands.[71] Most of the housing projects built by local housing authorities under the federal program have been located in urban areas and have consisted of groups of multifamily apartment houses. A small program of farm housing inaugurated prior to World War II was subsequently liquidated through sale to individual farm owners of the houses built by local housing authorities.[72]

Urban Renewal

A new program had its inception in the Housing Acts of 1949 and 1954, which authorized federal loans and grants to local-government agencies for slum clearance and urban renewal.[73] Urban renewal projects, as the term is now generally used, involve cooperative efforts on the part of local governments, the federal government, and private enterprise to eliminate and prevent slums and blight in both residential and nonresidential areas. Slum property is acquired through purchase or eminent domain and cleared of existing buildings. The land may then be resold to private investors to be redeveloped for residential or commercial purposes or may be redeveloped by a governmental agency as a public housing project or for other public purposes such as schools and parks. Sale to private investors must ordinarily be made at a monetary loss, with the difference between cost and selling price being met from public funds. Sometimes a renewal project includes, in addition to slum clearance, measures designed to rehabilitate areas which, although deteriorating, still lend themselves to restoration, and to protect some of the better properties from decay through building codes and safety and health regulations. The federal contribution to renewal projects is in some instances two-thirds of the cost and in others three-fourths.[74]

As of 1961, forty-five states had enacted legislation empowering local governments to participate in the urban renewal program with the aid of federal funds; and a few of these provided for direct state participa-

[71] Housing and Home Finance Agency, *Sixteenth Annual Report: 1962*, pp. 203-206.

[72] Cf. Rupert B. Vance and Gordon W. Blackwell, *New Farm Homes for Old;* "A Rural Slum Clearance Program Comes to an End," *Jour. of Housing*, XII, 278-280, 292 (Aug.-Sept., 1955).

[73] The term "urban renewal" was introduced by the 1954 act. Cf. James E. Lash, "Renewal: Area Problem," *Nat. Civic Rev.*, LI, 200-205 (Apr., 1962).

[74] Cf. Glenn H. Beyer, *Housing: A Factual Analysis,* Chap. 9; Urban Renewal Administration, *The Urban Renewal Program: Fact Sheet* (Urban Renewal Admin., Washington, Aug., 1963).

tion, through loans or grants, in the financing of renewal activities. At the local level the projects are administered in some instances by local public housing authorities, in others by separate urban renewal agencies, and in still others by departments of the city government.[75] By the end of 1962, a total of 1,210 urban renewal projects in 636 cities had been given federal approval. These projects involved federal grants estimated in excess of $3 billion. Unlike public housing projects, which have been located principally in the larger cities, urban redevelopment projects have been undertaken by many municipalities of small or medium size. Indeed, of the 636 cities with approved projects, more than 66 percent had populations of less than 50,000 and about 20 percent had fewer than 10,000 inhabitants.[76]

REFERENCES

ABRAMS, Charles, *The Future of Housing* (Harper, New York, 1946).

BEYER, Glenn H., *Housing: A Factual Analysis* (Macmillan, New York, 1958).

———, and ROSE, J. Hugh, *Farm Housing* (Wiley, New York, 1957).

Committee on the Costs of Medical Care, *Medical Care for the American People* (Final Report of the Committee, Univ. of Chicago Press, Chicago, 1932).

DALAND, Robert T., *Government and Health: The Alabama Experience* (Bur. of Pub. Admin., Univ. of Ala., University, Ala., 1955).

DAVIS, Michael M., *Public Medical Services* (Univ. of Chicago Press, Chicago, 1937).

EMERSON, Haven, and LUGINBUHL, Martha, *Local Health Units for the Nation* (Commonwealth Fund, New York, 1945).

FREEMAN, Allen W., ed., *A Study of Rural Public Health Service* (Commonwealth Fund, New York, 1933).

GOLDMANN, Franz, *Public Medical Care: Principles and Problems* (Columbia Univ. Press, New York, 1945).

———, and LEAVELL, Hugh R., eds., "Medical Care for Americans," *Annals of Amer. Acad. of Polit. and Soc. Sci.*, CCLXXIII, Philadelphia, Jan., 1951.

Housing and Home Finance Agency, *Sixteenth Annual Report: 1962* (U.S. Govt. Printing Office, Washington, 1963).

McCOMBS, Carl E., *City Health Administration* (Macmillan, New York, 1927).

MOUNTIN, Joseph W., and FLOOK, Evelyn, *Guide to Health Organization in the United States: 1951* (U.S. Govt. Printing Office, Washington, 1953).

[75] National Association of Housing and Redevelopment Officials, *Housing and Urban Renewal Directory: 1961-1962*, pp. xiii, xiv; Advisory Commission on Intergovernmental Relations, *Performance of Urban Functions: Local and Areawide* (U.S. Govt. Printing Office, Washington, 1963), 241-251; Dorothy Gazzolo, "The States in Housing and Urban Renewal," *The Book of the States* (Council of State Govts., Chicago), 1962-63, pp. 456-459.

[76] Housing and Home Finance Agency, *op. cit.*, 280.

MOUNTIN, Joseph, and others, *Distribution of Health Services in the Structure of State Government: 1950* (U.S. Govt. Printing Office, Washington, 1954).

MUSTARD, Harry S., *Government in Public Health* (Commonwealth Fund, New York, 1945).

———, *Rural Health Practice* (Commonwealth Fund, New York, 1936).

———, and Stebbins, Ernest L., *An Introduction to Public Health* (Macmillan, New York, 4th ed., 1959).

National Association of Housing and Redevelopment Officials, *Housing and Urban Renewal Directory: 1961-1962* (The Association, Chicago, 1961).

National Health Assembly, *America's Health* (Harper, New York, 1949).

Public Administration Service, *A Housing Program for the United States* (Pub. Admin. Service, Chicago, 1935).

SCHAFFTER, Dorothy, *State Housing Agencies* (Columbia Univ. Press, New York, 1942).

SMILLIE, Wilson G., *Public Health Administration in the United States* (Macmillan, New York, 3rd ed., 1947).

STERN, Bernhard J., *Medical Services by Government, Local, State, and Federal* (Commonwealth Fund, New York, 1946).

STRAUS, Michael W., and WEGG, Talbot, *Housing Comes of Age* (Oxford Univ. Press, New York, 1938).

TOBEY, James A., *Public Health Law* (Commonwealth Fund, New York, 3rd ed., 1947).

United States Bureau of the Census, *U.S. Census of Housing: 1960*, Vol. I: *States and Small Areas, United States Summary* (U.S. Govt. Printing Office, Washington, 1963).

United States Department of Health, Education, and Welfare, *Annual Report: 1962* (U.S. Govt. Printing Office, Washington).

———, *Handbook on Programs of the U.S. Department of Health, Education, and Welfare* (U.S. Govt. Printing Office, Washington, annually).

———, *Health, Education, and Welfare Trends* (U.S. Govt. Printing Office, Washington, annually).

VANCE, Rupert B., and BLACKWELL, Gordon W., *New Farm Homes for Old: A Study of Rural Public Housing in the South* (Univ. of Ala. Press, University, Ala., 1946).

WALKER, Mabel L., *Urban Blight and Slums* (Harvard Univ. Press, Cambridge, 1938).

WOOD, Edith Elmer, *Introduction to Housing: Facts and Principles* (U.S. Housing Authority, Washington, 1940).

WOODBURY, Coleman, ed., *Urban Redevelopment: Problems and Practices* (Univ. of Chicago Press, Chicago, 1953).

20

Education

Education as a Governmental Function

Everywhere in the United States today the provision of free elementary and secondary schools is recognized as a proper function of government. In addition, providing for free or heavily subsidized higher education by government is well accepted. Widespread education is the bulwark of democracy, and it is therefore essential that educational opportunities be available to all of the country's inhabitants. For this reason, the provision of school facilities cannot be left to private individuals and institutions, but must be undertaken as a public service. Though many private and sectarian schools exist throughout the nation, more than 85 percent of the country's school children and some 60 percent of its college and university students now attend institutions maintained at public expense.

In delegating powers to the national government, the United States Constitution makes no mention of education, and consequently provision of public educational facilities is left, by virtue of the Tenth Amendment, primarily to the states. The national government, it is true, has displayed an active interest in education, and its role is expanding. Early in our history there were federal grants of land and money to the states for school purposes, and more recently the national government has undertaken many activities concerned directly or indirectly with the promotion of education. The United States Office of Education collects and publishes educational statistics and various types of information concerning schools and colleges, conducts research studies on educational problems, and provides an advisory and consultative service to state and local school officials.

Congress provides federal funds in aid of state agricultural colleges, vocational education in high schools, school lunches, and various other special educational programs.[1] Since World War II and the Korean conflict, the funds available to veterans for educational purposes under the GI Bill of Rights have encouraged millions of ex-service men and women to pursue academic training further than they would otherwise have done. Under the National Defense Education Act of 1958, the federal government provides student loans and graduate fellowships designed to improve the teaching of science, mathematics, and modern languages in the nation's schools and colleges. Nevertheless, the providing of education remains primarily a function of the respective states, to be performed by the state governments themselves or passed on to the local governmental units. In practice, as we shall see, most states have chosen to impose responsibility for the function at the elementary and secondary levels, in large measure, upon their local subdivisions.

Public Schools

Public education is the largest single enterprise engaged in by the state and local governments. During the school year 1962-63, more than 40 million pupils—well over a fifth of the total population of the nation—were enrolled in public elementary and secondary schools. School enrollment has responded to the general population growth and, because of the increasing emphasis that is being placed on school attendance, it has risen somewhat more rapidly than the school-age population. In 1962-63 the public schools of the country were manned by an instructional staff of 1.6 million —an impressive number notwithstanding a current teacher shortage which is expected to become more acute. At the same time, annual expenditures for public-school purposes were estimated at over $19 billion.[2] Education regularly constitutes the largest single item of local-government expenditure, and occupies a prominent place in state budgets as well. These various facts give some indication of the gigantic proportions of the task of providing public-school facilities in the United States.

The expansion of public educational services over the years has involved not only the providing of facilities for progressively larger numbers of pupils, but also the offering, especially in the larger schools, of enlarged

[1] There is a growing demand for federal financial aid to elementary and secondary schools generally and, as noted in an earlier connection (Chap. II, "Federal Grants-in-Aid"), Congress is currently giving serious consideration to the inauguration of such a program. For discussion of the issue see Sidney C. Sufrin, *Issues in Federal Aid to Education* (Syracuse Univ. Press, Syracuse, N.Y., 1962). A review of existing federal education programs is to be found in Committee on Education and Labor, House of Representatives, Eighty-Eighth Congress, *The Federal Government and Education*.

[2] J. Alan Thomas, "State Public School Systems," *The Book of the States* (Council of State Govts., Chicago), 1964-65, pp. 323-329, and appended tables.

and enriched curricula. A century and a half ago, educational opportunity in America was confined to a mechanistic and rudimentary study of reading, writing, arithmetic, English grammar, and spelling. Today the elementary schools afford training in a broad range of subjects including, among others, health, safety, science, music, art, and homemaking. High school curricula have been expanded until some schools now offer courses in almost every cultural, civic, and vocational field. To administer this enriched program modern school systems employ, in addition to teachers and supervisors, librarians, nurses, doctors, dentists, janitors, business managers, cafeteria managers, and dietitians. Public colleges and universities offer training in almost every field of human endeavor. In addition to this extension outward to include additional curricular offerings, educational services have been extended downward, to include nursery schools for children of preschool age, and upward, to include opportunities for adult education. As a result of these developments, it is scarcely an overstatement to say that education "from the cradle to the grave" is now provided at public expense for those persons who wish to avail themselves of the opportunities offered.

Units for Public-School Administration

Each state determines by law what governmental unit shall assume primary responsibility for the financing and administration of elementary and secondary schools, and there is considerable variety among the states with respect to the unit used. For purposes of discussion, it is helpful to classify the states into groups on the basis of the type of governmental unit so employed. In Delaware and Hawaii, responsibility for providing schools has been so far centralized in the state government itself as to justify characterization of their organizations as a state-unit system. In all other states, primary responsibility for providing schools is imposed upon local governmental units of one kind or another. Of these 48 states, by rule-of-thumb classification,[3] 15 use the county unit as the predominant type of administrative organization,[4] 9 use the town or township unit,[5] and 24 employ the district system.[6] It should be emphasized, however, that few states use a single type of primary unit to the exclusion of all

[3] Cf. American Association of School Administrators, *School District Organization*, Chap. 4; National Commission on School District Reorganization, *Your School District* (Nat. Education Assn., Washington, 1948), 258-261; Chris A. DeYoung, *American Education* (4th ed.), Chaps. 3, 4.

[4] Alabama, Florida, Georgia, Kentucky, Louisiana (parish-unit), Maryland, Mississippi, Nevada, New Mexico, North Carolina, South Carolina, Tennessee, Utah, Virginia, and West Virginia.

[5] Connecticut, Indiana, Maine, Massachusetts, New Hampshire, New Jersey, Pennsylvania, Rhode Island, and Vermont.

[6] Alaska, Arizona, Arkansas, California, Colorado, Idaho, Illinois, Iowa, Kansas, Michigan, Minnesota, Missouri, Montana, Nebraska, New York, North Dakota, Ohio, Oklahoma, Oregon, South Dakota, Texas, Washington, Wisconsin, and Wyoming. The

others. For example, some independently incorporated school districts are frequently found in states where one of the larger units is more commonly employed as the basic administrative area. The suggested classification, therefore, is made only on the basis of the type of school unit which *pre-dominates* in the respective states. It is to be noted further that, where the county, town, or township unit prevails, the schools are frequently operated through separate school corporations, legally distinct from, but co-terminous with, the general-purpose units, and often known officially as school districts. As employed in this chapter, however, the term *district system* designates that plan of school organization under which a district is typically smaller in area than the overlying general-purpose unit, whether county, township, or town; and the term *district state* refers to a state where the district system, as thus defined, prevails.

The School District. Under the district system, responsibility for providing elementary and high schools rests primarily upon school districts organized and operated under state law. As recently as 1942 well over 100,000 such districts existed in the United States. Though consolidation programs reduced this number by two-thirds during the succeeding two decades,[7] 1962 found nearly 30,000 districts still in existence in the 24 district states. Nebraska led the list with over 3,000 districts, and each of a dozen other states had more than 1,000. Only in the sparsely populated western states of Alaska, Arizona, Idaho, and Wyoming was the number less than 300.[8] Though some districts in urban communities have large populations, and the number of consolidated districts in rural areas is constantly growing, small rural districts, many of them but a few square miles in area and including only a few families, remain in the majority.

In most districts the principal governing authority is an elective board, most commonly of three members, which has custody of school property, hires teachers, and exercises general administrative control over school affairs. District finances are controlled in some states by the district board and in others by the district's voters in annual school meetings. The organization of school-district government has been described at some length in an earlier chapter.[9]

Inadequacies of the District System. The district system was devised early in our national history with a view to making basic educa-

---

term *school district* is used here and elsewhere in this discussion to mean an incorporated special-purpose unit charged by law with important powers and duties concerning the administration and financing of public schools. In quite a different sense the term is sometimes used to refer to a mere attendance area, within a county, township, or incorporated school district, which is served by a particular school building.

[7] See above, Chap. XVI, "School Consolidation."

[8] For further data concerning the number of districts in the respective states, see above, Chap. XII, "Number of Units."

[9] Above, Chap. XV.

tional facilities available to all children of school age notwithstanding primitive means of transportation and communication. As new states were organized, the system gained widespread favor as being well-adapted to the needs of frontier communities. Under present-day conditions, however, the district system displays many serious weaknesses. A principal product of the system, with its large number of small units, has been the one-room, one-teacher school. It is true that the number of such schools has been dramatically reduced during recent years, from more than 75,000 in 1948 to slightly less than 20,000 in 1961.[10] But, notwithstanding this remarkable reduction, with a majority of the school districts in rural America still operating such institutions, the problem of the one-room school has by no means been fully solved.[11]

In its traditional form and as it still operates in many communities, the one-room school is housed in an antiquated building lacking proper facilities for heating, ventilation, lighting, and sanitation. In this building a single teacher, who is often both inexperienced and underpaid, teaches all subjects in the eight elementary grades. In addition she (the teacher is usually a woman) is responsible for whatever limited extracurricular activities are carried on, such as social events for school patrons, and frequently she must be her own school janitor as well. Under such circumstances it is manifestly impossible to carry on a satisfactory educational program. Yet, in spite of these gross inadequacies, the per-pupil cost of education in such schools, because of the small enrollments, is often amazingly high. Poor physical plant, burdensome teaching loads, and frequently inadequate financial support, conspire to foster inefficiency in one-room rural schools. Only the tireless energy, the resourcefulness, and the selfless devotion displayed by thousands of country teachers make possible anything approaching even tolerable educational standards.

Another disadvantage of the district system lies in the inequality of financial resources available to the various districts for the support of schools. From the standpoint of value of taxable property, some districts are relatively wealthy while others are poor, and this without any reference to the number of school-age children within the respective units. In wealthy communities a relatively low tax rate for school purposes may produce sufficient revenue to provide the best facilities that other circumstances permit, whereas in poorer districts even a burdensome rate may

[10] Cf. Council of State Governments, *The Forty-Eight State School Systems,* 194; *The Book of the States,* 1962-63, p. 317.

[11] In addition to the one-room schools, there are many districts which maintain no school at all but pay the tuition of their pupils in schools of neighboring districts. These nonoperating units are sometimes referred to as "tax-protective" districts since tax advantage is commonly the principal reason for their preservation. The tax levy needed to raise funds for tuition payments is usually less than would be required if the district operated its own school or if its territory were consolidated with an operating district.

fail to yield enough to provide the barest essentials. Thus it happens, when school financing is left entirely to the respective districts, that some children will have much better educational opportunities than others because of the merely fortuitous circumstance that they live in a district containing taxable property of relatively high value. In a country that emphasizes democratic ideals, such inequality of opportunity is deplorable, and fortunately it is now rectified to some extent by state financial assistance to the poorer districts.[12]

The weaknesses of the one-room elementary school are found also, in forms only slightly less extreme, in the small rural high school. Because of the small teaching staff in such institutions, instructors are required to teach subjects in which they are not properly prepared. Curricula are narrow, buildings and equipment are inadequate, and unit costs are likely to be high. The substandard work done in thousands of small elementary and high schools is readily seen when students from those schools enter college or university. While there are exceptions, such students in general give evidence of training inferior to that of students from larger and more modern schools. Even more serious are the results of the inferior quality of the small schools when viewed from the standpoint of the millions of young Americans who receive all of their formal education there and never enter any institution of higher learning.

The most obvious means of overcoming the disadvantages of the district system is, of course, the adoption of larger units for school administration. One method of accomplishing this is through the consolidation of numerous small districts into fewer units of greater area. During recent decades many states have carried through consolidation programs of varying comprehensiveness, and the consolidation movement is still under way.[13] Consolidated districts, with their greater financial resources and larger numbers of pupils, are able to provide better physical plants, broader curricula, and improved instruction, and in general to operate school systems superior to those of the smaller districts which they supersede. When all elements of cost are considered, including transportation of pupils to the consolidated school, it is doubtful whether school consolidation results in most instances in monetary savings. Indeed, until new buildings have been paid for, the more efficient and modern consolidated schools may actually cost somewhat more. But costs are more equitably distributed, and there seems to be little doubt that the improvement in educational facilities fully justifies some slight increase in school expenditures as well as the fact that some of the more distant pupils may have to spend a longer time than might otherwise be desirable in traveling to and from the consolidated school. A method more extreme than consolidation of avoiding the shortcomings of the small school district is the

---

[12] See below, "Public-School Finance."
[13] See above, Chap. XVI, "School Consolidation."

adoption of one of the larger areas of local government—township or county—as the principal unit for school purposes.

Towns and Townships. In the six New England states the town, and in New Jersey, Pennsylvania, and Indiana the township, is the primary unit for school administration. Under the New England town system, educational affairs in each town are managed by a central elective body usually known as the school committee. Ordinarily this committee manages the schools within villages as well as those in strictly rural areas, though some of the larger municipalities have city boards of education.[14] In New Jersey and Pennsylvania, each township constitutes a school district, with a board of education for administering all schools except those within areas (for the most part municipalities) which are separately incorporated for school purposes. Each civil township in Indiana is incorporated also as a school township, and an elective township trustee is charged with management of the rural schools therein.

It is to be noted that use of the town or township as the basic educational unit does not necessarily mean the elimination of the small one-room school. Even though they are managed and financed on a town or township-wide basis, one-room schools serving small attendance areas may still exist if state laws permit and the local school authorities desire. Nevertheless, the town or township plan of school administration tends to encourage use of larger attendance areas and the operation of larger, better-equipped, and better-staffed schools than are ordinarily found under the district system.

The County. Fifteen states, principally in the South but including the western states of Nevada, Utah, and New Mexico, employ the county-unit plan of school administration. Under this plan, schools are managed and financed on a countywide basis. Administrative organization for school purposes varies somewhat among these states, but usually there is a county board of education with a county superintendent of schools appointed by and responsible to the board. The superintendent, as the executive officer of the board, is charged with management of the rural schools of the county. City schools in some instances are under the jurisdiction of the county unit, but in others are separate units with their own school boards and superintendents.

Like the town or township unit, the county unit does not assure the elimination of small, inefficient schools. It does, however, provide a more equitable basis for school financing than the district system or even the town or township plan. Because of both financial and administrative advantages, there is a distinct trend today toward larger school units than those commonly used in the past, and the county unit is steadily gaining

[14] Ellwood P. Cubberley, *State School Administration* (Houghton, Boston, 1927), 186.

in favor among educators and students of school administration. Even some of the present-day counties are too small for the most efficient and economical administration of educational affairs and might well be merged with others to form still larger school units.[15]

Many states which do not use the county-unit system of administration nevertheless provide for a county school superintendent charged with supervising, in various respects, the rural schools within his county.[16]

The State. Only in Delaware and Hawaii are the administration and financing of local schools so highly centralized as to be considered state-unit systems. In every state, however, the state government has assumed important functions in the field of education. These functions, for purposes of convenience, may be grouped into four principal categories: (1) the enactment of legislation establishing and regulating a system of public schools; (2) supervision and control of local schools through state administrative agencies; (3) contribution of financial support to elementary and secondary schools; and (4) maintenance of state colleges and universities. State functions within the last two of these groups are discussed in subsequent sections of this chapter. Activities falling in the first two groups will be considered briefly at this point.

It is the state legislature which enacts the basic laws governing the public-school system. Through a succession of statutes, sometimes referred to collectively as the state school code, the legislature determines what local units shall be responsible for providing schools, how those units shall be organized and governed, what officers the local units shall have and how they shall be chosen, and what taxing and other powers the local units shall possess. Various state officers and boards are commonly established with supervisory authority over local schools and school officers. Standards for teacher certification are fixed, and the minimum length of the school term prescribed. The subjects to be taught in the schools, and in some states the textbooks to be used, are determined in large measure by the state, either directly by statute or through the supervisory agencies. Compulsory-attendance laws require school attendance by children of specified ages, with the age limits of seven to sixteen years being fairly common. A majority of the states have established minimum salary standards for public-school teachers; and these standards have been important, if not altogether successful, factors in enabling the public schools to secure and hold capable teachers. The average salary for the country as a whole increased from $1,440 in 1939-40 to an estimated $5,735 in 1962-63.[17]

[15] Cf. Alonzo O. Briscoe, *The Size of the Local Unit for Administration and Supervision of Public Schools* (Teachers Coll., Columbia Univ., New York, 1935), 106-107.

[16] See above, Chap. XIII, "The County Superintendent of Schools."

[17] A tabular analysis of public school teachers' salaries may be found in *The Book of the States,* 1964-65, p. 333.

Nevertheless, teachers' salaries in some states are still shamefully low. All states now make provision for some sort of teacher-retirement system.[18]

Every state has one or more state boards with educational functions, and in nearly all states one such agency, commonly called the state board of education, exercises some degree of control over elementary and secondary schools.[19] The state board of education is established in some states by constitutional provision and in others by statute. In some instances its membership is entirely ex officio, in others the members are appointed or elected, and in still others part of the members are ex officio and part appointive or elective. The most widely used method of selecting board members is appointment by the governor. In each state there is also a chief state school officer, provided for by the constitution in about two-thirds of the states and elsewhere by statute. The most common title is superintendent of public instruction, though commissioner of education or some other title is used in certain states. The chief school officer is elected by popular vote in 22 states, but in other states is appointed by the governor or by the state board of education. The trend in the last decade has been toward appointment, rather than election, of both the state board and state superintendent. There is a great deal of variation among the states with respect to the powers conferred upon state educational agencies as well as the division of those powers between the state board of education and the state superintendent. Functions commonly performed by one agency or the other include enforcement of various school laws, determination of educational policies, supervisory control over elementary and secondary schools, determination of courses of study, adoption of textbooks, certification of teachers, and distribution of state school funds. In some instances, the state board of education controls the administration of part or all of the state institutions of higher learning.[20]

The state governments, over the years, have assumed an ever broader responsibility in the field of elementary and secondary education. At one time decisions as to what school facilities should be provided, and also the financing of those facilities, were left almost entirely to the local school authorities. Gradually, however, it has been realized that education in a democratic society is too important to be left solely to the local communities.[21] Moreover, with increased mobility of population more and more persons live as adult citizens in localities other than those in

---

[18] Council of State Governments, *The Forty-Eight State School Systems*, 87.

[19] See *The Book of the States*, 1964-65, p. 336. Special boards, sometimes several in a single state, deal with individual phases of educational work. Examples are vocational education boards, library commissions, textbook commissions, and teacher retirement boards.

[20] Fred F. Beach and Robert F. Will, *The State and Education* (U.S. Office of Education, Washington, 1955).

[21] Cf. Ward G. Reeder, *The Fundamentals of Public School Administration* (4th ed.), 44-47.

which they received their schooling, and hence the educational standards of a given community cease to be of purely local interest. It is therefore no matter for surprise that state governments today, though in most instances leaving primary responsibility for school administration with the local governmental units, nevertheless prescribe and enforce minimum educational standards for local schools and provide state funds to assist the local communities in meeting those standards.

Public-School Finance[22]

At one time American schools depended for their support almost entirely upon the proceeds from a local property tax, and, taking the country as a whole, this tax is still the largest single source of local school revenue. During recent decades, however, in recognition of the statewide interest in elementary and secondary education, the states have assumed a substantial part of the burden of school finance. Every state now provides some state aid for schools, and the tendency is toward a constant increase in the amount.[23] During the school year 1962-63, nearly 40 percent of all local school revenues in the United States came from state sources, while 57 percent came from local sources and less than 4 percent from the federal government.[24] The percentage of total revenues derived from the respective levels of government varies widely among the individual states. It was recently reported that in eighteen states more than 50 percent of all school revenues was derived from the state and federal governments, while in four less than 15 percent of the total came from these sources.[25]

State financial grants enable local school units both to improve their educational facilities and to reduce the burden of the local property tax for school purposes. State grants may be made to the local units at a fixed rate per pupil in average daily attendance or on some other predetermined basis, or they may be apportioned according to need. When the latter plan is followed the term *equalization grant* is sometimes used, since the purpose of the state assistance is to equalize educational opportunities between the poorer and more wealthy districts. A system of equalization grants in common use provides that, if a local school corporation levies a specified minimum rate of property tax for school purposes, the state will supplement the proceeds from this local levy by whatever amount is necessary to enable the local unit to maintain a school or schools of state-prescribed standards. State educational funds, equalization and otherwise, are usually distributed to the local school units, in accordance with the provisions of state law, by the chief state school officer, with the

22 On the subject in general, see Paul R. Mort, Walter C. Reusser, and John W. Polley, *Public School Finance* (3rd ed.).
23 Cf. Reeder, *op. cit.*, 284.
24 *The Book of the States*, 1964-65, p. 338.
25 Mort, Reusser, and Polley, *op. cit.*, 197.

county superintendent in some states acting in an intermediary capacity. The amounts to which the respective local units are entitled are determined on the basis of reports, covering such matters as school attendance and local revenues and expenditures, which are made by local school officers to the state or county authorities. Some states distribute part of their school funds to the local units on a flat per-pupil basis and another part, as equalization grants, on the basis of need.

Higher Education

Education above the secondary-school level is provided by a wide variety of institutions, some supported at public expense and some by private or sectarian organizations. Though public institutions in this field have not supplanted private facilities to as large an extent as in the case of elementary and secondary schools, they now enroll more than 60 percent of the nation's 5 million college students, and undoubtedly will handle an increasing proportion of the higher education load in the future.[26]

All states maintain state institutions of higher education, usually including one or more universities.[27] These institutions vary widely with respect to such matters as size of enrollment, amount of financial support, and extent of educational facilities provided. The larger universities are commonly organized to include, in addition to a four-year college of liberal arts and sciences, a number of professional schools or colleges such as agriculture, forestry, business administration, education, fine arts, engineering, journalism, law, medicine, dentistry, pharmacy, social work, and veterinary medicine. There is usually also a graduate school which provides training leading to advanced degrees in various fields.

Every state maintains one or more "land-grant" colleges. These are institutions which receive federal aid under the Morrill Act of 1862 and subsequent legislation providing grants of land and money to state colleges specializing in agriculture and the mechanic arts. In about half of the states, the principal land-grant college is organized as a unit of the state university, while elsewhere it is a separate institution. The land-grant colleges carry on three principal activities: (1) resident instruction, (2) the conducting of agricultural experiment stations, and (3) agricultural extension work. Resident courses emphasize such subjects as agriculture, engineering, and home economics, but the curricula do not exclude other scientific and literary studies. Especially noteworthy in the field of agricultural extension is the cooperation of the colleges with county gov-

---

[26] Cf. William L. Frederick, "Higher Education," *The Book of the States*, 1962-63, pp. 319-323; Elmer D. West, "Higher Education," *Ibid.*, 1964-65, pp. 339-343.
[27] See Allan Nevins, *The State Universities and Democracy*.

ernments in the employment of county agricultural agents and home demonstration agents. At the present time there are sixty-eight land-grant colleges and universities. Some of the institutions in the South were set aside originally for Negroes. Overall, land-grant institutions enroll 20 percent of the nation's undergraduate students and grant nearly 40 percent of all doctoral degrees.[28]

In addition to state universities and land-grant colleges there are numerous other state institutions of higher education. A few states maintain technical schools. State colleges for women are provided in several states, in some of which attendance at the state university is limited to men. Most numerous of all state-supported schools at the college level are the teachers' colleges or normal schools. Originally these were designed primarily for the training of teachers for elementary and secondary schools, but they are now attended by many students seeking a college education with no thought of entering the teaching profession. Some of the teacher-training institutions, with their curricula broadened to include other subjects, are now officially designated as universities. A 1960 survey found over 250 publicly supported four-year colleges in the United States. Of these, 16 each were in California and New York, 14 in Pennsylvania, 13 in Massachusetts, and 12 in Texas. It is difficult to classify these institutions, as well as other higher educational institutions, because their scope and programs are constantly changing. The 1960 survey found 783 publicly supported educational institutions of all kinds.[29]

The control of state institutions of higher education is usually vested in special governing boards, the composition and powers of which vary widely. Some of these boards are established by constitutional provision and others by statute. Though some are composed of members chosen by popular election, the large majority are appointed by the governor, either alone or with senatorial consent. Some are composed in part of ex officio members. In some states there is a separate board for each university or college, while in others a single board governs several or all institutions. In general, it has been the policy of the states to give the governing boards of their educational institutions a position of relative independence from the executive branch of government responsible for administering other state functions, and thus to reduce the likelihood of political control or influence. Where board members are chosen by gubernatorial appointment, it is often sought to attain this independence by giving board members staggered terms longer than the term of the governor. As a result of state administrative reorganization, however, the boards in

[28] See *The Idea of a Land Grant College,* a pamphlet prepared by the American Association of Land-Grant Colleges and State Universities, 1962, in celebration of the centennial of the Morrill Act.

[29] S. V. Martorana and Ernest V. Hollis, *State Boards Responsible for Higher Education,* 6, 183-197.

some states have in recent years been brought more fully under the jurisdiction of the governor and other state officials.[30]

Most state universities and colleges charge students who are residents of the state a tuition fee considerably smaller than that charged by similar private institutions, but exact a somewhat higher charge from nonresident students than from residents. Even the nonresident tuition, however, is ordinarily less than the fees charged by private schools. Sizable state appropriations are the main source for the additional operating funds, although the federal government is constantly providing additional money.

Local government makes its contribution to higher education principally through institutions of two types: (1) the junior college, and (2) the municipal college or university. The junior college, which is almost entirely a product of the present century, offers two years of education in advance of the regular secondary-school course.[31] Institutions of this character serve the dual purpose of lightening the load on four-year colleges and universities and of making the first two years of college work available locally and at small cost to students who otherwise might be unable to extend their studies beyond high school. Though some junior colleges are maintained by the state and the tendency is for the states to assume a more important share of responsibility for these institutions, many are operated by cities or school districts. Of the local institutions, some are supported entirely from local funds while others receive substantial assistance from the state government. Some charge tuition fees while others do not. The junior-college movement has made most headway in the western and midwestern sections of the country. In 1959-60 there were 390 publicly controlled junior colleges in operation plus 273 private institutions of similar nature.[32] The public group enrolled more than 80 percent of all junior-college students. The 1960 survey found public junior colleges in 38 states, with the states having the largest numbers being California with 63 and Texas and Wisconsin with 31 each.[33] In view of the current overcrowding in four-year colleges and universities, it appears certain that the future will see further expansion of the junior-college system.

Municipal colleges and universities are much less numerous than junior colleges and are declining in significance as a part of our public educational system. These institutions are operated by city governments to provide four years of study at the college level and may be in addition

[30] For a careful analysis of this relationship, see Malcolm Moos and Francis E. Rourke, *The Campus and the State.*

[31] Cf. Clarence S. Marsh, ed., *American Universities and Colleges* (Amer. Council on Education, Washington, 4th ed., 1940), 47; Leland L. Medsker, *The Junior College: Progress and Prospect,* Chap. 1.

[32] Ralph R. Fields, *The Community College Movement,* 42.

[33] Martorana and Hollis, *op. cit.,* 183-197.

to two-year colleges operated by the same cities. In the cities where munic-ipal colleges and universities have been established, the reasons assigned for setting up institutions of this nature have been quite varied. Most gen-erally emphasized has been the fact that a municipal university will en-able many persons to secure a college education who otherwise would be unable to do so. Other reasons have included the desire "to provide a more practical education than that afforded by existing colleges, to provide better means for the training of teachers, to provide a center of culture for the city, and to meet specific local educational needs. Local civic pride and rivalry with another city, the belief that a local college is of economic advantage to a city and that a municipal university can serve a city in many ways outside of classroom instruction, the existence of local educa-tional foundations whose consolidation to form a university was desirable, and the examples of other institutions have each been stressed in one or more cases." [34]

The largest city college system in the world is the City University of New York, which embraces within its organization four individual col-leges—City, Hunter, Brooklyn, and Queens.[35] Other municipal institutions include the universities of Louisville, Cincinnati, Toledo, Akron, and Omaha. Most municipal universities are under independent governing boards. In some instances the city board of education appoints some or all members of the university board. The New York system is governed by a board of twenty-one members appointed by the mayor.[36] Several of the larger municipal institutions provide various professional courses in addi-tion to the standard four-year course in the liberal arts and sciences. The city universities in Detroit (Wayne) and Wichita have recently been made part of the higher education systems of their respective states.

Adult Education

Modern programs of public education are not limited to the pro-vision of educational facilities for children and young people of school and college age. Educational opportunities of various kinds are being made available on a constantly wider scale to the general adult population. Some programs of adult education are administered by the public schools and others by state and municipal colleges and universities.[37] Instruction

[34] R. H. Eckelberry, *The History of the Municipal University in the United States* (U.S. Office of Education, Washington, 1932), 190-191.

[35] DeYoung, *op. cit.*, 157-158. In addition, there are three two-year community colleges that are part of both the city and state university systems. This has been called an "anomalous situation." See Board of Higher Education, *A Long-Range Plan for the City University of New York, 1961-1975* (The Board, New York, 1962), 44.

[36] The president of the city board of education is an ex officio member of the university governing board. *Ibid.*, 35.

[37] Various privately controlled educational institutions and other private organ-izations also provide adult-education facilities.

is provided through night classes in the buildings of the schools and colleges administering the programs, extension classes held in other communities, and correspondence courses. Both vocational and cultural subjects are covered. Some persons take courses for credit toward high school graduation or a college or university degree, others with a view to advancement in their business or profession, and still others merely for self-improvement. Many adult education programs, especially in urban communities, include classes in which immigrants, as well as native-born adults who have had little or no formal schooling, may acquire basic skills in reading and writing the English language. Some include Americanization classes designed to prepare immigrants for naturalization. Advice and assistance are also frequently afforded to individuals or groups not organized into formal classes. An outstanding program of this nature is the agricultural extension work of the land-grant colleges. Other examples are seen in the providing of speakers for civic organizations, and forum leaders for study groups.

In vocational education particularly, much use is coming to be made of the institute or "short course," consisting of concentrated instruction during a brief period, usually of only a few days' duration. Many of these courses are of a "refresher" nature, designed to enable persons in business and the professions to receive periodic instruction in new problems and methods in their respective fields. Examples are short courses for doctors, lawyers, insurance salesmen, and various groups of public officers and employees. The latter include, for instance, courses for policemen, firemen, highway officers, health officers, and tax assessors.

Especially active in adult education work are the extension divisions of state universities. For many years these agencies have provided extension and correspondence courses of an academic character. More recently the extension programs have been elaborated and extended. During World War II, some extension divisions made a significant contribution to the war effort by organizing and administering industrial-education projects for the training of war workers. So successful were some of these projects that training of this nature has become an accepted part of peacetime extension work. Traditionally, public educational activities have been limited in large measure to the operation of regularly-established schools and colleges which qualified persons have been expected to seek out and attend for specified periods. In the future, if present trends continue, many forms of adult education will be greatly expanded in an effort to "bring public education directly to the people."

Public Libraries

An institution which, though not a school, is rapidly becoming a standard element in our educational system, is the public library. Although a newcomer, comparatively speaking, in the field of public functions, the provision of library facilities is being recognized more and more as an essential service of state and local governments.[38] Not only is the provision of library facilities being undertaken by governmental units in ever increasing number, but the forms of library service offered are constantly expanding. At one time the public library was concerned almost exclusively with making books accessible to its patrons. Today the modern library, in addition, provides magazines and newspapers in profusion, and frequently also various types of films and recordings. The larger and more progressive libraries also offer various forms of informational and readers' advisory services.

City Libraries. Most larger municipalities and many smaller ones support city libraries. These institutions are administered in a variety of ways. Most commonly, the library is placed under an unpaid board of trustees which appoints the librarian and decides matters of library policy. Board members are in some cases popularly elected and in others appointed by the mayor or city council. In occasional instances they are selected by the school board.[39] Some city libraries are financed by a special library tax levied under statutory authority, and others by direct appropriations from the city treasury. The former method is generally preferred by librarians, since it makes the library financially independent of the city council. On the other hand, most political scientists believe, as in the case of schools and for the same reasons,[40] that library funds should be subject to council control, to the end that financial needs for library purposes may be considered and determined in their relation to needs for all other essential municipal services.

County and Regional Libraries.[41] Public library facilities for the inhabitants of rural areas developed later than those for urban dwellers. Today, however, many rural communities are served by county and regional libraries and state library extension, and the movement to provide adequate service for the country districts continues to make progress.

The federal government has stimulated rural library development under the Library Services Act of 1956, which provided for federal grants to the states for five years to aid in the extension of library facilities to rural communities. "When the act was adopted it was estimated that 26

[38] For a good discussion of organization for library services in governments generally, see Oliver Garceau, *The Public Library in the Political Process*, especially Chap. 5.

[39] Cf. William B. Munro, *Municipal Administration* (Macmillan, New York, 1934), Chap. 33.

[40] See above, Chap. XV, "The City-School District Financial Relationship."

[41] For a summary of state local-library laws, see American Library Association, *County, Regional, and District Library Laws*.

million rural residents were without any library service and that an additional 50 million citizens had access only to extremely inadequate service; 319 rural counties had no library services within their areas." By 1961 under the Act, "some 4 million citizens had libraries for the first time; 32 million were receiving greatly improved service; and 169 counties and townships, previously without service, had it available." [42] The Act has now been extended to 1966.

County libraries may be divided, according to governmental type, into three principal classes.[43] The first and most prevalent type may be called the independent county library. Libraries of this character are usually established by the county governing board, with or without popular approval at a referendum election as state law may require, and are operated as a part of the county government. Control of the library may be exercised directly by the county board or may be in the hands of a semi-autonomous library board. The latter plan is the more common, and is generally preferred on the assumption that it lessens political interference. A county library of this type may serve the residents of the entire county, or only the inhabitants of those parts of the county not served by city or other publicly supported libraries. Where the latter plan is used, taxes for the support of the county library are usually imposed only upon property within the areas served by it. A second type of county library service that is fairly common is the contract variety. Under this plan, the county board enters into a contract with an already existing library for supplying library service to county residents. The institution agreeing to provide such service is occasionally the library of another county, but is most frequently a city library—usually one located in the county seat or the county's largest city. The amount to be paid by the county may be computed upon any one or more of various bases, such as population of the territory served, number of borrowers, or cost of providing the service. Yet a third means of providing library service to rural inhabitants, less common than either of the two just described, is through a city-county library established and administered jointly by the two governmental units. Whichever of these several plans is followed, use is frequently made, for distributing purposes, of branch libraries or deposit stations, or both. Branches, like the main library, are manned by trained personnel and extend various forms of assistance to readers. Deposit stations, on the other hand, have neither trained personnel nor reading-room facilities. They consist merely of book collections, changed at regular intervals and located in convenient places such as schoolhouses, post offices, stores, gasoline stations or even

    [42] Eleanor A. Ferguson, "Library Services and Legislation," *The Book of the States,* 1962-63, pp. 329-332, at 331.
    [43] Eleanor Hitt Morgan, "The County Library," in Carleton B. Joeckel, ed., *Library Extension: Problems and Solutions,* 59-74. Cf. also Carleton B. Joeckel, *The Government of the American Public Library,* 264-271.

private homes, with some responsible person agreeing to keep a record of books borrowed and returned. Of growing importance as a distributing agency, especially in making books available to the inhabitants of isolated regions, is the bookmobile. This is a closed motor truck, especially equipped with book shelves, which visits rural homes on regular schedules and from which books may be borrowed to be returned on subsequent visits.[44]

The first county libraries were established about the turn of the present century, and during the first quarter of the century the county library was the most widely used device in extending library service to rural areas. More recently, however, growing use has been made of the multicounty or regional library.[45] Under this plan, two or more neighboring counties, through contractual agreement or the establishment of a library district, cooperate in providing library service for their respective inhabitants. The plan is especially well-adapted to use by relatively poor, sparsely settled counties which might find it impracticable to operate individual county libraries. Combining the populations of two or more such counties for library purposes may provide sufficient demand to justify the establishment of a modern library, at the same time that the pooling of financial resources makes practicable the support of such an institution. Various states have now enacted legislation authorizing counties to cooperate with each other in providing library service, and several regional libraries have been established, the movement having been most active in some of the southern states. Thus, during the decade from 1937 to 1947, thirteen regional libraries, serving from two to thirteen counties each, were organized in Kentucky, Tennessee, Alabama, Georgia, North Carolina, and Virginia. These libraries are variously financed by contributions from a number of sources, including county governments, school districts, state library extension funds, and the Tennessee Valley Authority.[46]

In some states, mainly in the Midwest, library services are provided by special district governments. The 1962 Census of Government lists 349 library districts, with over half of them (214) in Indiana.[47]

State Library Agencies. Provision of library service is not a function solely of local governments. Many states have one or more state libraries. These are of varied character, but for the most part are designed primarily for use by state officials and for the preservation of historical materials. Some, such as legislative-reference libraries, are of a specialized nature.

[44] Morgan, "The County Library," *loc. cit.*
[45] *Ibid.;* Helen M. Harris, "The Regional Library," in Carleton B. Joeckel, ed., *op. cit.,* 87-97.
[46] M. H. Satterfield, "Intergovernmental Coöperation in the Tennessee Valley," *Jour. of Politics,* IX, 31-58 (Feb., 1947).
[47] United States Bureau of the Census, *Census of Governments: 1962,* Vol. I: *Governmental Organization* (U.S. Govt. Printing Office, Washington, 1963), 66.

More important from the standpoint of citizens of the state generally are state activities for the promotion of local library service, usually through some sort of library-extension agency. Every state has some agency charged with library-extension activities. In some instances the state library includes library extension as one of its activities; in others, there is an independent library commission established for the primary purpose of promoting library extension; and, in still others, the library-extension agency is a division of the state department of education. Whatever its form, the extension agency ordinarily provides book service to local libraries, groups, and individuals, through both extension loans and traveling libraries; encourages the establishment of local libraries and the improvement of library personnel; provides various forms of advice and assistance to local libraries; and, in general, promotes the expansion of library coverage throughout the state.[48] Of growing importance also are state financial grants supplementing local library appropriations and making possible the improvement and expansion of local library services. By 1963 more than half of the states were providing some degree of financial aid to local governments for public library purposes.[49]

REFERENCES

ALLEN, H. K. (in collaboration with Richard G. Axt), *State Public Finance and State Institutions of Higher Education in the United States* (Columbia Univ. Press, New York, 1952).

American Association of School Administrators, *School District Organization: Report of the AASA Commission on School Reorganization* (The Association, Washington, 1958).

American Library Association, *County, Regional and District Library Laws* (The Association, Chicago, 1957).

BAILEY, Stephen K., FROST, Richard T., WOOD, Robert C., and MARSCH, Paul E., *Schoolmen and Politics: A Study of State Aid to Education in the Northeast* (Syracuse Univ. Press, Syracuse, N.Y., 1962).

BEACH, Fred F., DUNBAR, Ralph M., and WILL, Robert F., *The State and Publicly Supported Libraries* (U.S. Office of Education, Washington, 1956).

BOLLENS, John C., *Special District Governments in the United States* (Univ. of Calif. Press, Berkeley, 1957), Chap. 6.

BURKHEAD, Jesse, *State and Local Taxes for Public Education* (Syracuse Univ. Press, Syracuse, N.Y., 1963).

[48] Fred F. Beach, Ralph M. Dunbar, and Robert F. Will, *The State and Publicly Supported Libraries;* Julia Wright Merrill, comp., *The State Library Agency: Its Functions and Organization* (Amer. Library Assn., Chicago, 5th ed., 1945); Paul A. T. Noon, "The Role of the State Agency in Library Extension," in Carleton B. Joeckel, ed., *op. cit.,* 160-170.

[49] For a state-by-state summary of appropriations for state library agencies and grants-in-aid in 1963, see *The Book of the States,* 1964-65, p. 352.

CARLSON, William S., *The Municipal University* (Center for Applied Research in Education, Washington, 1962).

Committee on Education and Labor, House of Representatives, Eighty-Eighth Congress, *The Federal Government and Education* (U.S. Govt. Printing Office, Washington, 1963).

COOPER, Shirley, and FITZWATER, Charles O., *County School Administration* (Harper, New York, 1954).

COUNCIL of State Governments, *Higher Education in the Forty-Eight States* (The Council, Chicago, 1952).

———, *The Forty-Eight State School Systems* (The Council, Chicago, 1949).

DEYOUNG, Chris A., *American Education* (McGraw-Hill, New York, 4th ed., 1960).

FIELDS, Ralph, R. *The Community College Movement* (McGraw-Hill, New York, 1962).

GARCEAU, Oliver, *The Public Library in the Political Process: A Report of the Public Library Inquiry* (Columbia Univ. Press, New York, 1949).

HUTCHINS, Clayton D., and STEINHILER, Delores A., *Trends in Financing Public Education* (U.S. Office of Education, Washington, 1961).

JOECKEL, Carlton B., *The Government of the American Public Library* (Univ. of Chicago Press, Chicago, 1935).

———, ed., *Library Extension: Problems and Solutions* (Univ. of Chicago Press, Chicago, 1946).

JOHNS, Roe L., and MORPHET, Edgar L., *Financing the Public Schools* (Prentice-Hall, Englewood Cliffs, N.J., 1960).

KNEZEVICH, Stephen J., *Administration of Public Education* (Harper, New York, 1962).

MARTIN, Roscoe C., *Government and the Suburban School* (Syracuse Univ. Press, Syracuse, N.Y., 1962).

MARTORANA, S. V., and HOLLIS, Ernest V., *State Boards Responsible for Higher Education* (U.S. Office of Education, Washington, 1960).

MEDSKER, Leland L., *The Junior College: Progress and Prospect* (McGraw-Hill, New York, 1960).

Moos, Malcolm, and ROURKE, Francis E., *The Campus and the State* (Johns Hopkins Univ. Press, Baltimore, 1959).

MORT, Paul R., Reusser, Walter C., and Polley, John W., *Public School Finance* (McGraw-Hill, New York, 3rd ed., 1960).

NEVINS, Allan, *The State Universities and Democracy* (Univ. of Ill. Press, Urbana, 1962).

REEDER, Ward G., *The Fundamentals of Public School Administration* (Macmillan, New York, 4th ed., 1958).

RELLER, Theodore L., ed., "The Public Schools and other Community Services," *Annals of Amer. Acad. of Polit. and Soc. Sci.*, CCCII, Philadelphia, Nov., 1955.

ROSE, Ernestine, *The Public Library in American Life* (Columbia Univ. Press, New York, 1954).

United States Bureau of the Census, *Census of Governments: 1962*, Vol. IV, No. 1: *Finances of School Districts* (U.S. Govt. Printing Office, Washington, 1963).

21

Highways and
Natural Resources

HIGHWAYS

A traditional function of government which still holds a position of major importance is the provision of public avenues for travel. In early days, with travel principally on horseback and by horse-drawn vehicles, roads were primitive and provided only by local governmental agencies. But with the advent of automobile travel in the early years of the present century came a demand for improved, all-weather highways. Roads previously of local interest only, came to be traveled by, and therefore of concern to, persons living outside the locality in which they were situated. Moreover, the provision of modern, surfaced thoroughfares was frequently beyond the financial means of local governmental units. Hence there began a tendency, which has continued to the present day, to shift the duty of financing and administering public highways from smaller to larger areas of local government, and from local units to the states. Nevertheless, the provision of roads and streets devoted primarily to local travel remains, in varying degrees in the different states, a duty of local government. The present-day importance of the highway function is indicated in some degree by the extent and costliness of the highway system. Public roads and streets in the United States total some 3.5 million miles, and approximately $9.6 billion annually is spent on their improvement and maintenance. On this elaborate highway network some 80 million motor vehicles travel annually, on the average, almost 10,000 miles each—a total of nearly 740 billion vehicle miles.[1]

The National Government and Highways

There is in this country no national highway system in the sense of a nationwide network of thoroughfares built and maintained by the central government. During the first half of the nineteenth century, the famous Cumberland Road, or National Pike, was built by the national government. With Cumberland, Maryland, as its eastern terminus, this road was officially projected as far westward as Vandalia, Illinois. Construction, however, was not completed to that point, and the road was ultimately ceded to the respective states through which it passed.[2] The national government now has some 115,000 miles of highways under its jurisdiction in such places as national forests, parks, and reservations;[3] and, beginning in 1916, has made generous grants of financial assistance to the states for highway purposes. Congress has also cooperated in the construction of the Pan-American Highway by providing funds for surveys, for construction of the Alaskan segment, and for loans to various other American countries through which the highway passes. But the construction and maintenance of highways in the continental United States has always been, and remains today, a responsibility primarily of the states and their local governments.

Since 1925, under a cooperative arrangement between the American Association of State Highway Officials and the federal government, a nationwide system of principal connecting thoroughfares selected by a Joint Board on Interstate Highways has been given a uniform system of marking and numbering. Roads in this "national highway system" are marked with signs in the shape of a shield which bear the name of the state, the letters "U.S.," and the number of the route. East-west highways are designated by even numbers, and north-south routes by odd numbers.[4] It should be emphasized, however, that these "U.S. highways," though financed in part by federal-aid funds, are built and maintained by the respective states as parts of their state highway systems, and are given uniform marking and numbering solely for the convenience of the traveling public.

[1] United States Bureau of the Census, *Statistical Abstract of the United States* (U.S. Govt. Printing Office, Washington, 84th ed., 1963), 555 ff.

[2] For a brief historical account of the Cumberland Road, see T. R. Agg and J. E. Brindley, *Highway Administration and Finance*, 4-21.

[3] United States Bureau of Public Roads, *Highway Statistics: 1961*. Data on highway mileage, surfacing, and financing presented in the following discussion are drawn in large part from this report.

[4] John H. Bateman, *Introduction to Highway Engineering* (5th ed.), 6-7.

State and Local Responsibility

Except that states and counties sometimes assist in building and maintaining streets which constitute segments of state or county highways, the providing of city streets is a function of municipal government. Legal responsibility for the construction and maintenance of rural highways, however, varies from state to state. In a few instances the states themselves have assumed complete responsibility for all rural highways. More commonly, however, the responsibility is apportioned by statute between the state and its counties or townships, or among all three levels of government. A survey of several years ago [5] showed that four states—Delaware, North Carolina, Virginia, and West Virginia—had centralized in the state government administrative and financial responsibility for all rural roads;[6] twenty-seven states [7] divided responsibility between the state government and the counties; the four New England states of Connecticut, New Hampshire, Rhode Island, and Vermont divided responsibility between the state and the towns; while the remaining thirteen states [8] made a three-way distribution of responsibility among the state, county, and town or township governments. Usually a particular scheme of distributing responsibility among the various levels of government is effective throughout a given state. Several states, however, have optional laws under which certain counties maintain all nonstate roads on a county-unit basis while others share the local highway function with townships or road districts. Each of these states, in the grouping just suggested, has been classified according to the scheme of responsibility predominant there. In some such states the centralization of local highway responsibility in the county is a result of the complete abandonment of the township as an area of government within the county, while in others a mere transfer of the highway function from the smaller to the larger unit is involved.

As previously noted, there has been a distinct tendency, especially during recent decades, to shift legal responsibility for providing rural highway facilities from smaller to larger governmental units. This shift has been due principally to the fact that, in practice, administration of the highway function by larger units has proved more efficient and economical. The transfer of highways from local to state control was most pronounced during the decade of the 1930's. During the six-year period from

---

[5] See tabular classification of states in Charles L. Dearing, *American Highway Policy*, 67.

[6] Except in three Virginia counties which, under optional statutory provisions, had elected to retain local control over secondary roads.

[7] All those not accounted for in the textual discussion or in footnote 8.

[8] Illinois, Kansas, Maine, Massachusetts, Minnesota, Missouri, Nebraska, New York, North Dakota, Ohio, Pennsylvania, South Dakota, and Wisconsin. At the time of the survey, Alaska and Hawaii had not been admitted to statehood.

the close of 1930 to the end of 1936, more than 200,000 miles of highways were transferred from local to state control, state mileage being thereby increased by more than 64 percent.[9] A major factor in bringing about this phenomenal increase in state-controlled mileage was the transfer of all local roads to the state in Delaware, North Carolina, West Virginia, and most Virginia counties; but the tendency toward a gradual increase in state mileage has been general throughout the country. Even more marked, when considered over an extended period, has been the removal of local roads from township jurisdiction. In 1920 it was estimated that probably as much as 70 percent of the total road mileage in the United States was under township administration,[10] while today township roads constitute only about 15 percent of the country's mileage. This significant shift has resulted in part from the statutory transfer in some states, such as Indiana, Iowa, and Michigan, of all township roads to county jurisdiction; in part from the adoption of the county-unit road system by individual counties in states, such as Kansas, which make county administration optional; and in part from the transfer, in areas where township control has not been entirely abandoned, of some township mileage to county highway systems.

At the end of 1961 the nation's highway mileage, exclusive of roads under federal control, was distributed approximately as follows: highways under state control, 700,000 miles;[11] county roads, 1,700,000 miles; town and township roads, 550,000 miles; and city streets, 400,000 miles.

Organization for Highway Administration[12]

Every state has a highway department or its equivalent. This fact reflects the recognized importance of the highway function, and also the requirement of federal-aid road laws that a state, in order to qualify for highway grants, have a central administrative agency empowered to deal with the agency of the national government (now the Bureau of Public Roads in the Department of Commerce) charged with the distribution of federal funds. The department is headed in some states by a commission and in others by a single commissioner or director.[13] In most states these principal highway officers are appointed by the governor, though in some instances they are elective or ex officio. The powers and duties of the high-

[9] Thomas H. MacDonald, "Financing of Local Roads and Streets," *Pub. Roads*, XIX, 1-8 (Mar., 1938).

[10] T. R. Agg, *American Rural Highways*, 14.

[11] Includes 136,000 miles of state-controlled county roads, principally in Delaware, North Carolina, Virginia, and West Virginia.

[12] Cf. Bateman, *op. cit.*, 493-495; Highway Research Board, *State Highway Administrative Bodies*.

[13] A 1952 survey reported that 14 states had single-headed agencies, 11 had administrative commissions, and 23 had some combination of the two organization plans. Highway Research Board, *op. cit.*

way department vary from state to state, but its principal functions commonly include the following:[14] selection of roads for inclusion in the state highway system, except insofar as such roads are designated by statute; construction and maintenance of highways in the state system; distribution to the local-government units of state-aid funds for highways; supervision of, and cooperation with, the local units of government in highway matters; and dissemination of highway information to the public. Other duties devolved upon the department in some states include the collection of motor-vehicle license fees, and the policing of highways for enforcement of the motor-vehicle laws.

County roads are in some states under the direct control of the county governing board, and in others are under a county highway commissioner or superintendent. The latter official in some instances is appointed by the county board and in others is popularly elected. The primary function of the county highway authorities is the construction and maintenance of roads and bridges in the county highway system. In those states which divide local road responsibility between counties and townships, it is usually provided that the county authorities shall select the roads to be included in the county system.

The principal road officer in the township is usually a highway commissioner or supervisor, who in some states is appointed by the township board and in others is popularly elected. It is the duty of this official to improve and maintain all local roads which do not fall under the jurisdiction of some other authority. Jurisdiction of the township highway officer ordinarily extends to the construction of bridges and culverts on township roads as well as to maintenance of the roadbed, though in some states such structures, or at least those costing in excess of a designated sum, are constructed by the county highway authorities or are under their supervision.[15]

City streets are usually built and maintained by a municipal street department, engineering department, or department of public works.[16] The head of this department is popularly elected in cities under the commission form of government and in some smaller cities under the mayor-council plan, but elsewhere is ordinarily appointed by the mayor or city manager.

Classes of Highways

On the basis of their predominant purpose, highways may be classified into four general categories, designated as (1) primary highways, (2)

[14] Bateman, *op. cit.*, 494-495.
[15] Agg, *op. cit.*, 13-15.
[16] Bateman, *op. cit.*, 9. On municipal highway departments and their work, see Agg and Brindley, *op. cit.*, Chap. 11, and the various standard textbooks in the field of municipal administration.

secondary highways, (3) farm-to-market roads, and (4) city streets. The first of these classes consists largely of interstate thoroughfares connecting the principal population centers of the country. Secondary highways are of an intercounty character and serve to connect the various cities within the state. Farm-to-market roads are designed principally to provide rural dwellers with access to local trade centers, as well as to railroads, schools, and churches. Most city streets are designed for local travel of an intra-municipal character, though some constitute segments of secondary or primary highway systems. It will readily be seen, of course, that this is by no means a hard-and-fast classification, since some highways serve more than a single purpose, and overlapping of the respective classes inevitably results. In a general way, control over highways of the four categories has been vested in the past, and to a considerable extent still remains, in the four respective classes of governmental units sharing in the highway function. Most of the primary-road mileage is included within the state highway systems. Both secondary and farm-to-market roads are controlled in some states by the counties and in others by the towns; but, where both counties and towns participate, secondary highways are ordinarily controlled by the former, and farm-to-market roads by the latter. A current tendency to shift farm-to-market roads from township to county control, and to transfer more and more secondary mileage to the state highway system, has already been noted. City streets are primarily a responsibility of the respective municipalities.

State Highway Systems

The state highway systems include the principal thoroughfares of the nation. Much of the mileage is heavily traveled and therefore requires surfacing of good quality. Of all state-controlled mileage at the end of 1961, approximately 45 percent was surfaced with high-type pavements, including Portland cement concrete, brick, and high-type bituminous pavement; 35 percent was provided with low-type bituminous surfacing; and 14 percent was surfaced with gravel, stone, or stabilized soil. Only about 6 percent was unsurfaced.

The earliest paved highways in rural areas were two-lane roads designed to "get the farmer out of the mud" and to facilitate rural mail delivery. But the Federal Highway Act of 1921 envisaged road-building as a means of stimulating travel and transportation, providing for state designation of interstate highways for improvement with federal-aid funds.[17] Twenty years later, the primary systems of rural state highways included 15,000 miles of three-lane roads and another 5,000 miles of four-, five-, and six-lane highways.[18] Good roads are even more essential in war-

[17] Thomas H. MacDonald, "Paving America," *State Govt.*, XVIII, 78-80 (May, 1945).

[18] G. Donald Kennedy, *The Role of the Federal Government in Highway Development,* 61-63.

time than in times of peace. In recognition of this fact, Congress, in the Defense Highway Act of 1941, made special appropriations to the states for "access" roads to military and naval establishments, defense industries, and essential raw materials, and for a system of "strategic" highways designated by the War Department as necessary to national defense. Under these provisions, hundreds of miles of new and improved roads were built to facilitate the movement of workers to armament plants, and to tap supplies of timber and minerals needed for war production.[19]

The Interstate System

A new program of arterial highways was authorized by Congress in 1944 but was first given major financial implementation by the Federal-Aid Highway Act of 1956. Officially designated as the National System of Interstate and Defense Highways but popularly known as The Interstate System, this program is intended to provide an integrated network of the nation's most heavily traveled roads, linking together the country's metropolitan areas and industrial centers and serving the national defense. Originally planned to embrace 40,000 miles of principal thoroughfares, the program was subsequently expanded to 41,000 miles. By September, 1963, more than 15,000 miles of the new system had been opened to traffic and it was expected that construction would be completed by 1972.

Highways within the system are marked with a blue-and-red shield bearing the word "Interstate," the name of the state, and the route number. Most of the mileage is 4-lane with a center dividing strip and limited access. A small portion of the mileage is 2-lane only, and a somewhat larger portion consists of 6 lanes or more. Like other portions of the state highway system, the roads of the interstate system are constructed and maintained by the respective states. However, the federal government contributes 90 percent of the construction costs as compared with 50 percent in the case of other federal-aid projects. The importance of the interstate system is indicated by the fact that, though comprising little more than 1 percent of the nation's mileage, it will, when completed, carry 20 percent of all traffic.[20]

A unique feature of the 1956 Highway Act was the provision for a federal incentive bonus to any state agreeing to regulate billboard advertising along the interstate system. By 1962, sixteen states had entered into agreements with the Secretary of Commerce for billboard regulation.[21]

---

[19] MacDonald, "Paving America," *loc. cit.*
[20] Cf. United States Bureau of Public Roads, *Highway Progress: 1962*, pp. 7-12. See below, "Federal Aid."
[21] *The Book of the States* (Council of State Govts., Chicago), 1962-63, pp. 336-337.

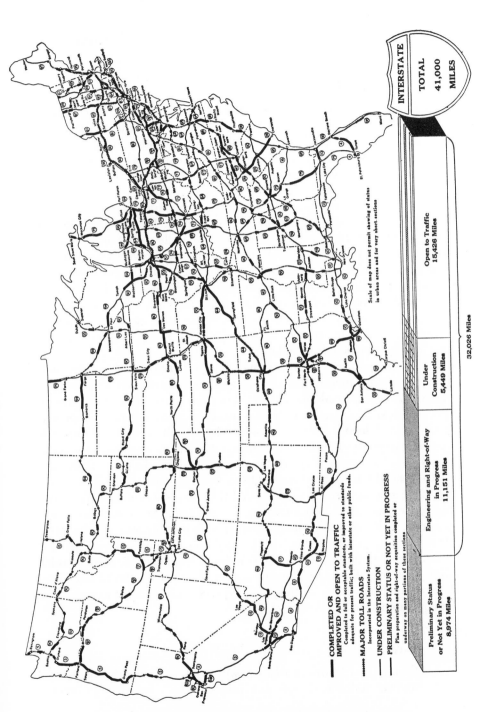

THE NATIONAL SYSTEM OF INTERSTATE AND DEFENSE HIGHWAYS

Status of Improvement as of September 30, 1963

U.S. Department of Commerce. Bureau of Public Roads.

Toll Roads

Another significant development of recent years has been the renewal of toll-road construction. During the early years of the 19th century, many intercity roads were toll roads, a few of them being operated by the states but most by private turnpike companies. These toll projects, however, encountered financial difficulties. By 1850 most of the turnpike companies had failed, with their roads being taken over by the states and assigned to local governmental units for maintenance. Nearly a century later, with current taxes proving inadequate for financing the vast highway construction programs required to handle mounting automobile traffic, the toll principle of highway financing was revived. In 1940 the Pennsylvania Turnpike was opened between Pittsburgh and Harrisburg. Subsequently this project was extended to reach the entire length of the state; and various other states followed Pennsylvania's lead in the construction of tollways. These roads were built by state agencies, frequently called toll road commissions, and were financed by the issuance of "revenue" bonds to be paid from toll income.[22]

In most instances the revenue from toll payments has been sufficient to meet payments on bond principal and interest; but several of the roads have experienced difficulties at times due to the fact that toll income has been less than was anticipated.[23] Recently some toll roads appear to have suffered income losses occasioned by the shifting of toll traffic to competitive freeways in the interstate system; and in some instances traffic losses have necessitated an increase in toll charges. In view of the fact that the need for arterial thoroughfares is increasingly being met by the interstate system, it seems unlikely that the immediate future will see any marked expansion of toll financing, though some toll construction will continue. Toll roads are usually planned with the intention of converting them to freeways when all of their bonded indebtedness has been paid. It is interesting to note that the 15,000 miles of the interstate system which were open to traffic in 1962 included more than 2,000 miles of toll roads, bridges, and tunnels which, though incorporated into the new system, were still operated as toll facilities.[24]

County and Township Roads

County and township roads comprise some 65 percent of the nation's highway mileage, though they probably carry less than 15 percent

[22] John F. Due, "The Rise and Decline of the Toll Principle in Highway Finance, 1940-1957," *Nat. Tax Jour.*, X, 97-113 (June, 1957).

[23] *Ibid.*

[24] United States Bureau of Public Roads, *Highway Progress: 1962*, p. 9.

of the total traffic. Of the 2.3 million miles in the county and township rural systems in 1961, some 1.5 million miles were surfaced. Of the surfaced roads, only 106,000 miles were of high-type pavement, the remainder being improved with gravel, stone, stabilized soil, and low-type bituminous materials. More than 800,000 miles of county and township roads, constituting about 35 percent of the nation's rural mileage, were unsurfaced. Though, as has been noted, these rural roads under county and township management carry only a small percentage of the nation's traffic, they are important both as farm-to-market roads and as "feeders" to the primary state systems.

City Streets

Of the 445,000 miles of streets and alleys in American cities, approximately 190,000 miles are improved with high-type pavement, 135,000 miles with low-type bituminous surfacing, and 80,000 miles with gravel, stone, or stabilized soil. The remaining 40,000 unsurfaced miles are for the most part graded and drained. City streets are commonly regarded as existing to provide access to business and residential property, and indeed in most cases this is their primary function. But some streets, totaling about 50,000 miles throughout the country, constitute segments of "through" highways carrying heavy traffic. On such streets, vehicles passing through the city aggravate traffic congestion and greatly increase the cost of street maintenance. Since streets of this character serve state and interstate traffic, as well as local, it is scarcely just to impose their full cost upon the local taxpayers, and both the federal and state governments provide some or all of the finances for these roads. Also, there are now more "by-passes" of major highways around cities than was the case years ago.

Highway Finance

Apart from the toll financing previously discussed, state and local highway revenues are derived principally from four sources: (1) property taxes, (2) special assessments, (3) various taxes on the users of motor vehicles, and (4) federal aid.[25]

Property Taxes. The property tax is an ad valorem levy at a uniform rate upon all taxable property or, more recently in some states, upon different classes of property at different rates.[26] Once the principal source of

[25] On the subject of highway finance generally, see Harry Tucker and Marc C. Leager, *Highway Economics,* Chaps. 4, 5; Dearing, *op. cit.,* Chap. 4; Denzel C. Cline and Milton C. Taylor, *Michigan Highway Fiscal Study, 1961;* Illinois Commission on Revenue, *Report* (Springfield, 1963), Chap. 17; Kentucky Legislative Research Commission, *Gasoline Tax Structure* (Ky. Legis. Research Comsn., Frankfort, 1958); MacDonald, "Financing of Local Roads and Streets," *loc. cit.*
[26] See below, Chap. XXIV.

highway revenue, the property tax has now yielded first place to user levies. It remains, however, an important source of local highway revenue, and is still employed to a limited extent by some states.

Special Assessments. Under the special-assessment plan, part or all of the cost of constructing a highway is made a charge against property abutting thereon or in close proximity thereto. It is assumed that a highway improvement, in addition to being of general benefit to the people of the city, township, county, or state, confers an additional special benefit upon nearby property, and that it is equitable to levy against such property assessments commensurate with those special benefits. A "benefit district" is laid out along the project and the costs to be assessed are apportioned among individual properties therein on various bases, such as area and proximity. Special assessments are widely used in financing the construction of city streets, but are employed only occasionally in the case of rural roads.

User Taxes. Recent decades have witnessed two outstanding developments in the field of highway finance.[27] One of these is the increased participation of the national and state governments in highway support. The other is the progressive shifting of the costs of road construction and maintenance to persons using the highways through the imposition of various user levies. Most important among these newer sources of highway revenue are motor fuel and motor-vehicle license taxes.[28] Every state now has a gallonage tax on gasoline used for highway travel and a system of license charges,[29] the revenue from which is used wholly or in part for highway purposes. Though in a few instances highway revenues from these sources are expended on state roads exclusively, most states now distribute substantial portions of such revenues to the local-government units. In 1961, highway-user revenues collected by the various states amounted to $5.5 billion. Of this sum, after payment of collection and administrative expenses, nearly $3.5 billion was expended for state highway purposes, $1.4 billion was distributed to local governments for roads and streets, and $424 million was devoted to nonhighway purposes.[30] About half of all state and local highway revenue is now derived from user levies,

[27] Cf. Dearing, *op. cit.,* 100.

[28] Other user levies include operators' license taxes, and ton-mile taxes on the travel of commercial vehicles.

[29] See below, Chap. XXIV, "Motor Fuel Taxes," "Motor Vehicle and Operators' License Taxes." These levies are employed also to a limited extent by city and county governments.

[30] In the opinion of many public officials the diversion of user revenues to nonhighway purposes is of doubtful propriety. See below, Chap. XXIV, "Motor Fuel Taxes."

and in some states such levies provide, apart from federal aid, almost the sole source of highway support.[31] Funds derived from federal aid and state user levies have enabled the state and local governments, during recent years, to effect vast improvements in their highway systems and at the same time to reduce substantially their property-tax levies for road purposes. In this connection it is to be further noted that Congress in 1956 established a Federal Highway Trust Fund into which is channeled the greater part of the proceeds from a 4-cents-per-gallon motor fuel tax and certain other federal user levies. From this fund, which now amounts to some $3 billion annually, are made all federal-aid highway payments including those for the interstate system. It will thus be seen that a very large proportion of overall highway costs in the nation is borne by motorists through user taxes.

Federal Aid. Prior to 1916, nonfederal highways in the United States were financed entirely from state and local funds. In that year Congress enacted the first Federal-Aid Highway Law, appropriating $75 million for cooperating with the states, over a five-year period, in the improvement of rural post roads. This act authorized the national government to pay up to 50 percent of the cost of approved projects, and provided for apportioning federal funds among the states on the three-fold basis of area, population, and mileage of rural delivery routes. Thereafter, financial aid to the states for highway purposes became an established federal policy, and the amount of aid provided steadily increased. In 1961, federal expenditures for highway aid amounted to $2.7 billion.

In the regular federal-aid program, grants are made to the states for construction purposes only, but failure on the part of any state to maintain a federal-aid road in accordance with federal standards renders the state ineligible for further construction grants. Regular federal-aid grants usually carry the requirement that they be matched, dollar for dollar, by nonfederal funds, though the match-fund requirement has not been applied to grants for elimination of railroad grade-crossings. As previously noted, the federal share of construction costs of highways in the interstate system is 90 percent. Prior to the depression, federal aid was limited to improvement of the primary-highway systems of the states. During the 1930's, however, federal funds were made available for urban extensions of federal-aid rural highways, for improving a limited mileage of secondary "feeder" roads, and for railroad grade-crossing elimination on highways of all classes; and this broadened aspect of the federal-aid program has been continuously expanded.[32]

[31] Cf. Dearing, *op. cit.,* 103, 104.
[32] United States Bureau of Public Roads, *Highway Progress: 1962,* pp. 21-24; Kennedy, *op. cit.,* 11-12; MacDonald, "Paving America," *loc. cit.*

Highway Bonds. Whether state and local highway funds are derived ultimately from property taxes, user taxes, or special assessments, it is commonly necessary, when new improvements involving heavy outlays are undertaken, to borrow money for the immediate defraying of construction costs. In such cases the state or local unit concerned usually issues and sells interest-bearing bonds to be paid from taxes or assessments subsequently collected. Highway debt thus incurred constitutes a substantial portion of all state and local indebtedness. In 1961 state indebtedness for highway purposes, to say nothing of local highway debt, amounted to more than $9.7 billion, though in that year eleven states had no indebtedness of this nature. Of the total indebtedness, less than one-third was secured by the general taxing power of the state, the remainder consisting of limited-obligation bonds secured by tolls or other road-user revenues.

AGRICULTURE AND CONSERVATION

Attaining the status of major governmental activities only during recent decades, but now gaining steadily in importance, are the promotion of agriculture and the conservation of natural resources. For many years the soil, timber, minerals, and other resources with which the American continent was so richly endowed were treated as if they were inexhaustible. Meager aids were provided for agriculture, and individual conservation projects were undertaken, but in general natural resources were exploited in a profligate manner. In time, however, wasteful practices took their toll and it came to be recognized that, if a reasonable proportion of the country's natural wealth was to be preserved for future generations, governmental action for its protection was imperative. Eventually, steps in this direction were taken by government at all levels. Though the agriculture and conservation programs of the national government have tended to take the spotlight, state and local activities in these fields are also of first-rate importance.

Under their police power and power to tax for the general welfare, states have passed many laws dealing with the protection of natural resources and related matters, such as conservation and recreation. Despite these laws and accompanying programs, however, one observer has concluded: "In most states some resource agencies are doing an effective job on some phases of resources administration, such as the development of state parks, the management of state lands, forest first prevention and the conservation of wild life; but no state is carrying on a well coordinated multiple-purpose program of resource administration." [33]

[33] Vincent Ostrom, "State Administration of Natural Resources in the West," *Amer. Polit. Sci. Rev.*, XLVII, 478-493 (June, 1953), at 493.

Administrative Organization

The state and local agencies concerned with agriculture and conservation vary considerably from state to state. The principal agency dealing with agriculture is usually either an agricultural board or a single-headed department of agriculture, the latter being now the more common. It is not to be inferred, however, that this agency carries on all of the state's agricultural functions and engages in no other activities. The board or department of agriculture is sometimes charged with the performance of nonagricultural functions, and in many instances some functions that would logically fall within its jurisdiction are lodged in other agencies. About half of the states have established a conservation department or commission in which conservation activities are more or less centralized. In other states conservation services are scattered among various independent agencies, and some use is ordinarily made of independent agencies even in states having conservation departments.[34] Closely related to state and local conservation services are the increasing number of public recreational activities.

At the local level, some functions pertaining to agriculture and conservation are performed directly by county and township governing boards. In most counties there is a county agricultural agent, and in many also a home demonstration agent. Some counties have a county veterinarian. In towns and townships there are sometimes found such local officers as surveyors of lumber, forest-fire wards, fish wardens, and weed commissioners. And, finally, there are the governing boards of special-purpose districts concerned with such matters as flood control, soil conservation, and weed control.

Education and Research

An important means of encouraging scientific agriculture and the conservation of natural resources is through the provision of educational and research facilities. Every state maintains an agricultural college [35] and in connection therewith an agricultural experiment station. Through these institutions the states offer agricultural education at the college level, conduct experiments in soil management and in the breeding and care of plants and livestock, carry on agricultural research and make the results thereof available in published form, and provide extension services of various kinds to farmers and stock raisers. A closely related activity is that of mapping and analyzing the natural resources of the state and conducting research with respect thereto. Work of this nature provides scientific infor-

---

[34] Clifford J. Hynning, *State Conservation of Resources*, 100-103.
[35] See above, Chap. XX, "Higher Education."

mation which aids the legislative authorities in determining public policy with respect to the state's resources and is generally useful in promoting their development and conservation. To carry on activities of this nature Illinois, for example, maintains a state geological survey, a state water survey, and a state natural history survey. All of these agencies have their principal offices on the campus of the state university and cooperate with related university departments in the performance of their respective functions.

Also primarily educational in nature is the counseling and demonstration work of the county agricultural agents and home demonstration agents. This work, carried on cooperatively by the county, state, and federal governments, is of vast importance in American rural life. The work of the agricultural agent concerns such matters as soil-use programs, the growing and marketing of farm crops, livestock improvement, boys' and girls' club work, and general farm management. County agents have participated actively in the program of land-use planning sponsored by the United States Department of Agriculture and the state agricultural colleges.[36] Home demonstration agents advise and instruct women concerning the selection and preparation of foods, balancing of diets, sewing, child care, gardening, poultry raising, and a large variety of related subjects.[37]

Regulation and Promotion of Agriculture

Regulatory and promotional activities in the field of agriculture vary from state to state and to some extent from community to community. Those found in a given state or community will depend in part upon the nature of the principal farm products and in part upon the attitude of those who make and administer the laws. So numerous are the activities engaged in that it is possible to mention here only some of those more generally pursued and a few others which, though less widespread, are of special interest.

Among the major activities of most state departments of agriculture are those concerned with the suppression and eradication of animal and plant diseases and insect pests. Control measures include information and inspectional services, and sometimes the destruction of infected plants and animals. In the case of livestock there are vaccination programs, frequently administered cooperatively by state and county vet-

---

[36] See John D. Lewis, "Democratic Planning in Agriculture," *Amer. Polit. Sci. Rev.*, XXXV, 232-249, 454-469 (Apr., June, 1941).

[37] See above, Chap. XIII, "Other County Officers and Boards." Further discussion may be found in Clyde F. Snider, *Local Government in Rural America* (Appleton-Century-Crofts, New York, 1957), 457-471.

erinarians. A common measure for plant protection is the licensing and inspection of nurseries. In the absence of federal quarantine regulations, states may establish quarantines to prevent the bringing in of diseases or pests from outside their borders.[38] The plant diseases and insect pests with which control programs of varying types are concerned include black stem rust, Dutch elm disease, the Japanese beetle, the European corn borer, and the Mexican fruitfly. Hoof-and-mouth disease, brucellosis (Bang's disease) in cattle, hog cholera, and bovine tuberculosis are among the animal diseases that are subjects of control measures.

Of particular value to farmers are the weed-control activities of state and local governments. State agricultural departments publicize information concerning noxious weeds and their control, and sometimes also engage directly in extermination activities.[39] Many states have laws requiring landowners to cut weeds on their premises and also, in some instances, those on adjoining highways. It is commonly provided that, where landowners fail to comply with such requirements, the work shall be performed by a designated public official, frequently a local weed commissioner. Costs of the work are then assessed against the land and collected in the same manner as taxes, or by such other procedure as the statutes may prescribe. In some states special weed-eradication districts are organized for carrying on weed-control work. Districts of this nature are functioning in such states as California, Utah, and Wyoming, and are extensively utilized in Nebraska.[40] The weeds against which particularly active campaigns are waged in various states include bindweed, Russian knapweed, Canada thistle, perennial peppergrass, puncture vine, hoary cress, leafy spurge, and barberry bushes.

A serious hazard of livestock and poultry raising, especially in the more sparsely settled western states, is the danger to flocks and herds from predatory animals.[41] As a means of lessening this hazard most states provide systems of bounties for the killing of predators, such as wolves, coyotes, mountain lions, and foxes. The bounty payments are often made by counties, and are sometimes financed from special levies upon the livestock and poultry to be protected. Thus, for bounty purposes, Wyoming counties levy an ad valorem tax on sheep, Utah counties an ad valorem tax on sheep and turkeys, and South Dakota counties a head tax on sheep and cattle. In some states, including Michigan and Missouri, the

[38] On the matter of federal and state quarantines, see George R. Taylor, Edgar L. Burtis, and Frederick V. Waugh, *Barriers to Internal Trade in Farm Products* (U.S. Govt. Printing Office, Washington, 1939), 85-97.

[39] An excellent technical treatise on control methods is Wilfred W. Robbins, Alden S. Crafts, and Richard N. Raynor, *Weed Control* (McGraw-Hill, New York, 1942).

[40] John C. Bollens, *Special District Governments in the United States* (Univ. of Calif. Press, Berkeley, 1957), 176-178.

[41] See Michael Norman, "The War Against the Predators," *Outdoor Life*, Vol. CIII, No. 3 (Mar., 1949), 37-39, 125-127.

laws authorize employment of state hunters to aid in predatory-animal extermination.[42]

State laws of various types seek to aid agricultural producers in marketing their products. Examples are statutes regulating the grading, packaging, and labeling of farm, dairy, and horticultural products, and the marketing of fresh fruits and vegetables through commission merchants. Laws of this nature are usually administered by the state department of agriculture. Of special interest in the marketing category, since it involves the application to agricultural production of proration principles applied in several states to oil and gas,[43] is a California law first enacted in 1933. This statute authorizes the establishment, by vote of the producers within marketing zones, of compulsory proration marketing programs for agricultural products. Enacted avowedly as a measure for conserving the state's agricultural wealth, another purpose of the law would seem to be maintenance of agricultural prices through production control. Some states regulate the price of milk.[44]

Several states at one time or another have financed, wholly or in part, advertising campaigns designed to stimulate sales of some of their major farm products. Among products which have been the beneficiaries of state advertising are milk in New York, New Jersey, and Massachusetts; dairy products in Wisconsin; poultry in Massachusetts; citrus fruits in Florida; apples in Michigan, Idaho, and Washington; wines in California; potatoes in Maine and Idaho; and sweet potatoes in Louisiana. In some instances the money expended by the states on such advertising has been appropriated from the state general fund, and in others it has been raised by special taxes on the sale of the products advertised.[45] An older form of agricultural promotion is the financial assistance frequently given to state and county fairs. Fairs thus subsidized by state and county governments seek to encourage scientific agriculture by offering prizes for the best exhibits of livestock, poultry, and farm produce.

Soil Conservation

One of the nation's most basic resources is its soil, and conservation of soil productivity is essential to the national economy. Soil is rendered nonproductive in two principal ways: (1) by depletion of fertility through

[42] Cf. Minnesota Legislative Research Committee, *The Control of Predatory Animals* (St. Paul, 1952). For a critique of the bounty system, see Edwin H. Cooper, "Is the Bounty System of Predator Control Practical?" *County Progress* (County Judges and Commissioners Assn. of Texas), Vol. XXXV, No. 12 (Dec., 1958), 9, 14.

[43] See below, "Oil and Gas."

[44] See above, Chap. XIX, "Sanitation." For an interesting discussion of milk price regulation in Florida, see Harmon Ziegler, *The Florida Milk Commission Changes Minimum Prices* (Interuniversity Case Program, Univ. of Ala. Press, University, Ala., 1963).

[45] Taylor, Burtis, and Waugh, *op. cit.*, 98-104; *Acts of La.*, 1942, No. 294.

continued cropping and (2) by actual loss of topsoil through erosion.[46] Of these, erosion is the more spectacular and ultimately the more serious. Land that is merely "crop poor" can be restored to productivity, and fairly quickly, by use of commercial fertilizers, the planting of leguminous and other soil-building crops, crop rotation, and other soil-building practices. But so slow is the natural process by which soil is formed from its parent materials—it is believed to require anywhere from 300 to 1,000 years or more to produce a single inch of topsoil—that land from which all the topsoil has been eroded may for practical purposes be regarded as permanently ruined.[47] When the country was first opened for settlement, forests, grass, and other natural cover provided adequate protection against erosion; but, with the removal of much of this protective cover and the placing of vast areas in cultivation, the soil, in the absence of proper conservation practices, became a ready prey to the two principal eroding forces—water and wind.

The extent to which erosion has already taken place in the United States and the rate at which it is now progressing are nothing short of appalling. It is reliably estimated that some 282 million acres of land have already been ruined by erosion, and that another 775 million acres have been moderately damaged.[48] Available measurements indicate that 3 billion tons or more of solid matter is washed annually from American fields and pastures—some 730 million tons being deposited each year in the Gulf of Mexico by the Mississippi river alone.[49] Wind erosion has been especially devastating during certain periods in the "dust bowl" area centering in western Oklahoma and Kansas and eastern Colorado, where thousands of acres of grassland have been plowed and planted to wheat. On a single day during the dust storm of 1934, according to one estimate, 300 million tons of rich topsoil were lifted from the Great Plains to be deposited in places where it would cause damage and discomfort.[50] The cost of erosion in diminished soil productivity in the United States was estimated some years ago at $400 million annually.[51]

The most comprehensive program for erosion prevention and soil conservation yet undertaken in this country is that carried on by local soil conservation districts in cooperation with the Soil Conservation Service of the United States Department of Agriculture.[52] This program had its be-

46 Cf. Stuart Chase, *Rich Land, Poor Land*, 37.

47 Hugh H. Bennett, *Soil Conservation*, 8.

48 Hugh H. Bennett, *Elements of Soil Conservation*, 28.

49 Bennett, *Soil Conservation*, 9.

50 Stuart Chase, "When the Crop Lands Go," *Harper's Mag.*, CLXXIII, 225-233 (Aug., 1936).

51 Bennett, *Soil Conservation*, 11.

52 A trenchant discussion of the program and of intergovernmental relationships involved therein may be found in Herman Walker, Jr., and W. Robert Parks, "Soil Conservation Districts: Local Democracy in a National Program," *Jour. of Politics*, VIII, 538-549 (Nov., 1946). See also, Bollens, *op. cit.*, 157-167.

ginning when, shortly after the creation of the Soil Conservation Service in 1935, the Department of Agriculture drafted and recommended to the states a model enabling act for the establishment of soil conservation districts. In 1937, twenty-two states enacted soil conservation district laws following rather closely the provisions of this model. Thereafter the enactment of enabling legislation and the organization of districts proceeded apace, and today every state has a soil conservation law. By 1963 more than 2,900 districts had been organized in the 50 states, embracing 97 percent of the nation's farms and ranches.[53] The work of these districts constitutes a major, if belated, step in protecting our vital soil resources.

Though the organization and powers of soil conservation districts vary in detail among the different states, most of the enabling statutes follow, at least in some measure, the model act of the Department of Agriculture, and the general pattern is much the same. Local districts are usually established, under the supervision of a state soil conservation agency, by vote of the owners or occupiers of land within the area concerned.[54] In some instances district boundaries are made to follow county lines, each district embracing one or more entire counties. In many cases, however, county lines are disregarded and an effort is made to include within a particular district land confronted with a common erosion problem. A district, for example, may consist of a watershed, a type-of-farming area, or an extent-of-erosion area, and thus embrace less than an entire county, or all or parts of several counties. This is only logical since erosion is no respecter of traditional political boundaries. The governing body of each local district is a board of supervisors or directors which in most states consists of five members, three being elected by the farmers of the district and two appointed by the state agency.

The powers of soil conservation districts are ordinarily of two kinds, districts being authorized: (1) to formulate and carry out cooperative erosion-control projects, and (2) to adopt compulsory land-use regulations. In practice, most districts have confined themselves to exercising powers of the first type, under which erosion-control programs are put into effect through voluntary agreements between the district and its farmers. Each district, through its boards of supervisors, enters into a "memorandum of understanding" with the Soil Conservation Service with respect to the district's program and work plan as a whole and the receiving of federal assistance. Cooperative agreements are then made between the district and individual landowners and occupiers concerning erosion-control work and soil-conservation practices on their respective

[53] Donald A. Williams, "Soil Conservation," *The Book of the States*, 1964-65, pp. 496-498.

[54] The state agency often includes in its membership the principal state agricultural officer and the director of the state's agricultural experiment station. Some states restrict voting on district matters to *landowners* while others extend the voting privilege to all occupiers of land, whether owners or tenants.

farms.[55] Measures and practices provided for under these agreements include such matters as terracing, contour plowing, strip cropping, and the return of natural cover. The more drastic power of enacting land-use ordinances can be exercised by the district supervisors only with the approval of the landowners or occupiers in a referendum election. When so approved, however, such regulations are enforceable by judicial process. Though some districts in the dust bowl have adopted compulsory regulations prohibiting the plowing of grassland, the ordinance power of soil conservation districts has on the whole been little used.[56] Although there are exceptions, most districts have neither taxing nor borrowing power. Labor, materials, and equipment necessary for district activities are contributed in part by the farmers benefited and in part by the state and county governments and the Soil Conservation Service. Staff members of the latter agency supply necessary technical assistance in making plans and surveys.

Recently there has been an effort to tie water conservation activities to the work of soil conservation districts. Under 1954 federal legislation some forty states have passed legislation tending to speed up soil and water conservation. More than a dozen states have provided for creation of subdistricts of soil conservation districts in watershed areas needing flood prevention and water management; and in some instances taxing and borrowing powers have been conferred upon districts for the financing of district or subdistrict programs. Of particular significance are the laws of several states authorizing counties, cities, and towns to participate in watershed protection and flood-prevention projects and to provide financial assistance for such activities.[57]

Forestry

Forest lands serve as sources of lumber, facilitate the impounding of water and the checking of erosion, provide natural habitat for wildlife, and afford recreational facilities. For all of these reasons it is highly desirable that forest resources be used wisely and protected from waste. The activities of state and local governments designed to further these ends fall into two principal categories: (1) promotion of private forestry, and (2) ownership and management of public forests.

The most common activities in the first of these classes is the protection of private forest lands from fire. Practically every state has a forestry department or its equivalent which, in cooperation with the fed-

[55] H. H. Bennett, "The Soil Conservation Service: Organization and Operations," *The Book of the States*, 1948-49, pp. 289-300. Cf. Bollens, *op. cit.*, 162-163.

[56] Cf. "Legal Techniques for Promoting Soil Conservation," *Yale Law Jour.*, L, 1056-1070 (Apr., 1941).

[57] Donald A. Williams, "Soil Conservation," *The Book of the States*, 1962-63, pp. 466-470.

eral government, provides such protection. It is estimated that, of 435 million acres of nonfederal forest and watershed lands in need of organized fire control, some 402 million acres are now protected under federal-state programs. Other functions of state forestry agencies have been broadened in recent years and now include such activities as insect and disease control, watershed protection, flood prevention, assistance in woodland management, and the administration of forest-practice laws.[58]

Most states provide at least some assistance to private forestry in the form of advice and demonstrations. Some maintain state nurseries from which trees for planting are supplied to private landowners at cost. A few states have laws for the control of cutting on privately-owned forest lands. A device employed by several states in an effort to foster conservation is the "forest crop law" deferring tax collections on privately-owned timber until the time of cutting.[59] Legislation of this character, under which timber is exempt from taxation as long as it stands but is taxed when cut, is designed to discourage premature cutting. In practice, however, the forest crop laws do not seem to have been highly successful in inducing better forestry management.[60]

State, county, and municipal forests serve both conservation and recreational purposes as described later in this chapter. State-owned forests exist in practically all important timber states and have a combined area, including forest parks, of more than 23 million acres. Leading states in state forest area are Minnesota, Michigan, New York, Oregon, Pennsylvania, and Washington, with more than a million acres each.[61] State forest lands in the eastern states have been acquired largely by purchase, and those in the West by federal grant and reversion through tax delinquency.[62] Counties in many states are empowered to establish county forests, in some instances by purchase, in others by setting aside tax-reverted lands, and in still others by either of these means. Leading the states in the actual establishment of county forests is Wisconsin where, by 1947, nearly 2 million acres of tax-reverted lands had been set aside as forests in twenty-seven counties.[63] County forests are to be found in various other states, but in no instance does the area within a single state approach that in Wisconsin. Numerous municipalities and park districts

[58] William J. Stahl, "State Forestry Administration," *The Book of the States,* 1962-63, pp. 480-485.

[59] A. D. Folweiler, "The Political Economy of Forest Conservation in the United States," *Jour. of Land and Pub. Util. Econ.,* XX, 202-216 (Aug., 1944).

[60] Cf. Charles H. Stoddard, Jr., "Future of Private Forest Land Ownership in the Northern Lake States," *Jour. of Land and Pub. Util. Econ.,* XVIII, 267-283 Aug., 1942).

[61] Stahl, *op. cit.*

[62] A. F. Gustafson and others, *Conservation in the United States* (2nd ed.), 231.

[63] F. G. Wilson, "County Forests of Wisconsin," *State Govt.,* XX, 116-117 (Apr., 1947).

over the country maintain forest areas as parts of local park systems. Some state forests are managed for the production of timber, and nearly all are used for recreational purposes. Most county and municipal forests are used as recreational areas, some also serving additional purposes such as the protection of local water supplies.[64]

Rural Zoning

Several states now permit counties, townships, or both to adopt rural zoning regulations designed, among other things, to preserve natural resources and discourage the cultivation of sub-marginal land. A typical zoning ordinance for rural areas divides the territory zoned into three classes of districts—forestry, recreational, and agricultural or unrestricted. By prohibiting the cultivation of lands situated in districts of the first two types, regulations of this character seek to prevent the despoiling of recreational, timber, and other natural values on land unsuited to agriculture. Zoning is also advantageous in restraining the settlement of farmers in remote places where schools, roads, and other essential public services can be provided only in inferior quality and at high unit costs. Rural zoning has been found especially valuable in some of the sparsely settled "cutover" regions of northern Michigan, Wisconsin, and Minnesota.[65]

Oil and Gas [66]

In the conservation of mineral resources, state activities have been principally concerned with oil and gas. The wasteful exploitation of those products which has necessitated regulatory action has been the result, in no small measure, of the widespread recognition in law of the "rule of capture." Under this rule, any landowner is free to take from a pool underlying his and neighboring properties whatever oil and gas he can draw off through wells drilled on his premises. When, therefore, a well drilled

[64] Cf. Gustafson and others, *op. cit.*, 231-232.

[65] Cf. W. A. Rowlands and F. B. Trenk, *Rural Zoning Ordinances in Wisconsin* (Extension Service, Coll. of Agr., Univ. of Wis., Madison, 1936); Louis A. Wolfanger, *Your Community and Township Zoning* (Agricultural Experiment Station, Mich. State Coll., East Lansing, 1945); P. A. Herbert, "Michigan Enacts a Rural Zoning Law," *Jour. of Land and Pub. Util. Econ.*, XI, 309-310 (Aug., 1935); William F. Musbach and Melville C. Williams, "Rural Zoning in Minnesota," *Ibid.*, XVI, 105-109 (Feb., 1940). For a discussion of the related subject of planning (primarily Wisconsin experience), see Fred A. Clarenbach, "The Planning Function in Rural Government," *Amer. Jour. of Econ. and Sociol.*, XI, 261-279 (Apr., 1952).

[66] J. C. Hunter, "Conservation of Our Oil and Gas Resources," in Leonard M. Fanning, ed., *Our Oil Resources*, 53-70; Northcutt Ely, *Oil Conservation through Interstate Agreement*; Illinois Legislative Council, *Oil Legislation in Illinois* (Ill. Legis. Council, Springfield, 1938); Northcutt Ely, "The Conservation of Oil," *Harvard Law Rev.*, LI, 1209-1244 (May, 1938).

in a new region is found to yield oil or gas in paying quantities, the owners of other properties within the area of the pool are faced with the alternatives of having wells drilled on their premises or of seeing the underlying wealth drawn off through the wells of their neighbors. Confronted with this situation, the owners and lessees of land in the vicinity of that on which a discovery has been made usually hasten to drill on their properties. Moreover, since the amount of oil and gas that can be produced within a relatively short time depends in considerable measure upon the number of wells in production, each producer tends to crowd his property with wells. The drilling of wells in excessive number, thus encouraged by the rule of capture, is a wasteful practice in two respects. In the first place, undue amounts of money are expended on drilling, since the oil and gas could ultimately be recovered through a smaller number of wells; and, secondly, an excessive number of wells in a given pool actually reduces the total amount of oil which can eventually be recovered. Oil is forced into wells by pressure of gas associated with the oil, and of water underlying the oil and pressing upward on it. When the rock cap overlying a pool is penetrated by wells in large number, the reservoir pressure is thereby dissipated and the amount of oil ultimately recoverable is reduced. On the other hand, moderation in drilling conserves reservoir pressure and increases ultimate recovery.

During the early years of the oil and gas industry, waste was rampant. This was especially true of gas, the operators being primarily interested in oil production. Billions of cubic feet of gas were blown into the air in an effort to bring oil into the wells, the escaping gas sometimes being burned in giant flambeau lights. Other wasteful practices included failure to protect oil sands from water penetration and to plug abandoned wells. Estimates indicate that prior to 1918 the waste of natural gas in many years equaled the consumption.[67]

The earliest state regulatory laws relative to oil and gas merely sought to prohibit wasteful practices such as those just mentioned and to require the observance of conservation measures, and this is the type of legislation most widely in effect even today. Examples of such legislation are provisions, enacted in Texas as early as 1899, which require the plugging of abandoned wells and the casing off of water-bearing strata, and prohibit the permitting of gas to escape into the air or to be burned in flambeau lights.[68] To reduce well-crowding, several states have enacted spacing legislation conferring upon administrative agencies authority to regulate the distance between wells. A special problem in connection with spacing requirements is presented by small parcels of land and tracts of irregular shape. Some states seek to meet this problem by providing for

[67] National Resources Committee, *Energy Resources and National Policy* (U.S. Govt. Printing Office, Washington, 1939), 188.

[68] Hunter, "Conservation of Our Oil and Gas Resources," *loc. cit.*, 55.

the "pooling" of such properties, either by voluntary agreement or on order of a state regulatory agency. Under such a system, for example, if one well is permitted for each twenty acres, tracts of less than that area are pooled with lands of an adjoining owner or owners so as to form a twenty-acre unit. The owners of the properties in this unit then share proportionately in the expense of drilling and operation and in the production.

A more recent and more drastic type of state regulation is production control in the form of proration—the enforcement of a system of production quotas fixed by a designated administrative agency. The proration process involves two steps: (1) assigning production quotas to the respective oil and gas fields of the state, and (2) allocating the total production of each field among the producing wells therein. The total outlet for a particular field may be fixed, depending upon statutory provision, either at the market demand or at the quantity that the field can produce without physical waste. Well quotas are determined variously on the basis of comparative potential production of the wells, relative acreage per well, well pressures, a flat rate per well, or other factors or combination of factors.[69] Proration has a two-fold objective. It seeks: (1) to conserve reservoir pressure and thus bring about more economical production, and (2) through production limitation to effect a balance between supply and demand and thus maintain crude-oil prices. Beginning with Oklahoma in 1915, several of the leading oil-producing states have enacted proration legislation applicable to oil, gas, or both.

Because of the interstate character of the market, effective oil and gas regulation requires that somewhat comparable standards be observed in all states of major production. If a single state requires scientific conservation practices or imposes drastic production limits, its producers will suffer thereby in competition with those of other states. In recognition of this fact, an interstate compact for the conservation of oil and gas was put into effect in 1935 among the states of Colorado, Illinois, Kansas, New Mexico, Oklahoma, and Texas.[70] Additional states subsequently adhered to the compact, and by 1963 thirty states, together producing most of the nation's gas and crude oil, were parties thereto. Member states reciprocally pledged themselves to enact and enforce conservation legislation. Consisting of a representative from each compacting state, an Interstate Oil Compact Commission holds meetings for the discussion of conservation problems, appoints committees to make special studies, and makes recommendations to the respective states.[71] Also deserving of mention as

[69] Ely, *Oil Conservation through Interstate Agreement*, 131.

[70] Wilfred D. Webb, "The Interstate Oil Compact—Theory and Practice," *Southwestern Soc. Sci. Quar.*, XXI, 293-301 (Mar., 1941).

[71] Arthur S. Davenport, "The Interstate Oil Compact Commission," *The Book of the States*, 1948-49, pp. 40-43. Three additional states had adhered to the compact

an instrument for strengthening state conservation programs is the federal law, first enacted in 1935 and known as the Connally Hot Oil Act,[72] which prohibits the interstate transportation of oil produced in excess of state restrictive regulations.

Fish and Game

State laws for the protection of wildlife have their basis not only in the police and taxing powers which support legislation for the conservation of other natural resources but also in the legal theory that the state owns all wild game within its borders,—that it has, in other words, a property right which it holds in trust for its inhabitants. The ownership theory is especially important because it enables states to reserve the privilege of hunting and fishing within their respective borders to their own residents exclusively, or to extend it to nonresidents on special conditions. Were it not for the doctrine of ownership, discriminatory measures of this nature would be invalid as violating the "interstate citizenship" clause of the United States Constitution.[73]

The most widely-used means of affording protection to wildlife is through prohibitions or restrictions upon the taking and killing of fish and game. State laws and regulations establish "closed seasons," during which the taking of specified varieties of fish and game is prohibited, and fix "bag limits," restricting takings during open seasons. Fishermen, hunters, and trappers are required to obtain licenses, issued by a state conservation department or fish and game commission but usually obtainable from designated local offices. Fees charged for licenses are almost universally higher for nonresidents of the state than for residents. In most states provision is made for a force of state game wardens charged with patrolling the fields, woods, and streams and enforcing the provisions of the fish-and-game code.

Another major method of preserving wildlife is through propagation activities. These ordinarily take two forms: (1) the establishment of refuges, and (2) the operation of fish hatcheries and game farms and, in Massachusetts, a lobster hatchery. A game refuge is an area set aside and

---

as associate members. Member states and associate members are listed in *Ibid.*, 1962-63, p. 274. Concerning the compact and its administration, see Blakely M. Murphy, "The Interstate Compact to Conserve Oil and Gas: An Experiment in Coöperative State Production Control," *Miss. Law Jour.*, XVII, 314-346 (Mar.-May, 1946); Blakely M. Murphy, "The Administrative Mechanism of the Interstate Compact to Conserve Oil and Gas: The Interstate Oil Compact Commission, 1935-1948," *Tulane Law Rev.*, XXII, 384-402 (Mar., 1948); Richard H. Leach, "The Interstate Oil Compact: A Study of Success," *Okla. Law Rev.*, X, 274-288 (Aug., 1957).

[72] Cf. Hunter, "Conservation of Our Oil and Gas Resources," *loc. cit.*, 59.

[73] Robert H. Connery, *Governmental Problems in Wild Life Conservation* (Columbia Univ. Press, New York, 1935), Chap. 4.

administered for the protection and propagation of game animals. Refuges vary widely in size and character. There are, for example, big-game refuges, small-game refuges, waterfowl refuges, and refuges in which all wildlife is protected. Most states now maintain several refuges, some of them of vast extent. Some refuges are located on land owned or leased by the state—in some instances on state-park lands—while others are maintained on privately-owned land closed to hunting. Often particular areas, in an effort to replenish a depleted game population, are closed to hunting for a limited number of years only. The practice of temporary closure is also commonly employed with respect to fishing in particular lakes and streams or parts thereof as a means of restoring depleted fishlife.[74] The purpose of refuges is to afford protected areas wherein wildlife may propagate without molestation. Much of the stock reared therein ultimately overflows into surrounding territory, where it is available, during open seasons, to hunters and fishermen. The supply of fish and game, as it is depleted by fishing and hunting, is replenished to some extent from fish hatcheries and game farms. Most states operate one or more fish hatcheries, and from these millions of young fish annually are placed in the country's streams and lakes. Some states have established state game farms, principally for breeding game birds, while others buy stock for release from farms which are privately owned.[75]

Yet another phase of wildlife preservation is the extermination of predatory animals, considered earlier in this chapter in its relation to domestic poultry and livestock. Many predators are enemies of game birds and animals as well as of farm fowls and domestic livestock, and their extermination, through bounties or otherwise, is as essential to wildlife conservation as to agriculture.

RECREATION

Scientific advances in agriculture, commerce, and industry have progressively made possible the production and distribution of more goods with less human effort. Shortened work days and weeks, together with labor-saving devices in the home, have greatly increased the amount of leisure at the disposal of the nation's populace, and the use of this leisure has become one of our major social problems. Properly used, leisure promotes the health, culture, and general well-being of a people; misused, it is likely to foster delinquency and crime. For this reason, promotion of the pleasant and profitable use of leisure is now recognized as

[74] Ira N. Gabrielson, *Wildlife Conservation* (2nd ed.), Chap. 16; Ira N. Gabrielson, *Wildlife Refuges*, Chap. 15. The latter chapter includes a brief description of state refuges in the respective states.

[75] Connery, *op. cit.*, 198-199.

a legitimate objective of government, and government at all levels has undertaken recreation activities designed to encourage the wholesome employment of leisure hours. The problem of providing recreation facilities is most acute in urban areas, and it is therefore not surprising that the cities have taken the lead in public recreation work. Nevertheless, the recreation activities of states and counties are also significant.

One type of governmental activity in the recreation field is the licensing and regulation of commercial recreation establishments such as motion picture houses, dance halls, billiard parlors, and bowling alleys. Such regulatory activities are for the most part in the hands of the city governments. However, some places of amusement are located in rural areas, and in numerous instances others have been established just beyond city boundaries to escape municipal regulation. For these reasons, many states now confer upon counties the authority to regulate amusement establishments outside the limits of incorporated municipalities. Although government regulation of commercial recreation is important, it tends at present to be overshadowed by the provision of recreation facilities at public expense.[76]

Public Park Systems

The most common type of public recreation facility is the public park. Parks vary widely in size and character. Some are a city block or less in area, while others comprise many acres. Some have been preserved in their natural state as "wild" parks, whereas others have been highly developed by planting and landscaping. Some are maintained principally for their scenic beauty, while others are equipped with various play facilities to encourage active forms of relaxation. The park movement in this country is almost entirely a matter of the last hundred years, and during recent decades especially it has made rapid progress. Park areas have expanded enormously, and at the same time the variety of recreational facilities provided in parks has greatly increased.

Municipal Parks. A 1960 survey by The National Recreation Association reported 24,710 municipal and county parks and other nonschool public recreation areas with a total area of more than a million acres.[77]

---

[76] Good general treatises on the subject are George Hjelte and Jay S. Shivers, *Public Administration of Park and Recreational Facilities;* Harold D. Meyer and Charles K. Brightbill, *Recreation Administration: A Guide to its Practices.* See also Jay B. Nash, "Standards of Play and Recreation Administration," *Nat. Mun. Rev.,* XX, 485-506 (July, 1931, Supp.); Arthur M. Williams, "Postwar Planning for Recreation," *Pub. Management,* XXVI, 40-44 (Feb., 1944); Garrett G. Eppley, "State Government's Role in Recreation," *State Govt.,* XXI, 107-109 (May, 1948).

[77] Arthur Williams, "Parks and Recreation—Developments in 1961," *The Municipal Year Book* (Int. City Mgrs'. Assn., Chicago), 1962, pp. 468-471.

There is a rough rule of thumb widely accepted by park administrators to the effect that an adequate municipal park system requires an acre of park land for each one hundred city inhabitants. In practice, many cities still fall far short of this standard, though the number meeting it is constantly increasing and some cities have exceeded it. Adequacy of a city's park system, however, is not a matter of acreage alone but depends fully as much upon such factors as the number, type, size, distribution, and development of individual parks.[78] Since different types of parks serve different purposes, variety is essential, and the park properties should be distributed over the city so as to be as generally accessible as possible.

Among the types of properties commonly included in a city park system are small and large in-town parks, neighborhood parks, children's playgrounds, and recreation areas of various kinds. Some systems include outlying forest parks and parkways. Recreation activities provided by municipal parks are many and varied. Those most frequently engaged in are baseball, softball, tennis, picnicking, swimming, horseshoes, and band concerts. Others less common include football, basketball, volleyball, winter sports, social dancing, community sings, nature study, motion pictures, boating, and organized hiking.[79]

County Parks. Relatively few American counties maintain public parks. However, in a survey of some years ago 152 counties reported 779 park properties with an aggregate area of almost 200,000 acres, and it is known that some additional counties have park areas. In general, county parks are larger and less highly developed than city parks. Though some are located within municipalities, and are then likely to be similar to city parks, it is probable that more than two-thirds of all county parks are outside city limits. Where park facilities are provided by all three governments, county parks tend to bridge the gap between city park systems on the one hand and state parks on the other.[80]

State Parks. State park systems, varying widely in nature and extent, are now maintained in all states. At the end of 1960, it was reported that there were 2,664 state parks and related types of recreational areas in the fifty states, embracing a total of more than 5.6 million acres. State parks provide places for citizens to camp, fish, and indulge in various other forms of sport. Many also provide excellent hotel facilities for vacationers. The extent to which these areas serve the recreational needs of the public is indicated in some measure by the fact that they are currently

[78] National Recreation Association, *Municipal and County Parks in the United States, 1940* (Nat. Recreation Assn., New York, 1942), 2-5.
[79] *Ibid.*, 5, 23.
[80] *Ibid.*, 47.

attracting visitors at the rate of some 260 million annually.[81] Though public forests, as indicated earlier in this chapter, are maintained primarily
for conservation purposes, they are important also as recreation areas.
Many state and county forests include campgrounds and picnic areas, and
some permit hunting and fishing.

Other Recreation Activities

Public playgrounds other than those maintained in connection with
parks are quite common.[82] In many cities, school playgrounds are opened
to the public during the summer months. Recreation supervisors for such
areas may be provided by the school authorities, by a city recreation department, or cooperatively by the two agencies. The larger cities in growing number maintain, under the jurisdiction of their park departments or
otherwise, such specialized recreation facilities as golf courses, swimming
pools, camping grounds, auditoriums, and stadiums. Less frequently found
are municipal museums and zoological gardens.

Organized recreation programs are now publicly supported in
many communities. Though in some instances these programs are administered by park or school authorities, the separate municipal recreation
commission or department is rapidly becoming more common. The activities comprising public recreation programs, in order to have as wide an
appeal as possible, are extremely varied in character. In addition to those
mentioned above as being provided by municipal parks, they include
reading rooms, table games, dramatics, arts and crafts, and many others.
Among the physical facilities for the various activities are public parks
and playfields, community-center buildings, and school buildings. In some
instances, state recreation agencies have been established to encourage
and assist local communities in the provision of organized recreation.

Some conception of the variety and extent of present-day community recreation facilities may be gained from statistical data compiled by
the National Recreation Association. As of 1960, report was made to the
Association of public recreation facilities being provided by 2,762 local-
government agencies exclusive of counties. These various recreation programs were administered by nearly 100,000 employed recreation leaders
and 277,000 volunteer workers, and involved operating expenditures by
2,208 reporting cities of $357 million.[83] Clearly, public recreation is rapidly
becoming a major governmental function.

[81] *The Book of the States,* 1962-63, pp. 486-490; Gustafson and others, *op. cit.,*
275.

[82] On playgrounds and their administration, see Jay B. Nash, *The Organization
and Administration of Playgrounds and Recreation* (A. S. Barnes & Co., New York,
1927); National Recreation Association, *Playgrounds; their Administration and Operation* (A. S. Barnes and Co., New York, 1936).

[83] Williams, "Parks and Recreation—Developments in 1961," *loc. cit.*

PLANNING

A governmental activity which touches on many aspects of state and local government is that of planning. Physical planning in particular touches on several of the programs considered in this chapter. Planning has different meanings to different persons, but generally it is designed to provide orderly physical, social, and economic development, to aid government to anticipate future needs, and to develop priorities.

Official planning agencies have now been established by many state and local governments. The number of state agencies and programs is increasing, and this is true also at the municipal level. Special federal programs have been designed to encourage planning at all levels of government. At the local level, planning and zoning are often thought to be closely related, although professional planners would emphasize that these are two distinct activities.

State Planning

Recently there has been considerable expansion of state activities in the related fields of planning and economic development. Over the years, planning at both the state and local levels has met with mixed reactions, primarily because planning is inherently long-range in nature. Often its results in the form of economies in services or facilities, and better arrangement of land use, seem unspectacular. "Thus, the planning process offers no immediate dramatic and novel exhibit comparable to the interstate highway system nor does it capture the news as did Sputnik I." [84]

For state governments, and for other governments as well, planning services mean assistance to the chief executive and the legislative body in fulfilling the following obligations: [85]

1. Determination of short- and long-range objectives.
2. Getting all relevant information and securing an adequate understanding of the problems.
3. Deciding on priority and balance of programs within a flexible schedule.
4. Coordination of effort for the most effective and economical accomplishment of aims.

One of the most comprehensive state plans was adopted recently in the new state of Hawaii. There a department of planning and research

[84] Harold V. Miller, "State Planning and Development," *The Book of the States*, 1962-63, pp. 451-455.
[85] Council of State Governments, *Planning Services for State Governments*, 7.

has been established, headed by a director with cabinet rank. The Hawaii General State Plan for 1960-80 treats on a statewide basis such elements as physical conditions, existing land use, future land use and subdivision, population distribution, public facilities, parks, and the development and utilization of fresh-water resources.[86]

Closely related to state planning efforts are the new state programs in economic development. Some of these are aimed at stimulating industrial development, while others are intended to encourage tourism.[87]

Local Planning

Planning at the local level has had a long history. One small New England town (Walpole, Massachusetts) adopted a comprehensive long-range plan as early as 1913. Such plans for individual communities provide guidance in making decisions on such matters as location of new schools, parks, utility extensions, and street improvements, and the design and construction of new subdivisions.

Most cities of any considerable size now have plans and planning agencies. In a 1961 survey of cities of over 10,000 population, 645 of the 1,227 cities reporting had comprehensive plans for community development, and an additional 406 said that such plans were in the process of preparation. Only 176 cities reported that they had no plan, and that none was in process. The survey also showed that 1,226 of 1,311 cities reporting had official planning agencies, and that 401 of these had full-time planning directors. As would be expected, more large cities than small had such directors.[88]

As previously mentioned, one reason for increased local planning activities has been the stimulus afforded by federal programs. Federal aid is now available for open-space planning activities, for the planning of mass transportation, and for urban renewal planning, as well as for the development of comprehensive urban plans.[89] In addition, state government agencies and programs have been designed to encourage local planning. For nearly twenty years, Alabama has been assisting in the development of water plans and their implementation. Wisconsin's department of resource development has for twenty-five years drafted ordinances and prepared maps, subdivision regulations, and building codes.[90]

State planning agencies are most frequently charged only with the responsibility of encouraging and assisting local planning. Some states, however, give limited supervisory powers affecting localities to the state

[86] Miller, op. cit.
[87] Recent programs of this nature are summarized in Ibid., 453-455.
[88] The Municipal Year Book, 1962, pp. 305-306.
[89] Frank S. So, "Urban Planning Developments in 1961," Ibid., pp. 301-304.
[90] Council of State Governments, State Technical Assistance to Local Governments (The Council, Chicago, 1962), 29-32.

planning agency. In Tennessee, the state planning commission grants extraterritorial regional jurisdiction to municipal planning commissions. The commission may also require its approval of staff appointments and expenditures of regional agencies, though it is reported that this power is seldom exercised. The Maine department of economic development may initiate local planning programs, but in practice emphasizes advice and cooperation.[91]

Planning is coming to be especially widespread in metropolitan areas. A 1963 survey of metropolitan planning agencies revealed the existence of 142 such agencies in the nation's 212 standard metropolitan statistical areas. The typical agency was found to be nine years old, and to consist of a 16-member commission. Some commission members represent governmental units, such as counties and cities, and include both elected and appointed officials. Most members, however, are lay citizens. Money for financing these agencies is derived principally from county and federal sources, with lesser amounts coming from city and state governments and private contributions. The planning programs concentrate on general planning studies, including population and economic analyses, land-use studies, and transportation studies, with some activity in the fields of zoning and subdivision control. Some metropolitan planning agencies have conducted studies on flood control, storm drainage, water pollution, waste disposal, and other area-wide environmental problems.[92]

REFERENCES

AGG, T. R., *American Rural Highways* (McGraw-Hill, New York, 1920).

———, and Brindley, J. E., *Highway Administration and Finance* (McGraw-Hill, New York, 1927).

AUMANN, Francis R., *Ohio Government and Conservation: Legislation, Program, and Administration* (Agricultural Experiment Station, Ohio State Univ., Columbus, 1953).

BATEMAN, John H., *Introduction to Highway Engineering* (Wiley, New York, 5th ed., 1948).

BENNETT, Hugh H., *Elements of Soil Conservation* (McGraw-Hill, New York, 2nd ed., 1955).

———, *Soil Conservation* (McGraw-Hill, New York, 1939).

CHASE, Stuart L., *Rich Land, Poor Land* (Whittlesey House, New York, 1936).

CLINE, Denzel C., and TAYLOR, Milton C., *Michigan Highway Fiscal Study, 1961* (Mich. Legis. Highway Study Committee, East Lansing, 1962).

Council of State Governments, *Planning Services for State Government* (The Council, Chicago, 1956).

[91] *Ibid.*, 30.

[92] See United States Senate, Committee on Government Operations, *National Survey of Metropolitan Planning.*

DEARING, Charles L., *American Highway Policy* (Brookings Inst., Washington, 1942).

ELY, Northcutt, *Oil Conservation Through Interstate Agreement* (Fed. Oil Conservation Board, Washington, 1933).

FANNING, Leonard M., ed., *Our Oil Resources* (McGraw-Hill, New York, 1945).

FIETZ, Louise A., *The Role of the States in Recreation* (Bur. of Pub. Admin., Univ. of Calif., Berkeley, 1947).

GABRIELSON, Ira N., *Wildlife Conservation* (Macmillan, New York, 2nd ed., 1959).

———, *Wildlife Refuges* (Macmillan, New York, 1943).

GUSTAFSON, A. F., and others, *Conservation in the United States* (Comstock Pub. Co., Ithaca, N.Y., 2nd ed., 1944).

Highway Research Board, *State Highway Administrative Bodies* (The Board, Washington, 1952).

HJELTE, George, and SHIVERS, Jay S., *Public Administration of Park and Recreational Facilities* (Macmillan, New York, 1963).

HYNNING, Clifford J., *State Conservation of Resources* (Nat. Resources Committee, Washington, 1939).

KENNEDY, Donald G., *The Role of the Federal Government in Highway Development* (U.S. Govt. Printing Office, Washington, 1944).

MARSHALL, Hubert, and YOUNG, Robert J., *Public Administration of Florida's Natural Resources* (Pub. Admin. Clearing Service, Univ. of Florida, Gainesville, 1953).

MEYER, Harold D., and BRIGHTBILL, Charles K., *Recreation Administration: A Guide to its Practices* (Prentice-Hall, Englewood Cliffs, N.J., 1956).

Outdoor Recreation Resources Review Commission, *Outdoor Recreation for America* (U.S. Govt. Printing Office, Washington, 1962).

OWEN, Wilfred, *Automotive Transportation* (Brookings Inst., Washington, 1949).

———, and Dearing, Charles, *Toll Roads and the Problem of Highway Modernization* (Brookings Inst., Washington, 1951).

TUCKER, Harry, and LEAGER, Marc C., *Highway Economics* (International Textbook Co., Scranton, Pa., 1942).

United States Bureau of Public Roads, *Highway Progress: 1962* (Annual Report of the Bureau, U.S. Govt. Printing Office, Washington, 1962).

———, *Highway Statistics: 1961* (U.S. Govt. Printing Office, Washington, 1963).

United States Senate Committee on Government Operations, *National Survey of Metropolitan Planning* (U.S. Govt. Printing Office, Washington, 1963).

22

Government
and Business

REGULATION OF BUSINESS

Government and Economic Enterprise

A major political problem at all times is the relation of government to economic activities. The nature of this relation has varied from time to time with changing economic conditions and social attitudes. During the latter part of the 18th century and the first half of the 19th, the predominating laissez-faire philosophy kept public regulation of business at a minimum. More recently, with increasing industrialization, there has been a progressive expansion of governmental control in the economic field. In the United States, growing participation of the national government in business regulation during recent decades has had the effect of obscuring to some extent the importance of state and local regulatory action. Nevertheless, state and local regulations continue to constitute a vital part of the overall control program.

All business enterprises, in common with other private activities, are subject, under the police power, to whatever governmental regulation may be reasonably required to protect the public health, welfare, safety, and morals. It has long been customary, however, to regard certain business as being "affected with a public interest" and therefore subject to a higher degree of regulation than business in general.[1] Property, declared the United States Supreme Court at an early date, becomes "clothed with

---

[1] For a comprehensive discussion of the "public interest" concept, see Ford P. Hall, *The Concept of a Business Affected with a Public Interest.*

a public interest when used in a manner to make it of public consequence, and affect the community at large. When, therefore, one devotes his property to a use in which the public has an interest, he, in effect, grants to the public an interest in that use, and must submit to be controlled by the public for the common good, to the extent of the interest he has thus created."[2] Businesses commonly held to be affected with a public interest include public utility enterprises, common carriers of all kinds, public warehousing, banking, insurance, and innkeeping. The reasons assigned for placing particular enterprises in the "public interest" category are varied. Utilities are so classified because they provide essential services under public franchise and usually under monopolistic conditions, while banks and insurance companies act in a fiduciary capacity which justifies regulation. In other instances, however, such as that of innkeeping, the classification seems to be largely a matter of long tradition.

Since, in the final analysis, the public is concerned to some extent with almost every form of economic enterprise, any distinction between businesses regarded as affected with a public interest and those not so regarded is in reality one of degree only. The businesses assigned to the "public interest" group are merely those which seem to be of *more vital* public interest than others, and the extent of the public regulation permitted depends upon the *degree* of public interest. Finally, it should be noted that the "public interest" classification is not static, but changes with changing conditions, and indeed that the entire concept is gradually losing importance in determining the extent of permissible regulation. Thus in 1934 the United States Supreme Court, without declaring the milk industry affected with a public interest, upheld state regulation of milk prices under the police power. "It is clear," said the Court in that case, "that there is no closed class or category of businesses affected with a public interest, and the function of courts . . . is to determine in each case whether circumstances vindicate the challenged regulation as a reasonable exertion of governmental authority or condemn it as arbitrary or discriminatory. . . . The phrase 'affected with a public interest' can, in the nature of things, mean no more than that an industry, for adequate reason, is subject to control for the public good." [3] In line with this view there is a tendency on the part of the courts at present to disregard the traditional concept of businesses affected with a public interest and to permit, under the police power, such regulation of *any* business as may be reasonably necessary to protect the public health, morals, safety, and general welfare.

Entry into Business: Corporations

Some types of business may be engaged in at will by any and all persons wishing to pursue them, while others may be entered only with

---

2 *Munn* v. *Illinois,* 94, U.S. 113, at 126 (1877).
3 *Nebbia* v. *New York,* 291 U.S. 502, at 536 (1934).

governmental permission. As will be seen presently, several of the businesses mentioned above as affected with a public interest, such as banking, insurance, and the operation of transportation and other utilities, may not be entered until a permit has been secured from the appropriate public authority. The same is true of corporate enterprise in all its forms. Individuals wishing to organize a corporation must do so by securing a charter, the source of which in most instances is the state.[4] Every state has a general corporation law setting forth the conditions under which a corporation may be organized and the procedure to be followed. A corporation is considered as "domestic" in the state where it is incorporated and as "foreign" in all other states. Since corporations are not citizens within the meaning of the interstate citizenship clause of the federal constitution,[5] a corporation may do intrastate business in any state other than the one in which it is chartered only after being licensed therein, and states are free to impose upon foreign corporations, as prerequisite to licensing, whatever conditions they may wish to prescribe. In most states the chartering of domestic corporations and the licensing of foreign ones is a function of the secretary of state or of some subordinate in his office, though some states have a special corporation commission or delegate the function to some other administrative agency. When one considers the widespread use of the corporate form of business in manufacturing, merchandising, and other fields,[6] it is clear that chartering and licensing corporations constitute a potentially major factor in the regulation of business enterprise.

In practice, most state corporation laws, as actually administered, are relatively ineffective as regulatory measures. Applicants for corporate charters are required to submit information concerning such matters as the name of the proposed corporation, the location of its principal office, the kind or kinds of business in which it is desired to engage, and the proposed capitalization. Usually, however, when the information required by law has been filed and the required fees paid, a charter is issued as a matter of course, with little or no investigation of the character of the incorporators.[7] Since the state which charters a corporation may impose a franchise tax upon it, some states, with a view to increasing their revenues, virtually invite incorporators to organize therein by making their requirements even more lax than those in other states. For this reason a particular corporation may organize in a state offering attractive conditions of incor-

---

[4] Corporations of certain kinds are created by the national government. Examples are national banks and such government-owned corporations as the Tennessee Valley Authority.

[5] See above, Chap. IV, "Interstate Citizenship."

[6] On the extent and operation of corporate enterprise in the United States, see Leverett S. Lyon and others, *Government and Economic Life*, Vol. I, Chap. 4 and Appendix A.

[7] Harold Koontz and Richard W. Gable, *Public Control of Economic Enterprise*, 597.

poration even though it expects to do all of its business in other states. Under such circumstances, the concessions made by the chartering state may more than offset any special obligations to which the corporation may be subjected as being foreign to the states wherein it operates.[8] The diversity of state laws is a source of considerable vexation to corporations doing business in several jurisdictions, and their general laxity opens the way to many abuses. By various means it is frequently possible, for example, for large groups of stockholders to be virtually excluded from the management of a corporation and its profits diverted to "insiders." As a partial remedy for the existing laxity in state standards, it has sometimes been suggested that Congress require federal licensing of all corporations engaged in or affecting interstate commerce.[9]

State Occupational Licensing

Most of the professions, as well as various other callings and trades, can be practiced only under state license. A report on a 1952 survey indicated that more than 1,200 occupational licensing laws were in effect in the states. All states provided for the licensing of accountants, architects, attorneys, chiropodists, dentists, dental hygienists, embalmers, engineers, nurses, optometrists, osteopaths, pharmacists, physicians, teachers, and veterinarians. Other occupational groups licensed in many states included barbers, beauticians, insurance brokers, real estate brokers, and surveyors; while still other callings in large numbers were licensed in some states.[10]

State laws governing occupational licensing ordinarily prescribe certain general qualifications to be possessed by applicants for license, and provide for determining the occupational competence and fitness of applicants by examination. General qualifications relate to such matters as education or training and minimum age, and usually include the requirement that the applicant be of good moral character. Sometimes there are also residence and citizenship qualifications. The examination of applicants is usually conducted by an examining board composed wholly or partly of members of the profession or occupation concerned. Licenses, once granted, are ordinarily subject to revocation for various specified causes such as incompetency, malpractice, or unprofessional conduct. In

[8] See John T. Flynn, "Why Corporations Leave Home," *Atlan. Monthly,* CL, 268-276 (Sept., 1932).

[9] Koontz and Gable, *op. cit.,* 597-598.

[10] Council of State Governments, *Occupational Licensing Legislation in the States.* The report is summarized in "Occupational Licensing Legislation in the States," *State Govt.,* XXV, 275-280 (Dec., 1952). Concerning licensing in two individual states, see Robert J. Frye, *Government and Licensing: The Alabama Pattern;* Ruth B. Doyle, "The Fence-Me-In-Laws [in Wisconsin]," *Harper's Mag.,* Vol. CCV, No. 1227 (Aug., 1952), pp. 89-91.

some states, as in Illinois, administration of many or all of the regulatory statutes in the occupational field, and in connection therewith the granting and revocation of licenses, is the function of a single administrative department assisted by an examining board for each profession or occupation.

State occupational licensing has its constitutional justification in the police power as a means of protecting the public health, morals, safety, and welfare. It is based upon the theory that the public interest will suffer unless the qualifications and activities of persons engaged in the occupations concerned are properly regulated and controlled. This theory, however, fails to explain why in a given state certain occupations are subjected to licensing requirements while other comparable callings are not, or why a particular occupation is regulated in some states but not in others. The explanation of this rather illogical situation doubtless lies in the fact that occupational regulation is still in the stage of progressive development and that pressure from within or without the group to be regulated is frequently a determining factor in the enactment of licensing statutes. On the whole, the present tendency is toward the licensing and regulation of more and more occupational groups.[11]

Local Licensing

Municipalities make the securing of licenses prerequisite to engaging in various sorts of business enterprise, such licensing requirements serving both revenue and regulatory purposes. In practice, the revenue feature of municipal licensing seems generally to be emphasized, though the license system has high potentialities as a regulatory device.[12] Licenses may be denied to applicants of questionable character, the license requirement facilitates inspectional activities, and licensees may have their permits revoked for law violations or fraud. Under some circumstances, the threat of being put out of business through license revocation may be more effective in securing compliance with municipal regulations than would be the imposition of a fine for violations.[13] Enterprises commonly licensed by municipalities include hotels and restaurants, taverns, barber shops and beauty parlors, laundries, taxicabs, pawnbrokers, dealers in second-hand goods, and amusement places such as motion-picture theaters, dance halls, poolrooms, and bowling alleys. Similar establishments outside municipalities are frequently licensed by county governments.

[11] Marketing Laws Survey, *State Occupational Legislation*, 3.

[12] Blanche Davis Blank, "Licenses Can Be Policemen," *Nat. Mun. Rev.*, XXXVII, 73-76 (Feb., 1948).

[13] Charles M. Kneier, "The Licensing Power of Local Governments in Illinois," *Univ. of Ill. Law Forum*, Vol. 1957, pp. 1-18 (Spring, 1957). See also Louis Ancel and Jack M. Siegel, "Licensing as a Regulatory Device," *Ibid.*, 61-86.

Antitrust Laws

Most of the states have statutes, and many have constitutional provisions as well, aimed at preventing monopolistic practices in business enterprise.[14] Because early monopolistic combinations were frequently effected through the business device of the trust, it has become customary to refer to all business combinations, especially if they result in substantial curtailment of competition, as trusts, and to the legislation directed against such combinations as antitrust laws. Notwithstanding variations in terminology, the fundamental purpose of all such laws is substantially the same, namely, the outlawing of contracts, combinations, and arrangements designed to restrict trade with a view to increasing prices or curtailing production.[15]

Provisions of the state antitrust acts are similar in many respects to those of federal antitrust legislation, but apply to intrastate practices, whereas the national laws are directed at trade restraint among the states or with foreign nations. Many state laws, in addition to proscribing monopolies in general, contain explicit prohibitions of specific monopolistic or predatory practices such as interlocking directorates of corporations, intercorporate stockholding, exclusive dealing arrangements, and price discrimination. Violations of state antitrust laws are commonly made crimes punishable by fine and imprisonment. State attorneys general are usually charged with the duty of instituting injunction proceedings to restrain violations of the acts, and in many instances injunction suits by private individuals are also authorized. In some states domestic corporations violating antitrust provisions are subject to forfeiture of their charters, while violations by foreign corporations are cause for ouster from the privilege of doing business in the state. Private parties injured by violations are commonly authorized to sue the offending individuals or corporations for double or treble damages. Some states, in addition to antitrust laws of a general nature, have special laws prohibiting monopolistic practices in particular kinds of businesses such as railroads, other public utilities, stockyards, and the text-book business.[16]

Though antitrust laws thus occupy a prominent place in state statute books, authorities are in substantial agreement that they have had relatively little effect in preventing or breaking up monopolistic combinations. For one thing, since there is ordinarily no special administrative agency charged with enforcing these laws, the task falls to the state attorney general as a part of his general law-enforcement work. Frequently

[14] The constitutional and statutory provisions of this nature in each state, as of 1940, are analyzed in Marketing Laws Survey, *State Antitrust Laws.*

[15] Koontz and Gable, *op. cit.,* 328.

[16] Marketing Laws Survey, *State Antitrust Laws,* Scope Note.

the attorney general has neither the staff nor the funds for effective work in this field, and it is therefore not surprising that efforts at enforcement have been intermittent and haphazard. Perhaps the fatal weakness of the laws lies, however, in the fact that state authorities are without jurisdiction over business transactions of an interstate character. With so much of modern business involving operations in more than a single state, it has been only natural that the national government should be looked to for leadership in the prevention and suppression of monopolistic practices.[17]

Price-Control Legislation

During the 1930's a new type of state legislation in the economic field appeared in the form of resale price maintenance laws, commonly called "fair trade acts." The first such statute was enacted by California in 1931, and by the end of the decade laws of this nature had been enacted by more than forty states.[18] This legislation permits manufacturers of trade-marked or branded goods to fix the prices at which their products shall be sold by wholesalers and retailers. Contracts providing for price-fixing of this kind are legalized and the statutes, through "nonsigners' clauses," make prices so fixed binding even upon wholesalers and retailers who are not themselves parties to such agreements. The legislation seeks to protect manufacturers against exploitation of the goodwill embodied in their trademarks or brands by distributors who would use trademarked products as "leaders" for price-cutting, and also to protect small independent retailers from price-cutting by large department and chain stores. It will be noted that, whereas the antitrust laws seek to preserve competitive price-making by prohibiting arrangements and agreements in restraint of competition, the fair trade acts legalize as socially desirable a certain variety of price-fixing which had previously been held in several states to be violative of either the common law or the antitrust statutes. The fair trade laws do not ordinarily provide any criminal penalty for their violation, but make violators subject to civil suits for damages by manufacturers or other persons injured by their actions. Some of the statutes also provide for injunctive relief. Though state resale price-control

---

[17] Koontz and Gable, *op. cit.*, 328-329; Merle Fainsod and Lincoln Gordon, *Government and the American Economy* (rev. ed.), 449-450; Ford P. Hall, *Government and Business* (3rd ed.), 323-324.

[18] This legislation is analyzed, as of 1940, in Marketing Laws Survey, *State Price Control Legislation*, and the following discussion is based primarily on the Scope Note of that volume. Two supplements to the 1940 survey, entitled respectively *Regulation of Price Competition* and *Special Price Legislation*, were published in 1942 by the Work Projects Administration, Los Angeles. See also Stanley A. Weigel, *The Fair Trade Acts;* Ewald T. Grether, *Price Control under Fair Trade Legislation;* S. Chesterfield Oppenheim and Irwin Lechliter, "State Price Control Laws," *State Govt.*, XIII, 174-176, 187-189 (Sept., 1940); Earl R. Boonstra, "Trade Regulation—State Fair Trade Acts and Supplementary Federal Legislation," *Mich. Law Rev.*, XLVII, 821-831 (Apr., 1949).

laws apply only to intrastate trade, the federal antitrust laws were amended in 1937 to permit price maintainance contracts in interstate transactions when such a contract is valid under the state laws of the state in which the product is to be resold. In 1951 the United States Supreme Court construed the 1937 amendment as not legalizing nonsigners' clauses in interstate commerce;[19] but the following year Congress again amended the federal statutes to extend express approval to such clauses in interstate transactions. Nevertheless, the fair trade acts have been found difficult to enforce. In several states they have now been repealed by the legislature or nullified by the state supreme court, wholly or in part, as violative of state constitutional provisions.[20] On the whole, the fair trade legislation has proved to be much less effective than originally expected in the maintenance of retail price.

Other types of price-control legislation found in most states, either as provisions of the antitrust laws or as separate statutes, are those prohibiting sales below cost and prohibiting price discrimination between localities. Laws forbidding sales below cost are directed principally against the "loss leader" practice by which merchants seek to attract customers by advertising and selling certain standard-brand products at less than cost. Antidiscrimination statutes ordinarily prohibit the selling of commodities at a lower price or the buying of commodities at a higher price in one section or community of the state than in another, due allowance being made for differentials in transportation, when the effect would be to lessen competition or to create a monopoly. Sales-below-cost and antidiscrimination laws are fundamentally different in nature from the fair trade acts. The latter, as has been seen, legalize price-control practices of a vertical nature, i.e., restrictions applicable to different planes of the marketing process, such as resale price restrictions imposed by manufacturers upon wholesalers or retailers. In contrast, prohibitions of sales below cost and price discrimination strike at price control on a horizontal plane—for example, between manufacturers or between retailers. Another essential difference lies in the fact that the fair trade acts are merely permissive statutes, with civil remedies, whereas sales-below-cost and antidiscrimination laws, while usually also authorizing civil damage suits by injured parties, are mandatory in nature and carry criminal penalties for their violation.

Securities Regulation

All of the states except Delaware and Nevada have laws regulating the sale of corporate securities, with a view to assuring honesty in securi-

[19] *Schwegmann Bros.* v. *Calvert Distillers Corp.,* 341 U.S. 384 (1951).
[20] Cf. Cornelius P. Cotter, *Government and Private Enterprise,* 139-140; Vernon A. Mund, *Government and Business* (3rd ed.), 415.

ties transactions.[21] These statutes, commonly called "blue-sky laws," [22] do not have as their purpose the outlawing of all speculation in securities, but seek to make available to prospective purchasers reliable information concerning securities offered for sale, and to prevent the sale of those which are fraudulent rather than merely speculative in character. Some states have securities commissions charged with administering such regulatory laws. Elsewhere the duty of administration is imposed upon some other administrative officer or agency, such as the secretary of state, the banking department, the insurance department, the corporation commission, or a department of business regulation.

Provisions of state blue-sky laws are of three principal types: (1) those which require the licensing of securities dealers; (2) those which require the registration of securities offered for sale; and (3) those which authorize the designated regulatory agency or the attorney general to obtain court injunctions against the issuance or sale of fraudulent securities. These are commonly referred to as "licensing," "registration," and "fraud" provisions, respectively. Though a few laws have provisions of but a single type, that is not usually the case. Most present-day statutes contain both licensing and registration provisions, and a majority include provisions of all three types.

Applicants for dealer licenses are required to submit information concerning the plan and nature of their business and their previous business record. Licenses must ordinarily be renewed each year and may be revoked by the regulatory agency, after notice and hearing, for fraudulent practices or violations of the statutes. An issuing company desiring to register securities for sale in a given state must usually file a description of the securities concerned, and indicate the amount of securities to be offered in the state and the price at which they are to be offered. Some states also require the filing of comprehensive information concerning the character of the business of the issuing company, and its financial structure. Both issuing companies and dealers are required in some cases to file copies of prospectuses and circulars used in offering securities to the public. Information filed in registration statements constitutes a public record which may be consulted by prospective purchasers of securities and other interested persons. In most states, the regulatory agency is empowered to deny registration to any security which it believes, on the basis of facts

[21] The discussion in this section is based largely on Jacob Murray Edelman's *Securities Regulation in the 48 States.* See also Emanuel Stein, *Government and the Investor,* 63-73; Louis Loss and Edward M. Cowett, *Blue Sky Law,* Chap. 1. Rhode Island, in 1910, enacted the first state securities law of general applicability. However, the Kansas statute of the following year, which has frequently been credited with being the first such act, was of a more drastic nature and more influential in determining the course of subsequent legislation. Edelman, *op. cit.,* 1-2.

[22] From the fact that they seek to prevent the sale of securities having no more substantial basis than "a piece of the blue sky."

disclosed by the registration application, to be of a fraudulent nature; and registrations, in the same manner as licenses, may be revoked for cause.

All blue-sky laws, in addition to whatever provisions they may have for enjoining fraudulent practices and revoking licenses and registrations, make violators subject to criminal prosecution. A majority of the states impose civil liability as well, a typical provision being that any sale of securities in violation of the regulatory statute shall be voidable at the option of the purchaser, who may recover in a civil action any money that he has paid. It may be noted that certain kinds of securities are ordinarily exempted from provisions of the state regulatory laws. Among the classes most commonly exempted are government bonds, bank securities, the securities of nonprofit corporations, and securities of public utilities under federal or state control.

In their actual administration the blue-sky laws have revealed much the same weaknesses as state antitrust laws, namely, inadequacy of staffs and appropriations and inability to control interstate transactions. Largely as a result of these weaknesses, the national government entered the field of securities regulation in the early 1930's with the enactment of the Securities Act and the Securities Exchange Act. Under these laws the Securities and Exchange Commission, a national regulatory agency, now exercises jurisdiction over security sales in interstate or foreign commerce or through the mails.[23]

Public Utilities

The business enterprises which are subjected to the most stringent regulation are the public utilities.[24] No fully satisfactory definition of a public utility has ever been formulated,[25] and no hard-and-fast list can be made of the enterprises to be included in that category. For most purposes, a public utility may be considered as an enterprise which, usually under monopolistic conditions, supplies an essential and widely-used service to the public and, if privately owned,[26] enjoys grants of special privilege from government. The special privileges thus conferred upon

[23] The federal legislation is described in Stein, *op. cit.*, 73-147. See also Thomas Z. Wright, "Correlation of State Blue Sky Laws and the Federal Securities Acts," *Cornell Law Quar.*, XXVI, 258-295 (Feb., 1941).

[24] On the general subject of utility regulation, see William E. Mosher and Finla G. Crawford, *Public Utility Regulation;* Irston R. Barnes, *The Economics of Public Utility Regulation;* G. Lloyd Wilson, James M. Herring, and Roland B. Eutsler, *Public Utility Regulation;* Herman H. Trachsel, *Public Utility Regulation;* Emery Troxel, *Economics of Public Utilities;* Russell E. Caywood, *Electric Utility Rate Economics.*

[25] Cf. Howard R. Smith, "The Rise and Fall of the Public Utility Concept," *Jour. of Land and Pub. Util. Econ.*, XXIII, 117-131 (May, 1947).

[26] Public ownership of utilities and other forms of business enterprise is considered in a subsequent portion of this chapter.

utility companies ordinarily include use of the power of eminent domain for the acquisition of needed property from private owners and, in the case of urban utilities, use of the streets for their tracks, lines, or conduits. Also included in most instances, though not always, is the *exclusive* privilege of supplying the service concerned during the continuation of the franchise. Utility enterprises are regarded as "natural monopolies" with respect to which competition under most circumstances is wasteful and unwise. For example, parallel tracks of competing street railways result in traffic congestion and make it necessary for patrons to pay fares which will support two systems. Such being the case, the public interest is usually served by giving a single utility company a legal monopoly, in the form of an exclusive franchise, for supplying a particular service, and then subjecting the company to rigid public control. The enterprises which at present are most commonly regarded as public utilities within the regulatory jurisdiction of the state and local governments are those that provide electric light and power, water, gas, telephone and telegraph service, and public transportation facilities such as railroads, street railways, motorbuses, and trolley buses. With respect to all such utilities, the public is primarily interested in satisfactory service at reasonable rates, and the protection and promotion of this interest is the basic purpose of all regulatory measures.

Franchise Regulation

Down to the beginning of the present century, urban public utilities were regulated for the most part through franchise provisions. A public utility franchise, as the term is here used, is a grant by a municipality to a utility company of the privilege of using the streets and other public places in supplying some essential community service.[27] The grant may be made in perpetuity, for a fixed number of years, or for an indeterminate period. Enacted by the municipal council in the form of an ordinance, the franchise, when accepted by the grantee, becomes a binding contract upon the municipality and the utility company. It describes the nature and extent of the use of streets and alleys which the company is entitled to make, and usually specifies the payments to be made by the company to the municipality for the privileges granted. Early franchises, in addition, contained detailed specifications relating to the nature of the services to be provided by the company and the rates to be charged therefor. In practice, provisions of this character proved unsatisfactory because of their inflexibility. They frequently operated as impediments to the introduction of improved services made possible by technological advances,

---

[27] Cf. John Bauer, *The Public Utility Franchise: Its Functions and Terms under State Regulation,* 1. The discussion of franchise regulation which follows is based largely on this monograph.

and rates which were fair when the franchise was granted became too high or too low with changes in the general price level. Discontent became especially acute in the later years of the 19th century when, notwithstanding declining prices and costs, franchise regulation failed to bring about rate reductions.

As a result of general dissatisfaction with the franchise type of regulation, there developed a widespread demand that the state governments undertake the regulation of utility rates and services under their police power. State administrative commissions for the regulation of railroads had already been established quite generally and, in response to popular demand, the commission form of regulation was now extended to other forms of utility enterprise. During the early 1900's most of the states either established new regulatory bodies or extended the jurisdiction of their railroad commissions to various utilities which had theretofore been subject only to local regulation. In the latter case the name of the regulatory agency was frequently changed from railroad commission to public utilities commission or public service commission. By 1920 or thereabouts, the local franchise had been supplanted by the state utilities commission as the primary instrument of utility regulation. Utility companies are still required to obtain local franchises for use of the streets, but before beginning operation must also secure a license, usually called a "certificate of convenience and necessity," from the state commission.[28] The present-day utility franchise is in most cases little more than a permit for use of the streets and other public places. Some franchises, however, still contain regulatory provisions, and it would seem that provisions of this nature, if carefully drawn and properly administered, could be used much more widely and effectively than they now are to supplement state regulation.

Commission Regulation

Every state but Delaware now has, under one name or another, a public utilities commission with regulatory jurisdiction over intrastate operations of some or all of the principal forms of utility enterprise.[29] These state commissions naturally vary with respect to organization and functions.[30] Though chosen by popular election or otherwise in some states, commission members are most often appointed by the governor,

[28] For a comprehensive discussion of the certificate of convenience and necessity as a regulatory instrument, see Ford P. Hall, *State Control of Business through Certificates of Convenience and Necessity*.

[29] See Kentucky Legislative Research Commission, *Public Utilities Regulatory Bodies*. Most interstate aspects of utility operations are regulated by federal agencies such as the Interstate Commerce Commission, Federal Communications Commission, and Federal Power Commission.

[30] See C. O. Ruggles, *Aspects of the Organization, Functions, and Financing of State Public Utility Commissions* (Bur. of Bus. Research, Harvard Univ. Grad. School of Bus. Admin., Boston, 1937).

usually with the advice and consent of the state senate. The three-member commission is most common, as is the six-year staggered term. In general, the commission has jurisdiction over most privately-owned urban utilities, though some states exempt one or more types of utility from commission control. Municipally-owned utilities are subject to commission regulation in some states and not in others.[31] In addition to its jurisdiction over urban utilities, the state commission usually has regulatory authority over certain intrastate aspects of the business of railroads, motor carriers, pipe lines, and telephone and telegraph companies.

The regulatory powers of state utilities commissions extend to practically every phase of utility operations. Before a utility company may inaugurate service in a given community, it must, as we have seen, secure from the commission a certificate of convenience and necessity. Such a certificate will be granted only if, after thorough investigation, the commission is convinced that the proposed service would be in the public interest, and ordinarily it will not be granted if another company is already providing satisfactory service. A permit from the commission must likewise be secured before a company may extend its lines or services into areas not covered by the original certificate, or discontinue service in a given area. Consolidations and mergers of utility companies are subject to commission control. Utilities must follow accounting practices approved or prescribed by the commission, and must usually secure commission approval before they can issue new securities. Since utility rates are expected to produce sufficient revenue to cover, among other things, bond interest and stock dividends, the public interest requires that securities be issued only in necessary amounts and on reasonable terms. In a majority of the states, utility securities are regulated by the utilities commission rather than under the terms of the blue-sky law governing corporate securities generally.

One of the most important functions of the utilities commission, and in many respects the most difficult of all its functions, is the regulation of rates. State regulatory statutes usually stipulate that rates shall be *reasonable*. As construed by commissions and courts, this requirement means that rates are to be fixed at a point where they will cover all operating costs and yield a *fair return* on a *fair value* of the property devoted to public use. This doctrine, however, immediately raises the questions of what constitutes a fair return and what constitutes a fair value. The rate of return deemed reasonable on utility investments will depend in part on the current level of interest rates generally, and in part on the degree of risk involved in the particular enterprise concerned. Since utilities deal

---

[31] Seward P. Reese, "State Regulation of Municipally Owned Electric Utilities," *George Washington Law Rev.*, VII, 557-594 (Mar., 1939); Charles M. Kneier, "State Supervision over Municipally Owned Utilities," *Columbia Law Rev.*, XLIX, 180-200 (Feb., 1949).

in essential services for which there is always a demand, and since furthermore they are usually protected from competition by exclusive franchises, the financial risk involved is relatively small, and it is therefore reasonable that utility investors should be satisfied with a somewhat lower rate of return than is expected from competitive enterprises where the degree of risk is greater. In the 1920's, many commissions accepted 8 percent as a fair rate of return, but more recently a lower rate of around 6 percent, or in some cases less, has generally been allowed.[32]

Even more difficult to determine than the rate of return, is the valuation upon which that return is to be permitted. Numerous tests or bases have been employed, singly or in combination, for fixing the value of utility property for rate-making purposes, but no fully satisfactory formula has yet been devised. Among the rate bases more commonly used, in each case with appropriate deductions for depreciation, are those of (1) original cost, (2) reproduction cost, and (3) prudent investment. The first of these takes as the primary rate base the original or "historical" cost of the properties used for public service. This formula, in practice, has several disadvantages. For one thing, company records may not be in such form as to make possible an accurate determination of original cost. Again, this plan, taking into account the *entire* original cost, permits the capitalization for rate-making purposes even of cost items which may have been unwisely or wastefully incurred. And finally, the original cost plan, since it fails to take into consideration fluctuations in the general price level, is likely to result in rates that are too low in time of rising prices and too high in times of falling prices. The reproduction or "replacement" cost formula overcomes these difficulties in large measure by substituting for original cost the estimated cost of reproducing the plant at current price levels. One of the principal objections to this plan is the work and expense involved in its administration. The physical appraisal of public utility properties is a highly technical task calling for employment on a large scale of engineers, accountants, and other expert personnel. Moreover, since reproduction cost fluctuates with changes in the price level, frequent reappraisals are necessary if just rates are to be maintained.

According to the prudent investment principle, those who provide the capital for a utility enterprise are entitled to a return, after due allowance for depreciation, on every dollar that has been invested honestly and wisely in the business. By excluding from the rate base expenditures of a clearly imprudent or extravagant nature, this plan overcomes one of the basic weaknesses of the original cost formula, and by eliminating the necessity for periodic physical appraisals it surmounts the principal objec-

---

[32] William E. Mosher, "Defects of State Regulation of Public Utilities in the United States," *Annals of Amer. Acad. of Polit. and Soc. Sci.*, CCI, 105-110 (Jan., 1939). Cf. Koontz and Gable, *op. cit.*, 256. Concerning factors considered in determining a fair rate of return, see Caywood, *op. cit.*, 200-204.

tion to reproduction cost. Prudent investment, having once been determined, is relatively stable and can easily be kept up-to-date by appropriate accounting methods. Though none of the three rate bases discussed, nor any other, is in practice fully satisfactory, commissions and courts in recent years have looked with growing favor upon prudent investment as a useful and appropriate factor in the rate-making procedure. What the commissions ordinarily do in actual practice is to consider various rate bases, weigh each in whatever manner seems most appropriate, and attempt in that way to arrive at an estimated value which will be substantially fair to both the utility and its consumers.

For nearly a half-century after 1898, rate-making was rendered especially difficult by a rule of the United States Supreme Court requiring that regulatory commissions, in fixing valuations, give consideration, along with any other pertinent matters, to several specifically enumerated factors including original cost and reproduction cost. In 1944, however, the Court repudiated this rule, taking the position that, insofar as the federal constitution is concerned, commissions are free to determine valuations in any manner they may choose, without regard to any specific formula or combination of formulae, provided that the resulting rates are just and reasonable. The new rule broadens the discretion of utility commissions in the rate-making process by emphasizing the fact that the result reached, rather than the formula employed, is the important matter.[33] Some commissions, however, are still required by state law to give consideration to reproduction cost or other specific factors.[34]

State versus Local Regulation

Though there are occasional instances of municipal utilities commissions, commission regulation is for the most part state regulation. As has been seen, utility regulation since the turn of the century has shifted, in large measure, from municipal franchise regulation under the contract power to state commission regulation under the police power. Proponents of local regulation urge in its favor that local officials, because of their direct contact with local conditions, have better knowledge of local problems and needs. More than counterbalancing this factor, however, are various advantages of state regulation. In the first place, small municipalities cannot afford the cost of maintaining their own agencies with the technical staff necessary for carrying on regulatory activities. Again, many of the cases coming before utilities commissions involve controversies be-

---

[33] *Smyth* v. *Ames,* 169 U.S. 466 (1898); *Federal Power Commission* v. *Hope Natural Gas Company,* 320 U.S. 591 (1944). Cf. Bauer, *The Public Utility Franchise: Its Functions and Terms under State Regulation,* 4-6; Koontz and Gable, *op. cit.,* 248-253.

[34] Koontz and Gable, *op. cit.,* 253-255.

tween a utility company and a municipality or a large group of its citizens, and under such circumstances the propriety of having the merits of a case judged by a municipal agency is at best questionable. But perhaps the strongest argument for state regulation stems from the fact that many utilities operate in more than a single municipality, and sometimes in rural territory as well. A well-recognized principle of regulation requires that the jurisdiction of a regulatory body be as broad as the operations of the enterprise to be regulated, and in accordance with this principle nothing less than an agency of statewide jurisdiction is competent to deal with many of our present-day utility systems.[35] It may be, as has been suggested, that municipalities are legally competent to exercise, through franchise provisions, a somewhat larger degree of regulatory authority in the utility field than is now generally done. But there appears to be no doubt that the backbone of the regulatory program will remain in the future, as it is today, in the hands of state administrative commissions.

Air Transport

A relatively new form of public utility service which has grown rapidly in importance is that of commercial air transport. This service, together with other phases of civil aviation, is the subject of both national and state regulatory legislation; and, since so large a proportion of aviation activities are of interstate character or in some way related to interstate traffic, it is not surprising that the national government has taken the lead in regulation.[36]

Regulatory measures in the field of air transport are of two general kinds: *safety* regulations and *economic* regulations. Safety regulations have to do with such matters as examination and licensing of pilots, inspection and licensing of aircraft, investigation of accidents, establishment of safety standards, and prescribing air traffic rules. Under the Civil Aeronautics Act of 1938, the national government has assumed safety jurisdiction not only over interstate, overseas, and foreign air commerce, but also over all aircraft navigation which directly affects or may endanger the

[35] Wilson, Herring, and Eutsler, *op. cit.*, 35-40; William B. Munro, *Municipal Administration* (Macmillan, New York, 1934), 645.

[36] On the general problem of regulation and regulatory jurisdiction, see Charles S. Rhyne, "Federal, State and Local Jurisdiction over Civil Aviation," *Law and Contemp. Probs.*, XI, 457-487 (Winter-Spring, 1946); Frederick G. Hamley, "Appropriate Areas of State Economic Regulation," *Ibid.*, 488-507; Oswald Ryan, "Economic Regulation of Air Commerce by the States," *Va. Law Rev.*, XXXI, 479-531 (Mar., 1945); Wm. C. Green, "The War Against the States in Aviation," *Ibid.*, 835-864 (Sept., 1945); Sheldon B. Steers, "Development of State Aviation Agencies," *State Govt.*, XVIII, 8-9, 15 (Jan., 1945); George W. Starr, "The Position of the State in Economic Control and Regulation of Air Commerce," *Jour. of Air Law and Commerce*, XV, 127-155 (Spring, 1948). Pertinent legislation is summarized in Samuel H. Still, *State Aviation Laws: A Summary of the Laws of the Forty-Eight States* (Legis. Ref. Service, Library of Congress, Washington, 1947).

safety of such commerce. Pursuant to this law, a federal license is now required of every pilot and aircraft flying anywhere in the airspace above the United States. In view of this and other federal safety requirements, some authorities feel that the national government has so completely occupied the field of safety regulation that nothing remains to be done by the states except, perhaps, to cooperate in the enforcement of federal regulatory measures. Others, however, contend that there is still both room and need for supplementary state action in safety matters with respect to intrastate aviation. As a matter of fact, every state has enacted some sort of safety legislation,[37] and most of the states have established special aeronautics departments or commissions to administer their safety programs. With respect to licensing, most state laws merely require that aircraft and airmen have federal licenses, though a few provide for state licenses; and state air traffic regulations are in general similar to the federal rules.

Economic regulations are concerned with such matters as the issuance of certificates of convenience and necessity, supervision of rates, control of mergers and consolidations, and abandonment of service. In this field federal jurisdiction is exercised only over air transportation of interstate, overseas, or foreign character, and the transportation of mail by air, leaving to the states the regulation of nonmail air carriers operating wholly within a single state and carrying only intrastate traffic.[38] Though the jurisdiction left to the states is thus wider in the economic than in the safety field, it appears that the states have been less eager to exercise it. A number of states, it is true, have statutes containing economic regulations, but most of these seem to have been relatively ineffective as control measures. Some of these statutes antedate the Civil Aeronautics Act, and most of them are administered by the state public utilities commission rather than the aviation agency. Whether Congress will ultimately extend federal regulatory controls in the economic field, as it has in the field of safety, to cover all phases of intrastate air transportation in any way affecting interstate commerce, remains to be seen. If it does not, state economic regulation may be expanded and strengthened. On the whole, however, considering the long-distance nature of most air transport and the desirability of uniformity in regulatory measures, it seems likely that state regulation, in comparison with national, is destined to play a distinctly minor role.

Banking

The banking business is subjected to detailed governmental regulation. Banks not only provide a widely-used public service, but also

---

[37] Rhyne, *op. cit.*, 467.
[38] Ryan, *op. cit.*, 483.

serve as custodians of private savings, and consequently there is a vital public interest in their financial stability. Two commercial banking systems exist side by side in the United States, one controlled by the national government and the other by the states.[39] State banks are organized under state laws and are regulated, under statutory provisions, by state administrative agencies. Some states have banking departments, while others vest banking regulation in some other department or agency. In this discussion, the term *banking department* will be used in a generic sense to designate the state regulatory agency, whatever its official title.

State banking regulations concern such matters as the organization of banking institutions, the types of assets in which banks may invest their funds, reserve requirements, and provisions for examinations and reports.[40] State statutes prescribe minimum-capital requirements for state banks, what officers a bank shall have and what their respective functions shall be in the administration of the institution, and the types of financial activities in which banks may engage. Before a new bank is organized it must secure a charter from the banking department, and in some states the department has broad discretion in deciding whether or not to grant a charter. In determining whether the proposed bank would be in the public interest, consideration will ordinarily be given to such matters as the character and financial standing of the organizers, the qualifications and character of the proposed officers, and the need for the institution in the locality concerned.[41] Banks are usually strictly limited in their power to invest in nonliquid assets such as real estate and real-estate mortgages. In normal times a large proportion of the assets of commercial banks consists of loans to customers—manufacturers, farmers, merchants, etc.—on a short-term basis for use in their business enterprises. The statutes usually place a limit upon the amount which may be lent to any one individual or corporation, and prescribe standards with respect to the security which must be pledged by borrowers. To meet normal withdrawal demands, banks are required to keep a specified portion of their assets, expressed as a percentage of their deposits, in "reserve" as cash in their vaults or deposits in other banks.

An important feature of the regulatory system consists of provisions for bank examinations and reports. All state banks are subject to examination by the state banking department. Examiners from the department's staff make unannounced visits to banks, examine their records, inspect their cash and securities, and report thereon to the department. If an examination reveals irregularities, or laxity in the observance of prescribed standards, the department may require the bank to correct such condi-

---

[39] For a general discussion of federal and state banking regulation, see Hall, *Government and Business* (3rd ed.), Chap. 14.

[40] Cf. Lyon and others, *op. cit.*, Vol. I, p. 160.

[41] Hall, *Government and Business* (3rd ed.), 251.

tions. If there is evidence of criminal dishonesty, it may be turned over to the regular law-enforcement agencies for appropriate action. Banks are required to make reports of their financial condition to the banking department at regular intervals, and to publish statements of these reports in local newspapers. In addition, the department may at any other time call for the submission of reports and the publication of statements. The banking department is charged with administering the affairs of banks that have failed, and with supervising their reorganization or liquidation. State-chartered savings banks and building and loan associations are regulated in much the same manner as commercial banks, and usually by the same administrative agency. State banks which become members of the Federal Reserve System, and others which have their deposits insured by the Federal Deposit Insurance Corporation, are subject to federal as well as state examination.

Following the panic of 1907, several states, principally in the Midwest, established state guaranty funds for the protection of bank depositors. These arrangements, which involved the assessment of other "guaranteed" banks to pay the depositors of banks that had failed, worked satisfactorily as long as the only failures were those occurring occasionally as a result of dishonesty or mismanagement on the part of bank officers. However, they were unable to withstand the widespread bank failures resulting from the economic depression of the 1920's and early 1930's.[42] Today most state banks have their deposits insured, along with those of the national banks, by the Federal Deposit Insurance Corporation.

The Small-Loan Business

There is a substantial class of people whose credit needs are not adequately met by commercial banks and who desire to borrow, on personal security, relatively small sums of money to be repaid, frequently in instalments, within a period of a few weeks or months. Such borrowers have all too often been easy prey to the "loan sharks"—professional lenders of small sums who exact extortionate, and usually illegal, rates of interest. To afford some degree of protection against loan-shark tactics, most states have now enacted laws providing for a system of licensed and regulated small-loan or "personal finance" establishments. These statutes are administered either by the state banking department or by some other designated agency and, while varying in detail, are fairly uniform in their fundamental nature and purpose. The businesses regulated are commonly those which engage in lending sums of $800 or less at interest rates exceeding 6 percent per annum. Businesses in this class are required to be licensed and to submit to various regulatory measures. The latter concern

---

[42] Cf. Harold G. Moulton, *Financial Organization and the Economic System* (McGraw-Hill, New York, 1938), 359.

such matters as terms of the loan contract, rate of interest to be charged, records to be kept by the company, and forms of advertising. Licensed establishments are subject to examination by the regulatory agency and are required to make reports on prescribed forms. Licenses may be revoked for violations of the law, and violators, in addition, are subject to civil and criminal penalties.[43]

Insurance

One of the most strictly regulated categories of business enterprise is that of insurance. Every state has regulatory laws in this field, the enforcement of which is the duty of a department of insurance or some other designated administrative agency.[44] In this country insurance is the normal means of distributing the effects of various kinds of economic losses over a period of time, and life insurance has become a major form of investment. The objectives of insurance regulation include, among others, assurance that companies will pay claims for insured losses, protection of the public against unreasonable rates, and, in the case of life insurance, security of savings.

Insurance regulation takes many forms.[45] Ordinarily both an insurance company and its agents must obtain licenses before selling contracts in a given state. In some states the insurance department must issue a license to any company or agent complying with all legal requirements, while in others the department may deny a license if it believes such action to be in the public interest. Licenses may usually be revoked for violations of the regulatory laws and for various other reasons, such as failure to pay valid loss claims. Companies are strictly controlled with respect to investment of their assets. Some states permit investment only in securities of enumerated categories, whereas others permit any investments except those specifically prohibited. The forms of investment most commonly approved are government bonds; railroad, public utility, and industrial bonds; and real-estate mortgage loans. Some states require that insurance companies, especially those chartered in other states, deposit securities

---

[43] Symposium, "Combating the Loan Shark," *Law and Contemp. Probs.*, Vol. VIII, No. 1 (Winter, 1941). See especially the following articles in the symposium: F. B. Hubachek, "The Development of Regulatory Small Loan Laws," pp. 108-145; James M. Sullivan, "Administration of a Regulatory Small Loan Law," pp. 146-153; William Trufant Foster, "The Personal Finance Business under Regulation," pp. 154-172.

[44] On the organization of the regulatory agencies, see Edwin W. Patterson, *The Insurance Commissioner in the United States: A Study in Administrative Law and Practice* (Harvard Univ. Press, Cambridge, 1927), Chap. 2.

[45] On the subject generally, see Hall, *Government and Business* (3rd ed.), Chap. 13; Koontz and Gable, *Public Control of Economic Enterprise*, 437-443; Marshall E. Dimock, *Business and Government* (4th ed.), 413-418; Margaret Rohrer, *State Regulation of Insurance*.

with the insurance department or some other state agency to guarantee payment of loss claims incurred within the state. Insurance companies are subject to examination by the state regulatory department and are required to make periodic reports thereto.

State laws commonly require that the rates charged by insurance companies be reasonable and nondiscriminatory, but actual rate-making has not yet developed in this field to the extent that it has in that of public utilities. The fixing of fire insurance rates by public authority has been upheld by the courts,[46] and some states have conferred rate-making powers upon their insurance departments. In large measure, however, the rate-control functions of state insurance departments have been limited to the approval or disapproval of rate schedules fixed by private rating bureaus maintained by the insurance companies.

Public regulation of insurance was long regarded as being exclusively within the power of the states. The United States Constitution makes no mention of insurance, and it was decided by the Supreme Court in 1869 that insurance was not commerce.[47] On the basis of this decision, it appeared that insurance, not being commerce, was not subject, even in its interstate aspects, to congressional regulation under the commerce clause. In 1944, however, the Supreme Court reversed this earlier view, holding that insurance *is* commerce, and that insurance companies therefore might be prosecuted for violations of the federal antitrust laws.[48] Following this decision, Congress enacted legislation declaring continued state regulation of insurance to be in the public interest. Insurance companies were exempted temporarily from the federal antitrust acts; but it was provided that, beginning in 1948, those acts should apply to the insurance business to the extent that such business was not regulated by state law. Though the 1944 decision appears to establish firmly the power of the national government to regulate insurance under the commerce clause, direct regulation has thus far been left to the states. To what extent Congress may see fit in the future to enter the insurance field with regulatory legislation remains to be seen.[49] Since 1944, many states have strengthened their regulatory statutes in an effort to forestall federal regulation. The newer state provisions concern such matters as the regulation of private rating bureaus for the purpose of preserving competition in rate-making, and the prevention of various unfair and deceptive practices on the part of insurance companies and their agents.[50]

[46] *German Alliance Insurance Co.* v. *Lewis,* 233 U.S. 389 (1914).

[47] *Paul* v. *Virginia,* 8 Wall. 168 (1869).

[48] *United States* v. *Southeastern Underwriters Assn.,* 322 U.S. 533 (1944).

[49] Elmer W. Sawyer, *Insurance as Interstate Commerce* (McGraw-Hill, New York, 1945); Mund, *op. cit.,* 254-256; Edwin W. Patterson, "The Future of State Supervision of Insurance," *Tex Law Rev.,* XXIII, 18-38 (Dec., 1944).

[50] Lester B. Orfield, "Improving State Regulation of Insurance," *Minn. Law Rev.,* XXXII, 219-261 (Feb., 1948).

Liquor Regulation

With the repeal of National Prohibition in 1933, power to regulate the liquor trade was returned to the respective states; and the regulatory legislation which they have enacted, though quite varied in detail, reveals certain basic objectives as widely sought. Among these objectives are dissociation of the liquor business from organized crime and vice and from corrupt politics, prevention of the return of the old-time saloon, encouragement of moderation in the use of alcoholic beverages, and collection of substantial revenue from the liquor trade.[51] State liquor control systems are commonly considered as being of three types: (1) the prohibition system, (2) the public monopoly system, and (3) the licensing system.[52] Classified as to the type of control primarily employed, Mississippi alone remains a prohibition state.[53] Of the remaining states, seventeen [54] are regarded as monopoly states and thirty-two as licensing states. A given state, however, does not necessarily confine itself to a single type of control. Some licensing is usually to be found in both prohibition and monopoly states. Thus even a prohibition state, while forbidding the sale of intoxicating liquor for beverage purposes, ordinarily licenses the sale of certain "nonintoxicating" beverages of not more than a specified low percentage of alcoholic content.

The monopoly plan involves the sale of liquor through publicly owned and operated liquor stores. Fifteen of the seventeen monopoly states operate systems of state retail dispensaries, North Carolina operates a system of county dispensaries under state supervision, and Wyoming operates a state wholesale monopoly while licensing private retailers. As a matter of fact, the term *monopoly* as applied to this group of states is somewhat misleading. The monopoly system ordinarily applies only to hard liquors, with wines and beer being sold under the licensing system; and in some states the public dispensaries are "package" stores only, with restaurants and hotels licensed to serve hard liquor by the drink. Proponents of the monopoly system of control point out that it avoids tax-

---

[51] Paul Studenski, " Liquor Regulation: Success or Failure?" *Nat. Mun. Rev.*, XXXII, 180-184 (Apr., 1943).

[52] The state control laws are analyzed in Marketing Laws Survey, *State Liquor Legislation*. Tabular analyses of statutory provisions concerning the organization and powers of state control agencies may be found in *The Book of the States*, 1948-49, pp. 466-471. See also Symposium, "Alcoholic Beverage Control," *Law and Contemp. Probs.*, Vol. VII, No. 4 (Autumn, 1940); Dean E. McHenry, "Liquor Control Ten Years After Repeal," *State Govt.*, XVI, 208-210 (Oct., 1943); Alabama Legislative Reference Service, *A Comparative Analysis of State Liquor Monopoly Statutes* (Ala. Legis. Ref. Service, Montgomery, 1948).

[53] Kansas was in the prohibition category until 1949 and Oklahoma until 1959.

[54] Alabama, Idaho, Iowa, Maine, Michigan, Montana, New Hampshire, North Carolina, Ohio, Oregon, Pennsylvania, Utah, Vermont, Virginia, Washington, West Virginia, and Wyoming.

evasion problems inherent in the licensing system. The sale of liquor by government agencies is also commonly believed to promote temperance, since the profit motive, which naturally leads private dealers to make their sales as large as possible, is secondary to that of control and therefore less pronounced than in the case of private business. Actually, however, it appears doubtful that the monopoly system has been successful in discouraging alcohol consumption.

Under the licensing system employed in a majority of the states, liquor is manufactured and sold by private operators under government license. State licenses are ordinarily required of manufacturers, wholesalers, and retailers, and are subject to revocation for violations of the regulatory statutes. In some instances, licensing authority is conferred upon local governments also, most commonly with respect to retail establishments. Where this plan is employed, establishments within municipalities are usually licensed and regulated by the municipal government and those in unincorporated areas by the county. A few of the licensing states have some county or municipal liquor dispensaries.[55]

Some licensing states have established special officers or commissions to administer their liquor control laws, while others vest the control function elsewhere in the state government—frequently in the hands of some state fiscal agency. The latter plan is not illogical in view of the fact that liquor taxes constitute a major source of state revenue. Each monopoly state has a board or commission of some type to manage the public dispensaries. A large majority of the regulatory statutes in both licensing and monopoly states contain local-option provisions of one kind or another, and under these provisions some "dry" areas now exist in many of the nonprohibition states.[56]

The States and Atomic Energy

At its inception, atomic energy in the United States was a monopoly of the federal government, and it was not until 1954 that private development under federal license was authorized. Though the scope of state authority in the atomic-energy field has not yet been fully delineated, a majority of the states have already enacted related laws of some sort. Several states have established "coordinators of atomic energy activities" to coordinate the studies and proposals of various state departments and subdivisions of the states relating to atomic energy; to provide liaison with other states and with the federal Atomic Energy Commission; and to advise the governor and legislature concerning atomic industrial de-

[55] Municipal dispensaries are especially numerous in Minnesota, where 360 such establishments were in existence in 1952. C. C. Ludwig, "Liquor Sales Aid to Cities," *Nat. Mun. Rev.*, XLII, 497-501 (Nov., 1953).

[56] McHenry, *op. cit.* Liquor taxes are discussed below, Chap. XXIV.

velopment. Some states have gone further and enacted regulatory laws designed to protect the public health and safety. These provide various measures for the control of radiation hazards and for regulating the disposal of radioactive wastes. A substantial number of states have made injuries from excessive exposure to radiation compensable under their workmen's compensation or occupational diseases laws. Some states have established special administrative agencies for carrying on their atomic-energy activities, such as the "coordinators" mentioned above, atomic energy commissions, or offices of atomic development; while others have made those activities a duty of existing state agencies. Congressional legislation of 1959 authorizes the federal Atomic Energy Commission to enter into contracts with states for state performance of certain regulatory functions. And through the Southern Interstate Nuclear Compact, concluded in 1962, a dozen or so southern states have joined in establishing the Southern Interstate Nuclear Board to serve the member states in an advisory and informational capacity and to aid them in attracting and promoting nuclear industry.[57]

GOVERNMENT OWNERSHIP

An alternative to government regulation as a means of protecting the public interest in business enterprise is government ownership and operation. Government ownership by the states is less extensive than federal ownership, yet there are several fields in which some state business is found. Municipal ownership, especially in the public utility field, is not uncommon, and various other examples of public or quasi-public business at the local level are provided by counties, special-purpose districts, and consumers' cooperatives.

State Business in North Dakota

The state which has undertaken the greatest variety of business enterprises is North Dakota, where a program of governmental ownership was inaugurated during the years 1917 to 1922 under sponsorship of the Nonpartisan League. Public enterprises in that state include a flour mill,

[57] William A. W. Krebs and Robert L. Hamilton, "The Role of the States in Atomic Development," *Law and Contemp. Probs.*, XXI, 182-210 (Winter, 1956); William A. W. Krebs, Jr., "What are You Doing about Atomic Development?" *State Govt.*, XXIX, 79-82, 96-97 (May, 1956); Clinton P. Anderson, "The Atom—Everybody's Business or Nobody's Business?" *Ibid*, 243-247, 257-258 (Dec., 1956); William H. Berman and Lee M. Hydeman, "State Responsibilities in the Atomic Energy Field," *Ibid.*, XXXII, 114-120 (Spring, 1959); Robert H. Solomons, III, "The Southern Interstate Nuclear Compact and Board," *Ibid.*, XXXVI, 40-44 (Winter, 1963).

feed mill, and terminal elevator, all located in Grand Forks, and branch warehouses in several other cities. A state-owned bank, operated under the name of the Bank of North Dakota, serves as a depository for state funds, may receive deposits from other public or private sources, and is authorized to make loans to local governments and real estate loans to private individuals and corporations. The state's milling, elevator, and banking operations are administered by the state industrial commission, an ex officio body composed of the governor, the attorney general, and the commissioner of agriculture and labor. Three insurance enterprises are operated as divisions of the state insurance department. Through a state fire and tornado fund, fire and tornado insurance, together with certain other types of coverage, is provided for publicly owned state and local buildings and their contents; a state bonding fund provides surety bonds for state and local officers and employees; and insurance against hail damage to growing crops may be secured by farmers through a state hail insurance fund. A board of university and school lands administers extensive landholdings received from the federal government for educational and other purposes. During the 1920's, there was inaugurated a system of state farm loans, administered by a division of the Bank of North Dakota, under which funds raised through the sale of real estate bonds were used for making loans to farmers on farm-mortgage security. The financial consequences of North Dakota's business ventures seem to present no uniform picture. The state fire and tornado fund, though charging premiums no higher than private insurance companies, has been able, through accumulated surpluses, to provide free insurance for public property during certain periods. At times it has been found necessary to use state tax funds to cover deficits in the state's milling and elevator operations as well as defaults on its farm-mortgage loans, though in the past two decades both enterprises have been returning substantial surpluses or profits to the state general fund.[58]

State Docks and Terminals

Several seaboard states own and operate public dock facilities. The Alabama department of state docks and terminals operates piers, warehouses, a shipside cold storage terminal, and other terminal facilities at the port of Mobile. Wharves, warehouses, and a public grain elevator at the port of New Orleans are state-owned and operated by a state agency known as the board of commissioners of the port of New Orleans. The Maine state pier in Portland is operated by the Maine port authority.

[58] "State Business Operations in North Dakota," *The Book of the States,* 1945-46, pp. 393-401. Recent information provided by C. Emerson Murry, Director, North Dakota Legislative Research Committee.

Other states having port authorities include Georgia, South Carolina, and Virginia.[59]

The country's most extensive system of docks, terminals, and related facilities is operated by the Port of New York Authority, a bistate corporate agency established in 1921 under the terms of an interstate compact between New York and New Jersey. The governing body of this Authority is a board of twelve commissioners, six of whom are appointed by the governor of each state with the consent of the state senate. Responsibility for actual administration of the Authority's activities is in the hands of an executive director appointed by the board. Under the terms of the compact creating the agency, the Authority is empowered to construct, purchase, or lease, and to operate, self-supporting transportation or terminal facilities of any kind. Projects may be financed by the issuance of bonds, but the Authority has no taxing power. At present the Authority owns port and terminal facilities valued at more than a billion dollars and operates extensive additional properties under lease. For motor traffic between New York and New Jersey, the Authority operates the Holland and Lincoln tunnels under the Hudson river, the double-deck George Washington bridge over the river, and three Staten Island bridges —Goethals bridge, Bayonne bridge, and Outerbridge Crossing. Each year some 100 million vehicles cross these six toll bridges and tunnels. Also owned by the Authority are extensive port and dock facilities, a railroad freight station, bus and truck terminals, and a grain terminal. In 1947 the Authority, under long-term leases, undertook the development and operation of New York City's La Guardia and Idlewild (now Kennedy International) airports, and of Newark Airport in New Jersey. Subsequently, Teterboro Airport in New Jersey was added to the Authority's air terminal system; and in 1956 a commercial heliport was opened. Together, these various projects go a long way toward providing the metropolitan area with an integrated system of terminal facilities for land, sea, and air transport. Since 1945 the Authority has maintained a field office in Chicago to keep in touch with midwestern shippers and to encourage the routing of traffic through the New York-New Jersey gateway.[60]

[59] Henry W. Sweet, "Alabama State Docks," *State Govt.*, XX, 240-241, 254-255 (Sept. 1947); John B. Ferran, "State Ownership and the Port of New Orleans," *Ibid.*, 245-246, 255; Richard M. Hallet, "The Maine Port Authority," *Ibid.*, 251; Thomas J. Tobias, "South Carolina State Ports Authority," *Ibid.*, 252-256; L. Vaughan Howard, "Georgia's Port Development Plans," *Ibid.*, 242-243, 255; Harry A. Keitz, "The State Port Authority of Virginia," *Ibid.*, 253-254.

[60] Austin J. Tobin, "The Port of New York Authority," *State Govt.*, XX, 234-239 (Sept., 1947); *Time*, Vol. L, No. 18 (Nov., 3, 1947), 88, 90, 92; Sidney Goldstein, "The Port of New York Authority," *Jour. of Pub. Law*, V, 408-417 (Fall, 1956); J. D. Ratcliff, "Builder for the Future," *Nat. Mun. Rev.*, XLVI, 565-569 (Dec., 1957); Edward T. Chase, "How to Rescue New York from its Port Authority," *Harper's Mag.*, Vol. CCXX, No. 1321 (June, 1960), pp. 67-74. See also the Authority's annual reports.

State Liquor Stores

As a partial alternative to the regulation and taxing of privately owned liquor stores, sixteen states, as previously noted,[61] have established systems of state dispensaries for the sale of liquor. For the most part, these are retail package stores, though Wyoming sells at wholesale rather than at the retail level. In 1962, state liquor stores showed combined sales of more than a billion dollars and net revenues of nearly a quarter-billion.[62]

Other State Enterprises

About a third of the states operate systems of workmen's compensation insurance, some maintaining a state monopoly of this business and others permitting competition by private insurance companies.[63] Twenty-five airports were reported in 1962 as being owned and operated by state governments or state universities.[64] The state of Georgia owns a railroad—the Western and Atlantic—which it leases for private operation;[65] and a few states own and operate printing plants to supply the printing needs of their respective governments.[66]

Municipal Ownership

Public ownership is more common among the cities than elsewhere at the state and local levels, and is most widespread with respect to utility enterprises.[67] In the case of water utilities, municipal ownership actually predominates over private, more than two-thirds of all city water systems being municipally owned. The prevalence of public ownership in this field is probably to be explained in part by the close relationship between water supply and public health. Another contributory cause may be the fact that difficulties encountered in securing a safe and adequate water

---

[61] See above, "Liquor Regulation."

[62] Cf. Twiley W. Barker, Jr., "The States in the Liquor Business: Some Observations on Administration," *Quar. Jour. of Studies on Alcohol,* XVIII, 492-502 (Sept., 1957); United States Bureau of the Census, *Summary of State Government Finances in 1962* (U.S. Bur of the Census, Washington, 1963), 3.

[63] Cf. Frank Lang, *Workmen's Compensation Insurance* (Richard D. Irwin, Chicago, 1947), 15-17.

[64] *The Municipal Year Book* (Int. City Mgrs.' Assn., Chicago), 1962, pp. 362-363.

[65] T. N. Sandifer, "Airports, the New Monopoly," *Pub. Util. Fortnightly,* XXVI, 564-569 (Oct., 24, 1940); Howard, *op. cit.*

[66] Estal E. Sparlin, "Public Ownership versus State Purchasing: The Case of Printing," *Jour. of Polit. Economy,* XLVIII, 211-221 (Apr., 1940).

[67] Current statistics regarding municipal ownership of utilities in cities of over 5,000 population will be found in the "governmental data" section of the annual issues of *The Municipal Year Book.*

supply sometimes reduce the profits of such undertakings to a point where they fail to attract private capital.[68]

Next to water among the enterprises usually considered as utilities, municipal ownership is most common in the field of electric light and power. Some municipally owned electric systems generate their own power, while others are merely distribution systems which purchase their electricity wholesale. Though some large cities own electric utilities, a large majority of the municipal plants are found in small municipalities of less than 2,500 population. During the 1920's there was a substantial reduction in the total number of municipal electric utilities when many small cities, finding that they could obtain cheaper and more dependable service from the high voltage transmission lines of private companies, abandoned their municipal plants.[69] More recently, however, various programs of the national government have operated to encourage further extension of public and cooperative ownership in the electric utility field. Among these have been provisions for federal loans and grants to municipalities and public power districts for construction of generating plants and distribution systems; for capital loans to rural electric cooperatives by the Rural Electrification Administration; and for the wholesaling to municipalities and cooperatives of power generated by the Tennessee Valley Authority and other federal power projects.[70]

As a result, in no small part, of federal grants-in-aid for airport development, municipal ownership of airports is now widespread. In 1962 it was reported that 374 cities of over 10,000 population owned 439 airports, operating 291 and leasing 148 for operation.[71] A few gas utilities, street railway systems, and bus systems are municipally owned. Other business enterprises, of a utility nature or otherwise, which are operated by municipalities in varying number, include port facilities, ferries, toll bridges, traffic tunnels, steam heating systems, abattoirs, liquor stores, and markets.

County and Township Enterprises

Business enterprises owned by counties and townships are small in number as compared with those owned by municipalities, and recent data concerning most such enterprises are not available. In 1945, according to the United States Bureau of the Census, business enterprises operated by American counties included thirty-two alcoholic-beverage dispensaries (seven in Maryland and twenty-five in North Carolina), twenty-two

---

[68] Cf. Roland B. Eutsler, "Public and Private Ownership of Water Supply Utilities," *Annals of Amer. Acad. of Polit. and Soc. Sci.*, CCI, 89-95 (Jan., 1939).

[69] Cf. Trachsel, *op. cit.*, 507.

[70] See below, "Rural Electric Coöperatives," "Public Power Projects."

[71] *The Municipal Year Book*, 1962, p. 362. A few of the airports were owned jointly by a city and a county or by two cities.

water-supply systems, five electric light and power systems, five toll bridges, a telephone system, and a few other enterprises of miscellaneous nature. Some additional water-supply systems were operated by counties but, being financed from taxation or other general revenues, were not classified by the Census Bureau as business enterprises. Census data for 1942 report 110 water systems, sixteen electric systems, and a small number of other enterprises as being operated by townships and New England towns.[72] A field in which county ownership has been spreading during recent years is that of airport facilities, with 117 airports being reported as county-owned in 1962.[73]

Rural Electric Cooperatives

The cooperative form of business enterprise is not public or governmental in the strict sense, but in various respects partakes of the nature of public business. Thus consumer cooperatives, whether organized under the general corporation laws of the state or under other legislative authorization, represent a form of collective enterprise and are operated in the interest of their members on a nonprofit basis. In the case of most rural electric cooperatives, the public element is further emphasized by the fact that they are organized under the sponsorship of, and derive their initial capital as a loan from, a governmental agency—namely, the federal Rural Electrification Administration. Although some electric cooperatives operate generating plants, most of them operate distribution systems only. Electrical energy is purchased wholesale by distributing cooperatives from private utility companies, municipal plants, and federal power projects, and then retailed to rural consumers. A large majority of the establishments served by rural electric cooperatives are farms, the remainder consisting of rural nonfarm residences and other rural establishments such as stores, schools, and churches.[74]

Rural electric cooperatives, under the sponsorship of the Rural Electrification Administration, have proved an effective means of extending central station electric service to farm consumers. In large measure, the communities to which cooperative service has been extended have been in sparsely settled areas which private utility companies have been unwilling to supply because of the relatively unprofitable character of the business.[75] Today more than 95 percent of all American farms have electricity, as compared with 10 percent when the Rural Electrification Administration was established in 1935. While this dramatic spread of elec-

[72] United States Bureau of the Census, *County Finances: 1945* (U.S. Govt. Printing Office, Washington, 1947), 2, 12, 82-86; *Finances of Townships and New England Towns: 1942* (U.S. Govt. Printing Office, Washington, 1944), 10.

[73] *The Municipal Year Book*, 1962, p. 362.

[74] Cf. Frederick W. Muller, *Public Rural Electrification.*

[75] *Ibid.*

trification in rural areas is by no means the result solely of the REA program, more than half of the farms having electricity are served by REA borrowers.[76] With farm electrification now so nearly complete, some cooperatives are currently extending their services into suburban and urban areas; and such extensions, understandably, are encountering opposition on the part of privately-owned utilities. The REA lends federal money to the cooperatives at a rate of interest substantially below that simultaneously paid by the federal government on its own borrowings. This interest differential operates, in effect, as a subsidy to the cooperatives at the expense of the nation's taxpayers. Cooperatives also enjoy certain tax concessions which are not accorded to private utility companies.

Public Power Projects

Excluding the areas served by such federal projects as the TVA, public ownership of electric power facilities has had its most extensive development in the state of Nebraska. In the 1930's, with municipal ownership of electric utilities already widespread, a public power district and two power and irrigation districts were organized in different parts of the state to generate and sell electric power and to provide water for irrigation purposes. Later these three "hydros" were consolidated into the Nebraska Public Power System for the production and transmission of electricity, and the Consumers Public Power District was organized as a statewide distributing agency. Construction of hydroelectric projects was financed by loans and grants from the federal Public Works Administration, and the Consumers district, with funds raised from the issuance of revenue bonds, purchased most of the private utilities operating within the state. Eventually one of the power and irrigation districts originally included in the Nebraska Public Power System withdrew, and the system now consists of the Loup River Public Power District and the Platte Valley Public Power District. In 1946 the Omaha Public Power District was organized and when, in December of that year, this district completed purchase of the private utilities serving Omaha and vicinity, 100 percent public and cooperative ownership of electric utilities within the state was achieved. All consumers in Nebraska now purchase their electricity from public power districts, municipal plants, or rural electric cooperatives. The Nebraska Public Power System sells most of its power to the Consumers district, but also sells directly to some municipalities and rural cooperatives. The Consumers district wholesales power to municipalities and cooperatives and sells directly to consumers in some cities, a part of the energy which it distributes being generated in its own plants acquired from private owners. It is to be noted that the Nebraska system is not de-

[76] Jerry L. Anderson, ed., *Rural Electric Fact Book* (Nat. Rural Electric Coöperative Assn., Washington, circa 1960), 3, 7.

voted solely to the production and distribution of electricity but is essentially a multipurpose project, providing flood control and water for irrigation as well as cheap electric power.[77]

Extensive hydroelectric projects for flood control, public power, and other purposes have also been constructed, with federal financial assistance, by the states of South Carolina, Oklahoma, and Texas.[78] The New York Power Authority has recently developed a vast hydroelectric system on the Niagara and St. Lawrence rivers, generating electrical energy which is sold to industrial establishments, municipalities, rural electric cooperatives, private utility companies, and the state of Vermont.[79]

Pros and Cons of Public Ownership

The merits and weaknesses of publicly-conducted business have been debated at great length. In large measure the controversy has centered around municipal ownership of utility enterprises, and too often the arguments on each side have been based on sentiment and emotion rather than on logic and experience.[80] Opponents of public ownership have branded public business as socialistic, contrary to American ideals, and a universal failure. On the other hand, there are proponents of government in business who insist that public ownership is always preferable to private. Supporters of this doctrine often base their argument, as far as utility enterprises are concerned, upon the assumption that public regulation has failed and that the only alternative means of protecting the public interest is through government ownership. The weakness of this argument lies, of course, in the falsity of its basic premise. To be sure, utility regulation has failed in some instances, but in others it has achieved a high degree of success. The extent to which regulation is successful in protecting the interests of the public inevitably varies a great deal from place to place and from time to time, depending upon such factors as the nature of the regulatory statutes, the character of the personnel of the regulatory agency, and the adequacy of the funds provided for regulatory activities. But to say that regulation, because not always successful, has been a universal failure, is simply to ignore the facts.

[77] Judson King, "Nebraska, the Public Power State," *Pub. Util. Fortnightly,* XXXIX, 357-363, 419-426, 483-488 (Mar. 13, 27, Apr. 10, 1947); Emery Troxel, *Economics of Public Utilities,* 704-707. Recent information provided by Jack W. Rodgers, Director of Research, Nebraska Legislative Council.

[78] For descriptions of these projects, see Twentieth Century Fund, *Electric Power and Government Policy,* 559-564.

[79] Robert Moses, "The Niagara Power Project," *State Govt.,* XXXV, 155-157 (Summer, 1962).

[80] For discussions of the arguments for and against municipal ownership, see Munro, *op. cit.,* Chap. 46; Lent D. Upson, *Practice of Municipal Administration* (Century, New York, 1926), Chap. 31; Austin F. Macdonald, *American City Government and Administration* (Crowell, New York, 6th ed., 1956), Chap. 36; Wilson, Herring, and Eutsler, *Public Utility Regulation,* Chap. 19.

Much of the difficulty encountered in discussing the pros and cons of public ownership lies, it would seem, in an attempt to settle on the basis of principle a question which is in reality a matter of policy or expediency. Public ownership of business enterprise is not, inherently and universally, either good or bad. It is in practice desirable in some instances and not in others. Any debate over the relative merits of private and municipal ownership of utility enterprises in general is likely to be relatively barren of results. But the question as to whether a particular city, at a particular time, should own a particular utility, is one which should lend itself to solution on an objective basis. In determining whether it would be good policy for a given city to assume ownership of a utility which has been in private hands, various factors would require consideration. One of these would be the question of whether the citizens are receiving satisfactory service at reasonable rates under private ownership. If they are, the wisdom of shifting to municipal ownership would be more questionable than if service standards were unsatisfactory or rates unduly high. Another factor to be considered is the past record of the city government with respect to the more traditional functions. If the government in the past has provided streets, parks, and other municipal services in an efficient and economical manner, there is reason to believe that a municipal utility would be operated in a similar businesslike way. On the other hand, if the past record of the government has been one of waste and inefficiency, the wisdom of conferring additional duties and financial responsibilities upon it would be extremely doubtful. In other words, the question as to whether public or private ownership of a particular business enterprise is to be preferred is one which must be decided in each individual case after consideration of all pertinent circumstances.

Any attempt at broad comparison of municipal and private utilities with respect to relative efficiency is hazardous. In general, rates charged by municipal utilities appear to be somewhat, though not greatly, lower than those of private plants. A common plan is for municipal plants to keep their rates near the same level as those of private companies and contribute from their profits to the support of other municipal services.[81] Frequently these contributions are sufficient to offset the taxes which would be paid by the utilities if they were under private ownership, and in some instances they are sufficient to pay all the costs of municipal government. A number of municipalities which finance their governments solely from utility revenues have been given considerable publicity as "taxless" cities. That such a method of financing municipal activities represents sound policy is open to grave doubt, and in any event when used for advertising purposes to attract new residents and business the term *taxless* as here employed is misleading for two reasons. In the first

---

[81] John Bauer, "Public Ownership of Public Utilities in the United States," *Annals of Amer. Acad. of Polit. and Soc. Sci.*, CCI, 50-57 (Jan., 1939).

place, it is only the tax levy for city purposes that is replaced by utility revenues. Property within the city is still taxed for school, county, and other local purposes, and for state purposes if there is a state property levy; it is therefore far from taxless. In the second place, even the city government in such a municipality is by no means free to the inhabitants, as the term *taxless* might seem to imply. The costs of city government are merely assessed on the basis of utility service consumed rather than of value of property owned, and are paid through what may fairly be considered a hidden tax in the utility bills.

The Yardstick Principle

In conclusion, it may be pointed out that public ownership in the utility field is sometimes used, in part at least, for regulatory purposes. This is accomplished by operating publicly owned plants in competition with private plants, as is done in several cities.[82] Under such circumstances, the mere fact of competition tends to keep rates down to a reasonable level. In addition, the public plant is sometimes looked upon as a "yardstick" for determining what rates a private company, operating under similar conditions, would be justified in charging. Proponents of yardstick regulation believe that experience in the actual operation of a plant will indicate more accurately than the best estimate of a regulatory commission what rates will constitute reasonable charges for utility services. As a theory, yardstick regulation has much to commend it. In practice, however, the plan can operate effectively and honestly only if the public plant operates under conditions comparable to those to which the private plant is subject. This means that the publicly owned plant must pay taxes or make equivalent payments in lieu of taxes, pay interest on its capital investment, and in general follow accepted business and accounting practices. To whatever extent yardstick plants fall short of these standards, the plan fails to provide the honest measuring rod which its name implies, and is therefore worse than useless as a measuring device.[83]

[82] On the legal aspects of such competition, see Charles M. Kneier, "Competitive Operation of Municipally and Privately Owned Utilities," *Mich. Law Rev.*, XLVII, 639-654 (Mar., 1949).

[83] At the national level, the Tennessee Valley Authority has the yardstick objective as one of its several aims. For conflicting appraisals of this aspect of the Authority's program, see *Report of the Joint Committee on the Investigation of the Tennessee Valley Authority* (Sen. Doc. No. 56, 76th Cong., 1st Sess., 1939), 185-198, 285-290.

REFERENCES

BARNES, Irston R., *The Economics of Public Utility Regulation* (Appleton-Century-Crofts, New York, 1942).

BAUER, John, *The Public Utility Franchise: Its Functions and Terms under State Regulation* (Pub. Admin. Service, Chicago, 1946).

CAYWOOD, Russell E., *Electric Utility Rate Economics* (McGraw-Hill, New York, 1956).

COTTER, Cornelius P., *Government and Private Enterprise* (Holt, New York, 1960).

Council of State Governments, *Occupational Licensing Legislation in the States* (The Council, Chicago, 1952).

DIMOCK, Marshall E., *Business and Government* (Holt, New York, 4th ed., 1961.

EDELMAN, Jacob Murray, *Securities Regulation in the 48 States* (Council of State Govts., Chicago, 1942).

FAINSOD, Merle, and GORDON, Lincoln, *Government and the American Economy* (Norton, New York, rev. ed., 1948).

Federal Power Commission in cooperation with the National Association of Railroad and Utilities Commissioners, *State Commission Jurisdiction and Regulation of Electric and Gas Utilities* (Fed. Power Comsn., Washington, 1948).

FRYE, Robert J., *Government and Licensing: The Alabama Pattern* (Bur. of Pub. Admin., Univ. of Ala., University, Ala., 1958).

GRETHER, Ewald T., *Price Control under Fair Trade Legislation* (Oxford Univ. Press, New York, 1939).

HALL, Ford P., *Government and Business* (McGraw-Hill, New York, 3rd ed., 1949).

————, *State Control of Business through Certificates of Convenience and Necessity* (Bur. of Govt. Research, Ind. Univ., Bloomington, circa 1947).

————, *The Concept of a Business Affected with a Public Interest* (Principia Press, Bloomington, Ind., 1940).

Joint Committee of the States to Study Alcoholic Beverage Laws, *Alcoholic Beverage Control* (The Committee, Cleveland and New York, 1950).

Kentucky Legislative Research Commission, *Public Utilities Regulatory Bodies* (Ky. Legis. Research Comsn., Frankfort, 1958).

KOONTZ, Harold, and GABLE, Richard W., *Public Control of Economic Enterprise* (McGraw-Hill, New York, 1956).

LOSS, Louis, and COWETT, Edward M., *Blue Sky Law* (Little, Brown, Boston, 1958).

LYON, Leverett S., WATKINS, Myron W., and ABRAMSON, Victor, *Government and Economic Life*, Vol. I (Brookings Inst., Washington, 1940).

————, Abramson, Victor, and Associates, *Government and Economic Life*, Vol. II (Brookings Inst., Washington, 1940).

Marketing Laws Survey, United States Department of Commerce, *State Occupational Legislation* (U.S. Dept. of Commerce, Washington, 1942).

Marketing Laws Survey, Works Progress Administration, *State Antitrust Laws* (U.S. Govt. Printing Office, Washington, 1940).

————, *State Liquor Legislation* (U.S. Govt. Printing Office, Washington, 1941).

————, *State Price Control Legislation* (U.S. Govt. Printing Office, Washington, 1940).

MOSHER, William E., and CRAWFORD, Finla G., *Public Utility Regulation* (Harper, New York, 1933).

MULLER, Frederick William, *Public Rural Electrification* (Amer. Council on Pub. Affairs, Washington, 1944).

MUND, Vernon A., *Government and Business* (Harper, New York, 3rd. ed., 1960).

ROHLFING, Charles C., CARTER, Edward W., WEST, Bradford W., and HERVEY, John G., *Business and Government* (Found. Press, Brooklyn, 6th ed., 1953).

ROHRER, Margaret, *State Regulation of Insurance* (Bur. of Pub. Admin., Univ. of Calif., Berkeley, 1951).

STEIN, Emanuel, *Government and the Investor* (Farrar & Rinehart, New York, 1941).

TRACHSEL, Herman H., *Public Utility Regulation* (Richard D. Irwin, Chicago, 1947).

TROXEL, Emery, *Economics of Public Utilities* (Rinehart, New York, 1947).

Twentieth Century Fund, *Electric Power and Government Policy* (Twentieth Century Fund, New York, 1948).

WEIGEL, Stanley A., *The Fair Trade Acts* (Found. Press, Chicago, 1938).

WILCOX, Clair, *Public Policies toward Business* (Richard D. Irwin, Homewood, Ill., rev. ed., 1960).

WILSON, G. Lloyd, ed., "Ownership and Regulation of Public Utilities," *Annals of Amer. Acad. of Polit. and Soc. Sci.*, CCI, Philadelphia, Jan., 1939.

————, HERRING, James M., and EUTSLER, Roland B., *Public Utility Regulation* (McGraw-Hill, New York, 1938).

23

Government
and Labor

As long as the American economy was predominantly agricultural, there was no development of a "labor problem" in the sense in which that term is now generally understood. With the growth of industry and commerce, however, this situation changed. Tools of production and trade came to be owned by businessmen and corporations who employed workers in large numbers under conditions and on terms over which the employees had little control. Under these circumstances, problems and abuses arose which called for governmental regulation in the public interest.

Since the United States Constitution makes no mention of labor, responsibility for regulatory action in this field fell in the first instance to the states, and the earliest labor legislation was enacted by the states under their police power. More recently, and especially since the beginning of the New Deal in the 1930's, there has grown up a body of federal labor legislation, enacted for the most part under the power of Congress to regulate commerce and to prescribe labor standards for establishments supplying commodities or services to the United States Government under contract. Foremost among the federal labor statutes are the National Labor Relations (Wagner) Act of 1935 concerning collective bargaining, as modified in 1947 by the Labor-Management Relations (Taft-Hartley) Act, and the Fair Labor Standards Act of 1938 establishing minimum wages and a basic work week and prohibiting child labor. These acts, however, apply only to workers whose employment is related in some way to interstate or foreign commerce, and not to the millions of workers engaged in purely intrastate activities. While the candlestick maker whose product is sold in interstate commerce is covered by the federal laws, the butcher and baker producing solely for intrastate trade must look for protection to the respective state governments. Moreover, certain forms of protection, such as the requirement that workers be compensated for industrial accidents, are still provided by the states rather than the national government even for most employees associated with interstate or foreign commerce. Though federal labor legislation currently holds the spotlight of popular attention, it would therefore be a grave mistake to conclude that the states no longer play a vital role in labor regulation.[1]

Health and Safety Legislation

One of the earliest forms of state labor legislation was that designed to protect the safety and health of industrial workers. Some of this legislation goes back at least to the 1880's, though most of that now on the statute books is of more recent origin. Among the provisions found are requirements that dangerous machinery be equipped with guards; that accidents and occupational diseases be reported to designated state officials; that places of employment be provided with proper heating, lighting and ventilating facilities, and with fire escapes; and that there be adequate and sanitary toilets and dressing-rooms for employees.[2] Some of the early laws attempted to deal with each individual hazard in considerable detail, but the rigidity of such statutory provisions rendered that method unsatisfactory. The present tendency, therefore, is to enact statutes which merely require in broad terms that employers maintain reasonably safe and healthful working conditions and then confer upon administrative agencies authority to issue rules and regulations prescribing detailed standards. About half of the states now have safety codes established in this manner.[3]

A special health and sanitation problem is presented where employers supply individuals with raw materials to be processed in their homes. In the absence of public regulation, this "industrial homework" is often carried on under unsanitary and unhealthful conditions, and in an effort to meet these evils more than a third of the states have now enacted

[1] Cf. United States Department of Labor, *Why a State Wage-Hour Law Now?* (U.S. Dept. of Labor, Washington, 1941).

[2] See John R. Commons and John B. Andrews, *Principles of Labor Legislation* (4th ed.), Chap. 4.

[3] "Labor Legislation and Administration in the States," *The Book of the States* (Council of State Govts., Chicago), 1948-49, pp. 439-454.

regulatory measures.[4] The Illinois law of 1937, which may be taken as an example of this legislation, contains an outright prohibition of homework in processing articles of food or drink, drugs and medical supplies, fireworks and explosives, toys, and tobacco. Before any premises may be used for other kinds of industrial homework, the owner must secure a sanitary permit from the state department of labor. To qualify for such a permit, inspection must show that a specified minimum amount of floor space and air space is provided for each worker, and that workrooms meet prescribed standards with respect to heating, lighting, and ventilation. Every person employed as an industrial homeworker must secure from the department a worker's certificate, the statute specifying that no certificate shall be issued to any worker who has a contagious, infectious, or communicable disease or is less than sixteen years of age. Finally, every employer of industrial homeworkers must secure an employer's permit authorizing him to employ homeworkers in the specific industry concerned. No person may carry on industrial homework in a home other than that in which he resides. All permits and certificates issued under the law are valid for one year unless sooner revoked or suspended for cause. The requirement of annual renewal makes necessary the regular reinspection of all premises upon which homeworkers are employed, and the reexamination of all applicants for workers' certificates and employers' permits.

Workmen's Compensation

The form of social insurance legislation first adopted extensively in the United States was in the field of labor, and consisted of state "workmen's compensation" statutes relating to the compensation of workers by their employers for injuries sustained in the course of employment.[5] Adoption of such legislation began about 1910, and every state now has a compensation law.

At common law, an employer was liable to his employees or their dependents for accidental injury or death of an employee arising from failure of the employer to provide reasonably safe conditions of work or from other negligence on his part. Actual enforcement of this liability, however, was a difficult matter. If the employer refused to pay compensation due, the employee's only recourse was to a suit in the courts, which would ordinarily involve the hiring of a lawyer and all of the delay and expense usually attendant upon judicial process. Frequently the em-

---

[4] *The Book of the States,* 1962-63, p. 514.
[5] On the subject generally, see Herman M. Somers and Anne R. Somers, *Workmen's Compensation;* Marshall Dawson, *Problems of Workmen's Compensation Administration;* United States Bureau of Labor Standards, *State Workmen's Compensation Laws.*

ployee's lawyer would be no match for the specialist retained by the employer to handle injury cases, and if the employee was without ready cash he might have to hire his lawyer on a contingent-fee basis under which, in the event of success in recovering from the employer, a large part of the compensation award would go for attorney's fees. The employee's lawyer, in order to recover compensation for his client, was required to prove negligence on the part of the employer. In comparison, the task of the employer's lawyer was lightened by availability to the employer of three common-law defenses: (1) contributory negligence; (2) the fellow-servant doctrine; and (3) assumption of the risk. Establishment of any one of these defenses would absolve the employer from liability. Under the first and second, respectively, the employer was not liable if it could be shown that the injured employee's own negligence had contributed to the accident or that the accident had been caused by the negligence of a fellow-employee. Under the third defense, the employer was held not liable for injuries flowing from dangers ordinarily and inherently involved in the employment concerned, on the theory that the employee in accepting employment had voluntarily assumed all such risks. All in all, the situation was one where the employee's legal right to compensation was in practice often of little or no value.

Workmen's compensation laws have sought to remedy this unfortunate situation by abrogating the three common-law defenses and making employers liable to employees and their dependents for accidental injuries and death regardless of fault,[6] provided only that injury or death occurs in the ordinary course of employment. Most of the states now impose liability also for some or all occupational diseases.[7] Though in a few states the workmen's compensation law is enforced through the courts, in most instances enforcement is in the hands of some administrative agency, frequently a special board or commission established for this purpose. Where such an agency is provided, an employee or dependent, instead of having to sue in the courts, may have a contested claim for compensation heard and determined by the commission or board according to a simple procedure and without need of a lawyer.[8] Compensation awards are made in accordance with a schedule of benefits prescribed by the compensation statute or promulgated by administrative action under statutory authority. The amount of an individual award will depend upon such factors as the nature and seriousness of the injury or disease, the earnings of the employee concerned, and the number of his dependents.

[6] Except that injuries due to the employee's intoxication, willful misconduct, or gross negligence are in most states noncompensable.

[7] See Louise K. Steiner, *Recent Trends in Occupational Disease Legislation;* United States Bureau of Labor Standards, *State Workmen's Compensation Laws.*

[8] Appeal from decisions of the board or commission may ultimately be taken to the courts.

Employers are usually required to supply injured employees with necessary medical aid and hospitalization in addition to cash benefits.

Workmen's compensation is based on the theory that the cost of industrial accidents and occupational disease constitutes an integral part of the cost of production, which like other elements in production costs should be borne in the first instance by the employer and ultimately passed on to the consumer in the price of the goods produced. To make certain that benefit payments will be made when due, the compensation statutes require covered employers to take out workmen's compensation insurance. Though the greater part of this insurance coverage is provided by private insurance companies, state insurance funds have been established in eighteen states. In eleven of these, the state fund operates in competition with private insurance companies, with employers permitted to insure in either, while in the other seven the state fund has a monopoly of this type of insurance business. Most states permit covered employers, upon furnishing satisfactory proof of their financial responsibility, to carry their own risk instead of insuring with private companies or state funds, this practice being known as "self-insurance." [9]

Although workmen's compensation laws exist in every state, their coverage is by no means complete. Every law exempts some employments, with agricultural, domestic, and casual employments being most commonly exempted. Some laws apply only to employments considered hazardous or extrahazardous, and exempt all others; and in a majority of the states employers of less than a stipulated number of employees are exempt from coverage. Employers within the exempted categories are ordinarily permitted to come under the system by voluntary action, but many fail to do so. In about half of the states, furthermore, the compensation statute is elective rather than compulsory, thus permitting employers to choose whether or not they are to come under its terms. Since employers electing to remain subject to suit rather than to pay compensation under the workmen's compensation law are deprived of the common-law defenses, most nonexempt employers in such states accept the provisions of the statute as a matter of good business; yet some remain outside the system. All told, some 20 percent of the workers gainfully employed in the United States are still not protected by workmen's compensation.[10]

---

[9] Concerning the various types of insurance, see Frank Lang, *Workmen's Compensation Insurance;* Somers and Somers, *op. cit.,* Chap. 4. On state funds and their administration, see John B. Andrews, *Progress of State Insurance Funds under Workmen's Compensation* (U.S. Dept. of Labor, Washington, 1939). The states having competitive state funds are Arizona, California, Colorado, Idaho, Maryland, Michigan, Montana, New York, Oklahoma, Pennsylvania, and Utah. Those with monopolistic funds are Nevada, North Dakota, Ohio, Oregon, Washington, West Virginia, and Wyoming.

[10] United States Bureau of Labor Standards, *State Workmen's Compensation Laws.*

The economic security of the laboring class could therefore be further advanced by enlarging the present coverage of workmen's compensation laws. Another possible improvement in states where workmen's compensation is now administered through judicial proceedings would be a change to the commission plan, since an agency of the commission type is better adapted than are the courts to the administration of a compensation program in an efficient and expeditious manner.

Child Labor

Employment of children at too early an age, for excessive hours, or at tasks too heavy for their strength, may retard their physical development or injure their health, and their protracted employment is likely to interfere with proper schooling and recreation. Loss of schooling during childhood affects the ability of an individual in later life to earn a livelihood and participate intelligently in community affairs, while lack of sufficient playtime interferes with well-rounded development.[11] For these reasons, every state now has some sort of statute regulating child labor.

Though varying rather widely in the standards they establish and the occupations to which they apply, state child-labor laws follow a common general pattern. A basic minimum age is established, usually fourteen or sixteen years, at which a child may legally take a job, with many laws fixing a higher age requirement for hazardous occupations. In some states the age requirement is higher fcr employment during school hours than for work outside school hours or during vacations. Many laws, in addition to fixing a minimum age, require that the minor be physically fit for the job concerned, and some also provide that he must meet certain educational qualifications such as completion of a specified grade in school. Other provisions limit the number of hours per day and per week that young workers may be employed, restrict or prohibit night work, and prescribe a minimum amount of time to be allowed for meal periods.

Some of the child-labor statutes apply to all gainful employment; others exempt specified types of employment, such as agricultural work, domestic service, and the sale of newspapers and magazines; while still others apply only to designated classes of establishments, such as factories and stores. A cardinal factor in the administration of most laws is the requirement that employers secure, usually from local school officials, an employment certificate or work permit for each young worker. Before such a certificate or permit may be issued, the minor must present his birth certificate or other proof of age and establish that he meets any physical, educational, or other requirements which the law may prescribe. Certificate or permit systems of this nature serve not only to protect chil-

[11] Lucy Manning, *Why Child Labor Laws?* (U.S. Dept. of Labor, Washington, 1946), 1.

dren against improper employment, but also to protect employers against unknowingly violating the law.[12]

In the age limits and other standards which they impose, many of the present child-labor laws, measured in terms of modern needs, are wholly inadequate. In establishments producing goods for interstate or foreign commerce, the federal Fair Labor Standards Act now fixes a minimum age of sixteen for nonhazardous employment during school hours or in manufacturing, and eighteen for employment in hazardous occupations. Though these requirements are now generally recognized as the minimum acceptable age standards for child-labor legislation, many of the state statutes set age limits lower than sixteen for nonhazardous employment, while few if any states extend adequate protection to minors under eighteen against employment at hazardous work.[13] The laws of some states are rendered further inadequate by the narrow coverage resulting from numerous exemptions, and by lax enforcement. Currently, however, there is considerable interest in the improvement of child-labor laws, and it seems reasonable to expect a gradual raising of the standards presently established by state legislation.

Hours of Work

The first state statutes fixing maximum hours per day for industrial workers were enacted prior to the Civil War and applied only to children.[14] These were soon followed by laws applying to women, but legislation for adult men did not develop until a later period, and then applied for the most part only to men in certain hazardous occupations. Some of the earlier "hour" laws were invalidated by the courts as violations of the due-process clauses of state constitutions and the Fourteenth Amendment to the United States Constitution,[15] the judges taking the view that the statutes constituted an undue infringement upon the liberty of employers and employees to contract concerning hours of work. Thus the supreme court of Illinois, in 1895, declared an eight-hour law for women to be a violation of the state constitution;[16] and in 1905 the United States Supreme Court declared unconstitutional, as a violation of the Fourteenth Amendment, a New York statute limiting bakers to a ten-hour day.[17] Gradually,

---

[12] Lucy Manning and Norene Diamond, *State Child-Labor Standards;* Manning, *Why Child Labor Laws?,* 6-7; "Child-Labor Legislation," *The Book of the States,* 1948-49, pp. 455-464.

[13] Manning, *Why Child Labor Laws?,* 8.

[14] Commons and Andrews, *op. cit.,* 95-97.

[15] On the due-process clauses, see above, Chap. I, "The Bill of Rights"; Chap. II, "Due Process of Law."

[16] *Ritchie* v. *People,* 155 Ill. 98 (1895).

[17] *Lochner* v. *New York,* 198 U.S. 45 (1905).

however, the judicial attitude was altered and the concept of the police power broadened to permit maximum-hours legislation as a reasonable means of protecting the health and safety of the workers. In 1910, modifying its earlier attitude, the Illinois court upheld a ten-hour law for women;[18] and a 1917 decision of the United States Supreme Court sustained an Oregon statute establishing a ten-hour maximum day for men in general manufacturing work.[19] More recently, action of the national tribunal in upholding congressional regulation, through the Fair Labor Standards Act, of the hours and wages of employees, whether men or women, who are producing goods for interstate or foreign commerce,[20] further indicates that the states are now quite free to use their police power to regulate the hours of men, as well as women, in industrial employment generally.

At present, state child-labor laws [21] limit the daily hours of work for children to which they apply, usually providing for a maximum eight-hour day, and all but a few states have maximum-hours laws for women. Most of the statutes applicable to women establish a maximum work day of eight or nine hours, though a few permit a ten-hour day in some employments. With respect to both women and children a maximum work week is also usually established, this being generally, though not always, fixed at six times the daily limit. Maximum hours for men employed on public-works projects, state or local, are now prescribed in many states, these limitations frequently extending not only to public employees but also to workers on projects constructed for state or local governments by private contractors. Legislation regulating hours of work for men in private industry has as yet been limited for the most part to occupations, such as mining and smelting, in which long hours would be especially harmful to the health of the workers or would endanger their safety, and transportation work, such as the operation of street cars and buses, in which fatigue induced by prolonged work periods may, by increasing the likelihood of accidents, imperil the safety not only of the workers themselves but also of the traveling public. As long ago as the second decade of the present century, two or three states broke new ground by enacting maximum-hours laws for men in manufacturing establishments generally, but even now only a few states provide this broader coverage. Many states, in addition to fixing maximum daily and weekly hours for women and children, limit or prohibit night work by such persons, and a number have "six-

[18] *Ritchie* v. *Wayman*, 244 Ill. 509 (1910).
[19] *Bunting* v. *Oregon*, 243 U.S. 426 (1917).
[20] *United States* v. *Darby*, 312 U.S. 100 (1941). The federal statute, unlike most of the state laws, does not actually prescribe maximum hours but establishes a basic work week of forty hours and requires compensation at time-and-a-half rates for overtime.
[21] See above, "Child Labor."

day-week" laws, in some instances applicable to men also, requiring that employees be allowed one day of rest in seven.[22]

Wages

The method of paying industrial wages, as distinguished from the amount of the wage, has been a subject of state regulation from early times, and practically all of the states today have wage-payment laws of one kind or another. Among the early statutory provisions, still in effect in some instances, were requirements that wages be paid in cash rather than in scrip or orders on company stores, and that in the case of discharge or quitting payment should be made immediately or within a specified number of days. A widely prevalent type of provision in current legislation is that which regulates the frequency of wage payments. Though monthly payments are still permitted in some instances, most states now require the wages of some or all classes of industrial workers to be paid no less frequently than semi-monthly, and a few require weekly payments. Several states now have laws permitting workers unable to collect wages from employers to assign their claims to the department of labor or some other state agency for collection through court action or otherwise.[23]

Legislation prescribing minimum wages developed considerably later than that fixing maximum hours, and has spread less extensively. As in the case of maximum hours, minimum wages were first established for women and children. The first minimum-wage statutes were enacted during the second decade of the present century, with Massachusetts leading the way in 1912. In 1923, however, in the famous Adkins case, the United States Supreme Court declared unconstitutional, as wanting in due process of law, a minimum-wage statute for women enacted by Congress for the District of Columbia.[24] As a result of this decision, state minimum-wage legislation became for a number of years largely a dead letter. Few new laws were passed and some of those previously enacted were declared unconstitutional. Of the remaining statutes, some were repealed and little attempt was made to enforce most of the others. But when in 1937 the Supreme Court overturned the rule of the Adkins case in a decision upholding a Washington state statute providing minimum wages for women,[25] the states were enabled to resume the enactment and enforcement of legislation of this character.[26] By 1963, minimum-wage laws

[22] Commons and Andrews, op. cit., 99-140; Florence Peterson, Survey of Labor Economics, 460-462; "Labor Legislation and Administration in the States," loc. cit. See also The Book of the States, 1943-44, p. 240; Ibid., 1964-65, p. 542.

[23] Cf. Commons and Andrews, op. cit., 329-339; "Labor Legislation and Administration in the States," loc. cit.

[24] Adkins v. Children's Hospital, 261 U.S. 525 (1923).

[25] West Coast Hotel Co. v. Parrish, 300 U.S. 379 (1937).

[26] Commons and Andrews, op. cit., 54-58.

were in existence in thirty-three states. About half of these statutes applied to women and minors only, while the others were applicable to all workers, including adult men.[27]

Minimum-wage laws are of two principal types: (1) the flat-rate law under which minimum wage rates are fixed directly by statutory provision; and (2) the wage-board law which prescribes general standards, but leaves to the department of labor or some other administrative agency the task of fixing, by administrative order, specific minimum rates for individual industries. Because of their inflexibility, flat-rate laws have not proved satisfactory in operation and have now been quite generally replaced by statutes of the wage-board type.[28] Under present statutes, a minimum-wage scale for a particular industry is ordinarily established by administrative action upon recommendation, after full study and investigation, by a tripartite wage board composed of representatives of the employers, the workers, and the public.

In determining minimum-wage scales, two standards have been employed, singly or jointly—the "living wage" and the "value of the services performed." The earliest statutes adopted the standard of the living wage. However, this standard, as a *sole* basis for determining minimum wages to be required, has been frowned upon by the courts, and present laws therefore provide for taking into account the value of services rendered. Many of the recently-enacted statutes approach the problem by prohibiting the payment of *oppressive and unreasonable* wages, defined as wages which are *both* less than the fair and reasonable value of the services performed and less than sufficient to meet the minimum cost of living necessary for health. Provision is then made for the administrative establishment of "minimum fair wage" schedules to replace those found oppressive and unreasonable.[29] In practice, unfortunately, the "wage-floors" established under many of the statutes fall considerably below decent living standards.[30]

Some states require that employees on state and local public-works projects, whether constructed directly by the government concerned or by private contractors, be paid not less than the "prevailing rate" of wages for work of a similar character in the locality in which the work is performed. A type of regulation designed to afford further protection to women against exploitation in the matter of wages is the "equal pay" law prohibiting paying women employees lower wages than those paid to men for work of comparable character. As of 1963, statutes of this nature were reported to be in existence in twenty-four states.[31]

[27] *The Book of the States,* 1964-65, p. 541.
[28] Commons and Andrews, *op. cit.,* 64-68.
[29] *Ibid.,* 60-62.
[30] Glenn W. Miller, *American Labor and the Government,* 237-238.
[31] *The Book of the States,* 1964-65, p. 542.

Adjustment of Disputes

Peaceful settlement of industrial disputes should be a major element in any labor program. Success in making settlements tends to prevent strikes and lockouts, with their disruption of production and community life, as well as to foster amicable relations between management and labor generally. In seeking to effect the peaceful settlement of employer-employee controversies, governmental agencies make use of two principal procedures: (1) mediation or conciliation and (2) arbitration.

Although distinction is sometimes made between mediation and conciliation, their procedures are so similar, and the line between them is so indistinct, that most state statutes and many writers use the terms interchangeably;[32] and they are so used in this discussion. In mediation or conciliation, designated public officials or private citizens attempt to bring the parties concerned to an agreement which they will be willing to accept voluntarily. Both sides of the controversy are examined, investigations and inquiries are made, and the parties are encouraged to make mutual concessions. Neither mediator nor conciliator has any authority of a compulsory nature, or power to make a binding decision of any kind. Both are limited to the use of their "good offices" in seeking to bring about, through discussion and negotiation, a settlement which will be mutually acceptable to the parties on a voluntary basis.[33]

Arbitration, on the other hand, is to be clearly distinguished from mediation or conciliation. When a controversy is submitted to arbitration, the disputants agree in advance to abide by the arbitration award. The arbitrators then hear both parties, consider all available evidence, and hand down a binding decision. It will thus appear that arbitration is a much stronger form of adjustment procedure than mediation or conciliation; and this doubtless explains why it is less extensively used.

State Mediation and Arbitration Services

The first state law dealing directly with the adjustment of labor disputes appears to have been enacted by Maryland in 1878; and, during the quarter-century that followed, statutes or constitutional provisions concerning the subject were adopted in a majority of the states. Most of these early laws, however, were either administered in a perfunctory manner or subsequently repealed, only a few states—notably New York,

---

[32] Kurt Braun, *The Settlement of Industrial Disputes*, 29-31; John F. Duffy, Jr., *State Administrative Machinery for the Conciliation and Mediation of Labor Disputes* (Bur. of Pub. Admin., Univ. of Calif., Berkeley, 1945), 2.

[33] Cf. Commons and Andrews, *op. cit.*, 430.

Massachusetts, and Pennsylvania—having been continuously active in the adjustment of disputes since the turn of the century. In the 1930's, with a widespread upsurge of strikes and other labor difficulties, many states revived dormant agencies or established new ones, and the present era in mediation and arbitration activities was inaugurated.[34]

By 1958, according to the United States Bureau of Labor Standards, forty-four states had some kind of facilities, established by law or practice, for mediating labor disputes in industry generally.[35] In most instances mediation is a function of the state department of labor; but a few states have established special mediation boards independent of their labor departments. In some states the mediation authorities may undertake settlement of a labor dispute upon their own motion, while in others they may intervene only upon request of one or both parties to the controversy or under other circumstances specified by law. A few statutes make it the duty of the authorities to attempt mediation of a dispute upon learning of its existence, these laws also usually requiring that notice of intent to strike or lock out be filed with the mediation authority a specified number of days before such action is scheduled to take effect.[36]

The powers of mediation authorities vary considerably from state to state. Among those most commonly conferred are powers to engage in mediation and conciliation activities; employ special mediators and conciliators; establish procedures for the voluntary settlement of industrial disputes; investigate such disputes and promote their peaceful and voluntary settlement in all practicable ways; require advance notice of strikes and lockouts; hold hearings and make findings of fact and recommendations; and, in connection with investigations and hearings, subpoena witnesses, books, records, documents, and papers.[37] Some states make it the duty of the mediation agency to encourage voluntary arbitration of disputes not settled by the mediation process. Indeed, the official title of several state mediation boards is Board of Mediation (or Conciliation) and Arbitration. When both disputants agree to submit a controversy to arbitration, an arbitrator or a panel of arbitrators is appointed by the mediation agency or in such other manner as may be provided by law. The statutes of several states provide means for legal enforcement of arbitration awards.[38] State labor relations boards, which will be discussed presently, sometimes use mediation or arbitration in the settlement of labor disputes falling within their jurisdiction. The labor relations acts, how-

[34] Howard S. Kaltenborn, *Governmental Adjustment of Labor Disputes*, 171 ff.
[35] Some states have special mediation and arbitration agencies for settlement of disputes in the public-utility field.
[36] United States Bureau of Labor Standards, *A Guide to State Mediation Laws and Agencies* (U.S. Govt. Printing Office, Washington, 1958).
[37] Duffy, *op. cit.*, 13 ff.
[38] Commons and Andrews, *op. cit.*, 432.

ever, generally forbid those boards to engage in mediation or arbitration activities except in such cases.[39]

In some states the mediation and arbitration agency has functioned actively and vigorously, and has been successful in adjusting many controversies. In others, the work has been carried on in a perfunctory and desultory manner and with little effectiveness. Most of the statutory provisions, it will have been noted, carry little or no compulsion, and in this sense the legislation may be regarded as weak. Mediation in some instances may be undertaken only upon request of the parties concerned; mediators, having no authority to command, must rely upon persuasion; and arbitration, though resulting in a binding decision, is ordinarily possible only with the consent of both disputants. Yet, notwithstanding the general lack of compulsion, experience has shown that able and energetic mediators who can command the confidence and respect of management and labor alike can make substantial contributions toward preventing work stoppages and improving the tone of employer-employee relations.

Municipal Adjustment Plans

Municipal mediation agencies, official or unofficial, have been established in several cities.[40] Toledo, in 1935, pioneered the field by establishing an industrial peace board comprised of representatives of management, labor, and the public. This board operated with a considerable degree of success, settling a number of labor disputes both major and minor, but was discontinued during the war when mediation functions were largely centralized in national agencies. Early in 1946, as a means of promoting industrial peace in the post-war era, the Toledo city council enacted an ordinance establishing the municipality's present mediation agency—a labor-management-citizens committee appointed by the mayor as an official agency of the city government and consisting of eighteen nonsalaried members, six each from labor, management, and the public. Minor disputes are sometimes adjusted by the committee's executive secretary, but more serious controversies are submitted to a tripartite panel of mediators selected by its chairman. If the panel is unsuccessful in effecting a settlement, the dispute may be referred to the full committee. In addition to its mediation activities, the committee carries on some arbitration work, providing arbitrators upon request from among its public members or from outside. At the end of its first eight years of activity, the

[39] Charles C. Killingsworth, *State Labor Relations Acts*, 215.

[40] The discussion in this section is based primarily upon Institute of Labor and Industrial Relations, University of Illinois, *Municipal Mediation Plans*. See also Roy H. Owsley, *City Plans for Promoting Industrial Peace;* William L. Nunn, *Local Progress in Labor Peace;* Arthur W. Hepner, "Local and Unofficial Arrangements for Labor Dispute Settlement," *Law and Contemp. Probs.*, XII, 220-231 (Spring, 1947).

Toledo committee was reported to have settled 560 labor disputes, averted 153 strikes, and improved relationships between employers and employees generally.[41]

Another type of local mediation agency is exemplified by Boston's industrial relations council, established in 1941 by business and labor leaders. This council differs from Toledo's labor-management-citizens committee in being an unofficial agency having no connection with the city government. Another difference lies in the fact that the council's composition is primarily bipartite rather than tripartite. Though its executive committee includes one public member, most of the council's major organs consist simply of an equal number of union and company representatives. Like the Toledo committee, the Boston council offers both mediation and arbitration services.

The extent to which municipal mediation agencies may eventually be established, and their ultimate role in the adjustment of labor disputes, are matters for future determination. It would appear that, in general, the work of such agencies is likely to be found most valuable in states which do not themselves have effective mediation machinery. Indeed, where state adjustment facilities are adequate, the duplication and jurisdictional conflicts arising from a dual system may well render use of local agencies inadvisable except perhaps in unusual situations.

Unions and Collective Bargaining

"In union there is strength" is an axiom amply confirmed by the experience of labor. At one time workers could bargain only individually with their employers, and in such bargaining were inevitably at a disadvantage. Employers controlled the tools of production with which the laborers earned their daily bread, and thus were in a position to dictate terms and conditions of employment, which the individual laborer had little alternative but to accept. If proffered terms of employment were declined by one worker, they were likely to be accepted soon by another, perhaps a bit more hard-pressed than the first.

The obvious means of strengthening the hand of the laborer in the bargaining process was unionization, but the union movement and collective bargaining developed in their earlier stages in a fitful manner. Moreover, public opinion concerning unionism, as reflected in legislative action, has varied from time to time, with legislation tending to be pro-union in some periods and anti-union in others. To a large degree, state and national statutes have followed the same general trends, with sometimes the nation and at other times the states leading the way.

Early labor unions were relatively weak and were actively opposed

[41] Jerome Gross, "Industrial Peace in Toledo," *Nat. Mun. Rev.*, XLII, 507-511 (Nov., 1953).

by employers in a variety of ways. Among anti-union employer practices which were widespread were those of refusing to bargain with union representatives; "blacklisting" union leaders to prevent their employment; forcing employees to sign "yellow-dog" contracts;[42] and discriminating against union members in such matters as hiring, firing, and wages. Because of practices such as these, collective bargaining through labor unions made slow headway for many years. Indeed, as late as the early 1930's the attitude toward collective bargaining reflected in contemporary law was one of mere toleration, recognizing the right of such bargaining on the part of employees but providing no adequate means by which that right could be made effective.[43]

With the advent of the New Deal, however, the attitude of government toward unionization and collective bargaining shifted to one of positive encouragement, this shift being evidenced by the passage of the National Industrial Recovery Act, soon followed by the National Labor Relations Act and several state labor relations laws patterned after the national statute.[44] These earliest labor relations statutes, both national and state, were designed to give express confirmation to the right of laborers to organize and bargain collectively and to compel employers to respect that right. Eventually, however, as the result of both normal evolution and pro-union legislation, labor unions which had once been weak developed into powerful organizations and themselves engaged in practices deemed contrary to the general welfare. Accordingly, just as it had been found necessary at an earlier time to regulate the practices of "big business," it now became necessary, in the public interest, to regulate and restrict union activities. The response to this need was the enactment of restrictive state legislation and of the national Taft-Hartley Act of 1947, designed to outlaw certain union practices considered inimical to the public good. Thus public opinion and legislation seem to alternate in their nature between pro-union and anti-union, and the "happy mean" in labor-union legislation, which would protect the right of collective bargaining while reducing abuses to a minimum, has not yet been achieved.

Outstanding in the field of state legislation concerning labor unions and their activities have been the anti-injunction statutes and, more recently, the labor relations laws. These two principal types of regulatory action deserve consideration at this point.

Yellow-Dog Contracts and Anti-Injunction Laws

A favorite means of combating unionization in the early days was the yellow-dog contract in which the employee agreed, as a condition of

---

[42] See below, "Yellow-Dog Contracts and Anti-Injunction Laws."
[43] Commons and Andrews, *op. cit.*, 417-419.
[44] Cf. *Ibid.*, 419-429.

his employment, that he would not join a labor union.[45] Such a contractual provision was of value to the employer in that it might subsequently serve as the basis for an injunction against union representatives seeking to "organize" his plant. Since the employees had agreed not to become union members, organizational activities among those employees were held to violate the contractual rights of the employer and therefore to be a proper subject of prohibition by the courts. The injurious effect of the yellow-dog contract in obstructing unionization and collective bargaining resulted in the enactment by a dozen or more states of statutes outlawing such agreements and making their use a criminal offense.[46] These statutes, however, were held unconstitutional by the United States Supreme Court as violating the due-process requirement of the Fourteenth Amendment.[47]

Failing in their efforts to prohibit and penalize yellow-dog contracts, the legislatures next struck at the evil through their power to regulate the jurisdiction of state courts. Under this power, laws were enacted which, though not prohibiting yellow-dog contracts outright, provided that no state court should issue any injunction based upon their provisions. These statutes, which successfully made yellow-dog contracts unenforceable by judicial process, were regarded by labor as a substantial victory for the unionization movement. Eventually a majority of the states enacted anti-injunction laws of some kind applicable to labor disputes. Many of these statutes prohibit or limit the issuance of injunctions not only in connection with yellow-dog contracts, but also for various other purposes such as the prohibition of strikes or peaceful picketing. The federal anti-injunction law (Norris-LaGuardia Act) enacted by Congress in 1932 has served to some extent as a model for many of the more recent state statutes.

Labor Relations Acts

During the last three decades, the national Congress and several state legislatures have enacted statutes regulating in a fairly comprehensive manner collective bargaining and the respective rights of labor unions and management in the bargaining process. These laws are known as labor relations acts, and from the standpoint of their effect upon labor unions and union activities are of two fairly distinct types—the one protective and the other restrictive. In general, the earlier laws were of the protective type while those enacted more recently have been restrictive. Statutes which might properly be considered as labor relations acts were

[45] A variant form was that in which the employee agreed to join a "company" union dominated by the employer.

[46] Commons and Andrews, *op. cit.*, 407.

[47] *Coppage* v. *Kansas*, 236 U.S. 1 (1915).

in effect in 1961 in twelve states. Of these, the laws of New York, Massachusetts, Rhode Island, and Connecticut were of the protective type, while those of Minnesota, Michigan, Kansas, Hawaii, and Colorado were of the restrictive variety. In three states—Wisconsin, Pennsylvania, and Utah—early protective statutes had been revised in such a manner as to place them also in the restrictive category.[48]

The protective laws are patterned in large measure after the Wagner labor relations law of the national government and are sometimes referred to as "Baby Wagner Acts." They recognize the right of laborers to organize and bargain collectively through representatives of their own choosing, and prohibit certain "unfair labor practices" on the part of employers. Employer practices commonly proscribed include refusal to bargain with union representatives; domination of unions; and discrimination against workers, in hiring or firing, because of union activities. A labor relations board or similar agency is empowered to receive complaints of unfair labor practices, hold hearings, and issue cease-and-desist orders enforceable through the courts. Where an employee is found to have been discharged because of union membership or activities, the board may order his reinstatement with back pay. In case of a dispute between unions as to which shall represent a particular group of employees for bargaining purposes, an election may be conducted by the board among the employees concerned to determine the appropriate bargaining agency.

Statutes of the restrictive type ordinarily include most of the provisions contained in the protective acts, but in addition impose various limitations upon employees and their unions, some of which were ultimately incorporated at the national level into the Taft-Hartley Law. Whereas the protective acts seek to prevent unfair practices on the part of management, the restrictive statutes are concerned with unfair employee practices as well. Among the limitations imposed upon employees and unions in various states are those which forbid violence in labor disputes; prohibit sit-down strikes, mass picketing, and secondary boycotts; and outlaw or limit the use of various union-security devices such as the

---

[48] Charles C. Killingsworth, *State Labor Relations Acts*, Chap. 1; United States Bureau of Labor Standards, *State Labor Relations Acts*. Professor Killingsworth's book is a comprehensive study of state labor relations laws and their administration, and the discussion in this section is based in large measure upon his treatment of the subject. See also Agnes M. Brown and Mollie Margolin, *State Labor Relations Acts: An Analysis and Comparison;* Sanford Cohen, *State Labor Legislation: 1937-1947;* Edward F. Staniford, *Recent State Labor Legislation,* 1-24; Leifur Magnusson, *Government and Union-Employer Relations,* 12-22; Dale Yoder, "State Experiments in Labor Relations Legislation," *Annals of Amer. Acad. of Polit. and Soc. Sci.,* CCXLVIII, 130-137 (Nov., 1946); "State Regulation of Labor Unions," *Ill. Law Rev.,* XLII, 505-517 (Sept.-Oct., 1947); Richard H. Plock, "Methods Adopted by States for Settlement of Labor Disputes Without Original Recourse to Courts," *Ia. Law Rev.,* XXXIV, 430-479 (Mar., 1949), 462-476; Harold A. Katz, "Two Decades of State Labor Legislation: 1937-1957," *Univ. of Chicago Law Rev.,* XXV, 109-141 (Autumn, 1957).

closed shop, union shop, agency shop, and automatic checkoff.[49] Some of the laws require unions to register with, and submit reports to, designated state agencies, and regulate union finances and elections. A significant provision of most laws of the restrictive type is that which adds to the declared right of workers to organize and bargain collectively a coordinate right to *refrain from* union membership and collective bargaining—a provision designed to give nonunion laborers the same degree of protection against discrimination as that accorded to union members.

Most of the states which do not have statutes sufficiently comprehensive to be classed as labor relations acts have nevertheless singled out one or a few labor-union practices for prohibition or restriction. Practices banned in various states include sit-down, jurisdictional, and sympathy strikes; mass and stranger picketing; secondary boycotts; refusal to handle nonunion materials; coercion of employees to join the union; and the automatic checkoff of union dues.[50] During the 1940's and 1950's, some 20 states enacted "right-to-work" laws outlawing both closed-shop and union-shop contracts and in some instances agency-shop contracts as well.[51]

Notwithstanding the broad coverage of the National Labor Relations Act, large segments of industry are left to state regulation. To certain forms of business enterprise the national legislation does not apply, because interstate or foreign commerce is in no way involved; and in some cases jurisdiction possessed by the National Labor Relations Board is in practice not exercised for budgetary or administrative reasons. Among the enterprises in which labor relations thus fall principally to state regulation are retail stores, hotels and restaurants, laundries and dry-cleaning establishments, garages, hospitals, and local transportation and utility services.[52]

[49] Under a "closed-shop" contract the employer agrees to hire only union members. This form of contract is naturally favored by labor unions since it enables them to determine who shall be employed. The less extreme "union-shop" agreement permits the hiring of persons who are not union members but requires that workers so employed join the union within a specified period—frequently thirty days. Under an "agency-shop" contract, employees are not required to become union members but must pay to the union the equivalent of dues as a charge for its services as bargaining agent. A contractual provision for the automatic "checkoff" authorizes the employer to deduct union dues from the wages of employees and turn over the amounts so withheld to designated union officers.

[50] These laws are summarized in Killingsworth, *op. cit.*, Appendix A.

[51] United States Bureau of Labor Standards, *State "Right-to-Work" Laws* (U.S. Bur. of Labor Standards, Washington, 1959).

[52] Killingsworth, *op. cit.*, 3-4. Under the Taft-Hartley Act, moreover, the National Labor Relations Board may, by agreement, cede to a state regulatory agency jurisdiction over certain disputes affecting interstate commerce. See Labor Relations Information Bureau, *The Taft-Hartley Act in Operation* (Labor Rels. Inf. Bur., Washington, 1947), 35.

Fair Employment Practices Laws

A significant development in American labor law during the last two decades has been the enactment in a number of states of fair employment practices laws designed to prevent discrimination against Negroes and other minority groups. Legislation of this nature was enacted by New York and New Jersey in 1945, Massachusetts in 1946, and Connecticut in 1947; and by the end of 1961 some eighteen additional states had taken similar action.[53] Most of the laws follow the same general pattern. It is made an unlawful practice on the part of a covered employer[54] to refuse to hire any applicant for work, or to discharge or discriminate against any employee, because of race, creed, color, or national origin. Labor unions are likewise forbidden to exclude, expel, or discriminate against any person for such reasons; and discriminatory practices by employment agencies are prohibited.

Enforcement of the statutory provisions is placed in the hands of a fair employment practices commission (FEPC) or other administrative agency. The enforcement agency is authorized to make investigations on its own initiative, receive and investigate charges of discrimination, and endeavor to eliminate discriminatory practices by conference, conciliation, or persuasion. If these efforts are unsuccessful, the agency is empowered to hold formal hearings, subpoena witnesses and, if the evidence is found to substantiate the charges, issue cease-and-desist orders which, subject to appeal to the courts, are enforceable as law. Certain other states have declared discriminatory practices of the kinds mentioned to be contrary to public policy but have made no provision for compelling their discontinuance.

Experience with fair employment practices acts has not yet been sufficiently extensive to warrant a definitive appraisal of their results. Enforcement agencies seem generally to have emphasized investigatory activities and the informal adjustment of complaints, and this would appear to be wise policy. Yet enforcement provisions in such a statute seem desirable as a means of strengthening the hand of the administrative agency in informal proceedings. New York's early experience suggests that a fair employment practices act having enforcement provisions may be effectively administered in a large industrial state with little or no resort to actual compulsion. During the first two and one-half years of the New York law's effectiveness, though more than 1,000 complaints were filed

[53] Illinois Legislative Council, *State Fair Employment Practice Laws;* Illinois Legislative Council, *State "Educational" Fair Employment Practice Laws;* Beatrice McConnell, "Labor Legislation, 1960-1961," *The Book of the States,* 1962-63, pp. 491-497.

[54] Employers of less than a designated number of persons (six in several states) are exempted from coverage.

with the state commission against discrimination, the commission is reported to have been able, wherever it was found to have jurisdiction, to bring about elimination of the unlawful practices complained of through informal procedure without once resorting to formal hearings or criminal sanctions.[55]

Discriminatory employment practices being in large measure a problem of urban areas, their elimination, especially in jurisdictions which do not have adequate state laws on the subject, would seem to be an appropriate function of municipal government. As in other fields, of course, municipalities are able to act in such matters only if the necessary authority has been conferred by the state, either specifically or through some general grant of regulatory power. Pursuant to state authorization, several cities, including Chicago, Cincinnati, Milwaukee, Minneapolis, and Philadelphia, have enacted fair employment practices ordinances. Though some of the ordinances apply only to city employees, or to these and employees of firms awarded city contracts, others are applicable to municipal and private employment generally.[56]

Employment Agencies

One of the most serious economic hazards of the laborer is unemployment. Even in prosperous times, some workers suffer involuntary unemployment, and in periods of severe depression the number of unemployed is greatly increased. Traditionally, persons without means of support because of unemployment have been cared for through private charity or public-assistance payments (formerly known as poor relief). The depression of the 1930's however, with unemployment running far into the millions, revealed the utter inadequacy of assistance payments as a final answer to the unemployment problem. Not only is the stigma of charity likely to impair the morale of assistance recipients, but in times of widespread unemployment the burden on the taxpayers becomes so heavy that it may further aggravate the economic maladjustment. Efforts are therefore being made to supplement public assistance as a means of dealing with unemployment, and indeed to supplant it insofar as possible, by two principal instrumentalities—employment agencies and unemployment compensation.

An employment agency is a means of bringing together workers seeking employment and employers in need of workers. Unemployed workers are urged to register with the agency on blanks setting forth their

[55] Henry Spitz, "The New York State Law Against Discrimination," *N. Y. Bar Assn. Bull.*, XX, 8-13 (Feb., 1948).

[56] Cf. Alex Elson and Leonard Schanfield, "Local Regulation of Discriminatory Employment Practices," *Yale Law Jour.*, LVI, 431-457 (Feb., 1947); Public Administration Clearing House *News Bulletin* (Pub. Admin. Clearing House, Chicago), Release for June 28, 1949.

qualifications and experience, and may be interviewed by members of the agency's staff in order to determine further their abilities and personality traits. An effort is made to secure from employers information concerning jobs available, and it is then possible in many instances for the agency to refer a person seeking employment to an establishment having a vacancy which he is qualified to fill.

Regulation of Private Employment Agencies

Employment agencies financed by private philanthropy and making no charge for their services exist in most large cities, but are relatively limited in their facilities and effectiveness. Of more significance are the private agencies operated for profit and therefore charging fees for placement. Agencies of this nature abound in industrial centers and are found in many other municipalities as well. Though many of these agencies conduct their affairs in a completely ethical manner and perform a valuable social service, some have indulged in disreputable practices such as misrepresentation concerning wages and working conditions, charging extortionate fees, and fee-splitting with foremen—the latter encouraging frequent discharges and the making of replacements through favored agencies. Because of such abuses, most states have enacted legislation requiring that private employment agencies be licensed and bonded and regulating their practices. By 1963, forty-five states had laws of this nature. Among the common provisions of such statutes are those that prescribe the manner in which agency records shall be kept, require the filing of fee schedules with the state labor department, and prohibit fee-splitting. Some statutes limit the amount of the fees to be charged by the agencies for their services. Both license and bond are ordinarily made subject to forfeiture for violation of the regulatory laws. Though unethical practices have been reduced by this legislation, they have by no means been completely eliminated.[57]

State Employment Services

Most important among employment agencies today are the employment services operated by the state governments, ordinarily as units within their labor departments. Establishment of public employment agencies came about in part as an additional effort to remedy the abuses of private agencies, and in part as a recognition of the fact that aiding

[57] Commons and Andrews, op. cit., 5-12; John B. Andrews, Labor Problems and Labor Legislation (4th ed.), 13-16; United States Bureau of Labor Standards, State Laws Regulating Private Employment Agencies (U.S. Govt. Printing Office, Washington, 1960); United States Bureau of Labor Standards, Brief Summary of State Laws Regulating Private Employment Agencies (U.S. Bur. of Labor Standards, Washington, 1963).

the unemployed to find work is a legitimate governmental function. Led by Ohio in 1890, many states established public employment agencies of one kind or another. In the Wagner-Peyser Act of 1933 Congress inaugurated a program of grants-in-aid for state employment services meeting federal standards, and within a few years every state had acted to accept this offer of financial assistance.[58] Thereafter each state, as a recipient of federal aid, operated its employment service under the supervision of the national government; and at the beginning of 1942, as a part of the effort to mobilize civilian employees for maximum war production, the state employment services were completely federalized. During the war years, as a result of this action, the services were federally operated within the United States Employment Service, but in 1946 their operation was returned to the respective states. A state employment service ordinarily operates offices in each major city of the state, and sometimes part-time offices are maintained in less populous communities. Since the war, the activities of the state services have been expanded to include job counseling and special placement services for veterans.[59]

Unemployment Compensation

Unemployment compensation systems provide a means whereby, during the course of a worker's employment, funds are set aside through payroll taxes from which he may receive benefit payments during a period of unemployment. The availability of such benefits obviates, or at least postpones, the necessity of the unemployed worker's seeking assistance from public relief funds. Moreover, since unemployment compensation benefits are paid as a matter of right and not as a form of charity, the system tends to bolster the individual's morale during the period when he is out of work and seeking employment.

Like many other social problems, that of providing a system of unemployment compensation can scarcely be solved by the uncoordinated action of individual states. Payroll taxes increase production costs and therefore, if one state provides unemployment compensation and others do not, the industries of the state having this form of social insurance will be at a disadvantage when they sell their products on national and international markets in competition with products from other states. This may well be one of the principal reasons why only a single American state, Wisconsin in 1932, adopted an unemployment compensation law prior to the enactment of the federal Social Security Act in 1935.

The Social Security Act did not establish a national system of unemployment compensation, but included provisions designed to induce

[58] Commons and Andrews, *op. cit.*, 12-17.
[59] Cf. C. E. Rightor, "Recent Developments in State-Federal Relations," *The Book of the States*, 1948-49, pp. 53-61.

the states to establish compensation programs. A federal excise tax of 3 percent was imposed on the payrolls of all business concerns (except those in certain exempted categories) employing eight or more persons. Provision was then made that, in any state which established a system of unemployment compensation meeting federal approval, employers should be entitled to offset against their federal tax whatever amount they paid into the state system up to a maximum of 90 percent of the federal levy. Grants were also to be made from the federal treasury to the states to pay the costs of administering their programs. In somewhat simplified terms, this scheme meant that every nonexempt employer would be subject to a payroll tax; that, if a state established an approved system of unemployment compensation, the taxes paid by employers could be used, for the most part, by the state government to finance that program; but that, in any state not establishing an approved system, all receipts from the tax would go into the federal treasury.[60] Under this setup, a state desiring to establish a system of unemployment compensation could now do so without placing its industry at a disadvantage, since employers in states not levying a payroll tax for state use would nevertheless be subject to the federal tax. Indeed, the arrangement actually operated to penalize any state failing to provide a program of unemployment compensation, since payroll taxes paid by employers in such a state would be used for federal purposes instead of being used within the state for the benefit of the state's own unemployed. The efficacy of the federal scheme in bringing about state action is readily seen in the fact that within two years of the enactment of the Social Security Act every state had established an unemployment compensation program.[61] As a result of amendments to the federal legislation as originally enacted, the federal excise tax now applies to employers of four or more, and the rate of levy has been increased to 3.1 percent. However, the maximum tax offset allowed to employers operating under approved state systems continues at 90 percent of the original 3 percent levy—i.e., 2.7 percent. Thus a minimum tax of 0.4 percent must always be paid to the federal government. The federal tax, and the state tax in most states, applies to the first $3,000 of the annual wage of each covered employee.

Though every state now has a system of unemployment compensation meeting federal standards for tax-offset purposes, there is no federal requirement of absolute uniformity, and some variations are found in the

[60] Actually, unemployment compensation tax funds collected by the states must, under the terms of the Social Security Act, be turned over to the federal government and kept in a special trust fund upon which the respective states then draw for the payment of benefits.

[61] Edwin E. Witte, "Development of Unemployment Compensation," *Yale Law Jour.*, LV, 21-52 (Dec. 1945). For an analysis of state legislation, see United States Department of Labor, *Comparison of State Unemployment Insurance Laws as of January 1, 1962* (U.S. Govt. Printing Office, Washington, 1962).

state laws. The rate of payroll tax imposed by the states to finance unemployment benefits has varied somewhat, but at present the standard basic rate, in effect in most states, is 2.7 percent—the maximum amount which may be offset against the federal levy. However, the rate actually assessed against a particular employer may differ from the basic rate. Every state now uses some sort of "experience rating" system whereby an employer's rate of contribution may be less than the basic rate if his establishment has a past record of relatively little unemployment, or in some states may be more than the basic rate in case of an unfavorable record. Because of this system, the average rate of contribution actually paid by employers at present is in most states somewhat below the basic rate of 2.7 percent. The purpose of experience rating is two-fold: (1) to lessen unemployment by inducing employers to stabilize their operations, and (2) to impose the costs of unemployment upon the business concerns responsible for those costs.[62] Experience rating is in practice encouraged by the Social Security Act, since "merit" reductions permitted under state law operate to reduce the employer's federal tax. In most states unemployment compensation taxes are levied entirely upon the employers, only a very few requiring employee contributions.

To be eligible for unemployment compensation benefits under the typical state law, a worker must have earned a prescribed minimum amount of wages in covered employment during a specified prior period, and must be involuntarily unemployed and available for employment. He must make application for compensation and register with the state employment service as an applicant for work, and a brief "waiting period"—one week in most states—must then elapse before benefit payments begin. Weekly benefit rates, as well as the number of weeks for which benefit payments may be drawn, depend upon the aggregate amount of wages earned in the preceding base period. The statutes, however, ordinarily fix minimum and maximum benefit rates and the maximum duration of benefits in any year, the latter now being twenty-six weeks in most states. Since the compensation programs are designed to protect only persons who are unemployed through no fault of their own, some unemployed persons are disqualified for benefits. Thus compensation is usually denied, or benefits postponed or reduced, where unemployment results from the voluntary quitting of a job (except for good cause attributable to the employer), discharge for misconduct, refusal of suitable work, or work stoppage resulting from a labor dispute.[63]

One of the principal inadequacies of the present unemployment compensation programs, as in the case of workmen's compensation, is their

[62] Almon R. Arnold, "Experience Rating," *Yale Law Jour.*, LV, 218-241 (Dec., 1945).

[63] Ruth Reticker, "Unemployment Compensation in the United States," *Internat. Labour Rev.*, XLIX, 446-472 (Apr.-May, 1944).

limited coverage. Wages of agricultural workers, domestic servants, state and local government employees, and employees of nonprofit organizations are exempt from the federal payroll tax, and employees in these categories have generally been exempted by the states from their compensation provisions.[64] A majority of the states also follow the pattern suggested in the federal law in exempting employers of less than four, and thereby their employees, from compensation coverage. Other states, however, have lower numerical exemptions, with most of these covering employers of one or more. Notwithstanding that some of the state laws are thus broader in their coverage than the federal tax statute contemplates, and the further fact that more than 40 million workers are now covered, some 14 million American wage-earners are still excluded from the benefits of unemployment compensation.[65] Another serious shortcoming of the present programs is their failure, in most instances, to provide protection against unemployment due to disability. To be eligible for benefits under the system as it now operates in most states, an unemployed person must be *available for employment.* In most states, indeed, if a person actually drawing compensation becomes ill or otherwise incapacitated, he thereby becomes ineligible for continuation of benefits notwithstanding that his need, because of medical expenditures, is likely to be increased. Workmen's compensation, as we have seen, provides benefits for some employees while disabled from industrial accident or occupational disease, but affords no protection against accidents and sickness generally. Four states, however—California, New Jersey, New York, and Rhode Island—provide for disability benefits to persons unemployed because of nonoccupational illness or injury.[66]

Unemployment compensation is an essential element of a social security program, but at its best must be considered as only a palliative and not a cure. Benefit payments will be of considerable assistance to individual workers, especially in normal times when periods of unemployment are likely to be infrequent and of short duration. But when unemployment occurs on a large scale as the result of severe economic depression, a compensation program can only cushion and not avert its consequences. Prevention rather than compensation must be the basic answer to the problem of unemployment.

[64] Federal civilian employees and armed services personnel are covered by unemployment-compensation programs financed entirely from federal funds, and a majority of the state laws now require or permit coverage of some or all state and local employees.

[65] United States Department of Labor, *Unemployment Insurance: State Laws and Experience* (U.S. Govt. Printing Office, Washington, 1961).

[66] United States Department of Labor, *Comparison of State Unemployment Insurance Laws as of January 1, 1962,* Chap. 6.

Administrative Organization

In the absence of provision for special administrative agencies, enforcement of the earliest labor laws fell to the general law-enforcement officers of the state and local governments and was carried on, in many instances, in a desultory manner. The first administrative agencies to be established by the states in the labor field were mere fact-finding bodies known as bureaus of labor statistics. Though originally confined to the gathering and publication of labor information, these bureaus were eventually given the task of enforcing certain protective regulations. Somewhat later, factory inspectors were provided in many states, and the regulatory functions formerly lodged in local governments and state bureaus of labor statistics were rather generally transferred to these officials. Certain regulatory activities, however, remained where they had originally been placed, and as new state laws were enacted many established new and separate agencies for enforcement purposes. As a result, administrative activities in the labor field came to be scattered among a hodgepodge of state and local agencies. Little progress toward unified enforcement occurred until the second decade of the present century, when several states established central authorities for administering most or all of their labor legislation. Since that time, the movement toward integrated administration has advanced steadily. Local regulation of working conditions and local enforcement of state labor laws still exist in some instances, but are now of distinctly minor importance in comparison with the activities of the state governments.[67]

The principal agency for administering labor legislation in a majority of the states at present is a department of labor or industrial relations under a commissioner, director, or secretary. Other states have a bureau or division of labor within one of the principal departments, a labor commission, or some other type of administrative agency.[68] Administrative machinery is naturally more elaborate in the more highly industrialized states than in others. Even where there is a well organized labor department, however, it is usual to find some labor activities located in agencies outside the jurisdiction of the department's head. Workmen's compensation, for example, is frequently administered by an industrial commission or board which may either enjoy a high degree of autonomy within the labor department or be organized on a completely independent basis; and in many instances unemployment compensation is administered by an independent commission. Also usually enjoying a large measure of independence are the mediation boards, labor relations boards, and fair

[67] John B. Andrews, *Labor Laws in Action*, Chap. 2.
[68] United States Department of Labor, *Outline of State Agencies Administering Labor Laws*.

employment practices commissions found in some states; and in occasional instances certain activities in the labor field are administered by the agriculture, highway, welfare, or other state departments. Nothwithstanding numerous exceptions, however, there is a distinct tendency toward the consolidation of all labor services, except those of a quasi-judicial nature, in a state department under a single head. This process of integration, though still incomplete in a number of states, has made substantial progress during recent decades.

REFERENCES

ANDREWS, John B., *Labor Laws in Action* (Harper, New York, 1938).

————, *Labor Problems and Labor Legislation* (Amer. Assn. for Labor Legislation, New York, 4th ed., 1932 with 1940 supplement revision).

BRAUN, Kurt, *The Settlement of Industrial Disputes* (Blakiston, Philadelphia, 1944).

BROWN, Agnes M., and MARGOLIN, Mollie, *State Labor Relations Acts: An Analysis and Comparison* (Legis. Ref. Service, Library of Congress, Washington, 1947).

COHEN, Sanford, *State Labor Legislation: 1937-47* (Bur. of Bus. Research, Ohio State Univ., Columbus, 1948).

COMMONS, John R., and ANDREWS, John B., *Principles of Labor Legislation* (Harper, New York, 4th ed., 1936).

DAWSON, Marshall, *Problems of Workmen's Compensation Administration* (U.S. Dept. of Labor, Washington, 1940).

Illinois Legislative Council, *State "Educational" Fair Employment Practice Laws* (Ill. Legis. Council, Springfield, 1960).

————, *State Fair Employment Practice Laws* (Ill. Legis. Council, Springfield, 1957).

Institute of Labor and Industrial Relations, University of Illinois, *Municipal Mediation Plans* (Univ. of Ill., Urbana, 1947).

KALTENBORN, Howard S., *Governmental Adjustment of Labor Disputes* (Found. Press, Chicago, 1943).

KILLINGSWORTH, Charles C., *State Labor Relations Acts* (Univ. of Chicago Press, Chicago, 1948).

KING, Irving N., *Trends and Problems in Unemployment Insurance* (Inst. of Labor and Indus. Rels., Univ. of Ill., Urbana, 1950).

LANG, Frank, *Workmen's Compensation Insurance* (Richard D. Irwin, Chicago, 1947).

LEEK, John H., *Government and Labor in the United States* (Holt, New York, 1952).

MAGNUSSON, Leifur, *Government and Union-Employer Relations* (Pub. Admin. Service, Chicago, 1945).

MANNING, Lucy, and DIAMOND, Norene, *State Child-Labor Standards: A State-by-State Summary of Laws Affecting the Employment of Minors Under 18 Years of Age* (U.S. Dept. of Labor, Washington, 1949).

MILLER, Glenn W., *American Labor and the Government* (Prentice-Hall, New York, 1948).

NUNN, William L., *Local Progress in Labor Peace* (Nat. Mun. League, New York, 1941).

OWSLEY, Roy H., *City Plans for Promoting Industrial Peace* (Amer. Mun. Assn., Chicago, 1947).

PETERSON, Florence, *Survey of Labor Economics* (Harper, New York, 1947).

SOMERS, Herman M., and SOMERS, Anne R., *Workmen's Compensation* (Wiley, New York, 1954).

STANIFORD, Edward F., *Recent State Labor Legislation* (Bur. of Pub. Admin., Univ. of Calif., Berkeley, 1949).

STEINER, Louise K., *Recent Trends in Occupational Disease Legislation* (Inst. of Labor and Indus. Rels., Univ. of Ill., 1951).

United States Bureau of Labor Standards, *State Labor Relations Acts* (U.S. Govt. Printing Office, Washington, 1961).

————, *State Workmen's Compensation Laws* (U.S. Govt. Printing Office, Washington, 1960).

United States Department of Labor, *Outline of State Agencies Administering Labor Laws* (U.S. Dept. of Labor, Washington, 1941).

WHITE, R. Clyde, *Administering Unemployment Compensation* (Univ. of Chicago Press, Chicago, 1939).

VII

State and
Local Finance

24

Revenues

Securing revenue for the support of public services is a major problem of government at every level. For reasons suggested in the following chapter, governmental costs are steadily mounting, and the problem of providing funds is becoming ever more serious. In their efforts to finance public services at higher cost levels, the states and local units are increasing their rates of taxation, imposing new levies, and making constantly wider use of revenues from nontax sources.

The Taxing Power and Its Limitations

A tax may be defined as a compulsory contribution for the support of government, exacted without regard to individual benefits.[1] Taxes of various kinds constitute the principal source of governmental revenue. Power to levy taxes for state purposes rests with the respective state legislatures, and is subject only to such limitations as are imposed by the federal and state constitutions. Local governments possess only such taxing power as has been conferred upon them by the states. The local taxing power is subject to all limitations imposed upon the state by constitutional provision, as well as to any additional restrictions which the state legislature has seen fit to impose by statute.[2] State legislatures, therefore, may

[1] Cf. Merlin H. Hunter and Harry K. Allen, *Principles of Public Finance,* 169.
[2] Cf. Advisory Commission on Intergovernmental Relations, *State Constitutional and Statutory Restrictions on Local Taxing Powers.* Some local units in home-rule states possess certain taxing authority by virtue of state constitutional grant, and such authority of course is not subject to statutory abridgement.

levy any tax which they are not forbidden to impose, whereas local governmental units may impose only those taxes which they are empowered by the state to levy.

The principle implicit in the United States Constitution which forbids the states and local units to tax instrumentalities of the national government has been considered in an earlier chapter. Other significant limitations imposed by that document upon state and local taxing power flow from the "due process" and "equal protection" clauses of the Fourteenth Amendment.[3] To comply with the due-process requirement, tax measures must meet certain procedural standards, as, for example, in the matters of notice and hearing, and must not be confiscatory; while the equal-protection clause operates to prohibit arbitrary or discriminatory classification.

Limitations imposed upon the taxing power by state constitutions are of varied character. Constitutional provisions ordinarily exempt certain classes of property from taxation or specify what classes may be exempted by statute. Most commonly exempted is publicly-owned property and property used for educational, religious, or charitable purposes. A majority of the states provide exemptions of one kind or another for veterans. Some states have "homestead" exemptions under which owner-occupied homes are wholly or partially nontaxable; some exempt certain industrial and agricultural properties; and a few extend some degree of exemption to the property of elderly owners. All in all, exemptions have become so extensive that in many jurisdictions, particularly in urban communities, a substantial part of all real estate does not appear on the tax rolls.[4] As a result, property-tax revenues suffer serious curtailment unless the rates on nonexempt property are correspondingly increased. A number of constitutions still retain the requirement, once quite prevalent, that all nonexempt property be taxed at uniform and equal rates, and in some instances rate limitations of one kind or another are imposed.[5] Some constitutions enumerate at considerable length the businesses and transactions subject to privilege taxes, and such provisions may be interpreted by the courts to preclude the taxation of nonenumerated subjects.

The power of local governments to levy property taxes is frequently subject to percentage or millage limitations upon the rates that may be imposed for various purposes. For example, municipalities may be authorized to levy up to five mills on each dollar of assessed valuation for street purposes, three mills for health work, and two mills for parks. Sometimes it is provided that these maximum rates may be exceeded by action of the local voters in referendum elections. Authorizations for the imposition of

---

[3] See above, Chap. II, "Intergovernmental Tax Immunity," "Due Process of Law," "Equal protection of the Laws."

[4] It has been estimated that about one-sixth of all real estate in the country falls within the various exempt categories. K. P. Sanow, "Property Tax Exemption," *State Govt.*, XIX, 108-114 (Apr., 1946).

[5] See above, Chap. VIII, "Financial Limitations."

nonproperty taxes by local units are also usually accompanied by rate limitations.

In a special category in the property-tax field is the "overall" type of limitation adopted in several states by constitutional or statutory provision. These provisions fix maximum *total* rates, ranging from 10 to 50 mills on the dollar, which may not be exceeded by the *combined* levies, local and state, upon a single piece of property.[6] The total local rate permitted under an overall limitation may be apportioned among the taxing units concerned by statutory provision or, as is the more common practice, a designated administrative agency, say at the county level,[7] may be empowered to make the apportionment. In practice, overall limitations have proved to be of questionable merit. Faced with such drastic restrictions, local governmental units have sought in various ways to circumvent their effectiveness. In some instances assessed valuations have been raised to offset rate reductions, and in others borrowing for current expenses has been resorted to. Where efforts at evasion have failed, reductions in revenue resulting from the rate limitations have frequently necessitated curtailments in essential local services, such as police and fire protection and education.

Property Taxation

From the beginning of our existence as a nation, taxes on property have constituted the principal source of local revenue in the United States, and until recent decades such taxes were the chief source of state revenue also.[8] For purposes of taxation and otherwise, two broad classes of property are commonly recognized—real and personal. Real estate consists principally of land, buildings, and other improvements of a permanent nature. Personalty includes all property other than real estate and may be further divided into two categories—tangible and intangible. Among the more common forms of tangible personalty are household furnishings, automobiles, livestock, and farm and industrial machinery. Intangible personalty consists of such incorporeal forms of wealth as stocks and bonds, promissory notes, and bank accounts.

In its earliest form in this country, the property tax was a land tax of a fixed sum per acre or per hundred acres, with lands commonly divided into two or more classes or grades and the better grades taxed at higher rates. Supplementary to the land tax, levies were soon imposed upon specific kinds of personal property such as horses, cattle, and slaves. After

[6] Glen Leet and Robert M. Paige, eds., *Property Tax Limitation Laws* (Pub. Admin. Service, Chicago, 1934); A. Miller Hillhouse and Ronald B. Welch, *Tax Limits Appraised* (Pub. Admin. Service, Chicago, 1937).

[7] See Clyde F. Snider, "Fiscal Control at the County Level," *Nat. Mun. Rev.,* XXX, 579-586 (Oct., 1941).

[8] Cf. Jens P. Jensen, *Property Taxation in the United States,* 1.

about 1815, however, taxes on land and selected types of personalty were gradually expanded into the *general* property tax—an *ad valorem* levy upon all property not specifically exempted—and by the time of the Civil War the general property levy had been definitely established as the basic form of state and local taxation.[9] Implicit in the general property tax is the theory that every property owner should contribute to the support of government in direct proportion to the value of his property of whatever kind, the rate of levy being the same on property of all classes—real estate, tangible personal property, and intangible personalty.

Property-Tax Administration

Administrative agencies and procedures in the field of property taxation vary in detail from state to state, and sometimes within a single state, but the general picture is much the same throughout the country. Everywhere administration of the property tax is highly decentralized, though state supervision is gradually increasing.

The first step in the administrative process is that of assessment—the listing and valuation of the taxable property of each owner. Personal property is assessed annually. Assessment of real estate is made annually in some states, but in others at less frequent intervals, such as every two or four years. Though certain classes of property, such as public utilities, intangibles, and mineral and forest lands, are frequently assessed by state agencies, assessment is for the most part in the hands of locally-elected county, township, or city assessors. Some cities make their own separate assessments and impose their municipal levies thereon. The more common practice, however, is for a single assessment, made by a township or county assessor, to serve as the tax base for all levying units. In most jurisdictions assessment rolls prepared by local assessors subsequently pass through the hands of one or more local administrative boards for review and equalization, and in some instances there are state agencies of review and equalization as well. The review process involves the correction of clerical errors, the adding of omitted property, the hearing of complaints by aggrieved property owners, and the raising or lowering of individual assessments found to be out of line. Equalization involves the ordering of horizontal increases or decreases in the assessments of entire assessment districts or taxing jurisdictions so that similar properties will be treated substantially alike for valuation purposes regardless of where they are situated. After action by the various review and equalization agencies, the assessment rolls are turned over to a designated local officer, such as the county clerk, who makes the "extension of taxes" by multiplying each property owner's assessment by the sum of all rates imposed upon his

---

[9] Cf. William J. Schultz and C. Lowell Harriss, *American Public Finance* (7th ed.), 367.

property by the various taxing authorities and thus computing the individual tax bills.[10] The final step in the process is the collection by local collectors or treasurers of the taxes thus extended. Though occasionally individual local units collect their own levies, the more common plan is for a single collecting officer, frequently the county treasurer, to collect all property taxes and subsequently make remittance to the various levying units, including the state if a state property levy is imposed. Some states permit the payment of property taxes in two instalments with an interval of several months between.[11]

Practically every state has a state tax commission or equivalent administrative agency vested with some degree of supervisory authority over local tax administration.[12] Among the powers conferred upon the tax commission in various states are those of conducting tax research, advising and assisting local assessors, prescribing assessment forms, issuing rules and regulations concerning assessment procedure, removing local assessors from office, hearing and deciding appeals from local boards of review, acting as a state equalization agency, ordering reassessments where the original rolls are found to be faulty, and assessing in the first instance certain classes of property.[13] An additional service rendered by many tax commissions is the holding of periodic meetings at which local assessors are instructed concerning assessment procedures and problems. Some commissions also prepare manuals for the guidance of assessors in their work.

Criticisms of the General Property Tax

Though providing a lucrative and relatively elastic source of revenue, the property tax has numerous faults. Some of these are inherent in the very nature of the tax itself, while others are largely administrative shortcomings. In its basic theory, the general property tax errs in assuming that all property has the same taxpaying ability. Unless the tax base is to be impaired, taxes on property must be paid out of income therefrom, and in the final analysis, therefore, the taxpaying ability of property depends upon its ability to produce income. Actually, property varies widely in income-producing capacity. Some properties produce no income at all,

10 For a comprehensive account of assessment agencies and procedures, see National Association of Assessing Officers, *Assessment Organization and Personnel*.

11 Jensen, *Property Taxation in the United States*, 313.

12 The early development of these agencies is treated comprehensively in Harley L. Lutz, *The State Tax Commission* (Harvard Univ. Press, Cambridge, 1918). On the history and published reports of both regular and special commissions in the various states, see the series of articles by Lewis W. Morse entitled "State Tax Commissions—Their History and Reports" in various issues of volumes XVIII, XIX, XX, and XXI (1940-1943) of the magazine *Taxes* published by the Commerce Clearing House, Chicago.

13 National Association of Assessing Officers, *op. cit.*, 328-347; Jens P. Jensen, *Government Finance*, 260-261.

whereas others are highly productive; and between these extremes are all intermediate degrees of productivity. Yet the rate of taxation within a given jurisdiction is the same on all property, whether it produces much income, or little, or none at all.

Another weakness of the general property tax lies in the fact that, in practice, much nonexempt property actually escapes taxation. When this form of taxation first developed, America possessed a simple agricultural economy, and most property was in the form of real estate and tangible personalty which could readily be found and listed by assessors. Today, on the contrary, a large percentage of all property, particularly in urban areas, consists of intangibles which it is virtually impossible for the assessor to discover unless they are voluntarily listed by the owner. In practice, nonlisting of intangibles is widespread, and the same is true to a lesser degree of certain forms of tangible personalty, such as jewelry, which can easily be concealed. So prevalent, indeed, is the nonlisting of these types of property in some jurisdictions that practically all intangible property and much tangible personalty escapes taxation altogether. Under such circumstances, the general property tax ceases to be general except in theory, and actually becomes a tax on real estate and such tangible personalty as cannot be readily concealed. Thus persons whose property is largely in the form of intangibles escape their just share of the tax burden, and that burden becomes correspondingly heavier upon other property owners. It was estimated in 1961 that the assessed valuation of stocks and bonds owned by Illinois residents was only about one-third of 1 percent of their actual value.[14]

Administration of the property tax is rendered further unsatisfactory by the smallness of assessment districts and the methods by which assessors are chosen. In a considerable number of states, the township or some other area smaller than the county constitutes the primary assessment district, and the large majority of all local assessors are popularly elected.[15] The small districts make it necessary that assessors serve on a part-time basis, and popular election is not conducive to the choice of properly-qualified persons. All too often the assessor is a local politician with few or no qualifications for the difficult and technical task of assigning valuations to real and personal properties of every conceivable kind. Small assessment districts, moreover, encourage competitive undervaluation. Where, for example, township assessments constitute the base upon which county levies are imposed, there is a natural incentive for each assessor to seek to keep his valuations below those of neighboring townships, since success in doing so will correspondingly reduce the contribution his constituents will be required to make to the support of the county government. If, in addition, a state levy is imposed upon the township assessment,

[14] Illinois Commission on Revenue, *Report* (Springfield, 1963), 482-483.
[15] Cf. National Association of Assessing Officers, *op. cit.*, 35-43, 157-161.

the advantage flowing from undervaluation will be further increased. Such inequalities between townships may of course be adjusted in some measure by equalization agencies, but their complete elimination can scarcely be expected.

Satisfactory assessment administration would seem to require assessment districts of sufficient area to justify full-time assessors, and selection of those assessors under a system of examination designed to secure qualified personnel. Though such a plan would suggest selection by appointment, Kentucky applies an examination system to elective assessors.[16] Progress toward larger assessment districts and qualified assessing personnel has been slow in the past and is likely to continue so in the future, yet occasional steps in the right direction are being taken. Thus Iowa has abolished the office of township assessor and provided for county assessors appointed on the basis of examinations. Some 30 Illinois counties have appointive assessment supervisors to aid the township assessors in the performance of their duties. A few other states also have recently taken action along somewhat similar lines.

Classified Property Taxes

In an effort to overcome some of the weaknesses of the general property tax, many states now classify property in some manner for taxation purposes. The classified property tax has been defined by Dr. Simeon Leland as "the ad valorem taxation of property by its segregation into groups or types and the application to these various classes of different effective rates." [17] Though a few states permitted classification at an earlier date, the movement for classified property taxation has been for the most part a product of the 20th century, with one state after another amending its constitution to eliminate uniformity requirements. At present a majority of the states have constitutional authority for classification, and a substantial number have actually adopted classified property taxes in some form. A few states, with Minnesota as an outstanding example, have adopted fairly elaborate systems of classification. In most instances, however, classification has gone no further than placing intangibles in a class apart from real estate and tangible personalty for taxation at a special low rate. Proponents of classification seek its justification in part on the ground that it permits account to be taken of the varying taxpaying ability of different types of property. It is also contended that a low-rate tax on intangibles will draw that form of property out of hiding and secure its listing for

[16] *Ibid.*, 180.

[17] Simeon E. Leland, *The Classified Property Tax in the United States* (Houghton, Boston, 1928), 41. As Dr. Leland points out (*Ibid.*, 42), differentiation in effective rates may be secured either by uniform assessments and differential rates or by uniform rates and differential assessments.

taxation. Experience in this respect, however, has been somewhat disappointing. Although low rates, where applied, have resulted in a wider assessment of intangibles than before, they still have not eliminated wholesale evasion. In some instances, indeed, receipts from intangibles under classification appear actually to have been less than under the general property tax.[18]

Present Status of the Property Tax

At the state level the property tax, which at the turn of the century supplied about half of all tax revenue, has now become a distinctly minor factor. In 1962, 23 states levied no *general* property tax whatsoever for state purposes. In the 27 states imposing levies, their contribution to total state tax revenues ranged from less than 1 percent in seven states to 28 percent in Nebraska, with only Wyoming and Arizona, in addition to Nebraska, deriving as much as 10 percent of their tax revenue from this source. Some of the states which levy general property taxes and some which do not, impose *selective* levies on specified kinds of property such as motor vehicles, public utilities, and intangibles. In 1962, however, receipts from both general and selective property taxes constituted only about 3 percent of total tax revenues in the fifty states.[19] As a major source of state revenue, the property tax has definitely given way to various newer levies.

In local-government finance, on the other hand, the property tax has retained its preeminent position. Though its relative importance has declined somewhat during recent years as certain local units have adopted some of the newer forms of taxation, the property tax still produces between 80 and 90 percent of all local tax revenue. In 1957, according to that year's Census of Governments, property taxes provided approximately 94 percent of the local tax revenue for counties, towns, and townships throughout the county, 99 percent of that for school districts, and 100 percent of that for nonschool special districts. Since municipalities make more use than other local units of sales taxes, income taxes, and other nonproperty levies, property taxes constitute a somewhat smaller percentage of their total tax revenue. Some of the larger cities in particular now rely heavily upon various nonproperty taxes. Nevertheless, for cities generally, the property tax in 1957 yielded some 73 percent of all local tax revenue.[20] Because of the expanding role of state aid in the financing of local government, which is considered at a later point in this chapter, local taxes gen-

[18] Hunter and Allen, *op. cit.*, 338; Harold M. Groves, *Financing Government* (5th ed.), 85-87. Several states now exempt intangibles altogether from taxation as property.

[19] Advisory Commission on Intergovernmental Relations, *The Role of the States in Strengthening the Property Tax*, Vol. I, pp. 71-73.

[20] United States Bureau of the Census, *U.S. Census of Governments: 1957*, Vol. III, No. 5: *Compendium of Government Finances*, 17.

erally, and property taxes in particular, are relatively less important to-day than formerly in the overall local-revenue system. Yet in the early 1960's property levies were still supplying nearly half of all local-government revenue, tax and otherwise, in the United States.

Major Nonproperty Taxes

The levies which have supplanted the property tax as major sources of state revenue vary somewhat from state to state. A heavy producer in every state is the levy imposed upon employers for support of the unemployment compensation program discussed in the preceding chapter. However, since the proceeds from this levy are not available for general state purposes, being held in trust by the federal government for payment of benefits, the unemployment compensation tax may for ordinary purposes be omitted from a consideration of state revenue sources. For the states as a group, levies in each of six other categories now surpass the property tax in productivity. These respective taxes in 1963 produced approximately the following percentages of all state tax revenue for general purposes:[21] sales and use taxes, 25 percent; income taxes, 20 percent; motor fuel taxes, 18 percent; motor vehicle and operators' license taxes, 8 percent; tobacco taxes, 5 percent; and liquor taxes, 4 percent. Accordingly, the principal state taxes for general purposes at the present time are those on sales and incomes. Every state but Nebraska now imposes one or the other of these taxes,[22] with about half of the total number using both. Where both are used the sales tax usually is the more productive. Though motor fuel and license taxes together produce slightly more revenue than even the sales tax, income from these "highway-user" levies is earmarked in large measure for highway purposes. Tobacco and liquor taxes, while yielding less than the other levies, are nevertheless of substantial importance in the state revenue picture.

By and large, the states have been reluctant to empower their local governments to impose nonproperty taxes. Some states, however, do authorize local units of various types to impose one or more such taxes; and, where they are levied, they frequently constitute a significant element in the local revenue structure. Each of the six taxes mentioned in the preceding paragraph is now used to some extent by local governmental units.

Sales and Use Taxes

Thirty-seven states, in 1963, imposed sales taxes sufficiently broad in coverage to be considered in the category of general sales taxes as distinguished from selective levies on the sales of specific commodities such

[21] United States Bureau of the Census, *State Tax Collections in 1963*, 3.
[22] Cf. John F. Due, *State Sales Tax Administration*, 5.

as motor fuel, liquor, and tobacco.[23] Most state sales taxes apply to retail sales only. Some, however, apply also to sales by manufacturers and wholesalers [24] and even, in the case of the "gross receipts" and "gross income" levies, to receipts from various services, personal and otherwise. Rates of taxation of 2 or 3 percent are most common. Every sales-tax law provides for certain exemptions, but the classes of sales exempted vary widely. Many states, for example, exempt some or all farm products. Sales of motor fuel and tobacco products, where subject to special excise taxes, are frequently exempted. Some half-dozen states exempt sales of food for use in the home—an exemption which seriously curtails the productivity of a sales levy.

Beginning with New York City in 1934, a substantial number of municipalities and counties have imposed local sales taxes, with the most numerous adoptions occurring in the 1940's and 1950's. Though some local governments impose such levies in a dozen states, it is in California and Illinois that the tax has gained most widespread use. As of January 1, 1963, according to Professor John Due, sales taxes were imposed by all of California's counties and 353 of the state's municipalities; while in Illinois 67 counties and 1,148 municipalities used the tax. Other states having one or more local governments which imposed the tax included Alabama, Alaska, Arizona, Colorado, Louisiana, Mississippi, New Mexico, Utah, and Virginia. The rate of levy varies, but is most frequently ½ percent or 1 percent in states having state sales taxes and 2 or 3 percent in nonsales-tax states. The tax is collected locally in some instances and by state authorities in others. In 1961 local sales taxes produced $875 million, with more than half of the total being collected in New York City. Sales-tax proceeds in that year accounted for nearly 5 percent of all local tax revenue.[25]

Most of the states imposing sales levies, and some of the municipalities and counties, also levy, at the same rate as the sales tax, a compensating use tax. This is a tax on the use, consumption, or storage of articles purchased outside the taxing jurisdiction which, had they been purchased within that jurisdiction, would have been subject to the sales levy.[26] The use tax has as its principal objective the discouraging of buying outside the state or local-government unit concerned for the purpose of evading the sales tax. Because of the administrative difficulties, expense, and an-

[23] On the subject generally, see John F. Due, *Sales Taxation*, especially Chap. 14; Due, *State Sales Tax Administration;* Roy G. Blakey and Gladys C. Blakey, *Sales Taxes and Other Excises,* Chap. 1; Illinois Revenue Laws Commission, *op. cit.,* Chap. 20.

[24] The term *general sales tax* is sometimes reserved for levies having this broader coverage to distinguish them from the purely "retail" tax.

[25] Due, *State Sales Tax Administration,* Chap. 11.

[26] Maurice Criz, *The Use Tax;* Due, *State Sales Tax Administration,* Chap. 9. Nominally, the typical use tax applies to all nonexempt tangible personalty used, consumed, or stored within the taxing jurisdiction. However, since commodities upon which a sales tax has been paid to the taxing jurisdiction are exempted, the tax becomes in fact a levy only upon property purchased outside. Criz, *op. cit.,* 3.

noyance which would be entailed in an attempt to collect use taxes on every outside purchase of whatever amount, small purchases are ordinarily exempted, several states for example exempting total purchases each month up to a specified maximum sum. In general, enforcement of use taxes is sought principally on such relatively expensive items as automobiles, refrigerators, household furniture, and farm and industrial machinery. Use taxes yield only a small fraction of the amount of revenue produced by the companion sales levies, but the fiscal significance of a use tax is not to be measured alone by the amount of revenue which is derived directly. As has just been noted, the primary purpose of the use tax is the discouragement of outside buying for purposes of sales-tax evasion, and insofar as this purpose is successfully achieved the effect of the use tax is reflected in enlarged sales-tax revenues rather than in revenues from the use levy itself.

In its typical form of a retail levy with broad coverage, the sales tax is open to criticism as being, in effect, regressive. That is to say, the tax falls most heavily upon those persons who are least able, rather than those most able, to pay. The burden of a sales tax is ordinarily shifted from the seller to the consumer, and persons of low income spend a higher percentage of their income than do others for items, such as food and clothing, which are subject to the sales levy. But despite this objectionable regressiveness, which has caused sales taxes to be regarded as less equitable than levies on income, the sales tax has the important fiscal merit of high productivity. Even at a low rate, a sales levy produces a heavy yield. Now the largest single revenue source for the states as a group, this tax in some individual states provides half or more of all tax revenues. Municipal and county levies also have proved to be quite lucrative. Because of its remarkable productivity, the sales tax, while inappropriate as the sole means of financing a governmental unit, may well be justified as one element in a diversified tax program. Indeed, since the federal government already imposes a highly progressive income tax, sales taxes may in some instances be preferable to further income taxation for state or local purposes.

Though local administration of sales taxes has now been demonstrated to be quite possible, it appears that under most circumstances such levies can be more effectively and economically administered by the states. Where it is desired to provide funds for the support of local government from the sales tax, or other levies with respect to which state administration is preferred, this can readily be accomplished, and indeed is being accomplished in many instances, by having the taxes imposed and collected by the state with a part or all of the proceeds subsequently distributed to the local units through a system of tax sharing or grants-in-aid.[27] An alternative approach to the problem is the local supplement to the state levy. Where a given tax is already in use by the state, this device

[27] See below, "State Aid to Local Governments."

permits a local governmental unit so desiring to impose an additional or supplementary levy for local purposes, this levy then being collected by the state along with its own revenues and remitted, less collection costs, to the levying local government. Under such a scheme, local units needing additional revenue and willing to bear the burden involved may secure funds through the imposition of supplementary levies while other units, by refraining from imposition of such levies, may escape a corresponding increase in the local tax burden. Thus the plan of the supplementary levy preserves the principle of local home rule while at the same time eliminating duplication in collection machinery and securing the advantages of state tax administration.[28] California and Illinois, for example, use the plan for collection of all local sales taxes.

Income Taxes [29]

Next after levies on sales, income taxes constitute the largest source of state revenue. In 1963, some 33 states taxed the income of individuals and corporations, and a few others taxed either corporate income or individual income from specified sources only.[30] Under the laws for the taxation of individual income, certain classes of income are excluded from tax liability; and it is usual also to provide personal exemptions, up to specified amounts, for income that would otherwise be taxable. Most commonly excluded from the tax base are gifts, inheritances, and certain proceeds from life insurance, with other exclusions varying rather widely from state to state.[31] In personal exemptions there is also considerable variation, but exemptions of $600 to $1,000 for a single person and twice the single exemption for a married couple or family head are most common. Usually an additional exemption of some $600 is allowed for each dependent. All in all, exclusions and exemptions are ordinarily sufficiently broad to result in a substantial reduction in the tax base. Rates of taxation applied to individual income are in most states progressive, though less steeply so than in the case of the federal levy. From a minimum frequently as low as 1 percent on taxable income in the first "bracket," rates gradually increase to a maximum which in many states is in the neighborhood of 5, 6, or 7 percent and rarely is more than 10 percent. Levies on corporate income are usually, though not always, imposed at a flat rate. Most of the state laws require, as do those of the federal government, that em-

---

[28] Lewis H. Kimmel, *Governmental Costs and Tax Levels*, 116-117; John F. Sly, "Tax Supplements for Municipalities," *Tax Review*, Vol. VIII, No. 2 (Feb., 1947).

[29] On the subject generally, see Roy G. Blakey and Violet Johnson, *State Income Taxes;* Clara Penniman and Walter W. Heller, *State Income Tax Administration;* Robert A. Sigafoos, *The Municipal Income Tax: Its History and Problems.*

[30] Cf. United States Bureau of the Census, *State Tax Collections in 1963*, 10.

[31] Blakey and Johnson, *op. cit.*, 7-8.

ployers withhold the tax on wages and salaries.[32] Because of differences under state laws with respect to such matters as rates, exemptions, and classes of income excluded from taxation, there is much variation from state to state in income-tax productivity. In 1957, for example, income taxes yielded from less than 5 percent to more than 50 percent of the total tax revenue of the respective states imposing them, with an average yield for all income-tax states of 25 percent.[33]

A considerable number of municipalities and other local governments now impose income or payroll taxes, and the number of units using such levies is growing. Pioneering the income-tax field at the local level was Philadelphia, which, since 1938, has imposed a municipal tax on the salaries and wages of residents, the salaries and wages earned within the city by nonresidents, and the net profits of business and other activities. The rate of levy has varied from time to time from 1 percent to 1½ percent. Collected in large part through employer withholding, the tax has been highly productive, producing during recent years from a fourth to almost a third of the city's general revenues.[34]

Adoptions of local income taxes have been most numerous in Pennsylvania, Ohio, and Kentucky. Following the lead of Philadelphia, such levies are now imposed in Pennsylvania by Pittsburgh, some 30 additional cities, approximately 40 townships, and several hundred boroughs and school districts. Some 60 Ohio municipalities, including Toledo, Cincinnati, Dayton, and Youngstown, use the tax. In Kentucky income levies are imposed by Louisville and several other cities and by Jefferson county. St. Louis and Detroit are among the cities outside these three states which impose income taxes, Detroit having adopted its tax in 1963. Local income taxes typically differ from those of the states in being imposed at uniform low rates rather than on a graduated scale. Rates range from one-fourth of 1 percent to 2 percent, with 1 percent most common. In 1960, revenue from local income taxes amounted to $254 million.[35]

The graduated income tax is generally considered to be one of the most equitable of all forms of personal taxation. Flat-rate income levies such as those imposed by local governments are theoretically less equi-

[32] *Ibid.*, 33-36, 47-48; United States Bureau of the Census, *State Tax Collections in 1963*, 10; James T. McDonald, "Withholding of State Income Tax," *Your Govt.* (Govtl. Research Center, Univ. of Kan.), Vol. XVIII, No. 7 (Mar. 15, 1963). The first bracket of individual income in most states comprises the first one, two, or three thousand dollars, but in some instances embraces larger sums.

[33] Penniman and Heller, *op. cit.*, 10-11.

[34] Jewell Cass Phillips, "Philadelphia's Income Tax After Twenty Years," *Nat. Tax Jour.*, XI, 241-253 (Sept., 1958).

[35] Advisory Commission on Intergovernmental Relations, *Local Nonproperty Taxes and the Coördinating Role of the States*, 37-38. For appraisals of local income taxes, see Sigafoos, *op. cit.*, Chap. 6; Henry J. Frank, "Municipal Earned Income Taxes Appraised," *Current Economic Comment* (Bur. of Econ. and Bus. Research, Univ. of Ill.), Vol. XXI, No. 3 (Aug., 1959), 55-56.

table than progressive taxes, but even at low rates will produce large sums of money for local use.

Motor Fuel Taxes

Every state imposes a gallonage tax, usually collected from wholesale distributors, on the sale of gasoline for highway use. Most states tax diesel fuel also, and some tax other forms of fuel oil.[36] Though these levies are commonly referred to collectively as the gasoline tax, and gasoline provides all but a small fraction of the revenue therefrom, it will be seen that the term *motor fuel tax* is more accurate. Since the levy is generally considered as a highway-user tax, most states exempt from taxation motor fuels sold for nonhighway uses or, as is the more common practice, provide for the refunding of taxes paid thereon. Some states, however, have extended their levies to cover aviation gasoline, and this seems quite defensible if the states are to assist in financing airports. Almost all of the states have use taxes, supplementary to their motor fuel levies, applying to purchases made outside the state for resale or use within the state.[37] Revenues from motor fuel taxes are used for the most part for financing highway expenditures, the states commonly distributing a part of their revenue from this source to local governmental units for use in constructing and maintaining local roads and streets. In some instances, however, portions of motor-fuel revenue are used for schools, welfare, or general governmental purposes. In 1961, the rate of gasoline taxation by the states varied from 5 cents to 8 cents per gallon, with the rates of 6 and 7 cents most common.[38] During recent years the general trend of taxation on motor fuel has been consistently upward.

Motor fuel taxes of a local nature were imposed in 1961 by 375 municipalities in Alabama, Florida, Missouri, New Mexico, and Wyoming, and by 36 counties in Alabama, Hawaii, Mississippi, and Nevada. Rates under the local levies vary from a fraction of a cent to 5 cents, with the 1-cent rate most common. Some local units use their revenues from this source solely for street or road purposes, while others divert part or all to specified nonhighway purposes or to their general funds.[39]

State motor fuel taxes are relatively simple to administer and are extremely productive. Of all state taxes, only sales and income levies at the present time yield a larger amount of revenue. As a levy for highway pur-

[36] Finla G. Crawford, *Motor Fuel Taxation in the United States;* Blakey and Blakey, *op. cit.,* Chap. 3; Kentucky Legislative Research Commission, *Gasoline Tax Structure* (Ky. Legis. Research Comsn., Frankfort, 1958).

[37] Cf. Shultz and Harriss, *op. cit.,* 361-362.

[38] Illinois Commission on Revenue, *op. cit.,* 571.

[39] Advisory Commission on Intergovernmental Relations, *Local Nonproperty Taxes and the Coördinating Role of the State,* 36; A. M. Hillhouse and Muriel Magelssen, *Where Cities Get Their Money,* 79-83.

poses, the motor fuel tax has much to commend it. In the nature of a user levy, it is imposed more than most other taxes in accordance with benefits received, each taxpayer contributing roughly in proportion to his use of highway facilities. However, a levy on motor fuel as a means of financing nonhighway services is more difficult to justify. Motorists generally offer little objection to the tax as a method of providing highway revenues, but any widespread diversion to other uses might engender serious resistance. As yet, diversion has not been practised on more than a relatively limited scale.

Local taxes on motor fuels, even when used for highway purposes, are generally difficult to defend. As in the case of general sales taxes, evasion through outside buying is easier when motor fuel levies are imposed and administered locally than when the tax is statewide. Moreover, with motor fuel already taxed by the federal government [40] and every state, local levies add still further to the tax burden on motorists and result in triplication of administrative machinery. Insofar as it is desirable to retain local taxation of motor fuels, this might better be accomplished through local supplements to state levies than through local levies locally administered.

Motor Vehicle and Operators' License Taxes

Two other highway-user levies—one of major fiscal importance to the states—are the license taxes on motor vehicles and their operators. Schedules of state charges for motor vehicle licenses vary widely with respect to both bases and rates. Different schedules are commonly provided for passenger cars on the one hand and trucks and buses on the other, with such further variations as those between private and commercial vehicles. Weight of vehicle, horsepower, age, and value are among the bases of charge employed in the various states singly or in combination; with about a third of the states, however, charging a flat fee for all passenger cars. Annual license charges for private passenger automobiles range from a few dollars to more than $200. For buses and trucks the charges are higher, ranging upward to several thousand dollars for some of the heaviest diesel trucks.[41] Charges for operators' (drivers') licenses are relatively small—a few dollars at most—and the licenses in some instances require renewal only at intervals of several years. Consequently, revenue from this source is small in comparison with that from motor vehicle licenses. As in the case of the motor fuel tax, revenues from motor vehicle and operators' licenses are generally used for highway purposes, with some of the states distributing a portion to local units for such use.

About a dozen states empower municipalities to impose motor ve-

[40] The present (1964) federal rate on gasoline is 4 cents per gallon.
[41] Shultz and Harriss, *op. cit.*, 356-361; Illinois Commission on Revenue, *op. cit.*, 582.

hicle license taxes or, as they are sometimes called, wheel taxes, and similar authority is granted in a few states to counties. Under these authorizations, license taxes are currently imposed by a considerable number of local units, including more than 200 municipalities in Illinois. Local drivers' licenses are required also by some cities for operation of some or all classes of motor vehicles.[42]

State license taxes on motor vehicles and operators are much less productive than motor fuel levies. Nevertheless, in 1963 these held fourth place among sources of general state tax revenue, producing approximately 8 percent of the total. Local licenses of vehicles and operators, while yielding substantial amounts in individual municipalities, are employed in so few jurisdictions that they constitute a very minor item in the overall local-revenue picture. Like the motor fuel tax, license taxes on motor vehicles and operators, when imposed in reasonable amounts, afford an appropriate means for the partial financing of highway facilities, but would be inequitable if employed in any large measure for the support of governmental services generally.

Tobacco Taxes

Taxes on tobacco products—particularly cigarettes—have gained widespread use during recent decades.[43] In 1963, cigarettes were subject to a tax in 47 states,[44] with some 18 states also taxing certain other tobacco products such as cigars and smoking and chewing tobacco. These taxes are ordinarily collected through the sale of revenue stamps to be affixed to the products concerned. Most states, in addition, require that dealers pay a license tax for the privilege of selling tobacco products. The great bulk of tobacco-tax revenue comes, however, from the sales levy on cigarettes. State tax rates in 1963 ranged from 2 to 8 cents per package of twenty cigarettes, with rates of 5, 6, and 7 cents most common. In at least ten states cigarette and tobacco taxes are imposed by some local governments.[45]

In justification of tobacco taxes it may be said that these levies produce substantial sums of revenue in a relatively painless manner. Also of some significance is the fact that the taxes fall upon a consumption item which, in the opinion of some people at least, if not actually a luxury, is

[42] Hillhouse and Magelssen, *Where Cities Get Their Money*, 84-88; *Ibid.*, 1956 supplement, 6, 21-22.

[43] For general discussion of the subject, see Blakey and Blakey, *op. cit.*, Chap. 5; Illinois Commission on Revenue, *op. cit.*, 702-722.

[44] The states without cigarette taxes were Colorado, North Carolina, and Oregon.

[45] United States Bureau of the Census, *State Tax Collections in 1963*, 9; Advisory Commission on Intergovernmental Relations, *Local Nonproperty Taxes and the Coördinating Role of the State*, 33.

in the semiluxury class. On the other hand, it may be pointed out that the taxes are clearly regressive, since tobacco products are consumed heavily by persons in the low-income groups as well as those of higher income. Further to be noted is the fact that the federal government, which has occupied this field of taxation much longer than the states, imposes high tobacco taxes—the present (1964) federal tax on cigarettes being 8 cents per package. State and local taxation of tobacco products therefore results in double, or even triple, taxation.

Liquor Taxes

Except during periods of prohibition, taxes on alcoholic beverages have from colonial times been a source of considerable public revenue in this country.[46] Liquor taxes are of two principal types—license charges and excise levies on sales. Prior to National Prohibition, the states imposed only license taxes, with excise taxation of liquor left to the federal government,[47] but since repeal of the prohibition amendment the states have entered the excise field also. Today every state derives some revenue from alcoholic beverage taxation. Even the prohibition state of Mississippi licenses the sale of certain beverages of low alcoholic content, and each of the monopoly states, while relying for its liquor revenue primarily upon profits from publicly-operated dispensaries, derives something from license charges, excise levies, or both. For the most part, however, it is the thirty-two "licensing" states, where the liquor traffic is carried on as private business under government license, which account for the largest amounts of state liquor-tax revenue.[48]

Charges for state liquor licenses are generally highest for manufacturers, next highest for wholesalers, and lowest for retailers. In the manufacturing field, distilleries are usually charged most and wineries least, with breweries occupying an intermediate position. Charges for wholesaling licenses are ordinarily less for beer than for distilled spirits and wines. At the retail level, a distinction is frequently made between on-sale licenses, which permit sale for consumption on the premises, and off-sale licenses to package stores, with a lower charge imposed for the latter. The actual amount of charge for licenses of the different categories varies widely, from $25 in a few instances for retailers' licenses and wholesale beer licenses to $1,000 or more in many states for distillery licenses. Rates of excise or "gallonage" taxes also vary considerably from state to state, with rate differentials according to alcoholic content common.

[46] Cf. Charles F. Conlon, "Taxation in the Alcoholic Beverage Field," *Law and Contemp. Probs.*, VII, 728-748 (Autumn, 1940).
[47] Blakey and Blakey, *op. cit.*, 90.
[48] On the different systems of liquor control in the states, see above, Chap. XXII, "Liquor Regulation."

Though there are numerous exceptions both upward and downward, rates most commonly imposed are in the neighborhood of $1.50 to $2.50 per gallon on spirits, 15 cents to 60 cents per gallon on wines, and 5 cents to 15 cents per gallon on beer.[49]

In addition to requiring state licenses, many states authorize local licensing of retail liquor establishments and some permit local licensing of manufacturers and wholesalers as well. A fairly common plan is for the local licensing power to be vested in municipalities with respect to establishments within their borders and in the county governments with respect to those in unincorporated areas. Local licensing of the liquor business by counties and cities is in practice widespread. Though local liquor excises are much less common, such levies are imposed by a number of municipalities, sometimes as a percentage of sales or, especially with regard to beer, at so much per gallon, bottle, or case.[50]

Liquor license taxes yield considerable sums at both state and local levels, and liquor excises constitute a lucrative source of revenue for the states. In addition to their productivity, taxes on alcoholic beverages, like tobacco taxes, have an advantage over many other levies in that they fall upon an article of consumption which is not a necessity of life. The use that may be made of liquor taxation by state and local governments, however, is somewhat limited for practical purposes by the substantial levies imposed by the federal government, and the related fact that unduly burdensome taxation is likely to encourage illicit traffic. Insofar as taxation of alcoholic beverages has had as one of its objectives the encouragement of moderation in consumption, its effectiveness is difficult to determine. Liquor consumption is influenced not only by tax rates but also by a composite of other factors, such as social attitudes and wage levels. To whatever extent liquor taxes actually result in the curtailing of consumption, their fiscal productivity is of course correspondingly reduced.

Other Taxes

Sundry license levies not previously mentioned produce varying amounts of state and local revenue. Included in the list at the state level are charges for corporation licenses, hunting and fishing licenses, occupational licenses,[51] and, less commonly, licenses of chain stores and race tracks. Business licenses have long constituted one of the principal sources of nonproperty-tax revenue for cities and villages. Among the business enterprises commonly licensed by municipalities are mercantile establish-

---

[49] Kansas Legislative Council, *Liquor Control: Licenses and Taxes in 45 States* (Kan. Legis. Council, Topeka, 1949), 4-5; Illinois Commission on Revenue, *op. cit.,* 722-745.

[50] Hillhouse and Magelssen, *Where Cities Get Their Money*, 68-78; *Ibid.,* 1956 supplement, 26-27.

[51] See above, Chap. XXII, "State Occupational Licensing."

ments, motion picture theaters and other places of commercial amusement, hotels, restaurants, and taxicabs. Some municipalities also license various occupations and professions.[52] Business establishments located in unincorporated areas are sometimes licensed by counties.

An ancient levy which still provides some revenue, though only in small amounts, is the poll tax—a head tax imposed upon adults at a flat rate. Persons above a specified maximum age, commonly in the neighborhood of fifty or sixty years, are ordinarily exempted, as also in some instances are specific groups, such as soldiers and sailors. In some states the tax is imposed only upon men, but in others it applies to women also. The amount of the levy ranges in most instances from one to four dollars. Poll taxes at present are authorized in about three-fourths of the states. In most cases, however, the levies are imposed and collected by local governments, with only a few states deriving any revenue whatsoever from this source.[53]

Taxes on public utilities, based on gross receipts or otherwise, are used by many states and municipalities and are becoming increasingly prevalent, particularly as a form of municipal levy. About half of the states impose severance taxes—levies upon the privilege of "severing" from the land certain natural resources such as coal, oil, and timber.[54] Taxes on admissions to theaters and other places of amusement constitute a minor source of revenue for some states and cities.[55] Other forms of taxation which provide varying amounts of state revenue include estate and inheritance levies, documentary and stock transfer taxes, and taxes on insurance companies and pari-mutuels.

Federal Aid

One of the outstanding developments in American public finance during recent decades has been the growth of intergovernmental aid—financial assistance granted by one government to another. For the most part, this has taken the form of federal aid to the states and state aid to local governmental units, though in some instances federal assistance is granted directly to local governments.[56] The nature and development of the federal-aid program were discussed at some length in the chapter devoted to federal-state relations, and something concerning the merits and

---

[52] Hillhouse and Magelssen, op. cit., 19-43.

[53] Shultz and Harriss, op. cit., 288-289; Groves, op. cit., Chap. 13; Harvey Walker, "The Poll Tax in the United States," Bull. of Nat. Tax Assn., IX, 46-50, 66-71 (Nov.-Dec., 1923). Poll-tax payment as a qualification for voting is considered above, Chap. V.

[54] Cf. Jensen, Government Finance, 350.

[55] George E. Lent, "The Admissions Tax," Nat. Tax Jour., I, 31-50 (Mar., 1948).

[56] There are also instances of aid by local governments to their respective states and to each other, but the amounts involved are relatively small.

weaknesses of the federal-aid system was said at that time.[57] At the present point, however, some further observations should be made concerning the program's fiscal aspects.

In its most prevalent form, federal aid consists of grants to the states in support of specific state functions, conditioned upon the states' meeting of federally-prescribed standards and submitting to federal supervision with respect to the activities concerned. Usually there is the further requirement that the states match the amounts of the federal grants, dollar for dollar or according to some other prescribed formula, from state or other nonfederal funds. Federal grants-in-aid are made to the states for a wide variety of purposes. With respect to amount granted, highway construction now heads the list. Large sums are provided also for old-age assistance, aid to dependent children, unemployment-compensation administration, veterans' services, agricultural extension work and experiment stations, vocational education and rehabilitation, and public-health services. Some of the other purposes for which grants are made were mentioned in the earlier discussion.[58] At the local level, federal grants are available for financing such functions as housing, planning, urban renewal, vocational education, and the construction of highways, hospitals, and airports.

Of distinctly minor importance in comparison with grants-in-aid, yet deserving of mention as parts of the federal-aid program, are shared revenues and payments in lieu of taxes. Certain federal revenues, such as those from national forests and from fees for grazing privileges on the national domain, are shared with the states or counties in which such lands are located to replace, at least in part, tax losses resulting from federal ownership and consequent tax-exemption of the properties concerned. Local governments also receive payments from the federal treasury, amounting to several million dollars annually, in lieu of taxes on federally-operated housing projects and on power properties of the Tennessee Valley Authority.[59] Though of prime importance to some of the local units involved, income from these sources is of distinctly minor significance as an element in state and local revenues generally.

Federal aid constitutes a major factor in the financing of state government, and one of ever increasing importance. Although occasional years have witnessed a decline in the amount of such aid in comparison with preceding periods, the overall trend has been consistently upward. Amounting at the turn of the century to only some $3 million annually, federal aid to the states had grown by 1932 to more than $200 million, and

[57] Above, Chap. II, "Federal Grants-in-Aid." See also Chap. III, "National-Local Relations."

[58] Above, Chap. II.

[59] Council of State Governments, *Grants-in-Aid and Other Federal Expenditures within the States* (rev. ed.), 18-20. See also above, Chap. II, "Coöperation between Nation and States."

during the depression and war years it increased by leaps and bounds. In 1962 federal aid to the amount of $7.4 billion constituted 24 percent of all state general revenue.[60] As yet, however, assistance from the federal government is only a minor element in local-government finance.

State Aid to Local Governments

Though receiving relatively little federal assistance, local units are treated with considerable generosity, taking the country as a whole, by the state governments. Whereas the federal assistance program is comprised, with only very minor exceptions, of grants-in-aid, state aid consists in part of grants along lines similar to those at the federal level, but in considerable part also of shared taxes.

In its typical form, the state grant-in-aid is an appropriation from general state funds for allocation to local governments according to population or local need, or on some other predetermined basis. Many state grants are of the "equalization" variety, designed to enable local units having little taxable property to maintain local services of prescribed minimum standards. A plan commonly applied to local schools, for example, requires that a school district, in order to qualify for state aid, levy a property tax at a specified minimum rate and provides that, if the proceeds from that levy are insufficient to maintain "standard" school facilities, whatever additional funds are necessary to make that possible will be supplied by the state. Under the tax-sharing plan, part or all of the proceeds from a specified tax levied and collected by the state are distributed to local governmental units. The amount allocated to a particular unit may depend upon the amount collected there, or may be determined by population or on some other basis. Among the taxes thus shared by various states with their local governmental units are motor fuel taxes, motor-vehicle license taxes, liquor taxes, income taxes, and sales taxes.[61]

Every state now provides some financial aid to local governments through grants-in-aid, shared taxes, or both. Though each plan is widely used, the grant-in-aid appears at present to be gaining in popularity over the shared tax. One of the principal objections to the shared tax lies in the fact that the amount of funds available for distribution to local units depends upon the productivity of the tax rather than upon local needs. In practice, local needs for state assistance may be greatest at the very time when, perhaps because of an economic depression, revenues from the tax concerned are at their lowest point. Another shortcoming of the shared tax

[60] United States Bureau of the Census, *Historical Review of State and Local Government Finances*, 13; *Compendium of State Government Finances in 1962*, 6. *General* revenue, as the term is employed by the Census Bureau, excludes certain special forms of revenue. See below, "Special Revenues."

[61] Cf. American Municipal Association, *State-Collected Municipally-Shared Taxes*.

is its instability as a local-revenue source. Tax yields always vary somewhat from year to year, and may vary widely with changing economic conditions. Therefore, where the amount of revenue to be received by local governments from the state depends upon the productivity of one or more specific taxes, there is inevitably present an element of uncertainty which makes it difficult for local governments to engage in proper financial planning. Grants-in-aid, consisting as they usually do of appropriations from the general state treasury, are not dependent in amount upon the productivity of any one or more designated taxes, and thus can be kept at a relatively stable point.

For many years state grants-in-aid were made to local governments almost exclusively in support of designated functions, and shared-tax funds were also in many instances earmarked for specific purposes. Where this practice is followed, it is usual to require that the local activities concerned be conducted in accordance with state-prescribed standards and subject to state supervision.[62] Though state aid for specified local purposes is still the predominant practice, there has in recent years been a growing tendency to provide state aid for the *general* financial support of local government. Many states now make substantial sums available to local units without explicit restriction as to the purposes for which the money may be used, and most states provide some aid of this nature.

State aid during recent years has increased at a remarkable pace. From $2.6 billion in 1947, the total amount of such aid paid by all states rose to $10.9 billion in 1962. In the latter year the states passed on to their local governmental units, principally as grants-in-aid and shared taxes, approximately one-third of their total general revenue. Now constituting by far the largest source of local revenue exclusive of the property tax, state aid in 1962 accounted for more than one-fourth of the total general revenue of local governments in the fifty states. Local services benefiting most from state-aid programs are those in the fields of education, highways, and public welfare. Of the $10.9 billion in state aid in 1962, $835 million was provided for the support of local-government services generally. Of the remainder, approximately $6.5 billion was granted for schools, $1.3 billion for highways, and $1.8 billion for various welfare functions. Health, hospitals, airports, and conservation of natural resources were among the other local services coming in for lesser amounts. Of the total $10.9 billion, approximately $2.9 billion was assigned to counties, $1.8 billion to cities, and $5.2 billion to school districts, with relatively small amounts going to towns, townships, and special districts.[63]

Concerning the merits of state aid there is some diversity of opinion. In opposition to its use it is argued that, since acceptance of state con-

[62] See above, Chap. III, "State-Local Relations—Grants-in-Aid."
[63] United States Bureau of the Census, *Compendium of State Government Finances in 1962*, 25, 26.

trol is usually a part of the price demanded for state assistance, the system endangers local self-government. Against undue extension of state-aid programs it is also urged that excessive reliance upon state financial assistance is not conducive to economy and a proper feeling of responsibility at the local level. Proponents of state aid, on the other hand, contend that, since many local services are of statewide as well as local interest, it is the duty of the state not only to participate in their financial support but to do so in a way that will equalize the local tax burden between, for example, units having much taxable property and those with little. Perhaps the strongest case for state aid, however, rests on the fact that the states, which control local taxing power, have rather generally preempted to their own use such lucrative taxes as those on sales and incomes while compelling local governments to rely largely upon the overworked property tax. Essential services performed at the local level are costing more and more and, until the states are willing to confer upon local governments greater power than most of them now possess to raise funds from non-property-tax sources, it is only reasonable to expect the state governments to make available to local units, through grants or tax sharing, a part of the revenues accruing from the lucrative state levies.

Nontax Revenues

Some 10 percent of all state general revenue and 15 percent of the revenue of local units comes from sources other than taxation and aid from other governments. Intergovernmental aid, while a nontax source from the standpoint of the receiving unit, ordinarily consists of funds secured by the paying government through taxation, and therefore has been considered as in a special category apart from nontax revenues in the strict sense. Nontax revenue sources are quite varied in character and only a few will be specifically mentioned at this point. Even when considered collectively, they account for but a small part of all state and local revenues.

One of the older sources of nontax revenue consists of fees imposed to defray the cost of certain governmental services which confer special benefits upon their recipients. Among the charges in this category may be mentioned fees for court costs, for the recording of land titles and transfers, for building inspection, and, at the state level, for examinations in connection with the licensing of regulated professions.[64] Fines for the violation of state statutes and local ordinance also produce some revenue.

In many local governments, one of the most important forms of nontax revenue is that from special assessments. A special assessment is a charge levied upon real estate to defray all or part of the cost of a public improvement which, over and above its benefits to the community at large,

[64] Cf. Shultz and Harriss, *op. cit.*, 445-449.

confers an additional special benefit upon the property concerned. The special assessment differs from a tax principally in being imposed for, and in proportion to, special benefits conferred. Municipalities employ special assessments more extensively than do other local units, using this method of financing quite commonly for such public improvements as streets, sewers, and parks. However, assessment financing is occasionally used by counties, particularly in connection with highway improvements; and special districts created for such purposes as irrigation, drainage, water-supply, and levee construction, often finance their work entirely through special assessments.[65] Though a special assessment is ordinarily imposed as a single charge, payment is commonly permitted to be made in instalments, with interest, over a designated number of years. In order to raise funds to meet construction costs at the time the improvement is made, it is usual to issue and sell special-assessment bonds which constitute a lien upon the property assessed. Retirement of these obligations then takes place as assessment instalments are paid from year to year.

"Service charges" are a significant source of revenue in many municipalities. These are charges imposed upon users for financing certain specific local services which have traditionally been supported from tax funds. By financing some functions in this manner, the tax funds formerly devoted to their support are released for other purposes and thus the pressure for increased local taxation may be somewhat relieved. During recent years cities in considerable number have adopted the service-charge method of financing sewage disposal and refuse collection. Another source of municipal revenue which may be included in the service-charge category, though it might with equal propriety be considered as a highway-user tax, is the charge for automobile parking collected through parking meters. Though from the legal standpoint parking meters are installed as a means of regulating traffic, they produce considerable revenue. For the most part, parking-meter revenues are devoted to the payment of traffic policemen, the provision of off-street parking facilities, and other purposes ancillary to traffic regulation.

Special Revenues

Revenues from two sources are, because of their nature, excluded by the Census Bureau from the category of *general* revenue. These are: (1) revenues collected for insurance trust funds such as those for unemployment compensation and retirement benefits; and (2) revenues derived from government liquor stores and public utility enterprises.

Every state levies a tax on the payrolls of covered employers to finance its program of unemployment compensation,[66] and state and local

---

[65] United States Bureau of the Census, *Property Taxation: 1941*, Chap. 2. On the subject generally, see A. E. Buck and others, *Municipal Finance*, Chap. 12.

[66] See above, Chap. XXIII, "Unemployment Compensation."

governments operate many public-employee retirement systems into which are channeled employee contributions and earnings on trust-fund investments. As pointed out in an earlier chapter, some state and local governments own and operate liquor dispensaries and there are many municipally-owned utilities.[67] Some of these enterprises operate at a deficit and therefore must be subsidized from general funds, while others pay their way and no more. Still others, however, make substantial profits from which they contribute to the support of their respective governmental units. Of the state business enterprises, state-owned liquor stores are the largest contributors. At the local level, municipally-owned utilities frequently make contributions to city general funds, and in some instances utility profits are sufficient to pay the entire cost of the city government. In 1962, state and local governments collected nearly $6 billion for insurance trust funds, and some $5.4 billion from utilities and liquor stores. These revenues are largely offset, however, by payments for unemployment-compensation and retirement benefits and the costs of liquor stocks and utility operations, with only net profits being available for financing governmental services generally.[68]

Summary and Trends

By way of conclusion, the relative importance of the various state and local revenue sources during recent years may be briefly summarized, and some of the major current trends reviewed. In 1962, the more than $31 billion in general revenue received by the fifty states was distributed as follows:[69]

DISTRIBUTION OF STATE GENERAL REVENUE BY SOURCE, 1962

SOURCE	MILLIONS	PERCENT
Sales and Use Taxes	$ 5,111	16.5
Income Taxes	4,036	13.0
Motor Fuel Taxes	3,665	11.5
Motor Vehicle and Operators' License Taxes	1,550	5.0
Tobacco Taxes	1,075	3.4
Liquor Taxes	831	2.7
Property Taxes	640	2.1
Other Taxes	3,653	11.8
Federal Aid [70]	7,480	24.0
Nontax Sources	3,116	10.0
Total	$31,157	100.0

[67] See above, Chap. XXII, "Government Ownership."

[68] United States Bureau of the Census, *Governmental Finances in 1962*, 2, 20.

[69] United States Bureau of the Census, *Compendium of State Government Finances in 1962*, 6.

[70] Includes a small amount of aid received by the states from their local governments.

At the local level, analysis is simplified by the continued predominance of the property tax. Local-government general revenue in 1962 exceeded $38 billion, distributed in the following manner:[71]

DISTRIBUTION OF LOCAL-GOVERNMENT GENERAL REVENUE BY SOURCE, 1962

SOURCE	MILLIONS	PERCENT
Property Taxes	$18,416	48.0
Other Taxes	2,547	6.6
State Aid	10,929	28.5
Federal Aid	750	1.9
Nontax Sources	5,717	15.0
Total	$38,357	100.0

Of the changes that have occurred in the state and local revenue system during the past half-century the most significant has been the decline in the position of the property tax. This is by no means to say that property taxes have decreased in absolute amount. On the contrary, total property-tax collections have consistently increased and are still increasing, partly because of growth in the amount and value of taxable property and partly because of higher rates. But as public expenditures have mounted and it has become necessary to obtain more and more funds, the unfairness and practical impossibility of financing both state and local governments principally from property taxation have become increasingly apparent. It has therefore been found expedient to find other taxes to replace or supplement in various degrees the revenues from property-tax sources; and, as income from these newer taxes has grown, property taxation has become of less *relative* importance in the overall system.

It is at the state level that the trend away from the property tax has been most marked. In large measure, the states have now relinquished property taxation to the local units. Some states have abandoned altogether the taxation of property for their own purposes, and in most others property taxes now constitute a distinctly minor revenue source. Supplying more than 40 percent of all state general revenue prior to World War I,[72] property taxation in 1962 provided less than 3 percent of such revenue. Among local governments the decline of the property tax, though less dramatic, has nevertheless been substantial, property taxation providing more than 70 percent of the general revenue of all local governments in 1913, but only 48 percent in 1962.

---

[71] United States Bureau of the Census, *Governmental Finances in 1962*, 20. The data are preliminary. Because figures have been rounded, individual items add to slightly more than total.

[72] United States Bureau of the Census, *Historical Review of State and Local Government Finances*, 14.

The taxes which have, for the most part, replaced the property levy as sources of state revenue are the sales and income taxes for purposes of general government and, for highway purposes, the motor fuel and motor vehicle license levies. Other levies frequently imposed for general purposes, though at times earmarked for the support of specific services, are those on tobacco products and alcoholic beverages. Each of the major nonproperty taxes employed by the states is imposed by some local governments, though for the most part the states have been reluctant to authorize widespread use of the newer taxes by local units.

Not unrelated to the decline of the property tax is the other major development in state and local revenues, namely, the growth of intergovernmental aid. Aid from the federal government, which does not use the property tax, has enabled the states to support certain services with less drain upon their own tax resources; and state aid to local governments has similarly made possible the financing of local functions with less revenue from property and other local taxes than otherwise would have been necessary. From a paltry $3 million in 1902 the amount of federal aid rose to $7.4 billion in 1962, while state aid increased during the same period from $58 million[73] to nearly $11 billion. Federal aid now constitutes nearly one-fourth of all state general revenue, and state aid comprises almost 30 percent of the general revenue of local governments. The greatest increases in intergovernmental aid have been largely a product of recent years, this being particularly true of state aid to local units. Local revenue needs, especially since World War II, have been increasing apace, and local units have of necessity looked to their respective states for means of meeting those needs. In general, the states as yet have been more disposed to attack the problem through liberalized state aid than through any comprehensive expansion of local taxing authority.

REFERENCES

Advisory Commission on Intergovernmental Relations, *Local Nonproperty Taxes and the Coördinating Role of the States* (The Commission, Washington, 1961).

———, *State Constitutional and Statutory Restrictions on Local Taxing Powers* (U.S. Govt. Printing Office, Washington, 1962).

———, *The Role of the States in Strengthening the Property Tax*, Vol. I (U.S. Govt. Printing Office, Washington, 1963).

American Municipal Association, *State-Collected Municipally-Shared Taxes* (Amer. Mun. Assn., Chicago, 1946), with 1948 *supplement*.

BIRD, Frederick L., *The General Property Tax: Findings of the 1957 Census of Governments* (Pub. Admin. Service, Chicago, 1960).

[73] *Ibid.*, 13.

BLAKEY, Roy G., and BLAKEY, Gladys C., *Sales Taxes and Other Excises* (Pub. Admin. Service, Chicago, 1945).

BLAKEY, Roy G., and JOHNSON, Violet, *State Income Taxes* (Commerce Clearing House, New York, 1942).

BUCK, A. E., and others, *Municipal Finance* (Macmillan, New York, 1926).

Council of State Governments, *Federal Grants-in-Aid* (The Council, Chicago, 1949).

————, *Grants-in-Aid and other Federal Expenditures within the States* (The Council, Chicago, rev. ed., 1947).

CRAWFORD, Finla G., *Motor Fuel Taxation in the United States* (Author, Syracuse, N.Y., 1939).

CRIZ, Maurice, *The Use Tax* (Pub. Admin. Service, Chicago, 1941).

DUE, John F., *Sales Taxation* (Univ. of Ill. Press, Urbana, 1957).

————, *State Sales Tax Administration* (Pub. Admin. Service, Chicago, 1963).

GROVES, Harold M., *Financing Government* (Holt, New York, 5th ed., 1958).

HILLHOUSE, A. M., and MAGELSSEN, Muriel, *Where Cities Get Their Money* (Mun. Finance Officers Assn., Chicago, 1945), with supplements.

HUNTER, Merlin H., and ALLEN, Harry K., *Principles of Public Finance* (Harper, New York, 1940).

JENSEN, Jens P., *Government Finance* (Crowell, New York, 1937).

————, *Property Taxation in the United States* (Univ. of Chicago Press, Chicago, 1931).

KIMMEL, Lewis H., *Governmental Costs and Tax Levels* (Brookings Inst., Washington, 1948).

LELAND, Simeon E., *The Classified Property Tax in the United States* (Houghton, Boston, 1928).

LUTZ, Harley L., *Public Finance* (Appleton-Century-Crofts, New York, 4th ed., 1947).

National Association of Assessing Officers, *Assessment Organization and Personnel* (Nat. Assn. of Assessing Offs., Chicago, 1941).

PENNIMAN, Clara, and HELLER, Walter W., *State Income Tax Administration* (Pub. Admin. Service, Chicago, 1959).

SHULTZ, William J., and HARRISS, C. Lowell, *American Public Finance* (Prentice-Hall, Englewood Cliffs, N.J., 7th ed., 1959).

SIGAFOOS, Robert A., *The Municipal Income Tax: Its History and Problems* (Pub. Admin. Service, Chicago, 1955).

Tax Foundation, *Facts and Figures on Government Finances: Twelfth Edition, 1962-1963* (Prentice-Hall, Englewood Cliffs, N.J., 1963).

TAYLOR, Philip E., *The Economics of Public Finance* (Macmillan, New York, 3rd ed., 1961).

United States Bureau of the Census, *Compendium of State Government Finances in 1962* (U.S. Govt. Printing Office, Washington, 1963).

————, *Governmental Finances in 1962* (U.S. Bur. of the Census, Washington, 1963).

————, *Historical Review of State and Local Government Finances* (U.S. Bur. of the Census, Washington, 1948).

————, *Property Taxation: 1941* (U.S. Bur. of the Census, Washington, 1942).

————, *State Aid to Local Governments* (U.S. Bur. of the Census, Washington, 1948).

————, *State Tax Collections in 1963* (U.S. Bur. of the Census, Washington, 1963).

————, *U.S. Census of Governments: 1957*, Vol. III, No. 5: *Compendium of Government Finances* (U.S. Govt. Printing Office, Washington, 1959).

25

Expenditures and Indebtedness

The Rising Cost of Government

For many years governmental costs at all levels have been rising, and during recent decades the increase has been spectacular. At the turn of the century, general expenditures[1] of the states, excluding expenditures for debt retirement, amounted to less than $200 million annually. By the late 1920's the total had risen to some $2 billion. During the depression decade of the 1930's this amount more than doubled, reaching $5 billion by 1939. Local expenditures have risen in much the same fashion. From $888 million in 1902, general expenditures of all local governments, exclusive of debt retirement, increased to $1.5 billion in 1913 and to $6.3 billion in 1942.[2]

During the years of World War II, though federal expenditures mounted rapidly, those of the state and local governments increased but little. With the war programs of the national government taking top priority, labor and materials were not available for civil construction except in circumstances of extraordinary urgency, and projects for the construction of highways, public buildings, and public works generally were for

[1] In Census Bureau terminology, *general* expenditures exclude expenditures of government-owned liquor stores and utility enterprises and those from insurance trust funds.
[2] United States Bureau of the Census, *Historical Review of State and Local Government Finances,* 16-20.

the most part postponed. With the war's end, however, this situation soon changed and capital outlays for construction were resumed. In the post-war period, governmental agencies, along with private enterprises, have been faced with the necessity of granting salary and wage increases to their officers and employees and paying constantly-rising prices for materials and equipment. Furthermore, there has been a growing demand on the part of the citizenry for the addition of new public services and the expansion of traditional programs. All factors considered, it is not sur-prising that state and local expenditures are currently increasing at an extraordinary rate.

Today governmental expenditures at all levels in the United States total some $175 billion annually. Federal expenditures, amounting to approximately $100 billion, naturally take the spotlight. But some 80 percent of the federal budget goes for military and defense programs and related purposes such as space exploration, foreign aid, veterans' services, and interest on the national debt. For functions of a strictly civil nature, the states spend more than the national government, as do the local governments also. In 1962, general expenditures of the states amounted to more than $31 billion and those of local governments exceeded $39 billion. At the local level, the largest expenditures are by municipalities and school districts, with counties next and townships and special districts spending lesser amounts. With allowance made for the $11 billion in state aid which figured in the expenditures first of the states and then of the local units, state and local expenditures for 1962 still totaled $59 billion or more than $300 per capita.

The vast increase in government expenditures over the years, as expressed in dollars, is of course attributable in part to the general rise in the price level and the corresponding decline in the purchasing power of the dollar. But even in terms of dollars of constant purchasing power the increase has been striking, as reflected in the relation between government costs and national product. Expressed as a percentage of the gross national product, government expenditures at all levels rose from 9.8 percent of that product in 1929 to 30.1 percent in 1961. The rise was most dramatic in the case of federal expenditures, which increased from 2.5 percent of the gross national product in 1929 to 19.7 percent in 1961. But the increase has also been substantial in state and local expenditures, which amounted to 10.4 percent of the gross national product in 1961 as compared with 7.3 percent in 1929.[3]

[3] Tax Foundation, *Facts and Figures of Government Finance: Twelfth Edition, 1962-1963*, 27. The rise, of course, has not been without fluctuations. In the war years of 1943 and 1944, for example, federal expenditures amounted to more than 40 percent of the gross national product and state and local expenditures to less than 4 percent.

Purposes of Expenditures

The purposes for which a government incurs expenditures reflect the activities it administers or provides with financial support. As previously suggested, expenditures of the national government, though including sums for a wide variety of activities, center to a large degree around services concerned with war and its aftermath, national defense, and the conduct of foreign relations. Since the activities of state and local governments are more varied than those of the national government, touching almost every phase of social and economic life, the purposes of state and local expenditures cover a correspondingly wider range. The following tables give some indication of the distribution of expenditures among various governmental functions. State items include, for each function, both direct state expenditures and the amount of any state aid which may have been granted for financing the function at the local level.

DISTRIBUTION BY FUNCTIONS OF STATE GENERAL EXPENDITURES, 1962 [4]

FUNCTION	MILLIONS	PERCENT
Education	$10,731	34.3
Highways	7,961	25.5
Public Welfare	4,285	13.7
Health and Hospitals	2,351	7.5
Natural Resources	992	3.2
Interest on General Debt	635	2.0
Other Functions	4,309	13.8
Total	$31,264	100.0

DISTRIBUTION BY FUNCTIONS OF LOCAL-GOVERNMENT GENERAL EXPENDITURES, 1962 [5]

FUNCTION	MILLIONS	PERCENT
Education	$17,675	44.8
Highways	3,706	9.5
Public Welfare	2,535	6.5
Health and Hospitals	2,205	5.6
Natural Resources	416	1.1
Housing and Urban Renewal	1,110	2.8
Interest on General Debt	1,361	3.5
Other Functions	10,283	26.2
Total	$39,292	100.0

Perhaps the most striking feature of state and local expenditure programs lies in the large amounts spent at both levels in the fields of edu-

[4] United States Bureau of the Census, *Summary of Governmental Finances in 1962*, 20.

[5] *Ibid.* Because figures are rounded, individual items do not quite add to total.

cation, public welfare, and highways. In the case of the states, not only do services in the categories mentioned account for approximately three-fourths of all general expenditures, but seven-eighths of all state aid to local governments is granted for expenditure in these fields. At the local level, education, welfare, and highway expenditures together comprise 60 percent of all general expenditures. In the overall state-local picture, educational expenditures, including those for institutions of higher learning as well as for elementary and secondary schools, easily take first place. Next come expenditures for state highways and local roads and streets. In third place are expenditures for welfare activities. All but a small portion of this item goes for support of the six major programs of public assistance—general assistance, old-age assistance, aid to the blind, aid to dependent children, aid to the disabled, and medical assistance for the aged.[6]

Health services and hospitals account for substantial expenditures at both state and local levels, with the cost of state mental hospitals rising rapidly in recent years. Though small in comparison with those for the functions thus far mentioned, expenditures for preservation and development of natural resources are significant. These include expenditures in the fields of agriculture, conservation, and forestry, as well as those for various promotional programs. Local governments, particularly cities, have recently begun to spend substantial amounts for housing and urban renewal. Interest on indebtedness constitutes a considerable item—more so at the local level than at the state since local governments borrow more extensively than do the states. Services not listed separately in the tables account for varying portions of total expenditures. Police and fire protection regularly account for major items in municipal budgets. "Protective" expenditures by the states include those for the support of state police and highway patrols and a variety of inspectional and regulatory services. In the field of correction are expenditures for penal and correctional institutions, and for pardon, probation, and parole boards. Cities spend considerable sums for sewerage and for other sanitation services such as street cleaning and refuse collection. Parks and recreation account for modest expenditures at both state and local levels.

Finally, attention may be called to the relatively small percentage of all expenditures devoted to activities classified by the Census Bureau under the headings "general control" and "financial administration." Included within these categories are expenditures for the legislative and judicial branches, the office of the chief executive, personnel administration, legal services, tax administration, accounting, auditing, budgeting, and the like. In 1962, all such functions combined accounted for only 4 percent of the general expenditures of state and local governments. Since items of this nature comprise so small a portion of total public expenditures, realistic attempts to effect drastic economy or retrenchment in government must ordinarily take into account reductions in the larger "serv-

[6] See above, Chap. XVIII.

ice" items and not confine themselves to expenditures for general control and financial administration. It may be noted, however, that in small and sparsely populated local units expenditures such as these tend to be higher than elsewhere in comparison with other governmental costs, and that under such circumstances the formation of larger units through consolidation might result in substantial overhead savings.[7]

Public Budgeting[8]

Down to the present century, public finance in the United States was the subject of little deliberate planning. Appropriation measures introduced into legislative bodies by individual members and various committees were considered and enacted independently of each other; and revenue measures were passed in a haphazard manner in the general hope that they would produce the funds necessary to meet authorized expenditures. Today, however, careful fiscal planning through formal budgeting procedure is recognized as essential to the efficient administration of government at whatever level. A public budget has been defined as "a complete financial plan for a definite period, which is based upon careful estimates both of the expenditure needs and of the probable income of the government."[9] Interest in budgeting on the part of American cities and states antedates by several years the inauguration of our national budget system in 1921, rudimentary budgetary procedures being adopted by New York City during the first decade of the century and by the states of California and Wisconsin in 1911. Since 1913, provision for systematic budgeting has made steady progress at both state and local levels. Every state now has some sort of budgetary system by virtue of statutory or, in a few instances, constitutional provision; and budgeting is required of many cities, counties, and other local units by charter provision or statute. Some states, indeed, have general statutes prescribing budgetary procedures for all of their local governments.[10]

In states with biennial legislative sessions, state budgets normally cover a two-year period. In states having annual legislative sessions and in local governments, the budget period is a single year. The budget year, of course, is the official *fiscal* year, which may or may not coincide with the calendar year. In all but a very few states, the fiscal year, like that of the national government, begins on July first.[11] School districts commonly

[7] See above, Chap. XVI.

[8] For general treatises, see A. E. Buck, *Public Budgeting;* Jesse Burkhead, *Government Budgeting.*

[9] A. E. Buck, *Budget Making,* 2.

[10] Buck, *Public Budgeting,* 13-16.

[11] States reported in 1963 as using some date other than July 1 as the beginning of the fiscal year were Alabama (Oct. 1), New York (Apr. 1), and Texas (Sept. 1). *The Book of the States* (Council of State Govts., Chicago), 1964-65, pp. 248-249.

begin their fiscal year on July first; but among local governments of other types the calendar year is the predominant fiscal period.[12]

The budgetary procedures of the state and local governments vary greatly in detail, yet the underlying principles of public budgeting are everywhere much the same. For purposes of analysis and discussion, the budgetary process may be considered as consisting of three fundamental steps: (1) the preparation of the budget; (2) its consideration and adoption, in the original or some modified form, by the legislative body; and (3) its execution.

The Budget-making Authority

According to the nature of the authority charged with preparation of the budget plan, public budget systems are of three principal types: (1) the executive budget; (2) the board-type budget; and (3) the legislative budget.[13] Under the first of these types, responsibility for formulating the budget plan for submission to the legislative body is assigned to the chief executive. Where the board type is employed, the budget is prepared by an administrative or administrative-legislative board or, in the case of some local governments, by a citizens' committee. A legislative budget is prepared by a committee of the legislative body of the government concerned.

Among the states the executive type of budget is by far the most prevalent. Though this type of budget system places upon the governor primary responsibility for formulating the state's financial plan, it is usual to provide the chief executive with some sort of staff agency to perform the actual budgetary work under his direction. This agency is most commonly a budget bureau or division located within a department of finance or administration.[14] No less than 43 states were reported in 1963 as employing budget systems of the executive type. In six states the budget was prepared by a board of administrators, or administrators and legislators, of which the governor in each case either appointed the chairman or himself served as chairman. The legislative budget system is now used only in Arkansas, where budget formulation is a function of the legislative council.[15]

---

[12] United States Bureau of the Census, *Historical Statistics on State and Local Government Finance: 1902-1953* (U.S. Govt. Printing Office, Washington, 1955), 9.

[13] Buck, *Public Budgeting*, 284-289.

[14] Cf. James W. Martin and Vera Briscoe, "Some Statutory Provisions for State Budgets," *State Govt.*, XVIII, 162-167 (Sept., 1945).

[15] For a tabular analysis of state budgetary authorities and practices, see *The Book of the States*, 1964-65, pp. 164-167. The states reported as having budgets of the board type were Florida, Indiana, Mississippi, North Dakota, South Carolina, and West Virginia. In Illinois, though the system is nominally of the executive type, an important role is played by a legislative budgetary commission. Concerning the Arkansas system, see Henry M. Alexander, *The State Budget System of Arkansas* (Inst. of Science and Technology, Univ. of Ark., Fayetteville, 1951).

At the local level, it is among municipalities that public budgeting has made most progress.[16] Many strong-mayor and manager-government cities have budget systems of the executive type, some of the larger municipalities having budget directors to assist the mayor or manager in the performance of his budgetary duties. In commission-governed cities, preparation of the budget is commonly a responsibility of the commission, acting through the commissioner of finance.[17] Among weak-mayor cities, budget systems, where they exist at all, are most often of the board or legislative variety.

Since most American counties are without a principal executive officer having overall administrative authority,[18] executive budgeting has made little headway in county government. However, those counties which do have a manager or some other form of chief administrator in most instances make provision for an executive budget. A number of other counties have been provided with budget boards or officers of one kind or another, and in some states the finance committee of the county board is designated as the budget-making authority. In townships having a principal administrative officer, that official is frequently charged with the budget-making function. Considerable use is made also at the township level of budget boards or, where the appropriating body is the town or township meeting, of citizens' budget committees. Attention has been called in an earlier chapter[19] to the growing use in New England towns of citizens' finance committees for budget-making purposes, and similar agencies are sometimes employed in midwestern townships. New England town managers, where the office exists, usually prepare the budgets of their respective towns.

All in all, modern budgeting procedures have as yet made less progress at the local level than among the states. Some local governments still have no formal budget system whatsoever, and in many others existing procedures amount to nothing more than the formulation of a single annual appropriation ordinance. Yet even the degree of planning involved in drawing a comprehensive ordinance represents a step in advance of the haphazard appropriation practices of earlier periods. Moreover, almost every year sees the enactment of legislation in one or more states establishing budget systems for additional local units or improving and strengthening existing systems.

Of the three types of budget, the executive type is generally to be preferred over the others, which indeed it is gradually supplanting. The chief executive, being charged with the day-to-day management of the government's administrative activities, is in a better position than legisla-

[16] On problems and procedures in local budgeting, see A. E. Buck, *Municipal Budgets and Budget Making;* A. E. Buck, *Budgeting for Small Cities;* John A. Perkins, "Preparation of the Local Budget," *Amer. Polit. Sci. Rev.,* XL, 949-958 (Oct., 1946).

[17] The various forms of city government are explained above, Chap. XIV.

[18] See above, Chap. XIII.

[19] Above, Chap. XV.

tors or lesser administrative officers to understand the financial needs of the respective services. Executive budgeting also has the advantage of centralizing in the hands of a single official responsibility for overall financial planning. To be sure, no thoughtful person who believes in democratic government would suggest that the executive be vested with power to *determine* matters of expenditure and taxation, but the *recommending* of financial measures is properly within his province. As we have seen, executive budgeting is now practiced by most states and many local governments. Budgeting of the board type, though generally less desirable, has in some instances produced gratifying results, and may be the most feasible plan in local governments where the lack of a central administrative officer makes effective executive budgeting virtually impossible. Furthermore, a budget board of the administrative-legislative type, by permitting legislator participation in budgeting at the preparation stage, may foster cooperation between the legislature and the administration and lessen hostility toward budgetary recommendations when they reach the stage of legislative consideration. The strictly legislative budget, however, is the least satisfactory of the three types and has consistently lost in favor.

Preparation of the Budget

The budget process typically begins with a request from the budget-making authority for "estimates" of needed expenditures for the ensuing fiscal year or biennium. This request is sent, several months in advance of the budget period, to the head of each administrative department and other spending agency of the government, and the estimates are submitted on blanks provided by the budget authority. For comparative purposes, these blanks usually require that there be indicated, in columns parallel to the itemized estimates, the amount actually expended for each item during the last completed period and the amount expected to be spent during the current period.

When the requested information has been received from all spending agencies, the estimates are reviewed and revised by the budget authority. This is one of the most important and difficult steps in the entire budget process. Each department head is primarily concerned with the needs of his own department. He is likely to see many ways in which additional funds could be used by his department in the expansion of desirable services, and to make his budgetary requests accordingly. But the granting to every spending agency of the full amount of money requested might involve an unreasonable increase in taxation. It is therefore the function of the chief executive or other budgetmaking authority to take an *overall* view of the fiscal needs of the government, considering the requests of each department in their relation to those of all others. The budget authority must be concerned with *relative* as well as absolute needs, and with keeping the total expenditures of the government within an amount which the taxpayers can reasonably bear. Revision of the budget estimates therefore ordinarily involves the scaling down of some or all requests. Suppose, for example, that a municipal fire department requests funds for four additional firemen and the police department asks for six additional patrolmen. It may well be that these requests in their entirety do not exceed the actual needs of the respective departments. Yet if the city is not in a position to bear the cost of all this additional personnel, it is the duty of the budget authority to revise one or both requests downward. Perhaps it will appear that the proper solution is to recommend for each department a part of the additional personnel requested. On the other hand, if it is felt that the fire department is now seriously undermanned while the police department is in a relatively better position, it may seem wise to approve for the one department all of its request and to deny to the other, for the time being, approval for any increase.

In the course of reviewing and revising the budget estimates, conferences are ordinarily held by the budget authority with the respective department heads. The latter may be questioned concerning their estimates, and they are afforded an opportunity to justify their requests. Sometimes there are also public hearings at which interested citizens may voice their approval of proposed expenditures or may register objections. On the basis of information gained through conferences, hearings, investigation, and study, the budget authority makes its revision of the original estimates, the revised estimates becoming the authority's program of proposed expenditures.

Certain estimates, it is to be noted, are sometimes exempt from revision by the budget authority. Under executive budget systems, for example, the budget-making agency is frequently forbidden to revise the estimates for the legislative and judicial branches, being required to include those items in the budget in their original form. Moreover, the earmarking of various revenues for specific purposes frequently operates as a serious restriction upon the discretion of the budget authority. In some states earmarking is practiced so extensively as to make anything approaching comprehensive budgeting quite impossible. Though exemptions and earmarkings appear to be less extensive in the case of the local governments, even there the necessity of providing for debt retirement and fixed charges may impair the revision power considerably.[20]

On the revenue side, budget-making entails the planning of income commensurate with proposed expenditures. Estimates of the revenue

[20] Concerning the extent and problems of earmarking, see Tax Foundation, *Earmarked State Taxes* (Tax Found., New York, 1955); Illinois Commission on Revenue, *Report* (Springfield, 1963), Chap. 24; Paul H. Wileden, "Earmarking: Good or Bad?" *State Govt.*, XXXIII, 251-255 (Autumn, 1960).

which may be expected during the budget period from existing taxes and nontax sources are prepared by the budget authority or submitted by the government's chief financial officer. If anticipated revenues are less than proposed expenditures, it is the duty of the budget authority to recommend a plan for raising additional funds in the required amount. Such a plan may include proposals for increased taxes, expansion of nontax revenue sources, borrowing, or some combination of these means. If it appears that revenues will exceed proposed current expenditures, recommendations should ordinarily be made for tax reduction or reduction in debt. When the expenditure and income sides of the budget have been properly correlated, the recommendations of the budget authority are organized into a formal document for transmission to the legislative body.

The Budget Document

The budget document should ordinarily contain at least three principal parts: (1) a budget message; (2) a budget summary; and (3) the detailed financial plan. The detailed plan, which constitutes the main body of the document, consists of page after page of statistical data and, though necessary for the purposes of legislators and administrators, is itemized far too minutely to be of interest to the ordinary citizen. Often the detailed appropriation recommendations cover several hundred pages. The budget summary presents, within the compass of a single page or at most a few pages, a tabular condensation of basic statistical data concerning such matters as available balances at the beginning of the budget period, estimated revenues, recommended expenditures, and the expected condition of the treasury at the end of the period. These summary statistics are sufficiently general in nature to be of interest to the private citizen as well as the public official.

In the budget message the budget-making authority gives a nontechnical explanation of the financial plan as set forth in the budget.[21] Here the current financial condition of the government should be explained, the proposed program of expenditures and revenue summarized, and the government's debt situation reviewed. Particular attention should be called to any proposals for major increases in expenditure items, or for new or increased taxes, and the reasons therefor made clear. Since the message, like the budget summary, is designed for popular as well as official enlightenment, it should be written in terms understandable to the layman. Though covering in a general manner all major aspects of the budget program, the message should if possible be brief enough that the leading newspapers of the state or community can print it in its entirety. In the case of executive budgets, the governor, mayor, or manager fre-

[21] See Buck, *Public Budgeting,* 57-60.

quently appears in person before the legislative body and delivers his budget message orally at the time the budget document is transmitted for legislative consideration. If ably prepared, the budget message should provide interested citizens, as well as public officials, with a clear overall picture of the financial situation and problems of the governmental unit concerned.

Budgetary proposals are of course merely recommendations, and can be made effective only as the result of legislative action. Under some budget systems it is therefore made the duty of the budget authority to prepare for introduction into the legislature the measures required to make the budget plan effective. These measures, referred to as the "budget bills," will include an appropriation bill, a revenue bill where changes in the revenue system are recommended, and sometimes a bill to authorize borrowing. Where provisions of this nature exist, the budget bills may be considered as constituting a fourth major part or division of the budget document.

The Budget Before the Legislature

As it comes to the legislative body from the budget-making authority, the budget is merely a plan for legislative guidance in financial matters. Only the representative legislature, or a primary assembly of the voters as in the case of the town meeting, can enact the measures necessary to make the budget effective. Moreover, certain forms of financial action, such as authorizing the incurring of bonded indebtedness, are at times even beyond the competence of the representative legislature and must receive voter approval in referendum elections. In a few states and strong-mayor cities, the legislative body, though permitted to reduce or strike out items in appropriation bills based upon the executive budget, is forbidden to increase or insert items. However, this situation, which substantially strengthens the position of the executive in financial matters, is distinctly the exception rather than the rule. In most instances the legislature is legally quite free to appropriate more or less than the amounts recommended in the budget, to strike out or insert items at will, or even to ignore the budget recommendations completely and enact an appropriation measure of its own design. Yet the mere fact that the budget represents a carefully planned program is likely to result in its carrying much weight with the legislative body, this being particularly true where the political party of the chief executive (in the case of an executive budget) is in control of the legislative branch.

With financial legislation, as in the case of legislation generally, committee consideration is ordinarily a vital step in the legislative process.[22] Where budget bills are not submitted as a part of the budget

[22] On matters of legislative procedure, see above, Chap. VIII.

document, appropriation and revenue bills are ordinarily drafted by the legislative committees within whose province those subjects fall, and when so drafted do not always follow budget recommendations. State legislatures usually have separate appropriations and revenue committees. Many local legislative bodies, on the other hand, have a single finance committee for the consideration of both appropriation and revenue measures, a plan which tends to integrate legislative action on budgetary matters. In bicameral state legislatures, budget bills are sometimes considered first by committees of the house of representatives, though it is not uncommon for committee consideration to take place in the two houses concurrently.[23] Public hearings on budget proposals are held by legislative committees in some states; and in the case of local budget hearings are quite commonly provided, either before a committee or before the entire legislative body. Where the executive veto exists, budget bills which have passed the legislature must, like other measures, be submitted to the chief executive for his approval or disapproval. In the case of appropriation bills, most state governors and the mayors of many cities are not limited to approving or disapproving such measures in their entirety, but may veto certain items while approving others. A few governors, indeed, may reduce items and approve them in such reduced amount. Here as elsewhere, of course, the executive veto may be overridden by subsequent legislative action.[24]

Appropriation acts may be of the lump-sum or of the itemized or segregated variety. Under the first of these plans, each spending agency is granted its funds as a single amount, to be spent according to the discretion of the agency's principal officer. Lump-sum appropriations have the advantage of affording flexibility, but are considered objectionable in that they do not encourage careful planning by department heads. In contrast to the strictly lump-sum method, the appropriation act may specify, within the total amount provided for each agency, how much may be spent for personal services, how much for materials and supplies, and so on. From that point, segregation may proceed to any degree, even to the extent of listing, within the personal-services item, each individual position and the salary therefor.

Itemization of appropriations fosters administrative planning, but if carried to an extreme prevents a desirable degree of flexibility in work programs. In general, highly detailed segregation is not presently favored where administrative means are available for assuring work planning and preventing the exhaustion of appropriations before the end of the fiscal period. One device through which this type of administrative control is now provided in many states and local units is the "allotment" system.

---

[23] In states having systems of joint committees, a single committee consideration serves both houses. See above, Chap. VII, "The Committee System."

[24] Buck, *Public Budgeting*, 383-393, 413-416. The item veto in the states is discussed above, Chap. IX, "The Veto Power."

Under this plan each department head is required, after his appropriation has been determined but before the beginning of the fiscal period, to divide his total appropriation into four or twelve parts, depending upon whether quarterly or monthly allotments are to be used. These parts need not be of equal amount, since the work of the department concerned may be heavier during some seasons of the year than others, but should reflect a thoughtfully planned work program. When the sums so determined have been certified to the chief executive and approved by him, they are reported to the government's chief accounting officer and become the department's official allotments. Thereafter, during a particular month or quarter, the accounting officer will not approve expenditures by the department in excess of the allotment for that period unless a revision of allotments has been requested by the department head and approved by the chief executive. Under such a plan, administrative controls in the financial field supplant detailed itemization of appropriations by the legislative body. When used in connection with lump-sum or only slightly segregated appropriations, the allotment system preserves flexibility while at the same time requiring careful administrative planning.

Execution of the Budget

The best of budgets, even after adoption by the legislative body, is of little or no value unless the actual carrying out of the plan, in practice, is assured. In the matter of execution or enforcement, American budget systems have in the past been notoriously weak, and while many governmental units now have effective enforcement procedures, laxity in this phase of budgeting is still widespread. Whereas adoption of the budget is strictly a legislative function, its execution is a duty of the administrative branch.

Every government of considerable size should have, within its administrative organization and responsible to the chief executive, a principal accounting officer charged with the duty of making a careful check of all receipts and disbursements.[25] Where such an officer presently exists, he is known by various titles, though that of comptroller is most accurately descriptive of the duties which he should perform. On the expenditure side, it should be the duty of the comptroller, when the annual or biennial appropriation measure has been enacted by the legislative body, to establish accounts in conformity thereto. It should then be required that every voucher drawn by a department head against his appropriation be countersigned by the comptroller before being paid by the treasurer; and like-

[25] A comprehensive discussion of the problems of budget execution will be found in Buck, *Public Budgeting*, Chaps. 14-17. See also Burkhead, *Government Budgeting*, 340-356.

wise that every proposed obligation, contractual or otherwise, be cleared with the comptroller before being incurred. When a voucher or proposed contract is presented to the comptroller, he should examine the appropriate account to determine whether the intended expenditure has actually been authorized by the legislative body and, if so, whether funds to the required amount are still available. If both of these questions are resolved in the affirmative, the comptroller then countersigns the document concerned and enters against the account the amount of the obligation thereby incurred. It should thus be possible for the comptroller to determine at any moment what part of an appropriation has been spent or obligated and the amount which remains as an unencumbered balance for future use. In this manner, misuse of funds and overdrawing of accounts should be largely prevented. The process whereby the comptroller examines and approves claims against appropriation accounts *before* payment is frequently referred to as the "preaudit" of expenditures, as opposed to the "post-audit" described in the next paragraph.

As a final step in budget enforcement there should be a post-audit of expenditures, *after* disbursement, by an agency outside and independent of the administration. The officer responsible for the post-audit is most appropriately entitled auditor. In many instances the auditor is now popularly elected, and this manner of selection removes him at least formally from responsibility to the administration. A better method of choice, however, is appointment by the legislative body, since the basic function of the auditor is the determination of whether the administrative agencies have expended public funds in accordance with legislative appropriations. Whereas preauditing is a continuous process, the postaudit is usually made only at stated intervals, commonly at the end of each fiscal year. If irregularities in accounts are found as a result of his examinations, it is the duty of the auditor to turn the matter over to the law-enforcement authorities for appropriate action.

Although the distinction between the administrative preaudit and the independent post-audit is fundamental to good accounting practice, it is widely ignored in the state and local governments.[26] In many instances the preaudit is made by an elective official. Even more regrettable is the fact that frequently the same officer, regardless of what he is called or how chosen, is charged with both preaudit and postaudit and thus is placed in the position, at the latter stage, of examining his own accounts.[27] Among local governments, the postaudit is often made by state examiners, or by private accountants employed by the legislative body. In the latter case, unfortunately, the amount of funds provided for the auditing

[26] On the post-audit in the states, see Vera Briscoe, "Guarding the States' Money," *Nat. Mun. Rev.*, XXXV, 233-239 (May, 1946).

[27] Concerning the necessity for separating preaudit and postaudit functions, see Lloyd Morey, Albert E. Jenner, Jr., and John S. Rendelman, *Report and Recommendations to Illinois Budgetary Commission* (Ill. Budgetary Comsn., Springfield, 1956), especially pp. 35-43.

service is frequently insufficient to provide for more than a superficial examination.

Budgetary Deficits and Surpluses

One of the fundamental purposes of budgeting is the coordination of expenditures and revenues, and ordinarily a balanced budget should be considered as the normal budget. This is not to say, however, that neither deficit financing nor the accumulation of a surplus is ever justifiable. Unusual circumstances may arise in which it is quite permissible, over a limited period, for expenditures to exceed current revenues. But expenditures in excess of revenues must ordinarily be covered by borrowing and, as will be explained later,[28] the debt-incurring power of most state and local governments is subject to strict legal limitations. Even in the absence of legal restrictions, moreover, economic limitations are likely to be operative so that prolonged borrowing to cover current deficits will ultimately impair the credit of the government concerned.

Surpluses in public treasuries tend to be frowned upon since they are an indication that government is taking from the people more money in taxes than is required for the support of current services. Surpluses also invite pressures for their expenditure for all sorts of purposes, some of which are often of questionable wisdom except perhaps from the standpoint of partisan politics. Yet there may be occasions when the accumulation of a surplus is permissible or even desirable.[29] During World War II, substantial surpluses were accumulated by many states and some local governments. High levels of employment and production resulted in greatly increased revenues from state sales and income taxes. At the same time, labor and material shortages necessitated drastic curtailments in capital outlays, while certain operating expenditures, particularly those for relief, also showed some decline. Some of the surplus moneys resulting from increased revenues and reduced expenditures accumulated in general and highway funds, but about half of the states established special reserve funds with the moneys therein earmarked for post-war construction, veterans' aid, or other specific purposes. Local governments, because of their heavy reliance upon property taxation, enjoyed no such increase in tax yields as did the states. Nevertheless, the local units shared in reduced expenditures for construction and relief, and some even imposed special property levies for the deliberate building up of reserve funds.

Accumulation of these wartime surpluses, as an alternative to tax

28 See below, "The Borrowing Power and Its Limitations."

29 There is some difference of opinion among economists and others concerning the desirability of government surpluses. For a discussion of various aspects of the subject, see C. E. Rightor and Hugh D. Ingersoll, "How to Use State Surpluses," *State Govt.*, XV, 57-58, 71-72 (Mar., 1942); V. J. Wyckoff, "The Surplus Concept in State Finance," *Ibid.*, XVI, 238-240, 251 (Dec., 1943); Harley L. Lutz, "Surpluses vs. Reduced Taxes," *Tax Digest*, XX, 365-368, 387-388 (Nov., 1942).

reduction, was believed by many to exert a wholesome influence in several directions. It was claimed that tax reduction, by releasing additional purchasing power at a time when many consumer goods were in short supply, would have aggravated the current inflation. Considerable amounts of the surplus funds were invested in federal securities, and this was felt to be a laudable contribution to the war effort. Finally, it was considered as wise financial planning to put aside, in times of high employment and income, funds to be used for construction or other purposes which would tend to provide employment in possible periods of post-war depression. Some use was made of surplus funds for debt retirement. However, where outstanding obligations were neither due nor callable, retirement could be effected only through their purchase on the open market, frequently at a premium. Under such circumstances, it was ordinarily thought to be better policy to await the maturity of outstanding debts and to make other use meanwhile of surplus funds.

At the end of fiscal 1947, balances in state general, highway, and post-war reserve funds amounted to more than $3 billion.[30] Thereafter, most of the surpluses, both state and local, were soon expended. Of the arguments urged in favor of the wartime accumulations, their anti-inflationary effect seems to be the most convincing, notwithstanding that this effect, in the overall situation, would necessarily have been mild. The sums amassed, though considerable in absolute amount, could scarcely have been of major significance in meeting post-war construction needs or providing employment in times of depression.

Capital Budgeting

Many states and cities now budget capital expenditures apart from those for current operations. Major improvements such as public buildings, parks, sewerage systems, and other public works must ordinarily be financed on a long-term basis which frequently involves borrowing; and the planning of their financing presents problems of methods and priorities somewhat different from those relating to regularly recurring expenditures. Capital and operating budgets may constitute distinct parts of the same budget document or may take the form of separate documents; they may be prepared by the same agency or by different agencies. Capital budgets, for best results, should be formulated to cover a longer span of time than a single year or biennium, though they may be reviewed and revised periodically. For greatest effectiveness, a capital budget should be closely correlated with a comprehensive plan for the physical development of the state or local unit concerned.[31]

[30] United States Bureau of the Census, *Balances in State General, Highway, and Postwar-Reserve Funds in 1947* (U.S. Bur. of the Census, Washington, 1948).
[31] See A. M. Hillhouse and S. Kenneth Howard, *State Capital Budgeting*, especially Chaps. 1, 2; Burkhead, *op. cit.*, 182-211; above, Chap. XXI, "Planning."

Governmental Purchasing

Closely related to budgeting is the matter of purchasing procedures.[32] Expenditures for supplies, materials, and equipment consume, in the average government, from 20 to 30 percent of the total operating budget[33]—being second in amount only to expenditures for personal services. Traditionally, each department or agency of a government made its own purchases in its own way. Now, however, many governments have introduced centralized purchasing systems as a means of fostering economy and efficient administration.

Centralized purchasing has been defined as "the delegation to one office of the authority to purchase supplies, materials and equipment needed for use by all the several operating branches of the organization." [34] Where purchasing is decentralized, buying is likely to be by amateurs, with each department filling its needs at retail prices. Central purchasing, on the other hand, permits the employment of professional buyers skilled in the prediction of market trends and in purchasing technique. Pooling of departmental requirements results in larger orders, which may frequently be filled at wholesale and which facilitate the use of competitive bidding. As a result of these various factors, unit costs are often substantially reduced. "It has been estimated by students of public procurement that moving from wholly decentralized or independent buying to centralized and organized buying has effected savings to as much as 25 percent." [35]

In the early 1960's, forty-five states were reported as having central purchasing agencies charged with buying for the major needs of most state agencies.[36] In a majority of the states the purchasing agency constitutes a division within an integrated department of administration.[37] Many cities now practice centralized purchasing, as do some counties. Apart

---

[32] A standard treatise on the subject is Russell Forbes, *Governmental Purchasing.* See also Russell Forbes, *Centralized Purchasing* (rev. ed.); Council of State Governments, *Purchasing by the States;* Russell Forbes and others, *Purchasing for Small Cities;* Lewis C. Bell and Donald G. Rhodes, "Governmental Purchasing in the Fifty States," *Pub. Admin. Survey* (Bur. of Govtl. Research, Univ. of Miss.), Vol. IX, No. 6 (July, 1962).

[33] Forbes, *Centralized Purchasing* (rev. ed.), 5.

[34] *Ibid.*

[35] William E. Stevenson, "The Place of Purchasing in State Government," *State Govt.,* XXXV, 40-44 (Winter, 1962), at 42. Concerning various other advantages of centralized purchasing, see Forbes, *Centralized Purchasing* (rev. ed.), 6 ff; Forbes, *Governmental Purchasing,* 4-10.

[36] For a tabular analysis of purchasing organization and practices in the states, see *The Book of the States,* 1962-63, pp. 170-171. The states without central purchasing systems were Arizona, Delaware, Hawaii, Iowa, and Mississippi. In some instances these states had centralized purchasing for certain departments or institutions. More recently, Mississippi has inaugurated a new purchasing program.

[37] See above, Chap. X, "Departments of Administration."

from municipalities, however, central buying has made relatively little headway at the local level.

Of particular interest during recent years has been the development of plans for meeting the purchasing needs of small local units unable individually to obtain the benefits of professional or large-scale buying. In some instances two or more local units have established joint purchasing agencies or have entered into arrangements, formal or informal, for cooperative buying. Thus a county, a city, and a school district may cooperate in the purchasing of various kinds of supplies and materials used by all. A number of state municipal leagues have inaugurated purchasing services whereby the needs of several municipalities for various items may be pooled and the benefits of quantity buying secured; and several states have authorized local units to make purchases through the state purchasing agency. Altogether, local governments in considerable number are now employing one or another of these means of improving their purchasing procedures.

The Borrowing Power and Its Limitations[38]

By the terms of the federal constitution, Congress is empowered, without restriction, to "borrow money on the credit of the United States." In marked contrast to this unlimited grant of authority, the debt-contracting powers of state and local governments are ordinarily subject to rigid restrictions. State legislatures, in pursuance of their residual powers, may borrow in whatever manner and amount they wish except as authority may be denied or restricted by their respective constitutions, but restrictive provisions are numerous and in many instances severe. Local governments, as agencies of delegated powers, have only such borrowing authority as is positively conferred upon them by the states, and the powers so conferred are hedged about by many limitations, both constitutional and statutory.

Most state legislatures are permitted to borrow at their discretion for certain unusual purposes, such as repelling invasion or suppressing insurrection, but in practice occasions for the exercise of such emergency borrowing power seldom arise. Also common is legislative authority to borrow for the refunding of existing indebtedness and to borrow specified sums, ordinarily relatively small, for meeting casual deficits. But the power to incur indebtedness in substantial amounts for public improvements or other ordinary governmental purposes is another matter. In about four-fifths of the states, borrowing of this nature must either be ap-

---

[38] On the problems of state and local borrowing generally, see Paul Studensky, *Public Borrowing;* B. U. Ratchford, *American State Debts;* Carl H. Chatters and Albert M. Hillhouse, *Local Government Debt Administration.*

proved by the voters in a referendum election or be authorized by constitutional amendment. Since amendments require popular ratification,[39] this means that in all of these states the borrowing power has virtually been taken from the legislature and vested in the electorate, with the legislature limited to making proposals for the exercise of the power. In addition to such provisions concerning location of the borrowing authority, many state constitutions impose still other limitations upon the contracting of indebtedness. These concern such matters as the amount of indebtedness that may be incurred, the maximum term for which bonds may be issued, and the mandatory imposition of taxes for payment of interest and principal. Common also is a prohibition against lending the state's credit for the benefit of individuals or private enterprises—a provision having its origin in the financial embarrassment experienced in the pre-Civil War period as a result of state borrowing in aid of canal, turnpike, and other public-improvement companies. In only a few states is the legislature free to borrow without quantitative or other restrictions.[40]

Local governments, as noted above, are subject to a myriad of debt restrictions. Most state constitutions contain provisions on the subject and, whether or not there are constitutional restrictions, there will usually be found an abundance of statutory limitations. The restrictive provisions naturally vary from state to state.[41] Usually there will be a limitation on the amount of indebtedness that may be incurred, expressed as a percentage of the assessed valuation of taxable property. Most states impose restrictions upon the purposes of borrowing, including a prohibition of lending credit to private persons or corporations. The length of term for which local-government bonds may run is commonly limited, as is also the rate of interest that may be paid. A majority of the states now require that the bonds of some or all local units be issued in serial form.[42] In a few states local borrowing is subject to some degree of state administrative control.[43] Finally, it is to be noted that, though in occasional instances the borrowing power is vested in the local governing body, this is the distinct exception. In the great majority of local units, debt may be

[39] Except in Delaware, which is one of the states where the borrowing power rests with the legislature.

[40] Ratchford, *op. cit.*, Chap. 17; B. U. Ratchford, "Constitutional Provisions Governing State Borrowing," *Amer. Polit. Sci. Rev.*, XXXII, 694-707 (Aug., 1938). A tabular analysis of state constitutional provisions limiting the borrowing power appears in each of these references. For a more recent analysis, see Tax Foundation, *Constitutional Debt Control in the States.* Cf. above, Chap. VIII, "Financial Limitations."

[41] For a recent analysis and appraisal, see Advisory Commission on Intergovernmental Relations, *State Constitutional and Statutory Restrictions on Local Government Debt.*

[42] See below, "Sinking Funds versus Serial Bonds."

[43] Examples are mentioned above, Chap. III, "Approval and Review."

incurred only with the approval of the voters in a referendum election. In a few states only taxpayers are eligible to vote in such elections.

This plethora of restrictions upon the power of state and local governments to incur indebtedness has doubtless operated as a deterrent to overborrowing and defaults.[44] Such negative provisions, however, cannot assure wise borrowing policy. Within constitutional and statutory limits, it is still possible to borrow for current expenses, for unnecessary improvements, or for other imprudent purposes. Unwise use of the debt-incurring power which exists can be prevented only through discreet and vigilant action of legislative bodies and of the voters in approving or disapproving borrowing proposals.

Purposes of Borrowing

The purposes for which governments most commonly borrow are: (1) in anticipation of revenues; (2) for expenditures arising from emergencies; and (3) for construction of public improvements. In many governments the fiscal year and tax calendar are so poorly synchronized that tax revenues are not due and payable until the fiscal year is several months advanced. When this is the case, it is ordinarily necessary for the government to borrow funds to meet its payroll and other expenditures until tax moneys begin to reach the treasury.

At the national level, the exigencies of war and the threat of war constitute the primary occasion for what may be classed as emergency borrowing, accounting, directly or indirectly, for all but a relatively small part of our present federal debt. Since state and local governments do not participate directly in expenditures for waging war, they do not borrow for that purpose. But the states in post-war periods frequently issue bonds for the payment of bonuses or "adjusted compensation" to their citizens who have served in the armed forces. During the 1930's many states and local units, as well as the national government, borrowed to meet relief costs and other expenditures flowing from the depression emergency. Fire, tornado, flood, and earthquake are among the other causes of occasional widespread disaster which may call for emergency borrowing by state and local governments.

Almost any government may at times find it desirable to borrow for financing public improvements. School buildings, county courthouses and city halls, major highway improvements, and irrigation and reclamation projects call for construction expenditures in such amounts that it is usually not feasible to attempt to meet them from current revenues. When projects of this nature are undertaken, funds are ordinarily borrowed to meet construction costs, and the loan is then repaid from tax revenues over

[44] Limitations upon the debt-incurring power of local governments are sometimes virtually nullified by the establishment of special districts coterminous, or overlapping with, the general-government units. See above, Chap. XII, "Special Districts."

a period of several years. When borrowing for a public improvement, bond maturities should normally be so arranged that the loan will be repaid in its entirety within the useful life of the improvement concerned; and in practice it may frequently be wise policy, in times of prosperity, to liquidate public-improvement indebtedness well in advance of the end of this period of usefulness.

Types of Indebtedness

Public borrowings are commonly said to be of two classes: short-term and long-term. Short-term borrowings, or temporary borrowings as they are sometimes called, are usually in anticipation of taxes or the proceeds from bond issues, or to meet emergency expenditures unforeseen when the budget was adopted.[45] Borrowings of this nature are represented by bank loans, tax-anticipation warrants, and other short-term instruments; and are ordinarily repaid during the current fiscal year or, at the latest, early in the following year. Short-term borrowings normally constitute only a very small percentage of a government's total indebtedness. Along with unpaid bills and any other demand or short-term obligations, they make up the "floating" debt of the government concerned, in contrast to its more permanent "funded" or "bonded" debt.[46]

Long-term borrowing is usually effected through the issuance of bonds to be redeemed from revenues of future years. Government bonds are of two principal types: general-obligation bonds and revenue bonds. General-obligation bonds are secured by a pledge of the full faith and credit of the issuing government. Revenue bonds, which are most commonly issued for the financing of a public utility or some other income-producing enterprise, are secured only by a pledge of the revenues accruing from the enterprise concerned, supplemented in some instances by a lien upon the enterprise property. Like special-assessment bonds, revenue bonds are usually not subject to ordinary debt limits, and therefore may be issued after the government concerned has exhausted its general constitutional or statutory borrowing power. However, because of the limited nature of their security, revenue bonds are commonly considered as less desirable investments than general-obligation bonds, and therefore must often bear a higher rate of interest. Revenue bonds have long been used to a considerable extent for financing municipally-owned utilities, but until recently were of distinctly minor importance in state borrowing. During the last two decades, however, there has been a marked increase in revenue-bond financing at the state level. The most important single factor in this development has been the issuance in large amounts of toll-

---

[45] Studensky, *op. cit.*, 1; Chatters and Hillhouse, *op. cit.*, 165.

[46] Floating debt may be contrasted also with "fixed debt," a term that is broader than funded debt, including not only bonds but various other long-term obligations such as judgments and long-term notes. Chatters and Hillhouse, *op. cit.*, 494.

road bonds, these bonds now constituting about one-fourth of all state indebtedness. Overall, revenue bonds of one kind or another now constitute approximately half of the total state debt and about a third of all local-government indebtedness.

Sinking Funds versus Serial Bonds

Until comparatively recently, state and local bonds were ordinarily of the term or sinking-fund type. Under this plan, all bonds of a particular issue mature at the same time—say ten, fifteen, or twenty years after the date of issue. To provide for their retirement when due, a sinking fund is established into which a fixed sum is to be paid each year, and the moneys in which are invested in approved interest-bearing securities. The amount to be placed in the sinking fund annually is so calculated that, together with the interest earned by moneys in the fund, it should equal the face amount of the bond issue on the date of maturity. Bond interest, meanwhile, is paid from current revenues.

Term bonds proved generally unsatisfactory because of various weaknesses in the sinking-fund plan of retirement. In the first place, legislative bodies sometimes failed to levy the necessary tax for sinking-fund purposes or to make the required appropriation to the fund. Again, since sinking-fund moneys might not be needed for debt redemption for a number of years, there was constant temptation to borrow therefrom for seemingly more urgent purposes, and such borrowings were sometimes not repaid. Finally, if interest rates declined, securities purchased for the sinking fund were likely to produce less income than anticipated. For any or all of these reasons, when an issue of term bonds matured the moneys in the sinking fund might be inadequate for bond redemption. Because of difficulties such as these, sinking-fund bonds during recent decades have steadily declined in popularity and bonds of the serial type have gained in favor.

Serial bonds are retired from current revenues, maturities being staggered so that only a designated portion of an issue becomes due in any one year. Where it is desired, for example, to repay a particular loan over a period of twenty years, maturities may be arranged so that one-twentieth of the principal amount becomes due each year. In such a case, the bonds are known as *straight* serials. Since interest as well as payments on principal must be met from current revenues, the straight-serial plan places a heavier total burden upon the taxpayers during the earlier years of the repayment period than during later years when payments on principal have resulted in corresponding reductions in the interest item. In order to overcome this disadvantage and equalize the tax burden throughout the repayment period, maturities may be so arranged that principal payments are smaller during the early years when interest payments are heavy, and larger during later years when interest payments are lighter. Bonds issued under this arrangement, which seeks to make total annual payments for principal *and* interest approximately equal throughout the repayment period, are known as *annuity* serials. Because serial bonds eliminate the necessity of a sinking fund with all of its shortcomings, most bonds now issued by state and local governments are in serial form of one variety or another.

The Call Privilege

A special feature which may be included in either term or serial bonds is the "call" provision. Such a provision permits the issuing government or other agency, after a designated number of years but before their maturity date, to call and pay the bonds at par or, sometimes, at a specified small premium. The call privilege injects an additional element of flexibility into financial administration. If interest rates decline, substantial savings may sometimes be made by calling outstanding indebtedness and issuing new securities at lower interest rates. The call feature has long been quite common in bonds of private corporations and those of the federal government, but as yet has been employed but little in state and local-government securities. It deserves more extensive use in state and local borrowing.

Trends in Public Indebtedness

Prior to the First World War, public indebtedness in the United States was comparatively low. In 1912, total state and local debt amounted to less than $5 billion and the federal debt to but something more than $1 billion.[47] War financing brought the federal debt to a then high mark of some $26 billion, but this was reduced after the war to $16 billion. State and local indebtedness increased steadily during both war and post-war years, and the economic depression of the 1930's was the occasion for widespread borrowing by governments at all levels to finance vast expenditure programs for direct and work relief. Though state and local governments borrowed heavily for relief purposes, their debt limitations made it practically impossible for them alone to finance the depression programs. It was therefore almost inevitable, particularly in view of the national character of the emergency, that the federal government should exercise its unlimited borrowing power in aid of the states and localities. By 1940 total state and local indebtedness amounted to more than $20 billion —$3.5 billion state and $16.7 billion local—and the federal debt to nearly $43 billion.

During World War II federal indebtedness increased at a phe-

[47] The data in this section are based principally on Census Bureau reports. See also Tax Foundation, *Facts and Figures on Government Finance: Twelfth Edition, 1962-1963.*

nomenal rate, reaching nearly $280 billion by 1946. State and local indebtedness, on the other hand, was reduced by one-fifth during the war years. With labor and materials generally unavailable for ordinary civil construction, there was little new borrowing for capital outlays, and in some instances treasury surpluses resulting from high wartime tax yields were used for debt-reduction purposes. From $20 billion in 1940, total state and local debt had dropped by 1946 to less than $16 billion, state indebtedness amounting in the latter year to $2.3 billion and the indebtedness of local governments to $13.5 billion.

With the end of hostilities, some slight reduction was made in the federal debt and state and local indebtedness began a rise which has continued unabated to the present day. Major factors in the increase of state and local debt in the years immediately after the war were the resumption of construction work deferred during the war and the issuance by many states of bonds to provide bonus payments to veterans. Since 1950 there has been an occasional small reduction in the federal debt but the overall trend has been upward, with the total now (1964) exceeding $300 billion. State and local indebtedness has continued to rise rapidly. The states have borrowed large sums for toll roads and other highways, and for construction of buildings at state educational and welfare institutions. Municipalities have borrowed heavily for sewerage facilities and other public works, and for housing and urban renewal. School districts have increased their indebtedness enormously to provide new buildings and other facilities for soaring enrollments of public-school pupils. By 1962, the total amount of state and local long-term indebtedness exceeded $77 billion.

The following tables, based upon Census Bureau reports, show, as of 1962, the total and per capita indebtedness of the federal, state, and local governments; and the distribution of state and local debt among the various purposes for which it was incurred.[48]

Individual states and local units frequently vary, of course, from

GOVERNMENTAL DEBT, 1962

UNIT	AMOUNT IN BILLIONS	AMOUNT PER CAPITA
Federal	$298.2	$1,604
State	21.4	116
Local	55.8	300
Total	$375.4	$2,020

[48] United States Bureau of the Census, *Summary of Governmental Finances in 1962;* United States Bureau of the Census, *Long-Term Debt of State and Local Governments* (1962 Census of Governments, Preliminary Rept. No. 7, U.S. Bur. of the Census, Washington, 1962). Some of the data are estimates based upon samplings.

LONG-TERM DEBT OF STATE AND LOCAL GOVERNMENT BY PURPOSE, 1962

| | STATE | | LOCAL | |
| | AMOUNT IN | | AMOUNT IN | |
PURPOSE	MILLIONS	PERCENT	MILLIONS	PERCENT
Education	$ 4,004	18.6	$19,052	34.1
Highways	9,628	44.8	4,142	7.4
Local Utilities	xxxxxx	xxxx	12,581	22.5
Sewerage	xxxxxx	xxxx	5,304	9.5
Housing and Urban Renewal	659	3.1	4,559	8.2
Hospitals	263	1.2	950	1.7
Airports	xxxxxx	xxxx	1,196	2.1
Port and Terminal Facilities	317	1.5	748	1.3
State Veterans' Bonuses	929	4.3	xxxxxx	xxxx
Other and Unallocable	5,684	26.5	7,345	13.2
Total	$21,484	100.0	$55,877	100.0

the general trends noted. Because of differences in power and policy, some individual governments and classes of governments borrow more freely than others. Local-government indebtedness is consistently much greater than that of the states. This is due in part to the fact that some constitutions impose more rigorous debt limitations upon the state than upon local units, but it results in larger measure from the wider participation by local governments in public-works and other activities in connection with which borrowing is most common. Occasional state and local governments operate, for a time at least, entirely free of debt, but this is distinctly the exception rather than the rule.

An indebtedness of state and local governments exceeding $77 billion is a large sum, yet it may appear small in comparison with the debt of the national government. In reality, however, the very existence of the enormous federal debt should serve as a deterrent to any undue expansion of state or local borrowing. All governmental indebtedness, except that represented by revenue bonds, is an obligation of the taxpaying public, and therefore state and local debt should be viewed as a part of the overall financial picture. A total public debt of $375 billion—more than $2,000 per capita—is not to be taken lightly. Annual interest charges on the federal debt alone exceed $9 billion—twice the amount of the entire federal budget in years immediately preceding the depression of the 1930's; and interest on state and local debt amounts to $2 billion annually. Undoubtedly some additional borrowing will be necessary in the years ahead to enable the states and their local governments to provide the many programs of services demanded by their citizens. However, with the federal debt as large as it is and with little likelihood of its being reduced substantially in the immediate future, the conclusion seems inescapable that the state and local borrowing power should be exercised with more than ordinary care.

REFERENCES

Advisory Commission on Intergovernmental Relations, *State Constitutional and Statutory Restrictions on Local Government Debt* (U.S. Govt. Printing Office, Washington, 1961).

BUCK, A. E., *Budgeting for Small Cities* (Mun. Admin. Service, New York, 1931).

——, *Budget Making* (Appleton, New York, 1921).

——, *Municipal Budgets and Budget Making* (Nat. Mun. League, New York, 1925).

——, *Public Budgeting* (Harper, New York, 1929).

BURKHEAD, Jesse, *Government Budgeting* (Wiley, New York, 1956).

CHATTERS, Carl H., and Hillhouse, Albert M., *Local Government Debt Administration* (Prentice-Hall, Englewood Cliffs, N.J., 1939).

Council of State Governments, *Purchasing by the States* (The Council, Chicago, rev. 1956).

FORBES, Russell, *Centralized Purchasing: A Sentry at the Tax Exit Gate* (Nat. Assn. of Purchasing Agents, New York, rev. ed., 1941).

——, *Governmental Purchasing* (Harper, New York, 1929).

——, and others, *Purchasing for Small Cities* (Pub. Admin. Service, Chicago, rev. 1951).

HILLHOUSE, A. M., and HOWARD, S. Kenneth, *State Capital Budgeting* (Council of State Govts., Chicago, 1963).

Kentucky Legislative Research Commission, *State Purchasing in Kentucky* (Ky. Legis. Research Comsn., Frankfort, 1963).

RATCHFORD, B. U., *American State Debts* (Duke Univ. Press, Durham, N.C., 1941).

STUDENSKY, Paul, *Public Borrowing* (Nat. Mun. League, New York, 1930).

Tax Foundation, *Constitutional Debt Control in the States* (Tax Found., New York, 1954).

——, *Facts and Figures on Government Finance: Twelfth Edition, 1962-1963* (Prentice-Hall, Englewood Cliffs, N.J., 1963).

United States Bureau of the Census, *Compendium of State Government Finances in 1962* (U.S. Govt. Printing Office, Washington, 1963).

——, *Historical Review of State and Local Government Finances* (U.S. Bur. of the Census, Washington, 1948).

——, *Summary of Governmental Finances in 1962* (U.S. Bur. of the Census, Washington, 1963).

See also public finance textbooks included in reference list at end of the preceding chapter.

INDEX